Oh! 1001 Homemade Holiday Cookie Recipes

(Oh! 1001 Homemade Holiday Cookie Recipes - Volume 1)

Iva Alston

Copyright: Published in the United States by Iva Alston/ © IVA ALSTON

Published on October, 12 2020

All rights reserved. No part of this publication may be reproduced, stored in retrieval system, copied in any form or by any means, electronic, mechanical, photocopying, recording or otherwise transmitted without written permission from the publisher. Please do not participate in or encourage piracy of this material in any way. You must not circulate this book in any format. IVA ALSTON does not control or direct users' actions and is not responsible for the information or content shared, harm and/or actions of the book readers.

In accordance with the U.S. Copyright Act of 1976, the scanning, uploading and electronic sharing of any part of this book without the permission of the publisher constitute unlawful piracy and theft of the author's intellectual property. If you would like to use material from the book (other than just simply for reviewing the book), prior permission must be obtained by contacting the author at author@ashkenazirecipes.com

Thank you for your support of the author's rights.

Content

CHAPTER 1: VALENTINE'S DAY COOKIE RECIPES 15

1. Alsatian Chocolate Balls..............................15
2. Bethany's Favorite Valentine Cut Out Sugar Cookies 15
3. Boyfriend Brownies 16
4. Brownies V..16
5. Butter Crisps 17
6. Chef John's Chili Chocolate Cookies.........17
7. Cherry Cheesecake Hearts 18
8. Chocolate Black Tea Cake 19
9. Chocolate Chip Meringue 19
10. Chocolate Kiss Cookies 19
11. Chocolate Peppermint Meringue Drops ...20
12. Chocolate Pizzelles 20
13. Chocolate Wine Balls...................................21
14. Classic Butter Cookies II 21
15. Cookie Tulips..22
16. Cream Cheese Cut Outs I 22
17. Creme De Pirouline 23
18. Crispy Peanut Butter Chocolate Log 24
19. Dark Chocolate Macadamia Brownies......24
20. Egg Paint 25
21. Egyptian Rose Leaves..................................25
22. German Heart Cookies 25
23. Giant Heart Shaped Pan Cookie................26
24. Italian Pizzelles 27
25. Lesley's Valentine Brownies With Raspberry Coulis 27
26. Lollipop Cookie Valentines 28
27. Maraschino Cherry Almond Cookies 29
28. Mostaccioli (Mustaches)..............................29
29. Muddy Hearts 30
30. No Bake Chocolate Peanut Butter Bars 30
31. Old Fashioned Butter Valentine Cookies Dipped In Chocolate 31
32. Orange Almond Biscotti II.........................32
33. Pope's Valentine Cookies............................32
34. Raspberry Hearts..33
35. Raspberry Liqueur Valentine Cookies 33
36. Rose Pistachio Shortbread 34
37. So Pink Cereal Bars.....................................34
38. Stained Glass Sugar Hearts........................35
39. Sweet Chocolate Caramel Squares.............35
40. The Best Valentine Sugar Cookies 36
41. Two Hearts Together 36
42. Ultimate Double Chocolate Cookies 37
43. Valentine's Cinnamon Heart Shortbread Pan Cookies 38
44. Valentine's Day Cookies 38
45. Valentine's Slice And Bake Cinnamon Heart Shortbread Cookies...39
46. Wednesday Cookies 39

CHAPTER 2: EASTER COOKIE RECIPES 40

47. Almond Macaroon Nests...............................40
48. Annemarie's Lemon Bars............................40
49. Bird's Nests III 41
50. Bunny Cookies..41
51. Cardamom Rose Meringues 42
52. Carrot Cake Cookies...................................42
53. Chocolate Bunny Treats™ 43
54. Chrusciki I 43
55. Easter Bird's Nests.......................................44
56. Easter Egg Dipper Treat™ 44
57. Forgotten Kisses 45
58. Fresh Strawberry Cookies 45
59. Fruit Preserve Sandwich Cookies 46
60. Funfetti® Style Cookies 46
61. Gluten Free Easter Egg Cookies 47
62. Homemade Samoa Cookies 47
63. Honey Lavender Cookies 48
64. Jelly Bean Nests 48
65. Lavender Shortbread Cookies....................49
66. Lebanese Easter Cookies 49
67. Lemon Bars I 50
68. Lemon Bars II..51
69. Lemon Biscuits 51
70. Lemon Butter Cookies 52
71. Lemon Crisps..52
72. Lemon Curd Bars...52
73. Lemon Dream Bars 53
74. Lemon Drops 53
75. Lemon Kiss Cookies....................................54
76. Lemon Madeleines 54
77. Lemon Meltaways 55
78. Lemon Poppy Seed Biscotti 55
79. Lemon Whippersnappers.............................56
80. Lemon Yummies..56

81. Lemon Marmalade Cookie Sandwiches.....57
82. Macaron (Macaroon) 57
83. Meringue Cookies 58
84. Meringue Kisses II 58
85. Perfect And Delicious Royal Icing 59
86. Poppy Seed Hungarian Style Cookies 59
87. Quick Lemon Crisps 60
88. Rainbow Cookies 60
89. Raspberry Meringue Bars 61
90. Rhubarb Meringue Squares 61
91. Rose Pavlova Cakes 62
92. Spring Lime Tea Cookies 63
93. Strawberry Cake Cookies 63
94. Sugar Cookie Cups With Coconut Buttercream Frosting..............................63

CHAPTER 3: HALLOWEEN COOKIE RECIPES...64

95. Almond Joy® Cookies 64
96. Apple Crisp Cookies 65
97. Booger Cookies 65
98. Candy Bar Brownies 66
99. Candy Bar Squares 66
100. Caramel Apple Cookies.............................67
101. Cat Poop Cookies II 68
102. Chocolate Halloween Cookies 68
103. Chocolate Mice 69
104. Chocolate Toffee Cookies I 69
105. Cranberry Pumpkin Cookies 70
106. Crispy Rice Candy Corn Treats 70
107. Dianne's Pumpkin Cookie Cups................71
108. Edible Spiders 71
109. Halloween Chocolate Chip Cookies With Spiders...72
110. Halloween Ghosties..................................72
111. Halloween Shortbread Poppy Seed Cookie Fingers..73
112. Halloween Skeleton Cookies 73
113. Halloween Vegan Yacon Syrup Cookies ...74
114. Hoot Owl Cookies 75
115. Leftover Halloween Candy Cookies 75
116. Mary's Sugar Cookies...............................76
117. Meringue Bones 76
118. Mini Candy Bar Cookies 77
119. Mom's Walnut Bars 77
120. Owl Cookies 78
121. Pattern Cookies 78

122. Paul's Pumpkin Bars 79
123. Peanut Butter Crunch Cookies 79
124. Peanut Butter Spider Cookies 80
125. Peanut Candy Bar Cake.............................81
126. Peanutty Candy Corn Cereal Bars 81
127. Pumpkin Bars I 82
128. Pumpkin Bars II 82
129. Pumpkin Bliss Treats................................83
130. Pumpkin Chocolate Chip Brownies..........83
131. Pumpkin Chocolate Chip Cookies I 84
132. Pumpkin Chocolate Chip Cookies III 84
133. Pumpkin Cookies III.................................85
134. Pumpkin Cookies VI 85
135. Pumpkin Cookies With Cream Cheese Frosting (The World's Best!) 86
136. Pumpkin Funnel Cakes 86
137. Pumpkin Gobs 87
138. Pumpkin Oatmeal Chocolate Chip Cookies 88
139. Pumpkin Pecan White Chocolate Cookies88
140. Pumpkin Protein Cookies.........................89
141. Pumpkin Raisin Cookies 89
142. Pumpkin Spice Cookie 90
143. Pumpkin Pine Cookies 90
144. Root Beer Float Cookies..........................90
145. S'More Bars II..91
146. S'more Eyeballs 91
147. Spiderweb Brownies 92
148. White Chocolate Pumpkin Cookies 92
149. Witches' Hats...93

CHAPTER 4: THANKSGIVING COOKIE RECIPES...93

150. Acorn Candy Cookies..............................93
151. Anise Waffle Cookies 94
152. Apple Bars 94
153. Apple Brownies 95
154. Apple Butter Bars.....................................95
155. Apple Cinnamon Oatmeal Cookie 96
156. Apple Cookies 96
157. Apple Half Moons 97
158. Apple Hermits 97
159. Apple Oatmeal Bar Cookies.....................98
160. Apple Oatmeal Bars.................................98
161. Apple Oatmeal Cookies I 99
162. Apple Pie Bars 99
163. Apple Squares 100

164. Apple And Spice Cookies 100
165. Apple Cran Cherry Oatmeal Cookies 101
166. Applesauce Bars 101
167. Applesauce Brownies I 102
168. Applesauce Cookies I 102
169. Applesauce Oatie Cookies 103
170. Applesauce Oatmeal Cookies 103
171. Applesauce Raisin Bars 104
172. Applesauce Squares 104
173. Auntie's Persimmon Cookies 105
174. Autumn Harvest Cookies 106
175. Butterscotch Apple Cookies 106
176. Candy Turkeys 107
177. Caramel Apple Bars II 107
178. Caramel Apple Bars III 108
179. Caramel Apple Cookie Dessert 108
180. Chinese Style Peanut Cookie 109
181. Chocolate Cran Oat Cookies 109
182. Cranberry Cinnamon Cookies 110
183. Cranberry Cornmeal Linzer Cookies 110
184. Cranberry Kitchen Cookies 111
185. Cranberry Oat Bars 111
186. Cranberry Oatmeal Bars 112
187. Cranberry Oatmeal Drops 113
188. Cranberry Oats With Chocolate 113
189. Cranberry Orange Oat Cookies 114
190. Cranberry Orange Oatmeal Cookies 114
191. Cream Cheese Snowball Cookies 115
192. Cut Out Cookies In A Flower Pot 115
193. Danish Pastry Apple Bars I 116
194. Danish Pastry Apple Bars II 116
195. Easy Cheerio® Coconut Rum Balls 117
196. Easy Pecan Pie Bar Cookies 117
197. Erin's Fun Turkey Cookies 118
198. Espresso Biscotti 119
199. Graham Cracker Carmelitas 119
200. Iced Pumpkin Cookies 120
201. Light Holiday Tea Cakes 120
202. Linda's Cranberry Cookies 121
203. Make Ahead Cookie Mix 121
204. Mary's Salted Caramel Pecan Bars 122
205. Mocha Walnut Cookies 122
206. Moist Persimmon Cookie 123
207. Oatmeal Craisin Cookies 123
208. Oatmeal Cranberry White Chocolate Chunk Cookies 124
209. Oatmeal Dried Fruit Cookies 124
210. Oatmeal Raisin Cookies I 125
211. Old English Lemon Cranberry Cookies ..125
212. Orange Cranberry Biscotti 126
213. Orange Cranberry Drops 126
214. Peanut Butter Chews 127
215. Pecan Pie Bars I 127
216. Pecan Pie Bars II 128
217. Persimmon Cookies 128
218. Persimmon Cookies I 129
219. Persimmon Cookies II 129
220. Persimmon Raisin Cookies 130
221. Pumpkin Pecan Biscotti 130
222. Red Velvet Cheesecake Swirl Brownies ..131
223. Spiced Pecan Shortbread 132
224. Spicy Pear Cookies 132
225. Spicy Zucchini Oatmeal Cookies 133
226. Squash Cookies 133
227. Thanksgiving Cookies 134
228. Very Cranberry Chocolate Chip Cookies 134
229. White Chocolate Macadamia Cranberry Dreams 135
230. Yumkins 135

CHAPTER 5: CHRISTMAS COOKIE RECIPES 136

231. Almond Pretzels (Mandelplaetzchen) 136
232. Amariette Cookies 136
233. Anise Drops 137
234. Anisette Cookies I 137
235. Apple Pie Wedges 138
236. Applesauce Cookies II 138
237. Apricot Cookies 139
238. Apricot Cream Cheese Thumbprints 139
239. Apricot Fold Ups 140
240. Apricot Shortbread Bars 140
241. Aurilla's Anise Biscuit Mix Cookies 141
242. Austrian Jam Cookies 141
243. Baked Bottom Nanaimo Bars 142
244. Banana Oatmeal Cookie 143
245. Banana Rum Biscotti 143
246. Basic Gingersnap Cookies 144
247. Basic Sugar Cookies Tried And True Since 1960 144
248. Belgian Christmas Cookies 145
249. Best Chocolate Chip Cookies 145
250. Beth's Spicy Oatmeal Raisin Cookies 146
251. Betty's Sugar Cookies 146

252. Betz's Good Sugar Cookies 147
253. Big Soft Ginger Cookies 147
254. Biscotti 148
255. Black Walnut Balls 148
256. Black Walnut Cookies 149
257. Blue Ribbon Sugar Cookies 149
258. Bon Bon Christmas Cookies 150
259. Brooke's Best Bombshell Brownies 150
260. Brown Sugar Cookies 151
261. Brownie Mix In A Jar II 151
262. Buckeye Balls II 152
263. Butter Cookies IV 152
264. Butter Rich Spritz Butter Cookies 153
265. Butter Snow Flakes 153
266. Butter Tart Shortbread Bars 153
267. Candied Christmas Cookies 154
268. Candied Fruit Biscotti 154
269. Candy Cane Cookies III 155
270. Candy Cane Hot Chocolate Cookies 156
271. Caramel Brownies 156
272. Caramel Cashew Brownies 157
273. Caramel Filled Chocolate Cookies 157
274. Caramel Shortbread Squares 158
275. Cheesecake Topped Brownies 158
276. Chef John's Almond Biscotti 159
277. Cherry Bell Cookies 159
278. Cherry Mash Bars 160
279. Cherry Nanaimo Bars 161
280. Cherry Poppyseed Twinks 161
281. Cherry Shortbread Cookies 162
282. Cherry Almond Icebox Cookies 162
283. Chewy Chocolate Cookies I 163
284. Chewy White Chocolate Chip Gingerbread Cookies 163
285. Children's Gingerbread House 164
286. Chinese Christmas Cookies 165
287. Chocolate Brittle Surprise 165
288. Chocolate Caramel Brownies 166
289. Chocolate Cookie Mix In A Jar 166
290. Chocolate Cookie Nanaimo Bars 167
291. Chocolate Covered Orange Balls 168
292. Chocolate Crinkles II 168
293. Chocolate Pile Up Cookies 168
294. Chocolate Rum Balls I 169
295. Chocolate Snowballs 169
296. Chocolate Hazelnut Thumbprints 170
297. Christmas Cookie Cut Outs 170
298. Christmas Cookies II 171
299. Christmas Cornflake Wreath Cookies 172
300. Christmas Cut Out Cookies 172
301. Christmas Molasses And Ginger Cookies 173
302. Christmas Rocks 173
303. Christmas Stars 174
304. Christmas Wreaths 174
305. Cinnamon Stars 175
306. Classic Cup Christmas Cookies 176
307. Coconut Buffalo Chip Cookies 176
308. Coconut Cherry Surprise Cookies 177
309. Coconut Rum Balls 177
310. Cookie Mix In A Jar III 178
311. Cookie Pralines 178
312. Cookie In A Jar 179
313. Cowboy Cookie Mix In A Jar 179
314. Cracked Sugar Cookies I 180
315. Cranberry Almond Swirl Cheesecake Cookie Bars 180
316. Cranberry Bars 181
317. Cranberry Cashew Jumbles 182
318. Cranberry Hootycreeks 182
319. Cranberry Orange Cookies 183
320. Crazy Yummy Cranberry Pecan Cookies With Orange Glaze 183
321. Cream Cheese Christmas Cookies 184
322. Cream Cheese Sugar Cookies 185
323. Cream Tea Cakes 185
324. Crisp Anise Seed Butter Cookies 186
325. Crispy Golden Macaroons 186
326. Danish Peppernut Christmas Cookies (Pebernodder) 187
327. Date Rolls 187
328. Date Turnovers 188
329. Date And Orange Slice Bars 188
330. Date Nut Balls 189
331. Dawn's Easy Red Velvet Sandwich Cookies 189
332. Decorated Shortbread Cutouts With Nutella® Hazelnut Spread 190
333. Delicious Christmas Cookies 190
334. Dish Pan Cookies 191
335. Drommar 191
336. Dutch Cookies 192
337. Easy Lemon Cookies 192
338. Easy Nanaimo Bars 193

339. Easy Sugar Cookies 194
340. Easy Three Ingredient Gluten Free German Christmas Coconut Cookies 194
341. Easy Toffee Bars 194
342. Easy Vegan Gingerbread Cookies 195
343. Egg Yolk Painted Christmas Cookies 195
344. Eileen's Spicy Gingerbread Men 196
345. Esther's Christmas Cookies 197
346. Evelyn's Rolled Sugar Cookies 197
347. Fatty Natty's Peanut Butter Fudge Balls .198
348. Festive Fruit Squares 198
349. Festive Shortbread 199
350. Fig Filling For Pastry 199
351. Florentines II 199
352. French Peppermint Cookies With Chocolate Ganache 200
353. Fruit Meringues 201
354. German Lebkuchen 201
355. German Twists 202
356. German Walnut Shortbread Cookies 203
357. German X Mas Rum Crowns 203
358. Gingerbread Boys And Girls 204
359. Gingerbread Cookie Mix In A Jar 204
360. Gingerbread Cookies 205
361. Gingerbread Cookies I 205
362. Gingerbread Cookies II 206
363. Gingerbread Folk 207
364. Gingerbread Men 207
365. Gingerbread People From JELL O 208
366. Gluten Free Basic Sugar Cookies 208
367. Golden Honey Snaps 209
368. Gramma's Date Squares 210
369. Grandma Hasz's Christmas Cutouts 210
370. Grandma Minnie's Old Fashioned Sugar Cookies 211
371. Grandma's Cutout Sugar Cookies 211
372. Grandma's Drop Sugar Cookies 212
373. Grandma's Gingersnaps 212
374. Grandma's Raspberry Bars 213
375. Grandmom's Sand Tarts 213
376. Great Grandad's Sugar Cookies 213
377. Greek Butter Cookies 214
378. Gumbon Cookies 214
379. Hamantashen 215
380. Hatzic Bars 216
381. Hedgehog Cookies 216
382. Holiday Cookie Sandwich With Nutella® Hazelnut Spread 217
383. Holiday Lebkuchen (German Spice Cookies) 218
384. Hungarian Kiffles 218
385. Icelandic Pepper Cookies 219
386. Italian Chocolate Chip Cookies 219
387. Italian Christmas Cookies With Cocoa And Orange Liqueur 220
388. Jam Filled Butter Cookies 221
389. Jam Kolaches 221
390. Jill's World Famous Coffee Liqueur Brownies 222
391. Kolaczki 222
392. Kourambiathes (Greek Cookies) 223
393. Kourambiedes III 223
394. Krumkake I 223
395. Lebkuchen (Lep Kuchen) 224
396. Lebkuchen I 224
397. Lebkuchen II 225
398. Lebkuchen III 226
399. Liegnitzer Bomben 226
400. Lime Creams 227
401. Linzer Torte Cookies 228
402. Little Nut Cups 228
403. Macaron (French Macaroon) 229
404. Macaroons II 229
405. Magic Peanut Butter Middles 230
406. Mailaenderli 230
407. Mandelmakronen (Almond Meringues) ..231
408. Meatball Cookies 231
409. Medenjaci (Croatian Honey Spice Cookies) 232
410. Meringue Mushrooms 233
411. Meringue Springerle Cookies 233
412. Merry Cherry Bars 234
413. Michelle's Soft Sugar Cookies 235
414. Milano Style Cookies 235
415. Mint Nanaimo Bars 236
416. Minty Nanaimo Bars 236
417. Molasses Cookies VI 237
418. Molasses Crinkles 237
419. Mom's Peanut Butter Blossom Cookies ..238
420. Moravian Ginger Cookies I 238
421. Moravian Spice Cookies 239
422. Moravian Sugar Cookies 240
423. Mrs. P's Biscotti 240
424. Mrs. Ronzo's Lemon Balls 241

425. My Favorite Sugar Cookies 241
426. My Grandma's Fruitcake Cookies 242
427. Nanaimo Bars I 242
428. Nanaimo Bars II..............................243
429. No Bake Date Balls 244
430. Nonna's Pizzelle 244
431. Norway's Best Pepper Cookies 244
432. Norwegian Butter Cookies 245
433. Norwegian Krumkake 245
434. Nutella® Hazelnut Cookies 246
435. Nutella® Holiday Cookies 246
436. Oatmeal Chocolate Coconut Macaroons 247
437. Oatmeal Thumbprints..........................247
438. Old Fashioned Butter Cookies With Butter Frosting..248
439. Old Fashioned Sugar Cookies In A Jar ...248
440. Old German Polish Recipe For Lebkuchen (Christmas Cookies)..................................249
441. Oma Kiener's Hazelnut Christmas Cookies 250
442. One Oh One Cookies 250
443. Orange Cardamom Krumkake 251
444. Orange Drop Cookies II......................251
445. Orange Pizzelle 252
446. Orange Spiced Krumkake.......................252
447. Original Cheese Tempters 253
448. Original Nestle® Toll House Chocolate Chip Cookies 253
449. Peanut Butter Balls III 254
450. Peanut Butter Balls IV.......................254
451. Peanut Butter Bars I 254
452. Peanut Butter Christmas Mice 255
453. Peanut Butter Temptations II.................255
454. Peanut Butter And Jelly Thumbprint Cookies...256
455. Peanut Surprise Cookies 257
456. Pebber Nodder (Danish Christmas Cookies) 257
457. Pecan Turtles® Bars..........................258
458. Pennsylvania Snow Drops......................258
459. Pepparkakor I 259
460. Peppermint Bars..............................259
461. Peppermint Chocolate Chip Cookies 260
462. Peppermint Lace Cookies......................261
463. Peppermint Meringues 261
464. Peppermint Patties...........................262
465. Peppermint Rice Crispies Squares...........262

466. Peppermint Snowballs.........................263
467. Perfect Coconut Macaroons....................263
468. Perfect Double Chocolate Peanut Candy Cookies..264
469. Perfect Gingerbread Cookies..................264
470. Perfect Vegan Sugar Cookies 265
471. Persimmon Cookies III........................266
472. Pfeffernuesse Cookie Mix.....................266
473. Pfeffernusse 267
474. Pfeffernusse Cookies 267
475. Pfeffernusse Cookies II 268
476. Pfeffernusse Kuchen 268
477. Pistachio Cream Cheese Fingers...............269
478. Polish Christmas Cookies 269
479. Poppy Seed Pinwheels.........................270
480. Quick Mix Spritz.............................270
481. Raisin Coconut Treasure Cookies 271
482. Raisin Squares 271
483. Raspberry Thumbprint Cookies 272
484. Raspberry And Almond Shortbread Thumbprints..272
485. Raw Vegan Gingerbread Balls 273
486. Red Velvet Chocolate Chip Cookies........273
487. Red's Date Loaf With Coconut (Frying Pan Cookies)...274
488. Robin's Nests................................274
489. Romance Bars.................................275
490. Rosenmunnar..................................275
491. Rosettes I...................................276
492. Rum Balls I..................................276
493. Rum Balls III 277
494. Rum Sugar Cookies 277
495. Rum Or Bourbon Balls.........................278
496. Rumherzen....................................278
497. Russian Tea Cakes I..........................279
498. Sand Tarts 279
499. Scandinavian Almond Bars.....................280
500. Scandinavian Snowflake Cookies 280
501. Shorecook's Chocolate Peppermint Biscotti 281
502. Shortbread Christmas Cookies 282
503. Shulie Krinkles..............................283
504. Snow Balls In A Jar..........................283
505. Snow Flakes 283
506. Snowballs II 284
507. Soft Christmas Cookies.......................284
508. Sour Cream Cut Outs..........................285

509. Sour Cream Spritz 285
510. Speculaas Cookies Or Spicy Sinterklass Cakes 286
511. Spicy Ginger Cookies 286
512. Spoon Cookies 287
513. Springerle I 287
514. Springerle II 288
515. Springerle V 288
516. Springerle VII 289
517. Spumoni Chocolate Chip Cookies 289
518. Storybook Gingerbread Men 290
519. Strufoli I 290
520. Sugar Cookies IV 291
521. Sugar Cookies XII 291
522. Sugar Cookies With Buttercream Frosting 292
523. Sugar Free Christmas Cutouts 292
524. Sugar And Spice Cookies 293
525. Swedish Rye Cookies 293
526. Swedish Spritzs 294
527. Swedish Wedding Cakes 294
528. Swiss Hazelnut Taler 295
529. Tender Crisp Sugar Cookies 295
530. The Best Rolled Sugar Cookies 296
531. The Cookie Jar 296
532. Tina's Shortbread Chocolate Chip Cookies 297
533. Tiny Tarts 297
534. Tyler's Raspberry Thumbprints With White Chocolate Glaze 298
535. Vanilla Kifli 298
536. Vanille Kipferl I 299
537. Vanillekipferl 300
538. Vegan Chocolate Spelt Biscotti 300
539. Viennese Crescent Holiday Cookies 301
540. Wainachsrollen 302
541. Walnut Cheesecake Cookies 302
542. Walnut Tassies 303
543. White Chocolate Hazelnut Spread Bars ..303
544. White Chocolate Holiday Spritz Cookies 304
545. White Chocolate Thumbprint Cookies ...305
546. White Chocolate And Cranberry Cookies 305
547. Whole Wheat Ginger Snaps 306
548. Working Mom's Hamentashen 306
549. Yum Yum Squares 307

CHAPTER 6: AWESOME HOLIDAY COOKIE RECIPES 307

550. After Dinner Mint Delights 307
551. Almond Chocolate Cookies 308
552. Almond Crescent Cookies 308
553. Almond Macaroons 309
554. Almond Meringue Cookies 309
555. Almond Sugar Cookies 310
556. Ambrosia Bites 310
557. Anise Butter Cookies 311
558. Anise Cutout Cookies 311
559. Anise Spritz Cookies 312
560. Apple Butter Cookies 312
561. Apple Crisp Crescents 313
562. Apricot Tea Cookies 313
563. Apricot Thumbprints 314
564. Apricot Hazelnut Triangles 315
565. Behr Track Cookie Bars 315
566. Best Sour Cream Sugar Cookies 316
567. Best Ever Sugar Cookies 317
568. Black Forest Thumbprint Cookies 317
569. Black Walnut Butter Cookies 318
570. Blackberry Peekaboo Cookies 318
571. Blue Moon Crescent Cookies 319
572. Brandy Snap Cannoli 319
573. Brown Butter Spice Cookies 320
574. Brown Sugar Cutout Cookies 321
575. Brown Sugar Cutouts 321
576. Brownie Biscotti 322
577. Brownie Bourbon Bites 323
578. Butter Ball Chiffons 323
579. Butter Cookies 323
580. Butterscotch Eggnog Stars 324
581. Butterscotch Shortbread 324
582. Buttersweets 325
583. Buttery Potato Chip Cookies 326
584. Calypso Cups 326
585. Candied Cherry Hermits 327
586. Candy Cane Blossom Cookies 327
587. Caramel Chocolate Cookies 328
588. Caroling Fortune Cookies 328
589. Cashew Cookies 329
590. Cashew Sandwich Cookies 329
591. Cashew Tassie Cups 330
592. Chai Chocolate Chip Shortbread 330
593. Cherry & Macadamia Nut Cookies 331

594. Cherry Almond Chews 332
595. Cherry Bonbon Cookies 332
596. Cherry Cookies 333
597. Cherry Kiss Cookies 333
598. Cherry Pecan Chews 334
599. Cherry Surprise Cookies 334
600. Cherry Chocolate Coconut Meringues 335
601. Chevron Ornament Cookies 335
602. Chewy Almond Cookies 336
603. Chewy Chocolate Cookies 336
604. Chewy Fruit Cookies 337
605. Chocolate Almond Crescents 337
606. Chocolate Almond Drops 338
607. Chocolate Almond Wafers 338
608. Chocolate Cake Mix Cookies 339
609. Chocolate Caramel Kiss Cookies 339
610. Chocolate Cherry Cookies 340
611. Chocolate Chip Cherry Oatmeal Cookies 340
612. Chocolate Chip Meringue Cookies 341
613. Chocolate Chip Oat Cookies 342
614. Chocolate Chip Peanut Butter Cookies ... 342
615. Chocolate Chip Pistachio Cookies 343
616. Chocolate Coconut Neapolitans 344
617. Chocolate Double Chip Cookies 344
618. Chocolate Drops 345
619. Chocolate Fruit N Nut Cookies 345
620. Chocolate Gingerbread Cookie Mix 346
621. Chocolate Gingersnaps 346
622. Chocolate Hazelnut Shortbread 347
623. Chocolate Hazelnut Tassies 347
624. Chocolate Hazelnut Thumbprints 348
625. Chocolate Island Cookies 348
626. Chocolate Lebkuchen 349
627. Chocolate Lover's Drop Cookies 350
628. Chocolate Maple Cookies 350
629. Chocolate Marshmallow Meltaways 351
630. Chocolate Orange Checkerboard Cookies 351
631. Chocolate Orange Cookies 352
632. Chocolate Peanut Butter Thumbprints ... 352
633. Chocolate Peppermint Pinwheels 353
634. Chocolate Peppermint Snaps 354
635. Chocolate Pretzel Cookies 354
636. Chocolate Pretzels 355
637. Chocolate Thumbprints Cookies 355
638. Chocolate Almond Thumbprints 356
639. Chocolate Cherry Sandwich Cookies 356
640. Chocolate Cherry Thumbprint Cookies .. 357
641. Chocolate Covered Cherry Delights 358
642. Chocolate Covered Maraschino Cherry Cookies 358
643. Chocolate Dipped Cookies 359
644. Chocolate Dipped Macaroons 359
645. Chocolate Dipped Orange Spritz 360
646. Chocolate Dipped Spritz 361
647. Chocolate Dipped Triple Ginger Cookies 361
648. Chocolate Mint Cookie Cups 362
649. Chocolate Mint Hearts 363
650. Chocolate Raspberry Cutout Cookies 363
651. Chocolate Tipped Butter Cookies 364
652. Christmas Cookie Train 364
653. Christmas Cookies In A Jar 365
654. Christmas Eve Mice 366
655. Christmas Lights Sugar Cookies 366
656. Christmas Mice Cookies 367
657. Christmas Molasses Cookies 368
658. Christmas Wreath Cookies 368
659. Cinnamon Chocolate Minties 369
660. Cinnamon White & Dark Chocolate Chip Cookies 369
661. Classic Crisp Sugar Cookies 370
662. Cocoa Brownie Cookies 370
663. Coconut Cherry Sandies 371
664. Coconut Christmas Mice 372
665. Coconut Cranberry Yummies 372
666. Coconut Pecan Joys 372
667. Coconut Macadamia Biscotti 373
668. Cookie Jar Gingersnaps 374
669. Cookie Pops 374
670. Cookies With Pecans 375
671. Cornmeal Lime Cookies 375
672. Cran Orange Cookies 376
673. Cran Orange Oatmeal Cookies 376
674. Cranberry Almond Macaroons 377
675. Cranberry Chocolate Cookies With A Kick 377
676. Cranberry Cookies With Browned Butter Glaze 378
677. Cranberry Crispies 378
678. Cranberry Drop Cookies 379
679. Cranberry Orange Pinwheels 379
680. Cranberry Pecan Cookies 380

681. Cranberry Pecan Oatmeal Cookies 381
682. Cranberry Pecan Sandies............................381
683. Cranberry And Pistachio Biscotti 382
684. Cranberry Cashew Drop Cookies 382
685. Cranberry Chocolate Chip Cookie Mix ...383
686. Cranberry Pistachio Cookie Cups 383
687. Cranberry White Chocolate Cookies 384
688. Cream Cheese Cutouts...............................384
689. Cream Cheese Slice And Bake Cookies...385
690. Cream Filberts 386
691. Creepy Spiders 386
692. Crisp Lemon Cookies..................................387
693. Crispy Coconut Balls..................................387
694. Crispy Gingerbread.....................................388
695. Cutout Sugar Cookies.................................388
696. Daria's Best Ever Sugar Cookies 389
697. Date Nut Pinwheels....................................389
698. Decorated Butter Cookies 390
699. Decorated Sugar Cookie Cutouts............391
700. Deluxe Sugar Cookies 391
701. Diamond Almond Bars...............................392
702. Dipped Lemon Spritz.................................392
703. Dipped Spice Cookies 393
704. Double Butterscotch Cookies 394
705. Double Dipped Shortbread Cookies 394
706. Double Drizzled Biscotti 395
707. Dried Cherry Biscotti 395
708. Drizzled Gingerbread Biscotti 396
709. Dutch Speculaas 397
710. Dutch Spice Cookies 397
711. Easy Bizcochitos 398
712. Easy Chocolate Gingerbread Cutouts 398
713. Ellen's Edible Gingerbread House...........399
714. Fancy Butter Cookies 400
715. Fancy Sugar Cookies 401
716. Favorite Molasses Cookies 402
717. Festive Cranberry Oat Cookies................402
718. Fig Filled Cookies 403
719. Filled Chocolate Spritz 403
720. Flourless Peanut Butter Cookies 404
721. French Noisette Cups 404
722. French Toast Spirals...................................405
723. Frieda's Molasses Cookies 406
724. Frosted Anise Cookies 406
725. Frosted Cashew Cookies...........................407
726. Frosted Cherry Chip Cookies 407
727. Frosted Cutout Sugar Cookies.................408
728. Frosted Ginger Creams..............................408
729. Frosted Gingerbread Nut Cookies..........409
730. Frosted Oatmeal Cookies 410
731. Frosted Peanut Butter Cookies................410
732. Frosted Pumpkin Cookies 411
733. Frosted Sour Cream Cutouts 411
734. Fruit Filled Spritz Cookies........................412
735. Fruitcake Cookies With Rum Glaze 413
736. Fudge Filled Toffee Cookies....................413
737. Fudge Topped Orange Cookies 414
738. Fudgy Pinwheel Cookies...........................415
739. Full Of Chips Cookies 415
740. German Chocolate Tassies 416
741. German Chocolate Thumbprints 417
742. German Christmas Cookies 417
743. Ginger Diamonds 418
744. Ginger Shortbread Cookies 418
745. Ginger Macadamia Nut Snowballs..........419
746. Gingerbread Barn.......................................420
747. Gingerbread Boys 422
748. Gingerbread Christmas Cutouts 423
749. Gingerbread Cookie Bites 423
750. Gingerbread Cookie Wreath 424
751. Gingerbread Cookies With Buttercream Icing 425
752. Gingerbread Crisp Cutouts 425
753. Gingerbread Cutout Cookies 426
754. Gingerbread House Cookies 426
755. Gingerbread Oatmeal Cookies 427
756. Gingerbread Rings.....................................428
757. Gingerbread Snowflakes 428
758. Gingerbread Spritz.....................................429
759. Gingerbread Star Tree 430
760. Gingerbread Teddy Bears 431
761. Gingerbread Tree Recipe 432
762. Gingerbread Yule Logs 433
763. Gingersnap Cream Cookie Cups 433
764. Glazed Apple Cookies...............................434
765. Glazed Butter Cookies 435
766. Glazed Cherry Bon Bon Cookies 435
767. Glazed Maple Shortbread Cookies.........436
768. Gluten Free Almond Crispies 436
769. Gluten Free Peanut Butter Kiss Cookies 437
770. Gluten Free Sugar Cookies.......................437
771. Goblin Chewies..438
772. Golden Raisin Cookies..............................439
773. Golden Thumbprints 439

774. Good Fortune & Cheer Cookies 440
775. Grandma's Christmas Spice Cutouts 440
776. Grandma's Sugar Cookies 441
777. Harveys Coconut Macaroons 441
778. Hazelnut Chocolate Chip Pizzelle 442
779. Hazelnut Chocolate Cookies 442
780. Hazelnut Crescents 443
781. Hazelnut Shortbread Hearts 443
782. Hazelnut Mocha Bonbon Cookies 444
783. Holiday Bells 444
784. Holiday Biscotti 445
785. Holiday Butter Mint Cookies 446
786. Holiday Eggnog Snickerdoodles 446
787. Holiday Meringue Miniatures 447
788. Holiday Miniatures 447
789. Holiday Pinwheels 448
790. Holiday Sandwich Cookies 448
791. Holiday Shortbread 449
792. Holiday Spritz Wreaths 449
793. Homemade Honey Grahams 450
794. Homemade Lemon Sugar Cookies 450
795. Homemade Macaroon Kisses 451
796. Honey Crunch Cookies 451
797. Honey Date Pumpkin Cookies 452
798. Ice Cream Kolachkes 453
799. Icebox Sugar Cookies 453
800. Iced Orange Cutouts 454
801. Italian Lemon Cookies 454
802. Italian Sesame Cookies 455
803. Italian Spumoni Cookies 455
804. Jam Filled Wreaths & Hearts 456
805. Jelly Topped Sugar Cookies 456
806. Kipplens 457
807. Kris Humphries' Mom's Small Chocolate Chip Butter Cookies 457
808. Lace Cookies With Chocolate Middles 458
809. Lactose Free Chocolate Chip Cookies 458
810. Lemon Lover's Cookies 459
811. Lemon Pistachio Wreaths 460
812. Lemon Poppy Seed Cookies 460
813. Lemon Shortbread Cookies 461
814. Lemon Shortbread Trees 462
815. Lemon Snowballs Cookie 462
816. Lemon Stars 463
817. Lemon Thins 463
818. Lemon Cream Sandwich Cookies 464
819. Lemon Lime Butter Cookies 465
820. Lemony Bonbon Cookies 465
821. Lemony Coconut Bars 466
822. Lime Christmas Tea Cookies 467
823. Linzer Cookies 467
824. Macadamia Almond Delights 468
825. Macadamia Coffee Bean Cookies 469
826. Magic Stars 469
827. Maple Macadamia Nut Cookies 470
828. Maple Walnut Biscotti 470
829. Mayan Chocolate Biscotti 471
830. Midnight Moon Pies 472
831. Mini Baklava 472
832. Mini Cinnamon Roll Cookies 473
833. Mint Chocolate Snaps 473
834. Mint Chocolate Wafers 474
835. Minty Meringue Drops 474
836. Mocha Butterscotch Cookies 475
837. Mocha Fudge Cookies 475
838. Mocha Nut Balls 476
839. Mocha Pecan Butter Balls 477
840. Molasses Cookie Mix 477
841. Molasses Sugar Cookies 478
842. Mom's Old Fashioned Cutouts 478
843. Mom's Soft Raisin Cookies 479
844. Nativity Molasses Cookies 479
845. Nice 'n' Soft Sugar Cookies 480
846. No Bake Cookie Butter Blossoms 481
847. No Bake Peanut Butter Snowballs 481
848. Nut Filled Horns 481
849. Nutmeg Meltaways 482
850. Nutmeg Sugar Crisps 482
851. Nuts About You Cookie Sticks 483
852. Nutty Chocolate Batons 483
853. Nutty Maple Cookies 484
854. Oat & Coconut Icebox Cookies 484
855. Oatmeal Peanut Butter Chip Cookies 485
856. Oatmeal Pecan Cookie Mix 486
857. Oatmeal Sandwich Cookies 486
858. Old Fashioned Gingersnaps 487
859. Old Fashioned Mincemeat Cookies 487
860. Old Fashioned Oatmeal Cookies 488
861. Old Fashioned Oatmeal Raisin Cookies . 488
862. Olive Oil Cookies 489
863. Orange Cocoa Sandies 489
864. Orange Marmalade Linzer Tarts 490
865. Orange Sugar Cookies 490
866. Orange Cranberry Nut Tarts 491

867. Orange Cranberry Shortbread 492
868. Outrageous Chocolate Mint Cookies 492
869. Panforte Cookie Cups 493
870. Peanut Butter Blossom Cookies 493
871. Peanut Butter Chip Cookie 494
872. Peanut Butter Cookies 494
873. Peanut Butter Treats 495
874. Peanut Butter Filled Cookies 495
875. Peanut Chocolate Chip Cookies 496
876. Peanut Oat Cookies 496
877. Pecan Horns 497
878. Pecan Meltaways 497
879. Pecan Pie Cookies 498
880. Pecan Pie Thumbprints 499
881. Pecan Topped Sugar Cookies 499
882. Peppermint Biscotti 500
883. Peppermint Candy Cane Cookies 500
884. Peppermint Meltaways 501
885. Peppermint Ribbon Cookies 501
886. Peppermint Kissed Fudge Mallow Cookies 502
887. Pfeffernuesse Cookies 503
888. Pine Nut Thumbprints 503
889. Pistachio Cookies 504
890. Pistachio Pinwheels 505
891. Pistachio Cranberry Rugelach 505
892. Pistachio Mint Meringue Cookies 506
893. Poinsettia Pinwheel Cookies 506
894. Pumpkin Cookies With Cream Cheese Frosting 507
895. Pumpkin Cookies With Penuche Frosting 508
896. Pumpkin Pecan Tassies 508
897. Pumpkin Spice Cookies 509
898. Pumpkin Whoopie Pies 509
899. Pumpkin Chocolate Whoopie Cookies ... 510
900. Quick Cranberry Chip Cookies 511
901. Quick Fruitcake Cookies 511
902. Raisin Bran Chewies Cookies 512
903. Raisin Filled Cookies 512
904. Raspberry & Pink Peppercorn Meringues 513
905. Raspberry Almonettes 513
906. Raspberry Chocolate Rugelach 514
907. Raspberry Coconut Balls 515
908. Raspberry Cream Sugar Cookies 515
909. Raspberry Kisses 516
910. Raspberry Meringues 516
911. Raspberry Nut Pinwheels 517
912. Raspberry Pistachio Thumbprints 517
913. Red & Green Pinwheels 518
914. Refrigerator Cookies 518
915. Reindeer Track Cookies 519
916. Rosettes 519
917. Rugelach 520
918. Rum Balls 520
919. Sally Ann Cookies 521
920. Salted Butterscotch & Pecan No Bakes .. 522
921. Salted Caramel Fudge Drops 522
922. Salted Cashew Oatmeal Cookies 523
923. Santa's Coming Cookie Puzzle 523
924. Santa's Fruit & Nut Cookies 524
925. Santa's Sugar Cookies 524
926. Santa's Wake Up Cookies 525
927. Scottie Cookies 525
928. Scrumptious Sugar Cookies 526
929. Shortbread Ornament Cookies 527
930. Silver Bells 528
931. Simple Sugar Cookies 528
932. Sledding Teddies 529
933. Slice & Bake Chocolate Pecan Cookies ... 530
934. Slice & Bake Orange Spice Wafers 530
935. Snickerdoodles 531
936. Snow Day Cookies 531
937. Snow Capped Mocha Fudge Drops 532
938. Snow Topped White Chocolate Macadamia Cookies 532
939. Snowcapped Gingerbread Biscotti 533
940. Snowman Christmas Cookies 534
941. Snowman Cutouts 534
942. Snowy Mountain Cookies 535
943. Snowy Pinecones 536
944. Soft Buttermilk Sugar Cookies 536
945. Soft Chocolate Mint Cookies 537
946. Soft Lemon Ginger Cookies 537
947. Soft Macaroons 538
948. Soft Sugar Cookie Puffs 538
949. Soft Sugar Cookies 539
950. Soft And Chewy Molasses Cookies 539
951. Sour Cream Cutouts 540
952. Sour Cream Sugar Cookies 540
953. Special Oatmeal Chip Cookies 541
954. Spiced Brownie Bites 541
955. Spiced Christmas Cookies 542

956. Spiced Molasses Doughnut Cookies........543
957. Spicy Molasses Cookies..............................543
958. Spritz Wreaths 544
959. Star Anise Honey Cookies.........................544
960. Star Sandwich Cookies 545
961. Sugar Cookie Cutouts..................................545
962. Sugar Diamonds..546
963. Sugared Cherry Jewels.................................546
964. Super Chunky Cookies................................547
965. Super Snowman Cookies............................548
966. Surefire Sugar Cookies 548
967. Surprise Meringues 549
968. Surprise Sugar Stars 549
969. Swedish Spritz Cookies 550
970. Sweet Taste Of Victory Butterscotch Cookies 550
971. Sweetheart Slices 551
972. Tender Italian Sugar Cookies 551
973. Tender Sugar Cookies 552
974. Toasted Anise Strips.....................................552
975. Toffee Cranberry Crisps 553
976. Torcetti 553
977. Trail Mix Cookie Cups 554
978. Treasure Cookies...554
979. Triple Chip Cookies.....................................555
980. Triple Nut Snowballs...................................555
981. Two Minute Cookies 556
982. Two Tone Christmas Cookies 556
983. Vanilla Crescent Cookies 557
984. Vegan Chocolate Chip Cookies................557
985. Versatile Slice 'n' Bake Cookies 558
986. Vienna Triangles..558
987. Waffle Cookies 559
988. Walnut Filled Pillows...................................560
989. White Almond No Bake Cookies.............560
990. White Chocolate Chip Hazelnut Cookies 561
991. White Chocolate Cran Pecan Cookies.....561
992. White Chocolate Cranberry Cookies 562
993. White Chocolate Pumpkin Dreams 562
994. White Chocolate Star Sandwich Cookies 563
995. White Chocolate Cranberry Biscotti 564
996. Whoopie Cookies..564
997. Winning Cranberry Chip Cookies 565
998. Winter Wonderland Gingerbread Cottage 565
999. Yule Log Cookies..567
1000. Yummy Chocolate Double Chip Cookies 568
1001. "Home Sweet Home" Gingerbread Cottage 568

INDEX..571
CONCLUSION..576

Chapter 1: Valentine'S Day Cookie Recipes

***

1. Alsatian Chocolate Balls

Serving: 30 | Prep: | Cook: | Ready in:

Ingredients

- 2 eggs
- 2/3 cup white sugar
- 4 (1 ounce) squares unsweetened chocolate
- 1/2 teaspoon ground cinnamon
- 1 teaspoon vanilla extract
- 1/3 cup all-purpose flour
- 2 3/8 cups ground almonds
- 1/3 cup confectioners' sugar for decoration

Direction

- Beat sugar and eggs until fluffy and light. Grate the squares of chocolate and transfer to the egg mixture. Add the rest of the ingredients and beat thoroughly. Form into a ball. Refrigerate for at least 1 hour.
- Form the chilled dough into small balls (around 3/4 inch in diameter). Then roll each in the sifted confectioners' sugar.
- Put the balls in a greased baking sheet and let to dry in warm spot (kitchen) for about 4 to 5 hours. Bake for 3-5 minutes at 245 degrees C (475 degrees F). Let to cool for 10 minutes in baking pan.

Nutrition Information

- Calories: 129 calories;
- Total Fat: 9.1
- Sodium: 6
- Total Carbohydrate: 10.7
- Cholesterol: 12
- Protein: 3.9

2. Bethany's Favorite Valentine Cut Out Sugar Cookies

Serving: 12 | Prep: 15mins | Cook: 10mins | Ready in:

Ingredients

- 1 cup butter, softened
- 1 cup white sugar
- 1 egg, beaten
- 2 tablespoons milk
- 1 teaspoon vanilla extract
- 1/2 teaspoon almond extract
- 2 1/2 cups flour
- 1 teaspoon baking powder

Direction

- In a large bowl, cream almond extract, vanilla extract, milk, egg, sugar and butter together.
- Mix in baking powder and flour.
- Put into the refrigerator with a cover for 2 hours until firm.
- Turn on the oven to 400°F (200°C) to preheat.
- Cut the dough into 3 pieces. Roll out each piece on a lightly floured surface until they are 1/4-inch thick.
- Use a floured cookie cutter to cut cookies.
- On an ungreased baking sheet, place cookies 1-inch away from each other.
- Put into the oven to bake for 6-9 minutes until lightly golden.
- Allow to cool completely on a wire rack.

Nutrition Information

- Calories: 304 calories;
- Total Fat: 16.1
- Sodium: 157
- Total Carbohydrate: 36.8
- Cholesterol: 56
- Protein: 3.5

3. Boyfriend Brownies

Serving: 16 | Prep: 15mins | Cook: 45mins | Ready in:

Ingredients

- 1 1/2 cups all-purpose flour
- 1 teaspoon baking soda
- 1/2 teaspoon salt
- 1 1/2 cups white sugar
- 1/4 cup water
- 2/3 cup butter
- 1 (12 ounce) bag semisweet chocolate chips
- 2 teaspoons vanilla extract
- 4 eggs
- 1 (12 ounce) bag semisweet chocolate chips
- 1 cup coarsely chopped walnuts

Direction

- Set oven to 165°C (325°F). In a small bowl, mix salt, baking soda and flour; put aside. Grease a 9-in. square baking dish and dust with flour.
- In a saucepan, mix together butter, water and sugar. Place over medium heat, cook while stirring to melt butter and dissolve sugar. Take away from the heat and mix in vanilla extract and 1 bag of chocolate chips until chocolate is melted. Transfer the mixture to a mixing bowl; pour in eggs, one at a time, beating until smooth. Fold in flour mixture until combined; fold in walnuts and the remaining chocolate chips bag. Transfer to the prepped pan.
- Bake at 165°C (325°F) for 45-55 minutes, until edges begin to pull away from the pan's sides and the top is dry. Allow to cool entirely and slice into square pieces before serving.

Nutrition Information

- Calories: 451 calories;
- Protein: 5.7
- Total Fat: 26.4
- Sodium: 228
- Total Carbohydrate: 55.4
- Cholesterol: 67

4. Brownies V

Serving: 32 | Prep: 10mins | Cook: 45mins | Ready in:

Ingredients

- 1 cup butter
- 8 (1 ounce) squares unsweetened baking chocolate
- 4 eggs
- 1 1/2 cups packed brown sugar
- 1 1/2 cups white sugar
- 2 teaspoons vanilla extract
- 2 teaspoons orange zest
- 6 tablespoons brandy-based orange liqueur (such as Grand Marnier®)
- 1 1/2 cups all-purpose flour
- 1 cup semisweet chocolate chips
- 1 cup chopped walnuts (optional)

Direction

- Preheat the oven to 175°C or 350°F. Grease and spread flour onto a 9x13-in. baking dish.
- Melt butter over medium heat in a medium saucepan. Add in the unsweetened chocolate squares and stir till smooth and melted completely. Take away from the heat and put aside till cool.
- Beat eggs in a large bowl till fluffy and light then slowly add in white sugar and brown sugar. Keep beating for 3 minutes. Stir in Grand Marnier, orange zest, vanilla and the melted chocolate mixture. Gradually mix in flour on low speed then use your hand to fold

in nuts and chocolate chips. Evenly spread the batter in the prepped pan.
- Bake in the preheated oven for 45 minutes till the top feels firm when touched and the sides are slightly dry. Let the brownies cool then slice into squares. You can store these at room temperature, covered.

Nutrition Information

- Calories: 251 calories;
- Sodium: 55
- Total Carbohydrate: 31.1
- Cholesterol: 39
- Protein: 3.1
- Total Fat: 14.1

---

5. Butter Crisps

Serving: 12 | Prep: | Cook: |Ready in:

Ingredients

- 1 cup butter
- 1/2 (8 ounce) package cream cheese
- 1 cup white sugar
- 1 egg
- 1 teaspoon vanilla extract
- 2 1/2 cups all-purpose flour
- 1/2 teaspoon baking powder

Direction

- Cream butter and cream cheese together. Put in egg and sugar gradually, keep on beating until combined.
- Gradually put baking powder and flour into cream cheese mixture, then refrigerate dough about 1 to 2 hours.
- On a board coated with flour, roll out the dough and cut in preferred shapes. Bake at 175°C or 350°F until light brown, about 12 minutes. Use desired frosting to frost.

Nutrition Information

- Calories: 335 calories;
- Total Fat: 19.3
- Sodium: 163
- Total Carbohydrate: 36.9
- Cholesterol: 66
- Protein: 4.1

---

6. Chef John's Chili Chocolate Cookies

Serving: 12 | Prep: 20mins | Cook: 15mins |Ready in:

Ingredients

- 1/2 cup dried currants
- 2 tablespoons coffee flavored liqueur (such as Kahlua®)
- 4 ounces unsweetened chocolate
- 2 ounces bittersweet chocolate
- 3 tablespoons unsalted butter
- 1/2 cup all-purpose flour
- 1/2 teaspoon freshly ground black pepper
- 1/4 teaspoon baking powder
- 1/4 teaspoon salt
- 1/8 teaspoon ground cinnamon
- 1/8 teaspoon cayenne pepper
- 3/4 cup sugar
- 2 eggs
- 2 teaspoons vanilla extract
- 1 cup dark chocolate chips

Direction

- Preheat an oven to 175°C/350°F.
- Line silicone baking mats/parchment paper on 2 baking sheets.
- Heat coffee liqueur and currants in saucepan on low heat for 2 minutes till it starts to simmer; take off heat. Put aside.
- Mix butter, bittersweet chocolate and unsweetened chocolate in bowl; put bowl over saucepan with 1-in. water on low heat.

Occasionally mix chocolate mixture for 5 minutes till melted; take off heat. Put aside.
- Mix cayenne pepper, cinnamon, salt, baking powder, black pepper and flour in big bowl; put aside.
- Whisk egg and sugar till pale yellow, fluffy and light for 5 minutes in small bowl; whisk melted chocolate mixture and vanilla in slowly.
- Fold the flour mixture into chocolate and sugar mixture till combined.
- Mix liqueur soaked currants and dark chocolate chips in.
- Drop spoonfuls cookie dough on prepped baking sheets, 2-in. apart.
- In preheated oven, bake for 12 minutes till cookies are nearly set.
- Take out of oven; leave on baking sheets for 5 minutes to cool.
- Put on cooling rack; finish cooling for 5 minutes.

Nutrition Information

- Calories: 272 calories;
- Sodium: 74
- Total Carbohydrate: 36.4
- Cholesterol: 35
- Protein: 3.9
- Total Fat: 14.3

7. Cherry Cheesecake Hearts

Serving: 36 | Prep: 30mins | Cook: 8mins | Ready in:

Ingredients

- 1 cup butter, softened
- 1 (8 ounce) package cream cheese, softened
- 1 1/2 cups white sugar
- 1 egg
- 1 teaspoon vanilla extract
- 1 (0.13 ounce) package unsweetened cherry-flavored soft drink mix (such as Kool-Aid®)
- 1/2 teaspoon almond extract
- 3 1/2 cups all-purpose flour
- 1 teaspoon baking powder
- 1/4 teaspoon salt
- 1 teaspoon maraschino cherry juice, or as needed (optional)
- 1 teaspoon milk, or as needed (optional)
- 1 teaspoon lemon juice, or as needed (optional)

Direction

- In a bowl, mix cream cheese and butter until the mixture is creamy and smooth. Put in sugar; mix until fluffy and turning pale yellow in color. Put in almond extract, soft drink mix, vanilla extract and egg; beat thoroughly.
- In a bowl, sift salt, baking powder and flour. Pour into the beaten mixture; blend until fully combined. Pour in lemon juice, milk or maraschino cherry juice to make the dough loose; stir until combined. Split into 2 equal pieces; use plastic to wrap and chill for two hours or overnight.
- Set oven to 190°C (375°F) and start preheating. Use parchment paper to line two baking sheets.
- On a surface slightly dusted with flour, roll out cookie dough to 1/4 to 1/8-inch thick. Use a cookie cutter in a heart shape to cut out the dough; place on the baking sheets.
- Bake for 8-10 minutes at 190°C (375°F) until the cookies turn golden in color. Place on a wire rack to cool for 15 minutes.

Nutrition Information

- Calories: 146 calories;
- Total Fat: 7.5
- Sodium: 88
- Total Carbohydrate: 17.9
- Cholesterol: 26
- Protein: 2

8. Chocolate Black Tea Cake

Serving: 12 | Prep: 20mins | Cook: 1hours | Ready in:

Ingredients

- 4 eggs, separated
- 1 cup butter
- 1 2/3 cups white sugar
- 1 cup brewed black tea, cold
- 2 cups all-purpose flour
- 1 1/2 tablespoons baking powder
- 1/3 cup dry bread crumbs
- 1/3 cup unsweetened cocoa powder
- 1 cup chopped hazelnuts

Direction

- Set the oven at 360°F (180°C) and start preheating. Coat a 9-in. Bundt pan with grease and flour.
- Cream white sugar, butter and egg yolks together in a large bowl till fluffy and light. Slowly beat in black tea. Toss hazelnuts, cocoa powder, bread crumbs, baking powder and flour together; fold into the tea mixture till just incorporated.
- Whip egg whites till it forms stiff peaks in a large clean metal bowl or glass bowl. Fold the egg whites into the tea batter. Transfer the batter into the prepared pan.
- Bake in the preheated oven for 60-70 minutes, or till a toothpick comes out clean when inserted into the center. Allow the cake to cool for at least 20 minutes in the pan; remove and let cool completely on a wire rack.

Nutrition Information

- Calories: 421 calories;
- Sodium: 282
- Total Carbohydrate: 49.3
- Cholesterol: 103
- Protein: 6.7
- Total Fat: 23.5

9. Chocolate Chip Meringue

Serving: 24 | Prep: | Cook: | Ready in:

Ingredients

- 3 egg whites
- 1 cup white sugar
- 1/2 teaspoon distilled white vinegar
- 1/2 teaspoon vanilla extract
- 1 pinch salt
- 2 cups semisweet chocolate chips

Direction

- Set oven to 300° F (150° C) to preheat. Line baking sheets with parchment paper or grease them.
- Whip egg whites in a medium bowl until soft peaks form. Slowly put in the vanilla, vinegar and sugar while whipping until stiff peaks form. Fold in the chocolate chips. Drop onto the prepared cookie sheets by spoonfuls.
- Bake in the prepared oven for 20 to 25 minutes, until cookies turn dry.

Nutrition Information

- Calories: 102 calories;
- Sodium: 8
- Total Carbohydrate: 17.2
- Cholesterol: 0
- Protein: 1
- Total Fat: 4.2

10. Chocolate Kiss Cookies

Serving: 36 | Prep: 20mins | Cook: 12mins | Ready in:

Ingredients

- 1 cup margarine, softened
- 1/2 cup white sugar

- 1 teaspoon vanilla extract
- 1 3/4 cups all-purpose flour
- 1 cup finely chopped walnuts
- 1 (6 ounce) bag milk chocolate candy kisses
- 1/3 cup confectioners' sugar for decoration

Direction

- Whip margarine with vanilla and sugar in a big bowl until light and fluffy. Stir in walnuts and flour, whipping on low speed with an electric mixer until thoroughly combined. Cover and chill for 2 hours, or until hard enough to handle.
- Set oven to 375°F (190°C) to preheat.
- Discard chocolate kisses' wrappers. Form 1 tablespoon of dough around each chocolate kiss; completely cover the chocolate. Put cookies on an ungreased cookie tray.
- Bake in the prepared oven for 10 to 12 minutes. Toss them in confectioners' sugar while still warm.

Nutrition Information

- Calories: 127 calories;
- Total Fat: 8.6
- Sodium: 62
- Total Carbohydrate: 11.8
- Cholesterol: 1
- Protein: 1.5

---

11. Chocolate Peppermint Meringue Drops

Serving: 30 | Prep: 15mins | Cook: 30mins | Ready in:

Ingredients

- 3 egg whites
- 1/8 teaspoon cream of tartar
- 4 drops peppermint oil, or to taste
- 3/4 cup white sugar
- 1 drop red food coloring, or as needed (optional)
- 3 peppermint candy canes, crushed
- 1/2 cup chocolate chips

Direction

- Set the oven to 150°C or 300°F to preheat. Use parchment paper to line baking sheet.
- In a mixing bowl, use an electric mixer to beat together peppermint oil, cream of tartar and egg whites on medium-high speed until holds soft peaks. Beat in 1 tbsp. of sugar at a time, followed by food coloring, if you want, until the mixture holds stiff peaks and is glossy. Fold in chocolate chips and crushed candy canes extremely gently. Drop on prepped baking sheet with tablespoon of meringue.
- In the preheated oven, bake about 28-33 minutes, until dry. Allow cookies to cool on baking sheet on a rack about 20 minutes prior to taking out of parchment paper.

Nutrition Information

- Calories: 45 calories;
- Total Fat: 0.8
- Sodium: 7
- Total Carbohydrate: 9.5
- Cholesterol: 0
- Protein: 0.5

---

12. Chocolate Pizzelles

Serving: 12 | Prep: | Cook: | Ready in:

Ingredients

- 4 eggs
- 1/4 cup cocoa powder
- 1 cup white sugar
- 1/2 teaspoon ground cinnamon
- 1/4 teaspoon salt
- 1 tablespoon baking powder

- 1 cup unsalted butter
- 3/4 cup ground hazelnuts
- 2 cups all-purpose flour

Direction

- Whisk together salt, sugar and eggs until light. Melt butter and mix in egg mixture.
- Sift the entire leftover ingredients together excluding hazelnuts, and fold in.
- Stir hazelnuts in last.
- Heat Pizzelle iron and put on each imprint with 1 tsp. of batter, then close iron to bake about half a minute.
- Allow to cool on racks and sprinkle powdered sugar over top.

Nutrition Information

- Calories: 358 calories;
- Protein: 6
- Total Fat: 22.6
- Sodium: 197
- Total Carbohydrate: 35.5
- Cholesterol: 103

13. Chocolate Wine Balls

Serving: 48 | Prep: 30mins | Cook: | Ready in:

Ingredients

- 3 1/4 cups crushed vanilla wafers
- 3/4 cup confectioners' sugar
- 1/4 cup unsweetened cocoa powder
- 3 tablespoons corn syrup
- 1/2 cup full-bodied red wine (Cabernet Sauvignon, Cotes du Rhone, Zinfandel, Shiraz or Barolo)
- 1 cup red decorator sugar

Direction

- Mix red wine, corn syrup, cocoa powder, confectioners' sugar and vanilla wafers in a big bowl. Combine using your hands or a sturdy spoon to form a smooth dough. Form to an-inch balls and turn into the red decorator sugar. Keep refrigerated in container with cover. Bring to room temperature prior to serving.

Nutrition Information

- Calories: 88 calories;
- Protein: 0.6
- Total Fat: 2.4
- Sodium: 38
- Total Carbohydrate: 16.1
- Cholesterol: 0

14. Classic Butter Cookies II

Serving: 48 | Prep: | Cook: | Ready in:

Ingredients

- 2 1/2 cups all-purpose flour
- 1 cup butter
- 1/2 cup white sugar
- 1 egg
- 1/2 teaspoon almond extract

Direction

- Cream butter until light. Slowly add in sugar and beat until fluffy and light. Beat in almond extract and egg.
- Slowly mix in the flour. Cover up and allow to chill for at least 1 hour.
- Preheat the oven to 350°F (175°C).
- On a lightly floured surface, roll the dough out to the thickness of 1/8 inch. Cut into shapes as desired with lightly floured cookie cutters. Arrange the cookies on ungreased cookie sheets.
- Bake at 350°F (175°C) until golden, about 8-12 minutes. Transfer to wire racks for completely cooling. Decorate as desired.

Nutrition Information

- Calories: 67 calories;
- Cholesterol: 14
- Protein: 0.8
- Total Fat: 4
- Sodium: 29
- Total Carbohydrate: 7.1

15. Cookie Tulips

Serving: 12 | Prep: 45mins | Cook: 15mins | Ready in:

Ingredients

- 1/4 cup butter, softened
- 1/2 cup white sugar
- 7 tablespoons all-purpose flour
- 1 teaspoon vanilla extract
- 2 egg whites, beaten
- 1 (4 ounce) package cream cheese at room temperature
- 1 cup confectioners' sugar
- 1 teaspoon vanilla extract
- 1/2 (8 ounce) container frozen whipped topping, thawed
- 17 large fresh strawberries, divided

Direction

- Set the oven to 175°C or 350°F to preheat. Use a silicone sheet liner or parchment paper to line a baking sheet. Coat the outsides of twelve 2-in. baking glasses or small bowls with grease.
- In a bowl, mash white sugar and butter together until smooth, then mix in egg whites, 1 tsp. of vanilla extract and flour to form a smooth batter. Drop on the prepped baking sheet with 2 1/2 tbsp. of mixture, then spread dough out into an extremely thin circle with the diameter of 7 inches, using a spatula or spoon. Repeat process with leftover batter.
- In the preheated oven, bake for 7-9 minutes, until centers of cookie are set and edges are brown very slightly. Watch cookies carefully to prevent them from over-baking. Pull sheet from the oven and slip a spatula beneath each flat cookie instantly. Center and drape cookies over glasses coated with grease to harden into small wavy bowls. Let them cool fully.
- While cookies are cooling over their molds, in a bowl, beat together confectioners' sugar and cream cheese until smooth, then blend in 1 tsp. of vanilla extract. Take off green tops and cores from five strawberries, then put them into a small bowl and mash to a somewhat lumpy and juicy texture. Mix into cream cheese mixture with mashed strawberries, then fold into strawberry cream with whipped topping gently, until mixed well.
- Scoop 3 tbsp. of strawberry cream in every cookie bowl then place a beautiful fresh strawberry with green top on top of cream layer. Keep remaining cookies in a tightly sealed container and remaining cream in the fridge.

Nutrition Information

- Calories: 199 calories;
- Total Carbohydrate: 26.7
- Cholesterol: 21
- Protein: 2.1
- Total Fat: 9.6
- Sodium: 67

16. Cream Cheese Cut Outs I

Serving: 30 | Prep: | Cook: | Ready in:

Ingredients

- 1 cup butter, softened
- 1 (8 ounce) package cream cheese, softened
- 1/2 cup sifted confectioners' sugar
- 2 cups all-purpose flour

- 1/4 teaspoon salt

Direction

- Cream the cream cheese and butter till fluffy; slowly blend in the sugar. Whisk the salt and flour together; whisk to the creamed mixture. Keep covered; keep the dough chilled for a few hours or overnight.
- Preheat the oven to 190 degrees C (375 degrees F).
- Split the dough into thirds. Onto the lightly floured surface, roll the dough out, one section at a time. Keep other sections in the refrigerator. Using the cookie cutter, cut out to the shapes that you like.
- Add onto the ungreased cookie sheet. Bake for roughly 12 minutes or till firm yet not browned. If you want, sift more confectioners' sugar on the slightly warm cookies.

Nutrition Information

- Calories: 119 calories;
- Cholesterol: 24
- Protein: 1.5
- Total Fat: 8.8
- Sodium: 85
- Total Carbohydrate: 8.6

17. Creme De Pirouline

Serving: 36 | Prep: 25mins | Cook: 35mins | Ready in:

Ingredients

- 2 cups confectioners' sugar
- 1 1/4 cups all-purpose flour
- 1/8 teaspoon salt
- 5/8 cup unsalted butter, melted
- 6 egg whites
- 1 tablespoon heavy cream
- 1 teaspoon vanilla extract
- 1 1/2 teaspoons light corn syrup
- 4 ounces finely chopped bittersweet chocolate
- 1/4 cup unsalted butter

Direction

- Combine together the salt, flour, and confectioners' sugar in a large bowl. Form a well in the middle and then add vanilla, heavy cream, egg whites and melted butter. Combine until blended well. Cover the bowl and chill for at least two hours or overnight.
- Preheat an oven to 220 degrees C (425 degrees F). Use shortening or vegetable oil spray to coat two baking sheets.
- Pour a heaping tablespoon of the dough into 1 of the greased baking sheets. Smear batter into a very thin 6-inch by 3 1/2-inch oval with back of a spoon. Form as many as four for each baking sheet (work fast to shape them after baking).
- Bake for about 6 minutes until edges are turning brown. Transfer 1 cookie from baking sheet onto a clean surface with a spatula or long metal knife. Roll up the cookie, beginning from the long side, with a thin wooden dowel or chopstick. Repeat this with the rest of the cookies. In case the cookies become too stiff to roll, return the baking sheet to oven for around 30 seconds.
- Prepare the next sheet as the first bakes. Continue to bake while shaping the cookies until the batter has been used up. Let cool on wire rack.
- Mix the remaining 1/4 cup butter, corn syrup and chocolate in a bowl over simmering water. Mix sometimes until smooth and melted. Cool a bit. Immerse about one inch of the end of every cookie in chocolate sauce. Let cookies set up over waxed paper.

Nutrition Information

- Calories: 104 calories;
- Total Fat: 5.7
- Sodium: 19
- Total Carbohydrate: 12
- Cholesterol: 13

- Protein: 1.3

18. Crispy Peanut Butter Chocolate Log

Serving: 12 | Prep: 15mins | Cook: 5mins | Ready in:

Ingredients

- 1 (10 ounce) package large marshmallows
- 1/4 cup butter
- 1/4 cup peanut butter
- 5 1/2 cups crispy rice cereal (such as Rice Krispies®)
- 1 1/3 cups semi-sweet chocolate chips
- 3/4 cup butterscotch chips

Direction

- Line a 10x15x1-inch pan with waxed paper. Grease waxed paper.
- In a large microwave-safe bowl combine the marshmallows, peanut butter, and butter. Cover and heat the mixture in the microwave for about 2 minutes until marshmallows are melted. Mix well.
- Add in the rice cereal to marshmallow mixture and stir until well coated; place on the prepared pan.
- In a microwave-safe bowl mix butterscotch chips and chocolate chips. Heat about 2 minutes in the microwave oven until the mixture melts. Stir well.
- Place the chocolate mixture over rice cereal mixture, making sure to leave a 1-inch border around edges. Starting with the short side, roll the mixture jelly-roll style around the chocolate mixture. Take off the waxed paper while rolling. Transfer to a serving platter with the seam down. Refrigerate about 1 hour until set. Cut into thin slices.

Nutrition Information

- Calories: 338 calories;
- Cholesterol: 10
- Protein: 3.5
- Total Fat: 15.4
- Sodium: 182
- Total Carbohydrate: 50

19. Dark Chocolate Macadamia Brownies

Serving: 12 | Prep: 15mins | Cook: 30mins | Ready in:

Ingredients

- 8 ounces dark chocolate, broken into pieces
- 2/3 cup butter
- 4 eggs, lightly beaten
- 1/2 cup sour cream
- 1 teaspoon vanilla extract
- 1 1/2 cups superfine sugar (or granulated sugar, processed to fine texture in a food processor)
- 1 cup all-purpose flour
- 1 cup macadamia nuts, cut into quarters

Direction

- Set oven to 165°C (325°F) and start preheating. Use parchment paper to line a 9x11-in. baking pan.
- Heat butter and dark chocolate in a saucepan over low heat until melted. Using an electric mixer, beat the mixture on low speed until thoroughly incorporated; beat in flour, sugar, vanilla extract, sour cream and eggs until well blended. Mix in macadamia nuts and transfer mixture to the lined baking pan.
- Bake in prepared oven for 30-35 minutes until the crust cracks on top. Keep in pan and cool for 10 minutes, then transfer to a wire rack to cool completely.

Nutrition Information

- Calories: 451 calories;
- Sodium: 103
- Total Carbohydrate: 46.3
- Cholesterol: 94
- Protein: 5.5
- Total Fat: 28.6

20. Egg Paint

Serving: 1 | Prep: | Cook: | Ready in:

Ingredients

- 1 egg yolk
- 4 drops red food coloring

Direction

- Mix a small amount of food coloring with the egg yolk in small bowl or cup. Create designs on the cookies with a clean paintbrush before baking them.

Nutrition Information

21. Egyptian Rose Leaves

Serving: 36 | Prep: | Cook: | Ready in:

Ingredients

- 1/3 cup shortening
- 1 cup white sugar
- 2 eggs
- 1 teaspoon rosewater
- 2 cups all-purpose flour
- 1/4 teaspoon salt

Direction

- Combine together rose fluid, eggs, sugar and shortening until fluffy. Stir together salt and flour, then blend in butter mixture. The resulting dough will become soft; refrigerate for a few hours to overnight.
- Set the oven to 175°C or 350°F to preheat. Coat baking sheets lightly with grease or line them with parchment paper.
- Roll a third of dough at time into balls with the diameter of 3/4 inch while keeping the remaining dough chilled. Arrange dough balls on cookie sheets and use your hand to flatten until about half of the initial thickness. Imagine flattened cookie as a clock. Cut 2 slits in cookie with length of 1/2 inch each, at 10:00 and 2:00. Pinch the bottom to make base of petal, then sprinkle pink or red decorator's sugar over top.
- Bake at 175°C or 350°F until bottom turns brown slightly, about 8 to 10 minutes. Avoid browning tops of cookies.

Nutrition Information

- Calories: 68 calories;
- Total Fat: 2.2
- Sodium: 20
- Total Carbohydrate: 10.9
- Cholesterol: 10
- Protein: 1.1

22. German Heart Cookies

Serving: 50 | Prep: 45mins | Cook: 10mins | Ready in:

Ingredients

- 3 1/4 cups all-purpose flour
- 1 cup unsalted butter
- 2 tablespoons unsalted butter
- 1 cup white sugar
- 2 eggs
- Icing:
- 2 cups confectioners' sugar, divided
- 1 tablespoon lemon juice, or more as needed

- 1 tablespoon raspberry syrup, or more as needed

Direction

- In a large bowl, combine eggs, white sugar, one cup and two tablespoons butter and flour, then knead into a smooth dough. Form into a ball. Use plastic wrap to cover and flatten. Allow to sit for 120 mins in the refrigerator.
- Start preheating the oven to 375°F (190°C). Line parchment paper on 2 baking sheets or lightly coat with oil.
- Dust flour over a work surface; roll dough out to 1/4-in. thick. Using a heart-shaped cookie cutter, cut out hearts. Place the cut-out cookies onto prepared baking sheets.
- Bake in prepared oven for 10-15 mins, until browned lightly. Carefully take out of the baking sheets to the wire racks. Let it cool completely for 20 mins
- To make a thick icing: Mix one cup confectioners' sugar with as much lemon juice as needed. Add white icing to cover half of the hearts. Mix raspberry syrup with the remaining one cup of confectioners' sugar; then add pink icing to cover the other half. Allow the cookies to stand for around 120 mins or to overnight, until the icing completely dries.

Nutrition Information

- Calories: 105 calories;
- Protein: 1.1
- Total Fat: 4.4
- Sodium: 3
- Total Carbohydrate: 15.5
- Cholesterol: 18

23. Giant Heart Shaped Pan Cookie

Serving: 6 | Prep: 20mins | Cook: 18mins | Ready in:

Ingredients

- cooking spray
- 1/2 cup unsalted butter, softened
- 1/2 cup white sugar
- 1/4 cup firmly packed brown sugar
- 1 egg
- 1/4 teaspoon vanilla extract
- 1 cup all-purpose flour, or more as needed
- 1/4 teaspoon salt
- 1/4 teaspoon baking soda
- 1 cup candy-coated milk chocolate pieces (such as M&M's®), or to taste

Direction

- Draw the bottom of a heart-shaped aluminum pan over a sheet of parchment paper; snip along the tracing. Lightly grease the pan with cooking spray and line it with the prepared heart-shaped paper.
- Turn oven to 325°F (165°C) to preheat.
- In the bowl of a stand mixer fitted with the paddle attachment, beat together butter, brown sugar, and white sugar until creamy and smooth. Mix in vanilla and egg, approximately 50 strokes, or until batter is incorporated.
- In a small mixing bowl, combine baking soda, salt, and flour. Stir flour mixture into the batter, approximately 100 strokes, until thick but spreadable. Add milk chocolate pieces and fold gently. Transfer batter to the prepared pan, spreading evenly to within 1-inch of edges using a spatula.
- Bake in the center of the preheated oven until middle is firm and edges turn golden brown, for 18 to 23 minutes. Insert any remaining pieces of milk chocolate into the warm cookie for garnish.
- Allow to cool for 10 to 15 minutes in pan; remove to cooling rack and peel off parchment paper.

Nutrition Information

- Calories: 494 calories;

- Sodium: 187
- Total Carbohydrate: 66.3
- Cholesterol: 77
- Protein: 4.9
- Total Fat: 23.7

24. Italian Pizzelles

Serving: 18 | Prep: | Cook: | Ready in:

Ingredients

- 1/2 cup ground walnuts
- 2 1/4 cups all-purpose flour
- 1/4 cup unsweetened cocoa powder
- 1 tablespoon baking powder
- 3 eggs
- 1 cup white sugar
- 1/3 cup butter, melted
- 2 teaspoons vanilla extract

Direction

- Mix the baking powder, cocoa, flour and ground nuts in a medium bowl; put aside. Whip eggs on the high speed of an electric mixer in another bowl, put in the sugar gradually and stir until yellow and thick. Mix in the vanilla and melted butter. Mix in the flour mixture gradually, stirring enough just to combine.
- Heat up the pizzella iron until a drop of water sizzles on the surface, then turn down heat slightly. Drop a rounded tablespoon of batter for each cookie. Cover the lid and bake for about 2 minutes, based on your iron. Turn out cookie and cut off excess before cooling on racks.

Nutrition Information

- Calories: 161 calories;
- Total Fat: 6
- Sodium: 118

- Total Carbohydrate: 24.3
- Cholesterol: 40
- Protein: 3.3

25. Lesley's Valentine Brownies With Raspberry Coulis

Serving: 5 | Prep: | Cook: | Ready in:

Ingredients

- 1/4 cup butter
- 2 (1 ounce) squares unsweetened chocolate
- 1 cup white sugar
- 2 eggs
- 1/2 teaspoon vanilla extract
- 1/4 cup all-purpose flour
- 1/2 teaspoon salt
- 1 cup chopped walnuts (optional)
- 1 (10 ounce) package frozen raspberries
- 1 tablespoon raspberry juice
- 1 1/2 teaspoons cornstarch
- 1 tablespoon orange zest

Direction

- Set oven to preheat at 325°F (165°C).
- For the brownies: In a medium saucepan, melt chocolate and butter or margarine over medium heat; remove from the heat. Mix in vanilla, eggs and sugar; whisk well. If desired, mix in nuts, salt and flour.
- In an 8x8 inch greased baking dish, add the brownie mix.
- In the preheated oven, bake for 40 minutes or until toothpick comes out partly clean when slid into the middle of brownies.
- For the Raspberry Coulis: In a medium saucepan, cook raspberries over medium-high heat for 5 to 8 minutes; lower the heat to medium.
- In a small bowl, combine cornstarch and juice until a paste form; put into raspberries, stir continuously until thickened. Put in the rind and let cool.

- Add coulis onto a dessert plate in a pool and put brownie portion atop coulis; serve.

Nutrition Information

- Calories: 562 calories;
- Total Fat: 32.5
- Sodium: 330
- Total Carbohydrate: 67.6
- Cholesterol: 99
- Protein: 8.7

26. Lollipop Cookie Valentines

Serving: 6 | Prep: | Cook: |Ready in:

Ingredients

- 12 craft sticks
- 1/2 cup semisweet chocolate chips
- 1/2 cup butter, softened
- 1/3 cup packed light brown sugar
- 1/2 teaspoon vanilla extract
- 1 egg
- 2 cups all-purpose flour
- 1/4 cup unsweetened cocoa powder
- 1/4 teaspoon salt
- 12 (1 ounce) squares white chocolate
- 1 egg white
- 1 1/4 cups confectioners' sugar
- 3 drops red food coloring

Direction

- In a bowl of cold water, steep craft sticks for an hour.
- Stir chocolate chips in a small heavy saucepan on very low heat, until smooth and melted. Take away from the heat and allow to cool.
- Beat together vanilla, brown sugar and butter in a big bowl using an electric mixer at medium speed until fluffy. Beat egg in well, whip in cooled chocolate. Beat in salt, cocoa powder and flour using a mixer at low speed until smooth. Halve the dough.
- Set the oven to 190°C or 375°F to preheat. Coat 2 big cookie sheets with grease.
- Between two wax paper sheets, roll out each half of dough to the thickness of 1/8 inch. Freeze dough for 5 minutes in wax paper. Peel top sheets of wax paper off dough, then use a 3-inches heart-shaped cutter to cut out dough. Reroll scraps and freeze once more for 5 minutes, then cut out. Put 1/2 of the hearts on prepped cookie sheet, spacing 1-inch apart.
- Drain sticks and pat dry. Put on each heart with a stick to create 2 1/2-in. handle, press into dough slightly. Top with leftover hearts, then gently press edges together to seal. Bake until firm to touch, for 12 minutes, then allow to cool on wire racks.
- Stir white or milk chocolate in a 2-qt. heavy saucepan on extremely low heat or in the top of a double boiler placed over barely simmering water until smooth and melted. If you will use both kind of chocolate, melt in 2 different 1-qt. pans. Take away from the heat.
- Hold the handle of each lollipop and dunk in chocolate to coat both sides, allowing excess chocolate to drip back to pan. Put each lollipop once coated on cookie sheet lined with wax paper and chill until chocolate sets, about 20 minutes.
- For icing: Beat confectioners' sugar and egg white together on high speed of an electric mixer in a big bowl until extremely smooth. Transfer a small amount of icing to a separate bowl if you want and tint with drops of food coloring. Scoop colored icing in decorating bag with small writing tip and pipe preferred patterns over lollipops. Use decors and assorted candies to garnish using dots of icing to attach.

Nutrition Information

- Calories: 838 calories;
- Sodium: 293
- Total Carbohydrate: 111.2

- Cholesterol: 84
- Protein: 11.3
- Total Fat: 41

27. Maraschino Cherry Almond Cookies

Serving: 48 | Prep: 1hours | Cook: 12mins | Ready in:

Ingredients

- 1 cup unsalted butter, at room temperature
- 2/3 cup sifted confectioners' sugar
- 1 1/2 teaspoons almond extract
- 2 eggs, at room temperature
- 1/8 teaspoon salt
- 2 cups all-purpose flour
- 2/3 cup chopped drained maraschino cherries
- Royal Icing:
- 2 egg whites
- 2 teaspoons lemon juice
- 1/2 teaspoon vanilla extract
- 3 cups sifted confectioners' sugar

Direction

- In a mixing bowl, beat butter on high speed with an electric mixer, about 2 minutes, until creamy and smooth. Slowly beat in 2/3 cup of confectioners' sugar; beat in salt, eggs and almond extracts, about 3 minutes longer, until mixture is well incorporated and fluffy. Adjust speed to medium, and slowly beat in flour, about 1 minutes, until dough becomes smooth. Gently mix in maraschino cherries.
- Shape dough into two 1-inch diameter logs; roll each log in waxed paper or plastic wrap, and chill for a minimum of 2 hours until completely chilled.
- Set oven to 350°F (175°C) to preheat. Line parchment paper over several baking sheets.
- Slice each dough log into twenty-five of 1/2-inch-thick slices; arrange them by 1/2 inch apart on the prepared baking sheets.
- Bake cookies for 12 to 14 minutes in the preheated oven until firm but not browned. Transfer to cooling racks, and allow to cool to room temperature, approximately 15 minutes.
- For icing, beat egg whites and lemon juice together for about 1 minutes until frothy; whisk in vanilla extracts and 1 cupful of confectioners' sugar at a time until icing is spreadable and smooth. Spread over the top of each cookie with about 1 teaspoon icing; allow icing to harden before stacking.

Nutrition Information

- Calories: 98 calories;
- Total Fat: 4
- Sodium: 12
- Total Carbohydrate: 14.6
- Cholesterol: 18
- Protein: 1

28. Mostaccioli (Mustaches)

Serving: 30 | Prep: | Cook: | Ready in:

Ingredients

- 1 cup hazelnuts
- 1 cup walnuts
- 1/3 cup honey
- 1 egg white
- 1 tablespoon unsweetened cocoa powder
- 1/8 teaspoon ground cinnamon
- 1/8 teaspoon ground cloves
- 1 pinch salt
- 1/3 cup all-purpose flour
- 1/3 cup confectioners' sugar for decoration
- 1/2 cup confectioners' sugar
- 1 egg white, beaten
- 1/2 tablespoon orange liqueur

Direction

- Heat an oven to 275°F. Oil a baking sheet.

- Use a food processor to grind nuts finely. Put in salt, spices, cocoa, egg white and honey. Process into paste. Put in flour and combine with on/off turns barely to incorporate. The dough will turn sticky.
- Turn the dough onto work counter generously sprinkled with sifted confectioners' sugar. Sift top of dough with additional powdered sugar. Unroll dough gently into 3/8-inch thick. With knife sprinkled with powdered sugar, slice to 1x1 half-inch bars. Place, an-inch apart, on oiled sheet.
- Let cookies bake at 135°C or 275°F till set and surfaces seem dry, for approximately 25 minutes to half an hour. Let cookies cool fully on racks.
- Prep Icing: combine 2 teaspoons of egg white and half cup confectioners' sugar. Stir in sufficient liqueur to create a dense yet pourable icing. Place racks onto waxed paper; place cooled cookies, with edges touching, on racks. Sprinkle icing uneven lines on top of cookies. Split the cookies. Rest till icing dries. Keep in an airtight container.

Nutrition Information

- Calories: 82 calories;
- Total Fat: 5
- Sodium: 4
- Total Carbohydrate: 8.9
- Cholesterol: 0
- Protein: 1.6

29. Muddy Hearts

Serving: 12 | Prep: 20mins | Cook: 7mins | Ready in:

Ingredients

- 1 egg
- 1 cup crunchy peanut butter
- 1 cup white sugar
- 1 (12 ounce) package milk chocolate chips

Direction

- Preheat an oven to 175°C/350°F.
- Line parchment paper on baking sheet.
- Mix sugar, peanut butter and egg in bowl; the dough should be a bit dry, if it seems too wet, add small amounts of sugar.
- Put dough between 2 wax paper sheets; roll to 1/2-in. thick.
- Use heart-shaped cookie cutter to cut dough.
- Put hearts on prepped baking sheet.
- In preheated oven, bake for 7-10 minutes till edges are golden.
- Completely cool on baking sheet.
- At 30-sec intervals, melt chocolate chips in microwave in fully melted; mix between intervals.
- In melted chocolate, dip sides and bottom of each cookie.
- Put cookies on wax paper; dry.

Nutrition Information

- Calories: 348 calories;
- Total Fat: 20.6
- Sodium: 158
- Total Carbohydrate: 38.3
- Cholesterol: 25
- Protein: 7.6

30. No Bake Chocolate Peanut Butter Bars

Serving: 60 | Prep: 15mins | Cook: | Ready in:

Ingredients

- 2 cups peanut butter, divided
- 3/4 cup butter, softened
- 2 cups powdered sugar
- 3 cups graham cracker crumbs
- 1 (12 ounce) package NESTLE® TOLL HOUSE® Semi-Sweet Chocolate Mini Morsels, divided

Direction

- Grease 9x13-in. baking pan.
- In a big mixer bowl, whip butter and 1 1/4 cups of peanut butter till become creamy. Slowly whip in one cup of powdered sugar. Work in the half cup morsels, graham cracker crumbs and leftover powdered sugar using a wooden spoon or your hands. Press equally to the prepped baking pan. Using a spatula to smoothen the top.
- In a medium-sized and heavy-duty saucepan on the lowest possible heat, melt leftover morsels and leftover peanut butter while mixing continuously till smooth in consistency. Spread on top of graham cracker crust in the pan. Let chill in the refrigerator till chocolate becomes firm, for no less than 60 minutes; chop into bars. Keep in the fridge.

Nutrition Information

- Calories: 135 calories;
- Protein: 2.8
- Total Fat: 8.9
- Sodium: 91
- Total Carbohydrate: 12.4
- Cholesterol: 8

31. Old Fashioned Butter Valentine Cookies Dipped In Chocolate

Serving: 24 | Prep: | Cook: | Ready in:

Ingredients

- 3 cups all-purpose flour, sifted
- 1 teaspoon baking powder
- 1/2 teaspoon salt
- 1 cup butter, softened
- 3/4 cup white sugar
- 1 large egg
- 2 tablespoons milk
- 1 1/2 teaspoons vanilla extract
- 1/2 cup seedless raspberry jam
- 4 ounces semisweet chocolate chips
- 2 tablespoons butter

Direction

- In a bowl, sift together salt, baking powder and flour, then put aside.
- Beat together vanilla extract, milk, egg, sugar and 1 cup of butter in a separate bowl until well combined.
- Mix into butter mixture with flour mixture gradually.
- Form the dough into a disk, then use plastic wrap to wrap and chill for a minimum of 2 hours.
- Roll out a half of the dough at a time to the thickness of 1/8 inch.
- Use a big heart-shaped cookie cutter to cut into cookies, then repeat process with the leftover half of dough.
- Use a smaller heart-shaped cookie cutter to cut the center of half of the cookies.
- Top a whole cookie with an open centered cookie to make a sandwich. Place cookies on grease-free baking sheet and put aside.
- Set the oven to 200°C or 400°F to preheat.
- Put in a microwavable bowl with raspberry jam and heat for 35 seconds on high setting, until jam is runny.
- Use jam to fill the center of cookies and chill cookies about 10 minutes.
- In the preheated oven, bake for 5-8 minutes, until coolies are firm to the touch. Cookies will be pale in color.
- Remove cookies to a wire rack to cool through.
- In a microwavable ceramic or glass bowl, melt 2 tbsp. of butter and chocolate in 30-second intervals for 1-3 minutes, depending on your microwave, stirring after each melting until smooth.
- Scoop over half of each cookie decoratively with chocolate.
- Put cookie on a baking sheet lined with waxed paper and chill for 15 minutes, until chocolate is set.

Nutrition Information

- Calories: 202 calories;
- Total Fat: 10.4
- Sodium: 134
- Total Carbohydrate: 25.9
- Cholesterol: 31
- Protein: 2.2

32. Orange Almond Biscotti II

Serving: 12 | Prep: | Cook: |Ready in:

Ingredients

- 2 1/4 cups all-purpose flour
- 1 1/4 cups white sugar
- 1 pinch salt
- 2 teaspoons baking powder
- 1/2 cup sliced almonds
- 1 tablespoon orange zest
- 3 egg, beaten
- 1 tablespoon vegetable oil
- 1/4 teaspoon almond extract

Direction

- Turn on the oven to 350°F (175°C) to preheat. Prepare a baking sheet; grease and flour.
- Combine orange zest, almonds, salt, baking powder, sugar and flour in a large bowl. In the center, create a well and pour in almond extract and eggs oil. Use hand to mix or stir until the mixture turns into a ball.
- Divide the dough in half; roll each into an 8-inch long log. On the baking sheet, arrange logs and flatten to 3/4-inch thickness. Put into the oven to bake for 20-25 minutes. Let it cool slightly; take it out of the baking sheets. Use a serrated knife to cut into slices of 1/2-inch diagonally. Return the cookies on side onto the baking sheet; put them back into the oven to bake for another 10-15 minutes, turning over halfway through. The cookies should be crunchy and hard.

Nutrition Information

- Calories: 219 calories;
- Cholesterol: 46
- Protein: 4.8
- Total Fat: 4.6
- Sodium: 99
- Total Carbohydrate: 39.9

33. Pope's Valentine Cookies

Serving: 12 | Prep: | Cook: |Ready in:

Ingredients

- 1/2 pound butter, softened
- 2 1/2 cups sifted all-purpose flour
- 1 cup sifted confectioners' sugar
- 1 tablespoon milk
- 1 teaspoon vanilla extract

Direction

- Set the oven to 170°C or 325°F to preheat.
- In a mixer, mix butter until light, then put in leftover ingredients.
- Knead until velvety, then roll one half of dough at a time with the least quantity of flour possible to the thickness of 1/4 inch.
- Cut out dough and bake on a pan coated lightly with grease about 12 minutes. Cookies will become nearly white once cooked.

Nutrition Information

- Calories: 273 calories;
- Total Carbohydrate: 30.4
- Cholesterol: 41
- Protein: 2.9
- Total Fat: 15.6
- Sodium: 110

34. Raspberry Hearts

Serving: 12 | Prep: | Cook: |Ready in:

Ingredients

- 2 eggs
- 2 cups unbleached all-purpose flour
- 1/4 cup packed brown sugar
- 3/4 cup unsalted butter
- 2 egg yolks
- 1 tablespoon lemon zest
- 2 teaspoons ground cinnamon
- 1 pinch salt
- 1 (8 ounce) jar seedless raspberry jam
- 2 eggs
- 2 tablespoons water

Direction

- In a medium saucepan, put eggs (and water to cover). Heat water to a boil, take it off from heat and cool. Remove eggs shells and yolks. Push yolks through a sieve and put aside.
- Slice the butter into small pieces. In a mixing bowl, put in the salt, cinnamon, sugar, lemon zest, hard-boiled egg yolks, egg yolks and flour. Stir with your hands until the dough holds together and well combined. Cover in plastic wrap and chill for no less than 2 hours.
- On a lightly floured surface, shape the dough into 1/4-inch thick. Punch out as many hearts as possible with a 2 1/2 to 3-inch heart-shaped cookie cutter. Form the dough scraps into a ball, roll it again, and punch out more hearts. Cut out the centers of half the cookies with a smaller heart-shaped cookie cutter.
- Set the oven to 350°F (175°C) to preheat. Line baking trays with parchment paper.
- Using raspberry jam, spread thin coating on each whole heart. Garnish with the hearts with cut out centers. Keep working until all the dough has been used. Put the hearts 1 inch apart on the lined baking trays. In a small bowl, whip the 2 eggs with water and brush over the cookie frames lightly.
- Bake the cookies for 12 to 15 minutes just until light golden brown. Let cool on wire racks and put in an airtight container or in the freezer until ready to serve.

Nutrition Information

- Calories: 275 calories;
- Protein: 4.8
- Total Fat: 14.1
- Sodium: 28
- Total Carbohydrate: 33.2
- Cholesterol: 127

35. Raspberry Liqueur Valentine Cookies

Serving: 36 | Prep: 1hours30mins | Cook: 10mins |Ready in:

Ingredients

- 1/2 cup butter
- 1/2 cup vegetable shortening
- 1 cup confectioners' sugar
- 2 eggs
- 1/2 teaspoon vanilla extract
- 1/2 teaspoon lemon extract
- 2 3/4 cups all-purpose flour
- 1 tablespoon baking powder
- 1/2 teaspoon salt
- 2 tablespoons milk
- Frosting:
- 1 egg white, room temperature
- 3 cups confectioners' sugar
- 2 tablespoons milk, room temperature
- 2 tablespoons raspberry flavored liqueur
- 1 tablespoon cherry flavored Jell-O® mix
- 1 pinch salt

Direction

- Whisk 1 cup sugar, shortening, and butter together in a medium-sized bowl until creamy and smooth; and then add lemon extract, vanilla extract, and eggs. Combine baking powder, salt, and flour in a big bowl. Create a well in the center, and put the creamy mixture into it, folding the dry into the wet until blended. Mix in 2 tablespoons milk at the end. You can chill the mixture with a cover for 1 hour to a maximum of several days so that the rolling process will be easier.

- Start preheating the oven to 350°F (175°C). Roll the dough to 1/8 inch thickness on a surface lightly scattered with flour. Cut the dough into shapes with a heart-shaped cookie cutter. Put the cookies on a cookie sheet 2" apart.
- Put in the preheated oven and bake for 6-10 minutes. You can bake until the cookies turn light brown, but not needed. Take out of the cookie sheet and put on wire racks to cool.
- In the meantime, use an electric mixer to whisk egg white in a medium-sized bowl until foamy but not stiff. Slowly whisk in 1 1/2 cups sugar, and then 1/8 cup milk. Stir in cherry-flavored gelatin and raspberry liqueur. Slowly mix in a pinch of salt and the rest of the 1 1/2 cups sugar, blending until the ice resembles marshmallow fluff, but not stiff enough to form peaks. Spread over the tops of the cookies with the icing.

Nutrition Information

- Calories: 147 calories;
- Sodium: 99
- Total Carbohydrate: 22.1
- Cholesterol: 17
- Protein: 1.6
- Total Fat: 5.8

36. Rose Pistachio Shortbread

Serving: 24 | Prep: 20mins | Cook: 15mins | Ready in:

Ingredients

- 3/4 cup all-purpose flour
- 5 tablespoons confectioners' sugar
- 1 pinch salt
- 1/3 cup cold unsalted butter, cubed
- 1 egg yolk
- 3 tablespoons chopped pistachio nuts
- 2 teaspoons crushed dried rose petals

Direction

- In a bowl, mix salt, confectioners' sugar and flour. Add cubed butter; rub all together till it looks like fine breadcrumbs. Add the egg yolk; mix till you make a solid dough ball. Work in rose petals and pistachios.
- Roll dough to 1-in. diameter, 10-in. long log; wrap in plastic wrap. Chill for 2 hours – 5 days in the fridge.
- Preheat an oven to 165°C/325°F; line parchment paper on a baking sheet.
- When it is chilled and solid, remove plastic wrap from the dough. Unwrap; cut to 1/4-in. rounds. Put onto prepped baking sheet.
- In preheated oven, bake for 15 minutes till shortbread has light golden color. Cool; keep in airtight container.

Nutrition Information

- Calories: 51 calories;
- Total Carbohydrate: 4.8
- Cholesterol: 15
- Protein: 0.8
- Total Fat: 3.2
- Sodium: 11

37. So Pink Cereal Bars

Serving: 24 | Prep: 20mins | Cook: | Ready in:

Ingredients

- 2 tablespoons butter
- 1 (10 ounce) package large marshmallows

- 1/2 (3 ounce) package cranberry flavored Jell-O® mix
- 3 cups crispy rice cereal squares (such as Rice Chex ®)
- 3 cups toasted oat cereal rings (such as Cheerios®)
- 2/3 cup mini candy-coated chocolate pieces (such as mini M&M's®)
- 1/2 cup sweetened dried cranberries

Direction

- Coat a 12-inch x9-inch baking dish with butter.
- In a big nonstick pot, melt 2 tbsp. of butter on low heat.
- Mix in cranberry gelatin mix and marshmallows until the mixture is smooth and marshmallows melt.
- Stir in dried cranberries, mini candy-coated chocolate pieces, oat cereal rings and rice squares until mixed well.
- Pat the mixture quickly into prepped baking dish and let it cool.
- Slice into 2-inches squares.

Nutrition Information

- Calories: 98 calories;
- Sodium: 51
- Total Carbohydrate: 19.3
- Cholesterol: 3
- Protein: 1
- Total Fat: 2.3

38. Stained Glass Sugar Hearts

Serving: 96 | Prep: | Cook: | Ready in:

Ingredients

- 1 cup butter
- 1 cup shortening
- 1 cup confectioners' sugar
- 1 cup white sugar
- 2 eggs
- 1 teaspoon vanilla extract
- 4 1/2 cups all-purpose flour
- 1 teaspoon baking soda
- 1/2 teaspoon salt
- 1 teaspoon cream of tartar
- 1 cup crushed peppermint hard candies

Direction

- Cream the vanilla, eggs, sugars, shortening, and butter or margarine together. Put in the dry ingredients (but candy) and stir them well. The dough would be greasy.
- Use the floured surface and the rolling pin, roll the dough out. Chop out 2-in. heart-shape cookies. With one 1-in. heart-shaped cookie cutter, chop out a smaller heart in middle of bigger one. Add the cookies onto the foil-lined cookie sheet.
- Inside of the cut-out heart, dust the crushed candy crumbs, like candy canes or red life savers. Spread crumbs to inside edges of cookie.
- Bake at 175 degrees C (350 degrees F) for 10 to 12 minutes. Once the cookies have cooled down, take out of the sheets. Cookie could be frosted if desired.

Nutrition Information

- Calories: 82 calories;
- Total Fat: 4.2
- Sodium: 41
- Total Carbohydrate: 10.3
- Cholesterol: 9
- Protein: 0.8

39. Sweet Chocolate Caramel Squares

Serving: 24 | Prep: 20mins | Cook: 40mins | Ready in:

Ingredients

- 1 cup all-purpose flour
- 1/2 cup butter, softened
- 1/2 cup brown sugar
- 2 cups chopped pecans
- 1 cup flaked coconut
- 1 (14 ounce) can sweetened condensed milk
- 1 (11 ounce) package individually wrapped caramels (such as Hershey's®), unwrapped
- 2 tablespoons milk
- 1 cup chocolate chips

Direction

- Preheat the oven to 175 ° C or 350 ° F.
- In a bowl, combine butter, brown sugar and flour; pat into a baking dish, 9x13-inch in size.
- Bake for 12 to 15 minutes in prepped oven, till crust becomes slightly browned.
- Scatter coconut and pecans on top of crust. Top coconut and pecans with sweetened condensed milk.
- Bake for 25 minutes to half an hour in prepped oven till set.
- In small saucepan, heat milk and caramels over moderately-low heat for 2 to 3 minutes, till smooth. Top the baked sweetened condensed milk with caramel sauce. Scatter chocolate chips on top of caramel. Cool fully prior to slicing into bars.

Nutrition Information

- Calories: 283 calories;
- Total Fat: 15.9
- Sodium: 91
- Total Carbohydrate: 34.7
- Cholesterol: 17
- Protein: 3.7

40. The Best Valentine Sugar Cookies

Serving: 48 | Prep: | Cook: | Ready in:

Ingredients

- 7 cups all-purpose flour
- 2 cups white sugar
- 2 teaspoons salt
- 2 teaspoons baking powder
- 1 1/2 cups shortening
- 3 teaspoons almond extract
- 1 cup milk
- 3 eggs

Direction

- Turn on the oven to 375°F (190°C) to preheat.
- Combine baking powder, salt, sugar and flour in a large mixing bowl. Stir in shortening. When shortening is well-mixed, mix in milk and almond flavoring at the same time, then eggs. Use a floured rolling pin to roll the dough out on a floured surface. Roll thick. Cut cookies out; on a cookie sheet, place cookies.
- Put into the oven to bake at 375°F (190°C) just until the bottoms turn golden, 8-10 minutes.

Nutrition Information

- Calories: 163 calories;
- Cholesterol: 12
- Protein: 2.4
- Total Fat: 7
- Sodium: 124
- Total Carbohydrate: 22.6

41. Two Hearts Together

Serving: 36 | Prep: | Cook: | Ready in:

Ingredients

- 1 cup butter, softened
- 1 cup white sugar
- 1 (3 ounce) package cream cheese, softened
- 1 egg, separated
- 1 teaspoon almond extract
- 1/2 teaspoon salt

- 2 cups all-purpose flour
- 1 (14 ounce) can sweetened condensed milk
- 1/2 cup heavy whipping cream
- 1/4 cup pink decorator sugar

Direction

- Beat butter with salt, vanilla, 1/2 teaspoon almond extract, egg yolk, cream cheese, and granulated sugar in a mixer bowl until incorporated. Put in flour and mix until well combined. Refrigerate for 2 hours.
- Knead dough on a floured work surface until a smooth ball is formed. Split into 3 equal portions. Roll out each piece of dough to 1/8-inch thickness on a work surface lightly coated with flour. Using cookie cutter, cut out heart shapes.
- Arrange cookies 1 inch apart on unbuttered baking sheets. Lightly brush with beaten egg white and scatter with colored sugar. Bake cookies for 7 to 10 minutes at 375°F (190°C) in preheated oven. Allow to cool.
- Whisk the remaining 1/2 teaspoon almond extract, whipping cream, and condensed milk together in a saucepan. Cook and stir over medium-high heat until cream mixture comes to a boil. Lower heat to medium; cook, stirring, for 8 to 10 minutes, until thickened. Allow to cook. Spread one side of each heart with caramel mixture and top with another heart. Store cookies, tightly covered.

Nutrition Information

- Calories: 154 calories;
- Sodium: 93
- Total Carbohydrate: 18.3
- Cholesterol: 30
- Protein: 2.1
- Total Fat: 8.3

42. Ultimate Double Chocolate Cookies

Serving: 42 | Prep: 25mins | Cook: 10mins | Ready in:

Ingredients

- 1 pound semisweet chocolate, chopped
- 2 cups all-purpose flour
- 1/2 cup Dutch process cocoa powder
- 2 teaspoons baking powder
- 1 teaspoon salt
- 10 tablespoons unsalted butter
- 1 1/2 cups packed brown sugar
- 1/2 cup white sugar
- 4 eggs
- 2 teaspoons instant coffee granules
- 2 teaspoons vanilla extract

Direction

- On a double boiler or in the microwave, melt chocolate while stirring sometimes until smooth. Sift salt, baking powder, cocoa and flour together, then put aside.
- Cream brown and white sugars and butter together in a medium bowl until smooth. Beat in 1 egg at a time, then stir in vanilla and coffee crystals until well combined. Stir in melted chocolate. Stir in dry ingredients with a wooden spoon just until everything is blended. Place a cover and allow to stand about 35 minutes to help chocolate set up.
- Set the oven to 175°C or 350°F to preheat. Use parchment paper to line 2 cookie sheets. Form dough into balls with walnut size, or drop dough onto prepped cookie sheets by rounded tablespoonfuls, spaced 2 inches between.
- In the preheated oven, bake for about 8-10 minutes. Cookies will be set yet the centers are still extremely soft due to chocolate. Let cookies cool on baking sheet about 10 minutes prior to removing to wire racks to cool thoroughly.

Nutrition Information

- Calories: 148 calories;
- Protein: 2.2
- Total Fat: 6.8
- Sodium: 88
- Total Carbohydrate: 21.4
- Cholesterol: 25

43. Valentine's Cinnamon Heart Shortbread Pan Cookies

Serving: 40 | Prep: 15mins | Cook: 35mins | Ready in:

Ingredients

- 2 1/2 cups butter
- 1 1/4 cups confectioners' sugar
- 1 cup heart-shaped cinnamon candies, chopped finely
- 2 1/2 teaspoons vanilla extract
- 1/4 teaspoon cinnamon oil
- 1/4 teaspoon baking soda
- 1/4 teaspoon baking powder
- 5 cups all-purpose flour, or more as needed

Direction

- Set oven to 300 0 F (150 0 C) and preheat. Use parchment paper to line a jelly roll pan.
- In a large bowl, use electric mixer to cream butter until fluffy. Put in baking powder, baking soda, cinnamon oil, vanilla extract, cinnamon hearts and confectioner's sugar; mix with a wooden spoon. Pour in flour, a cup at a time, use hand to mix until the dough sticks together.
- Push the dough onto the lined pan, flattening the corners to create an even layer.
- Put in the prepared oven and bake for 35 to 40 minutes until corners begin to turn a light brown. Transfer to a wire rack to cool down for 10 minutes; hold onto the parchment paper to lift shortbread out of the pan. Slice into 2-inch squares.

Nutrition Information

- Calories: 196 calories;
- Cholesterol: 31
- Protein: 1.7
- Total Fat: 11.7
- Sodium: 95
- Total Carbohydrate: 21.1

44. Valentine's Day Cookies

Serving: 18 | Prep: 15mins | Cook: 15mins | Ready in:

Ingredients

- 1 1/4 cups all-purpose flour
- 1/4 cup white sugar
- 1/2 teaspoon baking soda
- 2 pinches salt
- 1/2 cup honey (optional)
- 1/3 cup milk
- 1/4 cup butter, softened
- 1/4 teaspoon vanilla extract
- 1/2 cup semisweet chocolate chips (optional)
- 1/2 cup vanilla chips
- 1/2 cup confectioners' sugar

Direction

- Set the oven to 175°C or 350°F to preheat.
- In a bowl, whisk salt, baking soda, white sugar and flour together.
- In a big bowl, beat together vanilla extract, butter, milk and honey until smooth.
- Stir into honey mixture with flour mixture until just mixed.
- Fold chocolate and vanilla chips in.
- Roll into walnut-sized balls and arrange on nonstick baking sheets, spacing 2 inches apart.
- In the preheated oven, bake about 15-18 minutes, until golden brown.
- Let cookies cool and sprinkle confectioners' sugar over top.

Nutrition Information

- Calories: 170 calories;
- Total Fat: 6
- Sodium: 70
- Total Carbohydrate: 28
- Cholesterol: 7
- Protein: 1.8

45. Valentine's Slice And Bake Cinnamon Heart Shortbread Cookies

Serving: 60 | Prep: 10mins | Cook: 10mins | Ready in:

Ingredients

- 1 cup butter, softened
- 1 teaspoon vanilla extract
- 1/2 cup confectioners' sugar
- 1/2 cup heart-shaped cinnamon candies, ground into a fine powder
- 1/4 cup cornstarch
- 1 3/4 cups all-purpose flour, divided

Direction

- In a large bowl, beat butter using a hand mixer until it turns fluffy. Add cornstarch, ground cinnamon candies, confectioners' sugar, and vanilla extract, mixing with a hand mixer until blended.
- Incorporate 1/4 cup flour at a time and mix using your hands until the dough comes together with all the flour.
- Divide into 2 and roll into 8 inch cylinders. Wrap them in waxed paper and freeze them for at least 1 hour to overnight until they become firm.
- Set an oven to 350 degrees F or 175 degrees C. Take the dough from the freezer. Let the dough thaw until just slightly soft.
- Cut the dough to 1/4 inch slices and place onto baking sheets.
- Bake in the oven for about 10 minutes until firm but edges are not brown. Cool on the baking sheets for 5 minutes then move to racks to completely cool.

Nutrition Information

- Calories: 54 calories;
- Sodium: 23
- Total Carbohydrate: 6.1
- Cholesterol: 8
- Protein: 0.4
- Total Fat: 3.1

46. Wednesday Cookies

Serving: 60 | Prep: | Cook: | Ready in:

Ingredients

- 1/2 cup butter
- 1 1/2 cups white sugar
- 2 eggs
- 1 cup sour cream
- 1 teaspoon vanilla extract
- 2 3/4 cups all-purpose flour
- 1/2 teaspoon baking powder
- 1/2 teaspoon salt
- 1/2 teaspoon baking soda
- 1 cup shortening
- 1/4 cup milk
- 2 egg whites
- 1/4 cup all-purpose flour
- 2 teaspoons vanilla extract
- 1 pound confectioners' sugar

Direction

- Cream sugar and butter together in a medium bowl, then stir in vanilla and eggs, followed by the sour cream. Sift together baking soda, salt, baking powder and flour, then mix into creamed mixture. Place a cover and refrigerate for a minimum of an hour.

- Set the oven to 175°C or 350°F to preheat.
- Drop on cookie sheets with heaping teaspoonfuls of cookies. In the preheated oven, bake about 10-12 minutes, then transfer to wire racks to cool. Use icing to frost the flat side once cool.
- For icing, in a medium bowl, mix together confectioners' sugar, vanilla, 1/4 cup flour, egg whites, milk and shortening using an electric mixer on high speed until fluffy. The icing will be fluffier if you mix it longer.

Nutrition Information

- Calories: 128 calories;
- Sodium: 52
- Total Carbohydrate: 17.6
- Cholesterol: 12
- Protein: 1.1
- Total Fat: 6

Chapter 2: Easter Cookie Recipes

***

47. Almond Macaroon Nests

Serving: 36 | Prep: 15mins | Cook: 20mins | Ready in:

Ingredients

- 2 cups all-purpose flour
- 1 tablespoon baking powder
- 1/4 teaspoon salt
- 3/4 cup butter, room temperature
- 1 (8 ounce) package cream cheese, room temperature
- 1 cup white sugar
- 3/4 teaspoon vanilla extract
- 2 cups flaked coconut
- 2 drops red food coloring (optional)
- 2 drops yellow food coloring (optional)
- 1 cup chocolate coated peanuts

Direction

- Set oven to 325°F (165°C) and start preheating. Grease cookie sheets.
- Sift salt, baking powder and flour together; put aside. In a medium bowl, cream sugar, cream cheese and butter together until smooth. Stir in vanilla; whisk in dry ingredients gradually.
- Separate coconut into 3 separate containers. Color one portion yellow, one red and leave one plain. Toss colored coconut with the plain together.
- Shape cookie dough into walnut-sized balls; coat with coconut mixture. Arrange them onto greased cookie sheet, 2 inches apart. Press a candy into each cookie's center.
- Bake in the prepared oven for 12 minutes; take out of the oven; place 2 more candies into each cookie's center and press. Put back in the oven and keep baking for 4-5 more minutes until golden brown. Cool cookies for a few minutes on baking sheet; place cookies on wire racks to completely cool.

Nutrition Information

- Calories: 146 calories;
- Total Carbohydrate: 16.1
- Cholesterol: 17
- Protein: 1.8
- Total Fat: 8.5
- Sodium: 117

48. Annemarie's Lemon Bars

Serving: 16 | Prep: 15mins | Cook: 40mins | Ready in:

Ingredients

- 1/2 cup butter, softened
- 1 1/3 cups all-purpose flour
- 1/4 cup white sugar
- 2 eggs
- 3/4 cup white sugar
- 2 tablespoons all-purpose flour
- 1/4 teaspoon baking powder
- 3 1/2 tablespoons lemon juice

Direction

- Set oven to 350°F (180°C) to preheat.
- For the crust: Combine butter, 1/4 cup sugar, and 1 1/3 cups flour using a fork until crumbly. Pat into an 8x8-inch baking pan; bake in the preheated oven for 20 minutes until crust has white color (do not brown).
- Combine lemon juice, baking powder, 2 tablespoons flour, 3/4 cup sugar, and eggs in a blender. Pulse until well combined. Pour filling into the pre-baked crust.
- Put bars back into the oven and bake for 20 minutes longer. Take out of the oven; scatter top with powdered sugar. Allow bars to cool until ready to cut.

Nutrition Information

- Calories: 151 calories;
- Total Fat: 6.5
- Sodium: 57
- Total Carbohydrate: 21.5
- Cholesterol: 39
- Protein: 2

49. Bird's Nests III

Serving: 6 | Prep: | Cook: | Ready in:

Ingredients

- 4 cups chow mein noodles
- 3 cups miniature marshmallows
- 3 tablespoons butter
- 30 small jellybeans

Direction

- Use foil to line a cookie sheet; use spray-on cooking oil to grease.
- In a large bowl, place noodles. Melt marshmallows and butter while stirring until smooth over medium heat. Place marshmallow mixture on top of noodles, stirring until coated well.
- Rub some butter on hands and shape noodle mixture into 6 round balls. Arrange balls on lined cookie sheet. Press the center of each ball with the back of a teaspoon to create a hollow indentation.
- Allow nests to set until firm. Fill small jelly beans into each. (You can use other kinds of small candies: chocolate covered peanuts, chocolate covered raisins, small gumdrops, M & M's, etc.)

Nutrition Information

- Calories: 307 calories;
- Sodium: 195
- Total Carbohydrate: 42.3
- Cholesterol: 15
- Protein: 3
- Total Fat: 15

50. Bunny Cookies

Serving: 48 | Prep: | Cook: | Ready in:

Ingredients

- 1 1/4 cups white sugar
- 2/3 cup shortening
- 2 eggs
- 3 1/2 cups all-purpose flour
- 1/2 teaspoon salt
- 2 teaspoons baking powder
- 2 1/2 teaspoons orange zest

- 1 tablespoon orange juice
- 1/4 cup cinnamon red hot candies

Direction

- Turn oven to 375°F (190°C) to preheat.
- Whisk together shortening and sugar in a large bowl. Whisk in eggs until incorporated. Mix in baking powder, salt, and flour until well combined. Stir in orange zest and orange juice.
- Flatten dough to a thickness of 1/4 inch on a work surface lightly coated with flour. Cut out rabbit shapes using a cookie cutter. Arrange rabbits onto a cookie sheet; position a cinnamon candies onto the rabbits for eyes. Bake cookies in the heated oven for 8 to 10 minutes. Add frosting if desired.

Nutrition Information

- Calories: 86 calories;
- Total Fat: 3.1
- Sodium: 48
- Total Carbohydrate: 13.4
- Cholesterol: 8
- Protein: 1.2

51. Cardamom Rose Meringues

Serving: 12 | Prep: 15mins | Cook: 1hours30mins | Ready in:

Ingredients

- 2 egg whites
- 1/4 teaspoon cream of tartar
- 2/3 cup white sugar
- 1/4 cup water
- 2 teaspoons rose extract
- 1/4 teaspoon ground cardamom
- 1/8 teaspoon salt
- 1 drop red food coloring (optional)

Direction

- Set the oven to 120°C or 250°F to preheat. Use parchment paper to line a baking sheet.
- Use an electric mixer to beat together cream of tartar and egg whites in a mixing bowl on high speed until the mixture holds stiff peaks.
- In a saucepan, add food coloring, salt, cardamom, rose extract, water and sugar, then bring to a simmer on low heat while stirring until sugar is dissolved. Simmer the mixture about 1-2 minutes while stirring continuously. Pour the syrup in a thin stream very gradually into egg whites while using electric mixer to beat continuously on high speed. Beat until the syrup is blended and meringue becomes shiny as well as stiff.
- Drop on prepped baking sheet by spoonfuls of meringue or pipe into rosettes with a star tip.
- In the preheated oven, bake about 1- 1 1/2 hours, until meringues become hard, then turn off the oven and let meringues cool inside oven to complete baking internal parts.

Nutrition Information

- Calories: 46 calories;
- Total Fat: 0
- Sodium: 34
- Total Carbohydrate: 11.2
- Cholesterol: 0
- Protein: 0.6

52. Carrot Cake Cookies

Serving: 36 | Prep: 10mins | Cook: 20mins | Ready in:

Ingredients

- 1/2 cup butter, softened
- 1 cup brown sugar
- 2 eggs
- 1 (8 ounce) can crushed pineapple, drained
- 3/4 cup shredded carrots
- 1 cup raisins
- 2 cups all-purpose flour

- 1 teaspoon baking powder
- 1/2 teaspoon baking soda
- 1/2 teaspoon salt
- 2 tablespoons ground cinnamon
- 1 cup chopped walnuts (optional)

Direction

- Set an oven to preheat to 175°C (350°F). Grease or line the cookie sheets with parchment paper.
- Cream together the brown sugar and butter in a big bowl, until it becomes smooth. Beat in the eggs, one by one, then mix in the raisins, carrots and crushed pineapple. Mix together the cinnamon, salt, baking soda, baking powder and flour, then mix it into the carrot mixture. If preferred, stir in the walnuts. Drop it on the prepped cookie sheets by rounded spoonfuls.
- Let it bake in the preheated oven for 15-20 minutes, until the cookies become set and the bottoms start to turn brown. Let the cookies cool for several minutes on the cookie sheets prior to transferring to wire racks to let it fully cool.

Nutrition Information

- Calories: 106 calories;
- Sodium: 85
- Total Carbohydrate: 14.4
- Cholesterol: 17
- Protein: 1.8
- Total Fat: 5.1

53. Chocolate Bunny Treats™

Serving: 4 | Prep: 20mins | Cook: | Ready in:

Ingredients

- 1 cup semi-sweet chocolate morsels
- 3 tablespoons butter or margarine
- 1 (10 ounce) package regular marshmallows
- 6 cups KELLOGG'S® RICE KRISPIES® cereal
- Canned frosting or decorating gel
- Assorted candies

Direction

- Melt butter and chocolate morsels in a big saucepan on low heat. Add the marshmallows; mix till melted completely. Take off heat.
- Add the KELLOGG'(R) RICE KRISPIES(R) cereal; mix till coated well.
- Evenly press the mixture into the 15x10x1-in. pan coated in cooking spray using wax paper or buttered spatula; slightly cool.
- Cut cereal mixture to shapes using rabbit head cookie cutter, a really small circle cookie cutter and a big circle cookie cutter coated in cooking spray. Attach 1 rabbit head shape on top of the big circle shape using frosting for each rabbit; to each, attach 1 small circle for tail. Use candies and/or frosting to decorate; best eaten the same day it is made.

Nutrition Information

- Calories: 694 calories;
- Sodium: 519
- Total Carbohydrate: 129.2
- Cholesterol: 23
- Protein: 5.6
- Total Fat: 22.3

54. Chrusciki I

Serving: 40 | Prep: 1hours | Cook: 30mins | Ready in:

Ingredients

- 12 egg yolks
- 1 egg
- 2 tablespoons white sugar
- 1 teaspoon salt
- 1 teaspoon vanilla extract

- 1 tablespoon whiskey (optional)
- 2 1/2 cups all-purpose flour, divided
- 1 quart vegetable oil for frying
- 1 cup confectioners' sugar for dusting

Direction

- Beat the whiskey, vanilla, salt, sugar, egg and egg yolks in a medium bowl, then mix in 2 cups of flour. Add the remaining flour if the dough is sticky. Knead for 5 minutes and split it into 3 parts. Use a plastic wrap to keep the dough pieces covered, until ready to use.
- In a big pan or deep fryer, heat the oil to 190°C (375°F), or you can melt 2 pounds of lard instead. The oil should be about an inch deep.
- Roll out a piece of the dough on a lightly floured surface until it becomes paper-thin. Slice it into long diamond (parallelogram) shape, then cut a slot in the middle using a sharp paring knife. Pull one point of the diamond through the slot, then put aside. Repeat the process with the leftover pieces.
- Depending on the size of the pan, fry 2-4 pieces at a time for about 5-10 seconds on each side. Cookies should not brown. Take out from the oil and let it drain on paper towels. When already cooled, dust with confectioner's sugar. Store the rest of the cookies in an airtight container.

Nutrition Information

- Calories: 256 calories;
- Cholesterol: 66
- Protein: 1.8
- Total Fat: 23.5
- Sodium: 62
- Total Carbohydrate: 9.8

55. Easter Bird's Nests

Serving: 10 | Prep: 15mins | Cook: 5mins | Ready in:

Ingredients

- 3 cups miniature marshmallows
- 1/4 cup creamy peanut butter
- 3 tablespoons butter
- 4 cups crispy chow mein noodles
- cooking spray
- 40 candy-coated milk chocolate eggs

Direction

- In a saucepan, cook and stir together butter, peanut butter and marshmallows on moderate heat for 5 minutes, until marshmallows are melted totally into the mixture.
- In a big bowl, add chow mein noodles, then place over chow mein noodles with marshmallow mixture and stir to coat well.
- Use cooking spray or butter to coat your hands to prevent noodles from sticking to your hands. Use an ice cream scoop to take the noodle mixture from bowl and shape into balls, hollowing the center out to make the nest. Place into each nest with 4 chocolate eggs.

Nutrition Information

- Calories: 365 calories;
- Total Fat: 21.1
- Sodium: 174
- Total Carbohydrate: 40.2
- Cholesterol: 17
- Protein: 4.6

56. Easter Egg Dipper Treat™

Serving: 24 | Prep: 20mins | Cook: | Ready in:

Ingredients

- 3 tablespoons butter or margarine
- 1 (10 ounce) package JET-PUFFED Marshmallows*
- 6 cups KELLOGG'S® RICE KRISPIES® Cereal

- 1 1/2 cups semi-sweet chocolate morsels or milk chocolate morsels
- 5 teaspoons shortening
- Multi-colored sprinkles

Direction

- Melt butter on low heat in big saucepan. Add marshmallows; mix till melted fully. Take off heat.
- Add the KELLOGG'S RICE KRISPIES CEREAL then mix till coated well.
- Divide the warm cereal mixture to portions with a 1/4-cup measuring cup coated in cooking spray. Form each portion to 2 1/2x1 1/2-in. egg shapes using buttered hands. Or, use cooking spray to coat the insides of the plastic snap-apart Easter eggs. Into eggs, press cereal mixture then remove the cereal mixture from the plastic eggs then cool.
- Mix shortening and chocolate morsels in small saucepan; cook on low heat, constantly mixing, till melted. Into chocolate, dip bottoms of the cereal eggs; use sprinkles to decorate. Put onto wax paper-lined baking sheet and refrigerate till chocolate is firm. Wrap in plastic wrap individually; best eaten the same day it is made.

Nutrition Information

- Calories: 135 calories;
- Total Fat: 5.7
- Sodium: 85
- Total Carbohydrate: 22.3
- Cholesterol: 4
- Protein: 1.1

57. Forgotten Kisses

Serving: 42 | Prep: | Cook: |Ready in:

Ingredients

- 3 egg whites
- 3/4 teaspoon cream of tartar
- 1/4 teaspoon salt
- 1 1/2 cups white sugar
- 3/4 teaspoon vanilla extract
- 2 cups semisweet chocolate chips
- 3 drops red food coloring

Direction

- Set the oven to 190°C or 375°F to preheat. Use non-stick spray to coat cookie sheets.
- Beat egg whites until they are frothy, then put in salt and cream of tartar. Beat the mixture until extremely stiff.
- Put in teaspoonful of sugar gradually and beat until glossy.
- Fold in chips, food coloring and vanilla.
- Drop on sheet coated with grease with spoonfuls of the mixture and put in the oven. Turn off the oven and leave until oven becomes cold. Avoid opening the door to peek as it will make cookies turn gummy.

Nutrition Information

- Calories: 70 calories;
- Sodium: 18
- Total Carbohydrate: 12.4
- Cholesterol: 0
- Protein: 0.8
- Total Fat: 2.3

58. Fresh Strawberry Cookies

Serving: 24 | Prep: | Cook: |Ready in:

Ingredients

- 2 cups fresh strawberries
- 2 cups blanched almonds
- 1 cup raisins

Direction

- Soak the almonds overnight in water.

- Soak the raisins for 5 minutes in boiling water and then drain. Then dice the strawberries and raisins.
- Grind the soaked almonds coarsely and then transfer to diced strawberry-raisin mixture. Combine thoroughly.
- Onto a dehydrator plastic tray, drop the batter by spoonfuls. Then dehydrate at 40 degrees C (105 degrees F) for 24 hours or until dry. Flip the cookies over in 8 to 12 hours or when one side looks dry enough.

Nutrition Information

- Calories: 91 calories;
- Total Carbohydrate: 8.1
- Cholesterol: 0
- Protein: 2.8
- Total Fat: 6.1
- Sodium: < 1

59. Fruit Preserve Sandwich Cookies

Serving: 10 | Prep: | Cook: | Ready in:

Ingredients

- 1 cup all-purpose flour
- 1/4 cup butter
- 1 egg
- 2 tablespoons ground almonds
- 1/4 cup white sugar
- 1 cup any flavor fruit jam
- 1/3 cup confectioners' sugar for decoration

Direction

- Set oven to 400°F (200°C) to preheat. Grease cookie sheets.
- Into a bowl, sift the flour and stir in the butter or margarine. Whisk in the sugar with almonds. Stir in the egg with a fork until dough is stiff.
- On a lightly floured surface, knead dough until smooth. Roll out to shape into a thin layer and slice into rounds, 2 inches wide. Roll trimmings again and slice until you have 20 rounds. Put rounds on cookie sheets.
- Bake in the preheated oven for 12 minutes, or until light brown. Cool on the sheet for about 3 minutes, then transfer onto wire racks.
- When biscuits are cold completely, spread a thin layer of preserves on half of the rounds and stick together. Sprinkle with confectioners' sugar.

Nutrition Information

- Calories: 223 calories;
- Total Fat: 5.9
- Sodium: 50
- Total Carbohydrate: 40.7
- Cholesterol: 31
- Protein: 2.3

60. Funfetti® Style Cookies

Serving: 48 | Prep: 10mins | Cook: 9mins | Ready in:

Ingredients

- 1 cup butter, softened
- 1 cup sour cream
- 1 cup white sugar
- 2 eggs
- 1/2 cup multicolored candy sprinkles
- 1/2 cup confectioners' sugar
- 1 tablespoon cornstarch, or more as needed
- 1 1/2 teaspoons vanilla extract
- 1 teaspoon almond extract
- 1 teaspoon baking powder
- 1/2 teaspoon baking soda
- 1/2 teaspoon salt
- 1/2 teaspoon nutmeg
- 1/2 teaspoon ground cinnamon
- 2 cups all-purpose flour, or more as needed

Direction

- Turn on the oven to 325°F (165°C) to preheat. Use parchment paper to line 2 baking sheets.
- In a large bowl, use an electric mixer to cream together eggs, white sugar, sour cream and butter until fluffy and light. Stir in cinnamon, nutmeg, salt, baking soda, baking powder, almond extract, vanilla extract, corn starch, confectioners' sugar and candy sprinkles for 1-2 minutes until fully incorporated. Beat in flour for another 1-2 minutes gradually until it forms sticky dough. On baking sheets, drop spoonfuls of dough, 2 inches apart.
- Put into the oven to bake for 9-13 minutes until the edges turn golden. Let it cool for 1 minute on the baking sheet before allowing to cool completely on wire rack.

Nutrition Information

- Calories: 98 calories;
- Total Fat: 5.5
- Sodium: 81
- Total Carbohydrate: 11.3
- Cholesterol: 20
- Protein: 1

61. Gluten Free Easter Egg Cookies

Serving: 12 | Prep: 20mins | Cook: 25mins | Ready in:

Ingredients

- 1 cup cassava flour (such as Amafil®)
- 1 cup potato starch
- 1 pinch stevia powder
- 6 tablespoons coconut milk
- 5 tablespoons coconut oil
- 4 egg yolks
- 2 tablespoons brandy-based orange liqueur (such as Grand Marnier®)
- 1 tablespoon honey
- 2 tablespoons peach jam
- 1 tablespoon colored sprinkles

Direction

- Turn the oven to 350°F (175°C) to preheat.
- In a bowl, mix together stevia powder, potato starch, and cassava flour; add honey, orange liqueur, egg yolks, coconut oil, and coconut milk and knead until the dough fully combines.
- On a work surface, use a rolling pin to roll the dough to 1/4-in. thick. With an egg-shaped cookie cutter, cut egg-shaped cookies. On a baking sheet, put the egg-shaped cookies. Spread each cookie with jam and put sprinkles on top.
- Put in the preheated oven and bake for 25 minutes until turning light brown around the edges. Let fully cool.

Nutrition Information

- Calories: 195 calories;
- Sodium: 6
- Total Carbohydrate: 27.1
- Cholesterol: 68
- Protein: 1.3
- Total Fat: 9

62. Homemade Samoa Cookies

Serving: 20 | Prep: 15mins | Cook: 15mins | Ready in:

Ingredients

- 2 cups butter, softened
- 1 cup white sugar
- 1 teaspoon salt
- 4 cups all-purpose flour, divided
- 1 large egg, lightly beaten
- 2 tablespoons vanilla extract
- 1 teaspoon milk
- 4 cups sweetened flaked coconut

- 22 ounces caramels (such as Kraft® Caramel Bits)
- 1 pound chocolate (such as CandiQuick®)

Direction

- Beat salt, white sugar and butter in bowl. Add 2 cups flour; mix. In butter mixture, beat 1 cup flour; mix till you make sticky dough.
- Whisk milk, vanilla extract and egg in bowl; beat egg mixture and leftover flour into dough. Use plastic wrap to cover bowl; refrigerate for 30 minutes.
- Preheat an oven to 175°C/350°F; line parchment paper on baking sheet.
- Break small dough portion off; roll out to 1/4-in. thick round on lightly floured work surface. Put round on prepped baking sheet; repeat with leftover dough.
- In preheated oven, bake cookies for 8-10 minutes till soft and slightly golden. Put cookies on wire rack; fully cool.
- Mix and cook coconut in big skillet on medium heat for 2-4 minutes till toasted and golden brown.
- Melt caramel bits in microwave-safe bowl for 2 minutes, mixing every 30 seconds, till smooth and melted; mix coconut into caramel. Press spoonful coconut-caramel mixture over top of every cookie.
- Melt chocolate in microwave-safe bowl for 1 minute, mixing every 30 seconds, till smooth and melted. Dip base of every cookie into melted chocolate; put dipped cookies onto parchment paper till chocolate sets. Drizzle chocolate on top of every cookie.

Nutrition Information

- Calories: 594 calories;
- Total Carbohydrate: 75
- Cholesterol: 60
- Protein: 5.9
- Total Fat: 32.4
- Sodium: 371

63. Honey Lavender Cookies

Serving: 24 | Prep: 15mins | Cook: 15mins | Ready in:

Ingredients

- 1/2 cup butter, softened
- 1/2 cup honey
- 1 egg
- 1 tablespoon lavender flowers
- 2 cups whole wheat flour

Direction

- Set the oven to 175°C or 350°F to preheat and use parchment paper to line baking sheets.
- In a bowl, use an electric mixer to beat butter until it is creamy. Beat into the creamed butter with lavender, egg and honey until blended. Stir into the butter mixture with flour, half cup of at once, until incorporated. On the prepped baking sheet, drop batter by spoonfuls with 2 inches apart.
- In the preheated oven, bake cookies for 15 minutes, until they are browned on the bottom.

Nutrition Information

- Calories: 92 calories;
- Total Fat: 4.2
- Sodium: 31
- Total Carbohydrate: 13.1
- Cholesterol: 18
- Protein: 1.7

64. Jelly Bean Nests

Serving: 12 | Prep: 25mins | Cook: 5mins | Ready in:

Ingredients

- 2 cups miniature marshmallows

- 1/4 cup butter
- 4 cups chow mein noodles

Direction

- Coat a 12-cup muffin tin with butter.
- In a saucepan, mix together butter and marshmallows on moderate heat, then stir mixture until both marshmallows and butter are melted. Stir in chow mein noodles and coat well. Coat your fingers with butter and press the mixture into bottom as well as sides of the prepped muffin tin. Chill until firm.

Nutrition Information

- Calories: 143 calories;
- Total Fat: 8.4
- Sodium: 104
- Total Carbohydrate: 15.5
- Cholesterol: 10
- Protein: 1.3

65. Lavender Shortbread Cookies

Serving: 24 | Prep: 20mins | Cook: 20mins | Ready in:

Ingredients

- 1 1/2 cups butter, softened
- 2/3 cup white sugar
- 1/4 cup sifted confectioners' sugar
- 2 tablespoons finely chopped fresh lavender
- 1 tablespoon chopped fresh mint leaves
- 1 teaspoon grated lemon zest
- 2 1/2 cups all-purpose flour
- 1/2 cup cornstarch
- 1/4 teaspoon salt

Direction

- Cream confectioners' sugar, white sugar and butter together in a medium bowl until fluffy and light. Stir in lemon zest, mint and lavender. Mix salt, cornstarch and flour. Stir into batter until blended well. Separate the dough into 2 balls, enclose in plastic wrap and then flatten to around one inch thick. Chill for about 1 hour until firm.
- Preheat an oven to 165 degrees C (325 degrees F). Roll out the dough to 1/4-inch thickness on a lightly floured surface. Use cookie cutters to cut into shapes. Also works well with cookie stamps. Transfer into the cookie sheets.
- Bake in the preheated oven for 18 to 20 minutes, just until the cookies start to brown at the edges. Let it cool for several minutes in baking sheets before placing onto wire racks so as to cool completely.

Nutrition Information

- Calories: 186 calories;
- Total Fat: 11.6
- Sodium: 107
- Total Carbohydrate: 19.3
- Cholesterol: 31
- Protein: 1.5

66. Lebanese Easter Cookies

Serving: 60 | Prep: 2hours | Cook: 10mins | Ready in:

Ingredients

- 1 1/2 pounds butter
- 4 cups white sugar
- 1 cup water
- 9 cups semolina flour
- 8 cups all-purpose flour
- 1 1/2 tablespoons quick rise yeast
- 1 teaspoon ground cinnamon
- 1/2 teaspoon freshly grated nutmeg
- 1/2 teaspoon ground cloves
- 1/2 teaspoon ground cardamom
- 1/2 teaspoon allspice
- 1 teaspoon ground mahleb
- 1/4 cup black sesame seeds
- 1/4 cup rose water

- 1/4 cup orange flower water
- 1 cup warm water

Direction

- Put the butter in a small saucepan and let it melt on low heat setting. Add in the water and sugar and keep stirring the mixture until the sugar has fully dissolved. There's no need to bring the mixture to a boil. Take away the pan from the heat and allow it to cool a bit.
- Measure the flours and put it in a big bowl. Put in the spices, melted butter, sesame seeds and yeast and mix gently for about 10 minutes until all ingredients have combined well. Use a plastic wrap to cover the mixture and let the dough mixture sit for 1 hour.
- Use a cooking spray to coat 3 baking sheets or line each baking sheet with parchment paper. Put the orange flower water and rose water in a small bowl. Put warm water in another small bowl. Get about 1 cup of the dough mixture and place it on a clean board that is covered with flour. Wet your fingers in the warm water and knead the dough for a couple minutes then dip the dough into the flower water and knead it again until the dough is soft and stretchy.
- Roll the dough ball into a rope using the palm of your hand until it is 12 inches in length and 1 inch in diameter. Slice the dough rope into 2 equal pieces and form each halved rope into a wreath, secure the ends by pinching them together. Put it in the prepared baking sheets. Once a baking sheet has been filled up with the wreath-shaped cookies, use a clean towel to cover the cookies and keep it in the fridge throughout the night to allow the dough to rest.
- Preheat the oven to 350°F (175°C). While the oven is preheating, take the baking sheets out of the fridge to let it warm up. Put the baking sheets in the preheated oven and let it bake for about 15 minutes until the cookies turn golden brown in color.

Nutrition Information

- Calories: 289 calories;
- Sodium: 67
- Total Carbohydrate: 44.6
- Cholesterol: 24
- Protein: 5.2
- Total Fat: 10

67. Lemon Bars I

Serving: 16 | Prep: | Cook: | Ready in:

Ingredients

- 1 cup all-purpose flour
- 1/4 cup confectioners' sugar
- 1/4 cup butter
- 1 cup white sugar
- 2 tablespoons all-purpose flour
- 1/2 teaspoon baking powder
- 2 eggs
- 3 tablespoons lemon juice
- 1 tablespoon lemon zest
- 1/3 cup confectioners' sugar for decoration

Direction

- Preheat an oven to 175°C/350°F.
- Bottom layer: Combine 1/4 cup of confectioners' sugar and 1 cup flour. Melt butter; mix into the flour mixture.
- Press it even and flat into 8x8-in. baking dish then bake it for 20 minutes.
- Make top layer as it bakes: Mix baking powder, 2 tbsp. flour and 1 cup sugar.
- Beat eggs; add to the mixture, mixing well. Add the lemon rind and juice; stir again.
- Put on bottom later; bake for 25 minutes at 350°. Slightly cool; while warm, cut to squares. Dust it with confectioners' sugar.

Nutrition Information

- Calories: 133 calories;

- Sodium: 45
- Total Carbohydrate: 24
- Cholesterol: 31
- Protein: 1.7
- Total Fat: 3.6

68. Lemon Bars II

Serving: 30 | Prep: | Cook: | Ready in:

Ingredients

- 3 cups all-purpose flour
- 1 cup confectioners' sugar
- 1 1/2 cups butter
- 4 egg whites
- 1 1/2 cups white sugar
- 3 tablespoons all-purpose flour
- 1 teaspoon baking powder
- 1/2 cup lemon juice

Direction

- Preheat an oven to 175°C/350°F; grease 9x13-in. pan.
- Mix confectioners' sugar and 3 cups flour in a medium bowl; use a pastry cutter/fork to cut in butter till coarse crumbs are formed. Press 1/2 mixture into bottom of greased pan; bake for 15 minutes.
- Mix white sugar and egg whites in a smaller bowl. Add baking powder and flour; mix till there are no lumps left. Mix in lemon juice. Put lemon mixture on baked crust; sprinkle leftover crust mixture on top evenly. Bake in preheated oven for 20-25 minutes; refrigerate until set before serving.

Nutrition Information

- Calories: 187 calories;
- Total Fat: 9.3
- Sodium: 89
- Total Carbohydrate: 24.5

- Cholesterol: 24
- Protein: 2

69. Lemon Biscuits

Serving: 24 | Prep: | Cook: | Ready in:

Ingredients

- 3 1/4 cups all-purpose flour
- 1/2 teaspoon baking soda
- 1 pinch salt
- 3/4 cup butter, melted
- 1 1/4 cups white sugar
- 1/4 teaspoon lemon extract
- 2 eggs

Direction

- Turn on the oven to 375°F (190°C) to preheat. Grease baking sheets.
- Combine dry ingredients through a sift. Combine extract, sugar and melted butter. Add eggs, beat well.
- On a board that is lightly floured, roll the dough to about 1/8-inch thickness. Cut into rounds or squares; arrange it on cookie sheet, 1 inch away from each other. Use granulated sugar to sprinkle on top.
- Put into the oven to bake until golden or in 10-12 minutes.

Nutrition Information

- Calories: 159 calories;
- Sodium: 80
- Total Carbohydrate: 23.4
- Cholesterol: 31
- Protein: 2.3
- Total Fat: 6.3

70. Lemon Butter Cookies

Serving: 12 | Prep: | Cook: |Ready in:

Ingredients

- 1/2 cup butter, softened
- 1/2 cup white sugar
- 1 egg
- 1 1/2 cups all-purpose flour
- 2 tablespoons fresh lemon juice
- 1 teaspoon lemon zest
- 1/2 teaspoon baking powder
- 1/8 teaspoon salt
- 1/3 cup granulated sugar for decoration

Direction

- In a big bowl, use an electric mixer to beat sugar and butter together until the mixture is creamy. Beat in egg until fluffy and light. Mix in salt, baking powder, lemon peel and juice, and flour. Cover and chill until firm, for 2 hours.
- Set the oven to 175°C or 350°F to preheat.
- On a work surface coated well with flour, roll out a small amount of dough at a time using a floured rolling pin into 1/4-inch thick while keeping the leftover dough in the fridge. Use a 3-in. round cookie cutter to cut, then remove to ungreased cookie sheet. Use sugar to sprinkle over.
- Bake until edges are browned slightly, about 8-10 minutes, then allow to cool on cookie sheets for a minute. Transfer to wire racks and let cool thoroughly. Keep in an airtight container.

Nutrition Information

- Calories: 185 calories;
- Total Fat: 8.2
- Sodium: 105
- Total Carbohydrate: 26.1
- Cholesterol: 36
- Protein: 2.2

71. Lemon Crisps

Serving: 48 | Prep: | Cook: |Ready in:

Ingredients

- 1 (18.25 ounce) package lemon cake mix with pudding
- 1 cup crisp rice cereal
- 1/2 cup butter
- 1 egg

Direction

- Set the oven to 180°C or 350°F to preheat.
- Melt margarine or butter on low heat.
- Stir all of ingredients together including margarine or butter, mixing well.
- Form dough into balls, 1-inch size, and arrange on a grease-free cookie sheets, spaced 2 inches apart. Use your thumb to press balls flat.
- Bake until edges turn golden, about 9 minutes. Allow to cool on cookie sheets for a minute. Transfer to wire racks to cool.

Nutrition Information

- Calories: 66 calories;
- Cholesterol: 12
- Protein: 0.8
- Total Fat: 3.3
- Sodium: 97
- Total Carbohydrate: 8.4

72. Lemon Curd Bars

Serving: 40 | Prep: | Cook: |Ready in:

Ingredients

- 1 cup unsalted butter
- 2 cups all-purpose flour

- 1 cup white sugar
- 1/2 teaspoon baking soda
- 1 (10 ounce) jar lemon curd
- 2/3 cup flaked coconut
- 1/2 cup toasted and chopped almonds

Direction

- Start preheating the oven to 375°F (190°C).
- Cream butter in a large mixing bowl. Put in baking soda, flour and sugar. Mix until mixture forms coarse crumbs.
- Pat 2/3 mixture into bottom of a 9x13 inch baking pan. Bake for 10 mins at 375°F (190°C). Take out, then cool slightly.
- Spread the baked layer with lemon curd. With remaining 1/3 crumb mixture, put in the almonds and coconut. Top with a sprinkle of lemon curd.
- Reduce the oven temperature to 350°F (175°C). Bake the bars until lightly browned, 25 mins.

Nutrition Information

- Calories: 121 calories;
- Protein: 1.1
- Total Fat: 6.3
- Sodium: 25
- Total Carbohydrate: 16
- Cholesterol: 17

73. Lemon Dream Bars

Serving: 12 | Prep: | Cook: | Ready in:

Ingredients

- 1/3 cup butter
- 1 cup all-purpose flour
- 2 tablespoons white sugar
- 2 eggs, beaten
- 1/2 cup packed brown sugar
- 3/4 cup flaked coconut
- 1/2 cup chopped walnuts
- 1/4 teaspoon salt
- 1/4 teaspoon baking powder
- 1/2 teaspoon vanilla extract
- 2 teaspoons lemon zest
- 2 tablespoons lemon juice
- 1 cup sifted confectioners' sugar

Direction

- Turn oven to 350°F (175°C) to preheat.
- Combine 1 cup of flour, and 2 tablespoon of sugar in a medium bowl. Cut 1/3 cup butter into mixture until crumbly. Press mixture firmly into the bottom of a 9-inch square baking pan. Bake crust in the preheated oven for 10 to 15 minutes. Put to one side and allow to cool.
- Combine baking powder, salt, and sugar in the same bowl. Put in vanilla and eggs and mix until well incorporated. Stir in chopped nuts and coconut until all ingredients are well coated. Spoon filling into the baked crust, spreading evenly. Put back into the oven and bake for 25 to 30 minutes longer.
- For icing: mix together confectioners' sugar, lemon juice, and lemon zest. Beat until no lumps remain. Pour icing over the hot bars right after they are out of the oven, spreading to distribute evenly. Allow to cool for 15 minutes before slicing into smaller bars.

Nutrition Information

- Calories: 233 calories;
- Cholesterol: 45
- Protein: 3.1
- Total Fat: 10.5
- Sodium: 123
- Total Carbohydrate: 32.9

74. Lemon Drops

Serving: 48 | Prep: | Cook: | Ready in:

Ingredients

- 1/2 cup butter
- 1/2 cup shortening
- 3/4 cup white sugar
- 1 tablespoon lemon zest
- 1/3 cup milk
- 2 cups all-purpose flour

Direction

- Set an oven to preheat to 190°C (375°F).
- Beat the shortening and butter for 30 seconds on high using an electric mixer. Add the lemon peel and sugar and beat it until blended, then beat in the milk.
- Beat in as much flour as possible, then mix in the leftover flour. Drop the dough onto ungreased cookie sheets by rounded teaspoons and place them 2 inches apart.
- Let it bake for around 10 minutes or until the edges turn light brown. Allow it to cool on wire racks. Frost it with lemon cream cheese frosting, then store it in the fridge with a cover.

Nutrition Information

- Calories: 68 calories;
- Total Fat: 4.1
- Sodium: 14
- Total Carbohydrate: 7.2
- Cholesterol: 5
- Protein: 0.6

75. Lemon Kiss Cookies

Serving: 60 | Prep: | Cook: | Ready in:

Ingredients

- 1 1/2 cups butter, softened
- 3/4 cup white sugar
- 1 tablespoon lemon extract
- 2 3/4 cups all-purpose flour
- 1 1/2 cups chopped almonds
- 60 milk chocolate candy kisses, unwrapped
- 1/3 cup confectioners' sugar for decoration
- 3 (1 ounce) squares bittersweet chocolate
- 2 teaspoons vegetable oil

Direction

- Beat lemon extract, 3/4 cup sugar and butter till fluffy and light in big bowl. Add almonds and flour; beat till well blended at low speed. Cover; refrigerate to easily handle for 1 hour minimum.
- Preheat an oven to 190°C/375°F.
- Form scant tbsp. dough around every kiss, fully covering; to make ball, roll in hands. Put on ungreased baking sheet; bake till bottom edges are light golden brown and set for 8-12 minutes. Cool for 1 minute; transfer to rack to fully cool. Sprinkle confectioners' sugar on cookies.
- Melt chocolate squares in small pan; mix oil in till smooth. Drizzle on each cookie.

Nutrition Information

- Calories: 122 calories;
- Total Fat: 7.9
- Sodium: 37
- Total Carbohydrate: 11.6
- Cholesterol: 13
- Protein: 1.6

76. Lemon Madeleines

Serving: 12 | Prep: | Cook: | Ready in:

Ingredients

- 2 eggs
- 1/2 cup white sugar
- 5 tablespoons unsalted butter
- 3/4 cup all-purpose flour
- 1 teaspoon baking powder

- 1/4 teaspoon vanilla extract
- 1/2 lemon, juiced and zested
- 1/3 cup confectioners' sugar for decoration

Direction

- Blend sugar and eggs in a large bowl. Then add butter and combine well. Blend in vanilla, lemon, baking powder and flour on low speed.
- Use towel to cover the bowl and leave to rest for 1 hour.
- Preheat an oven to 190 degrees C (375 degrees F). Butter and then flour the madeleine molds. Whisk the batter and ladle into molds 3/4 full. Bake for ten minutes. Take away from the molds and let cool. Sprinkle with confectioners' sugar.

Nutrition Information

- Calories: 129 calories;
- Sodium: 53
- Total Carbohydrate: 18
- Cholesterol: 44
- Protein: 1.9
- Total Fat: 5.7

77. Lemon Meltaways

Serving: 48 | Prep: 20mins | Cook: 12mins | Ready in:

Ingredients

- 3/4 cup butter, softened
- 1/3 cup confectioners' sugar
- 1 tablespoon lemon juice
- 1 teaspoon lemon zest
- 1 1/4 cups all-purpose flour
- 1/2 cup cornstarch
- 3/4 cup confectioners' sugar
- 1/4 cup butter, softened
- 1 teaspoon lemon juice
- 1 teaspoon lemon zest

Direction

- Cream 1/3 cup confectioners' sugar and 3/4 cup butter till smooth in a medium bowl; mix in 1 tsp. lemon zest and 1 tbsp. lemon juice. Mix cornstarch and flour; blend into lemon mixture to make a soft dough. Halve the dough; roll each half to a 1-in. diameter, 8-in. long log. Cover with plastic wrap; refrigerate till firm, 2 hours.
- Preheat an oven to 175°C/350°F. Cut each roll to 1/4-in. slices; put onto cookie sheet.
- In preheated oven, bake till set, 8-12 minutes; fully cool prior to frosting.
- Blend 1 tsp. lemon zest, 1 tsp. lemon juice, 1/4 cup butter and 3/4 cup confectioners' sugar with an electric mixer till smooth in a small bowl. Frost cookies; dry before storing/serving.

Nutrition Information

- Calories: 62 calories;
- Total Carbohydrate: 6.5
- Cholesterol: 10
- Protein: 0.4
- Total Fat: 3.9
- Sodium: 27

78. Lemon Poppy Seed Biscotti

Serving: 36 | Prep: | Cook: | Ready in:

Ingredients

- 2 cups all-purpose flour
- 3/4 cup white sugar
- 1/2 cup finely ground almonds
- 1/2 teaspoon baking powder
- 1/2 teaspoon baking soda
- 1 tablespoon lemon zest
- 3 tablespoons poppy seeds
- 1 egg
- 2 egg whites

- 1 teaspoon lemon extract

Direction

- Preheat the oven to 175 degrees C/350 degrees F. Line parchment paper on a baking sheet.
- Mix baking soda, baking powder, ground almonds, sugar and flour.
- Mix lemon extract, egg whites, egg, poppy seeds and lemon peel. Add dry mixture. Mix well. Shape dough to 2 logs.
- Put logs on prepped baking sheet. Bake for 30 minutes at 175 degrees C/350 degrees F. Slightly cool. Slice diagonally to 1/2-in. slices. Bake slices for 8-10 more minutes until dry. Completely cool. Keep in an airtight container.

Nutrition Information

- Calories: 60 calories;
- Protein: 1.6
- Total Fat: 1.5
- Sodium: 30
- Total Carbohydrate: 10.1
- Cholesterol: 5

79. Lemon Whippersnappers

Serving: 18 | Prep: | Cook: | Ready in:

Ingredients

- 1 (18.25 ounce) package lemon cake mix
- 2 cups frozen whipped topping, thawed
- 1 egg, beaten
- 1/2 cup confectioners' sugar

Direction

- Combine egg, whipped topping, and cake mix in a large mixing bowl until well incorporated. Refrigerate dough for a couple of hours (or wrap in plastic wrap and freeze) or overnight.
- Turn oven to 350°F (175°C) to preheat.
- Shape tablespoons of dough into 1-inch balls; roll them in confectioners' sugar to coat. Arrange cookies a few inches apart on parchment paper-lined or greased cookie sheet.
- Bake in the preheated oven until cookies are firm but not browned, for 10 to 12 minutes. Allow cookies to cool on a wire cooling rack.

Nutrition Information

- Calories: 164 calories;
- Protein: 2.2
- Total Fat: 5.8
- Sodium: 212
- Total Carbohydrate: 26.3
- Cholesterol: 18

80. Lemon Yummies

Serving: 30 | Prep: | Cook: | Ready in:

Ingredients

- 1 1/2 cups white sugar
- 1/2 cup low-fat lemon yogurt
- 1/3 cup vegetable oil
- 2 egg
- 1 teaspoon lemon zest
- 1 teaspoon fresh lemon juice
- 2 2/3 cups all-purpose flour
- 1/2 teaspoon baking soda
- 1 teaspoon baking powder
- 1 teaspoon salt

Direction

- Preheat the oven to 190 degrees C/375 degrees F. Grease the cookie sheets.
- Mix lemon juice, lemon zest, eggs, oil, yogurt and sugar in a big bowl. Mix until blended well. Sift together salt, baking powder, baking soda and flour. Add to wet mixture. Mix until smooth.

- By rounded teaspoonfuls, drop cookies on prepped cookie sheets. Bake for 8-10 minutes in preheated oven until edges are slightly brown. Cool cookies slightly then remove from cookie sheets.

Nutrition Information

- Calories: 109 calories;
- Total Fat: 2.9
- Sodium: 122
- Total Carbohydrate: 19.1
- Cholesterol: 13
- Protein: 1.8

81. Lemon Marmalade Cookie Sandwiches

Serving: 3 | Prep: | Cook: | Ready in:

Ingredients

- 1/2 cup butter, softened
- 1/2 cup sifted confectioners' sugar
- 2 teaspoons lemon zest
- 1 teaspoon vanilla extract
- 1 cup all-purpose flour
- 1/2 cup toasted hazelnuts
- 1/4 teaspoon salt
- 1/4 teaspoon ground cinnamon
- 3 tablespoons lemon marmalade

Direction

- Beat the 1/2 cup sugar and butter in a mixing bowl using an electric mixer until it becomes smooth, then beat in vanilla and lemon peel.
- Grind the cinnamon, salt, nuts and flour finely in a food processor, then add it to the butter mixture and stir just until the dough holds together.
- Gather the dough into a ball and flatten it into a disk. Wrap in plastic and let it chill for around an hour or until it becomes firm.

- Set an oven to preheat to 325 °F, then butter the cookie sheet.
- On a lightly floured surface, roll the dough into 1/4-inch thick. Use a 3-inch round cookie cutter to cut out the cookies. Gather the scraps into a ball and roll it once again into 1/4-inch thick. Cut out the cookies then form a total of twelve. Move the cookies to the cookie sheet.
- Cut out the middle of six cookies using a 1-inch round cookie cutter and take it out. Let it bake for around 20 minutes or until it turns golden in color. Allow it to cool for 5 minutes on a rack.
- Leave a 1/8-inch border and evenly spread 1 1/2 tsp. of marmalade on top of each cookie without a hole. Sift an extra of powdered sugar on top of the cookies with the holes. Put the cookies with the holes, sugar side facing up, on top of the jam-covered cookies.

Nutrition Information

- Calories: 700 calories;
- Total Fat: 44.8
- Sodium: 424
- Total Carbohydrate: 70.2
- Cholesterol: 81
- Protein: 8.1

82. Macaron (Macaroon)

Serving: 20 | Prep: 10mins | Cook: 12mins | Ready in:

Ingredients

- 3 egg whites
- 1 cup white sugar
- 1/2 cup ground almonds
- 2 tablespoons slivered almonds, or to taste (optional)

Direction

- Preheat an oven to 165 degrees C (325 degrees F). Line waxed paper onto 2 baking sheets.

- Use an electric mixer to beat the egg whites in a bowl until fluffy. Slowly add sugar and continue beating on high until firm peaks are formed. Gently fold in the ground almonds until incorporated into dough. Place tablespoonfuls of the dough into baking sheets, keeping two inches apart. Sprinkle slivered almonds over tops.
- Bake for 12 to 15 minutes in the prepared oven until golden.

Nutrition Information

- Calories: 57 calories;
- Protein: 1.8
- Total Fat: 0.9
- Sodium: 9
- Total Carbohydrate: 11
- Cholesterol: 0

83. Meringue Cookies

Serving: 12 | Prep: | Cook: | Ready in:

Ingredients

- 2 egg whites
- 1/8 teaspoon salt
- 1/8 teaspoon cream of tartar
- 1 teaspoon vanilla extract
- 3/4 cup white sugar
- 1 cup semisweet chocolate chips

Direction

- Set the oven to 150°C or 300°F to preheat. To avoid burning, you may bake on an air cushion baking sheet or put on a regular cookie sheet with parchment paper.
- Beat together vanilla, cream of tartar, salt and egg whites until extremely firm. Put in sugar slowly and mix well, then stir in chocolate chips.
- Drop on pan with teaspoonfuls of the mixture. Bake at 300° for about 25 minutes. They should just be browned lightly.

Nutrition Information

- Calories: 119 calories;
- Total Fat: 4.2
- Sodium: 35
- Total Carbohydrate: 21.4
- Cholesterol: 0
- Protein: 1.2

84. Meringue Kisses II

Serving: 12 | Prep: | Cook: | Ready in:

Ingredients

- 2 egg whites
- 1/4 cup white sugar
- 1 teaspoon almond extract
- 1/4 cup white sugar
- 1/3 cup toffee baking bits

Direction

- Set the oven to 130°C or 250°F to preheat. Use parchment paper to cover cookie sheets.
- Beat egg whites until extremely stiff and dry. Put in 1/4 cup of granulated sugar gradually and keep on beating until the mixture holds its shape.
- Put in flavoring extract. Fold in additional 1/4 cup of sugar and 1/3 cup finely crushed nut brittle or other crushed candy.
- Form or drop dough into preferred shapes on parchment covered the cookie sheet. You may sprinkle lightly with either additional powdered confectioner sugar or crushed candy, if wanted. Arrange in the oven until set and delicately brown for 30-35 minutes.
- To take baked kisses out of paper if a problem happens, lay out a hot, damp towel and put

paper with kisses on towel. Allow to stand for a minute and steam will help loosen kisses. Slip them off paper using a spatula.

Nutrition Information

- Calories: 74 calories;
- Protein: 0.6
- Total Fat: 2.5
- Sodium: 42
- Total Carbohydrate: 12.2
- Cholesterol: 5

85. Perfect And Delicious Royal Icing

Serving: 48 | Prep: 15mins | Cook: | Ready in:

Ingredients

- 1/2 cup water
- 1/4 cup meringue powder
- 7 cups confectioners' sugar
- 2 tablespoons light corn syrup (such as Karo®)
- 2 tablespoons shortening (such as Crisco®)
- 1 teaspoon vanilla extract

Direction

- In a large bowl, whip meringue powder and water for 7 to 10 minutes using an electric mixer on high speed until fluffy and soft peaks appear. Slowly add vanilla extract, shortening, corn syrup and confectioners' sugar while mixing with mixer on low speed. Raise the speed back to high and continue beating for about 3 minutes until smooth and well-combined.

Nutrition Information

- Calories: 82 calories;
- Cholesterol: 0
- Protein: 0.3

- Total Fat: 0.6
- Sodium: 4
- Total Carbohydrate: 19.4

86. Poppy Seed Hungarian Style Cookies

Serving: 12 | Prep: 30mins | Cook: 25mins | Ready in:

Ingredients

- 1/2 cup heavy cream
- 1 1/4 cups poppy seeds
- 1 1/2 cups whole wheat flour
- 1 teaspoon baking soda
- 1/2 teaspoon ground cinnamon
- 3/4 cup butter, softened
- 1/2 lemon, juiced
- 2/3 cup maple flavored syrup

Direction

- Preheat the oven to 175°C or 350°F. Place parchment paper or grease a baking sheet.
- In a small saucepan, mix together poppy seeds and cream. On medium heat, heat the poppy seeds mixture until hot but do not boil. Take off heat and let the mixture cool.
- Mix together cinnamon, flour, and baking soda in a medium bowl. Mix in syrup, lemon juice, and butter; blend well. Fold in the poppy seed mixture.
- Scoop small spoonfuls of mixture in the prepared baking sheet.
- Bake in the preheated oven for 20 minutes until the edges are golden brown. Let the cookies cool for 5 minutes in the baking sheet. Then move cookies onto a wire rack to completely cool.

Nutrition Information

- Calories: 309 calories;
- Protein: 5

- Total Fat: 21.7
- Sodium: 205
- Total Carbohydrate: 27.2
- Cholesterol: 44

87. Quick Lemon Crisps

Serving: 72 | Prep: 10mins | Cook: 10mins | Ready in:

Ingredients

- 2 cups all-purpose flour
- 3/4 teaspoon baking soda
- 1 pinch salt
- 3/4 cup shortening
- 1 cup white sugar
- 2 (3 ounce) packages instant lemon pudding mix
- 3 eggs

Direction

- Start preheating the oven to 375°F (190°C).
- Sift flour with salt and baking soda. Cream shortening, and then add pudding mix and sugar. Cream until fluffy and light. Add eggs and stir thoroughly, and then add the flour mixture. Stir until thoroughly combined. Onto the oil baking sheets, drop the dough by teaspoonfuls.
- Bake in the preheated oven for 8-10 minutes.

Nutrition Information

- Calories: 56 calories;
- Total Carbohydrate: 8
- Cholesterol: 8
- Protein: 0.6
- Total Fat: 2.4
- Sodium: 52

88. Rainbow Cookies

Serving: 96 | Prep: 45mins | Cook: 10mins | Ready in:

Ingredients

- 8 ounces almond paste
- 1 cup butter, softened
- 1 cup white sugar
- 4 eggs, separated
- 2 cups all-purpose flour
- 6 drops red food coloring
- 6 drops green food coloring
- 1/4 cup seedless red raspberry jam
- 1/4 cup apricot jam
- 1 cup semisweet chocolate chips, melted

Direction

- Set the oven to 350°F (175°C), and start preheating. Line parchment paper on 3 baking pans of 9x13 inches.
- In a large bowl, use a fork to break almond paste apart, then cream with egg yolks, sugar and butter together. Once the mixture is smooth and fluffy, mix in flour to shape a dough. Beat egg whites in a small bowl until forming soft peaks. Fold egg whites into the dough. Separate the dough into 3 portions of same size. Mix one portion with red food coloring, and one with green food coloring. Spread each portion into each prepared baking pan.
- Bake for 10 - 12 minutes in the preheated oven, until lightly browned. Slowly take away from pan and parchment paper, allow to cool completely on wire racks.
- Choose a piece of plastic wrap that is large enough to wrap all three layers, place green layer onto it. Spread raspberry jam onto green layer, then place uncolored layer on top. Spread apricot jam over the uncolored layer, and top with pink layer. Place layers to a baking sheet, and cover with plastic wrap. On top of wrapped layers, put a cutting board or heavy pan to compress. Let it chill in the fridge for 8 hours or overnight.

- Discard the plastic wrap. Sprinkle with melted chocolate chips, and chill in the fridge until chocolate is firm, about 1 hour. Cut into small squares then serve.

Nutrition Information

- Calories: 61 calories;
- Total Carbohydrate: 7.4
- Cholesterol: 13
- Protein: 0.8
- Total Fat: 3.3
- Sodium: 17

89. Raspberry Meringue Bars

Serving: 24 | Prep: | Cook: | Ready in:

Ingredients

- 1 cup butter, softened
- 1 1/2 cups white sugar
- 2 egg yolks
- 2 1/2 cups all-purpose flour
- 1 (10 ounce) jar seedless raspberry jam
- 4 egg whites
- 1/4 teaspoon salt
- 2 cups finely chopped walnuts

Direction

- Set the oven to 175°C or 350°F to preheat. Coat 15 1/2"x10 1/2"x1" jellyroll pan with grease.
- Cream together egg yolks, 1/2 cup of sugar and butter until well combined. Put in flour and mix well together. In the bottom of prepped pan, pat the dough evenly, then bake until browned slightly, about 15 to 20 minutes.
- Take the pan out of oven but leave oven on. Allow to cool about 5 minutes then spread jam over. Beat salt and egg whites together until firm but not dry. Fold in egg whites carefully with chopped nuts and leftover sugar.

- Spread egg whites mixture gently on top of the jam layer, ensuring to seal all corners and edges. Turn back to the oven and bake until turn golden brown, about 25 minutes more. While still warm, cut into bars 3x1-inch in size. Cake may be stored airtight for a maximum of 1 week in at room temperature or you can freeze it. Defrost with a cover at room temperature.

Nutrition Information

- Calories: 264 calories;
- Total Carbohydrate: 31.4
- Cholesterol: 37
- Protein: 3.7
- Total Fat: 14.5
- Sodium: 89

90. Rhubarb Meringue Squares

Serving: 12 | Prep: 30mins | Cook: 25mins | Ready in:

Ingredients

- CRUST:
- 1/4 cup butter
- 1/4 cup white sugar
- 1 egg
- 1 teaspoon vanilla extract
- 1 1/4 cups all-purpose flour
- 1 teaspoon baking powder
- 1/4 teaspoon salt
- FILLING:
- 3 cups chopped fresh rhubarb
- 3 tablespoons water
- 1/2 cup white sugar
- 1/2 teaspoon ground cinnamon
- 2 tablespoons water
- 3 tablespoons cornstarch
- TOPPING:
- 2 egg whites
- 1/2 cup white sugar
- 1/4 cup flaked coconut

Direction

- Start preheating the oven at 350°F (175°C). Oil an 8x8-inch square baking dish.
- In a medium bowl, whisk 1/4 cup of sugar and butter until smooth. Beat in vanilla and egg. Mix salt, baking powder, and flour; blend into the butter mixture until it forms stiff dough. Flatten the dough into the base and 1/2-inch up the sides of the greased pan.
- Bake crust about 15 minutes, until set.
- Mix 3 tablespoons of water, cinnamon, 1/2 cup of sugar, and rhubarb on medium heat in a saucepan. Heat to a boil, and cook about 10 minutes until rhubarb soften. Blend cornstarch and leftover 2 tablespoons water, and combine into the saucepan. Cook, stirring continually, until the sauce thickens. Take out from the heat, and scatter over the baked crust.
- Whisk egg whites in a medium metal or glass bowl until it has soft peaks. Slowly put in 1/2 cup leftover sugar, keep beating until it forms stiff peaks. Spread on the layer of rhubarb sauce with the meringue, and scatter top with coconut.
- Bake about 10 minutes in the prepared oven, until the meringue turns golden brown. Let cool completely before slicing into squares.

Nutrition Information

- Calories: 193 calories;
- Protein: 2.8
- Total Fat: 4.9
- Sodium: 127
- Total Carbohydrate: 35.1
- Cholesterol: 26

91. Rose Pavlova Cakes

Serving: 18 | Prep: 25mins | Cook: 1hours15mins | Ready in:

Ingredients

- 3 egg whites, at room temperature
- 1 teaspoon dried rose petal powder
- 1/2 cup white sugar, or more to taste
- 1 teaspoon vanilla extract, or to taste
- 1/2 teaspoon rose extract, or to taste
- 1 teaspoon cornstarch
- 1 1/2 tablespoons cream cheese
- 1 cup heavy whipping cream
- 2 tablespoons white sugar
- 1 tablespoon dried rose petals (optional)

Direction

- Preheat oven to 110 degrees C/225 degrees F. Line parchment paper on a baking sheet.
- In a stand mixer's bowl, beat rose petal powder and egg whites to form soft peaks. Begin by gradually beating 1/2 cup sugar in. Put speed on high. Beat to form glossy and stiff peaks. Mix in rose extract and vanilla extract. Very gently fold cornstarch in the meringue with a spatula.
- Spoon meringue in a piping bag that has a fine round tip. Pipe out to 18 individual rounds.
- Bake in preheated oven for 1 hour 15 minutes until edges look dry. Turn oven off. Keep pavlovas in the oven for 20-25 more minutes. Take out of the oven. Completely cool for about 30 minutes.
- In a bowl, beat cream cheese for 30 seconds. Add 2 tbsp. sugar and heavy cream. Beat it until fluffy. In another piping bag, spoon in whipped cream.
- Pipe the whipped cream on cooled pavlovas. Use dried rose petals to decorate.

Nutrition Information

- Calories: 81 calories;
- Sodium: 18
- Total Carbohydrate: 7.6
- Cholesterol: 19
- Protein: 1
- Total Fat: 5.3

92. Spring Lime Tea Cookies

Serving: 24 | Prep: 20mins | Cook: 10mins | Ready in:

Ingredients

- 2 teaspoons lime juice
- 1/3 cup milk
- 1/2 cup butter, softened
- 3/4 cup white sugar
- 1 egg
- 2 teaspoons lime zest
- 1 3/4 cups all-purpose flour
- 1 teaspoon baking powder
- 1/4 teaspoon baking soda
- 2 tablespoons lime juice
- 1/4 cup white sugar

Direction

- Preheat oven to 175 degrees C/350 degrees F. Mix 2 tsp. lime juice with milk. Stand for 5 minutes.
- Cream 3/4 cup sugar and butter together in a big bowl until fluffy and light. Beat egg in. Mix milk mixture and lime zest in. Mix baking soda, baking powder and flour then mix into creamed mixture. On ungreased cookie sheets, drop by rounded spoonfuls.
- Bake in preheated oven for 8-10 minutes until edges become light brown. Cool cookies for 5 minutes on baking sheets. Transfer onto a wire rack. Completely cool.
- Glaze: Mix sugar and leftover lime juice together. Brush it on cooled cookies.

Nutrition Information

- Calories: 105 calories;
- Protein: 1.4
- Total Fat: 4.2
- Sodium: 65
- Total Carbohydrate: 15.7
- Cholesterol: 18

93. Strawberry Cake Cookies

Serving: 30 | Prep: 10mins | Cook: 15mins | Ready in:

Ingredients

- 1 (18.25 ounce) package strawberry cake mix
- 2 eggs, beaten
- 1/2 cup chopped fresh strawberries
- 1 cup whipped cream

Direction

- Set oven to preheat at 175°C (350°F). Prepare cookie sheets by greasing them.
- Combine strawberries, eggs and the cake mix in a medium bowl until well mixed. Fold in the whipped cream until well incorporated. Drop the mixture by rounded spoonfuls onto the greased cookie sheets.
- Bake in the preheated oven for 8 to 10 minutes. Let cool for 5 minutes on baking sheet then take them out and place onto a wire rack to cool fully.

Nutrition Information

- Calories: 78 calories;
- Sodium: 114
- Total Carbohydrate: 14.4
- Cholesterol: 14
- Protein: 0.9
- Total Fat: 2

94. Sugar Cookie Cups With Coconut Buttercream Frosting

Serving: 24 | Prep: 20mins | Cook: 11mins | Ready in:

Ingredients

- cooking spray

- 1 (16.5 ounce) package refrigerated sugar cookie dough
- 1 tablespoon all-purpose flour, or as needed
- 3/4 cup unsalted butter, at room temperature
- 3 cups confectioners' sugar, sifted
- 3 tablespoons canned coconut milk, or more as needed
- 1 teaspoon coconut extract
- 1/4 cup colored sugar (optional)
- 1/4 cup candy sprinkles (optional)
- 1/4 cup shredded coconut (optional)

Direction

- Turn oven to 350°F (175°C) to preheat. Coat a mini muffin tin using cooking spray. Take out 2 tsp. of cookie dough and form into a ball, arrange the ball in the greased tin. Repeat procedure with the rest of cookie dough.
- Press each ball into a cup shape using the bottom of a short glass coated with flour; the top of each cup should be approximately 1/4 inch below the tin's rim.
- Bake for approximately 10 minutes in the heated oven, until golden. Reinforce the cup shape by pressing the cookies one more time using the shot glass. Keep baking for approximately 1 more minute or until cooking cups are extremely lightly browned. Allow to cool for 5 minutes in the tin. Gently remove to a wire rack to cool entirely.
- In a mixing bowl, mix butter until fluffy using an electric mixer. Put in confectioners' sugar, 1 cup at a time, mixing until well distributed. Add coconut extract and coconut milk; beat at high speed until frosting is fluffy and light. If the frosting looks too thick, put in 1 tablespoon coconut milk.
- Pipe or spoon frosting into each cookie cup. Garnish with shredded coconut, candy sprinkles, and colored sugar.

Nutrition Information

- Calories: 232 calories;
- Total Fat: 12.1
- Sodium: 72
- Total Carbohydrate: 30.9
- Cholesterol: 17
- Protein: 0.9

Chapter 3: Halloween Cookie Recipes

***

95. Almond Joy® Cookies

Serving: 36 | Prep: 20mins | Cook: 8mins | Ready in:

Ingredients

- 4 1/2 cups all-purpose flour
- 2 teaspoons baking soda
- 1 teaspoon salt
- 1 1/2 cups white sugar
- 1 1/2 cups brown sugar
- 1 ripe banana
- 4 eggs
- 1 tablespoon vanilla extract
- 5 cups chocolate chips
- 2 cups sweetened flaked coconut
- 2 cups chopped almonds

Direction

- Start preheating the oven to 375°F (190°C). Lightly oil baking sheets.
- Combine salt, baking soda, and flour in a bowl.
- Beat banana, brown sugar, and white sugar in another bowl until creamy and smooth; beat in 1 egg at a time until well-mixed. Mix in vanilla extract.

- Stir the banana mixture into the flour mixture until batter is well-blended; fold in almonds, coconut, and chocolate chips. Drop batter onto the prepared baking sheets by rounded spoonfuls.
- Bake in the prepared oven for 8 to 10 minutes until edges of cookies start to crisp. Let cookies cool on baking sheet for 5 minutes before removing to a wire rack to cool fully.

Nutrition Information

- Calories: 285 calories;
- Total Carbohydrate: 44.9
- Cholesterol: 21
- Protein: 4.6
- Total Fat: 11.5
- Sodium: 159

96. Apple Crisp Cookies

Serving: 24 | Prep: 30mins | Cook: 10mins | Ready in:

Ingredients

- 2 cups whole wheat flour, plus
- 2 tablespoons whole wheat flour
- 1 1/2 teaspoons ground cinnamon
- 1 teaspoon baking powder
- 1 teaspoon salt
- 1/2 cup butter, softened
- 1/2 cup demerara sugar
- 1/2 cup brown sugar
- 7 tablespoons apple butter
- 2 eggs
- 1 teaspoon vanilla extract
- 3 tablespoons apple juice
- 2 cups quick cooking oats
- 1 apple, finely chopped

Direction

- Heat oven to 375°F (190°C). In a large bowl, stir cinnamon, baking powder, salt with all of the whole wheat flour together.
- Mash the brown sugar, demerara sugar, and butter together in another bowl until well mixed, then mix in the apple butter until smooth. Mix in apple juice, vanilla extract, and eggs until thoroughly combined; put the apple juice mixture into the dry mixture about a third cup at a time, mixing after each addition. Stir in the oats and sliced apple.
- Form the dough into balls, 2 teaspoons each and place onto ungreased baking trays about 2 inches apart.
- Bake in the heated oven about 10 minutes until the cookies are lightly brown and firm in the centers; rest for about 2 minutes to cool on baking trays until taking out to cool completely on wire racks.

Nutrition Information

- Calories: 148 calories;
- Protein: 3
- Total Fat: 4.9
- Sodium: 155
- Total Carbohydrate: 24.1
- Cholesterol: 26

97. Booger Cookies

Serving: 24 | Prep: 35mins | Cook: 10mins | Ready in:

Ingredients

- 1 cup margarine, softened
- 1/3 cup confectioners' sugar
- 1 egg
- 1 teaspoon vanilla extract
- 3/4 teaspoon almond extract
- 1 (3 ounce) package instant pistachio pudding mix
- 2 cups all-purpose flour
- 1/2 cup semisweet chocolate chips

- 1 1/2 cups confectioners' sugar
- 1 teaspoon vanilla extract
- 1 tablespoon milk, or as needed
- 3 drops green food coloring, or as needed
- 24 milk chocolate candy kisses (such as Hershey's Kisses®), unwrapped

Direction

- Preheat the oven to 175°C or 350°F. Grease a baking sheet lightly.
- In a big bowl, beat 1/3 cup confectioners' sugar and margarine together using an electric mixer until smooth. Mix in almond extract, a teaspoon of vanilla extract, and egg until well blended. Stir in the pudding mix until the mixture is smooth. Mix in flour until just combined. Stir in chocolate chips just enough to blend evenly.
- Make 1-in balls from the cookie dough then arrange on the greased baking sheet. Form an indent into each cookies with your thumb.
- Bake for 10-14mins in the preheated oven until golden on the edges. Cool cookies for a minute on the baking sheet. Move to a wire rack to completely cool the cookies.
- Meanwhile, combine food coloring, 1 1/2 cups confectioners' sugar, milk, and a teaspoon of vanilla extract in a bowl to make the filling. Pour in more milk if necessary to make a smooth mixture. Scoop a bit of the green filling into each cooled cookie; add a candy kiss on top of each.

Nutrition Information

- Calories: 204 calories;
- Cholesterol: 9
- Protein: 1.9
- Total Fat: 10.4
- Sodium: 154
- Total Carbohydrate: 26.4

98. Candy Bar Brownies

Serving: 6 | Prep: | Cook: |Ready in:

Ingredients

- 1 (18.25 ounce) package German chocolate cake mix
- 3/4 cup melted butter
- 2/3 cup sweetened condensed milk
- 4 (2.16 ounce) bars chocolate-coated caramel-peanut nougat candy, chopped

Direction

- Combine condensed milk, melted margarine or butter, and cake mix. Pour the mixture in a 9 x 13-inch pan and spread evenly.
- Put inside the oven at 350°F and bake for 10 minutes.
- Slice candy bars into little pieces and put on the baked crust. To achieve a crumbly texture, add the leftover batter on the top of the sliced candy bars. Do not spread batter evenly.
- Bake again for 20 minutes in the oven.

Nutrition Information

- Calories: 841 calories;
- Total Carbohydrate: 112.3
- Cholesterol: 78
- Protein: 9.9
- Total Fat: 40.5
- Sodium: 940

99. Candy Bar Squares

Serving: 12 | Prep: | Cook: |Ready in:

Ingredients

- 1 cup butter, softened
- 1 cup white sugar
- 1/2 cup packed brown sugar
- 2 eggs

- 3 cups all-purpose flour
- 1 teaspoon baking soda
- 1 teaspoon salt
- 6 (2.1 ounce) bars chocolate-coated peanut and nougat candy, eg: Baby

Direction

- Preheat the oven to 350°F (175°C).
- Whisk the white sugar, brown sugar and butter or margarine together until the mixture becomes fluffy and light in texture. Combine in the eggs while thoroughly mixing everything together.
- Add in the baking soda, salt and flour and mix everything together. Keep 1/2 cup of the chopped candy bars aside to use for topping. Add the rest of the chopped candy bars into the combined egg-flour mixture and mix. In a 13x9-inch baking pan, put in the prepared batter mixture and spread it out in the pan. Top it off with the reserved chopped candy bars.
- Put it in the preheated oven and let it bake for 25-30 minutes until it turns light brown in color. Let cool in pan on wire rack; slice it into square-shaped pieces.

Nutrition Information

- Calories: 505 calories;
- Total Fat: 22.8
- Sodium: 490
- Total Carbohydrate: 69.1
- Cholesterol: 73
- Protein: 6.7

100. Caramel Apple Cookies

Serving: 24 | Prep: 10mins | Cook: 20mins | Ready in:

Ingredients

- 3/4 cup confectioners' sugar
- 2/3 cup butter, softened
- 3 tablespoons frozen apple juice concentrate, thawed, divided
- 1 1/2 cups all-purpose flour
- 1/4 teaspoon salt
- flat toothpicks
- 30 individually wrapped caramels, unwrapped
- 2 tablespoons water
- 3/4 cup finely chopped walnuts (optional)

Direction

- Preheat the oven to 175 ° C or 350 ° F.
- Use an electric mixer to whip butter, a tablespoon of apple juice concentrate and confectioners' sugar in bowl till fluffy and light; mix in salt and flour till dough is barely incorporated. Roll dough to make 3/4-inch balls and place on non-greased baking sheets.
- Bake for 12 to 17 minutes in prepped oven till edges turn pale golden brown. Quickly insert toothpicks in the middle of every cookie. Put the cookies on wire rack to fully cool.
- In a saucepan, mix 2 tablespoons of apple juice concentrate, water and caramels over low heat; cook and mix for 5 to 10 minutes, till mixture becomes smooth. Top every cookie with scoop of caramel sauce, allowing excess caramel sauce to drip off.
- Put the walnuts onto plate. Press the bottom of each caramel-coated cookie into walnuts and turn onto waxed paper sheet to set.

Nutrition Information

- Calories: 163 calories;
- Total Fat: 8.6
- Sodium: 92
- Total Carbohydrate: 20.7
- Cholesterol: 14
- Protein: 2

101. Cat Poop Cookies II

Serving: 18 | Prep: | Cook: |Ready in:

Ingredients

- 1/4 cup honey
- 1/4 cup molasses
- 2/3 cup butter
- 1 egg
- 2 1/3 cups whole wheat flour
- 1/2 teaspoon ground cinnamon
- 1/2 teaspoon ground ginger
- 1/2 teaspoon ground cloves
- 1 (32 ounce) package wheat and barley nugget cereal (e.g. Grape-Nuts™)
- 1/2 cup crushed ramen noodles

Direction

- Microwave honey in a medium bowl till it bubbles up to 1 minutes. Mix egg, butter and molasses in. Beat till smooth. Mix cloves, ginger, cinnamon and flour in till mixed. Add any of the following: peanuts, chocolate chips, ramen or coconut. Chill the dough till firm.
- Preheat an oven to 175°C/350°F. Roll dough to 3/4-in. diameter logs. Slice to pieces around the length of cat poop. In cereal, roll pieces. Put on unprepared cookie sheet. In preheated oven, bake for 10-15 minutes.
- In a disposable cat litter box with a bed of cereal and a new litterbox scoop, put cookies to serve. Put plastic flies in. for extra fun, dip litter scoop into chocolate.

Nutrition Information

- Calories: 328 calories;
- Total Fat: 8.5
- Sodium: 381
- Total Carbohydrate: 59.8
- Cholesterol: 28
- Protein: 8

102. Chocolate Halloween Cookies

Serving: 48 | Prep: 30mins | Cook: 10mins |Ready in:

Ingredients

- Cookies:
- 1 cup white sugar
- 2/3 cup butter, softened
- 1/3 cup milk
- 1 egg
- 1 1/2 teaspoons vanilla extract
- 1 1/2 cups all-purpose flour
- 1/2 cup cocoa powder
- 1/2 teaspoon baking powder
- 1/4 teaspoon salt
- 1 cup candy-coated peanut butter pieces (such as Reese's Pieces®)
- Frosting:
- 3 tablespoons melted butter
- 3 tablespoons cocoa powder
- 1 cup confectioners' sugar
- 2 tablespoons milk
- 1/2 teaspoon vanilla extract
- 1/4 cup candy-coated peanut butter pieces (such as Reese's Pieces®), or to taste

Direction

- Set oven to 350°F (175°C) to preheat.
- In a bowl, whip 2/3 cup softened butter and white sugar together with an electric mixer until creamy and smooth; stir in 1 1/2 teaspoons vanilla extract, egg and a third cup milk. Into creamed butter mixture, combine salt, baking powder, 1/2 cup cocoa powder and flour until just combined; fold in a cup peanut butter pieces coated with candy. Put dough onto a baking tray, 1 to 2 tablespoons per cookie.
- Bake in the prepared oven for 10 to 12 minutes until crispy on the edges. Let cookies cool on pans for 2 to 3 minutes before taking out to wire racks to fully cool.
- In a bowl, whip 3 tablespoons cocoa powder with 3 tablespoons melted butter with an

electric mixer until smooth and creamy; whip in 1/2 teaspoon vanilla extract, 2 tablespoons milk and confectioners' sugar until fluffy and smooth. Spread over cookies and sprinkle with more candy-coated peanut butter chunks.

Nutrition Information

- Calories: 97 calories;
- Protein: 1.4
- Total Fat: 4.7
- Sodium: 52
- Total Carbohydrate: 13.2
- Cholesterol: 13

103. Chocolate Mice

Serving: 12 | Prep: 20mins | Cook: | Ready in:

Ingredients

- 4 (1 ounce) squares semisweet chocolate
- 1/3 cup sour cream
- 1 cup chocolate cookie crumbs
- 1/3 cup chocolate cookie crumbs
- 1/3 cup confectioners' sugar
- 24 silver dragees decorating candy
- 1/4 cup sliced almonds
- 12 (2 inch) pieces long red vine licorice

Direction

- Melt chocolate; mix with sour cream. Stir in a cup of chocolate cookie crumbs. Chill in the fridge with a cover until firm.
- Roll into balls by level tablespoonfuls. Mold to a slight point at one end (the nose).
- Roll dough in chocolate cookie crumbs (for dark mice) and in confectioners sugar (for white mice). Place dragees, sliced almond and a licorice string in appropriate spots on each mouse for eyes, ears and tail.
- Chill in the fridge for at least 2 hours until firm.

Nutrition Information

- Calories: 176 calories;
- Protein: 2.3
- Total Fat: 7.2
- Sodium: 90
- Total Carbohydrate: 27.4
- Cholesterol: 3

104. Chocolate Toffee Cookies I

Serving: 12 | Prep: | Cook: | Ready in:

Ingredients

- 1 (18.25 ounce) package devil's food cake mix
- 1/3 cup vegetable oil
- 2 eggs
- 3/4 cup coarsely chopped chocolate-covered toffee candy bars

Direction

- Preheat an oven to 180 degrees C (350 degrees F).
- Mix the eggs, oil and cake mix in a large bowl. Then beat for 3 to 4 minutes with an electric beater until blended well. Mix in chopped candy with a spoon.
- Drop teaspoonfuls onto cookie sheets greased with nonstick baking spray by 2 inches apart. Bake for about 9 to 11 minutes or until cookies become firm. Transfer cookies onto a wire rack and cool completely.

Nutrition Information

- Calories: 303 calories;
- Total Fat: 15.9
- Sodium: 358
- Total Carbohydrate: 36.1
- Cholesterol: 44

- Protein: 4.7

105. Cranberry Pumpkin Cookies

Serving: 36 | Prep: 20mins | Cook: 12mins | Ready in:

Ingredients

- 1/2 cup butter, softened
- 1 cup white sugar
- 1 teaspoon vanilla extract
- 1 egg
- 1 cup solid pack pumpkin puree
- 2 1/4 cups all-purpose flour
- 2 teaspoons baking powder
- 1 teaspoon baking soda
- 1/2 teaspoon salt
- 1 cup fresh cranberries
- 1 teaspoon ground cinnamon
- 1 tablespoon orange zest
- 1/2 cup chopped walnuts

Direction

- Preheat the oven to 375°F (190°C). Coat the cookie sheets with oil.
- Cream the sugar and butter together in a big mixing bowl until the texture of the mixture becomes fluffy and light. Whisk in the egg, pumpkin and vanilla. Sift the baking soda, flour, cinnamon, baking powder and salt together then add it into the pumpkin mixture and mix everything together until thoroughly combined. Slice each of the cranberries into 2 equal portions then add it into the mixture followed by the walnuts and orange zest; mix well. Put teaspoonfuls of the prepared pumpkin-cranberry mixture onto the prepared cookie sheets.
- Put it in the preheated oven and let it bake for 10-12 minutes.

Nutrition Information

- Calories: 90 calories;
- Cholesterol: 12
- Protein: 1.3
- Total Fat: 3.9
- Sodium: 131
- Total Carbohydrate: 12.9

106. Crispy Rice Candy Corn Treats

Serving: 24 | Prep: 5mins | Cook: 10mins | Ready in:

Ingredients

- 9 cups miniature marshmallows
- 1/2 cup butter
- 10 cups crispy rice cereal
- 2 cups candy corn
- 3/4 cup mini chocolate chips

Direction

- Butter the 10x15-in. baking pan.
- In a big saucepan, melt butter and marshmallows on medium heat, mixing for 10 minutes till smooth.
- Mix chocolate chips, candy corn and cereal in a big bowl. Put marshmallow mixture into cereal mixture; mix till cereal is coated well. Spread in prepped pan; cool it to room temperature. Cut to squares.

Nutrition Information

- Calories: 225 calories;
- Total Carbohydrate: 42.9
- Cholesterol: 10
- Protein: 1
- Total Fat: 5.6
- Sodium: 142

107. Dianne's Pumpkin Cookie Cups

Serving: 32 | Prep: 30mins | Cook: 10mins | Ready in:

Ingredients

- 2 cups all-purpose flour
- 1 1/2 teaspoons baking powder
- 1/2 teaspoon salt
- 1/4 teaspoon ground nutmeg (optional)
- 1/2 cup unsalted butter, softened
- 1 cup white sugar
- 1 egg
- 2 tablespoons milk
- 1 (3 ounce) package cream cheese, softened
- 1 cup confectioners' sugar, divided
- 1/3 cup pumpkin puree
- 2 3/4 cups confectioners' sugar
- 1 1/2 teaspoons ground cinnamon
- 1/4 teaspoon ground nutmeg
- 1/4 teaspoon ground ginger
- 1 pinch ground cloves

Direction

- Heat oven to 200°C (400°F) beforehand. Greasing 32 miniature muffin cups.
- In a bowl, sift a quarter teaspoon of nutmeg, salt, baking powder, and flour. Using an electric mixer to cream sugar with unsalted butter in the second large mixing bowl till workable and smooth; beating in milk and egg. Setting the mixer to low speed and beating in flour mixture gradually, beat just till the dough comes together.
- Pinching off dough by tablespoon, rolling into a ball; in the prepared mini muffin cups, place balls.
- In the preheated oven, allow to bake for 8-10 minutes till edges begin to turn golden brown. Removing from oven; allow to rest for a minute. Pressing a small depression into the top of each cookie with the back of a rounded teaspoon measure. Before removing to finish cooling down on a rack, allow cookies to cool in pan for 5 minutes. It will give the cookies a little twist when you lift them out.
- In a bowl, using an electric mixer for beating a cup of confectioners' sugar with cream cheese till smooth. Beating in pumpkin puree slowly till mixed thoroughly. Beating in 2 and 3/4 cups of the remaining confectioners' sugar, a little at a time. Stirring in a pinch of cloves, a quarter teaspoon of ginger, a quarter teaspoon of nutmeg, and cinnamon. In every cookie cup, piping or spooning the pumpkin mixture.

Nutrition Information

- Calories: 149 calories;
- Sodium: 77
- Total Carbohydrate: 27.4
- Cholesterol: 16
- Protein: 1.3
- Total Fat: 4.1

108. Edible Spiders

Serving: 24 | Prep: 30mins | Cook: | Ready in:

Ingredients

- 1 cup semisweet chocolate chips
- 1 teaspoon butter
- 24 large marshmallows
- 1 (6 ounce) package chow mein noodles
- 1 (12 ounce) package mini candy-coated chocolate pieces

Direction

- Mix butter and chocolate chips in a microwave-safe bowl. Microwave until melted. Stir occasionally until chocolate becomes smooth. Pour the chocolate into a sealable plastic bag; put aside.
- Use wax paper to line a cookie sheet. Stick 4 chow mein noodles into each marshmallow's side to make legs; place on wax paper. Cut off the bag's corner (the bag with melted

chocolate) with scissors. Drizzle over the marshmallow spiders. Stick to each marshmallow 2 candies to make eyes. Chill to harden chocolate.

Nutrition Information

- Calories: 165 calories;
- Cholesterol: 3
- Protein: 1.7
- Total Fat: 7.7
- Sodium: 48
- Total Carbohydrate: 23.9

109. Halloween Chocolate Chip Cookies With Spiders

Serving: 48 | Prep: 30mins | Cook: 11mins | Ready in:

Ingredients

- 2 1/2 cups all-purpose flour
- 1 teaspoon baking soda
- 1 teaspoon salt
- 1/2 teaspoon baking powder
- 1 cup unsalted butter, at room temperature
- 3/4 cup white sugar
- 3/4 cup packed brown sugar
- 2 eggs
- 1 teaspoon vanilla extract
- 2 1/2 cups semisweet chocolate chips, divided

Direction

- Set oven to preheat at 350°F (175°C).
- Mix together the baking powder, salt, baking soda and flour in a large bowl and use a fork to combine the ingredients thoroughly.
- Mix together the brown sugar, white sugar, and butter in a large bowl; use an electric mixer to beat till smooth and creamy. Add the eggs and vanilla extract into the mixture and beat them till fluffy and smooth. Add in the flour mixture, 1 cup at a time, and use a spatula to mix till well incorporated. Fold 1 1/2 cups chocolate chips into the mixture till well incorporated.
- On ungreased baking sheets, drop the cookies. In a bowl, add 1/2 cup chocolate chips. On each cookie, press about 3 to 4 chocolate chips, tip-side down, to form the bodies of the spiders.
- In the preheated oven, bake till the edges are golden, 10 to 15 minutes. Let cool down on the baking sheet for 1 minute, then transfer to a wire rack.
- In a microwave-safe ceramic or glass bowl, melt the leftover 1/2 cup chocolate in 15-second intervals, stir after each melting, for 1 to 3 minutes. To create spider legs, spoon the melted chocolate into a piping bag fitted with a small tip and draw small legs on both sides of the spider bodies.

Nutrition Information

- Calories: 128 calories;
- Protein: 1.3
- Total Fat: 6.7
- Sodium: 112
- Total Carbohydrate: 17
- Cholesterol: 18

110. Halloween Ghosties

Serving: 24 | Prep: 40mins | Cook: | Ready in:

Ingredients

- 1 (12 ounce) package white chocolate chips, or as needed
- 24 peanut-shaped peanut butter sandwich cookies
- 48 miniature chocolate chips

Direction

- In a microwaveable bowl, put in the chocolate chips then put it inside the microwave and let

it heat up on low setting for 1 minute; give it a mix. Keep heating up the chocolate chips on low setting a few more times at 30 seconds each time while stirring the chocolate after every interval until the temperature of the white chocolate becomes warm and the consistency is already smooth.
- Dip each of the cookies into the melted white chocolate using 2 forks, then put the chocolate-coated cookies onto sheets of wax paper. To make the eyes, arrange 2 pieces of mini chocolate chips on 1 end of each of the cookies. Let the decorated cookies sit for about 20 minutes until the coating has set.

Nutrition Information

- Calories: 148 calories;
- Protein: 2.2
- Total Fat: 8
- Sodium: 67
- Total Carbohydrate: 17.3
- Cholesterol: 3

111. Halloween Shortbread Poppy Seed Cookie Fingers

Serving: 30 | Prep: 20mins | Cook: 7mins | Ready in:

Ingredients

- 1 1/2 cups all-purpose flour
- 1 teaspoon poppy seeds
- 1 teaspoon baking powder
- 1/8 teaspoon salt
- 1/2 cup butter, at room temperature
- 1/2 cup white sugar
- 2 teaspoons vanilla extract
- 1 teaspoon whiskey
- 1 tablespoon fruit jam
- 30 almond slices

Direction

- Preheat an oven to 190°C/375°F; line parchment paper on a baking sheet.
- Whisk salt, baking powder, poppy seeds and flour in bowl.
- Beat sugar and butter for 3-5 minutes till fluffy and light in a stand mixer; beat whiskey and vanilla extract in. Add flour mixture; beat just till dough is crumbly and combined.
- Chill dough for 10 minutes till set in fridge.
- Divide dough into 4 portions; roll 1 dough portion into a tube on floured work surface. Cut into 1-in. pieces; put on prepped baking sheet. Repeat with leftover dough; flatten dough pieces to 3/4 in. wide and 2 in. long.
- Use a butter knife's flat side to press into 1 end of dough pieces to create a small dent then dot with jam; put almond slivers on jam. Use knife to score 2 sets of slits to make knuckles.
- In preheated oven, bake for 7 minutes till golden; cool for 10 minutes. Transfer to a wire rack; fully cool, about 20 minutes.

Nutrition Information

- Calories: 69 calories;
- Total Fat: 3.4
- Sodium: 48
- Total Carbohydrate: 8.8
- Cholesterol: 8
- Protein: 0.8

112. Halloween Skeleton Cookies

Serving: 40 | Prep: 45mins | Cook: 8mins | Ready in:

Ingredients

- 1 1/2 cups white sugar
- 1 cup butter, softened
- 2 eggs
- 1 1/2 teaspoons vanilla extract
- 1 1/2 teaspoons almond flavoring
- 3 1/2 cups all-purpose flour

- 1 teaspoon baking powder
- 1/2 teaspoon salt
- 2 tablespoons confectioners' sugar
- Icing:
- 1 cup confectioners' sugar
- 2 teaspoons milk, plus more as needed
- 2 teaspoons light corn syrup, or more as needed
- 1/4 teaspoon vanilla extract
- 1 (1.5 ounce) tube black decorating gel

Direction

- Cream the butter and sugar in a bowl using the electric mixer till creamy. Put in the almond flavoring, 1.5 tsp. of the vanilla extract and eggs and stir them well.
- In the second bowl, whisk together the salt, baking powder, and flour. Put the flour mixture into creamed butter mixture and combine by mixing. Wrap in plastic wrap and keep chilled in fridge for 3 - 4 hours or overnight.
- Preheat the oven to 175 degrees C (350 degrees F). Use the parchment paper to line 2 baking sheets.
- Use 2 tbsp. of the confectioners' sugar to dust the working surface and roll the dough out into a quarter-in. -thick circle. Chop out figure shapes using the gingerbread man cookie cutter and arrange the cut-out cookies onto the prepped baking sheets.
- Bake in preheated oven for 8 - 10 minutes. Take out of the baking sheets gently and move onto wire racks. Let cool down totally for roughly 20 minutes.
- Whisk together the milk and 1 cup of the confectioners' sugar in a small-sized bowl till smooth. Whip in a quarter tsp. of the vanilla extract and corn syrup till the icing turns glossy and smooth. Pour in the extra corn syrup if the icing is too thick.
- Scoop the icing to a piping bag with the small plain tip. Draw a filled-out circle inside the head for skull and a skeleton on the body, include 3 horizontal lines for ribs. Allow the cookies to rest for roughly 2 hours (preferably overnight for the best) till the icing becomes dry totally.
- Use a black decorating gel to draw the eyes, a nose, and a mouth onto skull and allow the cookies to dry one more time for roughly 60 minutes.

Nutrition Information

- Calories: 131 calories;
- Cholesterol: 20
- Protein: 1.5
- Total Fat: 4.9
- Sodium: 95
- Total Carbohydrate: 20.4

113. Halloween Vegan Yacon Syrup Cookies

Serving: 30 | Prep: 25mins | Cook: 10mins | Ready in:

Ingredients

- Cookies:
- 2 1/2 cups gluten-free flour
- 1 teaspoon baking soda
- 1/2 teaspoon ground ginger
- 1/2 teaspoon ground cinnamon
- 1/4 teaspoon ground nutmeg
- 1 dash salt
- 1/2 cup coconut oil, or more as needed
- 1/2 cup yacon syrup
- Icing:
- 1/4 cup yacon syrup
- 2 1/2 tablespoons melted dark chocolate (85% cacao)

Direction

- Turn the oven to 340°F (170°C) to preheat. Use parchment paper to line a baking sheet.
- In a big bowl, mix together salt, nutmeg, cinnamon, ginger, baking soda, and flour. In another bowl, mix together yacon syrup and

coconut oil. Pour the oil mixture into the dry ingredients and stir to form a dough.
- Roll out the dough until having approximately 1/2-in. thickness. Cut out the cookies with Halloween-themed cookie cutters; put them on the prepared baking sheet.
- Bake for 10 minutes in the preheated oven.
- As the cookies are baking, mix together melted chocolate and yacon syrup.
- Take the cookies out of the oven and put on icing while they remain hot.

Nutrition Information

- Calories: 92 calories;
- Total Carbohydrate: 13.1
- Cholesterol: < 1
- Total Fat: 4.4
- Protein: 1.2
- Sodium: 55

114. Hoot Owl Cookies

Serving: 24 | Prep: 25mins | Cook: 12mins | Ready in:

Ingredients

- 1 cup white sugar
- 3/4 cup butter
- 1 egg
- 1 teaspoon vanilla extract
- 2 1/4 cups all-purpose flour
- 2 teaspoons baking powder
- 1/2 teaspoon salt
- 3 tablespoons unsweetened cocoa powder
- 1 cup semisweet chocolate chips
- 1 cup cashew halves

Direction

- Cream sugar and butter until fluffy. Whisk in vanilla and egg. Add salt and baking powder. Whisk well. Add flour; combine until blended. Take out 2/3 of dough. Pat or roll dough out to shape 2 10 x 4 inch rectangles. Add cocoa to the leftover 1/3 of dough. Combine until blended. Form chocolate dough into 2 10 inch long rolls. Put on rectangle and roll plain dough to completely cover chocolate dough, except the ends. Use plastic wrap to wrap; chill for 2 hours at least.
- Set oven to 350°F (180°C) and start preheating.
- Using a sharp knife, slice dough into 1/8 inch slices. On a cookie sheet, put 2 slices side by side to make the owl's face. Pinch upper "corners" to make ears. Place chocolate chips in each dark circle to make eyes and cashew in the center to make the beak.
- Bake in the prepared oven until browned lightly or for 8-12 minutes.

Nutrition Information

- Calories: 199 calories;
- Sodium: 170
- Total Carbohydrate: 24.2
- Cholesterol: 23
- Protein: 3
- Total Fat: 10.8

115. Leftover Halloween Candy Cookies

Serving: 36 | Prep: 15mins | Cook: 10mins | Ready in:

Ingredients

- 2 cups chopped candy bars, or more to taste
- 1 cup white sugar
- 1/2 cup butter
- 2 eggs
- 2 1/4 cups all-purpose flour
- 1 teaspoon baking soda
- cooking spray

Direction

- In a saucepan, put in the sugar, butter and candy bars and let it melt over medium heat setting. Remove the pan away from the heat and allow the mixture to cool down a little bit for about 5 minutes.
- Add and whisk in the eggs one by one until the consistency is smooth. Add in the baking soda and flour and mix everything together until you get a dough that has a sticky texture. Keep it in the fridge for about 1 hour until the texture of the dough allows you to scoop it with ease.
- Preheat the oven to 350°F (175°C). Use a cooking spray to grease 2 baking sheets.
- Form 1 1/2 teaspoonful of the chilled dough into ball shapes. On the prepared baking sheets, put in the dough balls 1 inch away from each other.
- Put it in the preheated oven and let it bake for 10-12 minutes until the dough balls have a fluffy texture and have turned brown in color.

Nutrition Information

- Calories: 115 calories;
- Total Carbohydrate: 16
- Cholesterol: 19
- Protein: 1.5
- Total Fat: 5.2
- Sodium: 61

116. Mary's Sugar Cookies

Serving: 30 | Prep: 15mins | Cook: 8mins | Ready in:

Ingredients

- 1 cup butter, softened
- 1 1/2 cups sifted confectioners' sugar
- 1 egg
- 1 teaspoon vanilla extract
- 1/2 teaspoon almond extract
- 2 1/2 cups all-purpose flour
- 1 teaspoon baking soda
- 1 teaspoon cream of tartar
- 1/4 cup granulated sugar for decoration

Direction

- Cream confectioners' sugar and butter together in a large bowl until smooth. Beat in egg and stir in almond extract and vanilla. Mix together cream of tartar, baking soda and flour; mix into the creamed mixture. Cover up and allow to chill for at least 2 hours.
- Preheat the oven to 375°F (190°C). Separate the dough in two. On a lightly floured surface, roll each half out to the thickness of 3/16 inch. Use cookie cutter to cut into desired shapes. On greased cookie sheets, place the cookies 1 1/2 inches apart. Sprinkle plain or colored granulated sugar over the cookies.
- Bake in the preheated oven for 8 minutes, until browned lightly. Cool on baking sheet for 5 minutes, then transfer to a wire rack for cooling completely.

Nutrition Information

- Calories: 126 calories;
- Total Fat: 6.4
- Sodium: 88
- Total Carbohydrate: 16
- Cholesterol: 22
- Protein: 1.4

117. Meringue Bones

Serving: 36 | Prep: 30mins | Cook: 1hours | Ready in:

Ingredients

- 6 egg whites
- 1/2 teaspoon cream of tartar
- 1 pinch salt
- 1 1/3 cups white sugar
- 2 teaspoons vanilla extract

Direction

- Set the oven to 225°F (110°C) and start preheating. Use aluminum foil to line 2 baking sheets; grease the foil.
- In a bowl, using an electric mixer, whisk egg whites with salt and cream of tartar until egg whites become foamy. Whisk in sugar gradually, a few tablespoons per time, whisking until sugar is dissolved in meringue; add more. Keep beating until meringue becomes glossy and shapes a sharp peak when you lift beaters straight up from the bowl; whisk in vanilla extract. Scoop meringue into a pastry bag fitted with a small tip.
- On the prepared aluminum foil, pipe meringue into small bone shapes. You must pipe all the shapes at once or the meringue will deflate.
- Put cookie sheets into prepared oven to bake for about an hour. During baking time, do not open oven door or peek. Turn off the oven and allow meringue bones to cool in the oven without opening door for an hour. Carefully and gently take cookies out of aluminum to avoid broken bones.

Nutrition Information

- Calories: 32 calories;
- Protein: 0.6
- Total Fat: 0
- Sodium: 9
- Total Carbohydrate: 7.5
- Cholesterol: 0

118. Mini Candy Bar Cookies

Serving: 60 | Prep: 45mins | Cook: 15mins | Ready in:

Ingredients

- 60 mini chocolate-coated caramel-peanut nougat candy bars (such as Snickers®)
- 2 (18.25 ounce) packages French vanilla flavored cake mix
- 2 eggs
- 2/3 cup vegetable oil
- 1/4 cup water

Direction

- Set the oven to 375°F (190°C), and start preheating. Line parchment paper on baking sheets. Open all the mini candy bars.
- In a large bowl, empty the 2 cake mixes; then stir in water, vegetable oil and eggs until the mixture is stiff. Roll tablespoons of dough in a heaping manner into balls of 1-inch. Insert a mini candy bar into the cookie ball, and cover carefully dough around the entire candy piece. If you can see any chocolate on the outside, the cookie will leak. On the prepared baking sheets, arrange filled cookies.
- Bake in the prepped oven for 11 minutes. Cookies should not look brown on top. Allow to cool on the baking sheets for 5 minutes before removing to cool on racks.

Nutrition Information

- Calories: 134 calories;
- Total Fat: 5.9
- Sodium: 135
- Total Carbohydrate: 19.3
- Cholesterol: 7
- Protein: 1.3

119. Mom's Walnut Bars

Serving: 18 | Prep: 20mins | Cook: 35mins | Ready in:

Ingredients

- 1 cup white sugar
- 1 pound ground walnuts
- 1 tablespoon orange zest
- 1 tablespoon fresh orange juice
- 3 egg whites
- 2 cups confectioners' sugar

Direction

- Start preheating the oven to 200°F (100°C).
- Combine 2 egg whites, orange juice, orange zest, ground walnuts, and white sugar. This mixture will be the same as paste and very sticky.
- Shape the paste into a long rectangle on a flat surface dusted with sugar in order not to stick. The rectangle should be about 16x4-inch.
- To make the frosting, mix confectioners' sugar with the remaining egg white. No need to beat the egg white first! You may need to pour in a little water or add a bit more powdered sugar to make a paste that is easily spread, but not runny.
- Spread over your rectangle with the frosting. With a knife coated with sugar, slice the rectangle into small 1x2-inch bars and arrange them on an ungreased cookie sheet.
- Bake for about 35 minutes in the prepared oven until frosting is firm but still white. Serve with a big glass of milk.

Nutrition Information

- Calories: 263 calories;
- Cholesterol: 0
- Protein: 4.5
- Total Fat: 16.5
- Sodium: 10
- Total Carbohydrate: 28.1

---
120. Owl Cookies

Serving: 36 | Prep: | Cook: |Ready in:

Ingredients

- 1 1/4 cups candy-coated milk chocolate pieces
- 2 tablespoons milk
- 24 ounces dry sugar cookie mix
- 1 cup cashew halves

Direction

- Mix together 3/4 cup of the candies and milk in a small saucepan. Liquefy over low heat, mixing till smooth. Take away from heat.
- Prepare cookie mixes following packaging instruction. Mix liquefied chocolate into 1/2 of the dough. Shape chocolate dough into two rolls of 12-inch in length and approximately 1 inch in diameter. Wrap using foil or wax paper. Refrigerate for 2 hours till firm.
- Split plain dough into two portions. Roll each plain half out to a 12 x 6-inch rectangle on a well-floured surface. On long edge, place a chocolate roll. Roll up, lightly pushing doughs together so plain dough surrounds chocolate roll. Repeat with the rest of the dough.
- In foil or wax paper, wrap each roll. Refrigerate for 2 hours till firm. Preheat the oven to 190°C or 375°F.
- Slice each roll into a-quarter-inch slices. Put 2 slices so they are touching on baking sheet that is greased. In the middle of every chocolate circle, put one of the leftover candies for eye. Place a cashew where the slices touch to create nose.
- Bake for 8 to 10 minutes till the plain cookie is browned lightly. Allow cookies to cool on baking sheets for 2 to 3 minutes. Take away and transfer to wire racks to cool.

Nutrition Information

- Calories: 151 calories;
- Total Fat: 7.2
- Sodium: 104
- Total Carbohydrate: 19.9
- Cholesterol: 7
- Protein: 1.9

---
121. Pattern Cookies

Serving: 12 | Prep: | Cook: |Ready in:

Ingredients

- 2/3 cup shortening
- 1 cup white sugar
- 2 eggs
- 1 teaspoon vanilla extract
- 1/3 cup milk
- 3 cups all-purpose flour
- 1 tablespoon baking powder
- 1/2 teaspoon salt

Direction

- Cream the sugar and shortening together in a medium-size bowl. Whip in eggs, one by one, then mix in milk and vanilla. Mix baking powder, salt and flour, and mix to wet mixture. Refrigerate with cover, approximately an hour.
- Heat the oven to 175 ° C or 350 ° F. Line parchment paper on baking sheets. Unroll dough on a slightly floured counter into thickness of 1/4 to 1/8 inch. Use cookie cutters to cut to preferred forms.
- Bake in prepped oven, about 8 - 10 minutes, till the center of cookie bounces back once tapped. Allow to cool on the wire racks. Ice with icing if wished.

Nutrition Information

- Calories: 296 calories;
- Total Fat: 12.6
- Sodium: 234
- Total Carbohydrate: 41.3
- Cholesterol: 32
- Protein: 4.5

---

122. Paul's Pumpkin Bars

Serving: 24 | Prep: 15mins | Cook: 30mins | Ready in:

Ingredients

- 4 eggs
- 1 2/3 cups white sugar
- 1 cup vegetable oil
- 1 (15 ounce) can pumpkin puree
- 2 cups all-purpose flour
- 2 teaspoons baking powder
- 1 teaspoon baking soda
- 2 teaspoons ground cinnamon
- 1 teaspoon salt
- 1 (3 ounce) package cream cheese, softened
- 1/2 cup butter, softened
- 1 teaspoon vanilla extract
- 2 cups sifted confectioners' sugar

Direction

- Preheat an oven to 175°C/350°F.
- Use an electric mixer to mix pumpkin, oil, sugar and eggs till fluffy and light in a medium bowl. Sift salt, cinnamon, baking soda, baking powder and flour together; mix into pumpkin mixture till combined well.
- Evenly spread batter into 10x15-in. ungreased jellyroll pan; bake in preheated oven for 25-30 minutes. Before frosting, cool.
- Frosting: Cream butter and cream cheese; mix in vanilla. A little at a time, add confectioners' sugar; beat till smooth. Evenly spread on cooled bars; cut to squares.

Nutrition Information

- Calories: 279 calories;
- Sodium: 282
- Total Carbohydrate: 34.1
- Cholesterol: 45
- Protein: 2.6
- Total Fat: 15.2

---

123. Peanut Butter Crunch Cookies

Serving: 30 | Prep: 15mins | Cook: 10mins | Ready in:

Ingredients

- 1/2 cup butter, softened
- 1/2 cup peanut butter
- 1/2 cup packed brown sugar
- 1/2 cup white sugar
- 1 egg
- 1/2 teaspoon vanilla extract
- 1 cup rolled oats
- 3/4 cup all-purpose flour
- 1/2 teaspoon baking soda
- 1/2 teaspoon baking powder
- 1/4 teaspoon salt
- 8 mini crisped rice chocolate bars (such as Nestle® Crunch bar), roughly chopped

Direction

- Preheat an oven to 175°C/350°F.
- Use electric mixer to beat peanut butter and butter till smooth and creamy in bowl; beat white sugar and brown sugar in till incorporated. Add vanilla and egg to creamed butter mixture; mix till smooth.
- Whisk salt, baking powder, baking soda, flour and oats in another bowl; mix into creamed butter just till incorporated. Fold chocolate bars carefully into dough; by rounded teaspoonfuls, drop dough on ungreased baking sheets.
- In preheated oven, bake for 8-10 minutes till edges are lightly browned.

Nutrition Information

- Calories: 117 calories;
- Cholesterol: 15
- Protein: 2.2
- Total Fat: 6.3
- Sodium: 97
- Total Carbohydrate: 13.8

124. Peanut Butter Spider Cookies

Serving: 48 | Prep: 45mins | Cook: 10mins | Ready in:

Ingredients

- 1/2 cup shortening
- 1/2 cup peanut butter
- 1/2 cup packed brown sugar
- 1/2 cup white sugar
- 1 egg, beaten
- 2 tablespoons milk
- 1 teaspoon vanilla extract
- 1 3/4 cups all-purpose flour
- 1 teaspoon baking soda
- 1/2 teaspoon salt
- 1/4 cup white sugar for rolling
- 24 chocolate candy spheres with smooth chocolate filling (such as Lindt Lindor Truffles), refrigerated until cold
- 48 decorative candy eyeballs
- 1/2 cup prepared chocolate frosting

Direction

- Preheat an oven to 190°C/375°F; line baking parchment on baking sheets.
- Use electric mixer to beat 1/2 cup white sugar, brown sugar, peanut butter and shortening till smooth in big bowl; beat egg into creamy mixture till incorporated fully. Mix vanilla extract and milk into mixture till smooth.
- Mix salt, baking soda and flour in small bowl; add to wet mixture in big bowl. Mix till incorporated fully to a dough. Divide then form dough to 48 balls.
- In wide shallow bow, spread 1/4 cup white sugar; roll dough balls in the sugar to coat. Put on prepped baking sheets, 2-in. apart.
- In preheated oven, bake for 10-12 minutes till golden brown; take out of oven. Press dimple quickly in center of every cookie using wooden spoon's blunt end. Cool cookies for 10 minutes on sheets. Transfer to wire cooling rack; fully cool.

- Cut every chocolate sphere to 2 hemispheres. Rounded side facing upwards, put 1 piece on each cookie.
- Put frosting in pastry bag with small round tip/plastic freezer bag with 1 end cut off. Dap small amount frosting on back of every candy eyeball; stick 2 onto every chocolate candy to make eyes. In 4 thin lines, pipe frosting, beginning at candy base, on every side over cookie to create spider legs.
- Let frosting harden for 30 minutes at room temperature; keep cookies in airtight container.

Nutrition Information

- Calories: 117 calories;
- Total Carbohydrate: 14.4
- Cholesterol: 7
- Protein: 1.7
- Total Fat: 6.3
- Sodium: 78

125. Peanut Candy Bar Cake

Serving: 24 | Prep: | Cook: | Ready in:

Ingredients

- 1 (18.25 ounce) package yellow cake mix
- 1/3 cup butter
- 3 cups miniature marshmallows
- 2/3 cup light corn syrup
- 1 egg
- 2 teaspoons vanilla extract
- 2 cups peanut butter chips
- 2 cups salted peanuts
- 1 1/2 cups crisp rice cereal
- 1/4 cup butter

Direction

- Set the oven to 175 °C (350 °F) to preheat.
- Combine the egg, 1/3 cup butter or margarine, and cake mix together. Into the bottom of one 9x13 inch pan, press down the mixture and bake at 175 °C (350 °F) for 12-18 minutes. Take out from oven and top with miniature marshmallows. Bring back to the oven for 1-2 minutes or until the marshmallows start to puff.
- In a saucepan, cook peanut butter chips, vanilla, 1/4 cup butter margarine, and corn syrup over medium heat until melted. Take away from heat and mix in the salted peanuts and puffed rice cereal. Pour over top of marshmallow-topped cake and spread to cover. Let cool before serving.

Nutrition Information

- Calories: 373 calories;
- Sodium: 349
- Total Carbohydrate: 43
- Cholesterol: 20
- Protein: 8.6
- Total Fat: 18.9

126. Peanutty Candy Corn Cereal Bars

Serving: 12 | Prep: 15mins | Cook: 5mins | Ready in:

Ingredients

- 1/4 cup margarine
- 1 tablespoon peanut butter
- 5 cups miniature marshmallows, divided
- 6 cups honey nut-flavored cereal squares (such as Honey Nut Chex®)
- 2 cups candy corn
- 1/2 cup peanuts

Direction

- Lightly coat a 9x13-in. baking pan with oil.

- In a saucepan, cook while stirring together peanut butter and margarine over medium heat for 2-3 mins until they become smooth. Put in 4 cups of the marshmallows to the margarine mixture. Then cook while stirring for 2-3 mins until the marshmallows melt. Discard the saucepan from the heat.
- Stir the cereal squares into the marshmallow mixture until slightly cooled and fully coated; then fold in the candy corn, the peanuts and the remaining one cup of the marshmallows. Transfer the mixture to prepared baking pan. Use a buttered wooden spoon or buttered hands to press down in an even layer. Let it cool completely before slicing into squares.

Nutrition Information

- Calories: 343 calories;
- Total Fat: 7.8
- Sodium: 226
- Total Carbohydrate: 63.9
- Cholesterol: 0
- Protein: 3.2

127. Pumpkin Bars I

Serving: 24 | Prep: 30mins | Cook: 25mins | Ready in:

Ingredients

- 2 cups all-purpose flour
- 2 teaspoons baking powder
- 2 teaspoons baking soda
- 2 teaspoons salt
- 2 teaspoons ground cinnamon
- 2 cups canned pumpkin
- 1 cup vegetable oil
- 4 eggs
- 2 cups white sugar
- 1 cup chopped walnuts

Direction

- Set oven to 350°F and start preheating. Prepare two greased 9x13" pans.
- Mix cinnamon, salt, baking soda, baking powder and flour together; put aside. Stir together sugar, eggs, vegetable oil and pumpkin in another bowl. Add in flour mixture and whisk until just blended. Stir in walnuts.
- Transfer batter to greased pan and bake in prepared oven for about 25 minutes until a toothpick inserted into the middle comes out without any streaks of batter. Place on a wire rack to cool, then top with cream cheese frosting.

Nutrition Information

- Calories: 235 calories;
- Sodium: 400
- Total Carbohydrate: 27.3
- Cholesterol: 31
- Protein: 3.1
- Total Fat: 13.3

128. Pumpkin Bars II

Serving: 12 | Prep: | Cook: | Ready in:

Ingredients

- 1 (15 ounce) can pumpkin puree
- 2 teaspoons ground cinnamon
- 1 teaspoon pumpkin pie spice
- 2 cups white sugar
- 2 cups all-purpose flour
- 2 tablespoons baking powder
- 1 tablespoon baking soda
- 1/4 teaspoon salt
- 1 cup vegetable oil
- 4 eggs
- 4 1/2 ounces cream cheese, softened
- 9 tablespoons butter, softened
- 1 1/2 teaspoons vanilla extract
- 3 cups confectioners' sugar

- 1 1/2 teaspoons milk

Direction

- In a medium bowl, mix together sugar, pumpkin pie spice, cinnamon and pumpkin.
- Sift salt, baking soda, baking powder and flour together.
- Slowly put the pumpkin mixture, eggs and oil into the flour mixture with an electric mixer.
- Combine; transfer onto a 17x11-in. pan coated with grease. Bake for 20-25 minutes, at 350°F (175°C). Allow to cool completely. Frost.
- To make the frosting: Cream together vanilla, 9 tablespoons of butter and cream cheese. Slowly put in milk and confectioners' sugar.

Nutrition Information

- Calories: 637 calories;
- Sodium: 789
- Total Carbohydrate: 83.5
- Cholesterol: 97
- Protein: 5.6
- Total Fat: 32.7

129. Pumpkin Bliss Treats

Serving: 12 | Prep: 10mins | Cook: 3mins | Ready in:

Ingredients

- cooking spray
- 3 tablespoons butter
- 1 (10 ounce) package miniature marshmallows
- 5 cups pumpkin spice-flavored toasted oat cereal (such as Pumpkin Spice Cheerios®)
- 1/2 cup candy corn, or to taste

Direction

- Spray cooking spray on a big spoon or 9-in. square baking dish.
- Melt butter on medium heat in a big saucepan. Add marshmallows; cook, constantly mixing, for 3 minutes till melted. Take off heat. Gently mix in cereal. Put mixture into prepped pan; put candy corn over. Use the sprayed spoon to evenly press mixture into pan. Fully cool for 30 minutes.
- Cut the mixture to bars.

Nutrition Information

- Calories: 181 calories;
- Total Fat: 3.6
- Sodium: 128
- Total Carbohydrate: 35.2
- Cholesterol: 8
- Protein: 1.4

130. Pumpkin Chocolate Chip Brownies

Serving: 12 | Prep: 5mins | Cook: 25mins | Ready in:

Ingredients

- 1 (16 ounce) package truffle brownie mix (such as Trader Joe's®)
- 1/2 cup butter, melted
- 2 eggs
- 1/2 cup pumpkin spice-flavored morsels (such as Nestle®)
- 2 tablespoons Halloween sprinkles, or to taste

Direction

- Set oven to 175°C (or 350°F). Prepare a greased 8" baking pan with 2-inch margins.
- Combine eggs, butter and brownie mix in a bowl until just incorporated. Whisk pumpkin spice morsels slowly into the mixture. Pour into the greased pan.
- Bake for 25-30 minutes in the prepared oven until top is dry and edges no longer stick to the sides of the pan. Put sprinkles on top. Chill for half an hour, then cut and take out of the pan.

Nutrition Information

- Calories: 302 calories;
- Sodium: 197
- Total Carbohydrate: 36
- Cholesterol: 52
- Protein: 3.4
- Total Fat: 17.3

131. Pumpkin Chocolate Chip Cookies I

Serving: 48 | Prep: 15mins | Cook: 15mins | Ready in:

Ingredients

- 1/2 cup shortening
- 1 1/2 cups white sugar
- 1 egg
- 1 cup canned pumpkin
- 1 teaspoon vanilla extract
- 2 1/2 cups all-purpose flour
- 1 teaspoon baking powder
- 1 teaspoon baking soda
- 1 teaspoon salt
- 1 teaspoon ground nutmeg
- 1 teaspoon ground cinnamon
- 1/2 cup chopped walnuts (optional)
- 1 cup semisweet chocolate chips

Direction

- Set the oven to 350°F (175°C), and start preheating. Coat cookie sheets with oil.
- Cream together sugar and shortening in a large bowl, until fluffy and light. Beat in egg, then mix in vanilla and pumpkin. Mix cinnamon, nutmeg, salt, baking soda, baking powder and flour together; slowly mix into the creamed mixture. Stir in chocolate chips and walnuts. Drop dough by teaspoonfuls onto the prepped cookie sheets.

- Bake in the preheated oven until light brown, about 15 minutes. Allow to cool down on wire racks.

Nutrition Information

- Calories: 95 calories;
- Total Fat: 4.2
- Sodium: 99
- Total Carbohydrate: 14.1
- Cholesterol: 4
- Protein: 1.2

132. Pumpkin Chocolate Chip Cookies III

Serving: 12 | Prep: | Cook: | Ready in:

Ingredients

- 1 cup canned pumpkin
- 1 cup white sugar
- 1/2 cup vegetable oil
- 1 egg
- 2 cups all-purpose flour
- 2 teaspoons baking powder
- 2 teaspoons ground cinnamon
- 1/2 teaspoon salt
- 1 teaspoon baking soda
- 1 teaspoon milk
- 1 tablespoon vanilla extract
- 2 cups semisweet chocolate chips
- 1/2 cup chopped walnuts (optional)

Direction

- Combine the egg, vegetable oil, sugar, and pumpkin. In a different bowl, stir the salt, ground cinnamon, baking powder, and flour together. Use milk to dissolve the baking soda and mix it into the mixture. Put the flour mixture into the pumpkin mixture and combine well.
- Add in the nuts, chocolate chips and vanilla.

- On greased cookie sheet, drop spoonfuls of the dough and bake to a light brown and firm at 175°C (350°F) for about 10 minutes.

Nutrition Information

- Calories: 405 calories;
- Protein: 4.8
- Total Fat: 21.4
- Sodium: 342
- Total Carbohydrate: 53.3
- Cholesterol: 16

133. Pumpkin Cookies III

Serving: 36 | Prep: 15mins | Cook: 15mins | Ready in:

Ingredients

- 1 cup white sugar
- 1 egg
- 1 cup shortening
- 1 teaspoon vanilla extract
- 2 cups all-purpose flour
- 1 teaspoon baking soda
- 1 teaspoon baking powder
- 1 teaspoon salt
- 1 teaspoon ground cinnamon
- 1 cup canned pumpkin
- 1/2 cup raisins (optional)
- 1/2 cup chopped walnuts (optional)

Direction

- Start preheating the oven to 350°F (175°C). Coat the cookie sheets with grease.
- Cream vanilla, shortening, egg and sugar together in a large bowl. Sift cinnamon, salt, baking powder, baking soda and flour together; then stir into creamed mixture. Mix in walnuts, pumpkin and raisins. Drop the dough by teaspoonfuls onto prepared cookie sheets.
- Bake in prepared oven for 10 to 15 mins.

Nutrition Information

- Calories: 119 calories;
- Total Fat: 7
- Sodium: 132
- Total Carbohydrate: 13.6
- Cholesterol: 5
- Protein: 1.3

134. Pumpkin Cookies VI

Serving: 24 | Prep: 10mins | Cook: 12mins | Ready in:

Ingredients

- 1 cup all-purpose flour
- 1/2 cup quick cooking oats
- 1/2 teaspoon baking soda
- 1/2 teaspoon ground cinnamon
- 1/4 teaspoon salt
- 1/2 cup butter, softened
- 1/2 cup brown sugar
- 1/2 cup white sugar
- 1 egg
- 1/2 teaspoon vanilla extract
- 1/2 cup canned pumpkin puree
- 1 cup raisins

Direction

- Set the oven to 175°C or 350°F to preheat. Mix together salt, cinnamon, baking soda, oats and flour, then put aside.
- Cream white sugar, brown sugar and butter together in a big bowl until smooth. Beat in vanilla and egg, then stir in pumpkin puree. Stir in dry ingredients gradually until well-combined. Stir in raisins. Drop on grease-free cookie sheets with rounded spoonfuls of dough.
- In the preheated oven, bake for about 8-10 minutes. Let cookies cool on baking sheet for

about 5 minutes prior to transferring to a wire rack to cool thoroughly.

Nutrition Information

- Calories: 105 calories;
- Total Fat: 4.2
- Sodium: 82
- Total Carbohydrate: 16.2
- Cholesterol: 18
- Protein: 1.2

135. Pumpkin Cookies With Cream Cheese Frosting (The World's Best!)

Serving: 36 | Prep: 30mins | Cook: 10mins | Ready in:

Ingredients

- 2 cups all-purpose flour
- 1 teaspoon baking powder
- 1 teaspoon ground cinnamon
- 1/2 teaspoon baking soda
- 1/2 teaspoon ground nutmeg
- 1/2 teaspoon ground ginger
- 1 cup butter
- 3/4 cup white sugar
- 3/4 cup brown sugar
- 2 teaspoons vanilla extract
- 1 egg
- 1 (15 ounce) can pumpkin puree
- 1 (3 ounce) package cream cheese, softened
- 1/4 cup butter, softened
- 1 teaspoon vanilla extract
- 2 cups confectioners' sugar

Direction

- Set an oven to 175°C (350°F) and start preheating. Coat baking sheets lightly with cooking spray.
- In a bowl, beat together ginger, nutmeg, baking soda, cinnamon, baking powder, and flour. In a different large bowl, use an electric mixer to whisk egg, 2 teaspoons of the vanilla extract, brown sugar, white sugar, and a cup of butter until the mixture becomes smooth. Whisk in pumpkin puree. Add dry ingredients into the pumpkin mixture and stir gradually. The batter will become moist.
- Place teaspoons of batter on the prepared baking sheets, 2 inches apart.
- In the preheated oven, bake for 10-12 minutes until the cookies are browned lightly. Allow the cookies to cool on the sheets for 5 minutes, then transfer onto the waxed paper to finish cooling.
- In a bowl, use an electric mixer to whisk a teaspoon of the vanilla extract, 1/4 cup of better, and cream cheese until they become creamy and soft. Whisk in 1/2 cup of confectioners' sugar at a time until the frosting becomes spreadable and smooth. Use cream cheese frosting to frost the cooled cookies.

Nutrition Information

- Calories: 152 calories;
- Protein: 1.3
- Total Fat: 7.5
- Sodium: 115
- Total Carbohydrate: 20.6
- Cholesterol: 25

136. Pumpkin Funnel Cakes

Serving: 4 | Prep: 15mins | Cook: 15mins | Ready in:

Ingredients

- 1 quart oil for frying
- 1 1/2 cups all-purpose flour
- 1/4 teaspoon baking powder
- 1 teaspoon baking soda
- 1 teaspoon cinnamon
- 1/4 teaspoon salt
- 1 egg

- 1/4 cup packed brown sugar
- 3/4 cup canned pumpkin puree
- 1 cup milk
- 3/4 teaspoon pumpkin pie spice
- 1/2 cup confectioners' sugar for dusting

Direction

- In a deep pan or deep pot, pour the oil and heat to 190°C (375°F).
- In a mixing bowl, Sift the pumpkin pie spice, salt, cinnamon, baking soda, baking powder and flour together.
- In a big bowl, beat together the milk, pumpkin puree, brown sugar and egg until well combined. Slowly stir in the flour mixture, mixing until the mixture becomes smooth.
- Close the opening with your fingers, and into a funnel with half an inch wide spout, pour 1/2 cup of the batter. Take off your finger and drizzle the batter in the hot oil on a circular motion, making 4-6 inch circle, then move across the circle to form a spiral pattern. Cook until it turns golden brown. To cook the bottom side, flip the cake over. Remove from the oil using a slotted spoon, then drain it on paper towels. Let it cool for 5 minutes then dust with confectioner's sugar liberally.

Nutrition Information

- Calories: 542 calories;
- Total Fat: 25.1
- Sodium: 649
- Total Carbohydrate: 71.6
- Cholesterol: 51
- Protein: 9

137. Pumpkin Gobs

Serving: 18 | Prep: | Cook: | Ready in:

Ingredients

- 1 1/2 cups solid pack pumpkin puree
- 1/2 cup butter, softened
- 1 cup white sugar
- 1 egg
- 1 teaspoon vanilla extract
- 2 cups all-purpose flour
- 1 teaspoon baking powder
- 1 teaspoon baking soda
- 1/2 teaspoon salt
- 1 teaspoon ground cinnamon
- 3/4 cup shortening
- 1 1/2 cups white sugar
- 2 teaspoons vanilla extract
- 1/2 cup prepared vanilla pudding

Direction

- Start preheating the oven to 350°F (190°C). Line parchment paper on baking sheets.
- Whisk sugar with margarine or butter. Whip in vanilla, egg, and pumpkin.
- Blend ground cinnamon, salt, baking powder, baking soda, and flour into the pumpkin mixture. Blend until combined.
- Drop dough by teaspoonfuls onto the paper-lined baking sheets. Bake for 12 to 14 minutes at 350°F (175°C). Allow cookies to cool completely; make a sandwich with two cookies and Vanilla Filling.
- To make Vanilla Filling: Mix 1 1/2 cups of white sugar and shortening for 10 minutes. Whip in vanilla pudding and vanilla. Whip until creamy.

Nutrition Information

- Calories: 303 calories;
- Total Fat: 14.4
- Sodium: 263
- Total Carbohydrate: 42.2
- Cholesterol: 24
- Protein: 2.2

138. Pumpkin Oatmeal Chocolate Chip Cookies

Serving: 72 | Prep: 15mins | Cook: 10mins | Ready in:

Ingredients

- 1 1/2 cups butter, softened
- 2 cups packed brown sugar
- 1 cup white sugar
- 1 (15 ounce) can pumpkin puree
- 1 egg
- 1 teaspoon vanilla extract
- 4 cups all-purpose flour
- 2 cups quick-cooking oats
- 2 teaspoons ground cinnamon
- 2 teaspoons baking soda
- 1 teaspoon baking powder
- 1 teaspoon salt
- 2 cups miniature chocolate chips

Direction

- Set an oven to 190°C (375°F) and start preheating.
- In a bowl, whisk together white sugar, brown sugar, and butter until they become creamy. Add the vanilla extract, egg, and pumpkin; whisk until they become smooth.
- In a different bowl, combine salt, baking powder, baking soda, cinnamon, oats, and flour; add into the creamed butter and stir until mixed. Fold the chocolate chips into the batter. For each cookie, drop 1-2 tablespoons of batter on a baking sheet.
- In the prepared oven, bake for 10-12 minutes until each cookie is browned lightly on the edges.

Nutrition Information

- Calories: 128 calories;
- Sodium: 119
- Total Carbohydrate: 19.2
- Cholesterol: 13
- Protein: 1.4
- Total Fat: 5.6

139. Pumpkin Pecan White Chocolate Cookies

Serving: 36 | Prep: 15mins | Cook: 22mins | Ready in:

Ingredients

- 2 1/4 cups all-purpose flour
- 1/2 teaspoon baking soda
- 1/2 teaspoon pumpkin pie spice
- 1 cup unsalted butter
- 1 1/2 cups dark brown sugar
- 1 cup solid pack pumpkin puree
- 2 eggs
- 1 teaspoon vanilla extract
- 10 ounces white chocolate, chopped
- 1/2 cup pecan halves

Direction

- Preheat an oven to 150°C/300°F then grease cookie sheets.
- Cream brown sugar and butter till smooth in big bowl; beat vanilla and eggs in. Mix pumpkin puree in till blended well. Mix pumpkin pie spice, baking soda and flour; mix into pumpkin mixture. Fold pecans and white chocolate in. By heaping spoonfuls, drop on prepped cookie sheets, 2-in. minimum apart.
- In preheated oven, bake for 20-22 minutes till bottoms brown lightly. Cool on baking sheets for 5 minutes. Transfer to wire racks; cool.

Nutrition Information

- Calories: 170 calories;
- Sodium: 50
- Total Carbohydrate: 20.2
- Cholesterol: 26
- Protein: 2
- Total Fat: 9.3

140. Pumpkin Protein Cookies

Serving: 14 | Prep: 15mins | Cook: 5mins | Ready in:

Ingredients

- 3/4 cup SPLENDA® Granular
- 1 cup rolled oats
- 1 cup whole wheat flour
- 1/2 cup soy flour
- 1 3/4 teaspoons baking soda
- 1/2 teaspoon baking powder
- 1/2 teaspoon salt
- 2 teaspoons ground cinnamon
- 1 teaspoon ground nutmeg
- 1/2 cup pumpkin puree
- 1 tablespoon canola oil
- 2 teaspoons water
- 2 egg whites
- 1 teaspoon molasses
- 1 tablespoon flax seeds (optional)

Direction

- Set an oven to 175°C (350°F) to preheat.
- Whisk together the nutmeg, cinnamon, salt, baking powder, baking soda, soy flour, wheat flour, oats and Splenda(R) in a big bowl. Stir in molasses, egg whites, water, canola oil and pumpkin. If preferred, mix in flax seeds. Roll into 14 big balls and flatten on a baking tray.
- Bake in the preheated oven for 5 minutes. Avoid overbaking; the cookies will become very dry if overbaked.

Nutrition Information

- Calories: 85 calories;
- Total Carbohydrate: 13.1
- Cholesterol: 0
- Protein: 4.2
- Total Fat: 2.2
- Sodium: 284

141. Pumpkin Raisin Cookies

Serving: 6 | Prep: | Cook: | Ready in:

Ingredients

- 1/2 cup shortening
- 1 cup packed brown sugar
- 1 egg
- 1 teaspoon vanilla extract
- 1 cup solid pack pumpkin puree
- 2 cups all-purpose flour
- 1 teaspoon baking soda
- 1/4 teaspoon salt
- 2 1/2 teaspoons pumpkin pie spice
- 1 teaspoon ground cinnamon
- 1/2 cup chopped walnuts
- 1 cup raisins
- 1 cup confectioners' sugar
- 2 tablespoons warm water
- 1/2 teaspoon ground cinnamon

Direction

- Set the oven to 350°F (175°C) and start preheating. Grease cookie sheets.
- Cream sugar and the shortening until smooth in a medium bowl. Add vanilla and egg; mix until fluffy. Stir in pumpkin. Sift cinnamon, baking soda, pumpkin pie spice, salt and flour together; stir into the pumpkin mixture. Lastly, stir in walnuts and raisins.
- Drop cookie dough onto the greased cookie sheets by heaping spoonfuls. Bake in the prepared oven for 10-12 minutes; the edges should turn light brown. Brush spice glaze over the cookies; remove to racks to cool.
- To prepare spice glaze: mix 2 tablespoons of warm water with confectioners' sugar until no lumps left. Stir in half teaspoon of cinnamon. Add a little more water if the glaze is too thick.

Nutrition Information

- Calories: 688 calories;

- Total Fat: 25
- Sodium: 432
- Total Carbohydrate: 112.6
- Cholesterol: 31
- Protein: 8.1

142. Pumpkin Spice Cookie

Serving: 24 | Prep: 15mins | Cook: 20mins | Ready in:

Ingredients

- 1 (18.25 ounce) package spice cake mix
- 1 (15 ounce) can solid pack pumpkin

Direction

- Set the oven to 175°C or 350°F preheat. Coat cookie sheets grease.
- Stir pumpkin and cake mix together in a big bowl until well-combined. Drop on prepared cookie sheet with rounded spoonfuls of dough.
- In the preheated oven, bake for about 18-20 minutes. Let cookies cool on baking sheet about 5 minutes prior to transferring to a wire rack to cool thoroughly.

Nutrition Information

- Calories: 98 calories;
- Total Carbohydrate: 17.2
- Cholesterol: 0
- Protein: 1.5
- Total Fat: 2.7
- Sodium: 188

143. Pumpkin Pine Cookies

Serving: 60 | Prep: 10mins | Cook: 8mins | Ready in:

Ingredients

- 2 cups all-purpose flour
- 1/2 teaspoon baking soda
- 1/2 teaspoon baking powder
- 1 teaspoon ground cinnamon
- 1/4 teaspoon ground cloves
- 1/2 cup butter, softened
- 1 1/3 cups white sugar
- 1 egg
- 1 1/2 cups canned pumpkin puree
- 1/4 cup heavy cream
- 1 cup rolled oats
- 1/2 cup crushed pineapple, drained
- 1 cup chopped pecans

Direction

- Set the oven to 200°C or 400°F to preheat. Coat cookie sheets with grease. Stir cloves, cinnamon, baking powder, baking soda and flour together, then put aside.
- Cream egg, sugar and butter together in a big bowl until smooth. Stir in cream and pumpkin. Blend in dry ingredients gradually until well-combined, then stir in pecans, pineapple and oats. Drop on prepared cookie sheets with tablespoonfuls of dough.
- In the preheated oven, bake for about 8-10 minutes, until bottoms start to brown. Let cookies cool on baking sheets about several minutes prior to transferring to wire racks to cool thoroughly.

Nutrition Information

- Calories: 72 calories;
- Total Carbohydrate: 9.7
- Cholesterol: 9
- Protein: 1
- Total Fat: 3.5
- Sodium: 26

144. Root Beer Float Cookies

Serving: 24 | Prep: 15mins | Cook: 8mins | Ready in:

Ingredients

- 3/4 cup butter
- 3/4 cup brown sugar
- 1/4 cup white sugar
- 1 (3.5 ounce) package instant vanilla pudding mix
- 2 eggs
- 1 teaspoon root beer concentrate
- 2 1/4 cups all-purpose flour
- 1 teaspoon baking soda
- 1 cup white chocolate chips, or more to taste

Direction

- Preheat an oven to 175°C/350°F then grease 2 baking sheets.
- Use electric mixer to beat white sugar, brown sugar and butter till creamy in bowl; beat pudding mix in. Add root beer concentrate and eggs; mix baking soda and flour in. Fold chocolate chips into dough.
- Drop dough spoonfuls on baking sheets, 2-in. apart.
- In preheated oven, bake for 8-10 minutes till golden.

Nutrition Information

- Calories: 182 calories;
- Cholesterol: 32
- Protein: 2.3
- Total Fat: 8.9
- Sodium: 167
- Total Carbohydrate: 23.5

---

145. S'More Bars II

Serving: 24 | Prep: 15mins | Cook: 15mins | Ready in:

Ingredients

- 1 1/2 cups butter, melted
- 4 cups graham cracker crumbs
- 6 (1.5 ounce) bars milk chocolate candy bars
- 2 cups miniature marshmallows

Direction

- Preheat an oven to 175°C/350°F then grease 9x13-in. pan.
- Mix graham cracker crumbs and melted butter in medium bowl; press 1/2 graham cracker mixture in bottom of prepped pan. Melt chocolate chips, frequently mixing till smooth, in microwave/metal bowl above pan with simmering water. Take off heat; spread on graham cracker layer. Refrigerate crust as chocolate melts to easily spread. Create marshmallow layer over chocolate; put leftover graham cracker crumbs over.
- In preheated oven, bake for 15 minutes. Cool; cut to squares.

Nutrition Information

- Calories: 230 calories;
- Protein: 1.7
- Total Fat: 16.3
- Sodium: 176
- Total Carbohydrate: 20.8
- Cholesterol: 33

---

146. S'more Eyeballs

Serving: 24 | Prep: 30mins | Cook: 10mins | Ready in:

Ingredients

- 8 whole graham crackers, crushed
- 6 tablespoons butter, melted
- 1/4 cup confectioners' sugar
- 2 (1.5 ounce) bars milk chocolate candy bars (such as Hershey's®)
- 12 large marshmallows, cut in half crosswise
- 1 dash red food coloring, or as needed
- 24 semisweet chocolate chips

Direction

- Preheat the oven to 350°F (175°C).
- In a bowl, mix the butter, confectioners' sugar and graham cracker crumbs together until the mixture has an evenly moist texture; push the prepared mixture into the bottom of a mini-muffin pan that is ungreased to create shallow cups.
- Put it in the preheated oven and let it bake for about 5 minutes until it is bubbling around the edges.
- Break the chocolate bars into 12 equally-sized smaller pieces and put 1 chocolate bar piece in each of the baked graham cracker cups.
- Use a red-colored food coloring to draw red lines and circles over each marshmallow so that they look like blood-shot eyes. Put each of the painted marshmallows, with the painted sides facing up, over the piece of chocolate bar in each of the graham cracker cups. In the middle of each of the marshmallows, press in 1 piece of chocolate chip.
- Put it in the preheated oven and let it bake for 1-2 minutes until the marshmallows become a little bit soft. Allow the baked graham cups to cool down in the muffin pan for 15 minutes before removing them from the muffin pan.

Nutrition Information

- Calories: 157 calories;
- Sodium: 55
- Total Carbohydrate: 20.1
- Cholesterol: 8
- Protein: 1.3
- Total Fat: 9.3

147. Spiderweb Brownies

Serving: 16 | Prep: 15mins | Cook: 40mins | Ready in:

Ingredients

- 1 (18.25 ounce) package chocolate brownie mix
- 2 (2.1 ounce) bars NESTLE® BUTTERFINGER® Original, chopped
- 1 (3 ounce) package cream cheese, at room temperature
- 1/4 cup granulated sugar
- 2 tablespoons milk

Direction

- Set oven to 350°F to preheat. Grease 9-inch or 10-inch round baking tray.
- Make brownie batter following package directions; mix in sliced Butterfinger. Scoop into greased tray.
- In a small mixer bowl, whip milk, sugar and cream cheese until smooth. On top of brownie batter, pipe cream cheese mixture into concentric circles. Drag a wooden pick or tip of knife through cream cheese from middle to last circle to make a spider web.
- Bake until wooden pick inserted near the middle comes out nearly clean, 40 mins. Let cool completely in pan on wire rack. Slice into wedges with a wet knife.

Nutrition Information

- Calories: 206 calories;
- Total Carbohydrate: 33.5
- Cholesterol: 6
- Protein: 2.3
- Total Fat: 8.1
- Sodium: 131

148. White Chocolate Pumpkin Cookies

Serving: 18 | Prep: | Cook: | Ready in:

Ingredients

- 2 1/4 cups all-purpose flour
- 1 teaspoon pumpkin pie spice
- 1/2 teaspoon baking soda

- 1 cup unsalted butter
- 1 1/2 cups packed brown sugar
- 1 cup solid pack pumpkin puree
- 2 eggs
- 1 tablespoon vanilla extract
- 2 cups white chocolate chips
- 1 cup chopped pecans

Direction

- In a small bowl, whisk the baking soda, pumpkin pie spice and flour together.
- In a medium bowl, cream sugar and butter using an electric mixer. Beat in the pumpkin pie puree. Beat in the vanilla and eggs. Beat in the flour mixture just until incorporated. Mix in the pecans and white chocolate.
- On an ungreased cookie sheet, drop rounded tablespoons of the dough 2 inches apart. Bake for 20-22 minutes at 150°C (300°F) just until set.

Nutrition Information

- Calories: 386 calories;
- Total Fat: 22.4
- Sodium: 104
- Total Carbohydrate: 43.3
- Cholesterol: 52
- Protein: 4.6

149. Witches' Hats

Serving: 32 | Prep: 1hours | Cook: | Ready in:

Ingredients

- 2 (16 ounce) packages fudge stripe cookies
- 1/4 cup honey, or as needed
- 1 (9 ounce) bag milk chocolate candy kisses, unwrapped
- 1 (4.5 ounce) tube decorating gel

Direction

- On a work surface, lay a fudge stripe cookie with the bottom-side up. Slather about 1/8 tsp of honey onto the base of a chocolate kiss; place the candy piece into the middle of the cookie and secure, covering the hole. Pipe a small bow at the bottom of the candy piece on the cookie using decorating gel. Repeat with the rest of the ingredients.

Nutrition Information

- Calories: 204 calories;
- Sodium: 170
- Total Carbohydrate: 28.5
- Cholesterol: 2
- Protein: 2.4
- Total Fat: 8.7

Chapter 4: Thanksgiving Cookie Recipes

***

150. Acorn Candy Cookies

Serving: 24 | Prep: 15mins | Cook: | Ready in:

Ingredients

- 1 tablespoon prepared chocolate frosting
- 24 milk chocolate candy kisses (such as Hershey's Kisses®), unwrapped
- 24 mini vanilla wafer cookies (such as Nilla®)
- 24 butterscotch chips

Direction

- On the flat bottom of a candy kiss, smear a little amount of frosting. Press onto the flat side of the vanilla wafer. On the flat bottom of a butterscotch chip, smear a little more frosting, and press it onto the rounded top of the cookie. Repeat with the rest of ingredients. Put aside for about 30 minutes to dry.

Nutrition Information

- Calories: 132 calories;
- Cholesterol: 1
- Protein: 0.5
- Total Fat: 6.7
- Sodium: 31
- Total Carbohydrate: 15.6

151. Anise Waffle Cookies

Serving: 36 | Prep: 15mins | Cook: 30mins | Ready in:

Ingredients

- 3 cups all-purpose flour, or as needed
- 1 tablespoon anise seed
- 1/2 teaspoon salt
- 1/2 cup shortening
- 1/2 cup white sugar
- 2 tablespoons white sugar
- 3 small eggs
- 1 drop anise oil
- 1/2 cup confectioners' sugar, or as needed

Direction

- Preheat a waffle iron following manufacturer's instructions. In a bowl, whisk salt, anise seed, and flour together.
- Mash the shortening in a separate bowl until creamy and stir with all of the anise oil, eggs, and sugar until mixed thoroughly. Mix the flour mixture into the wet ingredients to form a dough. Break off about 1 tablespoon of dough per cookie and roll into balls (1 inch in size).
- Use cooking spray to coat the waffle iron. Place dough balls on the iron, cover with a lid, and bake for 1 to 3 minutes until cookies are slightly golden brown and the iron stops emitting steam. Check after 1 minute. Take the cookies out of the iron and dust with confectioners' sugar while it is still warm. Place on wire rack to cool.

Nutrition Information

- Calories: 89 calories;
- Sodium: 37
- Total Carbohydrate: 13.3
- Cholesterol: 11
- Protein: 1.5
- Total Fat: 3.3

152. Apple Bars

Serving: 9 | Prep: 15mins | Cook: 40mins | Ready in::

Ingredients

- 1/2 cup melted butter
- 1 cup white sugar
- 1 egg
- 1 cup all-purpose flour
- 1/2 teaspoon baking soda
- 1 teaspoon ground cinnamon
- 1 cup apples - peeled, cored and finely diced
- 1 cup chopped walnuts

Direction

- Heat oven to 350°F (175°C) to preheat. Grease and flour an 8x8-inch baking pan.
- Stir melted butter with egg and sugar in a large bowl. Stir in cinnamon, baking soda, and flour, and then mix in walnuts and apple. Distribute batter evenly into the greased pan.

- Bake for about 40 minutes, or until a small knife pierced in the middle exits clean.

Nutrition Information

- Calories: 328 calories;
- Sodium: 151
- Total Carbohydrate: 36.8
- Cholesterol: 48
- Protein: 4.3
- Total Fat: 19.4

153. Apple Brownies

Serving: 12 | Prep: 25mins | Cook: 35mins | Ready in:

Ingredients

- 1/2 cup butter, melted
- 1 cup white sugar
- 1 egg
- 3 medium apples - peeled, cored and thinly sliced
- 1/2 cup chopped walnuts
- 1 cup all-purpose flour
- 1/4 teaspoon salt
- 1/2 teaspoon baking powder
- 1/2 teaspoon baking soda
- 1 teaspoon ground cinnamon

Direction

- To preheat: Set oven to 175°C (350°F). Grease a 9x9 inch baking dish.
- Put egg, sugar, melted butter in a large bowl then beat together till the mixture becomes fluffy. Fold in walnuts and apples. Sift together cinnamon, baking soda, baking powder, salt and flour in a different bowl. Put the flour mixture into the wet mixture then stir till both are blended. Spread the batter evenly in the greased baking dish.
- Put the baking dish into the preheated oven and bake for 35 minutes till you get a clean toothpick after inserting it in the center of the cake.

Nutrition Information

- Calories: 227 calories;
- Total Fat: 11.5
- Sodium: 177
- Total Carbohydrate: 30.3
- Cholesterol: 36
- Protein: 2.5

154. Apple Butter Bars

Serving: 18 | Prep: | Cook: | Ready in:

Ingredients

- 1/2 cup butter
- 1 1/2 cups all-purpose flour
- 1/2 cup packed brown sugar
- 1/4 cup white sugar
- 1 egg
- 3/4 cup apple butter
- 1/2 teaspoon baking soda
- 1/2 teaspoon apple pie spice
- 1 cup raisins
- 1 cup confectioners' sugar
- 1/4 teaspoon vanilla extract
- 2 tablespoons milk

Direction

- Heat oven to 350°F (175°C) to preheat. Grease a 13 x 9 x 2-inch baking dish.
- Whip margarine or butter until creamy. Put 1/2 of the apple pie spice, baking soda, apple butter, egg, white sugar, brown sugar and flour. Whip together until thoroughly combined. Whip in the remainder flour and mix in raisins. Distribute evenly in the greased baking dish.
- Bake for 20-25 minutes or until toothpick in the middle exits clean. Rest in pan on wire

rack to cool. Pour icing on top slowly. Slice into bars.
- Prepare Icing: Stir 1 - 2 tablespoons milk, 1/4 teaspoon vanilla and a cup confectioners' sugar. Stir until it reaches drizzling consistency.

Nutrition Information

- Calories: 193 calories;
- Cholesterol: 24
- Protein: 1.8
- Total Fat: 5.6
- Sodium: 81
- Total Carbohydrate: 34.9

155. Apple Cinnamon Oatmeal Cookie

Serving: 24 | Prep: | Cook: | Ready in:

Ingredients

- 1 cup apple cinnamon granola
- 3/4 cup all-purpose flour
- 1/2 cup packed brown sugar
- 1/2 cup shortening
- 1/4 cup white sugar
- 1 egg
- 1/2 teaspoon salt
- 1/2 teaspoon vanilla extract
- 1/2 teaspoon baking soda

Direction

- To preheat: Set oven to 190°C (375°F).
- In a medium size mixing bowl, mix baking soda, vanilla extract, salt, egg, white sugar, brown sugar, shortening, flour and granola together. Mix till everything is blended thoroughly.
- On baking sheets, pour mixtures by teaspoonfuls, spacing 1 1/2 inches apart.
- Put the baking sheet into the preheated oven and bake for 12 – 15 minutes or till golden brown. Allow to cool on wire racks.

Nutrition Information

- Calories: 101 calories;
- Total Fat: 5.3
- Sodium: 81
- Total Carbohydrate: 12.5
- Cholesterol: 8
- Protein: 1.1

156. Apple Cookies

Serving: 30 | Prep: | Cook: | Ready in:

Ingredients

- 1/2 cup shortening
- 1 1/3 cups packed brown sugar
- 1 egg
- 2 cups all-purpose flour
- 1 teaspoon baking soda
- 1/2 teaspoon salt
- 1/2 cup milk
- 1 cup chopped walnuts
- 1 cup raisins
- 1 cup chopped apples

Direction

- Set the oven to 200°C or 400°F to preheat. Coat cookie sheets with grease.
- Cream together egg, sugar and shortening, then put in 1/2 of the dry ingredients.
- Mix in the leftover dry ingredients and milk.
- Put in apples, raisins and nuts then mix well.
- Drop the mixture on cookie sheet coated with grease, then bake for 10-12 minutes. Allow to cool and spread with the Vanilla Glaze.

Nutrition Information

- Calories: 144 calories;
- Total Fat: 6.3
- Sodium: 88
- Total Carbohydrate: 21.1
- Cholesterol: 7
- Protein: 2

157. Apple Half Moons

Serving: 24 | Prep: | Cook: | Ready in:

Ingredients

- 1/3 cup sour cream
- 1 egg yolk, beaten
- 1 teaspoon vanilla extract
- 1 1/2 cups all-purpose flour
- 1/4 cup white sugar
- 3/4 cup butter
- 1 tablespoon butter
- 2 apple - peeled, cored, and chopped
- 1/4 cup raisins
- 1 tablespoon brown sugar
- 1 teaspoon apple pie spice

Direction

- Stir together vanilla extract, egg yolk and sour cream to blend. Stir together sugar and flour in a big bowl, then slice in 3/4 cup of margarine or butter until resembles coarse crumbs. Mix in sour cream mixture until well-mixed.
- Split the dough in 2 equal portions and refrigerate until easy to handle, 3 hours or so.
- For Filling: Melt 1 tbsp. of margarine in a small saucepan. Add in spice, brown sugar, raisins and apples, then cook until apples are fork-tender while stirring sometimes. Get rid of excess liquid and cool.
- Roll each dough piece to the thickness of about 1/8 inch and use a 2 1/2-inch round cookie cutter to cut. Put rounds on an ungreased cookie sheet with 1/2 inch apart. Put on each round a skimpy teaspoon of filling and fold in half, then use a fork to seal edges.
- Bake at 175°C or 350°F until browned lightly, about 10 to 12 minutes. Take out and allow to cool. Drizzle with lemon sugar icing. To make lemon sugar icing, mix together 1 tbsp. of water, 1 tsp. of lemon juice (fresh) and 1/2 cup of powdered sugar until get drizzling consistency. If icing is too thin, add somewhat more confectioners' sugar, if too thick, put in a little bit more water.

Nutrition Information

- Calories: 114 calories;
- Total Fat: 7.2
- Sodium: 47
- Total Carbohydrate: 11.6
- Cholesterol: 26
- Protein: 1.2

158. Apple Hermits

Serving: 60 | Prep: 30mins | Cook: 12mins | Ready in:

Ingredients

- 2 cups all-purpose flour
- 1 teaspoon baking soda
- 1 teaspoon ground cinnamon
- 1 teaspoon ground cloves
- 1/2 teaspoon ground nutmeg
- 1/2 teaspoon salt
- 1/2 cup softened butter
- 1 1/2 cups packed brown sugar
- 1 egg, beaten
- 1 cup chopped walnuts
- 1 cup chopped apples
- 1 cup raisins
- 2/3 cup confectioners' sugar
- 1 tablespoon milk

Direction

- Set an oven to 175°C (350°F) and start preheating. Use parchment paper to line

cookie sheets. Sift salt, nutmeg, cloves, cinnamon, baking soda, and flour together in a medium bowl. Cream the butter in a large mixing bowl until fluffy and light. Combine in egg and sugar. Then add in the flour mixture and stir thoroughly. Mix in raisins, apples, and nuts.
- Add a rounded teaspoon 1 1/2 inches apart to the prepared cookie sheets. Then bake for 12-14 minutes. Transfer onto a wire rack and allow to cool.
- Combine the confectioners' sugar together with milk in a small bowl to create a thin glaze. Spray on the cooled cookies.

Nutrition Information

- Calories: 77 calories;
- Protein: 0.9
- Total Fat: 2.8
- Sodium: 55
- Total Carbohydrate: 12.7
- Cholesterol: 7

159. Apple Oatmeal Bar Cookies

Serving: 36 | Prep: 15mins | Cook: 35mins | Ready in:

Ingredients

- 1/2 cup butter, softened
- 1 cup packed brown sugar
- 2 1/2 cups uncooked rolled oats
- 1 cup all-purpose flour
- 2 teaspoons ground cinnamon
- 1 teaspoon vanilla extract
- 1/4 cup applesauce
- 1 cup chopped walnuts

Direction

- Set the oven to 175°C or 350°F to preheat. Coat a 13"x9" baking pan slightly with grease.
- Cream brown sugar and butter together in a big bowl until smooth. Beat in vanilla, cinnamon, flour and oats, then fold in walnuts and applesauce. Remove the mixture to the prepped pan.
- In the preheated oven, bake until it turns golden brown, or about 35 minutes. Allow to cool in pan and cut into squares.

Nutrition Information

- Calories: 103 calories;
- Total Fat: 5.1
- Sodium: 20
- Total Carbohydrate: 13.2
- Cholesterol: 7
- Protein: 1.6

160. Apple Oatmeal Bars

Serving: 12 | Prep: | Cook: | Ready in:

Ingredients

- 2 cups all-purpose flour
- 1 teaspoon salt
- 1 teaspoon baking soda
- 1 cup packed brown sugar
- 1 cup rolled oats
- 1 cup butter
- 4 tablespoons butter
- 6 cups thinly sliced apples

Direction

- Combine together baking soda, salt and flour. Put in oatmeal and brown sugar, then blend well together. Cut in 1 cup of butter.
- Spread 1/2 of the crumb mixture in a 13"x9" pan coated with butter.
- Put apples on top of bottom layer, then use the leftover crumb mixture to cover and dot with 4 tbsp. of butter.

- Bake for 40-45 minutes at 175°C or 350°F. Serve together with ice cream for best flavor.

Nutrition Information

- Calories: 373 calories;
- Total Carbohydrate: 47.1
- Cholesterol: 51
- Protein: 3.4
- Total Fat: 19.9
- Sodium: 441

161. Apple Oatmeal Cookies I

Serving: 36 | Prep: 15mins | Cook: 15mins | Ready in:

Ingredients

- 1 cup all-purpose flour
- 1 teaspoon baking powder
- 1 teaspoon ground cinnamon
- 1/2 teaspoon salt
- 1/2 teaspoon ground nutmeg
- 1/2 cup shortening
- 3/4 cup white sugar
- 2 eggs
- 1 cup rolled oats
- 1 cup diced apple without peel
- 1 cup chopped walnuts

Direction

- Heat oven to 350°F (175°C) to preheat.
- Beat together the sugar and shortening in a large bowl. Blend in the eggs until well combined. Into the sugar mixture, beat the salt, nutmeg, cinnamon, baking powder, and flour until thoroughly combined. Fold in the apples, oats and walnuts. Put dough by spoonfuls about 2 inches apart onto an ungreased cookie tray.
- Bake in the preheated oven for 12 to 15 mins. Rest on wire racks to cool.

Nutrition Information

- Calories: 90 calories;
- Protein: 1.5
- Total Fat: 5.4
- Sodium: 50
- Total Carbohydrate: 9.4
- Cholesterol: 10

162. Apple Pie Bars

Serving: 18 | Prep: | Cook: | Ready in:

Ingredients

- 2 1/2 cups all-purpose flour
- 1 teaspoon salt
- 1 cup butter, chilled
- 1 egg yolk
- 2/3 cup milk
- 1 cup crushed cornflakes cereal
- 8 cups thinly sliced apples
- 1 cup white sugar
- 1 1/2 teaspoons ground cinnamon
- 1/2 teaspoon ground nutmeg
- 1 egg white
- 2 tablespoons white sugar
- 1/2 teaspoon ground cinnamon
- 1 cup confectioners' sugar
- 1 1/2 teaspoons milk
- 1/2 teaspoon vanilla extract

Direction

- Heat oven to 350°F (175°C) to preheat.
- Mix together the salt and flour in a medium bowl. Slice in a cup butter until it's mealy. Mix in the 2/3 cup milk and egg yolk with a fork. Split dough into two even parts. On a surface that has been lightly floured, stretch out a piece of dough into a big rectangle. Put on a 9x13 inch baking pan.
- Scatter cereal on the crust, then put the apples in a layer on the cereal. Mix together the 1 1/2 teaspoons of cinnamon and nutmeg and a cup

of white sugar; scatter on the apple layer. Stretch out another half of the dough and top everything in the pan. Brush the reserved egg white on the top crust and scatter with a combination of two tablespoons sugar, and half a teaspoon of cinnamon.
- Bake in the preheated oven for 45 minutes to an hour until top is lightly browned. Stir together the half teaspoon of vanilla, 1 and 1/2 tablespoons of milk and 1 cup of confectioners' sugar until smooth; pour over bars slowly while still warm.

Nutrition Information

- Calories: 272 calories;
- Sodium: 221
- Total Carbohydrate: 42.2
- Cholesterol: 39
- Protein: 2.8
- Total Fat: 11

163. Apple Squares

Serving: 16 | Prep: 25mins | Cook: 30mins | Ready in:

Ingredients

- 1 cup sifted all-purpose flour
- 1 teaspoon baking powder
- 1/4 teaspoon salt
- 1/4 teaspoon ground cinnamon
- 1/4 cup butter or margarine, melted
- 1/2 cup packed brown sugar
- 1/2 cup white sugar
- 1 egg
- 1 teaspoon vanilla extract
- 1/2 cup chopped apple
- 1/2 cup finely chopped walnuts
- 2 tablespoons white sugar
- 2 teaspoons ground cinnamon

Direction

- Set the oven to 175°C or 350°F to preheat. Coat a 9"x9" pan with grease. Sift 1/4 tsp. of cinnamon, salt, baking powder and flour together, then put aside.
- Using a wooden spoon, mix 1/2 cup of white sugar, brown sugar and melted butter in a big bowl until smooth, then stir in vanilla and egg. Mix in the flour mixture until just blended, then mix in walnuts and apples. Spread the mixture evenly into the pan. Stir together leftover sugar and cinnamon in a small bowl or cup, then sprinkle over top of bars.
- In the preheated oven, bake for 25-30 minutes. The resulted bars should spring back once touched lightly. Allow to cool in the pan then slice into squares.

Nutrition Information

- Calories: 143 calories;
- Sodium: 94
- Total Carbohydrate: 22.1
- Cholesterol: 19
- Protein: 1.8
- Total Fat: 5.7

164. Apple And Spice Cookies

Serving: 18 | Prep: | Cook: | Ready in:

Ingredients

- 2 cups sifted all-purpose flour
- 1 teaspoon baking soda
- 1/2 teaspoon salt
- 1 teaspoon ground cinnamon
- 1 teaspoon ground cloves
- 1 teaspoon ground nutmeg
- 1/2 cup shortening
- 1 1/3 cups packed brown sugar
- 1/3 cup apple juice
- 1 cup chopped walnuts
- 1 cup chopped apples
- 1 cup raisins

Direction

- Cream the brown sugar and shortening together, then stir in the spices, salt, baking soda and flour until moistened. Mix until it has a smooth consistency. The mixture will get very thick.
- Stir in raisins, apples and nuts.
- Drop it on a lightly greased cookie sheet by tablespoon and place 2 inches apart. Let it bake in a 205°C (400°F) oven for 8-10 minutes. Allow it to cool slightly, then take it out of the cookie sheet.

Nutrition Information

- Calories: 237 calories;
- Cholesterol: 0
- Protein: 2.7
- Total Fat: 10.2
- Sodium: 141
- Total Carbohydrate: 35.6

---

165. Apple Cran Cherry Oatmeal Cookies

Serving: 42 | Prep: | Cook: | Ready in:

Ingredients

- 1 cup butter, softened
- 1 1/2 teaspoons ground cinnamon
- 1/4 teaspoon ground cardamom
- 1 1/2 teaspoons baking soda
- 2 cups packed dark brown sugar
- 2 cups applesauce
- 2 cups all-purpose flour
- 6 cups rolled oats
- 1 1/2 cups dried cherries
- 1 1/2 cups dried cranberries

Direction

- Cream margarine or butter, brown sugar, baking soda, cardamom and cinnamon. Put in applesauce and mix. Blend in flour slowly then oats. Stir in dried. Allow dough to stand for an hour.
- Pour teaspoonful drops onto an ungreased baking sheet.
- Put the baking sheet into the oven and bake at 175°C (350°F) till edges of cookies become slightly brown, about 10-12 minutes. Place cookies on wire rack to cool down.

Nutrition Information

- Calories: 179 calories;
- Total Fat: 5.2
- Sodium: 81
- Total Carbohydrate: 31.3
- Cholesterol: 12
- Protein: 2.5

---

166. Applesauce Bars

Serving: 20 | Prep: 10mins | Cook: 25mins | Ready in:

Ingredients

- 1/4 cup butter or margarine, softened
- 2/3 cup brown sugar
- 1 egg
- 1 cup applesauce
- 1 cup all-purpose flour
- 1 teaspoon baking soda
- 1/2 teaspoon salt
- 1 teaspoon pumpkin pie spice
- 1 1/2 cups confectioners' sugar
- 3 tablespoons margarine, melted
- 1 tablespoon milk
- 1 teaspoon vanilla extract

Direction

- To preheat, set oven to 175°C (350°F). Grease a 9-by-13-inch baking pan.

- Put egg, brown sugar and butter in a medium bowl and mix together till smooth. Add applesauce and stir. Mix pumpkin pie spice, salt, baking soda and flour; stir the mixture into the applesauce mixture till both are well blended. Spread the combined mixture evenly into the greased pan.
- Put into the preheated oven and bake for 25 minutes, or till edges become golden. Allow to cool in the pan over a wire rack.
- Put margarine and confectioners' sugar in a small bowl and mix together. Add milk and vanilla; stir till the mixture becomes smooth. Spread on top of cooled bars before slicing into squares.

Nutrition Information

- Calories: 130 calories;
- Protein: 1.1
- Total Fat: 4.2
- Sodium: 162
- Total Carbohydrate: 22.5
- Cholesterol: 15

167. Applesauce Brownies I

Serving: 48 | Prep: | Cook: | Ready in:

Ingredients

- 1 1/2 cups white sugar
- 1/2 cup margarine
- 2 eggs
- 2 tablespoons unsweetened cocoa powder
- 1 1/2 teaspoons salt
- 2 cups applesauce
- 1 teaspoon baking soda
- 1 teaspoon ground cinnamon
- 2 cups all-purpose flour
- 2 tablespoons white sugar
- 1 cup semisweet chocolate chips
- 1 cup chopped walnuts

Direction

- Set the oven to 175°C or 350°F to preheat.
- Cream margarine and 1 1/2 cups of sugar together, then put in eggs. Sift flour ingredients, cinnamon, baking soda, salt and cocoa together, then put into the sugar mixture alternately with applesauce. Transfer into 10 1/2x15 1/2-in. jelly roll pan.
- Mix together 1 cup of chopped nuts, 1 cup of chocolate chips and 2 tbsp. of sugar, then sprinkle over batter. Bake for a half hour.

Nutrition Information

- Calories: 103 calories;
- Total Carbohydrate: 14.6
- Cholesterol: 8
- Protein: 1.4
- Total Fat: 4.8
- Sodium: 125

168. Applesauce Cookies I

Serving: 24 | Prep: | Cook: | Ready in:

Ingredients

- 3/4 cup shortening
- 1 cup packed brown sugar
- 1 egg
- 1/2 cup applesauce
- 2 1/4 cups all-purpose flour
- 1/2 teaspoon baking soda
- 1/2 teaspoon salt
- 3/4 teaspoon ground cinnamon
- 1 cup raisins
- 1/2 cup chopped walnuts

Direction

- Set oven to preheat at 375°F (195°C). Grease cookie sheets.
- In a large bowl, cream together the egg, sugar, and shortening. Mix in the applesauce. Sift

together the cinnamon, salt, baking soda, and flour; mix into the creamed mixture. Then mix in the nuts and raisins.
- Onto the prepared cookie sheets, drop the mixture by teaspoonfuls. Bake in the preheated oven for 10 to 12 minutes. Remove to cool on wire racks.

Nutrition Information

- Calories: 173 calories;
- Total Fat: 8.3
- Sodium: 81
- Total Carbohydrate: 23.7
- Cholesterol: 8
- Protein: 2.1

169. Applesauce Oatie Cookies

Serving: 60 | Prep: 15mins | Cook: 14mins | Ready in:

Ingredients

- 1 3/4 cups quick cooking oats
- 1 1/2 cups all-purpose flour
- 1 teaspoon baking powder
- 1 teaspoon baking soda
- 1 teaspoon salt
- 1 teaspoon ground cinnamon
- 1/2 teaspoon ground nutmeg
- 1/2 cup butter, softened
- 1 cup packed brown sugar
- 1/2 cup white sugar
- 1 egg
- 3/4 cup applesauce
- 1 cup semi-sweet chocolate chips
- 1 cup raisins
- 1 cup chopped walnuts

Direction

- Heat the oven to 375°F (190°C) to preheat. Grease cookie sheets. Mix together the nutmeg, cinnamon, baking soda, baking powder, salt, flour and quick oats in a medium bowl, put aside.
- Beat together the white sugar, brown sugar and butter in a large bowl until smooth. Whip in the applesauce and egg. Into the batter, mix the oatmeal mixture until well combined then fold in the walnuts, raisins and chocolate chips. Put by rounded spoonfuls onto the greased cookie sheets.
- Bake in the heated oven for 8 to 10 minutes. Let cool on baking sheet for 5 minutes before taking out to a wire rack to cool completely.

Nutrition Information

- Calories: 89 calories;
- Sodium: 79
- Total Carbohydrate: 13.3
- Cholesterol: 8
- Protein: 1.2
- Total Fat: 3.9

170. Applesauce Oatmeal Cookies

Serving: 12 | Prep: | Cook: | Ready in:

Ingredients

- 1/3 cup butter, softened
- 2/3 cup packed brown sugar
- 1/2 teaspoon ground cinnamon
- 1/4 teaspoon baking soda
- 1 egg
- 1/2 cup applesauce
- 1 1/4 cups all-purpose flour
- 1 1/4 cups rolled oats

Direction

- Beat butter until it becomes creamy in a bowl. Put in baking soda, cinnamon and brown sugar. Stir the mixture until everything is

combined. Add egg and applesauce then mix. Put in flour, a little at a time. Put in oats and stir.
- Lay dough on ungreased cookie sheets. Put into the oven and bake at 190°C (375°F) for 8-10 minutes or till lightly browned. Enjoy!

Nutrition Information

- Calories: 182 calories;
- Sodium: 73
- Total Carbohydrate: 28.9
- Cholesterol: 29
- Protein: 3.1
- Total Fat: 6.2

171. Applesauce Raisin Bars

Serving: 32 | Prep: 15mins | Cook: 25mins | Ready in:

Ingredients

- 1/4 cup shortening
- 2/3 cup brown sugar
- 1 cup applesauce
- 1 egg
- 1 cup all-purpose flour
- 1 teaspoon baking soda
- 1/2 teaspoon salt
- 1 teaspoon pumpkin pie spice
- 1/2 cup raisins
- 3 tablespoons butter
- 1 1/2 cups confectioners' sugar
- 1 teaspoon vanilla extract
- 1 tablespoon milk

Direction

- To preheat: Set oven to 175°C (350°F). Grease a 9x13 inch pan.
- Cream brown sugar and shortening together in a medium bowl until the mixture becomes smooth. Blend in egg and the applesauce. Mix together pumpkin pie spice, salt, baking soda, flour then stir into the applesauce mixture. Fold in raisins. Transfer the batter to the greased pan, spread the batter evenly.
- Put the pan into the preheated oven and bake for 20 – 25 minutes till firm. Making frosting: Put butter in a small saucepan and heat till it is melted and becomes golden brown. Blend in vanilla and the confectioners' sugar. Stir in the milk slowly till icing becomes spreadable and smooth. Before slicing into squares, spread frosting over cooled bars.

Nutrition Information

- Calories: 82 calories;
- Sodium: 87
- Total Carbohydrate: 13.8
- Cholesterol: 9
- Protein: 0.7
- Total Fat: 2.9

172. Applesauce Squares

Serving: 16 | Prep: | Cook: |Ready in:

Ingredients

- 1/2 cup butter
- 1 cup white sugar
- 1 egg
- 1 teaspoon vanilla extract
- 1 cup raisins
- 1 1/2 cups applesauce
- 1/2 teaspoon ground cinnamon
- 2 cups all-purpose flour
- 2 teaspoons baking soda
- 3/4 teaspoon salt
- 1 cup chopped walnuts

Direction

- Set the oven to 175°C or 350°F to preheat. Coat an 8"x8" baking pan with grease.

- Cream together vanilla, eggs, sugar and butter, then beat well together.
- Blend in salt, baking soda, flour and cinnamon, then put in applesauce, nuts and raisins. Mix well together.
- Into prepped baking pan, arrange the batter and bake at 175°C or 350°F for half an hour. Slice into squares and serve.

Nutrition Information

- Calories: 246 calories;
- Total Fat: 11
- Sodium: 314
- Total Carbohydrate: 35.3
- Cholesterol: 27
- Protein: 3.5

173. Auntie's Persimmon Cookies

Serving: 36 | Prep: 30mins | Cook: 14mins | Ready in:

Ingredients

- 1 1/2 cups persimmon pulp
- 1 teaspoon baking soda
- 1/2 cup butter, softened
- 1 cup white sugar
- 2 cups all-purpose flour
- 1 teaspoon ground cinnamon
- 1 teaspoon ground cloves
- 1 teaspoon ground nutmeg
- 1/2 teaspoon salt
- 1 egg
- 1 cup chopped pecans
- 1 cup golden raisins
- Maple Glaze:
- 1 cup confectioners' sugar
- 1/4 cup maple syrup
- 1 tablespoon melted butter
- 1/2 teaspoon vanilla extract
- 1/8 teaspoon salt
- Decoration:
- 2 green belt candy strips
- 1 cup white chocolate chips
- 1 teaspoon shortening (such as Crisco®)
- 36 red candy-coated chocolate pieces (such as M&M's®)

Direction

- Heat oven to 175 degrees C/350 degrees F. Line parchment paper on a baking sheet or use a silpat nonstick baking mat.
- In a small bowl, mash persimmon pulp. Mix in baking soda. Allow mixture to congeal.
- Beat half a cup of butter and white sugar in a big bowl using an electric mixer until fluffy and light. Mix salt, nutmeg, cloves, cinnamon, and flour in another bowl.
- Mix in persimmon mixture. Add flour mixture and persimmon mixture in the creamed butter mixture. Mix well until combined. Fold raisins and pecans in the batter.
- Drop the batter on prepared baking sheet with a medium sized cookie scoop.
- Bake for 13-15 minutes in the oven until puffy and slightly brown. Take out of oven and completely cool for 30 minutes on wire racks.
- Mix salt, vanilla extract, a tablespoon of melted butter, maple syrup, and confectioners' sugar in a bowl until glaze becomes smooth. Put a parchment paper sheet under the wire rack to get drips. Drizzle the maple glaze on the tops of the cookies with a spoon. Let it set for 30 minutes until glaze hardens.
- Slice green belt candy to small leaf shapes with kitchen scissors. Mix shortening and white chocolate in a ceramic or microwave-safe glass bowl. Melt in the microwave for 1-3 minutes in 15-second intervals, mixing it after each interval.
- Drip melted white chocolate on every cookie with a spoon. Put one red candy coated chocolate in the center of every cookie then place a green belt leaf on every side. Let it set for 30 minutes until frosting hardens.

Nutrition Information

- Calories: 178 calories;
- Total Fat: 7.6
- Sodium: 105
- Total Carbohydrate: 27
- Cholesterol: 14
- Protein: 1.9

174. Autumn Harvest Cookies

Serving: 42 | Prep: 15mins | Cook: 10mins | Ready in:

Ingredients

- 1 cup softened butter
- 1/2 cup brown sugar
- 1/2 cup white sugar
- 2 eggs
- 1/2 teaspoon orange extract
- 1/2 teaspoon vanilla extract
- 1 1/2 cups all-purpose flour
- 1/4 teaspoon salt
- 1 teaspoon baking powder
- 1 teaspoon pumpkin pie spice
- 2 1/2 cups rolled oats
- 1/2 cup chopped walnuts
- 1 cup dried cranberries

Direction

- Preheat the oven to 175 degrees C (350 degrees F). Use the parchment paper to line the baking sheet.
- Cream brown and white sugars with butter together in the bowl till smooth. Beat in orange extract, vanilla and eggs.
- In another bowl, mix pumpkin pie spice, baking powder, salt and flour; stir the flour mixture to sugar mixture. Put in cranberries, walnuts and rolled oats and stir thoroughly. With the small ice cream scoop/teaspoon, drop the rounded scoops of the dough to prepped cookie sheet.
- Bake in preheated oven for 8-10 minutes till edges turn golden. Let cookies cool down on baking sheet for 60 seconds prior to taking out onto the wire rack to let cool totally.

Nutrition Information

- Calories: 114 calories;
- Total Carbohydrate: 14.3
- Cholesterol: 20
- Protein: 1.7
- Total Fat: 5.9
- Sodium: 61

175. Butterscotch Apple Cookies

Serving: 18 | Prep: | Cook: | Ready in:

Ingredients

- 2 1/2 cups all-purpose flour
- 2 teaspoons ground cinnamon
- 1 teaspoon baking soda
- 1/2 teaspoon salt
- 1 1/3 cups packed brown sugar
- 10 tablespoons butter, softened
- 1 egg
- 2/3 cup apple juice
- 2 cups butterscotch chips
- 3/4 cup grated apple
- 3/4 cup chopped walnuts
- 2 tablespoons butter
- 1 cup confectioners' sugar

Direction

- Set oven to preheat at 175°C (350°F). Grease cookie sheets lightly.
- Mix together salt, baking soda, cinnamon and flour in medium bowl.
- In large mixer bowl, beat 1/2 cup butter and brown sugar until creamy. Beat in the egg. Mix in flour mixture gradually and alternately with

apple juice. Mix in 1/2 cup walnuts, apple and 1 1/2 cups butterscotch chips. Onto the lightly greased cookie sheets, drop the mixture by slightly rounded tablespoon.
- Bake until lightly browned, for 10 to 12 minutes. Let sit for 2 minutes; allow to cool down on wire racks.
- While the cookies cool down, prepare the butterscotch glaze: In small, heavy saucepan, melt the 2 tablespoons butter and the rest of butterscotch chips over lowest heat possible.
- When the chips and butter have melted, take the pan off the heat and mix in 1 1/2 tablespoon apple juice and 1 cup confectioners' sugar until the glaze becomes smooth. Spread the glaze atop the cooled cookies and sprinkle with the leftover walnuts on top.

Nutrition Information

- Calories: 369 calories;
- Total Fat: 16.7
- Sodium: 218
- Total Carbohydrate: 50.3
- Cholesterol: 31
- Protein: 3

176. Candy Turkeys

Serving: 24 | Prep: 5mins | Cook: | Ready in:

Ingredients

- 1 (16 ounce) package fudge striped shortbread cookies
- 1 (13 ounce) package chocolate covered caramel candies (e.g. Rolo TM)
- 1 (14 ounce) package individually wrapped caramels
- 1 (14 ounce) package candy corn
- 1 (16 ounce) container prepared chocolate frosting

Direction

- Stack on their sides candy corn, chocolate covered caramel candy and one caramel. Hold all together with a dab of frosting.
- On the back of caramel, put a dab of frosting and stick to the bottom of the top side of a cookie. Let it stand upright.

Nutrition Information

- Calories: 366 calories;
- Cholesterol: 3
- Protein: 2.9
- Total Fat: 12
- Sodium: 171
- Total Carbohydrate: 62.5

177. Caramel Apple Bars II

Serving: 48 | Prep: | Cook: | Ready in:

Ingredients

- 2 cups all-purpose flour
- 2 cups quick cooking oats
- 1 1/2 cups packed brown sugar
- 1 teaspoon baking soda
- 1 1/4 cups butter, melted
- 2 cups apples - peeled, cored and sliced
- 1/2 cup chopped walnuts
- 1 1/2 cups caramel ice cream topping
- 1/2 cup all-purpose flour

Direction

- Preheat the oven to 175 ° C or 350 ° F. Grease one jellyroll pan, 15x10 inch in size.
- Mix baking soda, brown sugar, quick cooking oats and flour in a big bowl. Mix in liquified butter. Combine to form a crumbly crust. Pat half of the mixture into prepped baking pan. Bake in prepped oven for 8 minutes.
- Mix leftover half cup flour and caramel topping in a small pan over moderate heat.

Mixing continuously, boil and cook the caramel filling for 3 minutes to 5 minutes.
- Scatter top of baked crust evenly with slices of apple. Scatter with nuts. Then top apple layer with caramel filling. Break up the rest of the crust mixture over all. Bake till golden brown in color, about 20 to 25 minutes more. Cool down prior to slicing to make bars.

Nutrition Information

- Calories: 141 calories;
- Total Fat: 5.9
- Sodium: 98
- Total Carbohydrate: 21.5
- Cholesterol: 13
- Protein: 1.5

178. Caramel Apple Bars III

Serving: 36 | Prep: 15mins | Cook: 25mins | Ready in:

Ingredients

- 1 cup packed brown sugar
- 1/2 cup butter, softened
- 1/4 cup shortening
- 1 3/4 cups all-purpose flour
- 1 1/2 cups quick cooking oats
- 1 (14 ounce) package individually wrapped caramels, unwrapped
- 1 teaspoon salt
- 1/2 teaspoon baking soda
- 4 1/2 cups apple - peeled, cored, and chopped
- 1 tablespoon lemon juice
- 3 tablespoons all-purpose flour

Direction

- Set the oven to 400°F (200°C), and start preheating.
- Cream together shortening, butter and brown sugar in a large bowl till smooth. Stir salt, baking soda, oats and 1 3/4 cups flour together and mix into the creamed mixture until well combined. Put aside 2 cups of the mixture. Press the rest into the bottom of ungreased 9x13 inch baking pan.
- Toss lemon juice with apples in a medium bowl, then toss with 3 tablespoons flour. Distribute the apple mixture evenly over the crust. In a small saucepan, melt caramels over medium heat, stirring often until smooth. Pour the melted caramels evenly over the apples. Drizzle the reserved oat mixture on top of apple layer. Press down gently.
- Bake in the oven for 25-30 minutes until the apples are tender and the top turns golden brown. Cut while slightly warm and store any leftover bars in fridge.

Nutrition Information

- Calories: 146 calories;
- Total Fat: 5.2
- Sodium: 129
- Total Carbohydrate: 24
- Cholesterol: 8
- Protein: 1.7

179. Caramel Apple Cookie Dessert

Serving: 10 | Prep: 13mins | Cook: 7mins | Ready in:

Ingredients

- 1 (18 ounce) package refrigerated sugar cookie dough
- 1 (18 ounce) container caramel dip
- 3 tablespoons white sugar
- 2 cups apple juice
- 3 Red Delicious apples - peeled, cored and sliced

Direction

- Heat oven to 350°F (175°C) to preheat. Grease a cookie sheet.
- In a bowl put apple slices and pour in apple juice to cover. Stretch out cookie dough onto the greased sheet. Scatter with sugar.
- Bake in heated oven 5 to 7 minutes, until firm.
- Heat the caramel dip up in the microwave and distribute most of it evenly on the cooled cookie. Take the apple slices out of the juice and put in rows on the caramel. Pour remaining caramel on apples. Slice into squares before serving.

Nutrition Information

- Calories: 509 calories;
- Total Fat: 19.9
- Sodium: 290
- Total Carbohydrate: 78.6
- Cholesterol: 13
- Protein: 2.7

180. Chinese Style Peanut Cookie

Serving: 48 | Prep: 12mins | Cook: 8mins | Ready in:

Ingredients

- 3/4 cup roasted peanuts, finely ground
- 1 cup all-purpose flour
- 1/4 cup corn flour
- 1 1/4 cups confectioners' sugar
- 1/2 cup vegetable oil
- 1 egg yolk, beaten (optional)

Direction

- Set the oven to 350°F (175°C) for preheating. Use parchment paper to line baking pans.
- In a large bowl, combine corn flour, confectioners' sugar, peanuts, and flour and mix them thoroughly. Make a hole in the center of the peanut mixture. Gradually pour vegetable oil into the hole. Mix the oil and peanut mixture to make a wet and slightly sticky dough. Take at least 2 teaspoons of dough and roll it to make a 1/2-inch diameter ball. Do the same with the remaining dough. Place the balls into the lined baking pans. You can coat each with egg yolk if you want.
- Bake the balls in the preheated oven for 6-8 minutes until the cookies are golden brown. Transfer the pan on racks to cool.

Nutrition Information

- Calories: 59 calories;
- Total Carbohydrate: 6.3
- Cholesterol: 4
- Protein: 0.9
- Total Fat: 3.5
- Sodium: < 1

181. Chocolate Cran Oat Cookies

Serving: 32 | Prep: 15mins | Cook: 10mins | Ready in:

Ingredients

- 1 cup butter
- 1 cup packed brown sugar
- 2 eggs
- 2 cups rolled oats
- 2 cups all-purpose flour
- 1 cup whole wheat flour
- 1 teaspoon baking soda
- 1/2 teaspoon salt
- 1 1/2 cups dried cranberries
- 1/2 cup white chocolate chips
- 1/2 cup semisweet chocolate chips

Direction

- Set oven to preheat at 190°C (375°F)
- In a medium bowl, cream the sugar and butter together. Beat in the eggs one by one. Combine

the salt, baking soda, flour, whole wheat flour, flour and rolled oats; mix into the creamed mixture slowly. Lastly, mix in the chocolate chips, white chocolate chips and cranberries. Drop rounded spoonfuls of the dough onto the prepared cookie sheet.
- In the preheated oven, bake for 8 to 10 minutes. Let cookies cool down on baking sheet for 5 minutes, then transfer to a wire rack to let cool thoroughly.

Nutrition Information

- Calories: 187 calories;
- Total Carbohydrate: 26.8
- Cholesterol: 27
- Protein: 2.8
- Total Fat: 8.3
- Sodium: 127

182. Cranberry Cinnamon Cookies

Serving: 60 | Prep: 15mins | Cook: 10mins |Ready in:

Ingredients

- 3 1/4 cups all-purpose flour
- 1 teaspoon ground cinnamon
- 1 cup butter, room temperature
- 2 1/8 cups white sugar
- 2 eggs
- 2/3 cup sweetened dried cranberries

Direction

- Sift cinnamon with flour in a bowl. Whisk sugar and butter in a different bowl. Beat in 1 egg thoroughly, and then beat in the next egg. Slowly blend the flour mixture into the butter mixture. Mix in cranberries.
- Form the dough into a 1 1/2 -inch diameter log; wrap in plastic; put into the freezer for a minimum of 1 hour.
- Start preheating the oven at 350°F (175°C). With a sharp knife, slice the cookie dough into 1/2-inch-thick slices. Place the cookies onto a large baking sheet.
- Bake in the prepared oven for about 10 minutes until edges seem brown.

Nutrition Information

- Calories: 86 calories;
- Total Fat: 3.3
- Sodium: 24
- Total Carbohydrate: 13.4
- Cholesterol: 14
- Protein: 0.9

183. Cranberry Cornmeal Linzer Cookies

Serving: 42 | Prep: 45mins | Cook: 10mins |Ready in:

Ingredients

- Cookies:
- 3/4 cup butter, softened
- 3/4 cup white sugar
- 1 egg
- 1 1/2 cups all-purpose flour
- 1/2 cup cornmeal
- 1 teaspoon baking powder
- 3/8 teaspoon salt
- 1 teaspoon vanilla extract
- Filling:
- 1 1/2 cups finely chopped cranberries
- 1/3 cup brown sugar
- 1/3 cup water
- 1 1/2 tablespoons butter
- 1 1/2 tablespoons lemon juice

Direction

- In a bowl, beat white sugar and 3/4 cup of butter together using an electric mixture until it becomes creamy, then beat in egg.

- Whisk salt, baking powder, cornmeal, and flour in a bowl, then gradually add into the butter mixture and stir. Beat in the vanilla. Form into a dough ball and tightly wrap using plastic wrap, then refrigerate for a minimum of 1 hour until the dough is firm.
- Set oven to 175 degrees C or 350 degrees F and grease baking sheets lightly.
- In a lightly floured surface, roll the dough to 1/8-inch thickness and cut with a Linzer or round cookie cutter; use smaller cutters to cut the centers from the tops. Place the tops and bottoms onto the baking sheets 1 inch apart.
- Bake for 10-12 minutes until the edges turn light gold, then move onto wire racks to cool.
- In a saucepan, stir water together with brown sugar and cranberries on medium-high heat, then cook for 10 minutes until cranberries become soft. Stir in lemon juice and butter, then take off the heat and let cool.
- Spread a bit of the cranberry mixture onto a side of the bottom cookie half, placing the top half over it. Repeat the process with the other cookies and leftover cranberry filling.

Nutrition Information

- Calories: 79 calories;
- Total Carbohydrate: 10.4
- Cholesterol: 14
- Protein: 0.8
- Total Fat: 3.9
- Sodium: 62

184. Cranberry Kitchen Cookies

Serving: 144 | Prep: 25mins | Cook: 10mins | Ready in:

Ingredients

- 1/2 cup butter
- 1 cup white sugar
- 3/4 cup packed brown sugar
- 1/4 cup milk
- 2 tablespoons orange juice
- 1 egg
- 3 cups sifted all-purpose flour
- 1 teaspoon baking powder
- 1/4 teaspoon baking soda
- 1/4 teaspoon salt
- 1 cup chopped walnuts
- 2 1/2 cups fresh cranberries, roughly chopped

Direction

- Set the oven to 190°C or 375°F to preheat. Coat cookie sheets with grease.
- Cream together brown sugar, white sugar and butter in a big bowl. Beat in egg, orange juice and milk. Mix salt, baking powder and flour together, then stir into creamed mixture. Mix in cranberries and chopped walnuts. Drop on prepared cookie sheets with teaspoonfuls of dough.
- In the preheated oven, bake for about 10-15 minutes, until edges turn golden. Allow to cookies to cool on cookie sheet for about 2 minutes prior to transferring to wire racks to cool thoroughly.

Nutrition Information

- Calories: 32 calories;
- Total Fat: 1.2
- Sodium: 14
- Total Carbohydrate: 4.9
- Cholesterol: 3
- Protein: 0.5

185. Cranberry Oat Bars

Serving: 16 | Prep: 15mins | Cook: 15mins | Ready in:

Ingredients

- 2 cups fresh or frozen cranberries
- 3/4 cup sugar

- 2 tablespoons orange zest
- 1 1/2 cups all-purpose flour
- 1 1/2 cups rolled oats
- 1 cup packed light brown sugar
- 1 teaspoon baking powder
- 1/2 teaspoon salt
- 3/4 cup butter

Direction

- In a small saucepan, mix orange zest, white sugar and cranberries over medium high heat. Heat to a boil, then lower the heat and cook until the mixture has evaporated to only about 1 cup.
- Set the oven to 350°F (175°C), and start preheating. Coat a baking pan of 9x9 inches with oil, line with foil, then coat the foil with oil.
- In a medium bowl, mix salt, baking powder, brown sugar, oats and flour together. Use your hands or a pastry blender to cut in the butter until the mixture looks like coarse crumbs. Press firmly 1/2 the mixture into the prepared pan. Spread evenly the cranberry sauce over the base, crumble the rest of oat mixture on top.
- Bake in the oven for 10 - 15 minutes, until the top is golden brown. Allow to completely cool then cut into bars.

Nutrition Information

- Calories: 243 calories;
- Sodium: 161
- Total Carbohydrate: 38.6
- Cholesterol: 23
- Protein: 2.4
- Total Fat: 9.3

186. Cranberry Oatmeal Bars

Serving: 12 | Prep: 15mins | Cook: 13mins | Ready in:

Ingredients

- 1/2 cup melted butter
- 1 egg
- 1/3 cup brown sugar
- 1 teaspoon vanilla extract
- 1 cup flour
- 1/4 teaspoon baking powder
- 1/4 teaspoon baking soda
- 1/4 teaspoon salt
- 1 teaspoon cinnamon
- 1/4 teaspoon ground nutmeg
- 1/4 teaspoon pumpkin pie spice
- 3/4 cup dried cranberries
- 3/4 cup pecans
- 3/4 cup old-fashioned rolled oats

Direction

- Set the oven to 350°F (175°C) and start preheating. Grease 11x7 inch baking pan lightly.
- Pour melted butter into a mixing bowl; whisk in vanilla extract, brown sugar and egg. In a separate mixing bowl, sift together pumpkin pie spice, nutmeg, cinnamon, salt, baking soda, baking powder and flour. Stir the flour mixture into butter mixture until blended thoroughly. Mix in oats, pecans and cranberries until blended evenly. Press mixture into greased baking dish.
- Bake in the prepared oven for 13-15 minutes until top turns dry and edges slightly pull away from the pan's sides. Cool then cut into squares.

Nutrition Information

- Calories: 225 calories;
- Sodium: 147
- Total Carbohydrate: 24.8
- Cholesterol: 36
- Protein: 3
- Total Fat: 13.4

187. Cranberry Oatmeal Drops

Serving: 14 | Prep: | Cook: | Ready in:

Ingredients

- 1 cup all-purpose flour
- 1 teaspoon baking powder
- 1/2 teaspoon ground cinnamon
- 1/4 teaspoon ground nutmeg
- 1/2 cup butter, softened
- 3/4 cup packed brown sugar
- 1 egg
- 1/4 cup milk
- 1 teaspoon orange zest
- 1 1/2 cups quick cooking oats
- 3/4 cup chopped cranberries
- 1/4 cup chopped walnuts
- 1 cup confectioners' sugar
- 1/2 teaspoon orange zest
- 1/4 teaspoon vanilla extract
- 2 tablespoons orange juice

Direction

- Start preheating the oven to 375°F (190°C). Grease the cookie sheets.
- Sift nutmeg, cinnamon, baking powder and flour together. Put aside. Cream sugar and butter in a medium bowl. Stir in orange zest, milk and egg. Put in the dry ingredients, then mix until blended well. Stir in nuts, cranberries and quick oats.
- Drop the dough by tablespoons about 2-inch apart onto prepared cookie sheets. Bake in prepared oven for 10-12 minutes, the cookies must be brown lightly. Transfer to cool on the wire racks.
- Stir vanilla, orange zest and confectioners' sugar together in a small bowl. Stir in orange juice, one tablespoon each time, until it reaches the preferred consistency. Sprinkle onto the cooled cookies.

Nutrition Information

- Calories: 227 calories;
- Total Fat: 9.1
- Sodium: 93
- Total Carbohydrate: 34.5
- Cholesterol: 31
- Protein: 3.1

188. Cranberry Oats With Chocolate

Serving: 24 | Prep: 10mins | Cook: 10mins | Ready in:

Ingredients

- 1 1/2 cups sweetened dried cranberries
- 1 cup orange juice
- 2/3 cup butter, softened
- 2/3 cup brown sugar
- 2 eggs
- 1 1/2 cups rolled oats
- 1 1/2 cups all-purpose flour
- 1/2 teaspoon baking soda
- 1/2 teaspoon baking powder
- 1/2 teaspoon salt
- 1 cup chopped white chocolate

Direction

- Soak dried cranberries in a small bowl with orange juice for half an hour to soften. Set the oven to 165°C or 325°F to preheat.
- Cream brown sugar and butter together in a big bowl until smooth, then beat in the egg. Mix salt, baking powder, baking soda, flour and oats together then stir into the creamed mixture. Drain cranberries and stir into the dough together with white chocolate ensuring not to over-mix and form tough cookies. Drop on ungreased cookie sheets with rounded spoonfuls of dough.
- In the preheated oven, bake for 10-12 minutes, then let cookies cool on baking sheet for 5 minutes prior to transferring to a wire rack to cool thoroughly.

Nutrition Information

- Calories: 183 calories;
- Total Fat: 8.3
- Sodium: 133
- Total Carbohydrate: 25
- Cholesterol: 31
- Protein: 2.6

189. Cranberry Orange Oat Cookies

Serving: 36 | Prep: 15mins | Cook: 10mins | Ready in:

Ingredients

- 1/2 cup butter, softened
- 1/2 cup white sugar
- 1 cup brown sugar
- 1/3 cup applesauce
- 2 eggs
- 2 tablespoons orange juice
- 1 teaspoon grated orange zest
- 2 cups all-purpose flour
- 1 teaspoon baking soda
- 1 teaspoon ground cinnamon
- 1 dash ground nutmeg
- 2 cups rolled oats
- 1 cup fresh cranberries, roughly chopped

Direction

- Preheat an oven to 175°C/350°F; grease the cookie sheets.
- Cream brown sugar, white sugar and butter till smooth in a big bowl; one by one, mix in orange zest, orange juice, eggs and applesauce, mixing well after each. Mix nutmeg, cinnamon, baking soda and flour; mix into orange mixture slowly. Fold in cranberries and oats. Dollop by rounded spoonfuls onto greased cookie sheets.
- In preheated oven, bake for 8-10 minutes; cool cookies for 5 minutes on baking sheet. Transfer onto wire rack; fully cool.

Nutrition Information

- Calories: 98 calories;
- Cholesterol: 17
- Protein: 1.7
- Total Fat: 3.2
- Sodium: 59
- Total Carbohydrate: 15.9

190. Cranberry Orange Oatmeal Cookies

Serving: 48 | Prep: 15mins | Cook: 10mins | Ready in:

Ingredients

- 1 cup butter, softened
- 1 cup packed brown sugar
- 1/2 cup white sugar
- 2 eggs
- 1 1/2 teaspoons vanilla extract
- 1 tablespoon grated orange zest
- 1 teaspoon orange extract
- 1 1/2 cups all-purpose flour
- 1 teaspoon baking soda
- 1 teaspoon ground cinnamon
- 3 cups rolled oats
- 1 cup dried cranberries

Direction

- Set an oven to 175°C (350°F) and start preheating.
- Cream white sugar, brown sugar, and butter together in a large bowl until they become smooth. Whisk in one egg at a time, then stir in the orange extract, orange zest, and vanilla. Mix cinnamon, baking soda, and flour; then add into the butter mixture and stir. Stir in cranberries and oats. Add on ungreased cookie sheets by rounded tablespoonfuls.
- In the preheated oven, bake until golden brown, for 10-12 minutes. On a baking sheet,

let the cookie cool for 2 minutes, then transfer onto a wire rack to completely cool.

Nutrition Information

- Calories: 104 calories;
- Sodium: 58
- Total Carbohydrate: 15.2
- Cholesterol: 18
- Protein: 1.4
- Total Fat: 4.4

191. Cream Cheese Snowball Cookies

Serving: 24 | Prep: 23mins | Cook: 6mins | Ready in:

Ingredients

- 1 cup confectioners' sugar
- 1/2 cup finely-chopped walnuts (optional)
- 1/2 cup vegetable shortening (such as Crisco®)
- 1/2 cup butter, softened
- 1/2 cup cream cheese, softened
- 1/2 cup white sugar
- 1/2 teaspoon almond extract
- 1/2 teaspoon vanilla extract
- 1 1/2 cups all-purpose flour

Direction

- Preheat the oven to 350°F (175°C). In a shallow bowl, sift the confectioners' sugar, mix in walnuts, and put aside.
- In a bowl, beat sugar, cream cheese, butter and shortening together until the mixture is creamy and completely blended. Add in flour, vanilla extract and almond extract and stir until combined. Scoop the dough up by rounded tablespoons, and roll into 1-in. balls in diameter. On ungreased baking sheets, arrange the balls approximately 1 1/2 inches apart.
- Bake in the preheated oven in about 6 minutes, until the edges are slightly golden. Cool the cookies in about 1 minute on the baking sheets, then roll in confectioners' sugar-and-walnut mixture while the cookies are still a little bit warm.

Nutrition Information

- Calories: 170 calories;
- Total Fat: 11.5
- Sodium: 42
- Total Carbohydrate: 15.8
- Cholesterol: 15
- Protein: 1.6

192. Cut Out Cookies In A Flower Pot

Serving: 72 | Prep: | Cook: | Ready in:

Ingredients

- 2 cups butter, softened
- 3 cups white sugar
- 4 eggs
- 1 tablespoon vanilla extract
- 1 tablespoon butter flavored extract
- 7 cups all-purpose flour
- 2 teaspoons baking powder
- 1 teaspoon salt

Direction

- Cream sugar and butter. Add in flavorings and eggs, stir well. Mix together salt, baking powder and flour. Add into batter and stir well.
- Allow to chill for 3-4 hours or overnight prior to doing the next steps.
- Roll cookies out with the thickness of about 1/4 inch; insert the cookie sticks at least one third to half way in the cookies.

- Bake at 350°F (175°C) for 8-10 minutes. This dough can be kept well in a covered container in the fridge for a couple of weeks. Decorate if desired. Arrange 3-7 cookies in a clay pot of 6 inches (considering the size of cookie). Weigh the pot down with some dried beans and cut a circle of Styrofoam to fit snugly on top of the pot. Decorate with ribbons and enjoy.

Nutrition Information

- Calories: 126 calories;
- Cholesterol: 24
- Protein: 1.7
- Total Fat: 5.5
- Sodium: 86
- Total Carbohydrate: 17.7

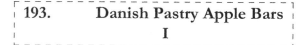

193. Danish Pastry Apple Bars I

Serving: 32 | Prep: | Cook: | Ready in:

Ingredients

- 2 1/2 cups all-purpose flour
- 1 teaspoon salt
- 1 cup shortening
- 1 egg yolk
- 1/2 cup milk
- 1 cup cornflakes cereal
- 8 cups tart apples - peeled, cored and sliced
- 1/2 cup white sugar
- 1 teaspoon ground cinnamon
- 1 egg white
- 1/3 cup sifted confectioners' sugar

Direction

- In a large mixing bowl, put salt and flour together; stir. Cut in shortening till the mixture looks like coarse crumbs. In a glass measuring cup, add egg yolks and beat lightly. Pour milk in to make 2/3 cup of liquid in total; mix thoroughly. Divide dough into 2 equal portions.
- Flour a surface then roll one half of the dough to a rectangle of 18x12 inches on the surface; fit the rectangle dough into and up sides of a baking pan with 15x10x1 inch in size.
- Use corn flake cereal to sprinkle over; use apples to top. Mix cinnamon and sugar, use the mixture to sprinkle over apples.
- Make a rectangle with the size of 16x12 inches by rolling the remaining dough; put over apples. Seal edges; make slits in the top for steam to escape. Put in the oven at 190°C (375°F) and bake till becoming golden brown, about 50 minutes. Allow to cool down on a wire rack.

Nutrition Information

- Calories: 131 calories;
- Total Fat: 6.8
- Sodium: 83
- Total Carbohydrate: 16.6
- Cholesterol: 7
- Protein: 1.5

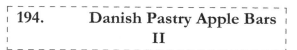

194. Danish Pastry Apple Bars II

Serving: 36 | Prep: 30mins | Cook: 50mins | Ready in:

Ingredients

- 2 1/2 cups all-purpose flour
- 1 teaspoon salt
- 1 cup butter
- 1 egg yolk
- 2/3 cup cold water
- 1 cup cornflakes cereal
- 10 apples - peeled, cored and sliced
- 3/4 cup white sugar
- 2 teaspoons ground cinnamon
- 1/2 cup confectioners' sugar
- 1 tablespoon milk

- 1/2 teaspoon almond extract

Direction

- Turn oven to 375°F (190°C) to preheat.
- Mix salt and flour together in a large bowl. Cut butter into flour mixture until crumbly. Beat egg yolk in a cup; whisk in cold water. Slowly whisk egg mixture into the flour mixture until dough can shape into a ball. Roll out 1 half of the dough on a clean dry surface until large enough to cover the sides and bottom of a 9x13-inch pan. Pack dough into the pan.
- Add cornflakes over the dough in the pan. Place apple slices atop cornflake layer. Scatter top with cinnamon and sugar. Roll the second half out just enough to cover the entire pan. Place over the filling; pinch edges of 2 crusts together. Beat egg white until frothy; bush over the top crust.
- Bake in the preheated oven until golden brown, for 45 to 50 minutes. Drizzle glaze over top while pie is still warm.
- For the glaze: beat milk, almond extract, and confectioners' sugar in a small bowl until no lumps remain.

Nutrition Information

- Calories: 124 calories;
- Protein: 1.2
- Total Fat: 5.4
- Sodium: 108
- Total Carbohydrate: 18.6
- Cholesterol: 19

195. Easy Cheerio® Coconut Rum Balls

Serving: 28 | Prep: 30mins | Cook: | Ready in:

Ingredients

- 3 cups honey-nut toasted oat cereal (such as Honey Nut Cheerios®)
- 1 cup confectioners' sugar, plus more for dusting
- 1/2 cup crushed cashews
- 1/2 cup crushed almonds
- 1/4 cup shredded coconut
- 3 tablespoons unsweetened cocoa powder
- 1/3 cup dark rum, or more as needed
- 3 tablespoons light corn syrup

Direction

- In a food processor, add cocoa powder, coconut, almonds, cashews, confectioners' sugar, and oat cereal; blend to an even crumb texture.
- In a bowl, mix corn syrup and rum together; put in cereal mixture. Mix until dough combines together. Pour in more rum if dough is dry. Shape dough into balls and put on a plate.
- Place rum balls in the refrigerator for at least an hour to allow flavors to blend. Dust with confectioners' sugar before serving.

Nutrition Information

- Calories: 74 calories;
- Total Fat: 2.4
- Sodium: 51
- Total Carbohydrate: 11.3
- Cholesterol: 0
- Protein: 1.1

196. Easy Pecan Pie Bar Cookies

Serving: 60 | Prep: 15mins | Cook: 40mins | Ready in:

Ingredients

- Crust:
- 3 cups all-purpose flour

- 3/4 cup butter
- 1/4 cup white sugar
- 2 tablespoons white sugar
- 3/4 teaspoon salt
- Filling:
- 1 1/2 cups light corn syrup
- 1 1/2 cups white sugar
- 4 eggs, beaten
- 3 tablespoons melted butter
- 1 1/2 teaspoons vanilla extract
- 2 1/2 cups chopped pecans

Direction

- Start preheating the oven to 350°F (175°C). Grease butter on a 10x15-inch baking pan.
- Combine salt, 1/4 cup plus 2 tablespoons of sugar, 3/4 cup of butter, and flour in a bowl until crumbly. Press into the buttered pan.
- Bake crust for about 20 minutes in the prepared oven until lightly browned. Take it out and leave the oven on.
- Mix vanilla extract, melted butter, eggs, 1 1/2 cup of sugar, and corn syrup in a bowl until blended. Mix in pecans. Pour the filling evenly over the baked crust.
- Bake in the hot oven for about 25 minutes until filling is firm. Let cool fully, then slice into squares.

Nutrition Information

- Calories: 129 calories;
- Cholesterol: 20
- Protein: 1.5
- Total Fat: 6.5
- Sodium: 59
- Total Carbohydrate: 17.8

197. Erin's Fun Turkey Cookies

Serving: 36 | Prep: 45mins | Cook: 10mins | Ready in:

Ingredients

- 6 1/2 cups all-purpose flour
- 2 cups white sugar
- 1 cup buttermilk
- 3 eggs
- 1 teaspoon vanilla
- 1 teaspoon salt
- 1 teaspoon baking powder
- 1 cup candy corn, or as needed
- 72 candy-coated milk chocolate pieces (such as M&M's®)
- 1/4 cup prepared white frosting, or as needed
- 4 pieces red string licorice (such as Twizzlers®), cut into 1-inch pieces

Direction

- In a bowl, beat together baking powder, salt, vanilla, eggs, buttermilk, sugar and flour until dough is blended thoroughly. Use plastic wrap to cover bowl and chill for at least an hour.
- Set the oven to 190°C or 375°F to preheat. Coat baking sheets with grease.
- Drop prepped baking sheets with 2 teaspoons of dough for each cookie, spaced 2 inches between.
- In the preheated oven, bake cookies for 10 minutes until turn light golden brown. Allow cookies to cool about 8-10 minutes prior to transferring to a plate to garnish.
- Press the top edge of the cookies with partway of candy corns, point-end first to look like feathers. Put in the center of each cookie the 2 candy-coated milk chocolate pieces to look like eyes of turkey. Make the mouth of turkey with a small amount of frosting. Press the bottom edge of cookie with 2 pieces of licorice to create the legs of turkey.

Nutrition Information

- Calories: 173 calories;
- Total Fat: 1.4
- Sodium: 98
- Total Carbohydrate: 36.9

- Cholesterol: 16
- Protein: 3.2

198. Espresso Biscotti

Serving: 24 | Prep: 25mins | Cook: 1hours | Ready in:

Ingredients

- 1/4 cup unsalted butter
- 3/4 cup white sugar
- 3 eggs
- 1 teaspoon vanilla extract
- 3 1/4 cups pastry flour
- 1 teaspoon ground cinnamon
- 1 teaspoon baking powder
- 1 teaspoon instant espresso powder
- 2 teaspoons grated orange zest
- 1/2 cup chocolate chips
- 1/2 cup dried apricots
- 1/2 cup dried cranberries
- 1/2 cup slivered almonds
- 1 egg white, lightly beaten

Direction

- Set the oven to 175°C or 350°F to preheat. Coat a cookie sheet with grease or use parchment paper to line it.
- In a bowl, cream sugar and butter together until fluffy and light, then beat in vanilla and eggs.
- In a separate bowl, sift baking powder, cinnamon and flour together. Mix flour mixture into the egg mixture, then stir in almonds, dried cranberries, dried apricots, chocolate chips, orange zest and espresso powder.
- Form dough into 2 even logs, 2 inches in diameter and 12 inches length. Put logs on baking sheet and flatten them to the thickness of approximately 1 inch. Use egg wash to brush over log.
- In the preheated oven, bake for 35-40 minutes, until the center becomes firm and edges turn golden. Once loaves are cooled enough to touch, cut the loaves diagonally into slices with the thickness of 1/2 inch, using a serrated knife. Put slices back to the baking sheet.
- Lower heat of oven to 165°C or 325°F and bake for 15-20 minutes, until they begin to turn light brown. Allow to cool thoroughly and transfer into an airtight container to store at room temperature.

Nutrition Information

- Calories: 150 calories;
- Total Fat: 5
- Sodium: 33
- Total Carbohydrate: 25.4
- Cholesterol: 28
- Protein: 3.3

199. Graham Cracker Carmelitas

Serving: 24 | Prep: 20mins | Cook: 10mins | Ready in:

Ingredients

- 12 whole graham crackers
- 1 cup margarine (such as Parkay®)
- 1 cup brown sugar
- 1 cup chopped pecans

Direction

- Set the oven to 175°C or 350°F to preheat.
- Break each graham cracker into four even pieces, make totally 48 pieces. Place closely together on a baking sheet with graham cracker pieces.
- In a heavy pan, melt margarine on moderate heat then put in brown sugar. Cook and stir the mixture until frothy and boiling. Boil about 2 minutes longer while stirring continuously. Take away from the heat and fold in pecans.

- Drizzle over graham crackers with caramel mixture and spread evenly.
- In the preheated oven, bake for 8-10 minutes, until caramel mixture is baked into graham crackers. Take out of the baking sheet instantly and allow cooling on an aluminum foil sheet.

Nutrition Information

- Calories: 163 calories;
- Total Fat: 11.5
- Sodium: 133
- Total Carbohydrate: 15.1
- Cholesterol: 0
- Protein: 1

200. Iced Pumpkin Cookies

Serving: 36 | Prep: 20mins | Cook: 20mins | Ready in:

Ingredients

- 2 1/2 cups all-purpose flour
- 1 teaspoon baking powder
- 1 teaspoon baking soda
- 2 teaspoons ground cinnamon
- 1/2 teaspoon ground nutmeg
- 1/2 teaspoon ground cloves
- 1/2 teaspoon salt
- 1/2 cup butter, softened
- 1 1/2 cups white sugar
- 1 cup canned pumpkin puree
- 1 egg
- 1 teaspoon vanilla extract
- 2 cups confectioners' sugar
- 3 tablespoons milk
- 1 tablespoon melted butter
- 1 teaspoon vanilla extract

Direction

- Start preheating the oven to 350°F (175°C). Mix salt, ground cloves, nutmeg, cinnamon, baking soda, baking powder and flour. Put aside.
- Cream white sugar and half cup butter together in a medium bowl. Put one teaspoon of the vanilla, egg and pumpkin into the butter mixture, then beat until it becomes creamy. Combine in the dry ingredients. Drop by tablespoonfuls on the cookie sheet and slightly flatten.
- Bake in prepared oven for 15-20 mins. Let cool the cookies. Use fork to drizzle glaze.
- For Glaze: Combine one teaspoon of the vanilla, one tablespoon of the melted butter, milk and confectioners' sugar. As needed, pour in milk to achieve the drizzling consistency.

Nutrition Information

- Calories: 122 calories;
- Total Carbohydrate: 22.4
- Cholesterol: 13
- Protein: 1.2
- Total Fat: 3.2
- Sodium: 120

201. Light Holiday Tea Cakes

Serving: 30 | Prep: | Cook: | Ready in:

Ingredients

- 3 egg whites
- 1 cup unsweetened applesauce
- 1/4 cup fat-free half-and-half
- 1 teaspoon vanilla
- 1 cup Splenda No Calorie Sweetener
- 1/2 cup whole wheat flour
- 1/2 cup all-purpose flour
- 1 teaspoon baking soda
- 1 tablespoon pumpkin pie spice
- 1 teaspoon cinnamon
- 1/2 cup chopped dried pineapple
- 1/2 cup dried cranberries, preferably orange flavored
- 1/2 cup chopped almonds or walnuts

Direction

- Set oven to 350° to preheat. Cream egg whites in a big bowl until stiff. Fold in vanilla, half-and-half and applesauce. Mix spices, baking soda, flour and Splenda in another bowl. Fold dry mixture into wet ingredients. Fold in nuts, cranberries and pineapple. Scoop batter into non-stick mini-muffin tins sprayed with cooking spray. Bake 12-15 minutes. Take it out, let cool. Sprinkle with confectioner's sugar (optional).

Nutrition Information

- Calories: 48 calories;
- Sodium: 51
- Total Carbohydrate: 8.2
- Cholesterol: < 1
- Protein: 1.5
- Total Fat: 1.4

202. Linda's Cranberry Cookies

Serving: 36 | Prep: 20mins | Cook: 10mins | Ready in:

Ingredients

- 2 1/4 cups all-purpose flour
- 1 teaspoon baking soda
- 1 cup butter
- 1/4 cup white sugar
- 3/4 cup brown sugar
- 1 (3.5 ounce) package instant vanilla pudding mix
- 1 teaspoon vanilla extract
- 2 eggs
- 1 (6 ounce) package white chocolate chips
- 1/2 (6 ounce) package dried cranberries

Direction

- Set the oven to 175°C or 350°F to preheat. Coat 2 baking sheets slightly with grease. Mix baking soda and flour in a bowl.
- In a big bowl, use an electric mixer to beat instant pudding, brown sugar, white sugar and butter together until smooth. Beat the first egg into the butter until mixed totally, then beat in the last egg and vanilla. Blend flour mixture into egg mixture until just combined. Fold in cranberries and white chocolate chips, mixing just enough to blend evenly. Drop dough onto prepped baking sheets by spoonfuls, 2 in. apart.
- In the preheated oven, bake for 9-12 minutes, until the cookies' edges turn golden brown. Allow to cool in the baking sheet for 10 minutes prior to transferring to cool thoroughly on a wire rack.

Nutrition Information

- Calories: 139 calories;
- Sodium: 120
- Total Carbohydrate: 17.5
- Cholesterol: 25
- Protein: 1.5
- Total Fat: 7.1

203. Make Ahead Cookie Mix

Serving: 24 | Prep: 15mins | Cook: | Ready in:

Ingredients

- 1 1/2 cups butter
- 1 tablespoon salt
- 2 teaspoons baking powder
- 6 cups all-purpose flour

Direction

- Mix baking powder, salt and butter in big bowl; mix flour in slowly. Keep in the fridge in covered container for up to 4 weeks.

Nutrition Information

- Calories: 216 calories;
- Protein: 3.3
- Total Fat: 11.8
- Sodium: 414
- Total Carbohydrate: 24
- Cholesterol: 31

204. Mary's Salted Caramel Pecan Bars

Serving: 24 | Prep: 10mins | Cook: 20mins | Ready in:

Ingredients

- cooking spray
- 1 cup chopped pecans
- 12 whole graham crackers
- 1 cup firmly packed brown sugar
- 3/4 cup butter, melted
- 2 tablespoons heavy whipping cream
- 1 teaspoon vanilla extract
- 1/4 teaspoon kosher salt

Direction

- Set oven to 175°C (350°F) and start preheating. Use aluminum foil to line a 10x15-in. jelly roll pan and coat with cooking spray.
- Place pecans in a shallow pan in one layer.
- Bake at 175°C (350°F) for 10-12 minutes, giving a stir after half the cooking time, until the pecans are fragrantly toasted.
- In the jelly roll pan, place graham crackers in one layer.
- In a heavy saucepan, mix together cream, butter and brown sugar; boil the mixture for 5 minutes, whisking once in a while, until sugar dissolves. Take away from the heat; mix in vanilla extract. Fold pecans into the mixture. Transfer over the cracker layer and even out until coated.
- Bake for 10-11 minutes at 175°C (350°F) until the topping bubbles. Take out of the oven;

scatter salt on top right away. Place on a wire rack together with the foil to cool for half an hour. Break the cookie into bars.

Nutrition Information

- Calories: 149 calories;
- Total Carbohydrate: 15
- Cholesterol: 16
- Protein: 1
- Total Fat: 10
- Sodium: 106

205. Mocha Walnut Cookies

Serving: 24 | Prep: | Cook: | Ready in:

Ingredients

- 2 cups semisweet chocolate chips
- 2 tablespoons instant coffee powder
- 2 teaspoons boiling water
- 1 1/4 cups all-purpose flour
- 3/4 teaspoon baking soda
- 1/2 teaspoon salt
- 1/2 cup butter, softened
- 1/2 cup white sugar
- 1/2 cup packed brown sugar
- 1 egg
- 1/2 cup chopped walnuts

Direction

- Start preheating the oven to 350°F (175°C).
- Heat 1/2 cup of the chocolate morsels over hot (not boiling) water until melted. Stir until smooth. Let cool to room temperature.
- Dissolve the instant coffee in 2 teaspoons of boiling water in a small cup. Put aside.
- In a small bowl, mix salt, baking soda, and flour. Put aside.
- In a large bowl, mix coffee, sugars, and butter. Beat until creamy. Add melted morsels and eggs. Combine well. Slowly pour in flour

mixture. Stir in walnuts and the remaining 1 1/2 cups of chocolate morsels. Shape into walnut-sized balls and arrange on ungreased cookie sheets.
- Bake for 10 to 12 minutes at 350°F (175°C). Let stand for 2 to 3 minutes before transferring from cookie sheets.

Nutrition Information

- Calories: 224 calories;
- Protein: 2.8
- Total Fat: 11.4
- Sodium: 119
- Total Carbohydrate: 28.2
- Cholesterol: 18

206. Moist Persimmon Cookie

Serving: 36 | Prep: 10mins | Cook: 12mins | Ready in:

Ingredients

- 2 persimmons
- 1/2 cup shortening
- 1 cup white sugar
- 1 egg
- 2 cups all-purpose flour
- 1/2 teaspoon salt
- 1 teaspoon baking soda
- 1 teaspoon ground cinnamon
- 1/2 teaspoon ground cloves
- 1/2 teaspoon ground nutmeg
- 1 cup chopped walnuts
- 1 cup raisins

Direction

- Peel then de-stem persimmons and process in a blender or food processor. You should have 1 cup of pulp. Heat oven to 175 degrees C or 350 degrees F. Grease the cookie sheets.
- Cream shortening and sugar in a medium bowl. Beat persimmon pulp and egg in. mix

nutmeg, cloves, cinnamon, salt, baking soda, and flour then mix in the persimmon mixture. Mix in raisins and chopped nuts. Place rounded spoonful on prepared cookie sheet.
- Bake in the oven for 8-10 minutes. Let cookies on for 5 minutes on the baking sheet then move them to a wire rack to completely cool.

Nutrition Information

- Calories: 108 calories;
- Total Fat: 5.2
- Sodium: 70
- Total Carbohydrate: 14.5
- Cholesterol: 7
- Protein: 1.5

207. Oatmeal Craisin Cookies

Serving: 24 | Prep: | Cook: | Ready in:

Ingredients

- 1 cup butter, softened
- 1 cup packed brown sugar
- 1 cup white sugar
- 2 eggs
- 1 teaspoon vanilla extract
- 2 cups quick cooking oats
- 2 cups all-purpose flour
- 1 teaspoon baking soda
- 1 teaspoon baking powder
- 1 teaspoon salt
- 1 cup raisins
- 1 cup dried cranberries

Direction

- Beat vanilla, eggs, sugars and butter for 5 minutes. Mix salt, baking powder, baking soda, flour and oats in another bowl; 1 cup at 1 time, add to butter mixture.
- Mix in craisins and raisins.

- By spoonfuls, drop onto greased cookie sheets; bake at 175°C/350°F for 12-14 minutes. Freeze well.

Nutrition Information

- Calories: 238 calories;
- Cholesterol: 36
- Protein: 2.8
- Total Fat: 8.7
- Sodium: 234
- Total Carbohydrate: 38.9

208. Oatmeal Cranberry White Chocolate Chunk Cookies

Serving: 30 | Prep: 20mins | Cook: 12mins | Ready in:

Ingredients

- 2/3 cup butter, softened
- 2/3 cup packed brown sugar
- 2 eggs
- 1 1/2 cups rolled oats
- 1 1/2 cups all-purpose flour
- 1/2 teaspoon salt
- 1 teaspoon baking soda
- 1 1/4 cups dried cranberries
- 2/3 cup coarsely chopped white chocolate

Direction

- Set the oven to 375°F (190°C) and start preheating.
- Cream butter and brown sugar together until fluffy and light in a medium bowl. Whisk in one egg at a time. Mix baking soda, salt, flour and oats; stir into butter mixture, a cup each time, mixing thoroughly after each increment. Stir in white chocolate and dried cranberries. Drop onto ungreased cookie sheets by rounded teaspoons.

- Bake in the prepared oven for 10-12 minutes or until it turns golden brown. Cool on wire racks.

Nutrition Information

- Calories: 134 calories;
- Sodium: 120
- Total Carbohydrate: 18.8
- Cholesterol: 24
- Protein: 1.9
- Total Fat: 6

209. Oatmeal Dried Fruit Cookies

Serving: 36 | Prep: 20mins | Cook: 10mins | Ready in:

Ingredients

- 1 1/4 cups butter or margarine, softened
- 1 1/4 cups brown sugar
- 1 egg
- 2 teaspoons vanilla extract
- 1 1/2 cups all-purpose flour
- 1 teaspoon baking soda
- 1 teaspoon salt
- 1 teaspoon ground cinnamon
- 1/2 teaspoon ground nutmeg
- 3 cups quick cooking oats
- 1 cup dried cranberries, or other dried fruit

Direction

- Set the oven to 190°C or 375°F to preheat.
- Cream sugar and butter together in a big bowl until fluffy and light. Beat in egg then stir in vanilla. Sift together nutmeg, cinnamon, salt, baking soda and flour then stir into the creamed mixture gradually. At last, stir in dried fruit and quick oats. Drop onto the unprepared cookie sheet with rounded spoonfuls of mixture.

- In the preheated oven, bake for 8-10 minutes. Let the cookies cool on baking sheet for 5 minutes prior to transferring to a wire rack to cool fully.

Nutrition Information

- Calories: 133 calories;
- Sodium: 149
- Total Carbohydrate: 16.4
- Cholesterol: 22
- Protein: 1.7
- Total Fat: 7

210. Oatmeal Raisin Cookies I

Serving: 48 | Prep: 15mins | Cook: 10mins | Ready in:

Ingredients

- 3/4 cup butter, softened
- 3/4 cup white sugar
- 3/4 cup packed light brown sugar
- 2 eggs
- 1 teaspoon vanilla extract
- 1 1/4 cups all-purpose flour
- 1 teaspoon baking soda
- 3/4 teaspoon ground cinnamon
- 1/2 teaspoon salt
- 2 3/4 cups rolled oats
- 1 cup raisins

Direction

- Set the oven to 375°F (190°C), and start preheating.
- In large bowl, cream brown sugar, white sugar and butter together until smooth. Beat in vanilla and eggs until fluffy. Stir salt, cinnamon, baking soda and flour together. Slowly beat into the butter mixture. Stir in raisins and oats. Drop the mixture by teaspoonfuls onto ungreased cookie sheets.

- Bake in the preheated oven until golden brown, about 8 - 10 minutes. Allow to cool down slightly, take away from sheet to wire rack. Allow to completely cool.

Nutrition Information

- Calories: 92 calories;
- Total Carbohydrate: 14.6
- Cholesterol: 15
- Protein: 1.3
- Total Fat: 3.4
- Sodium: 75

211. Old English Lemon Cranberry Cookies

Serving: 15 | Prep: 15mins | Cook: 10mins | Ready in:

Ingredients

- 2 cups all-purpose flour
- 1 cup white sugar
- 1 teaspoon baking soda
- 1/2 cup chopped walnuts
- 1/2 teaspoon ground cloves
- 1 egg
- 1/2 cup applesauce
- juice from 1 lemon
- 1 teaspoon vanilla extract
- 3/4 cup dried cranberries
- zest from 1 lemon
- 1/4 cup butter, softened
- 2 tablespoons confectioners' sugar

Direction

- Set an oven to 175°C (350°F) and start preheating. Coat 2 baking sheets with cooking spray.
- In a large mixing bowl, combine cloves, walnuts, baking soda, sugar and flour. In an individual bowl of an electric hand mixer, whisk together butter, lemon zest, cranberries,

vanilla, lemon juice, applesauce and egg; then add into the flour mixture and combine thoroughly. Drop the dough by spoonfuls onto the greased baking sheets by 2 inches apart.
- In the prepared oven, bake for 10 minutes until the edges turn golden. On the baking sheet, let the cookies cool for a minute, then transfer onto a wire rack to cool entirely. To serve, dust with the confectioners' sugar.

Nutrition Information

- Calories: 197 calories;
- Total Carbohydrate: 33.6
- Cholesterol: 21
- Protein: 2.8
- Total Fat: 6.2
- Sodium: 111

212. Orange Cranberry Biscotti

Serving: 20 | Prep: | Cook: | Ready in:

Ingredients

- 1/2 cup butter
- 3/4 cup white sugar
- 2 eggs
- 1 tablespoon orange zest
- 2 tablespoons orange liqueur
- 2 1/4 cups all-purpose flour
- 1 1/2 teaspoons baking powder
- 1/4 teaspoon salt
- 1 1/2 teaspoons ground cinnamon
- 1/4 cup chopped dried cranberries
- 3/4 cup toasted and chopped almonds

Direction

- Set oven to preheat at 350°F (175°C).
- Cream together the butter and sugar in a medium bowl. Beat egg into the mixture. Stir the orange zest and orange liqueur into the mixture. Sift together the cinnamon, baking powder, salt and flour, stir them into the creamed mixture, then stir the dried cranberries and almonds into the mixture.
- Divide the dough into halves on a lightly floured surface. Roll each half of dough to make a log of about 1 1/2 inches width and 10 inches length. Place the rolls on a baking sheet lengthwise no less than 3 inches apart, and slightly flatten them.
- In the preheated oven, bake for about 20 to 25 minutes until slightly brown on top and firm when touched.
- Let it cool down for 10 to 15 minutes, then at a diagonal, cut each log crosswise into slices of 1/2 inch width. Place them onto the baking sheet, cut side down and take back into the oven for 10 minutes, flip them and bake for another 10 minutes. Let it cool down on wire racks, for storage, keep in an airtight container. You can keep them for over a month.

Nutrition Information

- Calories: 169 calories;
- Total Carbohydrate: 21.4
- Cholesterol: 31
- Protein: 3.3
- Total Fat: 8
- Sodium: 106

213. Orange Cranberry Drops

Serving: 36 | Prep: 20mins | Cook: 10mins | Ready in:

Ingredients

- 1/2 cup white sugar
- 1/2 cup packed brown sugar
- 1/4 cup butter, softened
- 1 egg
- 3 tablespoons orange juice
- 1/2 teaspoon orange extract

- 1 teaspoon grated orange zest
- 1 1/2 cups all-purpose flour
- 1/2 teaspoon baking powder
- 1/4 teaspoon baking soda
- 1/4 teaspoon salt
- 1 cup dried cranberries

Direction

- Start preheating the oven to 375°F (190°C). Line the cookie sheets with parchment paper or lightly grease.
- Cream butter, brown sugar and white sugar together in the medium bowl. Stir in orange zest, orange extract, orange juice and egg. Sift salt, baking soda, baking powder and flour together. Then stir into orange mixture. Mix in dried cranberries. On the prepared cookie sheets, drop the cookie dough by heaping teaspoonfuls 2 inches apart.
- Bake until the edges are beginning to brown, about 10-12 mins. Cool for 5 mins on the baking sheets. Cool completely on a wire rack.

Nutrition Information

- Calories: 65 calories;
- Total Fat: 1.5
- Sodium: 44
- Total Carbohydrate: 12.7
- Cholesterol: 9
- Protein: 0.7

214. Peanut Butter Chews

Serving: 36 | Prep: 25mins | Cook: | Ready in:

Ingredients

- 1 cup corn syrup
- 1 cup white sugar
- 1 cup creamy peanut butter
- 4 1/2 cups cornflakes cereal
- 1 cup semi-sweet chocolate chips (optional)
- 1 cup butterscotch chips (optional)

Direction

- Mix white sugar and corn syrup in a large saucepan on medium heat. Boil and keep boiling for a minute, then take away from the heat. Add the peanut butter and stir until combined thoroughly. Combine in the cereal until it is coated evenly. Add onto the waxed paper by dropping spoonfuls.
- Melt the butterscotch chips and chocolate chips with a double boiler or in a glass bowl in the microwave, regularly stir until they become smooth. Sprinkle over the top of the cookies.

Nutrition Information

- Calories: 151 calories;
- Sodium: 63
- Total Carbohydrate: 22.6
- Cholesterol: 0
- Protein: 2.4
- Total Fat: 6.3

215. Pecan Pie Bars I

Serving: 48 | Prep: | Cook: | Ready in:

Ingredients

- 3 cups all-purpose flour
- 1/2 cup white sugar
- 1 cup butter
- 1/2 teaspoon salt
- 4 eggs
- 1 1/2 cups light corn syrup
- 1 1/2 cups white sugar
- 3 tablespoons margarine, melted
- 1 1/2 teaspoons vanilla extract
- 2 1/2 cups chopped pecans

Direction

- Set an oven to 175°C (350°F) and start preheating. Coat the bottom and sides of a 15x10-inch pan with cooking spray.
- Mix salt, butter or margarine, 1/2 cup of sugar, and flour in a large bowl until the mixture looks like coarse crumbs. Press in the prepared pan firmly.
- Bake at 175°C (350°F) for 20 minutes.
- Stir vanilla, melted margarine, 1 1/2 cups of white sugar, corn syrup, and eggs in a large bowl until combined. Add in the chopped pecans and stir.
- Add the filling onto the hot crust evenly. Bake at 175°C (350°F) until set, 25 minutes. Before cutting, allow to cool.

Nutrition Information

- Calories: 175 calories;
- Cholesterol: 26
- Protein: 1.9
- Total Fat: 9.1
- Sodium: 72
- Total Carbohydrate: 23

216. Pecan Pie Bars II

Serving: 12 | Prep: | Cook: | Ready in:

Ingredients

- 2 cups all-purpose flour
- 1 cup packed brown sugar
- 1/2 cup butter
- 1/2 cup margarine
- 5 eggs
- 1 cup dark corn syrup
- 3/4 cup white sugar
- 1 pinch salt
- 1 teaspoon vanilla extract
- 1 cup chopped pecans

Direction

- Start preheating the oven to 350°F (180°C).
- Mix brown sugar and flour. Cut in butter and margarine until mixture is the same as coarse crumbs.
- Press into a 9x13-inch pan and bake for 10 minutes.
- Except for pecans, combine the remaining ingredients and blend well. Mix in pecans. Spread over baked crust.
- Lower the oven temperature to 275°F (140°C). Bake for 50 minutes until firm. Let cool in the pan on wire rack. Slice into bars.

Nutrition Information

- Calories: 500 calories;
- Sodium: 232
- Total Carbohydrate: 69.1
- Cholesterol: 98
- Protein: 5.8
- Total Fat: 24

217. Persimmon Cookies

Serving: 48 | Prep: | Cook: | Ready in:

Ingredients

- 1/2 cup shortening
- 1 cup white sugar
- 1 egg
- 1/2 teaspoon vanilla extract
- 2 cups all-purpose flour
- 1/2 teaspoon baking soda
- 1/2 teaspoon baking powder
- 1/4 teaspoon salt
- 1/2 teaspoon ground cloves
- 1/2 teaspoon ground cinnamon
- 1/2 teaspoon ground nutmeg
- 1 cup raisins
- 1 cup chopped walnuts
- 1/4 teaspoon salt
- 1 cup persimmon pulp

Direction

- Heat oven to 175 degrees C/350 degrees F. Cream sugar and shortening together. Add vanilla and egg, mixing well.
- Sift nutmeg, cinnamon, cloves, 1/4 teaspoon of salt, baking powder, baking soda, and salt together. Mix flour mixture in the creamed sugar mixture.
- Mix in persimmon pulp, 1/4 teaspoon of salt, chopped nuts, and raisins. Mix well.
- Drop teaspoonfuls on parchment lined or greased cookie sheet. Bake for 12-15 minutes. Cool on wire racks.

Nutrition Information

- Calories: 87 calories;
- Cholesterol: 4
- Protein: 1.2
- Total Fat: 3.9
- Sodium: 44
- Total Carbohydrate: 12.6

218. Persimmon Cookies I

Serving: 18 | Prep: | Cook: | Ready in:

Ingredients

- 2 ripe persimmons, pureed
- 1 teaspoon baking soda
- 2 cups all-purpose flour
- 1/2 teaspoon ground cinnamon
- 1/2 teaspoon ground cloves
- 1/2 teaspoon ground nutmeg
- 1/2 teaspoon salt
- 1 egg
- 1 cup white sugar
- 1/2 cup butter
- 1 cup raisins
- 1 cup chopped walnuts

Direction

- Heat oven to 180 degrees C or 350 degrees F.
- In persimmon pulp, melt baking soda and put aside.
- Sift salt, spices, and flour together, put aside.
- Cream margarine or butter until it is fluffy, beat in persimmon and egg. Mix in dry ingredients. Mix in raisins and nuts.
- Place teaspoonfuls on a greased cookie sheet and bake for 15 minutes.

Nutrition Information

- Calories: 214 calories;
- Cholesterol: 24
- Protein: 3.1
- Total Fat: 9.9
- Sodium: 176
- Total Carbohydrate: 30.1

219. Persimmon Cookies II

Serving: 36 | Prep: | Cook: | Ready in:

Ingredients

- 2 ripe persimmons, pureed
- 1 cup white sugar
- 1/2 cup butter
- 1 egg
- 2 cups all-purpose flour
- 1 teaspoon baking soda
- 1 teaspoon ground cinnamon
- 1/2 teaspoon ground cloves
- 1/2 teaspoon ground nutmeg
- 1/2 teaspoon salt
- 1 cup chopped walnuts

Direction

- Heat oven to 190 degrees C/375 degrees F. Grease a baking sheet lightly or line with parchment paper.
- Mix salt, nutmeg, cloves, cinnamon, baking soda, and flour.

- Cream margarine or butter with sugar. Mix in persimmons and eggs. Add flour mixture then mix until combined, mix in chopped nuts. Drop in by teaspoonsfuls on prepared sheet, 2 inches apart.
- Bake at 190 degrees C/375 degrees F for 12-15 minutes.

Nutrition Information

- Calories: 95 calories;
- Protein: 1.4
- Total Fat: 4.9
- Sodium: 88
- Total Carbohydrate: 11.9
- Cholesterol: 12

220. Persimmon Raisin Cookies

Serving: 60 | Prep: 20mins | Cook: 12mins | Ready in:

Ingredients

- 2 cups white sugar
- 1 cup shortening
- 2 eggs
- 4 cups all-purpose flour
- 1 teaspoon salt
- 2 teaspoons baking soda
- 2 teaspoons ground cinnamon
- 2 teaspoons ground nutmeg
- 2 cups persimmon pulp
- 2 cups raisin paste
- 2 cups chopped walnuts

Direction

- Heat oven to 175 degrees C/350 degrees F. Grease 2 baking sheets lightly.
- Cream shortening and sugar in a big mixing bowl until fluffy and light. Beat eggs in, one by one. Mix in flour, nutmeg, cinnamon, baking soda, and salt, mixing well. Stir in walnuts, raisin paste, and persimmon pulp. Drop spoonsful on prepared cookie sheets then slightly spread out.
- Bake in the oven for 12-15 minutes until the tops of the cookies spring back when you touch it. Let cookies cool for 5 minutes on the baking sheet then completely cool on a wire rack.

Nutrition Information

- Calories: 148 calories;
- Sodium: 84
- Total Carbohydrate: 23.3
- Cholesterol: 6
- Protein: 1.9
- Total Fat: 5.9

221. Pumpkin Pecan Biscotti

Serving: 36 | Prep: 30mins | Cook: 45mins | Ready in:

Ingredients

- 2 3/4 cups all-purpose flour
- 3/4 cup white sugar
- 1/2 cup brown sugar
- 1 1/2 teaspoons baking powder
- 1 pinch salt
- 1 teaspoon ground cinnamon
- 1/2 teaspoon ground nutmeg
- 1/4 teaspoon ground ginger
- 2 eggs
- 1/2 cup pumpkin puree
- 1 teaspoon vanilla extract
- 1/4 cup finely chopped pecans

Direction

- Start preheating the oven to 350°F (175°C). Line parchment paper on a baking sheet. In a large bowl, combine ginger, nutmeg, cinnamon, salt, baking powder, brown sugar,

white sugar and flour until combined thoroughly.
- Beat eggs in a separate bowl with vanilla extract and pumpkin puree; stir in the pecans. Put in the dry ingredients, then stir to form a stiff dough. Separate the dough in half, shape each half into a 2-in. wide and 10-in. long log. Arrange logs onto parchment-lined baking sheet.
- Bake in prepared oven for 25-30 mins until browned lightly.
- Allow the logs to cool on baking sheet for 5 minutes. Transfer the logs to a work surface then slice into about 1/2-in. thick individual cookies. Cut up cookies in a light sawing motion with a sharp knife. Return cookies onto parchment-lined baking sheet.
- Place cookies back into oven, bake for around 8 mins until browned lightly. Flip over the cookies. Bake for 8 mins longer until crisp. Allow to cool on the wire racks.

Nutrition Information

- Calories: 74 calories;
- Total Fat: 1
- Sodium: 33
- Total Carbohydrate: 15
- Cholesterol: 10
- Protein: 1.5

222. Red Velvet Cheesecake Swirl Brownies

Serving: 12 | Prep: 20mins | Cook: 30mins | Ready in:

Ingredients

- 1/2 cup unsalted butter, melted
- 1 cup white sugar
- 1/4 cup unsweetened cocoa powder
- 1 ounce red food coloring
- 1 teaspoon vanilla extract
- 1 teaspoon distilled white vinegar
- 1/4 teaspoon salt
- 2 large eggs, slightly beaten
- 3/4 cup all-purpose flour
- 1 (8 ounce) package cream cheese at room temperature
- 1/4 cup white sugar
- 1 large egg
- 1/4 teaspoon vanilla extract

Direction

- Preheat an oven to 175°C/350°F then grease 8x8-in. baking dish.
- Whisk 1 cup sugar and melted butter in a big mixing bowl. One by one, mix salt, vinegar, 1 tsp. vanilla extract, red food coloring and cocoa into butter mixture, stirring well after every addition to prevent lumps. Mix 2 eggs into the mixture till combined thoroughly.
- Mix flour into the cocoa mixture till just combined; put 1/4 cup batter aside. Put leftover batter into prepped baking dish.
- Use an electric mixer at medium speed to beat cream cheese till fluffy and light in a bowl; beat 1/4 tsp. vanilla extract, 1 egg and 1/4 cup sugar into cream cheese for 3-4 minutes till there's only small lumps left and very well blended.
- In dollops, put cream cheese mixture on batter in pan; smooth the tops of dollops gently and even with batter with an offset spatula/knife. Don't overmix. Drizzle the reserved 1/4 cup batter on dollops of the cream cheese mixture. To make swirls, drag a skewer/knife through cream cheese mixture and batter.
- In preheated oven, bake for 30-35 minutes till an inserted toothpick in middle of pan exits clean. Fully cool; cut to bars. Keep refrigerated, covered.

Nutrition Information

- Calories: 265 calories;
- Sodium: 123
- Total Carbohydrate: 28.4
- Cholesterol: 87
- Protein: 4.2

- Total Fat: 15.7

223. Spiced Pecan Shortbread

Serving: 16 | Prep: 5mins | Cook: 25mins | Ready in:

Ingredients

- 2 cups all-purpose flour
- 1/2 cup packed dark brown sugar
- 1 teaspoon pumpkin pie spice
- 1/2 teaspoon ground cloves
- 1/4 teaspoon baking powder
- 1 cup butter, softened
- 1/2 cup chopped pecans
- 3 tablespoons confectioners' sugar

Direction

- Start preheating the oven to 350°F (175°C).
- In a medium bowl, stir baking powder, cloves, pumpkin pie spice, brown sugar, and flour. Combine in the butter with a fork until well-blended. The dough will be separated and flaky. Mix in pecans, then press into an 8-inch square pan.
- Bake in the prepared oven for 25 minutes until the top turns light brown. While still warm, slice into squares, but do not transfer from the pan. Allow to cool, then sprinkle with confectioners' sugar.

Nutrition Information

- Calories: 217 calories;
- Total Fat: 14.4
- Sodium: 90
- Total Carbohydrate: 20.8
- Cholesterol: 31
- Protein: 2.1

224. Spicy Pear Cookies

Serving: 15 | Prep: | Cook: | Ready in:

Ingredients

- 1/2 cup butter, softened
- 1 1/2 cups packed brown sugar
- 1 egg
- 1 teaspoon vanilla extract
- 2 cups all-purpose flour
- 1 1/2 teaspoons baking powder
- 1 teaspoon ground cinnamon
- 1 teaspoon ground ginger
- 1 pear - peeled, cored and diced
- 1/2 cup raisins
- 1/2 cup chopped walnuts
- 1 1/2 cups confectioners' sugar
- 2 1/2 tablespoons lemon juice

Direction

- Set oven to 175° C (350° F) and start preheating.
- Whisk sugar with margarine in a big bowl until smooth. Whisk in vanilla and egg. Combine ginger, cinnamon, baking powder, and flour; blend into batter. Mix in raisins, chopped nuts and chopped pears.
- By rounded tablespoonfuls, drop onto baking sheets, spacing 2 inches apart; bake until the center bounces back when slightly touched and the edges are golden brown, about 15 minutes. Transfer to wire racks, let cool.
- Mix together lemon juice and confectioners' sugar until smooth. Use a spoon to arrange icing over cookies.

Nutrition Information

- Calories: 299 calories;
- Sodium: 104
- Total Carbohydrate: 52.9
- Cholesterol: 29
- Protein: 3
- Total Fat: 9.2

225. Spicy Zucchini Oatmeal Cookies

Serving: 30 | Prep: 15mins | Cook: 15mins | Ready in:

Ingredients

- 1 1/4 cups all-purpose flour
- 1/2 teaspoon baking soda
- 1 1/2 teaspoons ground cinnamon
- 1/4 teaspoon ground cloves
- 1/2 cup butter, softened
- 2/3 cup packed brown sugar
- 1 egg
- 1 teaspoon vanilla extract
- 1 cup quick cooking oats
- 1 cup shredded zucchini
- 1/2 cup raisins

Direction

- Preheat the oven to 175 degrees C (350 degrees F). Grease the baking sheets.
- Stir cloves, cinnamon, baking soda and flour together in the bowl; put them aside. Beat brown sugar and butter using the electric mixer in the big bowl till creamy. Put in vanilla extract and egg. Stir in flour mixture and oats till just incorporated.
- Wring zucchini in the clean towel to get rid of any excess moisture. Stir raisins and zucchini into dough; stirring just enough to evenly mix. Drop the batter by rounded teaspoonfuls with 2-in. apart onto prepped baking sheets. Bake till bottom edges turn golden brown or for 14-16 minutes.

Nutrition Information

- Calories: 86 calories;
- Cholesterol: 14
- Protein: 1.3
- Total Fat: 3.5
- Sodium: 47
- Total Carbohydrate: 12.8

226. Squash Cookies

Serving: 30 | Prep: | Cook: | Ready in:

Ingredients

- 1/2 cup butter, softened
- 3/4 cup white sugar
- 3/4 cup packed brown sugar
- 2 eggs
- 1 1/2 cups mashed, cooked butternut squash
- 2 1/2 cups all-purpose flour
- 1 teaspoon baking soda
- 2 teaspoons ground cinnamon
- 1/2 teaspoon salt
- 1/2 teaspoon ground nutmeg
- 1/4 teaspoon ground ginger
- 1 cup raisins
- 1 1/2 cups chopped pecans
- 1/4 teaspoon ground allspice
- 2 1/2 teaspoons baking powder

Direction

- Start preheating oven to 375°F (190°C).
- Cream sugars and butter in a large mixing bowl until fluffy. Beat in squash and eggs. Sift spices, baking powder, baking soda and flour together. Then put into the mixture, stir until well blended. Mix in nuts and raisins. Spoon on the cookie sheets spacing cookies about 2-inch apart.
- Bake in the prepared oven for 10-12 mins or until the edges turn golden.

Nutrition Information

- Calories: 171 calories;
- Cholesterol: 21
- Protein: 2.3
- Total Fat: 7.8
- Sodium: 151
- Total Carbohydrate: 24.4

227. Thanksgiving Cookies

Serving: 32 | Prep: 30mins | Cook: 15mins | Ready in:

Ingredients

- 3 cups quick cooking oats
- 1 (14 ounce) can solid-pack pumpkin puree
- 1 (12 ounce) bag semisweet chocolate chips
- 1 3/4 cups all-purpose flour
- 1 cup butter, softened
- 1/2 cup white sugar
- 1 egg

Direction

- Set the oven to 190°C or 375°F to preheat.
- In a bowl, combine together egg, sugar, butter, flour, chocolate chips, pumpkin and oats until dough becomes thick and well combined. Form dough into 2 to 3-in. patties, then arrange on a baking sheet.
- In the preheated oven, bake for about 15-20 minutes, until patties are cooked through.

Nutrition Information

- Calories: 173 calories;
- Sodium: 75
- Total Carbohydrate: 21.1
- Cholesterol: 21
- Protein: 2.5
- Total Fat: 9.7

228. Very Cranberry Chocolate Chip Cookies

Serving: 12 | Prep: 20mins | Cook: 10mins | Ready in:

Ingredients

- 1/4 cup brown sugar
- 1/8 cup honey
- 1/8 cup butter
- 1/8 cup natural peanut butter
- 1/2 banana, mashed
- 1 teaspoon vanilla extract
- 5/8 cup whole wheat flour
- 1/8 cup oat bran
- 1/2 cup rolled oats
- 1/4 teaspoon baking soda
- 1/8 teaspoon salt
- 1 pinch pumpkin pie spice
- 1/2 cup dried cranberries
- 1/2 cup semisweet chocolate chips
- 2 tablespoons sunflower seeds

Direction

- Set oven to preheat at 350°F (175°C).
- Mix together the peanut butter, butter, honey and brown sugar in a medium bowl till smooth. Stir the banana and vanilla into the mixture. Mix together the pumpkin pie spice, salt, baking soda, oats, oat bran and whole wheat flour in a different bowl. Stir the dry ingredients into the liquid ones till a smooth dough forms. Mix the cranberries, chocolate chips and sunflower seeds into the mixture. Drop spoonfuls of the mixture onto an ungreased baking sheet.
- In the preheated oven, bake until cookies' edges are lightly browned, for 10 to 12 minutes.

Nutrition Information

- Calories: 148 calories;
- Protein: 2.6
- Total Fat: 5.9
- Sodium: 74
- Total Carbohydrate: 24
- Cholesterol: 5

229. White Chocolate Macadamia Cranberry Dreams

Serving: 36 | Prep: 40mins | Cook: 10mins | Ready in:

Ingredients

- 3 cups all-purpose flour
- 3/4 teaspoon baking soda
- 3/4 teaspoon salt
- 3/4 cup white sugar
- 1 cup packed light brown sugar
- 1 cup butter, softened
- 2 eggs, slightly beaten
- 1 tablespoon vanilla extract
- 1 cup vanilla baking chips
- 1 cup chopped macadamia nuts
- 1 cup dried cranberries

Direction

- Preheat an oven to 175°C/350°F.
- Mix salt, baking soda and flour in medium bowl; put aside. Cream butter (don't use shortening), light brown sugar and white sugar; mix vanilla and slightly beaten eggs in.
- Add flour mixture just till mixed; mix dried cranberries, macadamia nuts and vanilla chips in.
- By rounded teaspoon/small scoop, drop dough on ungreased cookie sheet. In preheated oven, bake for 10 minutes till cookies are just set. Take out of oven; cool. The cookies will slightly sink.
- Chocolate cookies: use 1/2 cup cocoa to replace for 1/2 cup flour. Refrigerator cookies: Roll dough to 2 rolls then use plastic wrap to wrap. Chill or freeze. Thaw dough for 1/2 hour minimum before cutting if freezing dough. Cut to 1-in. slices then cut to 4; put, point up, on baking sheet. Fancy cookies: On chocolate cookies, drizzle melted white chocolate and on white cookie, drizzle melted dark chocolate.

Nutrition Information

- Calories: 202 calories;
- Total Fat: 10.2
- Sodium: 131
- Total Carbohydrate: 25.7
- Cholesterol: 24
- Protein: 2.3

230. Yumkins

Serving: 12 | Prep: | Cook: | Ready in:

Ingredients

- 1 cup packed brown sugar
- 2 cups all-purpose flour
- 1 teaspoon baking soda
- 1 teaspoon baking powder
- 1/2 teaspoon salt
- 1 cup pumpkin puree
- 1 cup chopped walnuts
- 1 teaspoon vanilla extract
- 1 (3 ounce) package cream cheese
- 2 cups confectioners' sugar
- 1 tablespoon orange juice

Direction

- Set oven to 175°C (350°F) and start preheating. Coat 12 miniature muffin tins with grease.
- Combine vanilla, nuts, pumpkin, salt, baking powder, baking soda, flour and brown sugar. Scoop the dough by spoonful into the muffin tin.
- Bake in 175°C (350°F) for 15-20 minutes; put aside and let cool.
- Beat orange juice, sugar and cream cheese. Frost the top of yumkins.

Nutrition Information

- Calories: 318 calories;
- Total Fat: 9.1
- Sodium: 270
- Total Carbohydrate: 56.6

- Cholesterol: 8
- Protein: 4.4

Chapter 5: Christmas Cookie Recipes

***

231. Almond Pretzels (Mandelplaetzchen)

Serving: 26 | Prep: 30mins | Cook: 10mins | Ready in:

Ingredients

- 1 cup unsalted butter
- 1 cup white sugar
- 1/4 cup cultured sour cream
- 2 eggs
- 2 egg yolks, divided
- 2 1/2 cups all-purpose flour
- 1 teaspoon baking powder
- 1 teaspoon ground cinnamon
- 1 teaspoon lemon zest
- 8 tablespoons chopped blanched almonds
- 1 tablespoon white sugar

Direction

- In the bowl of a stand mixer fitted with the paddle attachment, beat butter until soft. Slowly mix in 1 cup of sugar until the mixture is creamy and very light. Beat in 1 egg yolk, eggs, and sour cream. Stir in flour until the dough pulls together. Stir in lemon zest, cinnamon, and baking powder.
- Divide dough into 2 portions; arrange each portion on a sheet of plastic wrap. Form each half into a 6-inch log of even thickness. Tightly wrap and place in the refrigerator for 4 hours to overnight.
- Start preheating the oven to 375°F (190°C). Grease 2 baking sheets.
- On a flat work surface, place the dough and let warm up slightly for about 10 minutes. Slice each log into 13 equal sections.
- With your fingers, roll sections back and forth to make 10-inch ropes. Shape each rope into a circle; overlap the left end over the right, twisting once, and press into a pretzel shape. Place pretzel cookies to the greased baking sheets.
- Whisk the leftover egg yolk in a small bowl; brush on cookies. Sprinkle 1 tablespoon of sugar and almonds on top.
- Bake for 10 to 15 minutes in the prepared oven until edges are dry. Let cool on the baking sheets for 5 minutes. Bring to a wire rack to cool.

Nutrition Information

- Calories: 169 calories;
- Protein: 2.7
- Total Fat: 9.8
- Sodium: 28
- Total Carbohydrate: 18.2
- Cholesterol: 50

232. Amariette Cookies

Serving: 24 | Prep: | Cook: | Ready in:

Ingredients

- 7 egg whites
- 2 1/2 cups white sugar
- 2 pounds ground almonds
- 2 tablespoons almond extract
- 1 cup chopped almonds
- 1/3 cup granulated sugar for decoration

Direction

- Turn on the oven to 350°F (175°C) to preheat.
- Beat together sugar and egg whites until it is fluffy. Mix in almond extract and ground almond until well-combined. Form the dough into walnut sized balls; roll into sugar and put a piece of candied cherry or almond on top.
- Put into the oven to bake at 350°F (175°C) until firm. The bottom should be light brown.

Nutrition Information

- Calories: 341 calories;
- Protein: 9.9
- Total Fat: 21.2
- Sodium: 17
- Total Carbohydrate: 31.9
- Cholesterol: 0

233. Anise Drops

Serving: 36 | Prep: | Cook: | Ready in:

Ingredients

- 3 eggs, beaten
- 1 cup white sugar
- 2 cups all-purpose flour
- 1/2 teaspoon baking powder
- 1/2 teaspoon cream of tartar
- 1 tablespoon anise seed

Direction

- Set oven to 350°F (175°C) to preheat.
- Mix the sugar with the beaten eggs and keep whipping for 15 minutes. Mix in the anise seeds, cream of tartar, baking powder and the flour.
- Drop by teaspoonfuls onto a cookie sheet, greased and bake for 15 minutes at 350°F (175°C).

Nutrition Information

- Calories: 54 calories;
- Total Fat: 0.5
- Sodium: 13
- Total Carbohydrate: 11
- Cholesterol: 16
- Protein: 1.3

234. Anisette Cookies I

Serving: 72 | Prep: | Cook: | Ready in:

Ingredients

- 7 eggs
- 2 cups white sugar
- 1/2 cup vegetable oil
- 3/4 cup orange juice
- 1 teaspoon almond extract
- 2 teaspoons vanilla extract
- 1 teaspoon lemon extract
- 1 teaspoon anise extract
- 5 teaspoons baking powder
- 7 cups sifted all-purpose flour

Direction

- Start preheating the oven to 350°F (175°).
- Whisk eggs in a big bowl. Mix in anise flavoring, lemon flavoring, vanilla flavoring, orange juice, and vegetable oil.
- Sift the flour with baking powder and sugar. Add to the egg mixture with the flour mixture. The dough should be sticky. Add extra flour until the dough is not sticky anymore and you can roll it.
- Cut off a walnut-sized piece of dough. Roll it into a rope and form it into a knot. Put the completed knots on a non-oiled baking sheet 2" apart.
- Put in the preheated oven and bake for 15 minutes at 350°F (175°) until the bottom turn light brown. Put the cookies on a wire rack to cool. Use confectioner's sugar icing to ice if you want.

Nutrition Information

- Calories: 88 calories;
- Cholesterol: 18
- Protein: 1.9
- Total Fat: 2.1
- Sodium: 41
- Total Carbohydrate: 15.2

235. Apple Pie Wedges

Serving: 16 | Prep: 45mins | Cook: 35mins | Ready in:

Ingredients

- 1 cup butter
- 2/3 cup white sugar
- 1 egg yolk
- 1/3 cup apple butter
- 2 1/3 cups all-purpose flour
- 1 teaspoon ground cinnamon
- 1/2 teaspoon apple pie spice
- 1/2 teaspoon vanilla extract

Direction

- Put sugar and butter in a large mixing bowl then beat at medium speed until the mixture becomes fluffy. Beat in apple butter and egg yolk. Put in vanilla, apple pie spice, cinnamon, flour. Beat at low speed till everything is thoroughly blended.
- Divide dough into 2 equal parts. On waxed paper, shape each half into a 6-inch disc. Put in the fridge for half an hour.
- To preheat: Set oven to 175°C (350°F).
- Invert 1 disc of dough into an ungreased 9-inch round pie plate. Lightly flour your hands then use them to press dough into plate, remember to cover plate completely. Use the handle of a wooden spoon to flute edges. Deeply score into 8 wedges. Use tines of fork to pierce surface. Repeat steps with the remaining disc of dough and a different pie plate.
- Put into the preheated oven and bake for 35 minutes till pies become golden brown. Get pies out of oven and put on wire rack. Allow pies to cool completely and chop into wedges.

Nutrition Information

- Calories: 215 calories;
- Cholesterol: 43
- Protein: 2.2
- Total Fat: 12
- Sodium: 83
- Total Carbohydrate: 25

236. Applesauce Cookies II

Serving: 60 | Prep: 15mins | Cook: 12mins | Ready in:

Ingredients

- 1 cup packed brown sugar
- 1 egg
- 3/4 cup shortening
- 1 cup applesauce
- 2 1/2 cups all-purpose flour
- 1/2 teaspoon baking soda
- 1/2 teaspoon salt
- 3/4 teaspoon ground cinnamon
- 1/4 teaspoon ground nutmeg
- 1/4 teaspoon ground cloves
- 1 cup chopped walnuts
- 1 cup raisins

Direction

- To preheat: Set oven to 165°C (325°F). Grease cookie sheets.
- Put shortening and brown sugar together in a medium bowl and cream them until the mixture becomes smooth. Mix in egg, then apple sauce till everything is well blended. Mix together cloves, nutmeg, cinnamon, salt, baking soda and flour; stir into the applesauce mixture. Put in raisins, walnuts and mix. Drop

mixture by teaspoonfuls onto the greased cookie sheets.
- Put the cookie sheets into the preheated oven and bake for 10-12 minutes till the edges start to brown. Allow the cookies to cool on the cookie sheets for a couple of minutes then transfer cookies to wire racks to cool completely.

Nutrition Information

- Calories: 78 calories;
- Cholesterol: 3
- Protein: 1
- Total Fat: 3.8
- Sodium: 33
- Total Carbohydrate: 10.5

237. Apricot Cookies

Serving: 24 | Prep: | Cook: | Ready in:

Ingredients

- 1 cup butter
- 1 cup white sugar
- 3 cups all-purpose flour
- 1 teaspoon baking powder
- 1/2 teaspoon salt
- 1 egg
- 1 teaspoon vanilla extract
- 1 cup apricot preserves
- 1/3 cup confectioners' sugar for decoration

Direction

- Preheat the oven to 175 degrees C (350 degrees F).
- Cream sugar and butter in the medium size mixing bowl. Stir the vanilla extract, egg, salt, baking powder and flour into the sugar-butter mixture. Let the dough cool down in the fridge for 60 minutes.
- On the surface that is floured a bit, roll the dough out into a quarter in. in thickness. Chop the dough into round-shape using the round cookie cutter/glass. With the tsp. tip, add a small drop of the apricot preserves into the center of the circle. Use water to brush the edges and fold the dough over in order to let cookie have the half-moon shape; seal the edges. Arrange onto the ungreased cookie sheets.
- Bake till turning golden brown or for 8 - 12 minutes. Use the powdered sugar to dust the cookies when still hot.

Nutrition Information

- Calories: 202 calories;
- Total Fat: 8
- Sodium: 127
- Total Carbohydrate: 31.2
- Cholesterol: 28
- Protein: 2

238. Apricot Cream Cheese Thumbprints

Serving: 84 | Prep: 15mins | Cook: 15mins | Ready in:

Ingredients

- 1 1/2 cups butter, softened
- 1 1/2 cups white sugar
- 1 (8 ounce) package cream cheese, softened
- 2 eggs
- 2 tablespoons lemon juice
- 1 1/2 teaspoons lemon zest
- 4 1/2 cups all-purpose flour
- 1 1/2 teaspoons baking powder
- 1 cup apricot preserves
- 1/3 cup confectioners' sugar for decoration

Direction

- Cream the cream cheese, sugar, and butter in a large bowl until smooth. Add the eggs, beat 1 at a time, then stir in the lemon zest and juice. Mix baking powder and flour; stir into the cream cheese mixture until just blended. Cover and chill until firm, for about 1 hour.
- Set the oven at 175°C (350°F) to preheat. Roll tablespoonfuls of the dough into balls; on ungreased cookie sheets, arrange them 2 inches apart. In the center of each ball, make an indention using your finger, then fill with a half teaspoon of apricot preserves.
- In the preheated oven, bake for 15 minutes, or until the edges are golden. Let the cookies cool for 2 minutes on the baking sheets before removing to cool completely on wire racks. Dust with confectioner's sugar.

Nutrition Information

- Calories: 89 calories;
- Total Carbohydrate: 11.8
- Cholesterol: 16
- Protein: 1.1
- Total Fat: 4.4
- Sodium: 43

239. Apricot Fold Ups

Serving: 48 | Prep: | Cook: | Ready in:

Ingredients

- 2 cups all-purpose flour
- 1 teaspoon salt
- 8 ounces cream cheese, cold
- 1 cup margarine, chilled
- 1 tablespoon milk
- 1 tablespoon distilled white vinegar
- 2 cups apricot preserves
- 3/4 cup confectioners' sugar
- 2 tablespoons water

Direction

- Whisk the salt and flour together in a medium bowl. Chop in margarine and cream cheese until the blend looks like coarse crumbs. Drizzle with vinegar and milk. Work the dough using hand until it sticks in a ball shape. Split the dough into 4 parts and chill for 2 hours in refrigerator.
- Preheat oven to 400°F (190°C).
- Roll out each piece of dough on a slightly floured surface into 7 1/2x10-inch rectangle. Chop the dough into squares of 2 1/2 inches. Put a 1/2 teaspoon dollop of apricot preserves on the middle of each square. Fold each corner to the middle and pinch together.
- Set cookies on an unprepared cookie sheet, then bake in the preheated oven for about 15 minutes. When cool, sprinkle with glaze.
- Mix 2 tablespoons of water and 3/4 cup of confectioners' sugar together in a small bowl until soft. Sprinkle over the cookies.

Nutrition Information

- Calories: 109 calories;
- Total Fat: 5.5
- Sodium: 112
- Total Carbohydrate: 14.6
- Cholesterol: 5
- Protein: 1

240. Apricot Shortbread Bars

Serving: 24 | Prep: 45mins | Cook: 15mins | Ready in:

Ingredients

- 2 cups all-purpose flour
- 1 cup packed light brown sugar
- 2/3 cup butter or margarine, softened
- 1 1/2 cups chopped dried apricots
- 2 teaspoons grated lemon zest
- 1 1/2 cups white sugar
- 4 teaspoons cornstarch
- 1 cup chopped walnuts

Direction

- Preheat the oven to 175 degrees C (350 degrees F). Mix the sugar and flour together in a medium-sized bowl. Chop in the butter till mixture looks like the coarse crumbs. Press into the bottom of the 9x13 in. pan.
- Bake in the preheated oven till becoming firm or for 12-15 minutes. When the crust is baking, add the apricots into the saucepan with enough of the water to cover. Boil, and cook for 10 minutes.
- Drain, saving half cup of liquid. Bring the reserved liquid and apricots back to the pan, and mix in lemon zest. Whisk the cornstarch and sugar together, and mix into the apricot mixture. Boil, and boil for 60 seconds. Take out of the heat and let it cool down. Spread on the prepped crust, and drizzle walnuts on top.
- Bake in the preheated oven till becoming firm to touch or for 20 - 25 minutes. Let it cool down fully prior to chopping into bars.

Nutrition Information

- Calories: 208 calories;
- Total Fat: 8.5
- Sodium: 39
- Total Carbohydrate: 32.6
- Cholesterol: 14
- Protein: 2.2

241. Aurilla's Anise Biscuit Mix Cookies

Serving: 30 | Prep: | Cook: | Ready in:

Ingredients

- 5 cups buttermilk baking mix
- 1 cup all-purpose flour
- 2 cups white sugar
- 2 egg
- 3/4 cup water
- 1 tablespoon anise extract
- 1 cup chopped pecans
- 2 cups confectioners' sugar
- 3 tablespoons water
- 1 teaspoon anise extract
- 3 drops red food coloring

Direction

- Set the oven to 350°F (175°C) to preheat.
- Mix nuts, sugar, flour, and buttermilk baking mix in a big bowl. Beat water, anise extract, and eggs in a separate smaller bowl. Pour liquid over the dry ingredients and whisk until fully blended. The dough should have a dry consistency similar to biscuit dough. Roll the dough into balls with the size of a walnut and put on a baking sheet. Bake for 12-15 minutes in the preheated oven. The cookies should turn pale golden brown. Transfer to a rack to cool. Once cool, use glaze to paint.
- To make the glaze: Combine food coloring and confectioners' sugar with anise extract. Add water, 1 tablespoon each time. Whisk until smooth. You can adjust the amount of water so the glaze can have a creamy paint-like consistency. Use a pastry brush to paint the cookies, or use a slotted spoon to dip them in the glaze. Put the cookies on cooling racks or waxed paper to dry. The texture of the cookies will turn rock-hard if you don't glaze them.

Nutrition Information

- Calories: 196 calories;
- Sodium: 390
- Total Carbohydrate: 39.5
- Cholesterol: 12
- Protein: 2.9
- Total Fat: 3.3

242. Austrian Jam Cookies

Serving: 36 | Prep: | Cook: | Ready in:

Ingredients

- 1/2 cup butter
- 1/2 cup white sugar
- 1 teaspoon vanilla extract
- 1 egg yolk
- 1 1/2 cups all-purpose flour
- 2/3 cup chopped almonds
- 1 cup raspberry jam

Direction

- Beat together the butter with sugar in a medium bowl. Put in the egg yolk and vanilla; stir until fluffy. Mix in the flour, and chill dough for 2 hours.
- Set oven to 300°F (150°C) to preheat. Grease cookie sheets.
- Measure out the dough by teaspoonfuls, and roll to shape into balls. Dip the balls into chopped almonds and place on the greased cookie sheet by an inch apart. Create an indention in each cookie using a finger, fill jam in the indention with a teaspoon or a pastry bag. Bake for 15 to 20 minutes in the prepared oven, until golden brown. Take out of the pan after baking to cool on a wire rack.

Nutrition Information

- Calories: 88 calories;
- Protein: 1
- Total Fat: 3.6
- Sodium: 19
- Total Carbohydrate: 13.3
- Cholesterol: 12

243. Baked Bottom Nanaimo Bars

Serving: 16 | Prep: 25mins | Cook: 15mins | Ready in:

Ingredients

- 1/2 cup unsalted butter at room temperature
- 1/4 cup white sugar
- 1 egg
- 1/4 cup unsweetened cocoa powder
- 1 1/4 cups graham cracker crumbs
- 1 cup flaked coconut
- 1/2 cup finely chopped almonds
- 3/4 cup semisweet chocolate chips
- 3 tablespoons butter
- 1 (5.1 ounce) package instant vanilla pudding mix
- 2 1/4 cups milk
- 1/4 cup flaked coconut

Direction

- Set oven to 350°F (175°C) to preheat. Grease an 8x8-inch square baking dish with butter.
- Whip unsalted butter and sugar for about a minute using an electric mixer in a big mixing bowl, until very creamy. Put in the egg and cocoa powder, and whip until the ingredients are well combined. Add the almonds, 1 cup coconut, and graham cracker crumbs, and whip on low speed until the ingredients are well blend. Press into the bottom of the greased baking pan.
- Bake for 12 minutes in the prepared oven and allow the crust to cool.
- In a saucepan over very low heat, melt 3 tablespoons of butter with chocolate chips, mixing until thoroughly combined. Take off from the heat, let it cool for a few minutes, then spread the chocolate mixture on top of the crust in a smooth layer. Chill the dish while you prepare the next layer.
- In a mixing bowl, whip the pudding mix with milk using an electric mixer about 2 minutes until thick and smooth. Spread the pudding on top of the chocolate layer; scatter the dish with 1/4 cup coconut, chill, cover loosely for at least 1 hour until firm and chilled.

Nutrition Information

- Calories: 249 calories;
- Total Carbohydrate: 27.4
- Cholesterol: 35

- Protein: 3.5
- Total Fat: 15.3
- Sodium: 221

244. Banana Oatmeal Cookie

Serving: 24 | Prep: | Cook: | Ready in:

Ingredients

- 1 1/2 cups sifted all-purpose flour
- 1/2 teaspoon baking soda
- 1 teaspoon salt
- 1/4 teaspoon ground nutmeg
- 3/4 teaspoon ground cinnamon
- 3/4 cup shortening
- 1 cup white sugar
- 1 egg
- 1 cup mashed bananas
- 1 3/4 cups quick cooking oats
- 1/2 cup chopped nuts

Direction

- Preheat the oven to 400°F (200°C).
- Sieve the baking soda, nutmeg, flour, cinnamon and salt together.
- Cream the sugar and shortening together and whisk it until it has a light and fluffy texture. Put in the oatmeal, egg, nuts and banana. Mix the mixture thoroughly.
- Put the dry mixture into the oatmeal mixture and stir the two mixtures thoroughly; put teaspoonfuls of the mixture onto an ungreased cookie sheet.
- Put it in preheated oven and let it bake for 15 minutes until the edges are slightly browned. Let the baked cookies cool down on a wire rack. Keep it in a covered container.

Nutrition Information

- Calories: 170 calories;
- Cholesterol: 8

- Protein: 2.4
- Total Fat: 8.8
- Sodium: 127
- Total Carbohydrate: 21.2

245. Banana Rum Biscotti

Serving: 36 | Prep: 20mins | Cook: 55mins | Ready in:

Ingredients

- 3 1/2 cups all-purpose flour
- 2 teaspoons baking powder
- 1/2 teaspoon salt
- 2 eggs
- 1 cup white sugar
- 3/4 cup mashed ripe banana
- 2 tablespoons vegetable oil
- 1 tablespoon rum
- 1/2 cup toasted, chopped pecans

Direction

- Set an oven to 350°F (175°C) to preheat. Line 2 baking trays using parchment paper.
- In a bowl, mix salt, baking powder, and flour thoroughly. Whip the eggs in a bowl lightly and put in the rum, oil, banana and sugar. Combine the banana mixture into the flour mixture, mix well, and put in the pecans, stirring them into the dough thoroughly. Shape the dough into 4 logs (about 1/2-in. thick), put them onto baking trays lined with parchment paper; bake for 25 minutes until they start to brown.
- Turn down the oven temperature to 250°F (120°C). Take the baking trays out of the oven and let cool for 10 minutes. Take the logs off the parchment paper and slice each log into 1/2-in. thick slices. Put the biscotti back onto the cookie trays and bake for 15 mins per side (30 mins total) until cookies start to brown. Take out to racks to cool. The biscotti will be soft at first but will harden as they cool.

Nutrition Information

- Calories: 92 calories;
- Protein: 1.8
- Total Fat: 2.3
- Sodium: 64
- Total Carbohydrate: 16.2
- Cholesterol: 10

246. Basic Gingersnap Cookies

Serving: 36 | Prep: 15mins | Cook: 8mins | Ready in:

Ingredients

- 6 cups all-purpose flour
- 1 teaspoon baking soda
- 1/2 teaspoon baking powder
- 1 1/2 teaspoons salt
- 4 teaspoons ground ginger
- 4 teaspoons ground cinnamon
- 1 1/2 teaspoons ground cloves
- 1 teaspoon ground black pepper
- 1 cup unsalted butter, softened
- 1 cup packed brown sugar
- 2 eggs
- 1 cup unsulfured molasses

Direction

- Sift together the baking powder, baking soda, flour, black pepper, salt, ginger, cinnamon, and cloves; put aside. Cream together the sugar and butter in a big bowl, or using a stand mixer attached with the paddle. Mix until smooth. Blend in the eggs one at a time, then mix in the molasses. Blend in the sifted ingredients moderately. Split the dough into three equal parts and use plastic wrap to wrap them. Leave in the fridge for at least 60 minutes.
- Set the oven at 175 degrees C (350 degrees F) to preheat.
- Lightly dust flour on a flat surface to roll the dough out until it becomes 1/8 inch thick. Using cookie cutters, cut out the dough into wanted shapes. Lay cookies 1 1/2 inches from each other onto baking sheets.
- Bake in the preheated oven to for 8 to 10 minutes, or until cookies are baked into a light crisp. Transfer cookies onto wire racks to cool thoroughly. Decorated as you wish.

Nutrition Information

- Calories: 176 calories;
- Cholesterol: 24
- Protein: 2.6
- Total Fat: 5.6
- Sodium: 147
- Total Carbohydrate: 29.2

247. Basic Sugar Cookies Tried And True Since 1960

Serving: 48 | Prep: 30mins | Cook: 15mins | Ready in:

Ingredients

- 3 cups self-rising flour
- 1 cup butter at room temperature
- 1 cup white sugar, or more to taste
- 2 eggs at room temperature
- 1 1/2 teaspoons vanilla extract
- 1/4 teaspoon salt

Direction

- In a bowl, mix thoroughly the sugar, salt, vanilla extract, butter, self-rising flour, and eggs. Whisk the mixture for at least 5 minutes. Store the dough inside the refrigerator for at least 2 hours to overnight.
- Set the oven to 275°F (135°C) for preheating.
- Using a lightly floured rolling pin, roll the dough out onto a floured work surface. Use

cutters to cut out cookies. Arrange the cookies into the baking sheets.
- Let it bake inside the preheated oven for about 15 minutes until the bottoms of the cookies are lightly golden brown.

Nutrition Information

- Calories: 81 calories;
- Sodium: 141
- Total Carbohydrate: 10
- Cholesterol: 18
- Protein: 1.1
- Total Fat: 4.1

248. Belgian Christmas Cookies

Serving: 30 | Prep: 20mins | Cook: 10mins | Ready in:

Ingredients

- 2/3 cup butter
- 1 teaspoon almond extract
- 1 cup packed brown sugar
- 2 eggs
- 1 2/3 cups all-purpose flour
- 1 1/2 teaspoons baking powder
- 1/2 teaspoon salt
- 1/2 cup finely chopped blanched almonds
- 1/2 teaspoon ground cinnamon
- 2 teaspoons red decorator sugar
- 2 teaspoons green decorator sugar

Direction

- Turn on the oven to 375°F (190°C) to preheat.
- Cream together brown sugar and butter in a large bowl. Put in one egg at a time, beating thoroughly after each addition. Mix in almond extract. Run salt, baking powder and flour through a sieve; mix into the creamed mixture until well-combined. Transfer to a greased 15x10x1 inch jelly roll pan; spread out to edges evenly.
- Use a mixture of cinnamon and almonds to sprinkle over batter; use a mixture of green and red sugars to sprinkle.
- Put into the oven to bake until the edges begin to loosen from the pan sides, 10-12 minutes. Slice into bars while it is still warm.

Nutrition Information

- Calories: 111 calories;
- Sodium: 100
- Total Carbohydrate: 13.7
- Cholesterol: 23
- Protein: 1.7
- Total Fat: 5.7

249. Best Chocolate Chip Cookies

Serving: 24 | Prep: 20mins | Cook: 10mins | Ready in:

Ingredients

- 1 cup butter, softened
- 1 cup white sugar
- 1 cup packed brown sugar
- 2 eggs
- 2 teaspoons vanilla extract
- 1 teaspoon baking soda
- 2 teaspoons hot water
- 1/2 teaspoon salt
- 3 cups all-purpose flour
- 2 cups semisweet chocolate chips
- 1 cup chopped walnuts

Direction

- Set the oven to 175°C or 350°F to preheat.
- Cream brown sugar, white sugar and butter together until the mixture is smooth. Beat in 1 egg at a time and then stir in vanilla. Dissolve in hot water the baking soda. Put into the

batter together with salt. Stir in chocolate chips, nuts and flour. Drop on grease-free pans with big spoonfuls of dough.
- In the preheated oven, bake until edges are browned beautifully, about 10 minutes.

Nutrition Information

- Calories: 298 calories;
- Total Carbohydrate: 38.8
- Cholesterol: 36
- Protein: 3.6
- Total Fat: 15.6
- Sodium: 166

250. Beth's Spicy Oatmeal Raisin Cookies

Serving: 36 | Prep: 15mins | Cook: 12mins | Ready in:

Ingredients

- 1/2 cup butter, softened
- 1/2 cup butter flavored shortening
- 1 cup packed light brown sugar
- 1/2 cup white sugar
- 2 eggs
- 1 teaspoon vanilla extract
- 1 1/2 cups all-purpose flour
- 1 teaspoon baking soda
- 1 teaspoon ground cinnamon
- 1/2 teaspoon ground cloves
- 1/2 teaspoon salt
- 3 cups rolled oats
- 1 cup raisins

Direction

- Set oven to 350°F (175°C), and start preheating.
- In a large bowl, cream vanilla, eggs, white sugar, brown sugar, butter flavored shortening and butter together until smooth. Mix salt, cloves, cinnamon, baking soda and flour into the sugar mixture. Add in raisins and oats; stirring. Drop the mixture by rounded teaspoonfuls onto clean and dry cookie sheets.
- Bake in the oven for 10 - 12 minutes until golden and light. Make sure not to overbake. Allow to cool for 2 minutes before taking out of cookie sheets for cooling completely. Place in an airtight container. The cookies cannot last too long.

Nutrition Information

- Calories: 144 calories;
- Total Fat: 6.3
- Sodium: 92
- Total Carbohydrate: 20.6
- Cholesterol: 17
- Protein: 1.9

251. Betty's Sugar Cookies

Serving: 48 | Prep: 15mins | Cook: 30mins | Ready in:

Ingredients

- 1 cup shortening
- 1/2 cup white sugar
- 1/2 cup brown sugar
- 2 eggs
- 1 1/2 teaspoons vanilla extract
- 2 1/4 cups all-purpose flour
- 1/2 teaspoon baking soda
- 1/2 teaspoon salt
- 1/4 cup colored sugar for decoration

Direction

- Heat the oven to 175 ° C or 350 ° F. Oil cookie sheets.
- Cream white sugar, brown sugar and shortening in a big bowl till smooth. Whip in eggs, one by one then mix in vanilla. Mix baking soda, salt and flour; mix to creamed mixture. Form dough into balls of 1/2-inch

and arrange them an-inch away on prepped cookie sheets. Press every ball a bit into flatten and scatter colored sugar over.
- Bake in prepped oven, about 8 to 10 minutes. Cool cookies for 5 minutes on baking sheet then transfer onto wire rack and fully cool.

Nutrition Information

- Calories: 80 calories;
- Protein: 0.9
- Total Fat: 4.5
- Sodium: 41
- Total Carbohydrate: 9.1
- Cholesterol: 8

252. Betz's Good Sugar Cookies

Serving: 48 | Prep: 20mins | Cook: 10mins | Ready in:

Ingredients

- 1 cup butter
- 1 1/2 cups white sugar
- 2 eggs
- 1 teaspoon vanilla extract
- 1 teaspoon lemon extract
- 2 cups all-purpose flour
- 1 teaspoon baking powder
- 1 pinch salt

Direction

- Cream sugar and butter together in a big bowl until fluffy. Whisk in the eggs, 1 egg each time, and then mix in lemon extracts and vanilla extracts. Mix salt, baking powder, and flour together; slowly mix into the creamed mixture to make a soft dough. Wrap or cover the dough, and chill overnight.
- Start preheating the oven to 400°F (200°C). On a surface scattered with flour, roll the dough into 1/4 inch thick. Use a cookie cutter to cut into the wanted shapes. Put the cookies on non-oiled cookie sheets 2" apart.
- Put in the preheated oven and bake until turning light brown, about 10 minutes. Put on wire racks to cool.

Nutrition Information

- Calories: 81 calories;
- Protein: 0.8
- Total Fat: 4.1
- Sodium: 40
- Total Carbohydrate: 10.3
- Cholesterol: 18

253. Big Soft Ginger Cookies

Serving: 24 | Prep: 15mins | Cook: 10mins | Ready in:

Ingredients

- 2 1/4 cups all-purpose flour
- 2 teaspoons ground ginger
- 1 teaspoon baking soda
- 3/4 teaspoon ground cinnamon
- 1/2 teaspoon ground cloves
- 1/4 teaspoon salt
- 3/4 cup margarine, softened
- 1 cup white sugar
- 1 egg
- 1 tablespoon water
- 1/4 cup molasses
- 2 tablespoons white sugar

Direction

- Preheat an oven to 175°C/350°F. Sift salt, cloves, cinnamon, baking soda, ginger and flour; put aside.
- Cream 1 cup sugar and margarine till fluffy and light in a big bowl; beat in egg. Mix in molasses and water. Mix sifted ingredients slowly into the molasses mixture. Form dough to walnut-sized balls; roll in leftover 2 tbsp.

sugar. Put cookies onto ungreased cookie sheet, 2-in. apart; slightly flatten.
- In the preheated oven, bake for 8-10 minutes; cool cookies for 5 minutes on a baking sheet. Transfer to a wire rack; fully cool. Keep in airtight container.

Nutrition Information

- Calories: 143 calories;
- Total Fat: 6
- Sodium: 147
- Total Carbohydrate: 21.1
- Cholesterol: 8
- Protein: 1.6

254. Biscotti

Serving: 42 | Prep: 15mins | Cook: 25mins | Ready in:

Ingredients

- 1/2 cup vegetable oil
- 1 cup white sugar
- 3 1/4 cups all-purpose flour
- 3 eggs
- 1 tablespoon baking powder
- 1 tablespoon anise extract, or 3 drops anise oil

Direction

- Set the oven to 375°F (190°C), and start preheating. Coat cookie sheets with oil or line with parchment paper.
- Beat together anise flavoring, sugar, eggs and oil in a medium bowl till well combined. Mix baking powder and flour together, stir into the egg mixture to create a heavy dough. Separate the dough into two pieces. Shape each piece into a roll equaling the length of your cookie sheet. Arrange on the prepped cookie sheet, and press down to the thickness of 1/2 inch.
- Bake in the preheated oven until golden brown, for about 25 to 30 minutes. Take away

from the baking sheet and let it cool on a wire rack. Once the cookies are cool enough to handle, cut each one into slices of 1/2 inch crosswise. On the baking sheet, arrange the slices with cut side up. Bake for 6 - 10 minutes longer per side, until lightly toasted.

Nutrition Information

- Calories: 83 calories;
- Cholesterol: 13
- Protein: 1.4
- Total Fat: 3.1
- Sodium: 40
- Total Carbohydrate: 12.3

255. Black Walnut Balls

Serving: 18 | Prep: | Cook: | Ready in:

Ingredients

- 1 cup butter, softened
- 2 cups sifted all-purpose flour
- 1/4 cup white sugar
- 1/2 teaspoon salt
- 2 teaspoons vanilla extract
- 2 cups chopped black walnuts
- 1/2 cup confectioners' sugar

Direction

- Start preheating the oven to 325°F (170°C).
- Blend vanilla, salt, white sugar, flour, and butter. Put in black walnuts and combine well.
- Form into 1-inch balls. Bake for 25 minutes on an ungreased cookie sheet. Take out of the oven and let cool.
- Roll in powdered sugar. Place flat - not stacked on top of each other to store.

Nutrition Information

- Calories: 252 calories;

- Total Fat: 18.6
- Sodium: 138
- Total Carbohydrate: 18.1
- Cholesterol: 27
- Protein: 4.9

256. Black Walnut Cookies

Serving: 48 | Prep: | Cook: | Ready in:

Ingredients

- 1 cup butter
- 1 cup sifted confectioners' sugar
- 3 tablespoons brandy
- 1 tablespoon vanilla extract
- 2 cups all-purpose flour
- 1/4 teaspoon salt
- 1 cup chopped black walnuts
- 1/8 cup confectioners' sugar

Direction

- Cream a cup confectioners' sugar and butter until fluffy. Mix in vanilla and brandy. Add nuts, salt and flour. Stir well.
- Form dough into 1-inch balls and arrange on an ungreased cookie sheet, 2-inch apart.
- Bake at 165 °C (325 °F) until light brown, about 20 minutes. Dust cookies with confectioner sugar.

Nutrition Information

- Calories: 84 calories;
- Total Carbohydrate: 7.2
- Cholesterol: 10
- Protein: 1.2
- Total Fat: 5.4
- Sodium: 40

257. Blue Ribbon Sugar Cookies

Serving: 48 | Prep: 35mins | Cook: 25mins | Ready in:

Ingredients

- 3/4 cup butter, softened
- 1 cup vegetable oil
- 1 cup confectioners' sugar
- 1 cup white sugar
- 2 eggs
- 1 teaspoon vanilla extract
- 1 1/2 teaspoons lemon extract
- 4 cups all-purpose flour
- 1 teaspoon cream of tartar
- 1 teaspoon baking soda
- 1 teaspoon salt
- 1/2 cup white sugar for decoration

Direction

- Start preheating the oven to 375°F (190 °C). Sift together salt, baking soda, cream of tartar, and flour. Put aside.
- Cream white sugar, confectioners' sugar, oil, and butter together in a big bowl until well mixed. Mix in lemon extracts, vanilla extracts, and eggs. Slowly stir in the dry ingredients until well mixed. Shape the dough into balls about the size of a walnut. Put the cookies on the baking sheet 2" part. Use a sugar-dipped bottom of a glass to flatten the cookies to 1/8 inch thickness. If you don't want to frost the cookies later, you can use colored sugar.
- Put in the preheated oven and bake until the edges turn golden brown, about 9-12 minutes. Let the cookies stay in the baking sheet to cool for 5 minutes, and then transfer to a wire rack to fully cool.

Nutrition Information

- Calories: 141 calories;
- Total Fat: 7.7
- Sodium: 98
- Total Carbohydrate: 16.8

- Cholesterol: 15
- Protein: 1.4

258. Bon Bon Christmas Cookies

Serving: 24 | Prep: | Cook: | Ready in:

Ingredients

- 1/2 (8 ounce) package cream cheese
- 1/2 cup butter flavored shortening
- 2 cups sifted all-purpose flour
- 1 1/2 cups sifted confectioners' sugar
- 2 (10 ounce) jars maraschino cherries, drained

Direction

- Stir cream cheese and shortening together in a medium bowl until they are well blended. Mix in flour, use your hands to help it shape into a dough. Put in a couple teaspoons water, if mixture is too dry. Let it chill with a cover several hours or overnight.
- Start preheating oven to 375°F (190°C). Grease the cookie sheets lightly.
- Heavily dust confectioners' sugar over rolling surface before rolling out the dough. Roll dough out to 1/8 in. thickness. Slice into 1x4 in. strips. Arrange 1 cherry on end of each strip. Roll up each strip beginning with the cherry. Put on the prepared cookie sheets, then dust with a little confectioners' sugar.
- Bake in prepared oven for 7-10 mins. The cookies should slightly brown. Dust with confectioners' sugar again. Let the cookies cool before enjoying, cherries are very hot!

Nutrition Information

- Calories: 151 calories;
- Sodium: 14
- Total Carbohydrate: 22.7
- Cholesterol: 5

- Protein: 1.5
- Total Fat: 6.2

259. Brooke's Best Bombshell Brownies

Serving: 24 | Prep: 15mins | Cook: 35mins | Ready in:

Ingredients

- 1 cup butter, melted
- 3 cups white sugar
- 1 tablespoon vanilla extract
- 4 eggs
- 1 1/2 cups all-purpose flour
- 1 cup unsweetened cocoa powder
- 1 teaspoon salt
- 1 cup semisweet chocolate chips

Direction

- Preheat the oven to 175°C / 350°Fahrenheit. Grease a 9x13-in baking dish lightly.
- In a big bowl, mix vanilla, sugar, and melted butter. Whisk in one egg at a time; mix the egg thoroughly after each addition until well combined.
- In a bowl, sift salt, cocoa powder, and flour; mix flour mixture into the egg mixture gradually until combined. Mix in chocolate morsels. Evenly spread the batter in the greased baking dish.
- Bake for 35-40 minutes in the preheated oven until an inserted toothpick comes out clean. Place pan on a wire rack to cool then slice.

Nutrition Information

- Calories: 248 calories;
- Total Fat: 11.2
- Sodium: 165
- Total Carbohydrate: 37.5
- Cholesterol: 51
- Protein: 2.9

260. Brown Sugar Cookies

Serving: 60 | Prep: 10mins | Cook: 10mins | Ready in:

Ingredients

- 2 cups brown sugar
- 1/2 cup unsalted butter, softened
- 2 large eggs
- 1 teaspoon vanilla extract
- 2 1/2 cups all-purpose flour
- 3/4 teaspoon baking powder
- 1/2 teaspoon salt
- 1 cup confectioners' sugar

Direction

- Set oven to 175°C (or 350°F) and begin preheating.
- In a bowl, cream together vanilla extract, eggs, butter and brown sugar with an electric mixer until creamy and smoothened.
- In another bowl, blend salt, baking powder and flour together. Combine flour mixture with butter mixture to fully incorporate the dough.
- Dust a large plate with confectioners' sugar. Drop dough, 1.5 teaspoons each cookie, over confectioners' sugar layer and roll until coated. Place dough onto a baking sheet.
- Bake in the prepared oven for 12-14 minutes until lightly browned around the edges. Let cookies cool for 2 minutes on baking pan, then cool thoroughly on a wire rack.

Nutrition Information

- Calories: 62 calories;
- Sodium: 30
- Total Carbohydrate: 10.8
- Cholesterol: 10
- Protein: 0.8
- Total Fat: 1.8

261. Brownie Mix In A Jar II

Serving: 24 | Prep: 20mins | Cook: | Ready in:

Ingredients

- 1 1/4 cups all-purpose flour
- 1 teaspoon baking powder
- 1 teaspoon salt
- 2/3 cup unsweetened cocoa powder
- 2 1/4 cups white sugar
- 1/2 cup chopped pecans

Direction

- In a quart jar, combine salt, baking powder and flour. Following the instructed order, layer remaining ingredients into the jar. Press firmly between layers. Note: Make sure to use a dry paper towel to clean the jar's inside after putting in cocoa powder to make other layers visible through the glass.
- Prepare a tag with this instruction and put on the jar: Brownie Mix in a Jar. 1. Set oven to 175°C (350°F) and start preheating. Grease a 9x13-in. baking pan and dust with flour. 2. Transfer the brownie mix from the jar to a big mixing bowl, whisk to combine. Stir in 4 eggs and three-fourths cup melted butter. Stir well. Pour batter equally into prepped baking pan. 3. Bake at 175°C (350°F) for 25-30 minutes. Cool fully in pan and slice into square pieces of 2 inches.

Nutrition Information

- Calories: 118 calories;
- Cholesterol: 0
- Protein: 1.3
- Total Fat: 2
- Sodium: 118
- Total Carbohydrate: 25.4

262. Buckeye Balls II

Serving: 30 | Prep: 45mins | Cook: 10mins | Ready in:

Ingredients

- 1 1/2 cups creamy peanut butter
- 1/2 cup butter, softened
- 1 teaspoon vanilla extract
- 4 cups sifted confectioners' sugar
- 6 ounces semi-sweet chocolate chips
- 2 tablespoons shortening

Direction

- Using waxed paper, line a baking sheet; put aside.
- Mix confectioners' sugar, vanilla, butter and peanut butter in a medium bowl, using hands to shape a smooth stiff dough. Form into balls with 2 teaspoons of dough per ball. Transfer to the lined pan, keep in the fridge.
- In a metal bowl set over a pan of lightly simmering water, melt chocolate and shortening together. Stir occasionally until smooth; take out of the heat.
- Take balls out of the fridge. Insert a wooden toothpick into a ball, and dip into the melted chocolate. Transfer back to wax paper with chocolate side down; get rid of toothpick. Do the same with leftover balls. Keep in the fridge for half an hour to set.

Nutrition Information

- Calories: 204 calories;
- Total Fat: 12
- Sodium: 81
- Total Carbohydrate: 22.8
- Cholesterol: 8
- Protein: 3.7

263. Butter Cookies IV

Serving: 18 | Prep: | Cook: | Ready in:

Ingredients

- 3 cups all-purpose flour
- 1 1/2 teaspoons baking powder
- 1/2 teaspoon salt
- 1 cup white sugar
- 1 cup butter
- 1 egg
- 3 tablespoons cream
- 1 teaspoon vanilla extract
- 2 1/4 ounces colored candy sprinkles

Direction

- Sift together sugar, salt, baking powder and flour, then mash in butter until the mixture looks like coarse crumbs. Stir in vanilla extract, cream and egg, then blend well. Use your hands to do this process best.
- Shape dough into flattened ball, then wrap and chill for a minimum of 24 hours. You can store this mixture for a few days.
- Set the oven to 205°C or 400°F to preheat.
- Roll dough out on a board coated with flour to the thickness of 1/4 -1/8 inch. Use a cookie cutter to cut out shapes and use different types of sprinkles to garnish.
- Bake about 5-8 minutes at 205°C or 400°F.

Nutrition Information

- Calories: 239 calories;
- Total Carbohydrate: 29.8
- Cholesterol: 41
- Protein: 2.7
- Total Fat: 12.3
- Sodium: 184

264. Butter Rich Spritz Butter Cookies

Serving: 36 | Prep: 10mins | Cook: 6mins | Ready in:

Ingredients

- 2 1/2 cups all-purpose flour
- 1/2 teaspoon salt
- 1 cup butter, softened
- 1 1/4 cups confectioners' sugar
- 2 egg yolks
- 1/2 teaspoon almond extract
- 1 teaspoon vanilla extract

Direction

- Preheat oven to 200°C or 400°Fahrenheit. Sift salt and flour together; set aside.
- Cream sugar and butter together in a medium bowl; mix in vanilla extract, almond extract and egg yolks. Mix in the sifted ingredients gradually. Pour dough in a cookie press until full then transfer the cookies on an ungreased cookie sheet, 1 1/2-in apart. Decorate with sprinkles or sugar at this time if desired.
- Bake in the preheated oven for 6-8 minutes.

Nutrition Information

- Calories: 96 calories;
- Protein: 1.1
- Total Fat: 5.4
- Sodium: 69
- Total Carbohydrate: 10.8
- Cholesterol: 25

265. Butter Snow Flakes

Serving: 36 | Prep: 15mins | Cook: 15mins | Ready in:

Ingredients

- 2 1/4 cups all-purpose flour
- 1/4 teaspoon salt
- 1/4 teaspoon ground cinnamon
- 1 cup butter
- 1 (3 ounce) package cream cheese, softened
- 1 cup white sugar
- 1 egg yolk
- 1 teaspoon vanilla extract
- 1 teaspoon orange zest

Direction

- Set an oven to 175°C (350°F) and start preheating. Sift cinnamon, salt, and flour together; then put aside.
- Cream the cream cheese and butter together in a medium bowl. Put in egg yolk and sugar then whisk until fluffy and light. Stir in orange zest and vanilla. Whisk in the dry ingredients gradually. Fill the dough into a pastry bag or cookie press, and on an ungreased cookie sheet, shape into cookies.
- In the prepared oven, bake until the bottoms and peaks of the cookies turn golden brown, or for 12-15 minutes. Take out from the cookie sheets altogether onto wire racks to cool.

Nutrition Information

- Calories: 105 calories;
- Protein: 1.1
- Total Fat: 6.1
- Sodium: 60
- Total Carbohydrate: 11.6
- Cholesterol: 22

266. Butter Tart Shortbread Bars

Serving: 16 | Prep: 15mins | Cook: 45mins | Ready in:

Ingredients

- 7/8 cup butter, softened, or as needed
- 1/4 cup confectioners' sugar
- 2 cups all-purpose flour

- 1/4 teaspoon salt
- 2 eggs
- 1 cup brown sugar
- 3 tablespoons butter, melted
- 1 tablespoon vanilla extract
- 1/2 cup raisins

Direction

- Prepare the oven by preheating to 350°F (175°C).
- In a large bowl, use a spoon to whisk confectioner's sugar and 7/8 cup butter until smooth. Mix in salt and flour. Transfer mixture to a 9-inch square baking pan and press.
- Place in the preheated oven and bake for about 14 minutes until lightly golden. Take off and cool for 10 minutes, keeping the oven on.
- In a bowl, whisk vanilla extract, 3 tablespoons melted butter, brown sugar, and eggs. Dust raisins over the cooled crust; put egg mixture over raisins.
- Place in the preheated oven and bake for about 30 minutes until top bounces back once touched. Cool fully before slicing into bars.

Nutrition Information

- Calories: 249 calories;
- Sodium: 137
- Total Carbohydrate: 31
- Cholesterol: 56
- Protein: 2.7
- Total Fat: 13

267. Candied Christmas Cookies

Serving: 72 | Prep: | Cook: | Ready in:

Ingredients

- 2 eggs
- 1/2 cup butter, softened
- 1 cup brown sugar
- 2 tablespoons orange juice
- 1 tablespoon bourbon
- 1 teaspoon baking soda
- 1 tablespoon milk
- 2 cups all-purpose flour
- 3 cups candied cherries
- 3 cups dates, pitted and chopped
- 4 cups chopped pecans

Direction

- Set oven at 350°F and start preheating. Use cooking spray to coat cookie trays.
- Cream the brown sugar, butter and eggs in a big mixing bowl. Combine the milk with baking soda and add to the mixture. Mix in bourbon and orange juice. Mix candied fruits with a little flour in a small bowl and toss lightly until the fruits can be detached easily. Add to the mixture. Add pecans, dates and flour. Mix until well combined. Divide the mixture into teaspoons and put them 2 inches away from another on the cookie tray.
- Let bake in the preheated oven for 8 to 10 minutes. Let them cool on baking tray for 5 minutes then take to a wire rack and let cool totally.

Nutrition Information

- Calories: 111 calories;
- Protein: 1.3
- Total Fat: 5.8
- Sodium: 34
- Total Carbohydrate: 14.5
- Cholesterol: 9

268. Candied Fruit Biscotti

Serving: 36 | Prep: | Cook: | Ready in:

Ingredients

- 1/2 cup butter
- 2 cups white sugar
- 1 1/2 teaspoons anise extract
- 6 egg
- 5 cups all-purpose flour
- 1 tablespoon baking powder
- 1/2 teaspoon salt
- 1 1/3 cups diced mixed candied fruit

Direction

- Beat together sugar and butter in a large bowl. Stir in anise extract and eggs. Put salt, baking powder and flour through a sieve; combine into the egg mixture. Mix in candied fruit. Put the dough into the refrigerator for 1 hour.
- Turn on the oven to 325°F (165°C) to preheat. Cut dough into 4 even portions. Roll each into 12-inch long log. On each cookie sheet, arrange 2 logs. Slightly press down; put into the oven to bake for 25-30 minutes.
- Take out of the oven; allow to cool for 5 minutes on the pans. Cut diagonally into slices of 1/2-inch thick. On baking sheet, arrange slices, cut side down and put back into the oven to bake until toasted lightly or for 16-18 minutes more. Remove to racks to cool; put into containers to store.

Nutrition Information

- Calories: 162 calories;
- Protein: 2.9
- Total Fat: 3.6
- Sodium: 103
- Total Carbohydrate: 29.9
- Cholesterol: 38

269. Candy Cane Cookies III

Serving: 48 | Prep: 25mins | Cook: 9mins | Ready in:

Ingredients

- 1 cup margarine
- 1/2 cup white sugar
- 1/2 cup confectioners' sugar
- 1 egg
- 1 teaspoon vanilla extract
- 1/2 teaspoon peppermint extract
- 2 1/2 cups all-purpose flour
- 1/2 teaspoon salt
- 1/2 teaspoon red food coloring
- 1/2 cup peppermint candy canes, crushed
- 1/2 cup white sugar for decoration

Direction

- Cream together the confectioners' sugar, white sugar, and margarine in a big bowl. Whisk in peppermint extracts, vanilla, and egg. Mix together salt and flour, mix into the creamed mixture until fully combined. Wrap or cover the dough and refrigerate for no less than 60 minutes.
- Turn the oven to 375°F (190°C) to preheat. Coat the baking sheets with oil. Split the dough into 2 portions. Blend 1 portion with the red food coloring to color. Roll a little of each dough into a long worm, about 2-inch. Make a twisted rope by rolling them together and bend the end to resemble a cane. Put on the prepared baking sheets.
- Bake in the preheated oven for 8-10 minutes. Combine the leftover white sugar and crushed candy cane in a small bowl. In the sugar mixture, put the hot cookies and roll.

Nutrition Information

- Calories: 90 calories;
- Total Fat: 3.9
- Sodium: 71
- Total Carbohydrate: 12.9
- Cholesterol: 4
- Protein: 0.8

270. Candy Cane Hot Chocolate Cookies

Serving: 60 | Prep: 15mins | Cook: 10mins | Ready in:

Ingredients

- 2 cups white sugar
- 1 cup butter, softened
- 2 eggs
- 1 teaspoon vanilla extract
- 1 teaspoon almond extract
- 2 cups all-purpose flour
- 3/4 cup hot chocolate mix (such as Carnation® Rich and Creamy)
- 1 teaspoon baking soda
- 1/2 teaspoon salt
- 1 2/3 cups chopped white chocolate
- 12 peppermint candy canes, crushed
- 1 (10.5 ounce) package miniature marshmallows

Direction

- Preheat an oven to 175°C/350°F.
- Use electric mixer to beat butter and sugar till creamy and smooth in bow; one by one, beat eggs in till incorporated. Mix almond extract and vanilla extract into butter mixture.
- Whisk salt, baking soda, hot chocolate mix and flour in another bowl; mix into butter mixture till dough is smooth. Fold white chocolate into dough then drop rounded dough teaspoonfuls on baking sheets, 2-in. apart. Sprinkle crushed candy canes generously on cookie dough.
- In preheated oven, bake for 8-10 minutes till cookie edges are slightly crisp. Put marshmallows on hot cookies immediately; cool till set on baking sheets. Put cookies on wire racks; completely cool.

Nutrition Information

- Calories: 143 calories;
- Protein: 1.1
- Total Fat: 4.9
- Sodium: 85
- Total Carbohydrate: 23.7
- Cholesterol: 15

271. Caramel Brownies

Serving: 24 | Prep: | Cook: | Ready in:

Ingredients

- 1 (18.25 ounce) package German chocolate cake mix with pudding
- 3/4 cup melted butter
- 1/3 cup evaporated milk
- 1 cup chopped pecans
- 13 ounces individually wrapped caramels, unwrapped
- 1/3 cup evaporated milk
- 1 cup semi-sweet chocolate chips

Direction

- Set oven to 350°F (175°C) to preheat. Grease a 9x13-inch pan with non-stick cooking spray.
- Stir a third cup evaporated milk, butter and cake mix. Stir thoroughly and put two thirds of the mixture into the pan.
- Push pecans into mixture and bake for 8-10 minutes.
- Mix 1/3 cup evaporated milk and the caramel in a saucepan over medium heat. Mix until melted and smooth; put on top of the rested cake mix.
- Scatter chocolate chips over the caramel and garnish with spoonful of leftover cake mix. Bake for 15 to 18 minutes more; let cool and slice.

Nutrition Information

- Calories: 269 calories;
- Total Carbohydrate: 34.9
- Cholesterol: 18
- Protein: 3.1
- Total Fat: 14

- Sodium: 244
- Total Carbohydrate: 27.1
- Cholesterol: 34
- Protein: 3.5

272. Caramel Cashew Brownies

Serving: 16 | Prep: 15mins | Cook: 30mins | Ready in:

Ingredients

- 18 caramels
- 1/3 cup butter
- 2 tablespoons milk
- 3/4 cup white sugar
- 2 eggs
- 1/2 teaspoon vanilla extract
- 1 cup all-purpose flour
- 1/2 teaspoon baking powder
- 1/4 teaspoon salt
- 1 cup chopped salted cashews

Direction

- Preheat the oven to 175°C or 350°F. Grease a square pan with 9 inches in size.
- In a big saucepan, cook over low heat and mix together milk, butter and caramels for 5 minutes till smooth and melted. Take off saucepan from heat and mix sugar into mixture till smooth.
- In a bowl, beat together vanilla extract and eggs; mix into caramel mixture.
- In a bowl, combine salt, baking powder and flour together; mix into caramel mixture till batter is just blended. Fold cashews into batter. Pour batter in the prepped pan.
- In the preheated oven, bake for 25 minutes till a toothpick pricked in the middle comes out clean.

Nutrition Information

- Calories: 202 calories;
- Total Fat: 9.5
- Sodium: 171

273. Caramel Filled Chocolate Cookies

Serving: 24 | Prep: 20mins | Cook: 10mins | Ready in:

Ingredients

- 1 cup butter, softened
- 1 cup white sugar
- 1 cup packed brown sugar
- 2 eggs
- 2 teaspoons vanilla extract
- 2 1/4 cups all-purpose flour
- 1 teaspoon baking soda
- 3/4 cup unsweetened cocoa powder
- 1 cup chopped walnuts
- 1 tablespoon white sugar
- 48 chocolate-covered caramel candies

Direction

- Whip butter till creamy. Slowly whip in brown sugar and white sugar. Whip in vanilla and eggs. Mix baking soda, cocoa and flour. Slowly put into mixture of butter, whipping thoroughly. Mix in a half cup of walnuts. Refrigerate with a cover for no less than 2 hours.
- Preheat the oven to 190 ° C or 375 ° F.
- Mix a tablespoon of sugar and leftover half cup of nuts. Split dough into 4 portions. Work one by one, keeping the rest refrigerated till needed. Split each part into a dozen pieces. Immediately press each dough piece around a chocolate covered caramel. Form into a ball. Dip tops in sugar mixture. Put 2-inch apart on baking sheets that is greased, sugar side facing up.
- Bake in the prepped oven for 8 minutes. Cool on baking sheets for 3 to 4 minutes prior to transferring to wire racks to fully cool.

Nutrition Information

- Calories: 253 calories;
- Cholesterol: 37
- Protein: 3.4
- Total Fat: 13
- Sodium: 128
- Total Carbohydrate: 33.1

274. Caramel Shortbread Squares

Serving: 40 | Prep: 10mins | Cook: 25mins | Ready in:

Ingredients

- 2/3 cup butter, softened
- 1/4 cup white sugar
- 1 1/4 cups all-purpose flour
- 1/2 cup butter
- 1/2 cup packed light brown sugar
- 2 tablespoons light corn syrup
- 1/2 cup sweetened condensed milk
- 1 1/4 cups milk chocolate chips

Direction

- Preheat the oven to 175°C or 350°F.
- Combine white sugar, flour and 2/3 cup butter in medium-sized bowl till crumbly evenly. Force into one square baking pan, 9-inch in size. Bake for 20 minutes.
- Mix sweetened condensed milk, corn syrup, brown sugar and half a cup of butter in a saucepan, 2-quart in size. Boil. Keep boiling for 5 minutes. Take off from heat and use a wooden spoon to whip vigorously for about 3 minutes. Add on cool or warm baked crust. Cool till it starts to firm.
- In microwavable bowl, add the chocolate. Allow to heat for one minute, then mix and keep heating and mixing at 20 second intervals till chocolate melts and smooth. Top caramel layer with chocolate and evenly smear to fully cover. Refrigerate. Slice into an-inch squares. These have to be in small portions because they are very rich.

Nutrition Information

- Calories: 119 calories;
- Sodium: 44
- Total Carbohydrate: 13.2
- Cholesterol: 17
- Protein: 1.1
- Total Fat: 7.3

275. Cheesecake Topped Brownies

Serving: 40 | Prep: 20mins | Cook: 45mins | Ready in:

Ingredients

- 1 (21.5 ounce) package brownie mix
- 1 (8 ounce) package cream cheese, softened
- 2 tablespoons butter, softened
- 1 tablespoon cornstarch
- 1 (14 ounce) can sweetened condensed milk
- 1 egg
- 1 teaspoon vanilla extract
- 1 (16 ounce) container prepared chocolate frosting

Direction

- Set oven to 175°C (or 350°F) and start preheating. Prepare a 9x13" baking pan coated with grease.
- Follow the package instructions in preparing brownie mix. Transfer to greased baking pan.
- Whip cornstarch, butter and cream cheese until fluffy in a medium bowl. Slowly beat in vanilla, egg and sweetened condensed milk until smoothened. Spread cream cheese evenly onto brownie batter.

- Bake for 45 minutes in prepared oven until top is browned a little. Cool, frost, and slice into bars. Cover and refrigerate, or arrange in 1 layer and put in the freezer for 2 weeks maximum.

Nutrition Information

- Calories: 170 calories;
- Total Carbohydrate: 24.4
- Cholesterol: 16
- Protein: 2.1
- Total Fat: 7.7
- Sodium: 102

276. Chef John's Almond Biscotti

Serving: 15 | Prep: 15mins | Cook: 1hours | Ready in:

Ingredients

- 2 cups all-purpose flour
- 1 teaspoon baking powder
- 1/4 teaspoon fine salt
- 3 tablespoons unsalted butter, room temperature
- 1 cup white sugar
- 1 tablespoon white sugar
- 1 tablespoon olive oil
- 2 large eggs
- 1/4 teaspoon vanilla extract
- 3/4 teaspoon almond extract
- 1/2 cup whole roasted almonds
- 1/2 cup chopped roasted almonds

Direction

- In a mixing bowl, stir salt, baking powder, and flour together.
- In another mixing bowl, put olive oil, a cup plus a tablespoon sugar and butter. Stir together well until mixture is creamy. Put in 1 egg; stir into butter and sugar mixture. Beat in almond extract, vanilla extract, and another egg; beat until smooth. Put in flour mixture. Stir until flour is combined. Put in whole and chopped almonds; stir in evenly. Cover the bowl using plastic wrap; chill for half an hour.
- Set oven to 350°F (175°C) to preheat. Line a rimmed baking sheet using a silicone mat.
- Split dough in half. Put each half on a length of plastic wrap and form into a log. Wrap using the plastic wrap and press into a shape about 1/2-inch-high and about 3 or 4 inches wide. Place both pieces onto prepared baking sheet, leaving about 3 or 4 inches among them for spreading.
- Bake in the middle of prepared oven for about 30 minutes until golden and an inserted toothpick exists clean from the middle. Cool 15 minutes before cutting.
- Turn down oven temperature to 325°F (165°C).
- Slice each piece into 1/2- to 1-inch thick slices at a slight angle using a serrated knife. Place pieces back to baking sheet in a layer. Bake 12 minutes; take out from oven and turn pieces over. Put the pan back to oven and bake for about 20 minutes until crunchy and golden brown.
- Place biscotti to a cooling rack; cool to room temperature.

Nutrition Information

- Calories: 200 calories;
- Total Fat: 8
- Sodium: 81
- Total Carbohydrate: 28.6
- Cholesterol: 31
- Protein: 4.3

277. Cherry Bell Cookies

Serving: 30 | Prep: | Cook: | Ready in:

Ingredients

- 3 cups all-purpose flour
- 1/2 teaspoon baking soda
- 1/2 teaspoon salt
- 1 teaspoon ground ginger
- 1/2 teaspoon instant coffee granules
- 1 cup butter
- 1 1/4 cups packed brown sugar
- 1/4 cup dark corn syrup
- 1 egg, beaten
- 1 tablespoon cream
- 1/3 cup packed brown sugar
- 1 tablespoon butter
- 3 tablespoons cherry juice
- 1 1/2 cups chopped walnuts
- 60 maraschino cherries, halved

Direction

- Sift together 1/2 teaspoon instant coffee, 1 teaspoon ginger, 1/2 teaspoon salt, 1/2 teaspoon baking soda, and 3 cups flour. Set aside.
- Cream 1 cup margarine or butter. Add 1 1/4 cups brown sugar. Cream thoroughly. Mix in cream, egg, and dark corn syrup. Add the dry ingredients and stir thoroughly.
- On a board scattered with flour, roll the dough out, 1/3 at a time, until having a 1/8-in. thickness. Slice the cookies into rounds, about 2 1/2-in. each. Put on a non-oiled cookie sheet.
- For the filling: mix together 3 tablespoons cherry juice, 1 tablespoon butter, and 1/3 firmly packed brown sugar. Mix in 1 1/2 cups finely chopped nuts.
- In the middle of each round, put 1/2 teaspoon filling. With a spatula, fold the sides of dough over the filling to form a bell shape. Make the bell top smaller than at the clapper end. To make the clapper, put 1/2 of a maraschino cherry at the open end of each bell with the cut-side down. Bake for 12-15 minutes at 350° F.

Nutrition Information

- Calories: 214 calories;
- Sodium: 117
- Total Carbohydrate: 28.1
- Cholesterol: 24
- Protein: 2.5
- Total Fat: 10.8

278. Cherry Mash Bars

Serving: 16 | Prep: 30mins | Cook: 30mins | Ready in:

Ingredients

- 2 tablespoons butter
- 1 cup white sugar
- 1/4 teaspoon salt
- 1/3 cup half-and-half cream
- 1 cup miniature marshmallows
- 1 cup cherry baking chips
- 1 cup semisweet chocolate chips
- 1/2 cup peanut butter
- 1 cup roasted Spanish peanuts

Direction

- Line waxed paper in an 8x8 or 9x9-in. square pan.
- Put half and half, salt, sugar and butter in a medium saucepan. Heat until it boils, occasionally stirring. Boil, stirring it enough to avoid scorching, for 5 minutes. Take off heat. Mix in cherry chips and marshmallows. Press mixture into prepped pan.
- In the microwave/metal bowl above a pan with simmer water, melt peanut butter and chocolate chips together, frequently mixing until smooth. Spread on top of mixture in pan. Keep in fridge for 2 hours then cut to squares.

Nutrition Information

- Calories: 286 calories;
- Cholesterol: 6
- Protein: 5.9
- Total Fat: 16.5

- Sodium: 130
- Total Carbohydrate: 32.1

279. Cherry Nanaimo Bars

Serving: 36 | Prep: 30mins | Cook: 10mins | Ready in:

Ingredients

- Bottom Layer:
- 1/2 cup butter
- 1/4 cup white sugar
- 1/3 cup unsweetened cocoa powder
- 1 egg, lightly beaten
- 1 3/4 cups graham cracker crumbs
- 1/2 cup shredded coconut
- 1/3 cup finely chopped walnuts
- Middle Layer:
- 1/4 cup butter, softened
- 2 cups confectioners' sugar
- 2 tablespoons maraschino cherry juice
- 1 teaspoon almond extract
- 1/3 cup chopped maraschino cherries, well drained
- Top Layer:
- 1 tablespoon butter
- 1/3 cup semisweet chocolate chips

Direction

- In a saucepan over medium heat, heat cocoa powder, white sugar, and 1/2 cup butter; cook, stirring, approximately 2 minutes, until butter is melted. Turn off the heat; whisk in beaten egg. Place the pan back onto the stove; cook, stirring, approximately 3 minutes, until slightly thickened. Put the saucepan off the heat.
- Whisk walnuts, coconut, and graham cracker crumbs into cocoa mixture. Pat mixture firmly into an unoiled 9-inch square baking pan.
- In a bowl, beat 1/4 cup butter with almond extract, cherry juice, and confectioners' sugar using an electric mixer until no lumps remain; mix in cherries. Drop cherry mixture over the base layer by spoonfuls, spreading evenly. Allow to sit for approximately 10 minutes or until cherry mixture is slightly set. Pat the cherry mixture layer until smooth using your hand.
- Melt 1 tablespoon butter over low heat in a small saucepan; mix in chocolate chips. Cook, stirring, approximately 3 minutes, until mixture is melted and smooth. Pour chocolate mixture over the cherry mixture layer. Quickly smoothen the chocolate layer using the back of a spoon. Refrigerate for about half an hour; cut into bars to serve.

Nutrition Information

- Calories: 118 calories;
- Total Carbohydrate: 14.3
- Cholesterol: 16
- Protein: 1
- Total Fat: 6.8
- Sodium: 57

280. Cherry Poppyseed Twinks

Serving: 30 | Prep: 25mins | Cook: 15mins | Ready in:

Ingredients

- 1 cup butter, softened
- 1 cup confectioners' sugar
- 1 egg
- 1 teaspoon vanilla extract
- 2 cups all-purpose flour
- 1/2 teaspoon salt
- 2 tablespoons poppy seeds
- 1/2 cup cherry preserves

Direction

- Preheat the oven to 150 degrees C/300 degrees F.

- Cream confectioners' sugar and butter together until fluffy and light. Beat vanilla and egg in. Mix in poppy seeds, salt and flour until blended well. From a teaspoon, drop dough on an ungreased cookie sheet. Create an indention in the center of every cookie using your finger. If it's too sticky, dip your finger in some water first. Fill every hole with 1/2 tsp. cherry preserves.
- Bake for 20-25 minutes in preheated oven until edges start to brown.

Nutrition Information

- Calories: 121 calories;
- Sodium: 86
- Total Carbohydrate: 14.5
- Cholesterol: 22
- Protein: 1.3
- Total Fat: 6.6

281. Cherry Shortbread Cookies

Serving: 12 | Prep: | Cook: | Ready in:

Ingredients

- 1 cup all-purpose flour
- 1/2 cup confectioners' sugar
- 1/2 cup cornstarch
- 1/2 cup chopped cherries
- 1 cup butter

Direction

- Start preheating the oven to 300°F (150°C).
- Cream together confectioners' sugar and butter. Add flour and cornstarch and stir thoroughly. Mix in chopped cherries. Drop the dough onto a baking sheet by teaspoonfuls, and then use the tines of a floured fork to press.
- Bake at 300°F (150°C) for 10-15 minutes, or until turning light brown.

Nutrition Information

- Calories: 218 calories;
- Total Carbohydrate: 18.8
- Cholesterol: 41
- Protein: 1.3
- Total Fat: 15.5
- Sodium: 110

282. Cherry Almond Icebox Cookies

Serving: 24 | Prep: 15mins | Cook: 20mins | Ready in:

Ingredients

- 1 cup butter, softened
- 1 cup brown sugar
- 2 cups all-purpose flour
- 1/2 cup sliced blanched almonds
- 1/2 cup chopped red candied cherries
- 2 ounces white chocolate (optional)

Direction

- Start preheating the oven to 350°F (175°C). Line parchment paper on sides and bottom of the 11-by 7-in. glass baking pan; leave the paper hanging over edges of pan so after baking, cookies can be lifted out.
- Using an electric mixer, beat together brown sugar and butter for approximately 2 mins or until fluffy and light. Stir the flour into the butter mixture till crumbly; then stir in cherries and almonds. Evenly press the mixture into prepared pan bottom.
- Bake in prepared oven for around 20 mins, until the edges are lightly golden. Use a sharp knife to score into bars while still warm and in pan; let cookies cool for approximately half an

hour. Then lift the cookies from the pan; then slice to divide along scored marks.
- In a ceramic or microwave-safe glass bowl, melt white chocolate in 30-sec intervals, for 1-3 mins (depending on microwave), stirring before melting the next one. Don't overheat or the chocolate will scorch. Then drizzle on top of the cookies with melted white chocolate or submerge 1/2 of each cookie into the melted white chocolate.

Nutrition Information

- Calories: 175 calories;
- Total Fat: 9.7
- Sodium: 62
- Total Carbohydrate: 21
- Cholesterol: 21
- Protein: 1.8

283. Chewy Chocolate Cookies I

Serving: 48 | Prep: 15mins | Cook: 10mins | Ready in:

Ingredients

- 1 1/4 cups butter, softened
- 2 cups white sugar
- 2 eggs
- 2 teaspoons vanilla extract
- 2 cups all-purpose flour
- 3/4 cup unsweetened cocoa powder
- 1 teaspoon baking soda
- 1/2 teaspoon salt
- 2 cups semisweet chocolate chips

Direction

- Set the oven to 175°C or 350°F to preheat.
- Cream sugar and butter together in a big bowl until fluffy and light. Beat in 1 egg at a time then stir in vanilla. Sift salt, baking soda, cocoa and flour together then stir flour mixture into creamed mixture. Fold in chocolate chips. Drop onto grease-free cookie sheets with teaspoonfuls of dough.
- In the preheated oven, bake for about 8-9 minutes. Cookies will be soft. Allow to cool a bit on cookie sheet then transfer to wire rack to cool thoroughly.

Nutrition Information

- Calories: 134 calories;
- Total Fat: 7.3
- Sodium: 89
- Total Carbohydrate: 17.5
- Cholesterol: 20
- Protein: 1.4

284. Chewy White Chocolate Chip Gingerbread Cookies

Serving: 24 | Prep: 20mins | Cook: 10mins | Ready in:

Ingredients

- 3/4 cup butter
- 1 cup white sugar
- 1 beaten egg
- 1/4 cup molasses
- 2 cups all-purpose flour
- 2 teaspoons baking soda
- 1 teaspoon ground ginger
- 1 teaspoon ground cinnamon
- 1/2 teaspoon ground cloves
- 1/2 teaspoon nutmeg
- 1/2 teaspoon salt
- 1 (12 ounce) package white chocolate chips
- 1/2 cup white sugar, for rolling

Direction

- Whisk the butter and 1 cup sugar together into a mixing bowl until smooth. Beat in the molasses and egg. Stir the baking soda, ginger, cloves, salt, flour, cinnamon, and nutmeg

together into a separate bowl. Combine into the molasses mixture half cupful at a time. Beat in white chocolate chips. Keep the dough into the refrigerator, 1 hour.
- Heat oven to 350°F (175°C).
- Spoon a large spoonful amount of dough and shape dough to form a ball. Roll the dough ball over the sugar and put into the unprepared baking pans. Flatten the balls slightly. Season a little amount of sugar on the cookies, if preferred. Do again with the remaining cookies.
- Place into the heated oven and bake until cookies turn to lightly brown for 10-15 minutes. Cool cookies on the baking pan, 1 minute. Transfer into the racks for complete cooling.

Nutrition Information

- Calories: 231 calories;
- Cholesterol: 26
- Protein: 2.4
- Total Fat: 11.1
- Sodium: 214
- Total Carbohydrate: 31.2

285. Children's Gingerbread House

Serving: 15 | Prep: | Cook: | Ready in:

Ingredients

- 3/4 cup butter
- 7/8 cup packed light brown sugar
- 1 teaspoon lemon zest
- 1 1/2 tablespoons lemon juice
- 1/2 cup molasses
- 2 eggs
- 3 cups all-purpose flour
- 2 teaspoons baking powder
- 1 tablespoon ground ginger
- 2 teaspoons ground allspice
- 6 egg whites
- 4 (16 ounce) packages confectioners' sugar, sifted

Direction

- First Template on thin cardboard: Cut out 4 1/2 by 8 inches for the side wall; 4 1/2 by 5 inches for the end wall; 4 1/2 by 3 by 3 inches for the triangular gable; and 4 1/2 by 9 inches for the rectangle roof. Tape the end wall rectangle piece into the gable triangle piece. Align 4 1/2 inches, the triangle's long side into one of the end wall sides, 4 1/2 inches.
- Whisk sugar and butter into a big bowl until mixture is fluffy and light. Beat in the lemon juice, molasses, and lemon zest. Slowly stir in 2 pieces of eggs. Sieve together the baking powder, spices, and flour. Beat flour mixture into the butter mixture to form the dough. Use parchment paper to wrap the dough and keep in the refrigerator, 1 hour.
- On a lightly floured working surface, roll the dough out to 6 pieces with the 2 pieces bigger than others. Roll the 4 smaller pieces out on the lightly floured working surface into a size same with the side and end wall using the gable patterns. Cut two of each out. Roll the rest of the dough out and cut out to 2 pieces of roof rectangles. Place the pieces into the greased baking pans.
- In heated oven to 375°F (190°C), bake until gingerbread is crisp, 10 minutes. Allow gingerbread to set for several minutes in the pan before transferring into the wire racks. Set aside overnight to get hard.
- Beat the 2 pieces of egg whites into a big bowl lightly. Gently stir in 5 cups of confectioner's sugar. Icing must be smooth and form firm peaks. On the cake board, pipe 9-inch line using the icing and push in one piece of the side walls to firmly adhere and stands vertically. Add a small amount of additional icing on both sides to strengthen it. Take the end wall and ice of both side corners. On the board. Pipe a line using the icing at the right angle from the first wall, pushing in the end

wall into place. Do again the instructions with the remaining 2 walls until all are in place. For 2 hours, let walls stand together until they harden. Place over the roof. Pipe a thick line using the icing at each wall's top, fixing pieces of the roof in place. The roof must overlap walls to form eaves. Add a little amount of icing into the roof's crest to adhere the two pieces together, firmly. Set aside overnight to firm.
- Prepare remaining icing for decorations. Lightly beat four egg whites into a big bowl. Beat in the rest of confectioner's sugar. Add snow into the roof by using the prepared icing. Use also the icing to adhere candies. Dust finely sieved confectioner's sugar for finishing.

Nutrition Information

- Calories: 736 calories;
- Sodium: 172
- Total Carbohydrate: 159.7
- Cholesterol: 49
- Protein: 5
- Total Fat: 10.3

286. Chinese Christmas Cookies

Serving: 24 | Prep: 15mins | Cook: | Ready in:

Ingredients

- 1 cup semisweet chocolate chips
- 1 cup peanut butter chips
- 1 cup chow mein noodles
- 1 cup dry-roasted peanuts

Direction

- In the top of a double boiler set over simmering water, melt peanut butter and chocolate chips while stirring often, until smooth.
- In a big mixing bowl, combine peanuts and chow mein noodles, then drizzle over noodles as well as peanuts with chocolate mixture, turning to coat well.
- Use waxed paper to line a baking sheet. Drop on prepared sheet with rounded tablespoonfuls of the mixture. Chill for 2 hours, until set.

Nutrition Information

- Calories: 136 calories;
- Total Fat: 8.5
- Sodium: 83
- Total Carbohydrate: 11.8
- Cholesterol: 0
- Protein: 4

287. Chocolate Brittle Surprise

Serving: 12 | Prep: | Cook: | Ready in:

Ingredients

- 35 unsalted soda crackers
- 1 cup butter
- 1 cup packed brown sugar
- 2 cups semisweet chocolate chips
- 1 cup chopped pecans (optional)

Direction

- To preheat: Set oven to 180°C (350°F). Use foil to cover cookie sheet then use cooking oil spray to spray foil.
- Lay crackers on foil in 5 x 7 inch rows.
- Put butter in the microwave and microwave on high for 2 minutes. Put brown sugar in and stir. Microwave on high in the microwave for 2 minutes longer, stir the mixture every 30 seconds.
- Pour mixture over crackers. Put in the oven and bake for 17 to 20 minutes (bubbles should form but there should not be any burning).

- Use chocolate chips to sprinkle over hot crackers. Wait for 2 minutes then spread the chocolate chips (by this time, the chips have softened). Use nuts to sprinkle on top.
- Chill in the fridge for an hour. Crack into pieces. This can be frozen in the freezer.

Nutrition Information

- Calories: 440 calories;
- Total Fat: 31.3
- Sodium: 184
- Total Carbohydrate: 43.2
- Cholesterol: 41
- Protein: 3

---

288. Chocolate Caramel Brownies

Serving: 15 | Prep: 15mins | Cook: 30mins | Ready in:

Ingredients

- 14 ounces caramels
- 1/2 cup evaporated milk
- 1 (18.25 ounce) package German chocolate cake mix
- 1/3 cup evaporated milk
- 3/4 cup butter, melted
- 1/4 cup chopped pecans
- 2 cups milk chocolate chips

Direction

- Take off the caramel wrappers and put them into a microwave-safe bowl. Stir 1/2 cup evaporated milk into the mix. Heat and stir till all caramels melt.
- Set oven to preheat at 350°F (175°C). Coat a 9x13-inch pan with grease.
- Mix together the chopped pecans, 1/3 cup evaporated milk, melted butter, and cake mix in a large mixing bowl. Put 1/2 of the batter into the prepared baking pan.
- Bake for about 8 minutes.
- Refrigerate the remaining batter. Take the brownies out of the oven and sprinkle the top with chocolate chips. Drizzle the caramel sauce onto the chocolate chips. Take the brownie mix out of the refrigerator. Use a teaspoon to make small balls out of the batter and smash them flat. Put them on top of the caramel sauce very carefully till the top is fully covered.
- Bake for another 20 minutes. Take them out and let cool.

Nutrition Information

- Calories: 460 calories;
- Cholesterol: 35
- Protein: 5.6
- Total Fat: 22.1
- Sodium: 398
- Total Carbohydrate: 64.1

---

289. Chocolate Cookie Mix In A Jar

Serving: 36 | Prep: 25mins | Cook: | Ready in:

Ingredients

- 1 3/4 cups all-purpose flour
- 1 teaspoon baking powder
- 1 teaspoon baking soda
- 1/4 teaspoon salt
- 3/4 cup dark brown sugar
- 1/2 cup white sugar
- 1/4 cup cocoa
- 1/2 cup chopped pecans
- 1 cup semi-sweet chocolate chips

Direction

- Mix salt, baking soda, baking powder, and all-purpose flour. Then put aside. Place chocolate chips, chopped pecans, cocoa, white sugar,

and dark brown sugar in a 1-quart wide mouth canning jar. Before adding the flour mixture, pack all ingredients firmly to snugly fit.
- Put a tag with these following directions: Chocolate Cookie Mix in a Jar: Set an oven to 175°C (350°F) and start preheating; transfer the cookie mix into a large bowl. Use hands to combine the mixture thoroughly. Combine in a teaspoon of vanilla, a lightly whisked egg, and 3/4 cup of margarine or softened butter. Form into walnut-sized balls, then arrange 2 inches apart from each other on a parchment-lined baking sheet. Bake for 11-13 minutes. On the baking sheet, allow to cool for 5 minutes, then transfer onto wire racks.

Nutrition Information

290. Chocolate Cookie Nanaimo Bars

Serving: 16 | Prep: 30mins | Cook: | Ready in:

Ingredients

- 1/2 cup butter
- 1/4 cup white sugar
- 1/4 cup cocoa powder
- 1 egg, beaten
- 1 1/4 cups crushed chocolate cream-filled sandwich cookies (such as OREO® Cookies)
- 1/2 cup butter
- 2 tablespoons instant vanilla pudding mix
- 3 tablespoons heavy cream
- 2 cups confectioners' sugar
- 1 cup semisweet chocolate chips
- 1 tablespoon vegetable oil

Direction

- Line parchment paper on the 9x9-in. square pan. Put half cup butter into top half of a double boiler, then melt over the simmering water. Mix in cocoa powder and sugar until the sugar is dissolved and mixture becomes smooth. Whisk in beaten egg; cook gently for around one min., until the mixture thickens up while whisking constantly. Take away the top of double boiler from heat, then stir in cookie crumbs until very well mixed. Press the crust into prepared dish. Place in the refrigerator at least half an hour, until chilled.
- Beat half a cup of butter with cream and vanilla pudding powder together in a mixing bowl, with an electric mixer until fluffy. Beat in confectioners' sugar slowly, keep beating for approximately 2 mins, until the mixture turns pale yellow and very creamy. Spread on top of the crust with filling, then put back to fridge for at least 30 mins longer.
- In top of the double boiler, melt vegetable oil with semisweet chocolate chips over hot water, then stir until very smooth. Take away the chocolate mixture from the heat, let it cool slightly, then transfer over layer of vanilla. Spread chocolate on top of vanilla layer completely using a spatula. Cool dish in fridge for around half an hour, until chocolate loses its gloss but is not hard completely.
- Cut, using a sharp knife, into five rows by five rows (25 squares), put back to the fridge. Let it chill for at least 15 mins to overnight. Enjoy cold.

Nutrition Information

- Calories: 285 calories;
- Total Fat: 18.3
- Sodium: 144
- Total Carbohydrate: 32.3
- Cholesterol: 46
- Protein: 1.6

291. Chocolate Covered Orange Balls

Serving: 18 | Prep: | Cook: | Ready in:

Ingredients

- 1 pound confectioners' sugar
- 1 (12 ounce) package vanilla wafers, crushed
- 1 cup chopped walnuts
- 1/4 pound butter
- 1 (6 ounce) can frozen orange juice concentrate, thawed
- 1 1/2 pounds milk chocolate, melted

Direction

- Mix together orange juice, butter, walnuts, vanilla wafers and confectioners' sugar in a big bowl. Combine well together and form into round balls with 1 inch size, then let balls dry about an hour.
- In the top of double boiler, add chocolate chips and stir often on moderate heat until chocolate is melted.
- Dunk into the melted chocolate with balls and transfer into decorative paper cups.

Nutrition Information

- Calories: 495 calories;
- Sodium: 124
- Total Carbohydrate: 66.3
- Cholesterol: 22
- Protein: 5
- Total Fat: 24.2

292. Chocolate Crinkles II

Serving: 72 | Prep: 20mins | Cook: 12mins | Ready in:

Ingredients

- 1 cup unsweetened cocoa powder
- 2 cups white sugar
- 1/2 cup vegetable oil
- 4 eggs
- 2 teaspoons vanilla extract
- 2 cups all-purpose flour
- 2 teaspoons baking powder
- 1/2 teaspoon salt
- 1/2 cup confectioners' sugar

Direction

- Mix vegetable oil, white sugar and cocoa in a medium bowl. One by one, beat in eggs; mix in vanilla. Mix salt, baking powder and flour; mix into the cocoa mixture. Cover the dough; chill for at least 4 hours.
- Preheat an oven to 175°C/350°F. Line parchment paper on cookie sheets. Roll dough to 1-in. balls. I use number 50 size scoop. In confectioners' sugar, coat each ball then put onto prepped cookie sheets.
- In the preheated oven, bake for 10-12 minutes; stand for 1 minute on cookie sheet. Put on wire racks; cool.

Nutrition Information

- Calories: 58 calories;
- Total Fat: 2
- Sodium: 34
- Total Carbohydrate: 9.8
- Cholesterol: 10
- Protein: 0.9

293. Chocolate Pile Up Cookies

Serving: 60 | Prep: 15mins | Cook: 10mins | Ready in:

Ingredients

- 2 cups all-purpose flour
- 3/4 cup unsweetened cocoa powder
- 1 teaspoon baking soda
- 1 teaspoon salt

- 1 cup unsalted butter, at room temperature
- 3/4 cup white sugar
- 3/4 cup brown sugar
- 2 eggs
- 2 teaspoons vanilla extract
- 2 tablespoons coffee-flavored liqueur
- 1 cup finely chopped toasted hazelnuts
- 1 cup semisweet chocolate chips
- 1 cup milk chocolate chips
- 1 cup white chocolate chips

Direction

- Prepare the oven by preheating to 375°F (190°C). Use parchment paper to line baking sheets. Combine the salt, baking soda, cocoa and flour in a bowl.
- In a bowl, whisk the brown and white sugar and butter using an electric mixer until creamy and soft, then mix in the coffee liqueur, vanilla extract and eggs. Slowly whisk the flour mixture into the butter-sugar mixture until incorporated. Mix in the white, milk and semisweet chocolate chips and hazelnuts until equally distributed through the dough. Then place by rounded teaspoons about 2 inches apart, onto prepared baking sheets.
- Place in the preheated oven and bake for 8-10 minutes until the edges are lightly browned. Let the cookies to cool on the baking sheet for 1 minute prior taking to a wire rack to fully cool.

Nutrition Information

- Calories: 133 calories;
- Total Fat: 7.7
- Sodium: 86
- Total Carbohydrate: 14.8
- Cholesterol: 16
- Protein: 1.7

294. Chocolate Rum Balls I

Serving: 48 | Prep: 45mins | Cook: | Ready in:

Ingredients

- 3 1/4 cups crushed vanilla wafers
- 3/4 cup confectioners' sugar
- 1/4 cup unsweetened cocoa powder
- 1 1/2 cups chopped walnuts
- 3 tablespoons light corn syrup
- 1/2 cup rum

Direction

- Combine nuts, cocoa, three-fourths cup of confectioners' sugar and crushed vanilla wafers in a big bowl. Beat in rum and corn syrup.
- Form mixture into 1-in. balls; roll balls in extra confectioners' sugar. Keep in a tightly sealed container for a few days to build the flavor. Prior to serving, roll in confectioners' sugar one more time.

Nutrition Information

- Calories: 99 calories;
- Total Fat: 4.8
- Sodium: 38
- Total Carbohydrate: 12.3
- Cholesterol: 0
- Protein: 1.2

295. Chocolate Snowballs

Serving: 72 | Prep: 15mins | Cook: 20mins | Ready in:

Ingredients

- 1 1/4 cups butter
- 2/3 cup white sugar
- 1 teaspoon vanilla extract
- 2 cups all-purpose flour
- 1/8 teaspoon salt

- 1/2 cup unsweetened cocoa powder
- 2 cups chopped pecans
- 1/2 cup confectioners' sugar for decoration

Direction

- Cream together sugar and butter in a medium-sized bowl until fluffy and light. Mix in vanilla. Sift together cocoa, salt and flour; mix into the creamed mixture. Stir in pecans until thoroughly combined. Put a cover on and refrigerate for a minimum of 2 hours.
- Turn the oven to 350°F (175°C) to preheat. Roll to shape the chilled dough into 1-in. balls. Put on unoiled baking sheets by 2-inch apart.
- Bake in the preheated oven for 20 minutes. Once cooled, roll in the confectioners' sugar.

Nutrition Information

- Calories: 74 calories;
- Total Carbohydrate: 6.1
- Cholesterol: 8
- Protein: 0.8
- Total Fat: 5.5
- Sodium: 27

296. Chocolate Hazelnut Thumbprints

Serving: 24 | Prep: 20mins | Cook: 14mins | Ready in:

Ingredients

- 2 cups flour
- 1/2 teaspoon MAGIC Baking Powder
- 1 cup butter, softened
- 1/2 cup packed brown sugar
- 2 eggs, separated, divided
- 1 teaspoon vanilla extract
- 1 cup chopped hazelnuts
- 1 (250 g) package PHILADELPHIA Chocolate Brick Cream Cheese, softened

Direction

- Prepare the oven by preheating to 350°F (175°C).
- Combine baking powder and flour. In a large bowl, whisk sugar and butter using mixer until fluffy and light. Mix in vanilla and egg yolks. Slowly stir in flour mixture until combined. Form into 48 balls, applying about 1 tablespoon for each.
- Lightly whisk egg whites. Dunk dough balls, 1 at a time, in egg whites, then roll in nuts until equally covered. Then set 1-inch apart on baking sheets lined with parchment paper. Push your thumb into middles to indent.
- Place in the preheated oven and bake for 12 to 14 minutes or until edges are golden brown. Let cool for 5 minutes on baking sheet. Take to wire racks; fully cool.
- Scoop cream cheese into pastry bag fitted with star tip. Apply to pipe cream cheese onto cookies, putting about 1 teaspoon each.

Nutrition Information

- Calories: 188 calories;
- Protein: 2.8
- Total Fat: 13
- Sodium: 104
- Total Carbohydrate: 15.6
- Cholesterol: 46

297. Christmas Cookie Cut Outs

Serving: 24 | Prep: 30mins | Cook: 10mins | Ready in:

Ingredients

- 3 cups all-purpose flour
- 2 teaspoons cream of tartar
- 1 teaspoon baking soda
- 1 teaspoon ground nutmeg
- 1 pinch ground cinnamon

- 1 cup butter, softened
- 1 cup white sugar
- 3 eggs, beaten
- 1 teaspoon vanilla extract
- Frosting:
- 4 cups confectioners' sugar
- 1/2 cup butter, softened
- 1 tablespoon vanilla extract
- 1/4 cup milk
- any color food coloring (optional)

Direction

- In a bowl, sift the cinnamon, nutmeg, baking soda, cream of tartar and flour together; put aside. Use an electric mixer to whip the sugar and butter till smooth in a big bowl. Put in eggs, one by one, blending each egg into mixture of butter prior to putting the next. Whip in vanilla including the final egg. Stir in flour mixture barely to incorporate. Chill dough with cover overnight.
- Heat the oven to 175 ° C or 350 ° F. On floured counter, unroll dough to half-inch thickness. Use Christmas cookie cutters to cut out shapes. Arrange cookies on unprepped cookie sheets an-inch away.
- Bake for 8 to 10 minutes in prepped oven till edges turn golden. Lower the baking time in case using cutters with small appendages, like reindeer legs, otherwise they will burn. Transfer cookies to wire rack and fully cool.
- Use an electric mixer to whip confectioners' sugar and butter in a big bowl, mixture will become firm. Put in vanilla and gradually stir in milk, a small amount at one time to attain a spreadable consistency. Mix food coloring in, if wished. Ensure cookies are fully cool to frost.

Nutrition Information

- Calories: 282 calories;
- Total Fat: 12.4
- Sodium: 145
- Total Carbohydrate: 40.7
- Cholesterol: 54
- Protein: 2.6

298. Christmas Cookies II

Serving: 48 | Prep: | Cook: | Ready in:

Ingredients

- 1 cup butter
- 1 1/2 cups white sugar
- 3 eggs
- 1 tablespoon cocoa
- 1 teaspoon ground cinnamon
- 1 teaspoon ground mace
- 1 teaspoon ground nutmeg
- 1/2 teaspoon ground cloves
- 1/2 teaspoon ground allspice
- 3/4 teaspoon baking soda
- 1/2 cup chopped, peeled apple
- 1 cup golden raisins
- 1/2 pound candied pineapple
- 1/4 pound chopped candied orange peel
- 1/4 pound candied lemon peel
- 8 ounces dates, pitted and chopped
- 1 pound chopped pecans
- 1 tablespoon bourbon
- 3 cups all-purpose flour

Direction

- Cream the sugar, eggs and butter together. Add in the cocoa, soda, mace, cinnamon, flour, cloves, nutmeg and allspice and whisk it together.
- While the creamed mixture is mixing on one side, let the lemon peel, candied pineapple and orange peel soak in bourbon.
- Mix the raisins, soaked fruits, apples, dates and pecans into the creamed mixture until well-combined.
- Scoop cookies half the size of a dollar on a cookie sheet that is greased, 1/2 inch away from each other.
- Put in the preheated 350°F (175°C) oven and let it bake for 12 to 15 minutes.

Nutrition Information

- Calories: 208 calories;
- Total Fat: 11.1
- Sodium: 57
- Total Carbohydrate: 27
- Cholesterol: 22
- Protein: 2.4

299. Christmas Cornflake Wreath Cookies

Serving: 18 | Prep: | Cook: | Ready in:

Ingredients

- 1/2 cup butter
- 4 cups miniature marshmallows
- 1 teaspoon green food coloring
- 1/2 teaspoon almond extract
- 1/2 teaspoon vanilla extract
- 4 cups cornflakes cereal
- 1 (2.25 ounce) package cinnamon red hot candies

Direction

- Heat butter and marshmallows in the microwave for 2 minutes on high power. Whisk well, then heat on high power in the microwave, 2 minutes longer. Whisk. (If you do not have a microwave, use a double boiler instead).
- Put and quickly mix in food coloring, extracts and cornflakes, consecutively. Drop mixture onto greased waxed paper by spoonfuls; garnish each with 3 red hots.
- Once cookies are cooled, remove to a lightly greased storage/serving tray using lightly oiled fingers.

Nutrition Information

- Calories: 117 calories;
- Cholesterol: 14
- Protein: 0.7
- Total Fat: 5.2
- Sodium: 92
- Total Carbohydrate: 17.9

300. Christmas Cut Out Cookies

Serving: 48 | Prep: 30mins | Cook: 12mins | Ready in:

Ingredients

- 1 cup shortening
- 1 cup light brown sugar
- 2 eggs
- 1 teaspoon anise extract
- 4 cups all-purpose flour
- 1 tablespoon baking powder
- 1 teaspoon salt
- 1/2 cup milk

Direction

- Start preheating the oven at 350°F (175°C). Oil cookie sheets.
- In a large bowl, combine sugar and shortening until smooth. Whisk in the eggs, one at a time; blend in the anise extract. Mix salt, baking powder, and flour; mix into the creamed mixture alternately with the milk. Combine until well-blended. Do not overmix or cookies would be tough.
- Roll out the dough to 1/4 -inch thick on a lightly floured surface. With cookie cutters, cut into the wanted shapes. Arrange cookies at least 1-inch apart onto the prepared cookie sheets.
- Bake in the prepared oven for 12 to 15 minutes until set. Cookie will not have a golden-brown color. If they have, they are over-done. Remove onto the rack to cool. If frosting, wait until cool.

Nutrition Information

- Calories: 92 calories;
- Total Fat: 4.6
- Sodium: 74
- Total Carbohydrate: 11.1
- Cholesterol: 8
- Protein: 1.4

301. Christmas Molasses And Ginger Cookies

Serving: 36 | Prep: 20mins | Cook: 10mins | Ready in:

Ingredients

- 1 1/3 cups molasses
- 2/3 cup packed brown sugar
- 2/3 cup butter, softened
- 5 1/2 cups all-purpose flour
- 2 eggs
- 4 teaspoons ground cinnamon
- 2 teaspoons baking soda
- 2 teaspoons ground ginger
- 1 teaspoon salt

Direction

- In a bowl, combine butter, brown sugar and molasses; beat together until smooth. Stir in salt, ginger, baking soda, cinnamon, eggs and flour to incorporate. Use plastic wrap to cover the bowl and put it into the refrigerator in 1 hour.
- Turn on the oven to 375°F (190°C) to preheat. Use parchment paper to line a baking sheet. Use generous amount of flour to sprinkle on the cloth-covered work surface.
- Put dough on the floured cloth and roll so that it forms cookies shape of 1/4-inch thickness. Use cookie cutter to cut the dough to your interest. On the baking sheet, place cookies, each stands 1-inch apart from the other.
- Put into the oven to bake for about 8 minutes until the cookies are firm when you touch. Let them cool for 10 minutes in the pans and then let them cool completely on wire rack.

Nutrition Information

- Calories: 155 calories;
- Total Fat: 3.9
- Sodium: 169
- Total Carbohydrate: 27.9
- Cholesterol: 19
- Protein: 2.4

302. Christmas Rocks

Serving: 96 | Prep: | Cook: | Ready in:

Ingredients

- 1 1/2 cups white sugar
- 1 cup butter
- 3 eggs
- 3 cups all-purpose flour
- 1 tablespoon unsweetened cocoa powder
- 1/2 teaspoon ground ginger
- 1/2 teaspoon ground allspice
- 3/4 teaspoon baking soda
- 1 teaspoon ground cinnamon
- 1 teaspoon ground mace
- 1 teaspoon ground nutmeg
- 1 tablespoon strong brewed coffee
- 1/2 cup currants
- 1 cup raisins
- 1 pound pecan halves
- 1/4 cup candied cherries
- 1/4 pound candied pineapple, coarsely chopped
- 1/4 pound chopped candied citron
- 1/4 pound pitted dates
- 1/4 pound chopped candied orange peel

Direction

- Cream the sugar and butter till becoming light and fluffy. Whip the eggs till becoming foamy,

pour to the mixture. Sift soda, cocoa and spices with the flour. Reserve half cup flour mixture. Put in the remaining of the flour mixture to the butter mixture. Mix in the coffee.
- Chop the fruits into the small slivers and dredge the fruit and chopped pecans a bit in the reserved flour. Put to the fruit and remaining of the flour to the batter, stirring completely
- Preheat the oven to 170 degrees C (325 degrees F). Grease the cookie sheets.
- Drop by teaspoon onto the cookie sheet. Don't position them too close together. Bake for 12 - 15 minutes. Don't overbrown. Keep the cookies stored in the jars.

Nutrition Information

- Calories: 100 calories;
- Protein: 1.2
- Total Fat: 5.6
- Sodium: 31
- Total Carbohydrate: 12.5
- Cholesterol: 11

303. Christmas Stars

Serving: 24 | Prep: 30mins | Cook: 15mins | Ready in:

Ingredients

- 3/4 cup butter, softened
- 1 cup white sugar
- 2 egg
- 1 teaspoon vanilla extract
- 2 1/2 cups all-purpose flour
- 1 teaspoon baking powder
- 1/4 teaspoon salt
- 6 tablespoons strawberry jam
- 1/4 cup green decorator sugar (optional)

Direction

- Cream sugar and butter together in a big bowl until fluffy and light. Put in vanilla and eggs gradually, mixing well. Sift together salt, baking powder and flour, then stir into butter mixture until well mixed. Split dough in half and use plastic to wrap dough. Chill dough in the fridge about 3 hours.
- Set the oven to 175°C or 350°F to preheat. Coat 2 cookie sheets with grease or use parchment paper to line them.
- Roll out 1/2 of the dough on a surface coated with flour to the thickness of 1/8 inch. Use a 3- to 4-in. star cookie cutter to cut dough into star shapes. Cut a star into the center of half of the big stars with a 1- to 2-in. star cookie cutter. Put the full stars on a cookie sheet and tops which are cookies with the center cutouts on another sheet. Sprinkle in the star tops with colored sugar, if you want.
- In the preheated oven, bake for 6-8 minutes, until edges turn golden brown. Let cookies cool thoroughly. You can reroll for a mini stars cutout of the centers or bake them 5 minutes separately. Repeat process with leftover cookie dough.
- Once cookies are cooled completely, spread in the center of each full star cookie with 1 tsp. of preserves, then put on top of the preserves layer with the cut-out cookie. Pack cookies between waxed paper in a covered tin to conserve their freshness.

Nutrition Information

- Calories: 158 calories;
- Total Fat: 6.3
- Sodium: 92
- Total Carbohydrate: 23.7
- Cholesterol: 31
- Protein: 1.9

304. Christmas Wreaths

Serving: 18 | Prep: 5mins | Cook: 10mins | Ready in:

Ingredients

- 1/2 cup butter
- 30 large marshmallows
- 1 1/2 teaspoons green food coloring
- 1 teaspoon vanilla extract
- 4 cups cornflakes cereal
- 2 tablespoons cinnamon red hot candies

Direction

- In a big saucepan, put in the butter and let it melt over low heat setting. Put in the marshmallows and let it cook while stirring it continuously until the marshmallows have melted. Remove the pan away from the heat then add in the vanilla, cornflakes and food coloring and mix everything together.
- Put large tablespoonfuls of the prepared marshmallow-corn flakes mixture on a wax paper immediately after cooking, then use your fingers that are covered with a little bit of oil to carefully shape the mixture into a wreath. Use red hot candies to garnish the wreath-shaped mixture right away. Let the mixture cool down until it gets to room temperature then take it from the wax paper and put it in an airtight container to store.

Nutrition Information

- Calories: 112 calories;
- Sodium: 91
- Total Carbohydrate: 16.7
- Cholesterol: 14
- Protein: 0.7
- Total Fat: 5.2

305. Cinnamon Stars

Serving: 18 | Prep: | Cook: | Ready in:

Ingredients

- 2 2/3 cups finely ground almonds
- 1 tablespoon ground cinnamon
- 1 teaspoon lemon zest
- 1/3 cup egg whites
- 1/8 teaspoon salt
- 2 1/2 cups confectioners' sugar
- 1 3/4 teaspoons lemon juice

Direction

- Mix lemon zest, cinnamon and the almonds together until combined.
- Whisk the egg whites and salt until it forms soft peaks. Gradually sift in the confectioner's sugar, keep beating until the mixture is stiff. Put aside 1/3 cup of the egg white mixture to make the glaze. Fold in the almond mixture.
- Set oven to 325 0 F (170 0 C) and preheat. Use parchment paper to line the cookie sheets.
- On a surface scattered with confectioners' sugar, roll the dough out to 1/4 inch thickness. Cut out the cookies using a 2 1/2-inch star cookie cutter and arrange them onto the cookie sheets.
- To prepare the glaze, pour the lemon juice into the reserved egg white mixture, blending until smooth. Lightly brush the glaze over the tops of the cookies. (If the glaze begins to thicken, put in a few extra drops of lemon juice.)
- Put in the prepared oven and bake for 20 to 25 minutes. When finish, the center will turn light brown and soft. Take out of the oven and cool on wire racks.

Nutrition Information

- Calories: 190 calories;
- Total Fat: 10.7
- Sodium: 24
- Total Carbohydrate: 21.2
- Cholesterol: 0
- Protein: 5

306. Classic Cup Christmas Cookies

Serving: 12 | Prep: | Cook: |Ready in:

Ingredients

- 1 cup unsalted butter
- 1 1/2 cups confectioners' sugar
- 1 egg
- 1/2 teaspoon orange extract
- 4 teaspoons orange zest
- 2 1/4 cups all-purpose flour
- 2 teaspoons baking powder
- 1 1/2 cups dried cherries
- 1/2 cup chopped pistachio nuts
- 4 ounces vanilla flavored confectioners' coating, melted

Direction

- Cream the confectioners' sugar together with butter in a medium bowl. Put in orange zest, orange extract and egg; stir until smooth. Sift the baking powder and flour together; mix into the creamed mixture. Then, mix in the chopped pistachios and dried cherries. Roll the dough into a 10-inch long log nearly 2 1/2-inches in diameter, wrap in wax paper or plastic, then freeze about 2 hours. If dough is too hard to shape a log, refrigerate for an hour first.
- Preheat oven to 190°C (375°F). Coat 2 cookie sheets with cooking spray.
- Chop the roll into 1/2-inch slices then put onto the cookie sheet. Bake in the preheated oven for 10 to 12 minutes. Cool for 1 to 2 minutes on the cookie sheet before transfer onto a wire rack to cool. Use melted candy coating to sprinkle on the cookies in a striped pattern when they're entirely cool.

Nutrition Information

- Calories: 427 calories;
- Sodium: 122
- Total Carbohydrate: 53.2
- Cholesterol: 58
- Protein: 5.8
- Total Fat: 21.5

307. Coconut Buffalo Chip Cookies

Serving: 30 | Prep: 20mins | Cook: 10mins |Ready in:

Ingredients

- 2 cups all-purpose flour
- 3 tablespoons unsweetened cocoa powder
- 1 teaspoon baking powder
- 1 teaspoon baking soda
- 1 cup coconut oil
- 1 cup lightly packed brown sugar
- 1 cup white sugar
- 2 eggs
- 1 1/2 teaspoons vanilla extract
- 1 cup rolled oats
- 1 cup crushed corn flakes
- 1 cup chocolate chips
- 1/2 cup shredded coconut
- 1/2 cup raisins

Direction

- Preheat the oven to 350°F (175°C). Coat 2 baking sheets with oil.
- In a bowl, combine the baking powder, flour, baking soda and cocoa powder together.
- In another bowl, whisk the brown sugar, white sugar and coconut oil together until it is smooth and creamy in consistency. Whisk the vanilla extract and eggs into the coconut oil mixture. Add in the flour mixture and mix well until combined. Put in the chocolate chips, rolled oats, raisins, corn flakes and shredded coconut and fold it into the batter mixture.
- On the prepared baking sheet, put in rounded tablespoonfuls of the prepared batter mixture.
- Put it in the preheated oven and let it bake for 10-12 minutes until the cookies are thoroughly

cooked in the center and the edges have turned light brown in color. Allow the baked cookies to cool down on the pans for 10 minutes then put the cookies on a wire rack to let them fully cool down.

Nutrition Information

- Calories: 199 calories;
- Total Fat: 10.2
- Sodium: 76
- Total Carbohydrate: 27.1
- Cholesterol: 12
- Protein: 2.2

308. Coconut Cherry Surprise Cookies

Serving: 36 | Prep: 40mins | Cook: 16mins | Ready in:

Ingredients

- 36 maraschino cherries, drained and juice reserved
- 1/2 cup slivered almonds
- 1 (8 ounce) package shredded coconut
- 3 drops green food coloring
- 3 drops red food coloring
- 1 cup butter, softened
- 1/2 cup confectioners' sugar
- 1 tablespoon water
- 1 teaspoon almond extract
- 2 cups all-purpose flour
- 1/2 cup quick cooking oats
- 1/4 teaspoon salt
- 1 (16 ounce) package confectioners' sugar

Direction

- Start preheating the oven to 350°F (175°C). Use parchment paper to line a cookie sheet.
- On a paper towel, put strained cherries.
- In a food processor, grind slivered almonds. Remove into a bowl.
- In the food processor, put coconut and grind to finely chop. Remove 1 cup to a resealable plastic bag; add green food coloring by 3 drops, close the bag, and shake. Add to a bowl. Remove the leftover coconut to another resealable plastic bag, add red food coloring by 3 drops. Add to another bowl.
- In a big bowl, use an electric mixer to whisk 1/2 cup sugar and butter until fluffy and light. Whisk in almond extract and water.
- In a bowl, mix together salt, oats, ground almonds, and flour. Slowly add the flour mixture to the butter mixture, the dough should be crumbly.
- Pack around each cherry with 1 tablespoon of dough, making a ball. Put on the prepared cookie sheet, about 2-in. apart.
- Put in the preheated oven and bake for 16-18 minutes, or until the cookies turn light brown on the bottoms. Put on a wire rack to cool.
- Use waxed paper to line a cookie sheet. In a bowl, put 16-ounce package sugar, stir in a sufficient amount of the saved cherry juice to achieve a smooth dipping consistency. Dip the tops of the cooled cookies in the icing, then in the colored coconut. Put on the waxed paper for 20 minutes, or until set.

Nutrition Information

- Calories: 189 calories;
- Sodium: 55
- Total Carbohydrate: 23.9
- Cholesterol: 14
- Protein: 1.7
- Total Fat: 10.1

309. Coconut Rum Balls

Serving: 4 | Prep: | Cook: | Ready in:

Ingredients

- 1 (12 ounce) package vanilla wafers, crushed

- 1 1/3 cups flaked coconut
- 1 cup finely chopped walnuts
- 1 (14 ounce) can sweetened condensed milk
- 1/4 cup rum
- 1/8 cup confectioners' sugar

Direction

- Mix together nuts, coconut and crumbs in a big bowl, then put in rum and sweetened condensed milk, mixing well. Refrigerate about 4 hours.
- Form the mixture into balls, about 1-inch size, then roll them into sugar. Keep in covered container in the fridge about 24 hours prior to serving.

Nutrition Information

- Calories: 1063 calories;
- Total Fat: 50.8
- Sodium: 453
- Total Carbohydrate: 133.7
- Cholesterol: 33
- Protein: 16.6

310. Cookie Mix In A Jar III

Serving: 36 | Prep: 20mins | Cook: | Ready in:

Ingredients

- 1 cup all-purpose flour
- 1 teaspoon ground cinnamon
- 1/2 teaspoon ground nutmeg
- 1 teaspoon baking soda
- 1/2 teaspoon salt
- 3/4 cup raisins
- 2 cups rolled oats
- 3/4 cup packed brown sugar
- 1/2 cup white sugar

Direction

- Mix salt, baking soda, ground nutmeg, ground cinnamon and flour; put aside.
- In a 1-qt. wide mouth canning jar, layer ingredients in the following order; flour mixture, the raisins, rolled oats, the brown sugar then white sugar. Firmly pack down every layer before adding the next layer; it'll be a tight fit.
- With the following instructions, attach a tag: Oatmeal Raisin Spice Cookies. Preheat an oven to 175°C/350°F. Line parchment paper on cookie sheets. Into a big mixing bowl, empty cookie mix jar; thoroughly mix with your hands. Mix in softened 3/4 cup margarine/butter. Mix in 1 tsp. vanilla and 1 slightly beaten egg till fully blended. To finish mixing, you need to use your hands. Form to walnut-sized balls; put onto parchment lined cookie sheets, 2-in. apart. In the preheated oven, bake till edges are lightly browned for 11-13 minutes; cool on cookie sheet for 5 minutes. Put onto wire racks; finish cooling.

Nutrition Information

- Calories: 67 calories;
- Cholesterol: 0
- Protein: 1.1
- Total Fat: 0.4
- Sodium: 69
- Total Carbohydrate: 15.4

311. Cookie Pralines

Serving: 12 | Prep: 20mins | Cook: 25mins | Ready in:

Ingredients

- 1 cup packed dark brown sugar
- 1 tablespoon all-purpose flour
- 1/4 teaspoon salt
- 1 egg white
- 1 teaspoon vanilla extract
- 2 cups chopped pecans

Direction

- Set oven to 275° F (135° C) to preheat. Line a baking sheet with parchment paper or grease it.
- Whisk salt, flour and sugar; put aside.
- Beat egg white in separate bowl until stiff. Then fold in the sugar mixture. Put in vanilla and pecans. Then gently stir.
- Drop onto the prepared baking sheet by teaspoonfuls. Bake for 25 to 30 minutes in the prepared oven until browned. Let cool on baking sheet for 5 minutes, then transfer to wire rack until completely cool.

Nutrition Information

- Calories: 200 calories;
- Cholesterol: 0
- Protein: 2.1
- Total Fat: 13.1
- Sodium: 58
- Total Carbohydrate: 21.1

312. Cookie In A Jar

Serving: 12 | Prep: 20mins | Cook: |Ready in:

Ingredients

- 1/2 cup white chocolate chips
- 1/2 cup crispy rice cereal
- 1 1/2 cups all-purpose flour
- 3/4 teaspoon baking soda
- 1/4 teaspoon baking powder
- 1/2 cup packed brown sugar
- 1/2 cup semisweet chocolate chips
- 1/2 cup rolled oats
- 1/2 cup white sugar

Direction

- Layer ingredients in listed order in 1-qt. jar; firmly packing down with every addition.
- Attach tag with these instructions: Cookie in Jar. Preheat an oven to 175°C/350°F. Cream 1/2 cup margarine till fluffy and light in big bowl. Mix 2 tbsp. water and 1 egg in. Add entire jar contents. Mix till blended well. By rounded spoonfuls, drop on ungreased cookie sheet. In preheated oven, bake for 10-12 minutes. Transfer from baking sheets onto wire racks. Cool.

Nutrition Information

- Calories: 217 calories;
- Protein: 3
- Total Fat: 5.1
- Sodium: 109
- Total Carbohydrate: 41.2
- Cholesterol: 2

313. Cowboy Cookie Mix In A Jar

Serving: 18 | Prep: 25mins | Cook: |Ready in:

Ingredients

- 1 1/3 cups rolled oats
- 1/2 cup packed brown sugar
- 1/2 cup white sugar
- 1/2 cup chopped pecans
- 1 cup semisweet chocolate chips
- 1 1/3 cups all-purpose flour
- 1 teaspoon baking powder
- 1 teaspoon baking soda
- 1/4 teaspoon salt

Direction

- In a 1 quart jar, layer the ingredients in the given order. Before placing the next layer, press the previous layer firmly in place.
- Include a card with the following instructions: Cowboy Cookie Mix in a Jar 1. Set oven to 3500 F (1750 C) to preheat. Coat cookie sheets

with grease. 2. In a medium bowl, blend 1 teaspoon of vanilla, 1 egg and 1/2 cup of melted butter or margarine. Mix in the entire contents of the jar. Use your hands to finish the mixing. Form into walnut sized balls. On greased cookie sheets, place 2 inches apart. 3. Put in the prepared oven and bake for 11 to 13 minutes. Move away from cookie sheets and put on wire racks to cool.

Nutrition Information

- Calories: 167 calories;
- Total Fat: 5.5
- Sodium: 133
- Total Carbohydrate: 29.1
- Cholesterol: 0
- Protein: 2.4

314. Cracked Sugar Cookies I

Serving: 24 | Prep: | Cook: |Ready in:

Ingredients

- 1 1/4 cups white sugar
- 1 cup butter
- 3 egg yolks
- 1 teaspoon vanilla extract
- 2 1/2 cups all-purpose flour
- 1 teaspoon baking soda
- 1/2 teaspoon cream of tartar

Direction

- Set oven to 350°F (180°C) to preheat. Lightly oil 2 cookie sheets.
- Whisk together butter and sugar. Whisk in vanilla and egg yolks.
- Stir in cream of tartar, baking soda, and flour.
- Shape dough into walnut-sized balls; lay the balls on the greased cookie sheets, placing them 2 inches apart. Do not press dough down. Bake cookies in the preheated oven until tops are cracked and colored, approximately 10 to 11 minutes.

Nutrition Information

- Calories: 163 calories;
- Sodium: 108
- Total Carbohydrate: 20.5
- Cholesterol: 46
- Protein: 1.8
- Total Fat: 8.4

315. Cranberry Almond Swirl Cheesecake Cookie Bars

Serving: 16 | Prep: 20mins | Cook: 47mins |Ready in:

Ingredients

- cooking spray
- 1 3/4 cups graham cracker crumbs
- 1/2 cup butter, melted
- 2 tablespoons white sugar
- 3/4 cup fresh cranberries
- 1/4 cup water
- 3/4 cup white sugar, divided
- 2 (8 ounce) packages cream cheese, at room temperature
- 2 eggs, at room temperature
- 5 tablespoons milk, at room temperature
- 1 tablespoon lemon juice
- 1 1/2 teaspoons almond extract
- 1/3 cup sliced almonds, or to taste

Direction

- Turn on the oven to 350°F (175°C) to preheat. Use aluminum foil to line a 9x13-inch baking dish; use cooking spray to grease lightly.
- In a bowl, mix together 2 tablespoons of sugar, melted butter and graham cracker crumbs, stir until the crumbs are well-coated with butter. Pour into the baking dish; flatten to form an even layer.

- Put into the oven for 8-10 minutes until lightly browned. Leave the oven on; take out the crust and allow to cool.
- In a saucepan, add 1/4 cup of sugar, water and cranberries over medium-high heat. Boil the mixture. Cook for about 7 minutes until the mixture thickens and the cranberries burst. Allow to cool for 15 minutes. In a food processor or blender, place the sauce and puree till smooth; adding more water to adjust the consistency to thin if needed.
- In a bowl, mix together cream cheese and the remaining sugar. Use an electric mixture to beat till smooth for about 4 minutes in total, scraping down the sides every 90 seconds. Beat in 1 egg at a time; make sure to beat well after each addition. Pour in almond extract, lemon juice and milk. Beat the batter until well-combined on medium-low.
- Transfer the batter to cooled crust and spread out. Add spoonfuls of cranberry sauce on top; swirl it through the batter with a knife. Scatter almonds evenly onto the cheesecake.
- Put into the oven to bake for 27-33 minutes until set. Allow to cool for at least 30 minutes. Put into the refrigerator overnight or for at least 8 hours. Slice into bars the next day.

Nutrition Information

- Calories: 257 calories;
- Total Carbohydrate: 20.1
- Cholesterol: 70
- Protein: 4.2
- Total Fat: 18.2
- Sodium: 190

316. Cranberry Bars

Serving: 24 | Prep: 30mins | Cook: 40mins | Ready in:

Ingredients

- 1 (12 ounce) package whole cranberries
- 1 cup white sugar
- 3/4 cup water
- 1 (18.25 ounce) package yellow cake mix
- 3/4 cup butter, melted
- 2 eggs
- 1 cup rolled oats
- 3/4 cup packed light brown sugar
- 1 teaspoon ground ginger
- 1 teaspoon ground cinnamon

Direction

- In a saucepan, mix together the cranberries, white sugar, and water over medium heat. Cook and stir sometimes until the mixture is thick and all of the cranberries have popped, about 15 minutes. Take away from heat, and put aside to cool.
- Set oven to preheat at 350°F (175°C).
- Mix together the cake mix, melted butter, and eggs in a large bowl. Stir the cinnamon, brown sugar, ginger and oats into the mixture. Save about 1 1/2 cups of the mixture, and spread the remainder into a 9x13 inch baking dish's bottom. Press it down to make a solid crust, as evenly as possible. Spread the cooled mixture of cranberry onto the crust. Pinch out pieces from the reserved mixture and evenly arrange atop the cranberry layer.
- In the preheated oven, bake for 35 to 40 minutes till the top is light brown. Let it cool down in the pan for about 40 minutes, then cut into bars.

Nutrition Information

- Calories: 228 calories;
- Sodium: 191
- Total Carbohydrate: 36.1
- Cholesterol: 31
- Protein: 2
- Total Fat: 8.9

317. Cranberry Cashew Jumbles

Serving: 48 | Prep: 30mins | Cook: 10mins | Ready in:

Ingredients

- 2 cups unbleached all-purpose flour
- 3/4 teaspoon baking powder
- 1/4 teaspoon baking soda
- 1 cup packed light brown sugar
- 1/2 cup butter, softened
- 1/2 cup sour cream
- 1 egg
- 2 teaspoons grated orange zest, or more to taste
- 1 teaspoon vanilla extract
- 1 cup chopped salted cashews
- 1 (6 ounce) package dried cranberries, chopped
- 1 1/2 cups confectioners' sugar
- 3 tablespoons orange juice

Direction

- Preheat oven to 375 °F (190 °C). On baking sheets, line with parchment paper.
- In a bowl, whisk baking soda, baking powder and flour together.
- In a bowl, beat butter and brown sugar together by using an electric mixer on medium speed till creamy and smooth; put in egg, sour cream, vanilla extract and orange zest; beat until mixed well. Mix flour mixture into brown sugar mixture until dough is smooth. Fold cranberries and cashews into dough; on prepared baking sheets, drop by rounded teaspoons placing 2 inches apart.
- In the preheated oven, bake for around 10 to 12 minutes until browned lightly. Allow 10 minutes for cooling on the pans before taking away to a wire rack to cool completely.
- In a bowl, whisk confectioners' sugar and orange juice together till glaze is smooth. Drizzle glaze over cookies.

Nutrition Information

- Calories: 103 calories;
- Total Fat: 3.9
- Sodium: 50
- Total Carbohydrate: 16.5
- Cholesterol: 10
- Protein: 1.2

318. Cranberry Hootycreeks

Serving: 18 | Prep: 25mins | Cook: | Ready in:

Ingredients

- 5/8 cup all-purpose flour
- 1/2 cup rolled oats
- 1/2 cup all-purpose flour
- 1/2 teaspoon baking soda
- 1/2 teaspoon salt
- 1/3 cup packed brown sugar
- 1/3 cup white sugar
- 1/2 cup dried cranberries
- 1/2 cup white chocolate chips
- 1/2 cup chopped pecans

Direction

- In the order listed, layer ingredients in 1 liter/1quart jar.
- Attach tag with these instructions: Cranberry Hootycreeks. 1. Preheat an oven to 175°C/350°F. Grease or line parchment paper on cookie sheet. 2. Beat 1 tsp. vanilla, 1 egg and 1/2 cup softened butter till fluffy in medium bowl. Add entire jar of ingredients. By hand, mix till blended well. By heaping spoonfuls, drop on prepped baking sheets. 3. Bake till edges begin to brown or for 8-10 minutes. Transfer to wire racks to cool or cool on baking sheets.

Nutrition Information

- Calories: 126 calories;

- Protein: 1.7
- Total Fat: 4.2
- Sodium: 106
- Total Carbohydrate: 21.2
- Cholesterol: 1

319. Cranberry Orange Cookies

Serving: 48 | Prep: 20mins | Cook: 14mins | Ready in:

Ingredients

- 1 cup butter, softened
- 1 cup white sugar
- 1/2 cup packed brown sugar
- 1 egg
- 1 teaspoon grated orange zest
- 2 tablespoons orange juice
- 2 1/2 cups all-purpose flour
- 1/2 teaspoon baking soda
- 1/2 teaspoon salt
- 2 cups chopped cranberries
- 1/2 cup chopped walnuts (optional)
- 1/2 teaspoon grated orange zest
- 3 tablespoons orange juice
- 1 1/2 cups confectioners' sugar

Direction

- Preheat your oven to 375°F (190°C).
- Cream the white sugar, brown sugar and butter together in a big bowl until it is smooth in consistency. Add in the egg and whisk it altogether until well-combined. Add in 2 tablespoons of orange juice and 1 teaspoon of orange zest and mix well. Mix the baking soda, salt and flour together and add it into the orange mixture; mix well. Put in the walnuts (if available) and cranberries and mix everything together until the nuts and berries are well-distributed in the mixture. On ungreased cookie sheets, put in drops of rounded tablespoonfuls of the dough mixture at least 2 inches away from each other.
- Put it in the preheated oven and let it bake for 12-14 minutes until the edges of the cookies turn golden in color. Take the baked cookies from the cookie sheets and place it onto wire racks to let them cool down.
- Combine 3 tablespoons of orange juice, confectioners' sugar and 1/2 teaspoon of orange zest together in a small bowl; mix well until it is smooth in consistency. Coat the top of each cooled down cookies evenly with the prepared glaze mixture and allow it to rest until the glaze has set.

Nutrition Information

- Calories: 110 calories;
- Sodium: 67
- Total Carbohydrate: 16.2
- Cholesterol: 14
- Protein: 1.1
- Total Fat: 4.8

320. Crazy Yummy Cranberry Pecan Cookies With Orange Glaze

Serving: 48 | Prep: 25mins | Cook: 10mins | Ready in:

Ingredients

- Cookie:
- 2 1/4 cups all-purpose flour
- 1 teaspoon baking soda
- 1 teaspoon salt
- 1 cup butter
- 3/4 cup white sugar
- 3/4 cup brown sugar, packed
- 1 teaspoon vanilla extract
- 2 eggs
- 1 cup chopped pecans
- 1 cup rolled oats
- 1 cup sweetened dried cranberries (such as Ocean Spray® Craisins®)

- Glaze:
- 1 1/2 cups confectioners' sugar
- 1/2 cup freshly squeezed orange juice
- 1 orange, zested
- 1 tablespoon butter

Direction

- Preheat the oven to 190 degrees C (375 degrees F). In a bowl, sift together the salt, baking soda and flour.
- In a big bowl, whip the vanilla extract, brown and white sugars, and butter together using an electric mixer till the mixture is well combined and creamy. Whip in one egg at a time, and then slowly whip in flour just till mixture forms a soft dough. Whisk in cranberries, rolled oats and pecans, and drop by heaping the spoonfuls to the ungreased baking sheets.
- Bake in preheated oven for 10-12 minutes till cookies become set and edges turn browned a bit. Allow cookies to cool down for 60 seconds on the baking sheets prior to taking out onto wire racks to finish the cooling process. Glaze the cookies when they are still slightly warm.
- Add orange juice and confectioners' sugar into a microwave-safe bowl, and whisk to dissolve sugar. Whisk in butter and orange zest, and let microwave on the medium power for roughly half a minutes till butter is melted and mixture is warmed. Whisk warm glaze till smooth, and pour on top of the cookies.

Nutrition Information

- Calories: 131 calories;
- Sodium: 108
- Total Carbohydrate: 18.6
- Cholesterol: 19
- Protein: 1.4
- Total Fat: 6.1

321. Cream Cheese Christmas Cookies

Serving: 60 | Prep: | Cook: | Ready in:

Ingredients

- 1 cup butter, softened
- 1 (8 ounce) package cream cheese
- 1 cup white sugar
- 1/2 teaspoon vanilla extract
- 2 1/2 cups all-purpose flour
- 1/2 teaspoon salt
- 1/2 cup chopped pecans
- 1/2 cup green sugar crystals
- 1/2 cup red sugar crystals
- 1 cup pecan halves

Direction

- Cream the cream cheese and butter together. Put in the vanilla and sugar; whip till light and fluffy.
- Mix salt and flour; slowly put into the creamed mixture, whip till well-blended. Whisk in the chopped pecans. Keep the bowl covered using plastic wrap and keep in the refrigerator for 15 minutes.
- On four sheets of aluminum foil, form the dough into four 6-in. rolls, 1.5 in. in the diameter. Wrap each of the roll tightly in the foil and keep in the refrigerator overnight.
- Preheat the oven to 165 degrees C (325 degrees F). Use foil to line the cookie sheets. Take the rolls of the dough out of the refrigerator, one at a time. Use the green/red sugar crystals to coat each of the rolls; slice the dough out into a quarter in. slices.
- Add onto the prepped cookie sheets; add a pecan half on each of the cookies. Bake till the bottom of the cookies become brown a bit when being lifted or for 15 - 18 minutes.

Nutrition Information

- Calories: 105 calories;
- Total Fat: 6.5

- Sodium: 52
- Total Carbohydrate: 11.1
- Cholesterol: 12
- Protein: 1.1

322. Cream Cheese Sugar Cookies

Serving: 72 | Prep: 15mins | Cook: 10mins | Ready in:

Ingredients

- 1 cup white sugar
- 1 cup butter, softened
- 1 (3 ounce) package cream cheese, softened
- 1/2 teaspoon salt
- 1/2 teaspoon almond extract
- 1/2 teaspoon vanilla extract
- 1 egg yolk
- 2 1/4 cups all-purpose flour

Direction

- Mix together the butter, sugar, cream cheese, vanilla extracts, almond, egg yolk and salt in a big bowl. Beat the mixture until the consistency turns smooth. Add in flour and stir until completely incorporated. Keep the dough inside the fridge to chill for 8 hours, or up to overnight.
- Set the oven for preheating to 375°F (190°C).
- Dust your work surface lightly with flour. Roll out the dough 1/3 at a time to 1/8 inch in thickness, keeping the remaining dough in the fridge until ready to use. Form into preferred shapes using a lightly floured cookie cutters. Arrange the cookies an inch apart on the cookie sheets that's ungreased. Leave them plain for frosting, or brush them up with slightly beaten egg white and decorate with colored sugar or candy sprinkles.
- Let it bake inside the oven for 7 to 10 minutes, or until the cookies becomes light and golden brown in color. Allow them to cool through before decorating with frosting.

Nutrition Information

- Calories: 53 calories;
- Protein: 0.6
- Total Fat: 3.1
- Sodium: 38
- Total Carbohydrate: 5.8
- Cholesterol: 11

323. Cream Tea Cakes

Serving: 9 | Prep: 30mins | Cook: 10mins | Ready in:

Ingredients

- 1 cup margarine
- 3/4 cup white sugar
- 2 1/4 cups self-rising flour
- 4 tablespoons custard powder
- 1 egg
- 1 pinch salt

Direction

- Preheat the oven to 175 degrees C/350 degrees F.
- Beat sugar and margarine in a medium sized mixing bowl until very soft. Put salt, flour, custard powder and beaten egg. Knead it well on a floured surface.
- Roll it out. Cut using a plain biscuit cutter. Bake them until pale brown for 10 minutes.

Nutrition Information

- Calories: 375 calories;
- Protein: 4
- Total Fat: 20.8
- Sodium: 638
- Total Carbohydrate: 43.6
- Cholesterol: 21

324. Crisp Anise Seed Butter Cookies

Serving: 50 | Prep: 20mins | Cook: 8mins | Ready in:

Ingredients

- 4 cups all-purpose flour
- 1 tablespoon baking powder
- 1/8 teaspoon salt
- 1 cup butter, softened
- 1 cup white sugar
- 2 eggs
- 1 teaspoon vanilla extract
- 3 tablespoons anise seeds
- 1/4 cup white sugar for decoration
- 1 teaspoon ground cinnamon

Direction

- Sift together salt, baking powder, and flour; put aside. Cream together 1 cup sugar and butter in a big bowl until smooth. Whisk in eggs, 1 egg each time, then mix in vanilla. Slowly stir in anise seeds and the sifted ingredients until fully combined. Put the cover on and refrigerate for a few hours to overnight.
- Set the oven to 400°F (200°C) to preheat. Coat baking sheets with oil. On a surface lightly sprinkled with flour, roll out the dough into 1/4-in. thickness. Use cookie cutters to cut into your favorite shapes. On the baking sheets, put the cookies 1 1/2 in. apart. Sprinkle a mixture of cinnamon and the leftover 1/4 cup of sugar over the tops.
- Bake in the preheated oven for 8-10 minutes until they turn light brown. Leave on the cookie sheets to cool, about a couple of minutes, then transfer to wire racks to fully cool. Happy Holidays!

Nutrition Information

- Calories: 93 calories;
- Total Fat: 4
- Sodium: 55
- Total Carbohydrate: 12.9
- Cholesterol: 17
- Protein: 1.4

325. Crispy Golden Macaroons

Serving: 12 | Prep: | Cook: | Ready in:

Ingredients

- 2/3 cup low-fat sweetened condensed milk
- 1 cup cornflakes cereal
- 1 cup crisp rice cereal
- 3/4 cup flaked coconut

Direction

- Preheat the oven to 190°C or 375°Fahrenheit. Grease a cookie sheet lightly.
- Combine flaked coconut, crisp rice cereal, and flaked corn cereal in a medium bowl; mix in sweetened condensed milk until well blended.
- Drop a tablespoon of dough on the greased cookie sheet, about 2-in apart. Bake for 8-10 minutes until golden brown. Cool for a minute in the cookie sheet then transfer to wire racks; completely cool.

Nutrition Information

- Calories: 96 calories;
- Sodium: 66
- Total Carbohydrate: 16.7
- Cholesterol: 2
- Protein: 1.8
- Total Fat: 2

326. Danish Peppernut Christmas Cookies (Pebernodder)

Serving: 200 | Prep: 20mins | Cook: 10mins | Ready in:

Ingredients

- 1 cup butter, softened
- 1 cup white sugar
- 2 eggs
- 1 teaspoon ground cardamom
- 1 teaspoon ground cinnamon
- 1/2 teaspoon ground nutmeg
- 1/4 teaspoon ground cloves
- 1 teaspoon salt
- 2 3/4 cups all-purpose flour, or as needed

Direction

- Turn on the oven to 350°F (175°C) to preheat. Prepare 2-3 baking sheets and grease lightly.
- In a mixing bowl, combine sugar and butter; beat until it is fluffy and light. Add eggs, one at a time; beat well to combine after each addition. Add salt, cloves, nutmeg and cinnamon into the cardamom; stir well to combine. Add in flour, one cup at a time; mix well to gather the dough. Pinch off small, 1/2 teaspoon amounts of dough with floured hand; roll so that it forms tiny balls, transfer into baking sheets.
- Put into the oven for 10-12 minutes until the cookies bottom are lightly tanned. Let it cool on baking sheets for 15 minutes. Transfer into airtight container to store.

Nutrition Information

- Calories: 19 calories;
- Protein: 0.3
- Total Fat: 1
- Sodium: 19
- Total Carbohydrate: 2.3
- Cholesterol: 4

327. Date Rolls

Serving: 36 | Prep: | Cook: | Ready in:

Ingredients

- 1 cup shortening
- 1 cup white sugar
- 1 cup packed brown sugar
- 3 eggs
- 1 teaspoon vanilla extract
- 1 tablespoon water
- 4 cups all-purpose flour
- 1 teaspoon baking soda
- 1 teaspoon salt
- 1 pound dates, pitted and chopped
- 1/2 cup white sugar
- 1 cup water

Direction

- Cream shortening, 1 cup of brown sugar and 1 cup of white sugar. Mix in 1 tablespoon of water, vanilla and eggs.
- Sift the salt, soda and flour together two times then add them to the sugar mixture. Divide the dough into 2 or 3 portions.
- Cook dates with 1 cup of water and half a cup of white sugar over low heat, stir regularly until it turns into a smooth paste. Let cool.
- Roll each portion out into rectangles with 1/4 to 1/2-inch thickness.
- Add filling on the rectangles, spread out and roll into jelly-roll style. Cover and let chill for 2 to 3 hours to get firm dough.
- Set oven at 180°C (350°F) and start preheating. Divide the dough into 1/4 to 1/2 inch thick slices. Bake them for 10 to 12 minutes.

Nutrition Information

- Calories: 198 calories;
- Cholesterol: 16
- Protein: 2.3
- Total Fat: 6.3

- Sodium: 108
- Total Carbohydrate: 34.4

328. Date Turnovers

Serving: 12 | Prep: 45mins | Cook: 15mins | Ready in:

Ingredients

- 2 cups pitted dates, chopped
- 1/2 cup water
- 1/4 cup brown sugar
- 1 tablespoon cider vinegar
- 1/2 cup milk
- 2 cups all-purpose flour
- 1 teaspoon baking soda
- 2 1/2 cups regular rolled oats
- 1 1/2 cups brown sugar
- 1/2 cup melted butter
- 1/2 cup butter-flavored shortening (such as Crisco®), melted

Direction

- Add 1/4 cup of brown sugar, water and dates into a saucepan, heat over medium heat; cook for about 5 minutes until dates get totally soft. Let cool to room temperature and put aside.
- Mix milk with vinegar in a bowl; let curdle for 10 minutes and put aside.
- In a big bowl, mix the baking soda and flour, mix in 1 1/2 cups of brown sugar and oats. Mix in the milk mixture, shortening and butter; cover the dough and let chill in fridge for about 60 minutes until firm.
- Set oven at 175°C (350°F) and start preheating. Use parchment paper to line baking trays.
- Take the dough to a light-floured surface, roll it out into about 1/8-inch thick; divide into rounds using a round cookie cutter. Add about 1 tablespoon of the date mixture at the middle of each rounds; fold in half and pinch to seal edges. Put them on the lined baking trays.
- Put the cookies in the preheated oven and bake for about 10 minute until they turn golden. Take to a wire rack and let cool.

Nutrition Information

- Calories: 497 calories;
- Sodium: 175
- Total Carbohydrate: 81.5
- Cholesterol: 21
- Protein: 5.6
- Total Fat: 18.2

329. Date And Orange Slice Bars

Serving: 24 | Prep: 30mins | Cook: 30mins | Ready in:

Ingredients

- 8 ounces chopped pitted dates
- 1/2 cup white sugar
- 2 tablespoons all-purpose flour
- 1 cup water
- 3/4 cup shortening
- 1 cup packed brown sugar
- 2 eggs
- 1 teaspoon vanilla extract
- 1 teaspoon baking soda
- 2 tablespoons hot water
- 1 3/4 cups all-purpose flour
- 1/4 teaspoon salt
- 2 (10.5 ounce) packages orange slice candies, cut in half lengthwise

Direction

- Mix the water, 2 tablespoons of flour, 1/2 cup of sugar and dates in a saucepan. Boil, and let cook for 10 minutes till thickened. Take off heat, and reserve to cool.
- Preheat an oven to 165 °C or 325 °F. Oil a baking dish, 9x13 inch in size.

- Cream together brown sugar and shortening in medium bowl till smooth. Mix in eggs one by one, then mix in vanilla. In hot water, melt baking soda, then mix into creamed mixture. Put together the salt and 1 3/4 cups flour; mix into batter barely till incorporated.
- In the base of prepped pan, scatter 1/2 of batter. Arrange orange slice candy to cover, then scatter date mixture on top of orange candy. Top with the rest of the batter to cover.
- In the prepped oven, let bake for half an hour, or till golden brown. Allow to cool, and slice into bars.

Nutrition Information

- Calories: 271 calories;
- Cholesterol: 16
- Protein: 1.8
- Total Fat: 7
- Sodium: 96
- Total Carbohydrate: 51.9

330. Date Nut Balls

Serving: 48 | Prep: 15mins | Cook: 10mins | Ready in:

Ingredients

- 14 tablespoons butter
- 1 cup pitted chopped dates
- 1 cup white sugar
- 2 cups crispy rice cereal (such as Rice Krispies®)
- 1 cup chopped pecans
- 2 tablespoons confectioners' sugar, or as needed

Direction

- Melt the butter on medium heat in the sauce pan; cook and stir the white sugar and dates in melted butter for 10-15 minutes or till becoming thickened and golden brown. Take the saucepan out of the heat and mix in the pecans and crispy rice cereal. Allow the mixture to cool down till becoming easy to handle, for 5 - 10 minutes.
- Shape the mixture into small balls with your hands.
- Add the confectioners' sugar to the resealable bag; put in nut-date balls and shake the bag a bit till the balls become coated.

Nutrition Information

- Calories: 76 calories;
- Protein: 0.4
- Total Fat: 5
- Sodium: 33
- Total Carbohydrate: 8.1
- Cholesterol: 9

331. Dawn's Easy Red Velvet Sandwich Cookies

Serving: 24 | Prep: 25mins | Cook: 8mins | Ready in:

Ingredients

- 1 (18.25 ounce) box red velvet cake mix
- 2 eggs, lightly beaten
- 1/2 cup vegetable oil
- 1 tablespoon bourbon
- Icing
- 1 (8 ounce) package cream cheese, softened
- 1/4 cup butter, softened
- 2 teaspoons evaporated milk
- 1 teaspoon vanilla
- 1/2 cup flaked coconut
- 4 cups confectioners' sugar
- 1/2 cup chopped pecans

Direction

- Set oven to 190°C (375°F) and start preheating.
- In a big bowl, combine bourbon, oil, eggs and cake mix. Roll cookie dough into walnut-sized

balls. Arrange onto ungreased baking sheets, placing each 2 in. away from each other.
- Bake for 8 minutes at 190°C (375°F) until starting to crack on the top. Keep in baking sheets to cool for 10 minutes, then transfer to a wire rack and let cool fully.
- Mix together coconut, vanilla, evaporated milk, butter and cream cheese in a big bowl. Put in confectioners' sugar, one cup at a time, stirring thoroughly between additions. If the dough becomes too stiff, put in additional milk.
- In a bowl, add the chopped pecans. For each cookie, generously spread icing on the bottom and attach to another cookie to make a sandwich, firmly pressing to spread the icing all over until the edge. Roll the edges in the chopped pecans. Repeat the same steps to the rest of the cookies.

Nutrition Information

- Calories: 292 calories;
- Total Carbohydrate: 39.9
- Cholesterol: 29
- Protein: 2.5
- Total Fat: 14.3
- Sodium: 182

332. Decorated Shortbread Cutouts With Nutella® Hazelnut Spread

Serving: 20 | Prep: 30mins | Cook: 10mins | Ready in:

Ingredients

- 1 1/3 cups flour
- 1/4 cup granulated sugar
- 7 tablespoons butter, room temperature
- 1 pinch salt
- 3/4 teaspoon gingerbread spice mix
- 1/3 cup Nutella® hazelnut spread
- Cookie cutter or a stencil made out of cardboard

Direction

- Combine all the ingredients in a bowl for 1 to 2 minutes, but the Nutella® hazelnut spread, until the dough turns workable. Between two sheets of baking paper, roll out the dough until it achieves around 1/8-inch of thickness.
- Use a cookie cutter or a stencil to cut out the dough.
- Place in the refrigerator for 30 minutes
- Prepare the oven by preheating to 325°F and place the baking rack in the center of the oven.
- Use baking paper to line a baking tray and place the cookies on it. Place in the preheated oven and bake for 10-11 minutes. Take from the oven and allow them to cool down on the tray. Stuff a piping bag fitted with a small nozzle (approx.1/16 inch) with the Nutella® hazelnut spread and pipe 1/2 tablespoon on half of the cookies and assemble with the other half.
- Complete your cutout cookies with Nutella® hazelnut spread.

Nutrition Information

- Calories: 103 calories;
- Total Fat: 5.7
- Sodium: 39
- Total Carbohydrate: 11.7
- Cholesterol: 11
- Protein: 1.2

333. Delicious Christmas Cookies

Serving: 54 | Prep: 15mins | Cook: 9mins | Ready in:

Ingredients

- 1 1/2 cups graham cracker crumbs

- 1/2 cup all-purpose flour
- 2 teaspoons baking powder
- 1 (14 ounce) can sweetened condensed milk
- 1/2 cup butter, softened
- 1 1/2 cups sweetened, flaked coconut
- 2 cups red and green candy-coated chocolate

Direction

- Set an oven to preheat to 190°C (375°F).
- Mix together the baking powder, flour and graham cracker crumbs in a medium bowl.
- Mix together the butter and condensed milk in another big bowl, then beat it until it becomes smooth. Mix in the graham cracker mixture and stir well. Stir in the chocolates and coconut.
- Drop it by rounded teaspoonfuls onto ungreased cookie sheets.
- Let it bake for 7-9 minutes in the preheated oven or until it turns light brown. Let the cookies cool for 1 minute on the baking tray prior to transferring to a wire rack to fully cool.

Nutrition Information

- Calories: 100 calories;
- Total Fat: 4.8
- Sodium: 59
- Total Carbohydrate: 13.2
- Cholesterol: 8
- Protein: 1.3

334. Dish Pan Cookies

Serving: 60 | Prep: 15mins | Cook: 1hours30mins | Ready in:

Ingredients

- 2 cups white sugar
- 2 cups light brown sugar
- 4 eggs
- 2 cups vegetable oil
- 2 teaspoons vanilla extract
- 4 cups all-purpose flour
- 2 teaspoons baking soda
- 2 teaspoons salt
- 4 cups cornflakes cereal
- 1 1/2 cups rolled oats
- 1 cup flaked coconut
- 1 cup chopped pecans
- 1 cup chopped dates
- 1 cup raisins

Direction

- Set the oven to 165°C or 325°F to preheat. Coat a cookie sheet lightly with grease.
- In a big bowl or dishpan, cream together vanilla, vegetable oil, eggs, brown sugar and white sugar. Mix together salt, baking soda flour in another bowl. Stir into the creamed sugar with the flour mixture and mix until well-blended.
- Stir into the dough with raisins, dates, pecans, coconut, oats and corn flakes. Mix everything thoroughly using your hands. Form the dough into balls with 1 1/2-2 inches in size. On a cookie sheet coated with grease, press balls down slightly.
- In the preheated oven, bake at 165°C or 325°F until turn golden, about 10-14 minutes.

Nutrition Information

- Calories: 206 calories;
- Cholesterol: 14
- Protein: 2.1
- Total Fat: 10.4
- Sodium: 140
- Total Carbohydrate: 27.3

335. Drommar

Serving: 25 | Prep: 45mins | Cook: 12mins | Ready in:

Ingredients

- 1 cup butter
- 3/4 cup white sugar
- 1 teaspoon baking powder
- 2 teaspoons vanilla extract
- 1/2 teaspoon ground cardamom
- 2 cups all-purpose flour
- 50 blanched whole almonds, toasted

Direction

- Set oven to 180 degrees C (350 degrees F) to preheat.
- Cook butter in a big heavy skillet over medium-low heat for about 15 minutes without stirring, until butter appears light tan in color. Transfer into mixing bowl. Chill over a bowl of cold water until it firms.
- Beat in cardamom, vanilla, baking powder and sugar until well blended. Stir in flour.
- Cut dough into balls of 1 inch size. Arrange each ball on a cookie sheet that's not greased so they are 1 inch apart from each other. Garnish each with an almond; press almond into a dough slightly.
- Bake for 12 to 15 minutes, until it appears golden brown.
- Take it out of the oven and cool on a wire rack.

Nutrition Information

- Calories: 140 calories;
- Total Fat: 8.7
- Sodium: 73
- Total Carbohydrate: 14.2
- Cholesterol: 20
- Protein: 1.6

---

336. Dutch Cookies

Serving: 40 | Prep: | Cook: | Ready in:

Ingredients

- 1/2 cup butter
- 1/2 cup shortening
- 1 cup white sugar
- 2 cups all-purpose flour
- 1/2 teaspoon baking soda
- salt to taste
- 1 teaspoon vanilla extract
- 1 cup semi-sweet chocolate chips

Direction

- Set an oven to preheat to 175°C (350°F).
- Cream together the vanilla, sugar, shortening and butter.
- Sift together the salt, baking soda and flour, then add it to the sugar mixture and stir well. Be cautious not to overmix.
- On ungreased cookie sheet, drop heaping teaspoonfuls of dough and flatten each using the tines of a fork (submerge the fork into a small bowl of water so that the dough will not stick to the fork). Do this 1-2 times. It depends on the size of the fork and cookie.
- Let it bake for 13-15 minutes. After each pan has taken out of the oven, put 5-6 chocolate chips carefully on top of each cookie while they are still hot. Spread with a knife when the chocolate is soft and glossy.

Nutrition Information

- Calories: 107 calories;
- Total Fat: 6.1
- Sodium: 32
- Total Carbohydrate: 12.5
- Cholesterol: 6
- Protein: 1

---

337. Easy Lemon Cookies

Serving: 36 | Prep: | Cook: | Ready in:

Ingredients

- 1 (18.25 ounce) package lemon cake mix
- 2 eggs
- 1/3 cup vegetable oil
- 1 teaspoon lemon extract
- 1/3 cup confectioners' sugar for decoration

Direction

- Set an oven to 190°C (375°F) and start preheating.
- Place the cake mix into a large bowl. Stir in lemon extract, oil, and eggs until combined thoroughly. Add into a bowl with confectioners' sugar by dropping teaspoonfuls of dough. Roll around to cover them lightly. Arrange them onto an ungreased cookie sheet when sugared.
- In the prepared oven, bake for 6-9 minutes. The insides will become chewy and the bottoms will turn light brown.

Nutrition Information

- Calories: 87 calories;
- Cholesterol: 14
- Protein: 1.2
- Total Fat: 4
- Sodium: 107
- Total Carbohydrate: 11.6

338. Easy Nanaimo Bars

Serving: 16 | Prep: 25mins | Cook: | Ready in:

Ingredients

- 1/2 cup butter
- 2 (1 ounce) envelopes instant hot chocolate mix
- 1 teaspoon vanilla extract
- 1 egg, beaten
- 2 cups graham cracker crumbs
- 1 cup flaked coconut
- 1/2 cup chopped walnuts
- 1/4 cup cream cheese, softened
- 1/4 cup milk, or as needed
- 2 tablespoons instant vanilla pudding mix
- 2 cups confectioners' sugar
- 4 (1 ounce) squares milk chocolate
- 1 tablespoon butter

Direction

- Use grease to coat a 9x9-in. square pan. Place a saucepan on low heat; melt 1/2 cup of butter; mix in egg, vanilla extract and cocoa mix. Whisk together for around 1 minute, or till the mixture is thickened (do not boil); take away from the heat; mix in walnuts, 1 cup of coconut and graham cracker crumbs. Stir well; press onto the bottom of the prepared pan. Keep chill for around 1 hour.
- In a mixing bowl, beat cream cheese using an electric mixer till fluffy and smooth. Beat in confectioners' sugar, vanilla pudding mix and milk to form a creamy and spreadable mixture. Add in more milk, 1/2 teaspoon per time, if the mixture seems too stiff to spread easily. Spread the filling over the crust, in an even layer; return back to the refrigerator. Keep chilled for around 1 hour, or till firm.
- Place a saucepan on very low heat; melt while stirring constantly 1 tablespoon of butter and milk chocolate till the mixture is well-combined and smooth. Evenly spread the toppings over the vanilla layer; place in the refrigerator till the topping is firm but not hard, around 1/2 hour. Cut into bars; return back to the refrigerator for at least 1/2 hour longer to finish the chilling. Serve cold.

Nutrition Information

- Calories: 285 calories;
- Total Fat: 15.1
- Sodium: 188
- Total Carbohydrate: 35.6
- Cholesterol: 35
- Protein: 3.1

339. Easy Sugar Cookies

Serving: 48 | Prep: 15mins | Cook: 10mins | Ready in:

Ingredients

- 2 3/4 cups all-purpose flour
- 1 teaspoon baking soda
- 1/2 teaspoon baking powder
- 1 cup butter, softened
- 1 1/2 cups white sugar
- 1 egg
- 1 teaspoon vanilla extract

Direction

- Set an oven to 190°C (375°F) and start preheating. Stir baking powder, baking soda, and flour in a small bowl. Then put aside.
- Cream sugar and butter together in a large bowl until they become smooth. Whisk in vanilla and egg. Combine in the dry ingredients gradually. Roll rounded teaspoonfuls of dough to form into balls, then transfer onto ungreased cookie sheets.
- In the prepared oven, bake until golden, or for 8-10 minutes. Allow to stand on the cookie sheet for 2 minutes, then transfer onto wire racks to cool.

Nutrition Information

- Calories: 86 calories;
- Protein: 0.9
- Total Fat: 4
- Sodium: 60
- Total Carbohydrate: 11.7
- Cholesterol: 14

340. Easy Three Ingredient Gluten Free German Christmas Coconut Cookies

Serving: 45 | Prep: 25mins | Cook: 15mins | Ready in:

Ingredients

- 4 egg whites
- 1 cup white sugar
- 2 cups unsweetened coconut flakes

Direction

- Set oven to 300 0 F (150 0C) and preheat. Use parchment paper to line 2 baking sheets.
- In a glass, metal, or ceramic bowl, whisk egg whites until forming stiff peaks. Slowly combine in sugar, one tablespoon at a time, and keep beating. Use a spatula to fold in coconut flakes.
- Place onto the baking sheets little mounds of coconut mixture by 2 inches apart using 2 teaspoons.
- Put into the prepared oven and bake for 15 to 20 minutes, until lightly browned, depending on the size of the cookies. Let them cool on baking sheet for a few minutes, then carefully move onto a wire rack to cool completely.

Nutrition Information

- Calories: 46 calories;
- Total Carbohydrate: 5.4
- Cholesterol: 0
- Protein: 0.6
- Total Fat: 2.7
- Sodium: 6

341. Easy Toffee Bars

Serving: 24 | Prep: 5mins | Cook: 15mins | Ready in:

Ingredients

- 1 cup butter
- 1 cup packed brown sugar
- 1 (10 ounce) package saltine crackers
- 1 (12 ounce) package semisweet chocolate chips

Direction

- Set an oven to preheat to 200°C (400°F).
- Melt the butter with brown sugar in a small saucepan on medium-high heat, then boil and take it out of the heat.
- On a jelly roll pan, lay out the crackers, salt side facing up. Pour the butter mixture on top of the crackers.
- Let it bake for 5 minutes in the preheated oven.
- Take it out of the oven and sprinkle chocolate chips on top of the crackers. Let it bake for 5 minutes more.

Nutrition Information

- Calories: 220 calories;
- Total Fat: 13.2
- Sodium: 184
- Total Carbohydrate: 26.1
- Cholesterol: 20
- Protein: 1.8

342. Easy Vegan Gingerbread Cookies

Serving: 24 | Prep: 10mins | Cook: 8mins | Ready in:

Ingredients

- 1 1/2 cups all-purpose flour
- 1 teaspoon baking powder
- 1 teaspoon ground cinnamon
- 1/2 teaspoon baking soda
- 1/2 teaspoon ground ginger
- 1/2 teaspoon ground allspice
- 1/4 teaspoon salt
- 1/2 cup coconut oil, at room temperature
- 1/3 cup molasses
- 1/4 cup white sugar
- 1 teaspoon vanilla extract

Direction

- Set the oven to preheating at 350°F (175°C). Prepare two baking pans and line them with parchment paper.
- Sift cinnamon, allspice, salt, baking soda, baking powder, flour, and ginger into a bowl.
- Use an electric mixer to cream sugar, molasses, and coconut oil in a bowl. Stir in vanilla extract. Add the flour mixture and whisk until the dough is sticky, for about 2 minutes. Use a plastic wrap to cover the dough and let it chill for 2 hours.
- Dust flour on a working surface and roll out dough to 1/4-1/2-inch thick. Coat the cookie cutter with flour and use it cut the cookies. Place the cutout cookies into the prepared baking pans.
- Let it bake inside the preheated oven for 8-10 minutes until lightly golden.

Nutrition Information

- Calories: 90 calories;
- Total Fat: 4.6
- Sodium: 73
- Total Carbohydrate: 11.7
- Cholesterol: 0
- Protein: 0.8

343. Egg Yolk Painted Christmas Cookies

Serving: 24 | Prep: 10mins | Cook: 15mins | Ready in:

Ingredients

- 1/2 cup butter, softened
- 1/2 cup shortening

- 1 cup sifted confectioners' sugar
- 1 egg
- 1 teaspoon vanilla extract
- 2 1/2 cups all-purpose flour
- 1 teaspoon salt
- 1 egg yolk
- 1/4 teaspoon water
- assorted colors of paste food coloring

Direction

- Cream shortening and margarine or butter; slowly put in the sugar, whipping till fluffy and light. Put in the vanilla and egg; whip thoroughly.
- Mix salt and flour; mix into the creamed mixture. Split the dough in half; refrigerate with cover for not less than 1 hour.
- Unroll a dough portion on a cookie sheet slightly dusted with flour into thickness of 1/8 inch. Use with assorted cutters to cut dough out; take the dough trimmings. Use small paintbrush and Egg Yolk Paint to paint various patterns over cookies. Bake about 9 to 10 minutes, at 190 ° C or 375 ° F. Transfer onto wire racks and let cool. Redo the process with the rest of the dough.
- Prep Egg Yolk Paint: mix water and egg yolk; combine thoroughly. Distribute mixture to a few custard cups; color as wished using paste food coloring. Put on cover till set to use. Put several drops of water in case paint thickens, and stir thoroughly. Makes 1 1/2 tablespoons.

Nutrition Information

- Calories: 145 calories;
- Cholesterol: 26
- Protein: 1.8
- Total Fat: 8.6
- Sodium: 128
- Total Carbohydrate: 15.2

344. Eileen's Spicy Gingerbread Men

Serving: 30 | Prep: 20mins | Cook: 10mins | Ready in:

Ingredients

- 1/2 cup margarine
- 1/2 cup sugar
- 1/2 cup molasses
- 1 egg yolk
- 2 cups sifted all-purpose flour
- 1/2 teaspoon salt
- 1/2 teaspoon baking powder
- 1/2 teaspoon baking soda
- 1/2 teaspoon ground cinnamon
- 1 teaspoon ground cloves
- 1 teaspoon ginger
- 1/2 teaspoon ground nutmeg

Direction

- Cream the margarine and sugar in a large bowl until smooth. Stir in egg yolk and molasses. Combine baking powder, cinnamon, ginger, nutmeg, cloves, baking soda, salt, and flour. Pour the dry mixture into the molasses mixture and mix until smooth. Cover and let it chill for at least 60 minutes.
- Set the oven to 350°F or 175°C to preheat. Roll the dough in a lightly floured surface to form a 1/4-inch thick dough. Use the cookie cutter to cut the dough according to your desired shape. Place the cookies into the ungreased cookie sheets, arranging them 2-inches away from each other.
- Let it bake inside the preheated oven for 8-10 minutes until the cookies are set. Transfer the cookies on wire racks and allow them to cool completely. Frost or decorate the cookies once cooled.

Nutrition Information

- Calories: 88 calories;
- Total Fat: 3.3
- Sodium: 103

- Total Carbohydrate: 14
- Cholesterol: 7
- Protein: 1

345. Esther's Christmas Cookies

Serving: 144 | Prep: 45mins | Cook: 14mins | Ready in:

Ingredients

- 1 1/2 cups butter
- 6 cups white sugar
- 3 eggs
- 1 teaspoon vanilla extract
- 1/2 cup milk
- 1 pound candied cherries, chopped
- 1/2 pound candied pineapple, coarsely chopped
- 5 cups chopped walnuts
- 1 pound golden raisins
- 6 cups self-rising flour
- 1 cup rolled oats
- 1 cup shredded coconut
- 1 tablespoon ground nutmeg

Direction

- Cream sugar and butter together in an extremely big bowl until smooth. Beat in 1 egg at a time, then stir in milk and vanilla. Put in nuts mixed with flour, raisins, pineapple and candied cherries. Stir in coconut and oatmeal. Form balls with the size of a big walnut and flatten a little. Arrange onto ungreased cookie sheets.
- On the middle rack of oven, bake at 150°C or 300°F, 1 pan at a time, until bottoms are browned slightly, or about 10-12 minutes. Cookies will have underdone appearance.
- Use nutmeg to sprinkle over cookie and leave them on cookie sheet for 10 minutes to complete cooking. Remove to cooling rack and prepare a lot of containers to store.

Nutrition Information

- Calories: 123 calories;
- Cholesterol: 9
- Protein: 1.5
- Total Fat: 5
- Sodium: 87
- Total Carbohydrate: 19.1

346. Evelyn's Rolled Sugar Cookies

Serving: 36 | Prep: | Cook: | Ready in:

Ingredients

- 1 1/2 cups white sugar
- 1 cup shortening
- 3/4 cup milk
- 2 eggs
- 1 teaspoon baking powder
- 1 teaspoon baking soda
- 1/2 teaspoon salt
- 3 1/2 cups all-purpose flour

Direction

- Preheat oven to 375°F (190°C).
- Cream sugar and the shortening together. Mix in eggs and beat well.
- Sift the baking powder, flour, salt and baking soda together in a separate bowl. Add in flour mixture in thirds. Add 1/4 cup of the milk after each third and mix well. Dough will be soft.
- On well-floured surface, place dough and knead in enough additional flour in order for it to be rolled. Use your favorite cookie cutter to cut.
- Bake the dough on the parchment-lined baking sheet for approximately 10 minutes. Rotate the sheets, baking each sheet for around 5 minutes on middle, then another 5 minutes on top rack.

Nutrition Information

- Calories: 133 calories;
- Total Fat: 6.2
- Sodium: 87
- Total Carbohydrate: 17.9
- Cholesterol: 11
- Protein: 1.8

347. Fatty Natty's Peanut Butter Fudge Balls

Serving: 20 | Prep: 15mins | Cook: | Ready in:

Ingredients

- 2 cups confectioners' sugar
- 1 cup peanut butter
- 1/4 cup butter, melted
- 2 tablespoons cocoa powder
- 2 tablespoons marshmallow cream (such as Marshmallow Fluff®)
- 1 teaspoon vanilla extract

Direction

- In a bowl, mix together vanilla extract, marshmallow creme, cocoa powder, butter, peanut butter and confectioners' sugar, until they become smooth. Roll to form into 2-inch balls. Arrange in a sealed container. Place in the refrigerator at least half an hour until set.

Nutrition Information

- Calories: 147 calories;
- Total Fat: 8.9
- Sodium: 76
- Total Carbohydrate: 15.3
- Cholesterol: 6
- Protein: 3.4

348. Festive Fruit Squares

Serving: 36 | Prep: | Cook: | Ready in:

Ingredients

- 2/3 cup mixed candied fruit
- 1/4 cup all-purpose flour
- 1/2 cup butter
- 1/2 cup white sugar
- 2 tablespoons frozen orange juice concentrate
- 1 egg
- 1/4 teaspoon almond extract
- 1 1/2 cups all-purpose flour
- 1/2 teaspoon baking soda
- 1/4 teaspoon salt
- 1/2 cup chopped walnuts
- 1 1/2 cups confectioners' sugar
- 3 tablespoons butter
- 2 tablespoons orange juice

Direction

- Turn on the oven to 350°F (175°C) to preheat. Prepare a 9x9-inch square pan and lightly grease.
- Mix together 1/4 cup of flour and glaceed fruit just enough for the fruit to be coated in a small bowl. Cream sugar and butter together in a medium bowl. Mix in orange juice concentrate, egg and almond extract. Run salt, baking soda and flour through a sieve; mix into the creamed mixture. Mix in walnuts and flour coated fruit.
- In the 9x9-inch pan, spread out the batter evenly. Put into the oven until bars start to loosen from the pan side, 20 minutes. Take it out of the oven and let it cool before frosting.
- For the frosting, in a small bowl, mix together orange juice, 3 tablespoons of butter and confectioners' sugar. Beat until fluffy and light. Transfer to cooled bars and spread out. Cut into squares to serve.

Nutrition Information

- Calories: 112 calories;

- Sodium: 74
- Total Carbohydrate: 16.7
- Cholesterol: 14
- Protein: 1.1
- Total Fat: 4.8

349. Festive Shortbread

Serving: 30 | Prep: | Cook: | Ready in:

Ingredients

- 2 cups butter, softened
- 1 3/4 cups sifted confectioners' sugar
- 4 1/2 cups sifted all-purpose flour

Direction

- Cream butter and mix in sugar, a little at a time. Put in flour, beating 1 part at a time. Use wax paper to wrap and refrigerate.
- Set oven to 150°C (300°F) and start preheating.
- Let the dough warm a little and knead the dough for a minute. On a board slightly dusted with flour, roll out the dough to 1/4-in. thickness and use cookie cutters to cut. Decorate as you like. Bake for 14 to 20 minutes at 150°C (300°F).

Nutrition Information

- Calories: 205 calories;
- Sodium: 88
- Total Carbohydrate: 21.6
- Cholesterol: 33
- Protein: 2.1
- Total Fat: 12.5

350. Fig Filling For Pastry

Serving: 24 | Prep: 25mins | Cook: 5mins | Ready in:

Ingredients

- 1 pound dried figs
- 1 orange, zested
- 1/2 cup semisweet chocolate chips
- 1/4 cup whiskey
- 1/2 cup chopped walnuts
- 1 teaspoon cinnamon
- 1/4 cup maple sugar

Direction

- Use scissors to remove fig stems. In batches, chop in food processor.
- Mix cinnamon, maple syrup, walnuts, whiskey, chocolate chips, orange zest and chopped figs in nonstick pan. Heat till chocolate melts, frequently mixing, on medium heat. Completely cool.

Nutrition Information

- Calories: 95 calories;
- Total Carbohydrate: 16.9
- Cholesterol: 0
- Protein: 1.1
- Total Fat: 2.9
- Sodium: 3

351. Florentines II

Serving: 30 | Prep: | Cook: | Ready in:

Ingredients

- 1/4 cup white sugar
- 3/4 cup heavy whipping cream
- 1/4 cup all-purpose flour
- 1/2 cup finely chopped almonds
- 8 ounces chopped candied orange peel
- 8 (1 ounce) squares semisweet chocolate

Direction

- Preheat an oven to 175°C/350°F.

- Blend cream and sugar; mix in orange peel, almonds and flour. By teaspoonfuls, drop onto heavily creased and floured cookie sheet. Use a spatula to spread mixture to thin circles.
- Bake for 10-12 minutes at 175°C/350°F till edges are light brown; cool for several minutes. Remove from cookie sheet; cool.
- Chop up chocolate to small pieces; melt the chocolate in microwave for 3 minutes on medium or on low heat. Flip cooled cookies upside down; spread melted chocolate on bottoms. Stand cookies for a minimum of 3 hours till chocolate is firm in room temperature. Keep in room temperature in covered container/refrigerated.

Nutrition Information

- Calories: 106 calories;
- Sodium: 2
- Total Carbohydrate: 13.5
- Cholesterol: 8
- Protein: 1.3
- Total Fat: 5.8

352. French Peppermint Cookies With Chocolate Ganache

Serving: 24 | Prep: 30mins | Cook: 1hours30mins | Ready in:

Ingredients

- 3 egg whites at room temperature
- 1/4 cup white sugar
- 1/4 teaspoon cream of tartar
- 1 dash peppermint extract, or to taste
- 2 cups confectioners' sugar, or as needed
- 1 (6 ounce) package semisweet chocolate chips
- 3/4 cup heavy whipping cream, or as needed
- 1 teaspoon white sugar, or to taste
- 1 peppermint candy cane, finely crushed

Direction

- Place the rack on the bottom of the oven and preheat an oven to 80 degrees C (175 degrees F). Line aluminum foil onto baking sheets.
- At the top of a double boiler that is set on simmering water, whisk 1/4 cup white sugar and egg whites until smooth. Then whisk peppermint extract and cream of tartar into the egg mixture. Beat until foamy. Slowly whisk the confectioners' sugar into the mixture while beating until the egg white meringue can hold stiff peaks.
- Spoon approximately one tablespoon meringue for each cookie and then transfer gently into the prepped baking sheets. Shape the meringue cookies into a football shape with two gently pointed ends using a spoon.
- Bake the cookies at the bottom rack of the prepared oven for about 1 1/2 hours until they are dry outside but still a bit soft in the middle. Cool completely prior to transferring from the baking sheets.
- At the top of double boiler above simmering water, melt the chocolate chips while stirring until melted and smooth. Slowly stir the cream into the chocolate until the mixture becomes thick but not pasty. Mix one teaspoon of white sugar into the chocolate ganache until the sugar is dissolved. Immerse the cookies into ganache. Put the dipped cookies onto a piece of parchment paper and drizzle with crushed peppermint candy. Allow the cookies to set. Chill the leftovers.

Nutrition Information

- Calories: 115 calories;
- Cholesterol: 10
- Protein: 0.9
- Total Fat: 4.9
- Sodium: 11
- Total Carbohydrate: 18.5

353. Fruit Meringues

Serving: 18 | Prep: | Cook: | Ready in:

Ingredients

- 4 egg whites
- 1/4 teaspoon cream of tartar
- 1/4 teaspoon salt
- 1 cup fructose (fruit sugar)
- 2 teaspoons vanilla extract
- 1/2 cup chopped walnuts
- 1/2 cup diced mixed candied fruit
- 1/2 cup flaked coconut

Direction

- Heat the oven to 135°C or 275°F. Line parchment paper on baking sheets.
- Beat egg whites in medium bowl, till foamy. Put in salt and cream of tartar. Keep beating to form soft peaks. Little by little put in sugar while beating, try to put in gently to ensure it will not fall to bowl bottom. Beat till mixture holds firm peaks. Fold in fruit, coconut and nuts. Drop rounded teaspoons of mixture to prepped cookie sheets.
- Bake in prepped oven till firm, about 45 minutes to 60 minutes. Cool away from drafts, on the baking sheets.

Nutrition Information

- Calories: 92 calories;
- Total Fat: 2.7
- Sodium: 51
- Total Carbohydrate: 16.8
- Cholesterol: 0
- Protein: 1.4

354. German Lebkuchen

Serving: 36 | Prep: 15mins | Cook: 12mins | Ready in:

Ingredients

- 1 egg
- 3/4 cup brown sugar
- 1/2 cup honey
- 1/2 cup dark molasses
- 3 cups sifted all-purpose flour
- 1/2 teaspoon baking soda
- 1 1/4 teaspoons ground nutmeg
- 1 1/4 teaspoons ground cinnamon
- 1/2 teaspoon ground cloves
- 1/2 teaspoon ground allspice
- 1/2 cup slivered almonds
- 1/2 cup candied mixed fruit peel, finely chopped
- 1 egg white, beaten
- 1 tablespoon lemon juice
- 1/2 teaspoon lemon zest
- 1 1/2 cups sifted confectioners' sugar

Direction

- Beat honey, brown sugar and egg in a large bowl until they become smooth. Mix in molasses. Combine allspice, cloves, cinnamon, nutmeg, baking soda and flour; stir into molasses mixture. Stir in candied fruit peel and almonds. Wrap or cover the dough, then chill overnight.
- Start preheating oven to 400°F (200°C). Lightly coat cookie sheets with oil. Roll dough out on a lightly floured surface to 1/4-in. thick. Then cut into rectangles, about 2x3-inches in size. Arrange cookies onto the cookie sheets, by 1 1/2-in. apart.
- Bake in prepared oven until firm, for 10-12 minutes. Brush lemon glaze over cookies while still warm.
- For glaze: Stir lemon zest, lemon juice and egg white together in a small bowl. Mix in confectioners' sugar until they become smooth. Then brush over the cookies.

Nutrition Information

- Calories: 120 calories;
- Total Carbohydrate: 26.6

- Cholesterol: 5
- Protein: 1.7
- Total Fat: 1.1
- Sodium: 24

355. German Twists

Serving: 24 | Prep: 1hours | Cook: 15mins | Ready in:

Ingredients

- 1 (.25 ounce) package active dry yeast
- 1/4 cup warm water
- 3 1/2 cups bleached all-purpose flour
- 1 teaspoon salt
- 1 cup butter, sliced
- 3/4 cup sour cream
- 1 large egg
- 2 large egg yolks
- 1 teaspoon vanilla extract
- 1 cup white sugar, or as needed

Direction

- In a bowl filled with warm water, put in the yeast and allow it to activate while you perform the other steps in this recipe.
- Use a food processor to pulse the salt and flour together 1 or 2 times until blended. Spread slices of butter on top of the flour-salt mixture and allow the food processor to run for about 1 minute until the butter has fully incorporated into the flour.
- In a bowl, combine the egg, yeast mixture, vanilla extract, sour cream and egg yolks together then add the mixture into the food processor. Pulse the mixture a couple times just until the dough has come together and clean the sides around the bowl (make sure not to overmix the dough). Take the dough from the food processor and separate it into 2 equal portions then shape each of the dough portions in the shape of a thick disk; use a plastic wrap to cover the disk-shaped doughs and keep it in the fridge for not less than 2 hours. Store it in the fridge throughout the night to get the best texture for the dough.
- Preheat the oven to 375°F (190°C). Use parchment paper to line a couple pieces of baking sheets.
- Cover a surface with a good amount of sugar and flatten out one of the disk-shaped doughs into a rectangle that is 8x16 inches in size. Cover the dough generously with sugar. Fold the rectangular dough into 3 equal parts just like how you would fold a letter then roll it out again. Fold the dough in the same way again and roll it out, do this twice more; coat the dough with sugar before each folding. Roll out the dough for the last time into a rectangle that is 4x14 inches in size and about 1/4 inch in thickness. Do the same procedure for the remaining disk-shaped dough.
- Cut 1/2- to 3/4-inch wide strips from the shorter side of the rectangular dough. Put the strips of dough onto the prepared baking sheets; twist each dough strip and stretch them a bit. You may also shape them like a horseshoe if you want.
- Put it in the preheated oven and let it bake for 12-15 minutes until the doughs turn light golden brown in color. The cookies will expand a little bit and it will show some subtle layers. Allow the baked cookies to cool down on baking sheets for about 5 minutes first before putting them onto the wire racks.

Nutrition Information

- Calories: 191 calories;
- Protein: 2.8
- Total Fat: 9.9
- Sodium: 159
- Total Carbohydrate: 22.8
- Cholesterol: 48

356. German Walnut Shortbread Cookies

Serving: 80 | Prep: 20mins | Cook: 15mins | Ready in:

Ingredients

- 3/4 cup unsalted butter, at room temperature
- 2 tablespoons unsalted butter, room temperature
- 3/4 cup confectioners' sugar
- 4 teaspoons confectioners' sugar
- 1 egg yolk
- 1 pinch salt
- 2 1/4 cups all-purpose flour
- 2 tablespoons all-purpose flour
- 3/4 cup chopped walnuts
- 2 tablespoons chopped walnuts

Direction

- Beat 3/4 cup and 2 tablespoons of butter in a large bowl with an electric mixer until creamy. Put in salt, egg yolk, and 3/4 cup and 4 teaspoons of confectioner's sugar; beat until smooth. Knead in 3/4 cup plus 2 tablespoons of walnuts and 2 1/4 cups plus 2 tablespoons of flour.
- Form dough into 2-inch thick rolls and flatten them into rectangles, with a flat item, such as a cutting board. Wrap in plastic wrap and put in the refrigerator for about 1 hour until set.
- Start preheating the oven to 375°F (190°C).
- Slice the dough into thin slices and arrange them on an ungreased baking sheet.
- Bake in the prepared oven for 10 minutes. Lower the heat to 250°F (120°C) and bake for extra 5 minutes until very lightly browned.
- Transfer from the baking sheet and let cool on a wire rack, for about 20 minutes.

Nutrition Information

- Calories: 45 calories;
- Sodium: 4
- Total Carbohydrate: 4.3
- Cholesterol: 8
- Protein: 0.6
- Total Fat: 3

357. German X Mas Rum Crowns

Serving: 36 | Prep: 15mins | Cook: 15mins | Ready in:

Ingredients

- 2 1/3 cups all-purpose flour, sifted
- 3 1/2 ounces semisweet chocolate, grated
- 1 pinch salt
- 3/4 cup confectioners' sugar
- 2/3 cup butter, cut into pieces
- 2 tablespoons rum
- 1 egg
- 1 egg yolk
- 1 tablespoon water
- 1/2 cup chopped pistachio nuts

Direction

- Mix the confectioners' sugar, salt, chocolate and flour in a big bowl. Stir in butter until the mixture is crumbly. Put in rum and egg and stir until forms a smooth dough. Wrap in plastic, and chill for no less than 1 hour.
- Set the oven to 400°F (200°C) to preheat. Grease cookie sheets.
- Roll to shape dough into thin 6-inch long ropes. Twist 2 ropes together and put the ends together to create a crown. Stir the egg yolk with water, brush on top of each crown, and scatter with chopped pistachios.
- Bake in the preheated oven for 15 minutes, or until set. Let cookies cool on wire racks.

Nutrition Information

- Calories: 98 calories;
- Protein: 1.7
- Total Fat: 5.4
- Sodium: 34

- Total Carbohydrate: 10.8
- Cholesterol: 20

358. Gingerbread Boys And Girls

Serving: 12 | Prep: | Cook: | Ready in:

Ingredients

- 1/3 cup shortening
- 1 cup packed brown sugar
- 1 1/2 cups dark molasses
- 2/3 cup cold water
- 7 cups all-purpose flour
- 2 teaspoons baking soda
- 1 teaspoon salt
- 1 teaspoon ground allspice
- 1 teaspoon ground ginger
- 1 teaspoon crushed cloves (optional)
- 1 teaspoon ground cinnamon
- 2 egg yolks
- 10 drops food coloring
- 1/2 teaspoon water
- 3/4 cup raisins

Direction

- Combine brown sugar, molasses, and shortening in a bowl. Add 2/3 cup of water and whisk. Mix salt, flour, spices, and soda. Add the flour mixture into the molasses mixture and mix thoroughly. Allow it to chill for 60 minutes.
- After 1 hour, roll the dough into 1/4-inch thick. Use boy and girl cookie cutters to cut the dough.
- Blend 1/2 tsp. of water and egg yolks to make egg yolk paint. Distribute the bowls among few bowls and fill each bowl with the desired food coloring. Paint boy and girl's clothes with the coloring and style them up if desired. Place the cookies into the lightly greased baking pan. Make a small hole on top of the cookies using a toothpick. Press raisins into the dough to form the mouth, nose, and eyes. Decorate the clothes with candied cherries for the coat buttons and strips of citron for the ties.
- Set the oven to 350°F or 175°C. Place the baking pan inside and bake for 10-12 minutes. Let the cookies cool in the pan for a few minutes before removing them carefully.

Nutrition Information

- Calories: 546 calories;
- Total Carbohydrate: 113
- Cholesterol: 34
- Protein: 8.4
- Total Fat: 7.3
- Sodium: 428

359. Gingerbread Cookie Mix In A Jar

Serving: 18 | Prep: 20mins | Cook: | Ready in:

Ingredients

- 2 cups all-purpose flour
- 1 teaspoon baking powder
- 1 teaspoon baking soda
- 1 1/2 cups all-purpose flour
- 2 teaspoons ground ginger
- 1 teaspoon ground cloves
- 1 teaspoon ground cinnamon
- 1 teaspoon ground allspice
- 1 cup packed brown sugar

Direction

- Combine baking soda, 2 cups flour, and baking powder together. Stir cinnamon, allspice, ginger, cloves, and the leftover 1 1/2 cups of flour together. Put ingredients in layers into 1-qt, wide mouth canning jar, beginning with the baking powder and flour mixture, following by brown sugar, and lastly

- the spice and flour mixture, firmly packing between the layers.
- Place card with the following instructions on the jar.
- Gingerbread man cookie.
- 1. Pour all contents from the jar into a big bowl. Mix until well combined. Beat in a 3/4 cup of molasses, 1 slightly beaten egg and a 1/2 cup of softened margarine or butter. Use your hand to mix if the dough is very stiff. Keep in the refrigerator with cover, 1 hour.
- 2. Heat oven to 350° F (175°C).
- 3. On a lightly floured flat working surface, roll the dough out into 1/4 inch. Using the cookie cutter, cut out shapes from the dough and put 2 inches apart on a cookie sheet that is lightly greased.
- 4. Bake in the heated oven, 10-12 minutes. Decorate cookies with your preference.

Nutrition Information

- Calories: 137 calories;
- Sodium: 101
- Total Carbohydrate: 31
- Cholesterol: 0
- Protein: 2.6
- Total Fat: 0.3

360. Gingerbread Cookies

Serving: 30 | Prep: | Cook: | Ready in:

Ingredients

- 1 1/2 cups dark molasses
- 1 cup packed brown sugar
- 2/3 cup cold water
- 1/3 cup shortening
- 7 cups all-purpose flour
- 2 teaspoons baking soda
- 1 teaspoon salt
- 1 teaspoon ground allspice
- 2 teaspoons ground ginger

- 1 teaspoon ground cloves
- 1 teaspoon ground cinnamon
- 1 (16 ounce) package chocolate frosting

Direction

- Heat the oven to 350°F (175°C). Grease lightly the one piece of the cookie sheet.
- Combine the water, molasses, shortening, and water.
- Sieve the baking soda, cinnamon, ginger, flour, cloves, allspice, and salt together. Mix into the sugar mixture, stirring well until combined. Keep in the refrigerator, 2 hours.
- Roll the dough out into 1/4-in. the thickness on a floured board. Using the floured gingerbread cutter, cut out cookies from the dough. Put on the cookies sheet, 2 inches apart. For 10 to 12 minutes, bake and allow cooling before decorating using frosting.

Nutrition Information

- Calories: 264 calories;
- Total Fat: 5.3
- Sodium: 199
- Total Carbohydrate: 51.7
- Cholesterol: 0
- Protein: 3.2

361. Gingerbread Cookies I

Serving: 60 | Prep: 30mins | Cook: 12mins | Ready in:

Ingredients

- 1 cup white sugar
- 2 teaspoons ground ginger
- 1 teaspoon ground nutmeg
- 1 teaspoon ground cinnamon
- 1/2 teaspoon salt
- 1 1/2 teaspoons baking soda
- 1 cup margarine, melted
- 1/2 cup evaporated milk

- 1 cup unsulfured molasses
- 3/4 teaspoon vanilla extract
- 3/4 teaspoon lemon extract
- 4 cups unbleached all-purpose flour

Direction

- Heat oven to 375°F (190°C). Prepare the cookies sheets by greasing lightly.
- Mix the ginger, salt, baking soda, sugar, cinnamon, and nutmeg together into the big bowl. Whisk in evaporated milk, melted margarine, vanilla, lemon extracts, and molasses. Beat in flour, a single cup at one time, stirring thoroughly after every addition. The dough must be stiff to handle and must not stick to the fingers. Prevent dough from sticking by increasing flour up to a 1/2 cup.
- If the dough is smooth enough to handle, roll into 1/4-inch thick onto a floured working surface. Cut out dough to cookies. Put into the prepared cookie sheets.
- Place in the heated oven to bake, 10-12 minutes until top springs back when lightly pressed. Transfer to wire racks for cooling.

Nutrition Information

- Calories: 89 calories;
- Total Fat: 3.3
- Sodium: 90
- Total Carbohydrate: 14.1
- Cholesterol: < 1
- Protein: 1

362. Gingerbread Cookies II

Serving: 72 | Prep: 20mins | Cook: 12mins | Ready in:

Ingredients

- 6 cups all-purpose flour
- 1 tablespoon baking powder
- 1 tablespoon ground ginger
- 1 teaspoon ground nutmeg
- 1 teaspoon ground cloves
- 1 teaspoon ground cinnamon
- 1 cup shortening, melted and cooled slightly
- 1 cup molasses
- 1 cup packed brown sugar
- 1/2 cup water
- 1 egg
- 1 teaspoon vanilla extract

Direction

- Sieve the baking powder, cinnamon, flour, nutmeg, ginger, and cloves. Put aside.
- Whisk the brown sugar, molasses, shortening, egg, vanilla, and water into a medium-sized bowl until smooth. Slowly mix into the dry ingredients until mixture is thoroughly absorbed. Portion the dough to 3 pieces and roll out into 1 1/2-inch. Use plastic to wrap and keep in the refrigerator, 3 hours.
- Heat oven to 350°F (175°C). Roll out the dough into 1/4-inch thick on a lightly floured working surface. Cut out the desired shapes using the cookie cutter. Put on an ungreased cookie sheet, 1-inch apart.
- Place into the heated oven to bake, 10-12 minutes. When cookies are all baked, it will be soft to touch but looks dry. Take out from baking pans and transfer on wire racks to cool. Decorate the cooled cookies using the frosting of your preference.

Nutrition Information

- Calories: 90 calories;
- Cholesterol: 3
- Protein: 1.2
- Total Fat: 3
- Sodium: 24
- Total Carbohydrate: 14.5

363. Gingerbread Folk

Serving: 15 | Prep: | Cook: | Ready in:

Ingredients

- 1 egg
- 1/4 cup honey
- 7/8 cup packed brown sugar
- 2 teaspoons ground ginger
- 1/2 cup butter
- 1 teaspoon baking soda
- 3 cups all-purpose flour
- 1/4 cup dried currants
- 2 tablespoons water
- 1 1/2 cups confectioners' sugar
- 3 drops red food coloring

Direction

- Heat oven to 375°F (190°C). Melt a bit of butter and brush the baking sheets to grease with a pastry brush.
- On low heat, combine honey, butter, and brown sugar into a pot, stirring until melted.
- In a mixing bowl, sieve the baking soda, flour, and ginger together. Pour in melted mixture and add the egg.
- Combine mixture together and form dough in a ball. Put the dough into a plastic bag and keep in the chiller, 30 minutes.
- Place a little flour on a clean, flat working surface and rolling pin. Roll out the dough until 1/4 inch thickness. Cut out people and shapes from the dough using a cookie cutter or knife. Transfer the cookies into the baking sheet and continue to cut out shapes from the remaining dough. Create the buttons and eyes by pressing currants to the dough. Place in oven to bake until golden brown, 10-15 minutes.
- Preparation for icing: In a bowl, sieve confectioner's sugar and pour a small amount of water at a time until the paste turns thick and smooth. In a small sized bowl, scoop a little icing and drop a little food coloring. Repeat with the remaining icing, adding different colors of food coloring. Add to fill the pastry bags with colored icing and create clothes by squeezing the pastry bag filled with colored icing to the cookies.

Nutrition Information

- Calories: 270 calories;
- Cholesterol: 29
- Protein: 3.2
- Total Fat: 6.7
- Sodium: 137
- Total Carbohydrate: 50.3

364. Gingerbread Men

Serving: 30 | Prep: 25mins | Cook: 12mins | Ready in:

Ingredients

- 1 (3.5 ounce) package cook and serve butterscotch pudding mix
- 1/2 cup butter
- 1/2 cup packed brown sugar
- 1 egg
- 1 1/2 cups all-purpose flour
- 1/2 teaspoon baking soda
- 1 1/2 teaspoons ground ginger
- 1 teaspoon ground cinnamon

Direction

- Add butter, brown sugar, and dry butterscotch pudding mix into a medium-sized bowl and cream together until texture is smooth. Add egg and stir together. Mix baking soda, cinnamon, ginger, and flour, and add into pudding mixture while stirring. Keep dough covered and chilled for around an hour until firm.
- Set oven temperature to 350 degrees F (175 degrees C) and leave aside to preheat. Prepare baking sheets with grease. Apply a coat of flour on a board, roll and flatten dough until

thickness is about 1/8 inch, and use a cookie cutter to cut out man shapes. Arrange cookies with 2 inches distance on the baking sheets.
- Bake until cookies have golden edges, or for 10-12 minutes. Leave aside to cool on wire racks.

Nutrition Information

- Calories: 79 calories;
- Sodium: 63
- Total Carbohydrate: 11.5
- Cholesterol: 14
- Protein: 1
- Total Fat: 3.3

365. Gingerbread People From JELL O

Serving: 20 | Prep: 20mins | Cook: 10mins | Ready in:

Ingredients

- 3/4 cup butter, softened
- 3/4 cup packed brown sugar
- 1 (3.4 ounce) package JELL-O Butterscotch Instant Pudding
- 1 egg
- 2 cups flour
- 1 teaspoon baking soda
- 1 tablespoon ground ginger
- 1 1/2 teaspoons ground cinnamon

Direction

- Whisk the dry pudding mix, sugar, egg, and butter into a big bowl using a mixer until combined well. Beat the rest of the ingredients and slowly stir in into the butter mixture. Whisk well after every addition and keep in the refrigerator until dough is firm or for 1 hour.
- Preheat oven to 350°F. On a working surface that is lightly floured, roll the dough out into 1/4-in. thick. Cut out the gingerbread shapes using a cookie cutter with 4-in. dimension. Roll again the scraps. Put the cutout cookies onto the baking sheets greased with cooking spray, 2 inches apart. Make a hole along each top of gingerbread with straw.
- For 10-12 minutes, bake until edges turn lightly browned. For 3 minutes, allow cooling onto the baking sheets. Transfer into wire racks for complete cooling. If desired, decorate cookies. Attach a ribbon into the holes so you can hang the cookies into the tree as decoration.

Nutrition Information

- Calories: 160 calories;
- Total Fat: 7.3
- Sodium: 195
- Total Carbohydrate: 22.4
- Cholesterol: 28
- Protein: 1.7

366. Gluten Free Basic Sugar Cookies

Serving: 24 | Prep: 35mins | Cook: 8mins | Ready in:

Ingredients

- Cookie Dough:
- 2 1/2 cups gluten-free all-purpose baking flour
- 2 teaspoons baking powder
- 1 teaspoon xanthan gum
- 3/4 teaspoon ground nutmeg
- 1/4 teaspoon salt
- 1 cup white sugar
- 1/2 cup shortening (such as Crisco®)
- 2 eggs, well beaten
- 1 tablespoon milk
- 1 teaspoon gluten-free vanilla extract
- 2 tablespoons confectioners' sugar, or as needed

- For Decorating:
- 1 egg yolk
- 1 drop blue food coloring, or as needed
- 1/4 teaspoon water, or as needed
- 2 tablespoons sugar sprinkles, or to taste

Direction

- In a large mixing bowl, combine salt, nutmeg, xanthan gum, baking powder, and gluten-free flour.
- In another large mixing bowl, beat shortening and sugar with an electric mixer until no lumps remain. Add vanilla extract, milk, and beaten eggs; beat for about 2 minutes or until airy and light. Put in gluten-free flour mixture, little by little; mix until just incorporated.
- Form dough into a ball, wrap in plastic wrap, and refrigerate for a minimum of 1 hour.
- Set oven to 375°F (190°C) to preheat. Line parchment paper over 2 baking sheets.
- Dust cookie cutters and a rolling pin with powdered sugar. Roll dough out to a thickness of 1/2 inch; cut out cookies; arrange them 2 inches apart on the prepared baking sheets.
- In a small mixing bowl, stir egg yolk with water and food coloring. Use a child's paintbrush to decorate cookies with colored yolk mixture. Scatter top with sugar sprinkles.
- Bake cookies for 8 to 12 minutes in the preheated oven until edges turn golden. Allow cookies to cool for 1 minutes on the baking sheets before transferring them to a wire rack to cool entirely.

Nutrition Information

- Calories: 135 calories;
- Sodium: 76
- Total Carbohydrate: 20.6
- Cholesterol: 24
- Protein: 2.1
- Total Fat: 5.6

367. Golden Honey Snaps

Serving: 12 | Prep: 20mins | Cook: 10mins | Ready in:

Ingredients

- 1/2 cup butter, softened
- 1/4 cup honey
- 3 tablespoons golden syrup
- 1 teaspoon baking soda
- 1 cup all-purpose flour
- 1/2 cup white sugar

Direction

- Set the oven at 350°F (175°C) and start preheating. Use parchment paper to line a baking sheet.
- In a saucepan, mix golden syrup, honey and butter together. Cook while stirring the mixture frequently over medium heat, till the ingredients are well-blended and the butter is melted. Mix in baking soda; take away from the heat.
- In a mixing bowl, measure sugar and flour; stir to blend. Transfer the butter mixture into the bowl with the flour; combine till blended evenly. Shape the dough into 1 in. balls; arrange on the prepared baking sheet.
- Bake for 10-12 minutes in the preheated oven, or till golden brown. Allow to cool for a few minutes on the baking sheet; then, take away and let cool completely on a wire rack.

Nutrition Information

- Calories: 174 calories;
- Total Fat: 7.8
- Sodium: 163
- Total Carbohydrate: 25.9
- Cholesterol: 20
- Protein: 1.2

368. Gramma's Date Squares

Serving: 12 | Prep: 25mins | Cook: 25mins | Ready in:

Ingredients

- 1 1/2 cups rolled oats
- 1 1/2 cups sifted pastry flour
- 1/4 teaspoon salt
- 3/4 teaspoon baking soda
- 1 cup packed brown sugar
- 3/4 cup butter, softened
- 3/4 pound pitted dates, diced
- 1 cup water
- 1/3 cup packed brown sugar
- 1 teaspoon lemon juice

Direction

- Set oven at 175°C (350°F) and start preheating.
- Mix the baking soda, 1 cup of brown sugar, salt, pastry flour and oats together in a big bowl. Cut butter in until the mixture turns crumbly. Press half of the mixture against a 9-inch square baking tray's bottom.
- Mix 1/3 cup of brown sugar, water and dates into a little saucepan over moderate heat. Boil them up, cook until the mixture gets thicker. Mix in lemon juice and take out from the heat. Add the filling into the foundation and spread out, pat the rest of crumb mixture over the top.
- Put the tray in the preheated oven and bake until the top gets toasted lightly, or for 20 to 25 minutes. Let cool then divide into squares.

Nutrition Information

- Calories: 363 calories;
- Sodium: 217
- Total Carbohydrate: 63.7
- Cholesterol: 31
- Protein: 3.7
- Total Fat: 12.5

369. Grandma Hasz's Christmas Cutouts

Serving: 20 | Prep: 20mins | Cook: 10mins | Ready in:

Ingredients

- 1 cup butter
- 1 1/2 cups sugar
- 2 eggs
- 1/4 teaspoon lemon extract
- 1/2 teaspoon vanilla extract
- 3 cups flour
- 1 teaspoon salt
- 1 teaspoon baking soda
- 2 cups oatmeal

Direction

- Start preheating the oven to 350°F (175°C). Lightly spray cookie sheets with grease.
- In a big bowl, cream sugar and butter together. Mix in vanilla extract, lemon extract, and eggs. In another bowl, sift baking soda, salt, and flour together. Gradually pour the flour mixture over the butter mixture, whisking constantly. Mix in the oatmeal.
- On a surface lightly scattered with flour, roll the dough out to approximately 1/8-inch thickness. Use cookie cutters to slice the dough into shapes and put them on the grease-coated sheets.
- Put in the preheated oven and bake for 10-12 minutes until the edges begin to turn brown. Put on a cooling rack to cool down and then start frosting.

Nutrition Information

- Calories: 245 calories;
- Protein: 3.7
- Total Fat: 10.4
- Sodium: 273
- Total Carbohydrate: 34.8
- Cholesterol: 43

370. Grandma Minnie's Old Fashioned Sugar Cookies

Serving: 78 | Prep: 20mins | Cook: 8mins |Ready in:

Ingredients

- 3 cups sifted all-purpose flour
- 1 1/2 teaspoons baking powder
- 1/2 teaspoon salt
- 1 cup white sugar
- 1 cup butter
- 1 egg, lightly beaten
- 3 tablespoons cream
- 1 teaspoon vanilla extract

Direction

- Start preheating the oven to 400°F (200°C).
- Sift sugar, salt, baking powder, all-purpose flour together over a large bowl. Cut in the butter then using a pastry blender, blend until the mixture resembles cornmeal. Mix in the vanilla, cream and lightly beaten egg. Blend well. If desired, chill the dough.
- Roll out the dough to 1/8-in. thickness on floured surface. Drizzle over with sugar. Slice into the preferred shapes. Place into unoiled baking sheets.
- Bake until delicately brown, or about 6-8 mins.

Nutrition Information

- Calories: 51 calories;
- Total Carbohydrate: 6.3
- Cholesterol: 9
- Protein: 0.6
- Total Fat: 2.7
- Sodium: 40

371. Grandma's Cutout Sugar Cookies

Serving: 72 | Prep: 10mins | Cook: 6mins |Ready in:

Ingredients

- 2 cups butter
- 1 1/2 cups white sugar
- 3 eggs
- 1 teaspoon vanilla extract
- 1 teaspoon almond extract (optional)
- 3 1/2 cups all-purpose flour
- 2 teaspoons cream of tartar
- 1 teaspoon baking soda
- 1/2 teaspoon salt

Direction

- Use an electric mixer to whip sugar and butter in a big bowl till smooth. Put in the initial egg while whipping continuously, completely blending the egg prior to putting another one and completely whipping to the mixture. Whip almond extract and vanilla extract into mixture including the third egg.
- In another bowl, stir together the salt, baking soda, cream of tartar and flour; put into wet mixture and whip to just combine wet and dry and form into a cookie dough. Collect dough to a ball, encase with plastic wrap, and chill till cold, for not less than 3 hours.
- Heat the oven to 175 ° C or 350 ° F.
- Unroll dough on a floured counter and use cookie cutters to cut dough. Place the cut cookies on baking sheets.
- Let cookies bake for 6 to 8 minutes in prepped oven till starting to brown on edges' surrounding.

Nutrition Information

- Calories: 87 calories;
- Cholesterol: 21
- Protein: 0.9
- Total Fat: 5.4
- Sodium: 73

- Total Carbohydrate: 8.9

372. Grandma's Drop Sugar Cookies

Serving: 48 | Prep: 10mins | Cook: 10mins | Ready in:

Ingredients

- 2 cups white sugar
- 2 cups butter, softened
- 3 cups all-purpose flour
- 1 cup coconut flakes
- 1 teaspoon vanilla extract
- 1 teaspoon salt
- 1/2 teaspoon baking soda

Direction

- Set oven to 350 0 F (175 0 C) and preheat.
- In a bowl, use an electric mixer to beat together sugar and butter until smooth and creamy. Stir baking soda, salt, vanilla extract, coconut flakes and flour into creamed butter mixture until dough is smooth. Spoon the dough onto a baking sheet.
- Put in the prepared oven and bake for about 10 minutes until edges of cookies are lightly browned.

Nutrition Information

- Calories: 136 calories;
- Total Fat: 8.2
- Sodium: 121
- Total Carbohydrate: 15.1
- Cholesterol: 20
- Protein: 0.9

373. Grandma's Gingersnaps

Serving: 36 | Prep: 15mins | Cook: 10mins | Ready in:

Ingredients

- 3/4 cup margarine
- 1 cup white sugar
- 1 egg
- 1/4 cup molasses
- 2 cups all-purpose flour
- 1 tablespoon ground ginger
- 1 teaspoon ground cinnamon
- 2 teaspoons baking soda
- 1/2 teaspoon salt
- 1/2 cup white sugar for decoration

Direction

- Set the oven to 350°F (175°C), and start preheating.
- In a medium bowl, cream 1 cup white sugar and margarine together until smooth. Beat in molasses and egg until well combined. Stir salt, baking soda, cinnamon, flour and ginger together; mix into the molasses mixture to create a dough. Roll the dough into 1-inch balls then roll into the remaining sugar. On ungreased cookie sheets, arrange cookies 2 inches apart.
- Bake for 8 - 10 minutes in the preheated oven. Cool for 5 minutes on baking sheet prior to transferring to a wire rack to cool completely.

Nutrition Information

- Calories: 100 calories;
- Sodium: 149
- Total Carbohydrate: 15.5
- Cholesterol: 5
- Protein: 1
- Total Fat: 4

374. Grandma's Raspberry Bars

Serving: 24 | Prep: 20mins | Cook: 30mins | Ready in:

Ingredients

- 3/4 cup butter, softened
- 1/2 cup white sugar
- 1/2 cup brown sugar
- 1 1/2 cups all-purpose flour
- 1 teaspoon baking powder
- 1/4 teaspoon salt
- 3/4 cup raspberry jam
- 1 1/2 cups rolled oats
- 1/2 cup chopped walnuts

Direction

- Start preheating the oven to 350°F (175°C). Oil a 9x13 inch baking dish.
- Combine salt, baking powder, flour, brown sugar, white sugar and butter in a medium bowl; mix well. Spread prepared pan with 2/3 of the mixture.
- Spread the mixture with jam.
- Combine walnuts and oats with the remaining mixture. Scatter over the jam layer.
- Bake for half an hour in the prepared oven.

Nutrition Information

- Calories: 169 calories;
- Cholesterol: 15
- Protein: 1.9
- Total Fat: 7.7
- Sodium: 81
- Total Carbohydrate: 23.8

375. Grandmom's Sand Tarts

Serving: 72 | Prep: 20mins | Cook: 10mins | Ready in:

Ingredients

- 2 pounds butter
- 2 cups white sugar
- 5 eggs
- 8 cups all-purpose flour, or as needed
- 1 egg white
- 1 tablespoon milk
- 1/4 cup cinnamon sugar
- 3/4 cup pecan halves

Direction

- Cream eggs, sugar and butter together. Add just enough flour to stiffen. Dough will be sticky slightly. Keep dough in the fridge; allow to chill overnight.
- Set the oven to 350°F (175°C) and start preheating. Mix milk and egg white in a very small bowl. Put aside.
- Take the small amount of dough out of the fridge and place on a lightly floured surface; roll it out very thin. Use a biscuit cutter or drinking glass dipped in flour to cut out rounds. Arrange cookies on a cookie sheet; brush egg white mixture over the top. Dust with cinnamon sugar and place a pecan half on top. Do the same with the rest of dough.
- Bake for 10 minutes at 350°F (175°C) until edges turn browned slightly. Be careful as they burn very easily.

Nutrition Information

- Calories: 178 calories;
- Sodium: 79
- Total Carbohydrate: 17.1
- Cholesterol: 40
- Protein: 2.1
- Total Fat: 11.5

376. Great Grandad's Sugar Cookies

Serving: 30 | Prep: 30mins | Cook: 10mins | Ready in:

Ingredients

- 6 cups all-purpose flour
- 1 tablespoon baking powder
- 1 teaspoon ground nutmeg
- 1 pinch salt
- 2 1/2 cups white sugar
- 1 1/2 cups shortening
- 1 teaspoon baking soda
- 1 cup sour milk
- 3 eggs, beaten
- 1 teaspoon vanilla extract

Direction

- Preheat the oven to 350°F (175°C). Use a parchment paper to line cookie sheets.
- Mix the nutmeg, 4 cups of flour, sugar, baking powder and salt together in a medium-sized bowl. Mash the shortening into the mixture until the texture is like that of coarse crumbs. Add in the beaten eggs, baking soda, vanilla and sour milk and mix everything together. Mix the mixture as little as you can, and put in the remaining flour if need be to turn the dough thick enough to unroll.
- Roll dough out onto a surface that is slightly covered with flour until it is 1/4 inch in thickness. Use cookie cutters to cut the flattened dough into whatever shape you like. On the prepared cookie sheets, put in the cut-out cookies 1 inch away from each other.
- Put it in the preheated oven and let it bake for 8-10 minutes. Allow the baked cookies to cool down on the cookie sheets.

Nutrition Information

- Calories: 258 calories;
- Total Carbohydrate: 36.4
- Cholesterol: 19
- Protein: 3.5
- Total Fat: 11.1
- Sodium: 107

377. Greek Butter Cookies

Serving: 48 | Prep: 10mins | Cook: 10mins | Ready in:

Ingredients

- 1 cup butter, softened
- 3/4 cup white sugar
- 1 egg
- 1/2 teaspoon vanilla extract
- 1/2 teaspoon almond extract
- 2 1/4 cups all-purpose flour
- 1/2 cup confectioners' sugar for rolling

Direction

- Set oven to 400° F (200° C) to preheat. Coat cookie sheets with grease.
- Cream the egg, sugar, and butter together in a medium bowl until smooth. Stir in the almond extracts and vanilla. Blend in the flour so that a dough forms. At the end, you may need to knead by hand. Take out and roll about a teaspoon of dough at a time to shape into 'S' shapes, logs or balls. On the prepared cookie sheets, arrange cookies with 1 to 2 inches apart.
- Bake in the preheated oven for 10 minutes, or until firm and slightly brown. Let cookies cool thoroughly before dusting confectioners' sugar over cookies.

Nutrition Information

- Calories: 74 calories;
- Cholesterol: 14
- Protein: 0.8
- Total Fat: 4
- Sodium: 29
- Total Carbohydrate: 8.9

378. Gumbon Cookies

Serving: 24 | Prep: 30mins | Cook: 15mins | Ready in:

Ingredients

- 1/2 cup unsalted butter
- 3/4 cup confectioners' sugar, sifted
- 2 1/2 teaspoons vanilla extract
- 1 1/2 cups all-purpose flour
- 1/8 teaspoon salt
- 1 teaspoon evaporated milk, or as needed (optional)
- 24 small spice-flavored gumdrop candies
- 1 cup confectioners' sugar, sifted
- 2 tablespoons evaporated milk
- 1 teaspoon vanilla extract
- 1 drop red or desired shade of food coloring - or as needed

Direction

- Set oven to preheat at 350°F (175°C). Use parchment paper to line a baking sheet.
- Beat together the unsalted butter, 2 1/2 teaspoons vanilla extract, and 3/4 cup confectioners' sugar in a bowl till creamy and smooth. Sift together flour and salt in a different bowl; beat the mixture of flour into the butter mixture till a workable dough forms. If the dough feels dry or crumbly, beat 1 teaspoon evaporated milk into the dough, or more if needed.
- Pinch out about 1 tablespoon of dough and roll it into a ball; use your finger to make a hole in the dough ball, and place in a gumdrop, fully enclose the ball by wrapping the dough around the gumdrop. Place the cookie, sealed side down, onto prepared baking sheet. Continue the process with the rest of the gumdrops and dough.
- In the preheated oven, bake until cookies are set and not brown, about 12 to 14 minutes.
- Mix together 1 teaspoon vanilla extract, 2 tablespoons evaporated milk, and 1 cup confectioners' sugar in a bowl till a smooth frosting forms. Split the frosting into 3 or 4 small bowls and tint each into a different color, if you wish. Frost the cookies while they are still warm; put aside to cool thoroughly before serving.

Nutrition Information

- Calories: 114 calories;
- Cholesterol: 11
- Protein: 1
- Total Fat: 4
- Sodium: 16
- Total Carbohydrate: 18.5

379. Hamantashen

Serving: 36 | Prep: 2hours | Cook: 15mins | Ready in:

Ingredients

- 1 1/2 cups butter or margarine, softened
- 1 cup white sugar
- 2 eggs
- 6 tablespoons orange juice
- 1 tablespoon vanilla extract
- 2 teaspoons baking powder
- 4 1/2 cups all-purpose flour
- 1 (12 ounce) can poppyseed filling

Direction

- Cream sugar and butter together in a big bowl until smooth. Beat eggs in, one by one, then mix in vanilla and orange juice. Mix in baking powder. Gradually mix in flour until the dough becomes a ball. Refrigerate, covered, for a minimum of 2 hours. I leave mine overnight.
- Preheat oven to 190 degrees C/375 degrees F. Grease the cookie sheets.
- Roll dough out on a lightly floured surface to 1/4-in. thick. Use a cookie cutter/drinking glass to cut 3-in. circles out. Put circles on prepped cookie sheets. Spoon 1 tsp. filling on the middle of every circle. Too much will make it ooze out. Pinch every circles' sides to make a triangle, covering as much of the filling as you can. You can freeze cookies on cookie

sheets if you want to keep the shape as you cook them.
- Bake in preheated oven for 8-10 minutes until light golden brown. They're better when slightly undercooked. Cool for a few minutes on the baking sheet. Transfer to wire racks. Completely cool.

Nutrition Information

- Calories: 184 calories;
- Total Fat: 8.9
- Sodium: 86
- Total Carbohydrate: 23.4
- Cholesterol: 31
- Protein: 2.5

380. Hatzic Bars

Serving: 18 | Prep: 20mins | Cook: 10mins | Ready in:

Ingredients

- 1 cup brown sugar
- 1/2 cup butter
- 2 (1 ounce) squares semisweet chocolate, chopped
- 1 egg
- 2 cups graham cracker crumbs
- 1 cup chopped walnuts
- 1 (8 ounce) package unsweetened shredded coconut
- 1/2 (14 ounce) can sweetened condensed milk
- 1 (16 ounce) package prepared chocolate frosting, or as needed

Direction

- Coat a 9x9-in. pan with grease.
- In the top of a double boiler, melt while stirring often the egg, chocolate, butter and brown sugar over simmering water, using a rubber spatula to scrape down the sides to prevent scorching.
- Stir walnuts and graham cracker crumbs into the chocolate mixture; evenly press onto the bottom of the prepared pan.
- In a bowl, mix condensed milk and shredded coconut together; evenly spread over the chocolate layer. Spread the frosting over the top of the coconut mixture. Place in the refrigerator till ready to serve.

Nutrition Information

- Calories: 413 calories;
- Cholesterol: 28
- Protein: 4.3
- Total Fat: 25.2
- Sodium: 166
- Total Carbohydrate: 47

381. Hedgehog Cookies

Serving: 24 | Prep: 1hours | Cook: 10mins | Ready in:

Ingredients

- 4 cups all-purpose flour
- 3/4 teaspoon baking powder
- 1/2 teaspoon baking soda
- 1/2 teaspoon salt
- 1 1/4 cups white sugar
- 1 cup butter-flavored shortening
- 1/4 cup corn syrup
- 2 eggs
- 1 tablespoon vanilla extract
- 1 cup pecans
- 1 cup chocolate chips

Direction

- In a bowl, mix salt, baking soda, baking powder and flour. In another bowl, mix vanilla extract, eggs, corn syrup, shortening and sugar. Stir sugar mixture into flour mixture just until combined. Keep dough in the fridge for 30-60 minutes until chilled.

- Set the oven to 350°F (175°C) and start preheating.
- Spoon cookie dough with a tablespoon or cookie scoop so that all cookies are equal; form dough into teardrop-shaped cookies. Make the pointed side of each cookie flat to shape the 'face'. Place cookies on baking sheets.
- Bake in the prepared oven for 10-12 minutes until golden. Cool for 10 minutes on baking sheets; place cookies on wire racks to completely cool.
- In a food processor, pulse pecans until chopped finely; place in a bowl.
- In the top of a double boiler over simmering water, melt chocolate chips; stir frequently and scrape down sides, using a rubber spatula, to prevent it from scorching.
- Coat top of each cookie with melted chocolate, spreading to coat the 'body' of each hedgehog fully. Press cookies with the side with chocolate down into the ground pecans to form the 'fur'. Place cookies on a sheet of waxed paper for about half an hour to set.
- Place the rest of melted chocolate in plastic bag with a corner snipped or pipping bag. Pipe chocolate onto the pointed end of each cookie for eyes and a nose.

Nutrition Information

- Calories: 280 calories;
- Cholesterol: 16
- Protein: 3.4
- Total Fat: 15.2
- Sodium: 99
- Total Carbohydrate: 34.2

382. Holiday Cookie Sandwich With Nutella® Hazelnut Spread

Serving: 25 | Prep: 30mins | Cook: 10mins | Ready in:

Ingredients

- 1 cup soft butter
- 3/4 cup confectioners' sugar
- 4 cups sifted all-purpose flour
- 1 egg
- 1 vanilla bean
- 1 pinch salt
- 1 cup Nutella® hazelnut spread

Direction

- Use a knife to divide the vanilla pod lengthwise and drag out the seeds or apply 2 teaspoons vanilla extract instead.
- Whisk salt, vanilla seeds, egg, confectioners' sugar, and butter in a bowl. Briefly whisk to combine until all the ingredients are mixed, but keep from overworking. Stir in the sifted flour and briefly blend again.
- Turn this mixture up into a ball, use plastic wrap to wrap it and allow the dough to rest for 1 hour in the fridge.
- Remove the dough from the fridge and use a knife to slice into 2 portions.
- Turn out each portion between 2 pieces of parchment paper to thickness of 1/4 of an inch. Place two layers in the fridge and let it rest for at least 10 minutes (preferably 1 hour).
- Take the 2 layers from the fridge. Cut out cookies with a round cookie cutter. Slice a shape out of the top cookies with smaller cutters. Place on the center shelf of the oven and bake for about 10 minutes at 350°F. Remove from the oven and allow to cool.
- Place 1/2 tablespoons of Nutella® hazelnut spread onto each cookie without a hole, using a pastry bag. And put the top cookie to cover.

Nutrition Information

- Calories: 222 calories;
- Protein: 3
- Total Fat: 11.6
- Sodium: 67
- Total Carbohydrate: 26.3
- Cholesterol: 27

383. Holiday Lebkuchen (German Spice Cookies)

Serving: 36 | Prep: 40mins | Cook: 15mins | Ready in:

Ingredients

- 2 cups whole almonds
- boiling water to cover
- 2/3 cup chopped dried apricots
- 8 Medjool dates, pitted and chopped
- 4 1/2 cups unbleached all-purpose flour
- 1 tablespoon ground cinnamon
- 2 teaspoons ground ginger
- 1 1/2 teaspoons baking powder
- 1 teaspoon ground cloves
- 1/2 teaspoon ground cardamom
- 1/2 teaspoon salt
- 2 eggs
- 1 cup brown sugar
- 1 cup honey
- 1/4 cup blackstrap molasses
- 1 tablespoon water
- 2 teaspoons almond extract
- 2 teaspoons grated orange zest
- 1 teaspoon grated lemon zest
- 3/4 cup confectioners' sugar
- 2 tablespoons whole milk
- 1 teaspoon lemon zest

Direction

- In a bowl, submerge almonds in boiling water. Allow to stand 1-2 minutes; drain. Wash with cold water, then drain again. Pat almonds dry; discard skin. Place almonds on paper towels to dry.
- In a food processor, put half the almonds; pulse until nicely chopped. Put in dates and apricots; pulse till fruit is chopped. Save the remaining 1 cup almonds.
- In a bowl, combine salt, cardamom, cloves, baking powder, ginger, cinnamon, and flour. In a big bowl, with an electric mixer, beat 1 teaspoon lemon zest, orange zest, almond extract, water, molasses, honey, brown sugar and eggs, until smooth. Pour in apricot mixture, mixing until distributed evenly. On medium speed, slowly whisk in flour mixture till dough comes together. Use plastic wrap to cover dough; keep in the fridge from 8 hours to all night.
- Set oven to 175° C (350° F) and start preheating.
- Turn dough onto a slightly floured surface; roll out to approximately 1/2-in. thick. Use a 2 1/2 to 3-in.-diameter cookie cutter to cut out cookies. Place cookies on unoiled baking sheets, spacing 1 inch apart.
- Into each cookie, slightly press 3 almonds with their tips facing the center, forming a star pattern.
- Place in the preheated oven and bake 12 minutes until cookies start to brown. Allow to cool in pans 10 minutes, then remove to a wire rack to cool.
- In the meantime, in a bowl, whisk together 1 teaspoon lemon zest, milk, and confectioners' sugar till glaze is smooth. Brush glaze on warm cookies; let cookies cool entirely.

Nutrition Information

- Calories: 188 calories;
- Cholesterol: 10
- Protein: 3.9
- Total Fat: 4.5
- Sodium: 61
- Total Carbohydrate: 34.8

384. Hungarian Kiffles

Serving: 36 | Prep: 15mins | Cook: 10mins | Ready in:

Ingredients

- 1 pound butter, softened
- 1 pound cream cheese, softened
- 4 cups sifted all-purpose flour

- 1 pound walnuts, ground
- 1 cup white sugar
- 2 tablespoons milk, or more as needed

Direction

- In a stand mixer's bowl, mix cream cheese and butter until creamy and pale yellow in color. Slowly add in two cups of flour until the dough is too thick for the mixer to process. Use your hands to mix in leftover 2 cups of flour in the mixture; knead until the dough falls off hand easily. Form dough into a ball and put in a bowl; use a plastic wrap to cover. Place in the refrigerator to chill for 8 hours to overnight.
- Preheat the oven to 190°C or 375°F.
- Combine sugar and walnuts in a bowl; add milk. Stir the mixture until it forms into a paste.
- Place dough on a floured surface and spread into preferred thickness. Slice dough into squares measuring 2 inches. Spread a teaspoon of walnut filling in the middle of each square dough. Roll up the squares starting in one corner, over the filling, and into the other corner. Place rolls on a baking sheet.
- Bake in the preheated oven for 10-15 minutes until the rolls are light brown.

Nutrition Information

- Calories: 289 calories;
- Cholesterol: 41
- Protein: 4.4
- Total Fat: 23
- Sodium: 111
- Total Carbohydrate: 18.3

385. Icelandic Pepper Cookies

Serving: 18 | Prep: | Cook: | Ready in:

Ingredients

- 1 1/4 cups butter, softened
- 1 1/4 cups white sugar
- 3/4 cup light corn syrup
- 2 small eggs
- 3 cups all-purpose flour
- 1 1/2 teaspoons baking powder
- 1 teaspoon baking soda
- 1/2 teaspoon salt
- 2 teaspoons ground cinnamon
- 2 teaspoons ground cloves
- 1 teaspoon ground ginger
- 1/4 teaspoon ground black pepper

Direction

- Whip butter with sugar in big bowl. Mix in eggs and corn syrup; beat well. Sift pepper, ginger, cloves, cinnamon, salt, baking soda, baking powder and flour together. Put dry ingredients into the butter mixture and stir until smooth. Chill dough overnight.
- Set oven to 350°F (175°C) to preheat.
- Shape dough into 1/4-inch thickness. Punch out cookies with a 2-inch round cookie cutter. Arrange at least 1 inch apart on cookie tray and bake in preheated oven for 8-10 minutes.

Nutrition Information

- Calories: 289 calories;
- Sodium: 281
- Total Carbohydrate: 40.9
- Cholesterol: 49
- Protein: 2.8
- Total Fat: 13.5

386. Italian Chocolate Chip Cookies

Serving: 168 | Prep: 30mins | Cook: 20mins | Ready in:

Ingredients

- 2 cups butter

- 4 cups milk
- 12 cups all-purpose flour
- 1 1/2 cups white sugar
- 1 cup unsweetened cocoa powder
- 2 1/2 teaspoons baking soda
- 1 teaspoon ground cinnamon
- 1 teaspoon ground nutmeg
- 1 teaspoon ground cloves
- 3 1/2 cups semisweet chocolate chips
- 2 cups chopped walnuts

Direction

- Set oven to preheat at 350°F (175°C). Grease the cookie sheets. In a medium saucepan, combine the milk and butter over medium heat. Cook until butter melts, stir from time to time. Put aside to cool.
- In a large bowl, stir together the cloves, nutmeg, cinnamon, baking soda, cocoa, sugar and flour. Mix in the mixture of milk by hand until the dough becomes firm but not tacky. Mix in the walnuts and chocolate chips. Roll the dough into balls of 1 1/2 inch and put onto the prepared cookie sheets. You can put cookies quite close together because they don't spread much.
- In the preheated oven, bake for 20 to 25 minutes until firm. Take out of the baking sheets to cool down on wire racks. To preserve freshness, glaze a thin confectioners' icing on top once cooled.

Nutrition Information

- Calories: 89 calories;
- Total Fat: 4.4
- Sodium: 37
- Total Carbohydrate: 11.6
- Cholesterol: 6
- Protein: 1.6

387. Italian Christmas Cookies With Cocoa And Orange Liqueur

Serving: 24 | Prep: 30mins | Cook: 10mins | Ready in:

Ingredients

- Cookies:
- 3 1/2 cups all-purpose flour, or as needed
- 4 teaspoons baking powder
- 1 cup white sugar
- 1/2 cup butter, softened
- 4 eggs
- 1 cup cocoa powder
- 2 tablespoons orange-flavored liqueur
- 2 teaspoons vanilla extract
- Icing:
- 2 cups sifted confectioners' sugar
- 2 tablespoons orange-flavored liqueur
- 2 tablespoons water
- 2 teaspoons vanilla extract

Direction

- Start preheating the oven to 375°F (190 °C). Lightly coat 2 baking sheets with oil.
- In a bowl, sift together baking powder and flour. In a separate bowl, beat together butter and white sugar with an electric mixer until they become creamy and smooth; beat in the eggs. Then stir 2 teaspoons of vanilla extract, 2 tablespoons of liqueur, cocoa powder and creamed butter mixture into the flour mixture just until the dough has combined.
- Place onto a lightly floured work surface and knead; if needed, putting in more flour to prevent dough from sticking to hands. Then roll dough in your hands, 1-2 tablespoons each cookie, make a log-shape; then twirl log into the preferred shape. Arrange cookies on prepared baking sheet.
- Bake in prepared oven for around 10 mins until cookies are browned lightly around the edges.
- In a bowl, stir together 2 teaspoons of vanilla extract, water, 2 tablespoons of liqueur and

confectioners' sugar until icing is creamy. Submerge cookies into the icing. Position a waxed paper piece under a wire rack; arrange cookies on wire rack to cool.

Nutrition Information

- Calories: 204 calories;
- Total Fat: 5.4
- Sodium: 122
- Total Carbohydrate: 36
- Cholesterol: 41
- Protein: 3.7

388. Jam Filled Butter Cookies

Serving: 36 | Prep: 30mins | Cook: 10mins | Ready in:

Ingredients

- 3/4 cup butter, softened
- 1/2 cup white sugar
- 2 egg yolks
- 1 3/4 cups all-purpose flour
- 1/2 cup fruit preserves, any flavor

Direction

- Preheat your oven to 375°F (190°C).
- Cream the white sugar, egg yolks and butter together in a medium-sized bowl. Add in a small amount of flour at a time while mixing it until you get a dough that has a soft texture. Shape the dough mixture into balls that are 1 inch in size. In case the texture of the dough is still too soft, keep it in the fridge for 15-20 minutes. On cookie sheets that are not greased, put in the dough balls 2 inches away from each other. Create a dent in the middle of each of the cookie balls using your finger or any tool with the same size. Put 1/2 teaspoon of preserves into each dent.
- Put it in the preheated oven and let it bake for 8-10 minutes until the bottom of each cookie turns golden brown in color. Remove the baked cookies from the cookie sheets and place them onto wire racks to let them cool down.

Nutrition Information

- Calories: 82 calories;
- Sodium: 29
- Total Carbohydrate: 10.5
- Cholesterol: 22
- Protein: 0.8
- Total Fat: 4.1

389. Jam Kolaches

Serving: 12 | Prep: 45mins | Cook: 15mins | Ready in:

Ingredients

- 1/2 cup butter, softened
- 3 ounces cream cheese, softened
- 1 1/4 cups all-purpose flour
- 1/4 cup strawberry jam
- 1/4 cup sifted confectioners' sugar

Direction

- In a mixer bowl, beat the cream cheese and butter until it turns fluffy and light. Slowly add in the flour, beating well after every addition.
- On a lightly floured surface, roll the dough to 1/8-inch thick, then cut into 2-inch rounds. Into the center of each circle, spoon 1/4 teaspoon of jam. Fold together the opposite edges, overlapping the edges slightly.
- On a greased cookie sheet, place it 2 inches apart. Bake for 15 minutes at 190°C (375°F). Transfer to a wire rack to allow it to cool. Dust with confectioner's sugar.

Nutrition Information

- Calories: 168 calories;

- Total Fat: 10.3
- Sodium: 76
- Total Carbohydrate: 17.3
- Cholesterol: 28
- Protein: 2

390. Jill's World Famous Coffee Liqueur Brownies

Serving: 20 | Prep: 20mins | Cook: 35mins | Ready in:

Ingredients

- 8 (1 ounce) squares unsweetened chocolate
- 1 cup butter
- 5 eggs
- 3 cups white sugar
- 1 tablespoon vanilla extract
- 1 1/2 cups all-purpose flour
- 1/2 cup coffee flavored liqueur
- 2 cups chopped walnuts

Direction

- Preheat the oven to 190°C or 375°F. Grease a 9x13-in. baking pan. Combine unsweetened chocolate and butter in a heavy saucepan. Cook while stirring constantly over low heat till well blended and smooth. Take away from the heat and put aside.
- Beat vanilla, sugar and eggs in a large bowl till pale and thick. Stir in coffee liqueur and chocolate mixture. Fold in the flour. If desired, add in chopped walnuts and stir. Evenly spread into the prepped pan.
- Bake till a toothpick comes out almost clean after being inserted in the middle, for 30-35 minutes. Don't overbake. Let cool for at least 30 minutes then slice into bars to serve.

Nutrition Information

- Calories: 407 calories;
- Protein: 5.9

- Total Fat: 24.1
- Sodium: 87
- Total Carbohydrate: 44.7
- Cholesterol: 71

391. Kolaczki

Serving: 24 | Prep: | Cook: | Ready in:

Ingredients

- 5 cups all-purpose flour
- 4 egg yolks
- 3 teaspoons baking powder
- 1 pound shortening
- 1 cup milk
- 4 (.25 ounce) packages active dry yeast
- 1 teaspoon salt
- 1 cup any flavor fruit jam
- 1/3 cup confectioners' sugar for decoration

Direction

- Warm the milk just to above the room temperature. In milk, dissolve yeast. Put aside. Stir baking powder, salt and flour together in medium bowl. Cut in shortening until mealy. Then stir in milk mixture and egg yolks. Knead dough together. Place in the refrigerator overnight.
- Preheat oven to 350°F (175°C).
- Dust confectioners' sugar over clean, dry surface. Knead dough for a few minutes. Roll dough out carefully to 1/4 in. thick. Using cookie cutter, cut out circles, put one teaspoon jam onto center of each circle, then fold dough over, use a fork to seal edge.
- Bake in the preheated oven, about 12-15 minutes. They will become soggy if you store it in the airtight container.

Nutrition Information

- Calories: 323 calories;

- Protein: 4
- Total Fat: 20.2
- Sodium: 169
- Total Carbohydrate: 31.8
- Cholesterol: 35

392. Kourambiathes (Greek Cookies)

Serving: 16 | Prep: 30mins | Cook: 15mins | Ready in:

Ingredients

- 1 cup butter, room temperature
- 1 egg yolk
- 2 teaspoons anise extract
- 1/4 cup confectioners' sugar
- 2 1/2 cups all-purpose flour
- 1/3 cup confectioners' sugar for dusting

Direction

- Preheat the oven to 175°C or 350°Fahrenheit. Oil baking sheets.
- Cream anise extract, egg yolk, and butter in a medium bowl until light. Mix in flour and a quarter cup confectioners' sugar until combined.
- Form dough into crescents then arrange on the greased baking sheets two inches apart.
- Bake for 15-20 minutes in the preheated oven until starting to brown on the edges and bottoms. Liberally dust with confectioners' sugar before they cool fully.

Nutrition Information

- Calories: 194 calories;
- Sodium: 83
- Total Carbohydrate: 19.3
- Cholesterol: 43
- Protein: 2.3
- Total Fat: 12

393. Kourambiedes III

Serving: 18 | Prep: | Cook: | Ready in:

Ingredients

- 1 cup unsalted butter
- 4 tablespoons confectioners' sugar
- 1 teaspoon vanilla extract
- 2 cups sifted all-purpose flour
- 1 cup chopped pecans
- 36 whole cloves
- 1/2 cup confectioners' sugar

Direction

- Start preheating the oven to 350°F (175°C).
- In medium bowl, cream together confectioners' sugar and butter. Stir in vanilla, followed by flour, and the pecans next.
- Form the dough into the walnut sized balls; insert 1 clove into each dough. Arrange on the unprepared cookie sheet; then bake in prepared oven, about 15-18 mins. While the cookies are still hot, roll them in the powdered sugar. Discard cloves or warn your guests to discard them.

Nutrition Information

- Calories: 209 calories;
- Sodium: 7
- Total Carbohydrate: 17.7
- Cholesterol: 27
- Protein: 2.2
- Total Fat: 14.8

394. Krumkake I

Serving: 12 | Prep: | Cook: | Ready in:

Ingredients

- 1 egg
- 1/2 cup white sugar
- 1 cup heavy whipping cream
- 1 1/4 cups all-purpose flour
- 1/2 teaspoon baking powder
- 1/4 teaspoon salt
- 1 teaspoon vanilla extract

Direction

- Whisk egg. Put in vanilla and sugar and stir well. Put in whipping cream. Put in dry ingredients and whip until smooth.
- When krumkake iron is hot, on the iron, add a teaspoon of batter and bake until light brown. Immediately roll on stick when still hot.

Nutrition Information

- Calories: 155 calories;
- Total Fat: 7.9
- Sodium: 82
- Total Carbohydrate: 19
- Cholesterol: 43
- Protein: 2.3

395. Lebkuchen (Lep Kuchen)

Serving: 24 | Prep: | Cook: | Ready in:

Ingredients

- 1 1/2 cups all-purpose flour
- 1 tablespoon ground cinnamon
- 1/2 teaspoon ground nutmeg
- 1/2 teaspoon ground cloves
- 1/2 teaspoon cream of tartar
- 2 eggs
- 1 cup packed dark brown sugar
- 1/8 pound chopped candied citron
- 1/8 pound chopped almonds

Direction

- Preheat the oven to 175 degrees C (350 degrees F). Coat a large baking sheet (about 14x16 or 11x17 inches) with grease.
- Sift together flour, cream of tartar, cinnamon, cloves and nutmeg.
- Combine sugar and eggs well. Mix this with flour mixture and then mix in almonds and citron.
- Onto a floured surface, roll out the dough to 1/4 inch thick. Chop the dough sheet to fit on the baking sheet.
- Bake for 15 minutes at 175 degrees C (350 degrees F). Chop into diamonds or squares while still warm. Then ice thinly with lemon or white frosting.

Nutrition Information

- Calories: 92 calories;
- Sodium: 16
- Total Carbohydrate: 17.7
- Cholesterol: 16
- Protein: 1.9
- Total Fat: 1.7

396. Lebkuchen I

Serving: 12 | Prep: | Cook: | Ready in:

Ingredients

- 1 1/3 cups honey
- 1/3 cup packed brown sugar
- 2 cups all-purpose flour
- 1 teaspoon baking powder
- 1/2 teaspoon baking soda
- 1 cup candied mixed fruit
- 1 tablespoon light sesame oil
- 1/4 teaspoon ground ginger
- 1/2 teaspoon ground cardamom
- 2 teaspoons ground cinnamon
- 1/4 teaspoon ground cloves
- 1/4 teaspoon ground allspice (optional)
- 1/4 teaspoon ground nutmeg (optional)

- 1 1/2 cups all-purpose flour

Direction

- Use nonstick spray to coat bottom and sides of a 15"x10" glass pan. Set the oven to 170°C or 325°F to preheat.
- Heat the honey and 1/3 cup of sugar in a 2-cup glass measuring cup in the microwave about one minute. Transfer this mixture into a medium mixing bowl.
- Sift together baking soda, baking powder and flour, then put into the honey mixture, stirring well.
- Put in candied fruit, spices and oil and mix well, working by hand.
- Put in more 1 1/2 to 2 cups of flour, then knead dough to blend and dough will become stiff. Spread dough into pan and bake until a toothpick exits clean, about 20 minutes.
- Slice into squares. You can eat plain or frost with sugar glaze. Store about 2 weeks for the best quality.

Nutrition Information

- Calories: 330 calories;
- Cholesterol: 0
- Protein: 4
- Total Fat: 1.6
- Sodium: 97
- Total Carbohydrate: 77.5

397. Lebkuchen II

Serving: 84 | Prep: | Cook: | Ready in:

Ingredients

- 3 cups honey
- 2 1/4 cups packed brown sugar
- 3 eggs
- 1 tablespoon lemon zest
- 3 tablespoons lemon juice
- 8 1/4 cups all-purpose flour
- 1 1/2 teaspoons baking soda
- 1 tablespoon ground cinnamon
- 1 1/2 teaspoons ground allspice
- 1 1/2 teaspoons ground nutmeg
- 1 teaspoon ground cloves
- 1 cup chopped candied citron
- 1 cup chopped pecans
- 2 cups sliced almonds
- 1 1/2 cups white sugar
- 3/4 cup water
- 1/3 cup sifted confectioners' sugar

Direction

- In a big Dutch oven, boil the honey; take off from heat, and partially cool. Mix in juice, lemon rind, beaten eggs and brown sugar.
- In a big mixing bowl, mix baking soda, spices and flour; slowly put into mixture of honey, mixing thoroughly. Mix in chopped pecans and citron, mixing thoroughly. Refrigerate overnight with cover.
- Heat oven to 200°C or 400°F.
- Form the dough making balls measuring an-inch; arrange onto oiled cookie sheets, spacing 2-inch apart. Push ball softly using base of glass dunked in cool water into quarter-inch-thick. Carefully push 1 almond slice in the middle of every cookie. Bake for about 10 minutes. Take cookie sheets out of the oven. Brush top of cookies with glaze; transfer onto wire racks and let cool down.
- Prep Glaze: in a heavy, small-size saucepan, mix water and 1 1/2 cups of sugar; let cook on low heat, mixing to dissolve the sugar. Cook, without mixing, on high heat, till mixture attains a temperature of 230°F or thread stage. Take off from heat; mix in confectioners' sugar, stirring thoroughly. Set on low heat, if need be, to keep the basting consistency.

Nutrition Information

- Calories: 154 calories;
- Total Fat: 2.4
- Sodium: 36

- Total Carbohydrate: 32.3
- Cholesterol: 7
- Protein: 2.1

398. Lebkuchen III

Serving: 30 | Prep: 15mins | Cook: 12mins | Ready in:

Ingredients

- 1 egg
- 1/2 cup brown sugar
- 1/2 cup honey
- 1/2 cup molasses
- 3 cups all-purpose flour
- 1 1/4 teaspoons ground cinnamon
- 1/2 teaspoon ground nutmeg
- 1/2 teaspoon ground cloves
- 1/2 teaspoon ground allspice
- 1/2 teaspoon baking soda
- 1/2 cup chopped almonds
- 1/2 cup chopped candied citron

Direction

- Set oven to 350°F (175°C) to preheat. Grease cookie sheets.
- Whisk the molasses, honey, brown sugar and egg in a big bowl until smooth. Mix the baking soda, allspice, cloves, nutmeg, cinnamon and flour; combine into the molasses mixture. Mix in the candied citron and almonds. With 1/4 of the dough at a time, roll out to shape the dough into 1/4 inch in thickness on a lightly floured surface. Slice into desired shapes using cookie cutters. Put the cookies at least an inch apart onto greased cookie sheets.
- Bake for 10 to 12 minutes in the prepared oven or until firm. Let it cool on wire racks and put in an airtight container to store at room temperature.

Nutrition Information

- Calories: 113 calories;
- Total Fat: 1.1
- Sodium: 38
- Total Carbohydrate: 24.3
- Cholesterol: 6
- Protein: 1.9

399. Liegnitzer Bomben

Serving: 24 | Prep: 40mins | Cook: 20mins | Ready in:

Ingredients

- 14 ounces honey
- 1 1/4 cups white sugar
- 9 tablespoons butter
- 6 tablespoons milk
- 4 cups all-purpose flour
- 1 tablespoon all-purpose flour
- 5 tablespoons unsweetened cocoa powder
- 2 1/2 teaspoons baking powder
- 3 eggs, lightly beaten
- 1 teaspoon lemon zest
- 1 pinch ground cardamom
- 1 pinch ground mace
- 1 pinch ground cloves
- 1 pinch ground cinnamon
- 3/4 cup dried currants
- 1 tablespoon dried currants
- 3/4 cup chopped almonds
- 1 tablespoon chopped almonds
- 3/4 cup chopped candied citron
- 3 tablespoons chopped candied citron
- 1 1/4 cups apricot jam
- 2 tablespoons water
- 3/4 cup confectioners' sugar
- 3 tablespoons unsweetened cocoa powder
- 4 tablespoons hot water

Direction

- Set an oven to preheat at 175°C (350°F). Grease the muffin pans for twenty-four cookies.

- In a saucepan, mix the milk, butter, sugar and honey on medium heat. Mix until the mixture is hot but not boiling and the butter and sugar are melted. Move to a mixing bowl and allow it to cool.
- Sift the baking powder, 5 tbsp. of cocoa powder and 4 cups plus 1 tbsp. of flour together.
- Stir in the cinnamon, cloves, mace, ground cardamom, cocoa and flour mixture, lemon zest or extract and eggs once the mixture has cooled down. Fold in the 3/4 cup plus 1 tbsp. chopped citron, 3/4 cup plus 1 tbsp. chopped almonds and 3/4 cup plus 1 tbsp. of currants.
- Fill the muffin cups 1/2 full of batter. Bake in the oven for 20-25 minutes, until an inserted toothpick in the middle exits clean. Cool for 10 minutes in the pans before removing to fully cool on a wire rack set on top of the rimmed baking tray.
- In a pan, mix the 2 tbsp. of water and apricot jam then boil. Take it out of the heat. Brush it with warm jam mixture once the cookies have cooled down.
- Sift 3 tbsp. of cocoa powder together with the confectioners' sugar. To give the glaze a good coating consistency, pour just enough hot water. Put the glaze on top of the cookies. Place the cookies in airtight containers once the glaze dries completely.

Nutrition Information

- Calories: 336 calories;
- Total Fat: 7.1
- Sodium: 126
- Total Carbohydrate: 67.6
- Cholesterol: 32
- Protein: 4.5

400. Lime Creams

Serving: 36 | Prep: 30mins | Cook: 12mins | Ready in:

Ingredients

- 1/3 cup white sugar
- 2 tablespoons lime juice
- 1 tablespoon grated lime zest
- 1 egg
- 1 drop green food coloring, or as desired
- 1/3 cup butter, softened
- 1/4 cup white sugar
- 1 egg
- 1 teaspoon vanilla extract
- 1 1/2 cups all-purpose flour
- 1/4 teaspoon salt
- 1 tablespoon confectioners' sugar for dusting

Direction

- In a saucepan, place 1 egg, lime juice, lime zest and 1/3 cup of sugar over low heat; whisk continuously until the mixture nearly reaches a simmer and starts to thicken. Next, remove from the heat, and tint with food coloring to get your desired green shade. Put the filling aside to cool.
- Set the oven at 165°C (325°F) to preheat.
- Cream butter and 1/4 cup of sugar in a bowl, then put in vanilla extract and 1 egg, continue to stir. Add salt and flour, mix until the dough is smooth. Roll to shape the dough into 1-inch balls. Next, place them on an ungreased baking sheet, leaving about 2 inches between the balls. In the center of each ball, make an indentation using your thumb. Scoop into each indentation with about 3/4 teaspoon of the lime filling.
- In the preheated oven, bake until the cookies are set (not browned), for 12-15 minutes. Then let the cookies cool for 1 minute on the baking sheet before transferring to wire racks to finish cooling. Once the cookies are cool, lightly scatter with confectioners' sugar.

Nutrition Information

- Calories: 52 calories;
- Cholesterol: 15
- Protein: 0.9

- Total Fat: 2
- Sodium: 32
- Total Carbohydrate: 7.6

- Calories: 288 calories;
- Total Fat: 12.5
- Sodium: 71
- Total Carbohydrate: 42
- Cholesterol: 37
- Protein: 3.4

401. Linzer Torte Cookies

Serving: 15 | Prep: | Cook: | Ready in:

Ingredients

- 3/4 cup butter, softened
- 1 cup white sugar
- 1 egg
- 1 teaspoon lemon zest
- 2 cups all-purpose flour
- 3/4 cup blanched slivered almonds, ground
- 1 teaspoon ground cinnamon
- 1/8 teaspoon ground cloves
- 1 cup raspberry jam

Direction

- Set oven to 350°F (175°C). Grease an 11x7 inch baking dish.
- Beat the butter with sugar in a medium bowl. Whisk in the lemon peel and egg. Mix the cloves, cinnamon, almonds and flour in a separate bowl. Mix the dry ingredients into the creamed mixture gradually. The dough will be stiff, so you may need to knead it by hand to stick it together. Press half of the dough into the bottom of the prepped pan.
- Press half of the dough into the bottom of the prepped pan. Evenly spread the preserves on top of the crust. Shape the leftover dough into long rope about 1/2 inch in diameter on a lightly floured surface. In a lattice pattern, put lengths of the rope across the top of the jam on top of the preserves.
- Bake until top is golden, or for 40 minutes. Let it cool in pan on wire rack. Slice into 2 by 1inch bars.

Nutrition Information

402. Little Nut Cups

Serving: 36 | Prep: 15mins | Cook: 15mins | Ready in:

Ingredients

- 1 cup butter, softened
- 2 (3 ounce) packages cream cheese
- 1/2 cup white sugar
- 2 cups all-purpose flour
- 2 teaspoons butter, melted
- 2 eggs
- 1/2 teaspoon vanilla extract
- 2 cups chopped pecans
- 1 1/2 cups brown sugar
- 1/2 cup honey

Direction

- Mix sugar, cream cheese, and butter in a medium bowl till smooth. Stirring in the flour and thoroughly mixing. Make sure the dough to be somewhat firm. Rolling into 36 small balls; on a plate, place the balls and let them sit for an hour in the refrigerator.
- In a medium bowl, make the filling. Beating brown sugar, vanilla, melted butter, and eggs till blended well and smooth. Stirring in the nuts. Heat oven to 190°C (375°F) beforehand. In mini muffin cups or tart pans, pressing the chilled dough balls into the bottom and up the sides. Place filling into each shell to fill almost to the top. If you have a squeeze top honey container, user it to drip onto the top of each cup with approximately half a teaspoon of honey.
- In the preheated oven, allow to bake till crust is browned lightly for 15-20 minutes. Before

removing, let it sit in the tins to cool down completely.

Nutrition Information

- Calories: 183 calories;
- Sodium: 58
- Total Carbohydrate: 18.9
- Cholesterol: 30
- Protein: 2.1
- Total Fat: 11.7

403. Macaron (French Macaroon)

Serving: 8 | Prep: 30mins | Cook: 10mins | Ready in:

Ingredients

- 3 egg whites
- 1/4 cup white sugar
- 1 2/3 cups confectioners' sugar
- 1 cup finely ground almonds

Direction

- Line a silicone baking mat on a baking sheet.
- In a stand mixer's bowl with a whisk attachment, beat egg whites until whites are foamy. Beat white sugar in. Keep beating until the egg whites hold soft peaks and are glossy and fluffy. In another bowl, sift ground almonds and confectioners' sugar. Fold almond mixture quickly into egg whites, around 30 strokes.
- Spoon a bit of batter in a plastic bag that has a small corner cut off. Pipe out a test disk of the batter on the prepped baking sheet, about 1 1/2-in. in diameter. If the disk of batter holds a peak and doesn't immediately flatten, fold batter gently several more times, then test again.
- When batter is mixed enough to immediately flatten to an even disk, spoon it into a pastry bag with a plain round tip. Pipe the batter in rounds on the baking sheet. Leave space between disks. Let piped cookies stand for about 1 hour at room temperature until a hard skin forms on top.
- Preheat the oven to 140 degrees C/285 degrees F.
- Bake cookies for about 10 minutes until set yet not browned. Completely cool cookies prior to filling.

Nutrition Information

- Calories: 189 calories;
- Total Fat: 2.6
- Sodium: 22
- Total Carbohydrate: 36.4
- Cholesterol: 0
- Protein: 6.9

404. Macaroons II

Serving: 36 | Prep: | Cook: | Ready in:

Ingredients

- 2 egg whites
- 1 tablespoon cornstarch
- 1/2 cup white sugar
- 1 teaspoon vanilla extract
- 1 cup flaked coconut

Direction

- Set the oven to 150°C or 300°F to preheat. Use parchment paper to line 2 baking sheets.
- Beat egg whites in a medium bowl until stiff yet still not dry, then stir in cornstarch. Remove to the top of a double boiler placed on low heat.
- Stir in sugar and cook until edges of mixture start to pull away from pan, about 3-4 minutes. Take away from the heat and stir in vanilla extract. Stir in coconut.

- Drop onto prepped baking sheets with spoonfuls of dough, spaced 1 1/2 inches apart. Bake until turn golden brown and firm to the touch, about 20-25 minutes. Allow to cool on pans on wire racks.

Nutrition Information

- Calories: 22 calories;
- Total Fat: 0.6
- Sodium: 9
- Total Carbohydrate: 4.1
- Cholesterol: 0
- Protein: 0.3

405. Magic Peanut Butter Middles

Serving: 15 | Prep: | Cook: | Ready in:

Ingredients

- 1 1/2 cups all-purpose flour
- 1/2 cup unsweetened cocoa powder
- 1/2 teaspoon baking soda
- 1/2 cup white sugar
- 1/2 cup packed brown sugar
- 1/2 cup soft margarine
- 1/4 cup peanut butter
- 1 teaspoon vanilla extract
- 1 egg
- 3/4 cup confectioners' sugar
- 3/4 cup peanut butter

Direction

- Blend baking soda, cocoa and flour in a small bowl. Mix until ingredients are well blended.
- In a large bowl, beat 1/4 cup peanut butter, butter or margarine, brown and white sugars, until fluffy and light. Add egg and vanilla, beat. Stir in the flour mixture until mixed. Set aside.
- For the filling: Combine 3/4 cup peanut butter and confectioner's sugar. Blend properly.
- Roll filling into 30 1-inch balls. Cover your hands with flour and form about 1 tablespoon dough around 1 peanut butter ball for each cookie, covering the filling fully. Arrange dough balls on an ungreased cookie sheet 2 inches apart. Roll a glass dipped in white sugar over the dough balls.
- Bake for 7 to 9 minutes at 375°F (190°C). Cookies should be set and cracked slightly when they are done.

Nutrition Information

- Calories: 289 calories;
- Sodium: 199
- Total Carbohydrate: 34.4
- Cholesterol: 12
- Protein: 6.7
- Total Fat: 15.5

406. Mailaenderli

Serving: 50 | Prep: 50mins | Cook: 20mins | Ready in:

Ingredients

- 4 eggs
- 1 1/4 cups white sugar
- 1 1/8 cups butter, melted and cooled to lukewarm
- 1 pinch salt
- 4 cups all purpose flour
- 1 1/2 teaspoons grated lemon zest
- 2 egg yolks, beaten
- seasonal colored sprinkles

Direction

- Whip eggs in one big bowl. Mix sugar in and whip for 10 minutes till mixture is pale and thick. Stir in the salt and melted butter. Slowly fold in lemon zest and flour. Chill with cover

for not less than one hour or overnight preferably.
- Heat the oven to 165 ° C or 325 ° F. Oil cookie sheet lightly.
- Unroll dough on a floured counter to thickness of 1/4 inch. Cut to preferred forms with cookie cutters. Arrange cookies on prepped cookie sheet. Brush with beaten egg yolks and jazz up using sprinkles.
- Bake for about 15 to 20 minutes in prepped oven till edges turn golden. Let cookies cool onto racks.

Nutrition Information

- Calories: 105 calories;
- Sodium: 36
- Total Carbohydrate: 13.4
- Cholesterol: 34
- Protein: 1.7
- Total Fat: 5

407. Mandelmakronen (Almond Meringues)

Serving: 48 | Prep: 20mins | Cook: 15mins | Ready in:

Ingredients

- 4 egg whites
- 1 cup white sugar
- 1 1/2 cups almond flour, or more as needed
- 1/4 teaspoon ground cinnamon

Direction

- Set the oven to 300°F (150°C) and start preheating. Use parchment paper to line 2 baking sheets.
- In a ceramic, metal or glass bowl, whisk egg whites until it forms stiff peaks. Add 1 teaspoon of sugar per time gradually while keeping beating at high speed. In a bowl, mix cinnamon and ground almonds; using a spatula, fold into egg white mixture. Add more ground almonds if the mixture is too runny.
- Place little mounds of almond mixture with 2 teaspoons onto lined baking sheets, 2 inches apart.
- Bake for 15-20 minutes in the prepared oven until baked through and lightly brown. Take out of the baking sheets carefully; cool on wire racks.

Nutrition Information

- Calories: 40 calories;
- Total Fat: 1.9
- Sodium: 5
- Total Carbohydrate: 5
- Cholesterol: 0
- Protein: 1.1

408. Meatball Cookies

Serving: 30 | Prep: | Cook: | Ready in:

Ingredients

- 3 cups all-purpose flour
- 2/3 cup unsweetened cocoa powder
- 1 1/2 teaspoons baking powder
- 1 1/2 teaspoons baking soda
- 1 teaspoon salt
- 1 cup chopped walnuts
- 1 teaspoon ground cloves
- 1 teaspoon ground allspice
- 1 teaspoon ground cinnamon
- 1/2 teaspoon ground nutmeg
- 1 1/2 cups white sugar
- 3 eggs
- 1/2 cup butter
- 2 teaspoons vanilla extract
- 4 cups confectioners' sugar
- 1/4 cup unsweetened cocoa powder
- 1/2 cup milk

Direction

- Preheat the oven to 180°C or 350°Fahrenheit. Oil the cookie sheets.
- Cream vanilla, eggs, white sugar and shortening or butter margarine.
- Combine spices, salt, baking soda, baking powder, 2/3 cup cocoa and flour in another bowl; combine with the butter mixture. Add more flour if the mixture is too sticky. Alternatively, pour in a bit of milk if the mixture is too dry. Mix in nuts by hand. You should be able to roll the mixture into mini 1/2 to 1-in balls.
- Form mini-balls once the cookie dough is in the perfect handling consistency by adjusting either milk or flour. Arrange on the cookie sheet; bake cookies for 10-12 minutes until firm. Avoid to overcook. Take the cookies out of the oven then let it sit for a few minutes in the sheet; move to a wax paper. Frost cooled cookies with cocoa and confectioners' sugar glaze.
- For the glaze, mix half cup of milk, a quarter cup of cocoa, and four cups of confectioners' sugar together; it should have a glaze-like consistency. Spread about a teaspoon of glaze on top of each cookie. While glaze still wet, decorate with sprinkles.

Nutrition Information

- Calories: 216 calories;
- Cholesterol: 27
- Protein: 3.2
- Total Fat: 6.7
- Sodium: 197
- Total Carbohydrate: 37.9

409. Medenjaci (Croatian Honey Spice Cookies)

Serving: 48 | Prep: 15mins | Cook: 10mins | Ready in:

Ingredients

- 1 cup butter
- 1 cup demerara sugar
- 3/4 cup honey
- 2 1/2 cups all-purpose flour
- 2 1/2 cups cake flour
- 3/4 cup whole wheat flour
- 3 eggs, lightly whisked
- 2 teaspoons ground cinnamon
- 1 teaspoon baking soda
- 1/2 teaspoon ground cloves
- 1/2 teaspoon ground nutmeg
- 1/2 teaspoon ground ginger
- 12 whole walnuts, divided into quarters

Direction

- In a big saucepan on low heat, mix honey, sugar and butter together till butter is melted and sugar is dissolved. Let cool for 10 minutes.
- In a bowl, stir together ginger, nutmeg, cloves, baking soda, cinnamon, whole wheat flour, cake flour and all-purpose flour.
- Into the cooled butter mixture, whisk eggs and flour mixture till a soft, smooth dough creates. Put aluminum foil to cover the saucepan and place in cool area for 1 to 3 days to ferment.
- Preheat an oven to 190 °C or 375 °F. Line silicone baking mats or parchment paper on baking sheets.
- Split dough to make long ropes approximately 2/3-inch diameter. Cut ropes to make 1 1/2-inch portions. Roll each dough portion into a walnut-size ball. On prepped baking sheets, put balls 1 1/2-inch apart. Into the surface of each cookie, press a piece of walnut midway.
- In prepped oven, let cookies bake for 10 to 12 minutes till slightly golden.

Nutrition Information

- Calories: 131 calories;
- Total Fat: 4.7
- Sodium: 60
- Total Carbohydrate: 20.7
- Cholesterol: 22

- Protein: 2.1

410. Meringue Mushrooms

Serving: 36 | Prep: 45mins | Cook: 1hours | Ready in:

Ingredients

- 1/2 cup egg whites
- 1/4 teaspoon cream of tartar
- 1/4 teaspoon salt
- 1 teaspoon vanilla extract
- 1 cup white sugar
- 1 tablespoon unsweetened cocoa powder
- 4 ounces chocolate confectioners' coating

Direction

- Set the oven to 225°F (110°C), and start preheating. Line aluminum foil or parchment paper on 2 cookie sheets.
- In a metal bowl or large glass, whip egg whites with an electric mixer until foamy. Put in vanilla, salt and cream of tartar. Keep whipping until the egg whites hold soft peaks. Slowly sprinkle with the sugar, make sure that it will not sink to the bottom; then keep whipping until the mixture has stiff shiny peaks.
- In a pastry bag, place a round tip and fill 1/2 bag with the meringue. On one of the prepped cookie sheets, squeeze out round mounds of meringue to pipe mushroom caps. Pull the bag off to the side to prevent forming peaks on top. To make stems, on another sheet, press out a little bit of meringue, then pull the bag up straight. They should look like the candy kisses. The mushrooms will look more natural when they are in different sizes so do not worry about whether they are of the same size or not. Lightly dust the caps with cocoa with a small strainer or sifter.
- Bake in the preheated oven for 1 hour, or till the caps are dry enough and can be easily removed from cookie sheets. Put aside to cool down completely. In a in a glass bowl in the microwave or metal bowl, melt the coating chocolate over simmering water until smooth while stirring occasionally.
- In the bottom of a mushroom cap, poke to make a small hole. Spread chocolate over the caps' bottom. Dip a stem tip in chocolate, and lightly press into the hole. They will hold together once the chocolate sets. Repeat the process. Store in a dry place or a tin at room temperature.

Nutrition Information

- Calories: 39 calories;
- Total Carbohydrate: 7.1
- Cholesterol: 0
- Protein: 0.6
- Total Fat: 1.3
- Sodium: 22

411. Meringue Springerle Cookies

Serving: 36 | Prep: | Cook: 10mins | Ready in:

Ingredients

- cooking spray
- 2 tablespoons anise seeds, crushed, or as needed
- 4 1/2 cups confectioners' sugar, plus more for dusting
- 1 1/2 teaspoons baking powder
- 6 egg whites
- 1 tablespoon vanilla extract
- 1 teaspoon anise oil
- 3 1/2 cups all-purpose flour, plus more for dusting

Direction

- Freeze the cookie molds. Line parchment paper on baking sheets then lightly spray with

the cooking spray. Lightly sprinkle on top of parchment paper with crushed anise seeds.
- Sift together baking powder and confectioners' sugar into a large bowl. Put aside.
- In the bowl of a stand mixer fitted with the paddle attachment, beat the egg whites on medium speed for 5-10 mins until it forms the stiff peaks. Fold in anise oil, vanilla extract, and sifted sugar carefully. Gradually put in flour; mixing until a stiff dough form.
- Turn out dough onto the work surface. Separate into three pieces, form into discs, then wrap in plastic wrap. Let them chill for 3 hours to overnight until firm.
- Take out the dough discs from the fridge; then divide, based on your molds size, into the smaller pieces. Coat confectioners' sugar over each piece; as you roll out, keep in the fridge, 1 piece at a time.
- Lightly dust flour over the pastry cloth or work surface. Roll out dough piece to a 1/4-in. thick circle. Lightly dust confectioners' sugar over the circle top. Heavily dust confectioners' sugar over cookie mold; then firmly press down to create clear, deep impressions. If dough sticks, use a moistened brush or toothpick (don't use a knife) to pry it out of the mold.
- Cut molded cookies apart with a knife or pastry cutter. Arrange cookies onto prepared baking sheets. Do the same with the remaining dough pieces, dusting confectioners' sugar over molds any time before using. Place cookies out to air dry, uncovered, for 8 hours to overnight.
- Start preheating the oven to 300°F (150°C).
- Bake cookies in prepared oven for 10-15 mins until dry and firm but remain pale. Let cookies cool completely on the cooling racks.

Nutrition Information

- Calories: 111 calories;
- Sodium: 30
- Total Carbohydrate: 25.2
- Cholesterol: 0
- Protein: 1.9
- Total Fat: 0.3

412. Merry Cherry Bars

Serving: 36 | Prep: 10mins | Cook: 30mins | Ready in:

Ingredients

- 1 cup butter, softened
- 1 cup white sugar
- 1 egg
- 1/2 teaspoon almond extract
- 2 cups all-purpose flour
- 1/4 teaspoon salt
- 3/4 cup chopped red and green candied cherries
- 1/2 cup crushed candy coated milk chocolates
- 1 cup sifted confectioners' sugar
- 5 teaspoons warm water

Direction

- Set oven to 300°F (150°C) to preheat.
- Beat butter with sugar in a large bowl until fluffy and light. Beat in almond extract and egg. Mix together salt and flour; mix into the creamed mixture until well combined. Stir in 1/2 cup of cherries. Press the dough into an unoiled 9x13-inch baking pan. Sprinkle top with crushed candies and the rest of cherries, and press lightly into the dough.
- Bake in the preheated oven for 30 to 35 minutes or until edges turn brown lightly. Allow to cool entirely in the pan before icing. For icing, stir water and confectioners' sugar together until mixture achieves a drizzling consistency.

Nutrition Information

- Calories: 131 calories;
- Total Carbohydrate: 18.6
- Cholesterol: 19

- Protein: 1.1
- Total Fat: 5.9
- Sodium: 59

413. Michelle's Soft Sugar Cookies

Serving: 60 | Prep: | Cook: | Ready in:

Ingredients

- 1 cup margarine
- 1 1/2 cups white sugar
- 3 eggs
- 1 teaspoon vanilla extract
- 3 1/2 cups all-purpose flour
- 2 teaspoons cream of tartar
- 1 teaspoon baking soda
- 1/2 teaspoon salt

Direction

- Cream margarine and gradually put in sugar. Beat until fluffy and light. Put in the eggs one at a time, stirring well after each of addition.
- Mix in vanilla. Gradually put in salt, baking soda, cream of tartar and flour to creamed mixture, stirring in with your hand. Chill the dough with a cover overnight.
- Start preheating the oven to 375°F (190°C). Line parchment on the paper baking sheets.
- Roll the dough out on the floured surface to 1/8 to a quarter inch thick and slice into favorite shapes. Arrange the cookies on prepared baking sheets.
- Bake for 6-8 mins at 375°F (190°C) or until the cookie is golden appearance.

Nutrition Information

- Calories: 77 calories;
- Total Fat: 3.3
- Sodium: 79
- Total Carbohydrate: 10.7

- Cholesterol: 9
- Protein: 1.1

414. Milano Style Cookies

Serving: 40 | Prep: 15mins | Cook: 10mins | Ready in:

Ingredients

- 1/2 cup butter, softened
- 1/2 cup vegetable shortening
- 1 cup confectioners' sugar
- 3 tablespoons water
- 1 egg
- 1 1/4 teaspoons vanilla extract
- 1/4 teaspoon almond extract
- 2 1/2 cups all-purpose flour
- 1/2 teaspoon salt
- 1 cup miniature chocolate chips

Direction

- Turn on the oven to 375°F (190°C) to preheat.
- In a bowl, beat together shortening and butter until creamy. Beat in almond extract, vanilla extract, egg, water and confectioners' sugar. Mix in salt and flour until it forms smooth dough. Mix chocolate chips into the dough. Use a small cookie scoop to scoop dough; on ungreased baking sheet, arrange cookies.
- Put into the oven to bake for about 9 minutes until the cookie edges turn light brown.

Nutrition Information

- Calories: 107 calories;
- Sodium: 48
- Total Carbohydrate: 11.8
- Cholesterol: 11
- Protein: 1.2
- Total Fat: 6.4

415. Mint Nanaimo Bars

Serving: 16 | Prep: 20mins | Cook: | Ready in:

Ingredients

- 1 cup mint chocolate chips
- 1/4 cup butter
- 1/4 cup confectioners' sugar
- 1 egg
- 1 1/2 cups graham cracker crumbs
- 1/4 cup butter
- 2 cups confectioners' sugar
- 2 tablespoons milk
- 1 drop green food coloring, or as needed
- 1 cup mint chocolate chips
- 1/4 cup butter

Direction

- In the top of a double boiler set over hot water, melt 1/4 cup of butter and 1 cup of mint chocolate chips while stirring to melt both ingredients into a smooth mixture. Take away from the heat and beat in egg and 1/4 cup of confectioners' sugar, beating well. Stir in graham cracker crumbs until well mixed and press mixture into an 8"x8" dish. Chill the crust for an hour in the fridge.
- Beat together milk, 2 cups of confectioners' sugar and 1/4 cup of butter in a mixing bowl using an electric mixer, until mixture becomes fluffy and smooth. Beat in 1 drop of green food coloring at a time, until filling reaches your preferred color. Spread over chilled crust with the filling and turn back to the fridge for a half hour.
- In the top of a double boiler set over hot water, melt 1/4 cup of butter and 1 cup of mint chocolate chips while stirring to get a warm not hot, spreadable and smooth mixture. Spread over filing with a single even layer of topping, then turn the dish back to fridge again. Refrigerate for 15 minutes, until topping is firm yet still not hard. Cut into squares and turn back to the fridge for 15 minutes more, then serve cold.

Nutrition Information

- Calories: 287 calories;
- Total Fat: 15.7
- Sodium: 114
- Total Carbohydrate: 37.1
- Cholesterol: 35
- Protein: 2.6

416. Minty Nanaimo Bars

Serving: 16 | Prep: 20mins | Cook: | Ready in:

Ingredients

- 1 cup mint chocolate chips
- 1/2 cup butter
- 1 1/4 cups chocolate wafer cookie crumbs
- 1 cup flaked coconut
- 1/2 cup chopped walnuts
- 1/4 cup butter, softened
- 2 cups confectioners' sugar
- 3 tablespoons milk
- 2 tablespoons custard powder
- 1/4 teaspoon peppermint extract
- 1 drop green food coloring, or as needed
- 3/4 cup mint chocolate chips
- 1 tablespoon butter

Direction

- In large saucepan, melt one cup mint chocolate chips with half cup of butter over the very low heat; combine by stirring. Stir in walnuts, coconut and chocolate wafer crumbs, then press into bottom of the 8x8-in. square pan. Let chill for at least half an hour or until crust has set.
- Add a quarter cup of softened butter into the mixing bowl, then beat in peppermint extract, custard powder, milk and confectioners' sugar until filling is thick and smooth. Beat in the green food coloring to reach preferred green color, about 1 drop at a time. Spread crust with

filling in smooth layer. Place in the refrigerator at least half an hour or until set.
- Melt one tablespoon of butter with 3/4 cup of the mint chocolate chips together in small saucepan over very low heat, mix thoroughly by stirring. Let it cool for several mins, then spread over the chilled mint filling layer. Place dish back to refrigerator, let chill at least 60 mins or until set then divide into squares to enjoy.

Nutrition Information

- Calories: 323 calories;
- Total Carbohydrate: 37.6
- Cholesterol: 25
- Protein: 2.8
- Total Fat: 19.5
- Sodium: 132

417. Molasses Cookies VI

Serving: 48 | Prep: 2hours10mins | Cook: 8mins | Ready in:

Ingredients

- 1 cup butter, softened
- 1 cup molasses
- 1/2 cup sour cream
- 1 cup brown sugar
- 1 tablespoon distilled white vinegar
- 4 1/2 cups all-purpose flour
- 1 tablespoon baking soda
- 1 teaspoon salt
- 1 teaspoon ground cinnamon
- 1 teaspoon ground ginger

Direction

- Set an oven to preheat to 165°C (325°F), then grease the cookie sheets.
- Stir together the vinegar, brown sugar, sour cream, molasses and butter in a big bowl until it becomes smooth and well combined. Mix together the cinnamon, ginger, salt, baking soda and flour and mix it into the molasses mixture. The dough will get very stiff once complete.
- Roll out the dough to 1/4-inch thick on a lightly floured surface, then cut it into preferred shapes using cookie cutters. Put the cookies onto the prepped cookie sheets and place it 1 1/2 inches apart.
- Let it bake in the preheated oven for 8 -10 minutes. Let the cookies cool for 5 minutes on the baking tray prior to transferring to a wire rack to fully cool. Once cooled, the cookies can be iced using any standard icing recipe.

Nutrition Information

- Calories: 113 calories;
- Total Carbohydrate: 17.2
- Cholesterol: 11
- Protein: 1.3
- Total Fat: 4.5
- Sodium: 154

418. Molasses Crinkles

Serving: 48 | Prep: | Cook: | Ready in:

Ingredients

- 3/4 cup shortening
- 1 cup packed brown sugar
- 1 egg
- 1/4 cup molasses
- 2 1/4 cups all-purpose flour
- 2 teaspoons baking soda
- 1/4 teaspoon salt
- 1/2 teaspoon ground cloves
- 1 teaspoon ground cinnamon
- 1 teaspoon ground ginger
- 1/3 cup granulated sugar for decoration

Direction

- Cream brown sugar and shortening. Mix in molasses and egg and combine thoroughly.
- Mix ginger, cinnamon, cloves, salt, baking soda and flour. To the shortening mixture, put flour mixture and combine thoroughly. Place a cover and refrigerate dough for a minimum of 2 to 3 hours.
- Preheat the oven to 175°C or 350°F. Oil the cookie sheets.
- Roll dough forming rounds to the size of big walnuts. Roll rounds in sugar and on the prepped baking sheets, set 3-inch away. Allow to bake for 10 to 12 minutes in the preheated oven. Allow to cool for a minute prior to putting to a wire rack to keep cooling.

Nutrition Information

- Calories: 79 calories;
- Protein: 0.7
- Total Fat: 3.4
- Sodium: 68
- Total Carbohydrate: 11.7
- Cholesterol: 4

419. Mom's Peanut Butter Blossom Cookies

Serving: 48 | Prep: 15mins | Cook: 10mins | Ready in:

Ingredients

- 3/4 cup peanut butter
- 1/2 cup shortening
- 1/3 cup white sugar
- 1/3 cup light brown sugar
- 1 egg
- 2 tablespoons milk
- 1 teaspoon vanilla extract
- 1 1/2 cups all-purpose flour
- 1 teaspoon baking soda
- 1/2 teaspoon salt
- 1 (8 ounce) package milk chocolate candy kisses (such as Hershey's Kisses®), unwrapped

Direction

- Preheat the oven to 375°F (190°C).
- In a bowl, beat together the shortening and butter with an electric mixer until creamy and smooth; add brown sugar and white sugar; beat until fluffy. Add vanilla extract, milk and egg to cream the mixture; beat until mixture is smooth.
- In a separate bowl, mix together the salt, baking soda and flour; beat into the creamed mixture gradually until dough is just mixed. Form into 1-inch balls and transfer onto a baking sheet.
- Bake for 8 to 10 minutes in the preheated oven, until cookies have the lightly brown color. Force one chocolate kiss into the middle of every cookie immediately. Move cookies to a wire rack and allow to cool.

Nutrition Information

- Calories: 94 calories;
- Sodium: 75
- Total Carbohydrate: 9.5
- Cholesterol: 5
- Protein: 1.9
- Total Fat: 5.8

420. Moravian Ginger Cookies I

Serving: 30 | Prep: | Cook: | Ready in:

Ingredients

- 3 tablespoons shortening
- 2 tablespoons brown sugar
- 1/3 cup molasses
- 1 1/4 cups all-purpose flour

- 1/4 teaspoon baking soda
- 1/2 teaspoon salt
- 1/4 teaspoon ground cinnamon
- 1/4 teaspoon ground ginger
- 1/4 teaspoon ground cloves
- 1 pinch ground nutmeg
- 1 dash ground allspice

Direction

- Cream together the molasses, brown sugar and shortening in a medium bowl until it becomes smooth. Sift together the allspice, nutmeg, cloves, ginger, cinnamon, salt, baking soda and flour, then blend it into the creamed mixture. Use your hands to work on the dough until well combined. Put cover and let it chill for around 4 hours. The dough should be thoroughly chilled to hold together.
- Set an oven to preheat to 190°C (375°F). Roll out the dough to paper thin, a little at a time. Use cookie cutters to cut it into your preferred shapes, then put it on the greased baking trays.
- Let it bake in the preheated oven for 5-6 minutes or until it turns light brown.

Nutrition Information

- Calories: 45 calories;
- Sodium: 51
- Total Carbohydrate: 7.7
- Cholesterol: 0
- Protein: 0.5
- Total Fat: 1.4

421. Moravian Spice Cookies

Serving: 36 | Prep: | Cook: | Ready in:

Ingredients

- 2 tablespoons butter
- 1/2 cup molasses
- 1/4 cup packed dark brown sugar
- 2 tablespoons corn oil
- 1 teaspoon ground cinnamon
- 1/2 teaspoon ground ginger
- 1/2 teaspoon ground cloves
- 1/2 teaspoon ground allspice
- 1/2 teaspoon baking soda
- 2 cups all-purpose flour

Direction

- On low heat, melt the margarine or butter until it turns light brown in color. Stir in brown sugar, oil, and molasses, mixing until sugar melts. Pour mixture in mixing bowl. Set aside for 5 minutes to cool.
- Beat in ginger, baking soda, cloves, allspice, and cinnamon; stir well. Pour a 1/2 cup of flour at a time, whisking just until incorporated.
- Prepare a big plastic wrap sheet and place dough. Shaped the dough into a disk by flattening. Wrap disk with the plastic. Before using, allow the dough to rest in room temperature, 1-2 hours. DO AHEAD: You can make the dough 3 days ahead and keep in the refrigerator. Place in room temperature before using.
- Heat oven to 350°F (180°C). Prepare cookie sheets by greasing lightly.
- Split the dough in half. Wrap again unused piece of the dough. Working on a floured flat surface, roll the dough out to less than 1/16 inch. Using small 2-in cutter, cut the cookies out and transfer into greased baking sheets, a 1/4 inch apart.
- Work in batches, bake cookies until starts to brown on edges and crisp, 8-10 minutes. Put into wire racks; cool. Do again with the rest of the cookie dough. Put cookies in a tightly sealed container. Cookies can be stored up to three weeks.

Nutrition Information

- Calories: 57 calories;
- Total Fat: 1.5

- Sodium: 24
- Total Carbohydrate: 10.3
- Cholesterol: 2
- Protein: 0.7

422. Moravian Sugar Cookies

Serving: 30 | Prep: | Cook: |Ready in:

Ingredients

- 4 1/2 cups all-purpose flour
- 1/4 teaspoon baking soda
- 1/4 teaspoon salt
- 1 teaspoon ground cinnamon
- 1/2 teaspoon ground cloves
- 1/4 teaspoon ground ginger
- 1 cup packed brown sugar
- 1/2 cup butter
- 1/2 cup shortening
- 1 1/2 cups dark molasses
- 1/2 teaspoon distilled white vinegar

Direction

- Combine ginger, cloves, cinnamon, salt, baking soda and flour.
- Beat shortening, butter and the brown sugar in another bowl. Put into the dry mixture and stir thoroughly. Put in vinegar and molasses. Stir thoroughly.
- Refrigerate while covered overnight.
- Roll out a little bit of dough to one-eighth (or less) inch thickness. Cut into shapes of your choice.
- Bake in 180°C (350°F) oven until the cookies are lightly browned, about 10 minutes.

Nutrition Information

- Calories: 201 calories;
- Sodium: 60
- Total Carbohydrate: 33.9
- Cholesterol: 8

- Protein: 2
- Total Fat: 6.7

423. Mrs. P's Biscotti

Serving: 40 | Prep: 15mins | Cook: 30mins |Ready in:

Ingredients

- 1 cup white sugar
- 1/4 cup softened butter
- 3 eggs
- 1 egg yolk
- 1 1/2 teaspoons vanilla extract
- 2 1/2 cups all-purpose flour
- 2 teaspoons baking powder

Direction

- Set oven to preheat at 350°F (175°C). Use parchment to line a baking sheet.
- Use an electric mixer to beat together sugar and butter in a large bowl till fluffy and light; beat eggs, egg yolk, and vanilla extract into the mixture. Whisk together flour and baking powder in a bowl. Stir the flour mixture into mixture of butter till a fairly sticky dough forms.
- Split the dough in half; wet your hands and shape the dough on the prepared baking sheet into two loaves, about 1-inch high at the center.
- In the preheated oven, bake until light brown, about 20 minutes; take out to cool down thoroughly on a wire rack, about 30 minutes.
- Cut 1/2-inch slices out of the loaves using a serrated knife. Put the cookie slices, cut sides up, back onto lined baking sheet.
- Raise the oven temperature to 450°F (230°C).
- In the preheated oven, bake until golden brown, turning only one time, about 3 to 4 minutes on each side.

Nutrition Information

- Calories: 65 calories;
- Total Fat: 1.7
- Sodium: 38
- Total Carbohydrate: 11.1
- Cholesterol: 22
- Protein: 1.4

424. Mrs. Ronzo's Lemon Balls

Serving: 48 | Prep: | Cook: | Ready in:

Ingredients

- 1 1/2 cups white sugar
- 1/2 cup shortening
- 3 eggs
- 1/2 teaspoon vanilla extract
- 1/2 cup milk
- 1 teaspoon lemon extract
- 3 cups all-purpose flour
- 3 teaspoons baking powder
- 1 pinch salt
- 2 cups confectioners' sugar
- 3 tablespoons water
- 1 teaspoon lemon extract

Direction

- Preheat an oven to 175°C/350°F.
- Blend shortening and white sugar till light; beat 1 tsp. lemon extract, vanilla, milk and eggs in. Mix till blended well.
- Mix salt, baking powder and flour; add flour mixture to shortening mixture. Stir till combined and dough is sticky. On parchment paper-lined baking sheets, drop spoonfuls of dough.
- Bake for 8-10 minutes at 175°C/350°F; cool cookies then frost using icing.
- Icing: Beat lemon extract to taste, water and confectioners' sugar till smooth and thick enough to spread over cooled cookies.

Nutrition Information

- Calories: 97 calories;
- Total Fat: 2.6
- Sodium: 36
- Total Carbohydrate: 17.4
- Cholesterol: 12
- Protein: 1.3

425. My Favorite Sugar Cookies

Serving: 12 | Prep: 30mins | Cook: 8mins | Ready in:

Ingredients

- 1 1/2 cups white sugar
- 2/3 cup shortening
- 2 eggs
- 2 tablespoons milk
- 1 teaspoon vanilla extract
- 3 1/4 cups all-purpose flour
- 2 1/2 teaspoons baking powder
- 1/2 teaspoon salt
- 1 egg white (optional)

Direction

- In a mixing bowl, mix shortening and sugar. Then beat at low speed until the mixture is smooth. Stir in vanilla, milk, and eggs.
- Whisk salt, baking soda and flour in a separate bowl. Add to the sugar mixture and then blend until mixed.
- Form the dough into a ball and then encase in plastic wrap or waxed paper. Chill for about 2 to 3 hours until easy to work on.
- Preheat an oven to 200 degrees C (400 degrees F). Line cookie sheets with parchment paper or coat lightly with grease.
- Onto a lightly floured surface, roll out 1/2 of dough at a time. Keep rest of the dough chilled. Roll paper-thin for crisp cookies. Roll 1/8 to 1/4 inch thick for softer cookies.

- Chop the dough into various shapes using floured cookie cutters. Then re-roll the dough trimmings to form a ball. Cover, chill and continue cutting the shapes with the chilled dough.
- Transfer the cookies into greased cookie sheets, placing 1/2 inch apart. To glaze, rub the tops of the cookies with an egg white beaten slightly with one tablespoon water or with heavy or whipping cream.
- Drizzle the cookies with toppings you like and then bake for about 8 minutes or until turns very light brown. Take out the cookies and let to cool completely.

Nutrition Information

- Calories: 337 calories;
- Total Fat: 12.6
- Sodium: 217
- Total Carbohydrate: 51.3
- Cholesterol: 31
- Protein: 4.9

426. My Grandma's Fruitcake Cookies

Serving: 144 | Prep: 20mins | Cook: 25mins | Ready in:

Ingredients

- 3 cups all-purpose flour
- 1 teaspoon ground cinnamon
- 1/2 teaspoon baking soda
- 1 cup butter, at room temperature
- 1 cup brown sugar, packed
- 3 eggs
- 1/2 cup milk
- 2 tablespoons vanilla-flavored cream sherry
- 7 cups chopped mixed nuts
- 2 cups chopped raisins
- 2 cups pitted chopped dates
- 1 pound candied pineapple, coarsely chopped
- 1 pound red and green candied cherries, chopped

Direction

- Pre heat the oven to 150 degrees C (300 degrees F). Grease a few baking sheets. Sift baking soda, cinnamon and flour together in a bowl; put aside.
- Whip brown sugar and butter together in a big mixing bowl for roughly 5 minutes till becoming fluffy. Whip in eggs, one at a time. Slowly whip flour mixture into the butter mixture, alternating each of the additions with roughly 2 tbsp. of the milk till all milk becomes incorporated and dough softens. Whip in sherry, and stir in cherries, pineapple, dates, raisins and nuts till mixed through. Drop dough by the rounded teaspoons onto prepped baking sheets.
- Bake in preheated oven for 20-30 minutes till bottoms become very slightly brown and cookies become set. Let it cool down on the wire racks.

Nutrition Information

- Calories: 100 calories;
- Total Fat: 5.3
- Sodium: 21
- Total Carbohydrate: 12.4
- Cholesterol: 7
- Protein: 1.7

427. Nanaimo Bars I

Serving: 12 | Prep: | Cook: | Ready in:

Ingredients

- 1/2 cup butter
- 1/4 cup white sugar
- 5 tablespoons unsweetened cocoa powder
- 1 egg
- 1 teaspoon vanilla extract

- 2 cups graham cracker crumbs
- 1 cup shredded coconut
- 1/2 cup chopped walnuts
- 1/4 cup butter
- 2 cups confectioners' sugar
- 2 tablespoons vanilla custard powder
- 3 tablespoons milk
- 4 (1 ounce) squares semisweet chocolate, chopped
- 1 tablespoon butter

Direction

- In a double boiler or a heavy saucepan, combine vanilla, egg, cocoa, white sugar and 1/2 cup of margarine or butter together. Stir over low heat till the mixture attains the consistency of a custard.
- Mix walnuts, coconut and graham crackers together; add into the melted mixture. Stir well; pack into 9-in. square cake pan greased with butter.
- Cream milk, vanilla custard powder, confectioners' sugar and 1/4 cup of butter together. Beat till creamy; spread over the melted base.
- Place in the refrigerator till hardened.
- Melt 1 tablespoon of butter and semi-sweet chocolate together; drizzle over the custard icing. Place in the refrigerator. Once totally hard, cut into square bars.

Nutrition Information

- Calories: 389 calories;
- Total Carbohydrate: 46.8
- Cholesterol: 49
- Protein: 3.8
- Total Fat: 22.6
- Sodium: 199

428. Nanaimo Bars II

Serving: 16 | Prep: 30mins | Cook: 10mins | Ready in:

Ingredients

- 1/2 cup butter
- 2 (1 ounce) squares semisweet chocolate
- 1/3 cup white sugar
- 1 1/2 tablespoons pasteurized egg
- 1 cup rolled oats
- 1 1/2 cups flaked coconut
- 1/2 cup chopped walnuts
- 1 teaspoon vanilla extract
- 2 cups confectioners' sugar
- 3 tablespoons butter, softened
- 1/2 teaspoon vanilla extract
- 2 1/2 tablespoons milk
- 1 tablespoon butter
- 2 (1 ounce) squares semisweet chocolate

Direction

- Melt half cup of margarine or butter with two squares chocolate in a saucepan. Remove from heat. Stir in one teaspoon of the vanilla extract, chopped nuts, coconut, rolled oats, egg and white sugar. Press the mixture into a 9-inch square pan that greased. Chill 60 mins.
- Mix milk, half teaspoon vanilla and 3 tablespoons of the softened butter with confectioners' sugar. Mix until it has the consistency like icing, spread over oat mixture in pan. Chill for 30 mins.
- Melt remaining of 2 squares chocolate with the remaining one tablespoon of margarine or butter. Spread over the bar tops. Let chill for 4-5 hours.
- Using a hot knife, cut into squares, then dip the knife in the hot water, let it melt through chocolate.

Nutrition Information

- Calories: 266 calories;
- Sodium: 85
- Total Carbohydrate: 30.8
- Cholesterol: 28
- Protein: 2.3
- Total Fat: 15.8

429. No Bake Date Balls

Serving: 12 | Prep: | Cook: |Ready in:

Ingredients

- 2 tablespoons butter
- 1 1/2 cups dates, pitted and chopped
- 1 cup confectioners' sugar
- 2 eggs, beaten
- 1/4 teaspoon salt
- 2 1/2 cups crisp rice cereal
- 1/2 cup chopped walnuts
- 1 teaspoon vanilla extract
- 2 cups flaked coconut

Direction

- Heat together salt, eggs, confectioners' sugar, chopped dates and butter in a double boiler. Stir continuously for 20 minutes, until very thick. Take away from the heat and allow to cool.
- Put in vanilla, chopped walnuts and crispy rice cereal, then blend well and shape into small balls. Roll in coconut and keep chilled.

Nutrition Information

- Calories: 230 calories;
- Cholesterol: 36
- Protein: 3
- Total Fat: 9.5
- Sodium: 154
- Total Carbohydrate: 36

430. Nonna's Pizzelle

Serving: 60 | Prep: 20mins | Cook: 1mins |Ready in:

Ingredients

- 3 1/2 cups all-purpose flour
- 2 teaspoons baking powder
- 6 eggs
- 1 1/2 cups white sugar
- 3/4 cup shortening (such as Crisco®), melted and cooled slightly
- 2 tablespoons shortening (such as Crisco®), melted and cooled slightly
- 1 tablespoon anise seeds, crushed
- 1 teaspoon vanilla extract (optional)

Direction

- Follow manufacturer's directions to preheat the pizzelle iron.
- In a bowl, combine baking powder and flour.
- Use a stand mixer fitted with a paddle attachment to beat sugar and eggs together in a bowl; beat over medium speed until combined thoroughly. Put in three-fourths cup plus 2 tablespoons of shortening, then beat until incorporated. Blend in flour mixture, then process over medium speed to combine. Using a spatula, fold in vanilla extract and anise seeds.
- Drop a teaspoon of batter onto the prepared iron. Bake for 30-40 seconds until golden (you can bake for several seconds more to make darker pizzelle).

Nutrition Information

- Calories: 80 calories;
- Protein: 1.4
- Total Fat: 3.6
- Sodium: 23
- Total Carbohydrate: 10.7
- Cholesterol: 19

431. Norway's Best Pepper Cookies

Serving: 30 | Prep: | Cook: |Ready in:

Ingredients

- 1 1/8 cups butter
- 1 cup white sugar
- 1/4 cup heavy whipping cream
- 1 teaspoon baking soda
- 3 1/4 cups all-purpose flour
- 1 teaspoon ground cinnamon
- 1 teaspoon ground black pepper
- 1 1/2 teaspoons ground cardamom
- 1 teaspoon baking powder

Direction

- Cream the sugar and the butter together until fluffy and light. Mix in cream. Pour in baking soda and some water (not more than two tablespoons) into butter mixture.
- Sift the flour, baking powder and spices into butter mixture. Then blend until you have a nice dough. Roll the dough into sausages of approximately 2-1/2 inches in diameter. Encase tightly and allow dough to chill well.
- Preheat an oven to 190 degrees C (375 degrees F). Take out the chilled dough and slice into thin pieces. Bake for 6 to 8 minutes on a lightly greased cookie sheet. Cool the cookies on wire rack.

Nutrition Information

- Calories: 144 calories;
- Sodium: 108
- Total Carbohydrate: 17.3
- Cholesterol: 21
- Protein: 1.5
- Total Fat: 7.8

432. Norwegian Butter Cookies

Serving: 12 | Prep: | Cook: | Ready in:

Ingredients

- 1/2 cup butter
- 2 eggs
- 1/4 cup white sugar
- 1 cup all-purpose flour
- 1/2 teaspoon vanilla extract

Direction

- Set the oven to 190°C or 375°F to preheat.
- Hard boil the eggs and split the yolks. Cream hard-boiled egg yolks and butter together, then beat in sugar and put in flour and vanilla extract, mixing well together. Push through a cookie press or arrange the mixture on grease-free cookie sheets by teaspoonfuls.
- Bake until browned slightly, about 10-12 minutes.

Nutrition Information

- Calories: 134 calories;
- Sodium: 66
- Total Carbohydrate: 12.2
- Cholesterol: 51
- Protein: 2.2
- Total Fat: 8.6

433. Norwegian Krumkake

Serving: 50 | Prep: 5mins | Cook: 30mins | Ready in:

Ingredients

- 1/2 cup unsalted butter
- 1 cup white sugar
- 2 eggs
- 1 cup milk
- 1 1/2 cups all-purpose flour
- 1/2 teaspoon vanilla extract
- 1/2 teaspoon butter flavoring, optional

Direction

- On stove over medium heat, heat krumkake iron. You may also use an electric krumkake or pizzelle iron.

- Whisk sugar and butter in a bowl. Include in eggs, one each time, and blend well with a spoon. Put in butter flavoring, vanilla, flour, and milk; blend well.
- Put a teaspoon of the batter on the heated iron, and press together. Cook about 30 seconds each side until brown, depending on the heat. Take out from the iron and quickly roll up around a stick or a cone before they become hard.

Nutrition Information

- Calories: 51 calories;
- Protein: 0.8
- Total Fat: 2.2
- Sodium: 5
- Total Carbohydrate: 7.1
- Cholesterol: 13

434. Nutella® Hazelnut Cookies

Serving: 12 | Prep: 30mins | Cook: 12mins | Ready in:

Ingredients

- 2 1/2 cups all-purpose flour
- 1/4 cup unsweetened cocoa powder
- 1 teaspoon baking soda
- 1 teaspoon salt
- 1 cup butter, room temperature
- 3/4 cup brown sugar
- 3/4 cup white sugar
- 2 large eggs
- 2 tablespoons vanilla extract
- 1/2 cup chocolate-hazelnut spread, such as Nutella®
- 1/2 cup chopped toasted hazelnuts
- 1 cup chocolate chips

Direction

- Prepare the oven by preheating to 350°F (175°C). Line a baking sheet with parchment paper or grease.
- In a bowl, mix the salt, baking soda, cocoa powder, and flour. Blend with a whisk to break up any lumps.
- In a large bowl, whisk white and brown sugar, and butter using an electric mixer until smooth. Mix in eggs, one at a time, until fully blended. Stir in chocolate-hazelnut spread and vanilla.
- Gradually add and stir in flour mixture until just blended. Add in chocolate chips and chopped hazelnuts then fold. Drop the dough by a cookie scoop or tablespoons onto prepared baking sheet.
- Place in the preheated oven and bake for about 12 minutes until edges appear dry and cookies are scented. Let it cool on baking sheet for 1 minute prior taking to a wire rack.

Nutrition Information

- Calories: 502 calories;
- Cholesterol: 68
- Protein: 6.1
- Total Fat: 26.7
- Sodium: 434
- Total Carbohydrate: 63.1

435. Nutella® Holiday Cookies

Serving: 28 | Prep: 15mins | Cook: 10mins | Ready in:

Ingredients

- 1 cup lightly packed brown sugar
- 1 cup chocolate-hazelnut spread (such as Nutella®)
- 1/2 cup dark chocolate chips (optional)
- 1 egg
- 1 teaspoon baking soda

Direction

- Set the oven to 175°C or 350°F to preheat. Use parchment paper to line 2 baking sheets.
- In a big bowl, combine together baking soda, egg, chocolate chips, chocolate-hazelnut spread and brown sugar. Drop the mixture onto prepped baking sheets by rounded teaspoons, spaced a minimum of 1 1/2 inches.
- In the preheated oven, bake for about 8-10 minutes, until cookies are cracked and puffed. Allow cookies to cool for 5 minutes on baking sheet until firm. Remove to a wire rack to cool thoroughly.

Nutrition Information

- Calories: 92 calories;
- Protein: 0.8
- Total Fat: 3.5
- Sodium: 58
- Total Carbohydrate: 15.2
- Cholesterol: 7

436. Oatmeal Chocolate Coconut Macaroons

Serving: 15 | Prep: 15mins | Cook: 5mins | Ready in:

Ingredients

- 2 cups quick-cooking oats
- 1 cup shredded coconut
- 1/4 cup unsweetened cocoa powder
- 2 cups white sugar
- 1/2 cup butter
- 1/2 cup milk

Direction

- In a bowl, combine together cocoa powder, coconut and oats.
- In a saucepan, bring milk, butter and sugar to a boil while stirring sometimes. Take away from the heat instantly and stir into the oat mixture.
- Drop onto a sheet of waxed paper with 15 spoonfuls of batter, then allow to cool to room temperature prior to serving.

Nutrition Information

- Calories: 228 calories;
- Protein: 2.2
- Total Fat: 8.6
- Sodium: 62
- Total Carbohydrate: 37.7
- Cholesterol: 17

437. Oatmeal Thumbprints

Serving: 30 | Prep: | Cook: | Ready in:

Ingredients

- 1/2 cup butter, softened
- 1/2 cup shortening
- 1 cup packed brown sugar
- 3/4 cup white sugar
- 2 eggs
- 2 1/2 cups all-purpose flour
- 1 teaspoon baking soda
- 1 teaspoon salt
- 1/2 teaspoon ground cinnamon
- 1/2 cup water
- 2 1/2 cups quick cooking oats
- 1/2 cup finely chopped walnuts
- 1 teaspoon almond extract
- 1/4 cup raspberry jam

Direction

- Set oven to 205°C (400°F) and start preheating.
- Cream sugars, shortening and butter together. Beat eggs into the mixture. Sift cinnamon, nuts, salt, baking soda and flour together in another bowl. Add into butter mixture

alternately with water. Mix in almond extract and oats.
- Drop teaspoons of batter onto ungreased cookie sheets. Create a small deep notch in each cookie. Fill it with preserves.
- Bake for 10 to 12 minutes.

Nutrition Information

- Calories: 193 calories;
- Total Fat: 8.7
- Sodium: 149
- Total Carbohydrate: 26.9
- Cholesterol: 21
- Protein: 2.7

438. Old Fashioned Butter Cookies With Butter Frosting

Serving: 72 | Prep: 30mins | Cook: 5mins | Ready in:

Ingredients

- 1 cup butter, softened
- 3/4 cup white sugar
- 1 egg
- 2 tablespoons whole milk
- 1 1/2 teaspoons vanilla extract
- 3 cups all-purpose flour
- 1 teaspoon baking powder
- 1/2 teaspoon salt
- Frosting:
- 1 cup butter, softened
- 3 cups confectioners' sugar
- 1 1/2 tablespoons vanilla extract
- 9 tablespoons evaporated milk, or more as needed
- 6 cups confectioners' sugar, or more as needed

Direction

- In a large bowl, beat white sugar with one cup of the softened butter until creamy. Beat one and a half teaspoons of vanilla extract, whole milk and egg into the butter mixture until they become smooth. In a separate bowl, whisk salt, baking powder and flour. Stir dry ingredients gradually into the moist ingredients to create the smooth dough. Let chill the dough for 2-3 hours in refrigerator.
- Start preheating the oven to 400°F (200°C). Generously dust flour over a kitchen towel or pastry cloth.
- On prepared pastry cloth, split the dough into 3 portions and roll each third out to 1/8-in. thick. Using cookie cutters, cut shapes out of rolled dough. Put the cookies onto unoiled baking sheets.
- Bake cookies in prepared oven for 5-8 mins or until barely browned. Allow the cookies to cool on baking sheets for 5 mins. Then cool completely on a wire rack.
- In a bowl, beat evaporated milk, 1 1/2 tablespoons of the vanilla extract, 3 cups of the confectioners' sugar and one cup of the softened butter, until they become smooth. Stir 6 cups of confectioners' sugar gradually into the mixture until combined. Beat the frosting hard until it is fluffy. If needed to reach preferred consistency, stir in more confectioners' sugar or evaporated milk. Frost the cooled cookies.

Nutrition Information

- Calories: 136 calories;
- Cholesterol: 17
- Protein: 0.8
- Total Fat: 5.4
- Sodium: 63
- Total Carbohydrate: 21.3

439. Old Fashioned Sugar Cookies In A Jar

Serving: 24 | Prep: 15mins | Cook: | Ready in:

Ingredients

- 3 cups all-purpose flour
- 1 teaspoon baking powder
- 1 teaspoon baking soda
- 1/8 teaspoon salt
- 1 1/2 cups white sugar
- 1 cup butter, softened
- 2 eggs
- 1 teaspoon vanilla extract
- 1/2 teaspoon lemon extract

Direction

- Combine salt, baking soda, baking powder and flour in a medium bowl. Set aside. Add sugar in a layer onto the bottom of a 1 quart large mouth jar and add flour mixture on top. Attach the tag with the following instructions:
- In a large bowl, pour in the contents of the jar. Add 1 cup of softened butter; cut until crumbly. Whisk 1/2 teaspoon of lemon extract, 1 teaspoon of vanilla and 2 eggs in a separate bowl until it reaches fluffy and light texture. Combine with the dry ingredients; stir to blend properly. Cover and let it chill for 1 hour.
- Turn on the oven to 350°F (175°C) to preheat. Roll the dough on a lightly floured surface so that it becomes 1/4 inch thick. Use cookie cutters to cut into preferred shapes. Arrange cookies on cookie sheets, 1 1/2 inches apart from each other.
- Put into the oven to bake until the edges starts to turn brown, 10-12 minutes. Use sugar for decorations before baking of frost after baking.

Nutrition Information

- Calories: 180 calories;
- Total Fat: 8.2
- Sodium: 140
- Total Carbohydrate: 24.5
- Cholesterol: 36
- Protein: 2.2

440. Old German Polish Recipe For Lebkuchen (Christmas Cookies)

Serving: 20 | Prep: 20mins | Cook: 15mins | Ready in:

Ingredients

- 1/2 cup butter
- 1 1/2 cups white sugar
- 1 cup honey
- 6 cups all-purpose flour
- 1 1/2 teaspoons ground cinnamon
- 1 teaspoon ground cloves
- 1 1/2 teaspoons baking soda
- 1/2 cup water
- 2 eggs, beaten

Direction

- In a big pan, melt the butter on medium heat, then mix in the honey and sugar and boil it. Let it cool for about 10 minutes.
- In a bowl, mix together the cloves, cinnamon and flour.
- In a bowl, mix together the water and baking soda, then stir it into the butter mixture. Stir in eggs then add the flour-spice mixture. Mix it well until the dough is incorporated. Use plastic wrap to cover, then let it chill in the fridge for 24-48 hours.
- Set an oven to preheat at 165°C (325°F).
- Roll out the dough and cut it into cookies; arrange it on a baking tray.
- Bake in the preheated oven for 10-12 minutes until it becomes golden in the edges. Let it cool on the baking tray for a minute and move it onto a wire rack to fully cool.

Nutrition Information

- Calories: 295 calories;
- Total Fat: 5.5
- Sodium: 136
- Total Carbohydrate: 57.8

- Cholesterol: 31
- Protein: 4.6

441. Oma Kiener's Hazelnut Christmas Cookies

Serving: 48 | Prep: 15mins | Cook: 12mins | Ready in:

Ingredients

- 1/2 cup butter, softened
- 1/2 cup white sugar
- 1 egg
- 1/2 teaspoon salt
- 1 1/2 cups all-purpose flour, sifted
- 1/4 teaspoon baking soda
- 1/2 cup ground hazelnuts
- 1 egg, beaten
- 1/4 cup multicolored candy sprinkles (jimmies), or amount needed (optional)

Direction

- In a mixing bowl, whisk salt, egg, sugar and butter until fluffy and light. Mix in the baking soda and flour, and whisk until combined. Stir in the hazelnuts.
- Onto a surface that is lightly floured, roll the dough out and form into 2 1/2 inch log. Use wax paper to wrap easily, then keep in the refrigerator for overnight.
- Prepare the oven by preheating to 375°F (190°C). Prepare baking sheets that are lightly greased. Remove the wrap and slice the log into 1/8 inch thick cuts. Set 2-inches apart on prepared baking sheets. Use beaten egg to brush the tops and, if wished, garnish with sprinkles.
- Place in the preheated oven and bake for 12-15 minutes until edges are lightly browned. Let cool on racks, and keep in an airtight tin.

Nutrition Information

- Calories: 52 calories;
- Total Fat: 2.8
- Sodium: 48
- Total Carbohydrate: 6
- Cholesterol: 13
- Protein: 0.8

442. One Oh One Cookies

Serving: 48 | Prep: | Cook: | Ready in:

Ingredients

- 1 cup white sugar
- 1 cup packed brown sugar
- 1 cup butter
- 1 cup vegetable oil
- 1 egg
- 1 teaspoon cream of tartar
- 3 teaspoons vanilla extract
- 1 cup flaked coconut
- 1 cup chopped walnuts
- 1 cup crisp rice cereal
- 1 cup rolled oats
- 3 1/2 cups all-purpose flour
- 1 teaspoon salt
- 1 teaspoon baking soda

Direction

- Start preheating oven to 350°F. Combine all ingredients in a large bowl until incorporated.
- Dollop batter onto greased cookie sheets and bake for 12-15 minutes.

Nutrition Information

- Calories: 175 calories;
- Cholesterol: 14
- Protein: 1.8
- Total Fat: 10.8
- Sodium: 114
- Total Carbohydrate: 18.5

443. Orange Cardamom Krumkake

Serving: 30 | Prep: 15mins | Cook: 45mins | Ready in:

Ingredients

- 1 1/2 cups all-purpose flour
- 2 teaspoons ground cardamom
- 1/2 teaspoon ground ginger
- 1/4 teaspoon ground cinnamon
- 1/4 teaspoon ground nutmeg
- 1 cup white sugar
- 1/8 teaspoon salt
- 2 teaspoons grated orange zest
- 1/3 cup butter, softened
- 2/3 cup half-and-half
- 2 eggs

Direction

- Use vegetable spray or oil to grease the krumkake iron. Over medium-low heat, heat iron. The iron should only be greased once. Follow the directions of manufacturer to preheat if using electric krumkake iron.
- In a large bowl, combine nutmeg, cinnamon, ginger, cardamom and flour; sift. Add orange zest, salt and sugar into the flour mixture; stir to blend well.
- In a microwave bowl, combine half-and-half and butter. Put into the microwave to cook with cover for about 25 seconds to warm. Let it cool slightly. Add eggs into the mixture, one at a time; whisk well. Add the cream mixture into the flour mixture; stir to blend well.
- Add 1 tablespoon of batter into each krumkake mold on the krumkake iron; scrape off the batter with a second spoon. Close the krumkake iron; cook for 30-60 seconds until the cookies are golden brown and the iron doesn't steam anymore. Take the krumkake cookie off the iron gently. Wrap the cookie round a wooden krumkake cone when it is still hot to form the corn shape. Hold in place for 10 seconds to set. Take it off and transfer to waxed paper to cool completely. Continue the process with the rest of the batter.

Nutrition Information

- Calories: 79 calories;
- Sodium: 31
- Total Carbohydrate: 11.9
- Cholesterol: 20
- Protein: 1.3
- Total Fat: 3.1

444. Orange Drop Cookies II

Serving: 18 | Prep: | Cook: | Ready in:

Ingredients

- 2/3 cup shortening
- 3/4 cup white sugar
- 1 egg
- 1/2 cup orange juice
- 1 teaspoon orange zest
- 2 cups all-purpose flour
- 1/2 teaspoon baking powder
- 1/2 teaspoon baking soda
- 1/2 teaspoon salt
- 2 cups confectioners' sugar
- 2 tablespoons butter
- 2 tablespoons orange juice
- 1 teaspoon orange zest

Direction

- Preheat an oven to 175 degrees C (350 degrees F). Coat the cookie sheets with grease.
- Combine together salt, baking soda, baking powder, and flour. Mix one teaspoon of rind and half cup of orange juice into flour mixture.
- Cream white sugar and shortening together. Stir egg into sugar mixture well. Gradually blend the flour mixture into egg and sugar mixture. Drop by teaspoonful onto the greased cookie sheet.

- Bake for about 8 to 10 minutes.
- Prepare the icing: Stir 2 tablespoons butter and confectioner's sugar together until smooth. Transfer 1 teaspoon orange rind and 2 tablespoons of orange juice into sugar and butter mixture; stir thoroughly. Once the cookies cool, generously smear the icing on tops of the cookies.

Nutrition Information

- Calories: 221 calories;
- Total Fat: 9.3
- Sodium: 127
- Total Carbohydrate: 33.2
- Cholesterol: 14
- Protein: 1.9

445. Orange Pizzelle

Serving: 24 | Prep: 20mins | Cook: 1mins | Ready in:

Ingredients

- 1 3/4 cups all-purpose flour
- 1 teaspoon baking powder
- 3 eggs, at room temperature
- 3/4 cup white sugar
- 1/2 cup butter, melted
- 1 tablespoon orange extract
- 2 teaspoons triple sec (orange-flavored liqueur)
- 8 drops yellow food coloring
- 4 drops red food coloring
- 2 teaspoons finely grated orange zest

Direction

- Sift baking powder with flour in a small bowl.
- Mix eggs in a large bowl using an electric mixer on medium speed, putting in sugar slowly until the mixture is thickened. Whisk in melted butter slowly until well-combined. Mix in red food coloring, yellow food coloring, triple sec, and orange extract. Carefully blend in baking powder and sifted flour until batter seems smooth and stiff. Fold in grated orange zest.
- Grease and preheat the pizzelle baker based on the manufacturer's instructions.
- With a small ice cream scoop or tablespoon cookie scoop, drop the batter onto the heated pizzelle baker. Bake for 30 to 40 seconds until browned. Remove to a cooling rack to cool fully.

Nutrition Information

- Calories: 103 calories;
- Total Fat: 4.5
- Sodium: 57
- Total Carbohydrate: 13.5
- Cholesterol: 33
- Protein: 1.8

446. Orange Spiced Krumkake

Serving: 30 | Prep: | Cook: | Ready in:

Ingredients

- 1 cup white sugar
- 1/2 cup butter, softened
- 2 eggs
- 1 teaspoon orange zest
- 1/4 teaspoon ground cloves
- 1/4 teaspoon ground cardamom
- 1 1/2 cups all-purpose flour
- 1 cup milk

Direction

- Cream the butter, eggs, orange peel, and sugar together in a medium bowl. Sift cardamom, cloves, and flour together. Alternately mix the flour mixture and milk to the creamed mixture until smooth.

- Use vegetable spray or oil to lightly grease the krumkake iron; place on medium-low heat. Just grease the iron once.
- Scoop a tablespoon of batter at a time in the middle of the krumkake iron; close and press firmly. Cook for 15-20sec, flip the iron halfway through. Take the krumkake out and form into a cone. Cook and form the remaining batter.

Nutrition Information

- Calories: 85 calories;
- Cholesterol: 21
- Protein: 1.4
- Total Fat: 3.6
- Sodium: 30
- Total Carbohydrate: 11.9

447. Original Cheese Tempters

Serving: 30 | Prep: | Cook: | Ready in:

Ingredients

- 1/2 cup butter, softened
- 1/2 pound shredded sharp Cheddar cheese
- 1/4 teaspoon salt
- 1 pinch ground cayenne pepper
- 1 1/8 cups all-purpose flour
- 2 cups pecan halves

Direction

- Blend cayenne pepper, salt, cheese and butter till combined well; mix in flour well. Form dough to 3 1 1/2-in. diameter rolls; wrap rolls in plastic wrap. Refrigerate till firm.
- Preheat an oven to 190°C/375°F.
- Cut rolls to 1/8-1/4-in. thick slices; put onto parchment paper-lined baking sheet. Press pecan piece/half onto top of every cookie.
- Bake at 190°C/375°F till set for 12 minutes; cool on wire racks. Keep in airtight container.

Nutrition Information

- Calories: 124 calories;
- Cholesterol: 16
- Protein: 3.1
- Total Fat: 10.8
- Sodium: 88
- Total Carbohydrate: 4.7

448. Original Nestle® Toll House Chocolate Chip Cookies

Serving: 60 | Prep: 15mins | Cook: 9mins | Ready in:

Ingredients

- 2 1/4 cups all-purpose flour
- 1 teaspoon baking soda
- 1 teaspoon salt
- 1 cup butter, softened
- 3/4 cup granulated sugar
- 3/4 cup packed brown sugar
- 1 teaspoon vanilla extract
- 2 large eggs
- 2 cups NESTLE® TOLL HOUSE® Semi-Sweet Chocolate Morsels
- 1 cup chopped nuts

Direction

- Set oven to preheat at 375°F.
- Combine salt, baking soda and flour in small bowl. Beat vanilla extract, brown sugar, granulated sugar and butter until creamy in a large mixer bowl. Add in the eggs, one by one, and beat well after each time you add. Beat in the flour mixture slowly. Mix in nuts and morsels. Drop rounded tablespoons of the dough onto ungreased baking sheets.
- Bake until golden brown, or 9 to 11 minutes. Allow to cool on the baking sheets for 2 minutes, then transfer to wire racks to cool thoroughly.

Nutrition Information

- Calories: 108 calories;
- Total Fat: 6.2
- Sodium: 85
- Total Carbohydrate: 12.7
- Cholesterol: 14
- Protein: 1.4

---

449. Peanut Butter Balls III

Serving: 24 | Prep: | Cook: |Ready in:

Ingredients

- 2 cups creamy peanut butter
- 1/2 cup butter
- 4 cups confectioners' sugar
- 3 cups crisp rice cereal
- 2 cups semisweet chocolate chips

Direction

- Melt butter and peanut butter in saucepan on low heat. Mix confectioners' sugar and crispy rice cereal well in big bowl. Put butter and melted peanut butter on sugar and cereal; thoroughly blend.
- Shape to 1-in./smaller balls then spread on cookie sheets. Chill in the fridge till firm (overnight is okay).
- In double boiler, melt chocolate and keep melted as you work with balls. A teaspoon works best when dipping balls into chocolate; dip well then put on cookie sheet. While dipping them, put them back on cookie sheet then keep chilled till firm.

Nutrition Information

- Calories: 318 calories;
- Total Fat: 18.9
- Sodium: 154
- Total Carbohydrate: 36
- Cholesterol: 10
- Protein: 6.3

---

450. Peanut Butter Balls IV

Serving: 30 | Prep: | Cook: |Ready in:

Ingredients

- 1/4 cup butter
- 1 1/2 cups peanut butter
- 4 cups confectioners' sugar
- 1 teaspoon vanilla extract
- 1 teaspoon maple flavored extract
- 2 cups semisweet chocolate chips

Direction

- Cream and knead maple flavoring, vanilla, confectioners' sugar, peanut butter and butter well.
- Melt chocolate chips on low heat; roll dough to 1-in. balls then dip into melted chocolate chips.
- Refrigerate for 15 minutes minimum – overnight on wax paper-lined cookie sheet.

Nutrition Information

- Calories: 206 calories;
- Total Fat: 11.4
- Sodium: 72
- Total Carbohydrate: 25.6
- Cholesterol: 4
- Protein: 3.7

---

451. Peanut Butter Bars I

Serving: 12 | Prep: 25mins | Cook: |Ready in:

Ingredients

- 1 cup butter or margarine, melted
- 2 cups graham cracker crumbs
- 2 cups confectioners' sugar
- 1 cup peanut butter
- 1 1/2 cups semisweet chocolate chips
- 4 tablespoons peanut butter

Direction

- Mix 1 cup peanut butter, confectioners' sugar, graham cracker crumbs and margarine/butter till well blended in medium bowl; evenly press in bottom of 9x13-in. ungreased pan.
- Melt chocolate chips and peanut butter, occasionally mixing till smooth, in metal bowl above simmering water/microwave. Spread on prepped crust; refrigerate for no less than 1 hour. Cut to squares.

Nutrition Information

- Calories: 532 calories;
- Total Carbohydrate: 49.2
- Cholesterol: 41
- Protein: 8.8
- Total Fat: 36.6
- Sodium: 320

452. Peanut Butter Christmas Mice

Serving: 60 | Prep: 30mins | Cook: 10mins | Ready in:

Ingredients

- 1/2 cup butter, room temperature
- 1 cup creamy peanut butter
- 1/2 cup packed light brown sugar
- 1/2 cup white sugar
- 1 egg
- 1 teaspoon vanilla extract
- 1/2 teaspoon baking soda
- 1 1/2 cups all-purpose flour
- 1 cup peanut halves
- 1/4 cup green candy sprinkles
- 60 3-inch pieces red shoestring licorice

Direction

- Mix peanut butter and butter in a big bowl; whip till becomes creamy. Put in white sugar and brown sugar and whip till fluffy. Whip in baking soda, vanilla extract and egg till well blended. Whisk in flour with mixer on low setting just till blended. Let chill with a cover till becomes firm for 60 minutes.
- Preheat oven to 175 degrees C or 350 degrees F.
- Form 1 level tbsp. of dough into 1 inch balls. Taper each ball at one end to the shape of teardrop. Flatten on one side. Set flat sides facing downward, 2 inches apart onto the ungreased cookie sheets. Press the sides of the dough in to raise the 'backs' of the mice, as dough will spread a bit while baking.
- Lightly press 2 peanut halves into each 'mouse' for ears, and 2 pieces of green candy for making eyes. Make a hole that is half an in. deep in the tail ends using a toothpick.
- Bake till becomes firm for 8-10 minutes in the preheated oven.
- Remove to a cooling rack and insert licorice pieces as tails.

Nutrition Information

- Calories: 118 calories;
- Total Fat: 5.2
- Sodium: 48
- Total Carbohydrate: 16.3
- Cholesterol: 7
- Protein: 2.4

453. Peanut Butter Temptations II

Serving: 18 | Prep: | Cook: | Ready in:

Ingredients

- 1/2 cup butter
- 1/2 cup white sugar
- 1/2 cup packed brown sugar
- 1/2 cup peanut butter
- 1 egg
- 1/2 teaspoon vanilla extract
- 1 1/4 cups all-purpose flour
- 3/4 teaspoon baking soda
- 1/2 teaspoon salt
- 36 miniature chocolate covered peanut butter cups, unwrapped

Direction

- Start preheating the oven to 375°F (190°C).
- Cream butter, white sugar and brown sugar together in a medium bowl. Mix in peanut butter, followed by egg then vanilla. Sift the salt, baking soda and flour together, then stir into the peanut butter mixture till dough comes together. Form into balls, about 1-inch, then press into cups of the unprepared mini muffin pan.
- Bake in prepared oven for 8-10 mins. Press down one mini chocolate covered the peanut butter cup, as soon as cookies come out of oven, into the middle of each cookie, only until top is showing. Let cookies cool completely. Then remove from pans.

Nutrition Information

- Calories: 248 calories;
- Total Fat: 13.8
- Sodium: 241
- Total Carbohydrate: 28.3
- Cholesterol: 25
- Protein: 4.7

454. Peanut Butter And Jelly Thumbprint Cookies

Serving: 30 | Prep: 30mins | Cook: 20mins | Ready in:

Ingredients

- 1 2/3 cups all-purpose flour
- 1/2 teaspoon baking soda
- 1/4 teaspoon salt
- 1/2 cup unsalted butter
- 2/3 cup creamy peanut butter
- 1/2 cup white sugar
- 1/2 cup brown sugar
- 1/2 teaspoon vanilla extract
- 1 egg
- 3/4 cup seedless raspberry jam

Direction

- In a bowl, sift salt, baking soda, and flour.
- In a separate bowl, beat vanilla, brown sugar, white sugar, peanut butter, and butter using an electric mixer for 1-2 minutes, or until fluffy and light. Use a rubber spatula to scrape sides of the bowl. Put the egg into the butter mixture and keep beating on medium speed until combined. Scrape down the side of the bowl again.
- On low speed, whip the flour mixture into the butter mixture until just blended. Then scrape the bowl and mix for a few more seconds.
- Scoop the dough into 2 tablespoon-sized balls and put on a baking sheet. Then cover the baking sheet and chill for at least 4 hours (overnight is better).
- Set the oven at 350°F (175°C) to preheat. Use parchment paper to line baking sheets and place the cookie balls on top of the paper.
- In the preheated oven, bake the cookies for 11 minutes, or until partially cooked.
- In a bowl, put raspberry jam and stir until it gets a syrup consistency.
- In the center of each cookie, force a cap of soda bottle till the cookies edges bulge and start to crack creating an indentation. Put about 1 teaspoon of jam to fill each indentation.

- Let the cookies bake for 7 minutes more, until the edges are lightly brown. Before moving the cookies to a wire rack, let them cool fully on the baking sheet.

Nutrition Information

- Calories: 132 calories;
- Sodium: 70
- Total Carbohydrate: 17.7
- Cholesterol: 14
- Protein: 2.4
- Total Fat: 6.2

455. Peanut Surprise Cookies

Serving: 42 | Prep: 10mins | Cook: 10mins | Ready in:

Ingredients

- 1/2 cup margarine, softened
- 1/2 cup peanut butter
- 1/2 cup white sugar
- 1/2 cup light brown sugar
- 1 egg
- 1 1/4 cups all-purpose flour
- 1/2 teaspoon baking powder
- 2/3 teaspoon baking soda
- 1/4 teaspoon salt
- 1 (8.75 ounce) bag chocolate covered creamy caramel candies
- 1/4 cup white sugar for decoration

Direction

- Cream brown sugar, half cup of white sugar, peanut butter, and margarine together in a big bowl till becoming smooth. Whip in the egg. Mix salt, baking soda, baking powder, and flour together; mix into the peanut butter mixture. Keep the dough covered and let chill for roughly half an hour till firm.
- Preheat the oven to 190 degrees C (375 degrees F). Roll chilled dough into 1 in. balls. Push a caramel candy into each ball's middle in order to cover the candy entirely with the dough. Roll balls in leftover sugar and put 2 in. apart on the ungreased cookie sheets.
- Bake in the preheated oven till becomes set, about 10 - 12 minutes. Allow to cool down on the baking sheets for 2 minutes prior to transferring to the wire racks to let it cool down totally.

Nutrition Information

- Calories: 99 calories;
- Sodium: 91
- Total Carbohydrate: 13.1
- Cholesterol: 4
- Protein: 1.5
- Total Fat: 4.8

456. Pebber Nodder (Danish Christmas Cookies)

Serving: 100 | Prep: 15mins | Cook: 10mins | Ready in:

Ingredients

- 1 cup butter
- 1 cup sugar
- 2 eggs
- 2 1/2 cups all-purpose flour
- 1 teaspoon ground cardamom
- 1 teaspoon ground cinnamon, or to taste

Direction

- Set the oven to 350°F (175°C), and start preheating.
- In a large bowl, combine sugar and butter together until smooth. Beat in eggs, one at a time, stirring until fluffy and light. Mix cinnamon, cardamom and flour together; stir into sugar mixture just until combined.
- Divide dough into 6 balls. On a lightly floured surface, roll each ball into a rope about as big

around as a finger. Cut into pieces of 1/2-inch, and arrange them on an ungreased baking sheet.
- Bake for 10 minutes in the preheated oven, or till lightly browned. Cool for a few minutes on baking sheets, then cool completely on wire racks.

Nutrition Information

- Calories: 37 calories;
- Total Fat: 2
- Sodium: 15
- Total Carbohydrate: 4.4
- Cholesterol: 9
- Protein: 0.5

457. Pecan Turtles® Bars

Serving: 48 | Prep: 20mins | Cook: 25mins | Ready in:

Ingredients

- 1 1/2 cups all-purpose flour
- 1 1/2 cups brown sugar, divided
- 1/2 cup butter, softened
- 1 cup pecan halves
- 2/3 cup butter
- 1 cup milk chocolate chips

Direction

- Start preheating the oven to 350°F (175°C).
- Mix softened butter, 1 cup of brown sugar, and flour in a large mixer bowl. Beat for 2 to 3 minutes at medium speed until mixture is similar to fine crumbs. Pat mixture evenly onto the bottom of the ungreased 13x9-inch baking pan. Scatter pecans evenly over the crumb mixture.
- Mix the remaining 1/2 cup of brown sugar and 2/3 cup of butter in a small saucepan. Over medium heat, cook and stir mixture until bubbling on the entire surface; cook, stirring constantly, for additional 1/2 to 1 minute. Transfer into the pan, pouring evenly over the crust.
- Bake in prepared oven for 18 to 20 minutes until bubbling on the entire surface. Take out of the oven; immediately drizzle with chocolate pieces. Allow to stand for 2 to 3 minutes to melt the chocolate; with a knife or small spatula, swirl chocolate slightly. Let cool fully in pan on a wire rack. With a sharp knife, slice into 48 bars.

Nutrition Information

- Calories: 114 calories;
- Protein: 0.9
- Total Fat: 7.3
- Sodium: 40
- Total Carbohydrate: 12.1
- Cholesterol: 13

458. Pennsylvania Snow Drops

Serving: 36 | Prep: 20mins | Cook: 25mins | Ready in:

Ingredients

- 1 cup butter
- 1/2 cup confectioners' sugar
- 2 teaspoons water
- 1/2 teaspoon salt
- 1 teaspoon vanilla extract
- 1 teaspoon orange extract (optional)
- 2 cups all-purpose flour
- 1 cup quick-cooking rolled oats
- 1 (16 ounce) package white confectionery candy coating pieces
- 1 cup flaked coconut
- 1 teaspoon colored candy sprinkles (optional)

Direction

- Set the oven to 350°F (175°C) to preheat. Use parchment paper to line cookie sheets.

- In mixing bowl, put confectioners' sugar and butter, then use an electric mixer to whisk until fully blended and creamy. Mix in quick rolled oats, flour, orange extract, vanilla extract, salt, and water to make a dry, crumbly dough. Pinch off approximately 1 1/2 tablespoon of dough for each cookie, roll into an approximately 1-in. ball. Put on the prepared cookie sheets, approximately 2 in. apart.
- Put in the preheated oven and bake for 20 minutes until the cookies turn light brown. Take out of the oven and let cool to warm temperature.
- As the cookies bake, in a microwave-safe bowl, put confectionery candy pieces; put in the microwave oven to cook on low power for approximately 10 seconds each time, whisking when the candy starts to melt, until the coating is warm (or hot), smooth, and liquid.
- Plunge the warm cookies in the white coating and cool on the prepared cookie sheet. While the coating remains liquid, sprinkle flaked coconut over each cookie. If you want, use candy sprinkles to garnish some cookies. While the cookies are still on the cookie sheet, you can also put the coating onto the cookies, then garnish with sprinkles and coconut.

Nutrition Information

- Calories: 164 calories;
- Total Fat: 10
- Sodium: 86
- Total Carbohydrate: 17.2
- Cholesterol: 16
- Protein: 1.9

459. Pepparkakor I

Serving: 60 | Prep: | Cook: | Ready in:

Ingredients

- 2/3 cup packed brown sugar
- 2/3 cup molasses
- 1 teaspoon ground ginger
- 1 teaspoon ground cinnamon
- 1/2 teaspoon ground cloves
- 3/4 tablespoon baking soda
- 2/3 cup butter
- 1 egg
- 3 1/2 cups sifted all-purpose flour

Direction

- In a large heatproof bowl, add butter. Heat molasses, spices and brown sugar in a medium saucepan just to boiling point. Stir in baking soda. Pour this mixture over the butter and mix until it dissolves.
- Whisk in egg; add a cup of flour at a time and grind thoroughly. Knead on a lightly floured board for 1-2 minutes. Refrigerate in a firmly wrapped waxed paper for about an hour, until it becomes firm.
- Heat oven to 170 degrees C (325 degrees F).
- Roll out on a lightly floured board to a thickness of approximately 1/8 inch, and cut into desired shapes.
- Bake on greased baking sheets for 8 - 10 minutes.
- Take out from the sheets and leave to cool on racks, it can be topped with piped icing or anything else.

Nutrition Information

- Calories: 66 calories;
- Total Carbohydrate: 10.8
- Cholesterol: 9
- Protein: 0.9
- Total Fat: 2.2
- Sodium: 62

460. Peppermint Bars

Serving: 12 | Prep: | Cook: | Ready in:

Ingredients

- 1 cup butter
- 1 cup white sugar
- 1 egg
- 1/4 teaspoon peppermint extract
- 5 drops red food coloring
- 2 cups all-purpose flour
- 1/4 teaspoon salt
- 2/3 cup finely crushed peppermint candy canes
- 1 cup semisweet chocolate chips
- 1/3 cup coarsely chopped peppermint candy canes

Direction

- Preheat an oven to 175°C/350°F then grease the 9x13-in. pan.
- Cream sugar and butter/margarine; beat in food coloring, peppermint extract and egg. Add salt and flour till blended well; mix in 2/3 cup of finely crushed candy.
- Evenly spread into greased pan and bake till firm for 25 minutes.
- Sprinkle chocolate chips immediately after removing from the oven; cover with the cookie sheet till melted for 1 minute. Evenly spread chocolate; sprinkle 1/3 cup of coarsely chopped candy. Before cutting, fully cool. You can use plain chocolate bars instead; you should get 10-5/8-ounce bars.

Nutrition Information

- Calories: 428 calories;
- Sodium: 173
- Total Carbohydrate: 61
- Cholesterol: 56
- Protein: 3.4
- Total Fat: 20.2

461. Peppermint Chocolate Chip Cookies

Serving: 36 | Prep: 15mins | Cook: 8mins | Ready in:

Ingredients

- 1 1/2 cups white sugar
- 1 cup butter, softened
- 2 eggs
- 1 egg yolk
- 10 drops green food coloring
- 1 teaspoon peppermint extract
- 3 1/4 cups all-purpose flour
- 2 teaspoons baking powder
- 1 teaspoon baking soda
- 1 teaspoon cream of tartar
- 1/2 teaspoon kosher salt
- 1 (12 ounce) bag dark chocolate chips

Direction

- In a big bowl, use an electric mixer to beat butter and sugar together until they are fluffy and light. Beat in peppermint extract, green food coloring, egg yolk and eggs until the mixture is smooth.
- In another bowl, mix together kosher salt, cream of tartar, baking soda, baking powder and flour, then blend into the egg mixture until the dough has come together. Fold in chocolate chips, then cover dough and chill for an hour, until it is firm enough to scoop.
- Set the oven to 175°C or 350°F to preheat and use parchment paper to line 2 baking sheets.
- Drop dough onto baking sheets by spoonfuls with 2 inches apart.
- In the preheated oven, bake for 8-10 minutes, until edges turn golden. Allow to cool on baking sheet about a minutes prior to transferring to a wire rack to cool totally.

Nutrition Information

- Calories: 169 calories;
- Sodium: 132
- Total Carbohydrate: 23.4

- Cholesterol: 30
- Protein: 2.1
- Total Fat: 8.1

462. Peppermint Lace Cookies

Serving: 36 | Prep: 15mins | Cook: 10mins | Ready in:

Ingredients

- 1 cup butter, softened
- 1 cup confectioners' sugar
- 2 teaspoons peppermint extract
- 1 1/4 cups all-purpose flour
- 1/2 teaspoon salt
- 1 cup rolled oats
- 1/3 cup crushed peppermint candies
- 2 tablespoons confectioners' sugar, or as needed
- 1 tablespoon very finely crushed peppermint candies, or as needed

Direction

- Start preheating oven to 165°C (325°F).
- In a large bowl, beat 1 cup of confectioners' sugar and butter until smoothened and creamy; mix peppermint extract into butter mixture. In a bowl, whisk salt and flour, then stir into butter mixture. Lightly fold one-third cup of crushed peppermint candies and rolled oats into the dough.
- Drop teaspoonful of dough 3-inch apart onto ungreased baking sheets; press down each cookie to 1/4-inch thick using fingertips.
- Bake for 10-12 minutes in the preheated oven until the edges are light brown. Allow cookies to cool for at least 5 minutes on baking sheets, then transfer to wire racks to cool thoroughly.
- In a small bowl, combine 1 tablespoon of very finely crushed peppermint candies with 2 tablespoons of confectioners' sugar; strain in a fine-mesh wire strainer. Dust peppermint candy mixture onto cooled cookies.

Nutrition Information

- Calories: 96 calories;
- Total Fat: 5.3
- Sodium: 70
- Total Carbohydrate: 11.3
- Cholesterol: 14
- Protein: 0.8

463. Peppermint Meringues

Serving: 48 | Prep: 20mins | Cook: 1hours30mins | Ready in:

Ingredients

- 2 egg whites
- 1/8 teaspoon salt
- 1/8 teaspoon cream of tartar
- 1/2 cup white sugar
- 2 peppermint candy canes, crushed

Direction

- Set an oven to 110°C (225°F) and start preheating. Use foil to line 2 cookie sheets.
- Whisk cream of tartar, salt, and egg whites in a large metal or glass mixing bowl until forming soft peaks. Put in sugar gradually and carry on whisking until stiff peaks form on egg whites. Dropping with spoonfuls by an inch apart onto the lined cookie sheets. Scatter on top of the cookies with the crushed peppermint candy.
- In the prepared oven, bake for 1 1/2 hours. Let the inside of meringues dry completely. Don't let them brown. Turn off the oven. Leave the oven open ajar and allow the meringues to sit in the oven until cool completely. Use metal spatula to loosen from foil. Then place in a dry and cool place for a maximum of 2 months while covering loosely.

Nutrition Information

- Calories: 13 calories;
- Cholesterol: 0
- Protein: 0.2
- Total Fat: 0
- Sodium: 9
- Total Carbohydrate: 3.2

464. Peppermint Patties

Serving: 28 | Prep: 45mins | Cook: 10mins | Ready in:

Ingredients

- 3/4 cup sweetened condensed milk
- 1 1/2 teaspoons peppermint extract
- 4 cups confectioners' sugar
- 3 cups semisweet chocolate chips
- 2 teaspoons shortening

Direction

- Mix together the peppermint extract and condensed milk in a big mixing bowl. Beat in enough confectioner's sugar, a little at a time, to create a stiff dough that is not sticky anymore. Shape it into 1-inch balls, then put it on the waxed paper and use your fingers to flatten it to form the patties. Allow the patties to dry for 2 hours at room temperature, flipping once.
- Melt the chocolate with the shortening in a medium saucepan on low heat, mixing frequently. Take it out of the heat. Dunk the patties into the chocolate, one at a time, by placing them on the tines of a fork and lower the fork on the liquid. Allow to cool on the waxed paper until it becomes set.

Nutrition Information

- Calories: 183 calories;
- Cholesterol: 3
- Protein: 1.4
- Total Fat: 6.5

- Sodium: 13
- Total Carbohydrate: 32.9

465. Peppermint Rice Crispies Squares

Serving: 16 | Prep: 10mins | Cook: 1mins | Ready in:

Ingredients

- 24 large marshmallows
- 1/4 cup butter
- 1 teaspoon vanilla extract
- 1/2 cup crushed peppermint candies
- 5 1/2 cups crispy rice cereal (such as Rice Krispies®)
- 1 tablespoon crushed peppermint candies, or to taste

Direction

- Mix the vanilla extract, butter and marshmallows in the big microwave-safe bowl; cook in the microwave for roughly 50 seconds or till melted; whisk.
- Stir half cup of the peppermint candies to the marshmallow mixture; put in the rice cereal and whisk till equally mixed.
- Press the mixture to the 9x13-in. plate. Drizzle 1 tbsp. of the peppermint candies on top.

Nutrition Information

- Calories: 129 calories;
- Sodium: 106
- Total Carbohydrate: 25.4
- Cholesterol: 8
- Protein: 0.9
- Total Fat: 3

466. Peppermint Snowballs

Serving: 60 | Prep: 20mins | Cook: 10mins | Ready in:

Ingredients

- 3 cups confectioners' sugar
- 1 1/4 cups butter, softened
- 1 teaspoon peppermint extract
- 1 teaspoon vanilla extract
- 1 egg
- 3 cups all-purpose flour
- 1 teaspoon baking powder
- 1/2 teaspoon salt
- 1 cup white sugar, or as needed
- 1 cup finely crushed peppermint candy
- 3 tablespoons milk

Direction

- Preheat the oven to 175 degrees C (350 degrees F). Slightly grease the baking sheets or use the parchment paper to line.
- Whip the egg, vanilla extract, peppermint extract, and butter together with 1.5 cups of the confectioners' sugar in the mixing bowl at the Medium speed for 2-3 minutes or till well-blended and creamy. Lower the speed to Low, and slowly stir in the salt, baking powder and flour for 1-2 minutes or till well-blended. Whisk in half cup of the crushed peppermint candy with the wooden spoon.
- Add white sugar into the shallow bowl. Roll a little of the cookie dough between hands to form the three-fourth in. diameter balls. Roll in the sugar. Put 1-inch apart onto the prepped baking sheets.
- Bake in the preheated oven for 10-12 minutes or till turning browned lightly. Take out and let cool down on the racks.
- At the same time, to make glaze, whisk leftover 1.5 cups of the confectioners' sugar together with milk in the bowl till smooth. Sprinkle the cooled cookies with glaze, and drizzle instantly with leftover crushed peppermint candy.

Nutrition Information

- Calories: 111 calories;
- Total Fat: 4
- Sodium: 58
- Total Carbohydrate: 18.1
- Cholesterol: 13
- Protein: 0.8

467. Perfect Coconut Macaroons

Serving: 18 | Prep: 20mins | Cook: 15mins | Ready in:

Ingredients

- 1 (14 ounce) package sweetened, flaked coconut
- 1/3 cup white sugar
- 1 tablespoon all-purpose flour
- 1/2 teaspoon vanilla extract
- 1/2 teaspoon almond extract
- 1 pinch salt
- 3 egg whites, room temperature
- 8 ounces semisweet chocolate chips

Direction

- Preheat an oven to 175°C/350°F.
- Line parchment paper on baking sheet.
- Blend salt, almond extract, vanilla extract, flour, sugar and coconut for 30 seconds till combined in a food processor.
- Beat egg whites till soft peaks form in a bowl.
- Fold coconut mixture into the egg whites just till combined.
- Wet your hands. Between palms, roll spoonfuls coconut mixture to golf ball-sized cookies; put on prepped baking sheet.
- In the preheated oven, bake cookies for 15 minutes till coconut is toasted and slightly golden. Put on wire rack; cool for 30 minutes.
- Line new parchment paper piece on baking sheet.

- Melt chocolate chips on top of double boiler above just-barely simmering water, scraping down sides to avoid scorching with a rubber spatula, frequently mixing.
- In chocolate, dip 1/2 of every cookie; put on prepped baking sheet. Put in fridge for 15 minutes till chocolate is set.

Nutrition Information

- Calories: 178 calories;
- Sodium: 73
- Total Carbohydrate: 23.2
- Cholesterol: 0
- Protein: 1.9
- Total Fat: 9.8

468. Perfect Double Chocolate Peanut Candy Cookies

Serving: 48 | Prep: 30mins | Cook: 10mins | Ready in:

Ingredients

- 1/2 cup butter, softened
- 1/2 cup vegetable shortening
- 3/4 cup white sugar
- 2/3 cup packed brown sugar
- 1 teaspoon vanilla extract
- 2 eggs
- 2/3 cup unsweetened cocoa powder
- 2 1/4 cups all-purpose flour
- 1 teaspoon baking soda
- 1/4 teaspoon salt
- 3/4 cup semi-sweet chocolate chips
- 1 1/4 cups candy-coated peanut butter pieces (such as Reese's Pieces®), divided

Direction

- Set oven to preheat at 175°C (350°F). Use parchment paper to line baking sheets.
- In a large bowl, use an electric mixer to beat together the shortening and butter until thoroughly incorporated. Beat the brown and white sugar into the mixture until creamy, then beat in the eggs and vanilla extract, finally, beat in the cocoa powder. Beat the mixture until it has an even color. In a different bowl, whisk the salt, baking soda, and flour together; mix the flour mixture into the mixture of cocoa until the dough is thoroughly combined. Mix in the 3/4 cup of peanut butter candies and chocolate chips. Save the remaining candy pieces.
- Use plastic wrap to cover the bowl and place it in the refrigerator until the cookie dough is chilled, for no less than 45 minutes. On the prepared baking sheets, drop tablespoons of the dough. In each cookie's top, press in a few more candy pieces gently.
- In the preheated oven, bake for 8 to 9 minutes; allow to cool down on the baking sheets for 1 to 2 minutes, then finish cooling on racks.

Nutrition Information

- Calories: 121 calories;
- Total Fat: 6.4
- Sodium: 65
- Total Carbohydrate: 15.5
- Cholesterol: 13
- Protein: 1.8

469. Perfect Gingerbread Cookies

Serving: 72 | Prep: 30mins | Cook: 30mins | Ready in:

Ingredients

- 6 cups all-purpose flour, or as needed
- 1 1/2 teaspoons baking soda
- 1/2 teaspoon baking powder
- 1 teaspoon salt
- 2 teaspoons ground cinnamon
- 1/2 teaspoon ground allspice
- 1/2 teaspoon ground cloves

- 2 pinches ground nutmeg
- 1 1/2 teaspoons ground ginger
- 1 cup white sugar
- 1 cup brown sugar
- 1 cup molasses
- 2 tablespoons softened butter
- 2 tablespoons canola oil
- 3/4 cup applesauce
- 1/2 cup water
- 1/4 cup liquid egg substitute (such as Egg Beaters®)
- 1 teaspoon vanilla extract
- 1 1/2 teaspoons ground cinnamon
- 1 1/2 teaspoons white sugar

Direction

- Preheat the oven at 350°F or 175°C. Put grease lightly on all of the baking sheets you'll use for baking. In a bowl, combine salt, cloves, ginger, allspice, baking soda, flour, baking powder, 2 tsp. of cinnamon, and nutmeg; set aside.
- In a large bowl, whisk molasses, water, vanilla extract, 1 cup of white sugar, canola oil, egg substitute, applesauce, brown sugar, and butter until well-combined. Add the flour mixture and whisk to form a dough with a thick, soft, but not very sticky texture. Cover the dough and place it inside the refrigerator for 30 minutes. In a small bowl, mix 1 1/2 tsp of white sugar and 1 1/2 tsp. of cinnamon; put it aside.
- Dust the working surface with flour and lay the dough. Roll it out into 1/4-inch thick. Use a cookie cutter to cut the dough into shapes. Place the cutout cookies into the prepared baking sheet and sprinkle them with a cinnamon-sugar mixture.
- Place the baking sheets inside the preheated oven and bake for 9-11 minutes until the bottoms are darker than the tops and all of the edges are golden. Transfer the cookies into the wire rack and cool. After 10 minutes, check if the cookies are already hard, same as the typical gingerbread cookies, but still lightly bendable, and soft on the inside.

Nutrition Information

- Calories: 83 calories;
- Protein: 1.2
- Total Fat: 0.9
- Sodium: 69
- Total Carbohydrate: 17.7
- Cholesterol: < 1

470. Perfect Vegan Sugar Cookies

Serving: 30 | Prep: 15mins | Cook: 10mins | Ready in:

Ingredients

- 2 cups all-purpose flour
- 1 teaspoon baking soda
- 1/4 teaspoon salt
- 3/4 cup white sugar
- 1/2 cup vegan margarine (such as Earth Balance®)
- 1 teaspoon vanilla extract
- 2 tablespoons coconut milk

Direction

- Set an oven to preheat to 175°C (350°F). Line parchment paper on 2 baking trays.
- Sift the salt, baking soda and flour into a bowl.
- In a bowl, cream the vegan margarine and sugar using an electric mixer for about 2 minutes, then add the vanilla extract. Mix in the flour mixture, then add the coconut milk, 1 tbsp. at a time, until the dough comes together. Wrap it using plastic wrap and let it chill for 30 minutes.
- On a floured surface, roll out the dough to 1/4 to 1/2-inch thick. Dip the cookie cutter in the flour, then cut out the cookies and put it on the prepped baking trays.
- Let it bake in the preheated oven for about 10 minutes, until it turns light golden in color.

Nutrition Information

- Calories: 71 calories;
- Total Fat: 2.5
- Sodium: 86
- Total Carbohydrate: 11.4
- Cholesterol: 0
- Protein: 0.9

471. Persimmon Cookies III

Serving: 72 | Prep: 20mins | Cook: 12mins | Ready in:

Ingredients

- 1/2 cup shortening
- 1 cup white sugar
- 1 egg
- 1 cup persimmon pulp
- 1 cup all-purpose flour
- 1/2 teaspoon baking powder
- 1/2 teaspoon baking soda
- 1/2 teaspoon ground cinnamon
- 1/4 teaspoon ground cloves
- 1/2 teaspoon salt
- 1/2 cup raisins
- 1/2 cup chopped walnuts

Direction

- Heat oven to 175 degrees C/350 degrees F. grease the cookie sheets.
- Cream sugar and shortening together in a big bowl. Mix in persimmon pulp and egg. Mix salt, cloves, cinnamon, baking soda, and flour. Mix this mixture in the persimmon mixture. Fold walnuts and raisins in. drop teaspoonfuls on prepared cookie sheets, 2 inches apart.
- Bake in the oven for 12-15 minutes until edges become firm. Cool on cookie sheets for a minute then completely cool on wire racks.

Nutrition Information

- Calories: 42 calories;
- Sodium: 29
- Total Carbohydrate: 5.9
- Cholesterol: 3
- Protein: 0.4
- Total Fat: 2.1

472. Pfeffernuesse Cookie Mix

Serving: 30 | Prep: | Cook: | Ready in:

Ingredients

- 4 cups all-purpose flour
- 1/2 teaspoon ground nutmeg
- 1/2 cup white sugar
- 3/4 cup light molasses
- 1 1/4 teaspoons baking soda
- 1/2 cup butter
- 1 1/2 teaspoons ground cinnamon
- 2 eggs
- 1/2 teaspoon ground cloves
- 1/3 cup confectioners' sugar for decoration

Direction

- Stir dash black pepper, flour, spices, baking soda, sugar together.
- Combine butter and molasses in a large saucepan. Heat while stirring until butter has melted. Let it cool to the room temperature.
- Mix in eggs. Put in dry ingredients to the molasses mixture; then mix well. Put on the cover. Let it chill several hours or overnight.
- Form into 1-inch balls. Arrange on a lightly oiled cookie sheet.
- Bake at 350°F (180°C) until the cookies have done, or for 12-14 mins. Take out then let it cool. Roll into powdered sugar.

Nutrition Information

- Calories: 135 calories;
- Sodium: 82
- Total Carbohydrate: 23.7

- Cholesterol: 21
- Protein: 2.2
- Total Fat: 3.6

- Protein: 0.9
- Total Fat: 2.2

473. Pfeffernusse

Serving: 96 | Prep: | Cook: | Ready in:

Ingredients

- 4 cups all-purpose flour
- 1 teaspoon baking powder
- 1/2 teaspoon baking soda
- 1 teaspoon ground white pepper
- 1 teaspoon ground cinnamon
- 1/2 teaspoon ground cardamom
- 1/2 teaspoon ground ginger
- 3/4 teaspoon salt
- 3/4 cup butter, softened
- 1 1/4 cups packed brown sugar
- 2 eggs
- 3/4 cup finely chopped almonds (optional)

Direction

- Set the oven at 350°F and start preheating.
- Mix together the dry ingredients; set aside.
- Beat sugar and butter together in a separate bowl, till light. Add in eggs, one per time, beating properly after each addition.
- Mix in the dry ingredients, 1/2 cup per time. Add almonds, if you want.
- Form into 1 in. balls; arrange on an ungreased baking sheet, 1 in. apart. Bake for 11-14 minutes. Allow to cool and place into airtight containers for storage to mellow the flavors, for about 3 days.

Nutrition Information

- Calories: 51 calories;
- Sodium: 42
- Total Carbohydrate: 7.1
- Cholesterol: 8

474. Pfeffernusse Cookies

Serving: 18 | Prep: 15mins | Cook: 15mins | Ready in:

Ingredients

- 1/2 cup molasses
- 1/4 cup honey
- 1/4 cup shortening
- 1/4 cup margarine
- 2 eggs
- 4 cups all-purpose flour
- 3/4 cup white sugar
- 1/2 cup brown sugar
- 1 1/2 teaspoons ground cardamom
- 1 teaspoon ground nutmeg
- 1 teaspoon ground cloves
- 1 teaspoon ground ginger
- 2 teaspoons anise extract
- 2 teaspoons ground cinnamon
- 1 1/2 teaspoons baking soda
- 1 teaspoon ground black pepper
- 1/2 teaspoon salt
- 1 cup confectioners' sugar for dusting

Direction

- In a saucepan, blend margarine, shortening, honey, and molasses on medium heat; cook and stir until creamy. Take it off the heat and let cool to room temperature. Stir in eggs.
- In a large bowl, mix salt, pepper, baking soda, cinnamon, anise, ginger, cloves, nutmeg, cardamom, brown sugar, white sugar, and flour. Pour in the molasses mixture and blend until well- combined. Put in the refrigerator for a minimum of 2 hours.
- Start preheating the oven at 325°F (165°C). Shape the dough into acorn-sized balls. Place on baking sheets at least 1-inch apart.
- Bake in the prepared oven for 10 to 15

minutes. Remove to a rack to cool. Sprinkle cooled cookies with confectioners' sugar.

Nutrition Information

- Calories: 284 calories;
- Total Fat: 6.3
- Sodium: 213
- Total Carbohydrate: 53.9
- Cholesterol: 21
- Protein: 3.7

475. Pfeffernusse Cookies II

Serving: 60 | Prep: | Cook: | Ready in:

Ingredients

- 3 cups all-purpose flour
- 1 teaspoon baking powder
- 1/2 teaspoon ground cinnamon
- 1/4 teaspoon ground nutmeg
- 1/4 teaspoon ground cloves
- 1/4 teaspoon salt
- 1 cup white sugar
- 3 eggs
- 1 1/2 tablespoons fresh lemon juice
- 1/2 teaspoon lemon zest
- 1/4 cup chopped hazelnuts
- 1 teaspoon brandy

Direction

- Mix together salt, spices, baking powder and flour.
- Beat eggs and sugar in a big bowl until the mixture becomes light in color and has a thick consistency. Mix in lemon juice. Mix in lemon zest. Mix in dry ingredients, little by little. Mix in hazelnuts. Chill while covered for 4 hours.
- Roll out dough on a surface dusted with flour until 1/2-in. thick. Cut out cookies with a 1 1/2-in. round cookie cutter; arrange 1 inch apart onto baking sheets that are slightly coated with grease. Use clean towels to cover the sheets and let stand for 4 hours.
- Set oven to 175°C (350°F) and start preheating.
- Flip the cookies; into the middle of each cookie, add a brandy drop. Bake until lightly colored, or about 8-10 minutes. Place on wire racks to cool.

Nutrition Information

- Calories: 43 calories;
- Total Fat: 0.7
- Sodium: 21
- Total Carbohydrate: 8.3
- Cholesterol: 9
- Protein: 1

476. Pfeffernusse Kuchen

Serving: 50 | Prep: | Cook: | Ready in:

Ingredients

- 4 eggs
- 2 1/4 cups white sugar
- 3 1/2 cups all-purpose flour
- 2 teaspoons ground cinnamon
- 1 teaspoon ground cloves
- 1 tablespoon ground black pepper

Direction

- Use an electric mixer to beat eggs and sugar for 20 minutes in a big mixing bowl. Sift pepper, cloves, cinnamon and flour together; mix into egg mixture. Roll dough to 1-in. balls; put onto lightly greased cookie sheet. Sit out cookies to dry overnight.
- Preheat an oven to 175°C/350°F. Bake cookies for 10-15 minutes; cool. Keep for 1 week to blend flavors in an airtight container.

Nutrition Information

- Calories: 73 calories;
- Protein: 1.4
- Total Fat: 0.5
- Sodium: 6
- Total Carbohydrate: 15.9
- Cholesterol: 15

477. Pistachio Cream Cheese Fingers

Serving: 100 | Prep: 30mins | Cook: 12mins | Ready in:

Ingredients

- 1 cup butter, softened
- 1 cup white sugar
- 1 (8 ounce) package cream cheese, softened
- 1 egg
- 1 teaspoon vanilla extract
- 2 1/4 cups all-purpose flour
- 1 (3 ounce) package instant pistachio pudding mix
- 1 teaspoon baking powder
- 1/2 teaspoon salt
- 3 (1 ounce) squares semisweet chocolate
- 1 teaspoon shortening

Direction

- Cream together cream cheese, sugar and butter in a big bowl until fluffy and light. Whisk in vanilla and egg. Combine salt, baking powder, dry pudding mix, and flour; mix into the creamed mixture. Cover the dough and chill in the fridge no less than 1 hour to handle easier.
- Set oven to 175° C (350° F) and start preheating. Oil cookie sheets. By teaspoonfuls, form dough into finger shapes, around 1 1/2 inches in length. Arrange cookies in on the prepared cookie sheets.
- Place in the preheated oven and bake until set and very slightly browned on bottoms, about 9-12 minutes. Let cool completely on a wire rack.
- Melt shortening and chocolate in a small saucepan on low heat, mixing continuously until well blended and smooth. Drizzle over each cookie with a small amount of chocolate. Let chocolate set; store.

Nutrition Information

- Calories: 51 calories;
- Sodium: 51
- Total Carbohydrate: 5.6
- Cholesterol: 9
- Protein: 0.6
- Total Fat: 3

478. Polish Christmas Cookies

Serving: 72 | Prep: | Cook: | Ready in:

Ingredients

- 1 cup butter
- 1 cup shortening
- 2 cups white sugar
- 5 eggs
- 7 1/2 cups all-purpose flour
- 6 teaspoons baking powder
- 1/2 teaspoon salt
- 1/2 ounce anise extract

Direction

- Start preheating the oven at 350°F (175°C).
- Beat sugar, shortening, and butter. Blend in eggs and keep beating. Put in the anise flavoring. Blend in salt, baking powder, and 7 cups of flour. Combine until the dough becomes soft. Put in an extra cup of flour if necessary. Let the dough chill.
- Roll out the dough on a lightly floured surface and use cookie cutters to cut. Arrange cookies on greased cookie sheets.
- Bake at 350°F (175°C) about 12 to 15 minutes. Frost and garnish when cookies are cool.

Nutrition Information

- Calories: 122 calories;
- Total Carbohydrate: 15.6
- Cholesterol: 20
- Protein: 1.8
- Total Fat: 5.9
- Sodium: 80

479. Poppy Seed Pinwheels

Serving: 12 | Prep: | Cook: | Ready in:

Ingredients

- 1/2 cup white sugar
- 1/2 cup butter
- 1 3/4 cups all-purpose flour
- 1/2 teaspoon vanilla extract
- 1/4 teaspoon salt
- 1 egg
- 1/2 cup poppy seeds
- 1/2 cup ground walnuts
- 1/4 cup honey
- 1/4 teaspoon ground cinnamon
- 3/4 teaspoon orange zest
- 4 tablespoons butter

Direction

- With a mixer on high speed, beat 1/2 cup butter and sugar in a big bowl until fluffy and light. Add egg, salt, vanilla and flour. Beat at low speed until it's blended, occasionally scraping the bowl.
- Form the dough to a ball. Wrap. Keep in the fridge for 1 hour until it's firm enough to be handled.
- Filling: Mix leftover ingredients and 4 tbsp. butter until it's mixed. Put aside.
- Roll half of the dough on waxed paper to 10x8-in. rectangle. Spread dough with half of poppy seed mixture. Beginning at the narrow side, roll it like a jellyroll fashion. Wrap. Keep in the fridge for an hour until firm. Repeat process with leftover filling and dough.
- Preheat the oven to 190 degrees C/375 degrees F.
- Slice a roll to 1/4-in. thick slices, crosswise. Put on an ungreased cookie sheet, 1/2-in. apart. Bake until lightly browned for 10-12 minutes. Cool on a wire rack. Repeat process with leftover dough.

Nutrition Information

- Calories: 280 calories;
- Sodium: 138
- Total Carbohydrate: 30
- Cholesterol: 46
- Protein: 4.1
- Total Fat: 16.8

480. Quick Mix Spritz

Serving: 30 | Prep: | Cook: | Ready in:

Ingredients

- 2 1/4 cups all-purpose flour
- 3/4 cup white sugar
- 1/2 teaspoon salt
- 1/4 teaspoon baking powder
- 1 cup shortening
- 1 egg
- 1 teaspoon vanilla extract
- 1/2 teaspoon almond extract

Direction

- Turn oven to 375°F (190°C) to preheat.
- Combine baking powder, salt, sugar, and flour. Cut in shortening until mixture becomes crumbly.
- Measure egg and pour in enough water to have 1/4 cup; beat well. Add egg to crumb mixture along with vanilla; stir to combine.

- Put through cookie press onto cookie sheets. Sprinkle top of cookies with colored sugar, if desired. Bake cookies for 10 to 12 minutes at 190 degrees C (375 degrees F) until firm and very light brown.

Nutrition Information

- Calories: 117 calories;
- Cholesterol: 6
- Protein: 1.2
- Total Fat: 7.1
- Sodium: 45
- Total Carbohydrate: 12.2

481. Raisin Coconut Treasure Cookies

Serving: 18 | Prep: | Cook: | Ready in:

Ingredients

- 1 1/2 cups finely ground graham cracker crumbs
- 1/2 cup all-purpose flour
- 2 teaspoons baking powder
- 1 (14 ounce) can sweetened condensed milk
- 1/2 cup butter, softened
- 1 1/2 cups raisins
- 1 1/3 cups flaked coconut
- 1 cup chopped walnuts

Direction

- Set oven to 375°F (190°C) and start preheating.
- Combine baking powder, flour and graham cracker crumbs. Whisk margarine and sweetened condensed milk until smooth. Add crumb mixture. Combine well. Stir in walnuts, coconut and raisins.
- Drop onto lightly greased cookie sheets by tablespoons. Bake until browned lightly or for 9-10 minutes. Cool 2-3 minutes. Take out of cookie sheets. Keep with a cover loosely at room temperature.

Nutrition Information

- Calories: 261 calories;
- Total Fat: 13.6
- Sodium: 178
- Total Carbohydrate: 33.3
- Cholesterol: 21
- Protein: 4.2

482. Raisin Squares

Serving: 16 | Prep: 10mins | Cook: 45mins | Ready in:

Ingredients

- 1/2 cup brown sugar
- 1/2 cup butter
- 1/2 cup all-purpose flour
- 3/4 cup rolled oats
- 2 eggs
- 1 cup brown sugar
- 1/2 cup all-purpose flour
- 1/4 teaspoon salt
- 1/2 teaspoon baking powder
- 1 teaspoon vanilla extract
- 3/4 cup raisins
- 1/2 cup flaked coconut
- 1/2 cup pitted sour cherries, drained with liquid reserved

Direction

- Prepare the oven by preheating to 350°F (175°C).
- Combine oats, 1/2 cup flour, butter, and 1/2 cup brown sugar in a medium bowl until crumbly. Transfer to a 9-inch square pan and press into the bottom. Bake in the preheated oven for 15 minutes.
- Stir vanilla, baking powder, salt, 1/2 cup flour, 1 cup brown sugar, and eggs in the same bowl

until well combined. Mix in the cherries, coconut, and raisins, putting in a little bit of the cherry juice to keep it from turning stiff. Place over the baked crust in the pan and spread.
- Bake in the preheated oven for 30 minutes or until lightly browned and firm. Cool and slice into bars.

Nutrition Information

- Calories: 227 calories;
- Total Carbohydrate: 36.4
- Cholesterol: 39
- Protein: 2.7
- Total Fat: 8.6
- Sodium: 106

483. Raspberry Thumbprint Cookies

Serving: 48 | Prep: 30mins | Cook: 10mins | Ready in:

Ingredients

- 1/2 cup butter at room temperature
- 1/2 cup vegetable shortening (such as Crisco®)
- 1/2 cup brown sugar
- 2 eggs, separated
- 1 teaspoon vanilla extract
- 2 cups all-purpose flour, sifted
- 1/2 teaspoon salt
- 1 1/2 cups finely chopped pecans
- 1 (8 ounce) jar raspberry jam, or as needed

Direction

- Set the oven to 190°C or 375°F to preheat.
- In a bowl, beat together brown sugar, vegetable shortening and butter until creamy and smooth, then beat in vanilla extract and egg yolks. Save egg whites for a later step. Stir 1 cup of flour at a time into the butter mixture, then mix in salt.
- In a separate bowl, beat egg whites and remove pecans to a shallow bowl. Pinch off and roll dough into balls, 1 inch in size, then dip each ball into the beaten egg white and coat by rolling in pecans. Put onto an ungreased baking sheet, then make an indentation on top of each cookie with your thumbs. Scoop a little raspberry jam into the indentation.
- In the preheated oven, bake for 10-12 minutes, until browned very slightly.

Nutrition Information

- Calories: 102 calories;
- Total Fat: 6.7
- Sodium: 41
- Total Carbohydrate: 9.8
- Cholesterol: 12
- Protein: 1.1

484. Raspberry And Almond Shortbread Thumbprints

Serving: 36 | Prep: 30mins | Cook: 18mins | Ready in:

Ingredients

- 1 cup butter, softened
- 2/3 cup white sugar
- 1/2 teaspoon almond extract
- 2 cups all-purpose flour
- 1/2 cup seedless raspberry jam
- 1/2 cup confectioners' sugar
- 3/4 teaspoon almond extract
- 1 teaspoon milk

Direction

- Start preheating the oven to 350°F (175°C).
- Cream white sugar and butter together in a medium bowl until they become smooth. Mix

in half teaspoon of almond extract. Mix in the flour until the dough comes together. Form the dough into 1 1/2 in. balls. Arrange on unoiled cookie sheets. In middle of each ball, create a small hole with your finger and thumb, fill the preserves into the hole.
- Bake in the preheated oven until lightly browned, about 14-18 mins. Allow to cool on a cookie sheet one minute.
- Mix milk, 3/4 teaspoon of the almond extract, and confectioners' sugar together in a medium bowl until they become smooth. Lightly drizzle over the warm cookies.

Nutrition Information

- Calories: 104 calories;
- Total Carbohydrate: 13.7
- Cholesterol: 14
- Protein: 0.8
- Total Fat: 5.2
- Sodium: 37

485. Raw Vegan Gingerbread Balls

Serving: 20 | Prep: 10mins | Cook: | Ready in:

Ingredients

- 3/4 cup gluten-free rolled oats
- 1/2 cup almond flour
- 1 tablespoon ground cinnamon
- 1 teaspoon ground ginger
- 1/2 teaspoon ground nutmeg
- 1/2 teaspoon vanilla extract
- 1 1/4 cups dates, pitted and chopped
- 3 tablespoons coconut sugar

Direction

- Blend almond flour, nutmeg, ginger, vanilla extract, cinnamon, and rolled oats in a blender until smooth. Blend in dates, little by little, until it forms a soft dough. Shape the dough into 1-inch balls and roll the balls in coconut sugar.

Nutrition Information

- Calories: 71 calories;
- Sodium: 1
- Total Carbohydrate: 13.5
- Cholesterol: 0
- Protein: 1.4
- Total Fat: 1.8

486. Red Velvet Chocolate Chip Cookies

Serving: 15 | Prep: 20mins | Cook: 10mins | Ready in:

Ingredients

- 1 1/2 cups all-purpose flour
- 1/3 cup unsweetened cocoa powder
- 1 teaspoon baking soda
- 1/2 teaspoon baking powder
- 1/2 teaspoon salt
- 1/2 cup butter, softened
- 3/4 cup brown sugar
- 1/4 cup white sugar
- 1 egg
- 1 1/2 tablespoons milk
- 1 1/2 teaspoons vanilla extract
- 2 tablespoons red food coloring
- 1 cup dark chocolate chips, or as needed

Direction

- In a bowl, combine salt, baking powder, baking soda, cocoa powder and flour.
- Using an electric mixer, beat butter for 2 minutes until fluffy; beat in white sugar and brown sugar for 1 minute, until the mixture is smooth. Beat vanilla extract, milk, egg into butter mixture; beat in food coloring until evenly tinted.

- Using an electric mixer on low speed, beat flour mixture little by little into butter mixture until blended; mix in a cup of chocolate chips. Use plastic wrap to cover the bowl and refrigerate for an hour or overnight.
- Set oven to 175°C (350°F) and start preheating. Use parchment paper to line baking sheets.
- Form dough into balls of 2 inches; slightly flatten onto lined baking sheets.
- Bake at 175°C (350°F) for 10 minutes until edges turn light brown. Sprinkle with several additional chocolate chips; wait until fully cool.

Nutrition Information

- Calories: 205 calories;
- Sodium: 232
- Total Carbohydrate: 28.9
- Cholesterol: 29
- Protein: 2.8
- Total Fat: 9.9

487. Red's Date Loaf With Coconut (Frying Pan Cookies)

Serving: 12 | Prep: 15mins | Cook: 5mins | Ready in:

Ingredients

- 1 1/2 cups pitted and finely chopped dates
- 1 cup white sugar
- 2 eggs, beaten
- 2 cups crispy rice cereal (such as Rice Krispies®)
- 1 teaspoon vanilla extract
- 1 pinch salt
- 2 cups shredded coconut

Direction

- Mix the eggs, sugar and dates in the skillet; position on the medium heat. Let cook and whisk for roughly 5 minutes or till the mixture becomes thoroughly cooked and thick. Take the skillet out of the heat and whisk the salt, vanilla extract, and rice cereal to the egg mixture. Roll the mixture into a log-shape.
- Drizzle the coconut on one sheet of the waxed paper. Roll the date log into coconut till coated. Use the aluminum foil to cover the date log and keep refrigerated for roughly 60 minutes or till set. Chop the log into a-quarter-in. slices.

Nutrition Information

- Calories: 213 calories;
- Sodium: 96
- Total Carbohydrate: 43.9
- Cholesterol: 31
- Protein: 2.3
- Total Fat: 4.4

488. Robin's Nests

Serving: 36 | Prep: 30mins | Cook: 12mins | Ready in:

Ingredients

- 1 cup butter, softened
- 1/2 cup firmly packed brown sugar
- 2 eggs, separated
- 1 1/2 teaspoons vanilla extract
- 2 1/4 cups all-purpose flour
- 1 1/2 cups walnuts, finely chopped
- 2 tablespoons butter, softened
- 3 tablespoons light corn syrup
- 2 drops blue food coloring
- 1 drop green food coloring
- 1 teaspoon almond extract
- 2 cups confectioners' sugar

Direction

- Set oven to 350°F (175°C) and start preheating.
- Cream brown sugar and butter until fluffy and

light in a large bowl. Whisk in egg yolks; stir in vanilla. Stir in flour; combine well.
- Whisk egg whites until foamy in a shallow dish, pie pan for example. Place walnuts on a plate or waxed paper and spread.
- Roll a teaspoon of dough into a ball; coat with egg whites, then with walnuts. Arrange 2 inches apart on a cookie sheet. Create a depression in each ball, using your thumb.
- Bake for 12 minutes in the prepared oven.
- In the meantime, cream the leftover 2 tablespoons butter with almond extract, green and blue food coloring and corn syrup. Stir in confectioners' sugar gradually. Roll half teaspoon of fondant mixture into egg-shaped balls. Put fondant eggs into hollows of baked cookies.

Nutrition Information

- Calories: 160 calories;
- Total Fat: 9.3
- Sodium: 47
- Total Carbohydrate: 17.9
- Cholesterol: 26
- Protein: 2

489. Romance Bars

Serving: 32 | Prep: 15mins | Cook: 40mins | Ready in:

Ingredients

- 1 cup all-purpose flour
- 1/2 cup butter, melted
- 1 tablespoon white sugar
- 1 cup brown sugar
- 2 tablespoons all-purpose flour
- 1 teaspoon baking powder
- 2 eggs, beaten
- 1 teaspoon vanilla extract
- 2/3 cup chopped walnuts
- 1 cup flaked coconut
- 1/2 cup chopped maraschino cherries
- 3 tablespoons butter, softened
- 1 cup confectioners' sugar
- 1 tablespoon boiling water
- 1 tablespoon milk
- 1/2 teaspoon almond extract
- 1/2 teaspoon vanilla extract

Direction

- Start preheating oven to 300°F (150°C). Mix one tablespoon of the white sugar and one cup of flour together in a medium bowl. Mix in the melted butter. Spread thinly over bottom of 9x13 in. pan.
- Bake in oven preheated for 20 mins or until firm. Stir baking powder, 2 tablespoons of the flour, and brown sugar together in a medium bowl. Mix in one teaspoon of vanilla and eggs until well blended. Stir in maraschino cherries, coconut and walnuts. Transfer mixture over prepared crust.
- Bake in the prepared oven for 20 to 25 mins or until top turns light brown. Before frosting, cool completely. Making frosting, mix confectioners' sugar and 3 tablespoons of the butter together. Beat in vanilla extract, almond extract, milk and water until they become smooth. Spread over the cooled bars. Allow to stand until firm. Cut into squares.

Nutrition Information

- Calories: 131 calories;
- Total Fat: 6.6
- Sodium: 53
- Total Carbohydrate: 17.2
- Cholesterol: 22
- Protein: 1.4

490. Rosenmunnar

Serving: 72 | Prep: 40mins | Cook: 15mins | Ready in:

Ingredients

- 1 cup butter, softened
- 1/2 cup white sugar
- 2 cups sifted all-purpose flour
- 1/2 cup any flavor fruit jam

Direction

- Set oven to 375°F (190°C) to preheat.
- Mix sugar and butter until it becomes fluffy and light. Mix in sifted flour properly. Shape dough into balls of 1 inch size and put on cookie sheets. Thumbprint in the center to make a hole of 1/2-inch.
- Fill the hole with your favorite preserves.
- Bake until the edges turn golden brown, or for 15 to 20 minutes.

Nutrition Information

- Calories: 47 calories;
- Total Carbohydrate: 5.6
- Cholesterol: 7
- Protein: 0.4
- Total Fat: 2.6
- Sodium: 19

491. Rosettes I

Serving: 30 | Prep: 15mins | Cook: 1hours30mins | Ready in:

Ingredients

- 2 eggs
- 1 tablespoon white sugar
- 1 cup sifted all-purpose flour
- 1 cup milk
- 1 teaspoon vanilla extract
- 1/4 teaspoon salt
- vegetable oil for frying
- sifted confectioners' sugar

Direction

- Beat salt, sugar, and eggs thoroughly; beat in the rest of the ingredients until smooth.
- Heat the rosette iron for 2 minutes in deep hot oil that reaches to 375°.
- Drain the extra oil from the rosette iron then submerge in batter, a quarter-inch from the rosette iron's top. Dip the iron right away in hot, 375°F oil.
- Fry rosette for half a minute until golden. Pull it out then upturn to drain. Push the rosette out of the iron using a fork; move on a rack set on top of paper towels.
- Reheat the iron for a minute then make another rosette.
- Sprinkle confectioners' sugar over the rosettes.

Nutrition Information

- Calories: 561 calories;
- Total Carbohydrate: 8.2
- Cholesterol: 13
- Protein: 1.1
- Total Fat: 59.2
- Sodium: 28

492. Rum Balls I

Serving: 36 | Prep: | Cook: | Ready in:

Ingredients

- 3 cups vanilla wafer crumbs
- 1/2 cup ground pecans
- 3 tablespoons cocoa
- 1 cup confectioners' sugar
- 3 tablespoons light corn syrup
- 1/3 cup water
- 2 teaspoons rum flavored extract
- 1/4 cup confectioners' sugar

Direction

- In a medium bowl, blend rum flavoring, water, corn syrup, 1 cup of confectioners'

sugar, cocoa, ground pecans, and vanilla wafer crumbs.
- Form the mixture into 1-inch balls, and then roll in the leftover confectioners' sugar. Keep, with cover, for a week before using.

Nutrition Information

- Calories: 102 calories;
- Sodium: 47
- Total Carbohydrate: 16.5
- Cholesterol: 0
- Protein: 0.8
- Total Fat: 3.8

493. Rum Balls III

Serving: 96 | Prep: 45mins | Cook: | Ready in:

Ingredients

- 1 (16 ounce) package vanilla wafers, crushed very fine
- 2 cups ground pecans
- 4 tablespoons unsweetened cocoa powder
- 1 (12 ounce) package miniature semisweet chocolate chips
- 1 cup corn syrup
- 1/2 cup rum
- confectioners' sugar for rolling

Direction

- Mix together the chocolate chips, cocoa, ground pecans and crushed vanilla wafers in a big bowl. Mix in the rum and corn syrup, then stir well into a thick dough.
- Use confectioner's sugar to coat the palms of your hand and roll the dough into balls not bigger than a quarter. Put it on a wax paper, foil or cookie sheet to dry.
- Allow the balls to dry for an hour. Roll it in confectioner's sugar and seal it in containers that are airtight.

Nutrition Information

- Calories: 64 calories;
- Total Fat: 3.3
- Sodium: 17
- Total Carbohydrate: 8.5
- Cholesterol: 0
- Protein: 0.6

494. Rum Sugar Cookies

Serving: 48 | Prep: 20mins | Cook: 9mins | Ready in:

Ingredients

- 3 cups all-purpose flour
- 1/2 teaspoon baking soda
- 1/2 teaspoon salt
- 1/2 teaspoon baking powder
- 1 cup butter
- 2 eggs
- 1 cup white sugar
- 1 teaspoon rum flavored extract
- 1/2 teaspoon almond extract
- 1/8 teaspoon ground nutmeg

Direction

- Combine butter, baking powder, salt, baking soda and flour until the mixture looks like cornmeal.
- Mix nutmeg, almond extract, rum extract, sugar and eggs together until well combined. Add the egg mixture into the flour mixture. Stir until well mixed. Separate the dough into two equally. Keep the dough in the fridge for 2 hours.
- Preheat the oven to 350°F (175°C).
- On a lightly floured surface, add dough. Roll out the dough to 1/8 inch thickness. Cut the dough into cookies with a cookie cutter (in any shapes you want). Arrange the cookies on an ungreased baking sheet.

- Bake in the preheated oven for 7-9 minutes, till the edges are golden. Cool the cookies on the baking sheet in 1 minute, then add onto a wire rack for cooling completely.

Nutrition Information

- Calories: 82 calories;
- Total Fat: 4.1
- Sodium: 73
- Total Carbohydrate: 10.2
- Cholesterol: 18
- Protein: 1.1

495. Rum Or Bourbon Balls

Serving: 24 | Prep: 10mins | Cook: 2mins | Ready in:

Ingredients

- 1 cup semisweet chocolate chips
- 1/2 cup white sugar
- 3 tablespoons corn syrup
- 1/2 cup rum
- 2 1/2 cups crushed vanilla wafers
- 1 cup chopped walnuts (optional)
- 1/3 cup confectioners' sugar

Direction

- In a microwavable medium bowl, add chocolate chips and heat in the microwave for a minute. Stir and keep on heating at 20-second intervals while stirring between each, until chocolate is smooth and melted. Stir in corn syrup and sugar, then mix in rum. Put in chopped nuts and crushed vanilla wafers, mixing until blended evenly. Place a cover and chill until firm.
- Roll the chilled chocolate mixture into balls with bite-size, then roll balls in a mixture of ground nuts and confectioners' sugar, or just coat with plain confectioners' sugar. Keep in a covered container for one week prior to serving to let flavors combine.

Nutrition Information

- Calories: 194 calories;
- Total Fat: 8.9
- Sodium: 58
- Total Carbohydrate: 26
- Cholesterol: 0
- Protein: 1.8

496. Rumherzen

Serving: 48 | Prep: 35mins | Cook: 8mins | Ready in:

Ingredients

- 4 cups all-purpose flour
- 2 tablespoons all-purpose flour
- 2 teaspoons baking powder
- 1 cup white sugar
- 1 cup finely ground almonds
- 2 eggs
- 3 tablespoons rum
- 1/2 teaspoon vanilla extract
- 9 tablespoons butter, cut into small pieces
- Icing:
- 1 cup confectioners' sugar
- 1 (1 ounce) bottle rum flavored extract
- 1 teaspoon hot water, or more as needed
- 48 blanched almond halves

Direction

- Preheat the oven to 175°C or 350°F. Line parchment paper on baking sheets.
- Sift baking powder and 4 cups plus 2 tbsp. of flour onto a pastry board.
- In the middle of the flour mixture, form a well then place in rum, eggs, almonds and white sugar. From the side of the well, mix in flour till a thick paste forms. Let the butter pieces

drop into the flour. Start kneading the dough from the center till smooth and firm.
- On a floured work surface, roll out dough to 1/8-in. thick. Using 3-in. cookie cutters to cut into shapes. Use a spatula to place onto the prepped baking sheets.
- Bake for 8-12 minutes in the preheated oven till golden on the edges. Place onto wire racks for 5 minutes till slightly cool.
- For icing, mix together water, rum flavoring and confectioners' sugar in a bowl. Spread over the warm cookies with icing. Top each cookie with 1 almond half.

Nutrition Information

- Calories: 119 calories;
- Sodium: 39
- Total Carbohydrate: 16
- Cholesterol: 13
- Protein: 2.4
- Total Fat: 4.9

497. Russian Tea Cakes I

Serving: 36 | Prep: 20mins | Cook: 12mins | Ready in:

Ingredients

- 1 cup butter
- 1 teaspoon vanilla extract
- 6 tablespoons confectioners' sugar
- 2 cups all-purpose flour
- 1 cup chopped walnuts
- 1/3 cup confectioners' sugar for decoration

Direction

- Preheat an oven to 175 degrees C (350 degrees F).
- Cream vanilla and butter in a medium bowl until smooth. Mix flour and six tablespoons of confectioners' sugar. Mix into butter mixture until just blended. Stir in chopped walnuts.
- Roll the dough to form one inch balls, then transfer them into an ungreased cookie sheet, placing two inches apart.
- Bake in the preheated oven for 12 minutes. Once cool, roll in the remaining confectioners' sugar. You also can roll in sugar a second time.

Nutrition Information

- Calories: 102 calories;
- Cholesterol: 14
- Protein: 1.3
- Total Fat: 7.3
- Sodium: 37
- Total Carbohydrate: 8.2

498. Sand Tarts

Serving: 24 | Prep: 15mins | Cook: 20mins | Ready in:

Ingredients

- 1 cup unsalted butter
- 1/2 cup confectioners' sugar
- 1 teaspoon vanilla extract
- 2 cups all-purpose flour
- 1 cup chopped walnuts
- 1/4 cup confectioners' sugar, or as needed

Direction

- In a large bowl, whisk butter until light. Whisk in vanilla and half cup confectioners' sugar. Add flour; combine just until blended. Stir in nuts. Form dough into a ball; make it flat into a disc. Use plastic wrap to wrap and chill in the fridge until cold.
- Set the oven to 325°F (170°C) and start preheating. Use parchment paper to line cookie sheets.
- Form dough into 1 inch balls. Arrange on lined sheets with even space in between. Bake until colored lightly and firm or for about 20 minutes.

- Sift 1/4 cup confectioners' sugar into a bowl. Place cookies on confectioners' sugar while still warm and roll gently to coat. Place cookies in a plastic bag immediately and seal (this helps cookies sweat and form an icing). Rest 5 minutes in the bag. Place on wire rack to cool.

Nutrition Information

- Calories: 153 calories;
- Total Carbohydrate: 12.5
- Cholesterol: 20
- Protein: 1.9
- Total Fat: 11
- Sodium: 1

499. Scandinavian Almond Bars

Serving: 48 | Prep: 10mins | Cook: 10mins | Ready in:

Ingredients

- 1/2 cup butter
- 1 cup white sugar
- 1 egg
- 1/2 teaspoon almond extract
- 1 3/4 cups all-purpose flour
- 2 teaspoons baking powder
- 1/4 teaspoon salt
- 1/2 cup sliced almonds
- 2 tablespoons milk
- 1 cup confectioners' sugar
- 1/4 teaspoon almond extract
- 1/4 cup milk

Direction

- Start preheating the oven to 325°F (165°C).
- Cream sugar and butter in a medium bowl. Put in almond extract and egg and stir until fluffy. Mix in salt, baking powder and flour and stir well.
- Cut the dough into 4 pieces, form each one into a 12-inch long log. Arrange two logs 4-5 inches apart per cookie sheet. Using your hand, flatten each roll until it has 3 inches wide. Brush milk over the flattened roll. Top with the sliced almonds.
- Bake for 12-15 mins in the prepared oven, until the edges are slightly browned. Cut the cookies crosswise at a diagonal while they are still warm, into about 1-inch wide slices. Once cool, drizzle with the almond icing.
- For almond icing: stir milk, almond extract and powdered sugar together in a small bowl, until smooth. Drizzle it over cookies.

Nutrition Information

- Calories: 68 calories;
- Sodium: 48
- Total Carbohydrate: 10.5
- Cholesterol: 9
- Protein: 0.9
- Total Fat: 2.6

500. Scandinavian Snowflake Cookies

Serving: 32 | Prep: 1hours30mins | Cook: 1hours | Ready in:

Ingredients

- 2 cups milk
- 4 cups all-purpose flour
- 1 teaspoon baking powder
- 1 tablespoon white sugar
- 1 tablespoon butter, softened
- 3 cups vegetable oil for frying
- 1 cup confectioners' sugar, or as needed

Direction

- Prepare baking sheets lined with waxed paper

- or you can also use a parchment paper, and dust it off with flour.
- Heat the milk in a saucepan just until up to the boiling point. Whisk the flour, baking powder and sugar together in a bowl until fully incorporated, then stir in the butter and pour in the hot milk little by little, whisking between adding the next portion, until the mixture makes a stiff dough.
- Lay the dough out on an oiled work area, and knead for roughly 5 minutes until the dough becomes smooth and cool. Slice the dough in 4 equal-sized portions, then slice those pieces into 4 parts, making 16 portions. Split each 16 pieces in half to form 32 equal-sized portions of dough. Cover the pieces of dough with a cloth, and let it rest for roughly 20 minutes.
- Work on a floured counter. Flatten every piece of dough into a thin circle measuring about 8 inches in diameter. Arrange the circles on the baking sheets and cover with a cloth; let them rest for half an hour.
- Fold every circle in half, then fold them in half once again. Use a sharp knife or you may also use a small cookie cutters to snip and form the shapes out of the folded dough the same as making a paper snowflake. Open the circle back up carefully, exposing the pattern. Stack the patterned snowflakes between the sheets of a waxed paper on a work surface.
- Pour the oil in a deep skillet and heat to 375°F (190°C). Ensure that the oil is about 2 inches deep.
- Lay the snowflake into the hot oil carefully while keeping it flat. Let it fry for about 1 minute for each side until it becomes golden brown and crisp. Flip the snowflakes lightly over using a tongs to avoid breaking them. Transfer the fried snowflakes on paper towels to drain, and dust it off with confectioners' sugar.

Nutrition Information

- Calories: 103 calories;
- Sodium: 24
- Total Carbohydrate: 17
- Cholesterol: 2
- Protein: 2.1
- Total Fat: 2.9

501. Shorecook's Chocolate Peppermint Biscotti

Serving: 32 | Prep: 1hours | Cook: 50mins | Ready in:

Ingredients

- 2 cups white sugar
- 1 cup butter, softened
- 1 cup unsweetened cocoa powder
- 4 eggs
- 1/3 cup chocolate liqueur (such as Godiva®)
- 2 teaspoons peppermint extract
- 4 1/2 cups all-purpose flour
- 4 teaspoons baking powder
- 3/4 teaspoon salt
- 1 2/3 cups mint chocolate chips (such as Hershey's®)
- 2 (14 ounce) packages white candy melts (confectioners' coating)
- 6 large peppermint candy canes, crushed

Direction

- Start preheating the oven at 350°F (175°C). Line parchment paper on 2 baking sheets.
- Whisk cocoa powder, butter, and white sugar using an electric mixer in a large bowl until smooth and creamy. Mix in eggs, one at a time, whisking well after each addition. Combine peppermint extract and chocolate liqueur into the sugar-egg mixture.
- Mix salt, baking powder, and flour in a different bowl. Slowly combine the flour mixture into the sugar-egg mixture until well combined; fold mint chocolate chips into the dough.
- Separate the dough into 4 equal parts and form into logs. Place the logs on the paper-lined baking sheets.

- Plunge a spatula in water and smooth the surface of the logs by running it over.
- Bake biscotti logs in the prepared oven for 30 to 35 minutes until set when touched. Let biscotti logs cool completely on wire racks.
- Lower the oven temperature to 300°F (150°C).
- Slice biscotti logs into 3/4-inch slices and place on baking sheets.
- Bake in the oven for about 10 minutes each side until biscotti are dry. Chill fully on wire racks.
- Put candy melts in a wide microwave-safe bowl; microwave for about 2 1/2 minutes until melted, stirring every 30 seconds.
- Dip the cooled biscotti in the melted white candy; scatter crushed candy canes over.

Nutrition Information

- Calories: 386 calories;
- Protein: 5.2
- Total Fat: 17.3
- Sodium: 190
- Total Carbohydrate: 54.1
- Cholesterol: 44

502. Shortbread Christmas Cookies

Serving: 36 | Prep: 25mins | Cook: 20mins | Ready in:

Ingredients

- 3 cups all-purpose flour
- 3/4 cup white sugar
- 1/4 teaspoon salt
- 1 1/2 cups cold butter
- 1/2 teaspoon rum extract
- 1/2 teaspoon almond extract
- 2 tablespoons cold water
- 2 cups confectioners' sugar
- 2 tablespoons milk
- 2 teaspoons milk
- 1 drop food coloring, or to desired shade (optional)
- 1 tablespoon colored edible glitter, or as desired

Direction

- In a big bowl, combine salt, sugar, and flour; chop in butter with a pastry cutter until the mixture looks like coarse crumbs. In a small bowl with water, add almond extract and rum extract and mix. Stir into the dry ingredients, a small amount each time, until the mixture forms into a ball when you squeeze it.
- On a work surface sprinkled with flour, put the dough; sprinkle flour over and roll out into a 1/4-in. thick sheet. Use floured cookie cutters to cut into shapes, then put on unoiled cookie sheets, about 1-in. apart. Use a layer of plastic wrap to cover and chill for 30 minutes.
- Set the oven to 325°F (165°C) to preheat.
- Bake the cookies for 15-18 minutes until the edges turn light brown. Leave the cookies on the sheets to cool for 2 minutes, then remove to wire racks to complete cooling. Let cool fully before garnishing.
- To prepare the frosting, in a bowl, combine milk and confectioners' sugar until smooth. If you want, split the frosting into small bowls and tint each bowl with your favorite food coloring. Frost completely cooled cookies and before the frosting sets, sprinkle edible glitter over.

Nutrition Information

- Calories: 149 calories;
- Total Carbohydrate: 18.9
- Cholesterol: 20
- Protein: 1.2
- Total Fat: 7.8
- Sodium: 71

503. Shulie Krinkles

Serving: 48 | Prep: 13mins | Cook: 12mins | Ready in:

Ingredients

- 2 (10.25 ounce) packages fudge brownie mix
- 1/2 cup butter, softened
- 1 egg
- 1 teaspoon vanilla extract
- 2 cups confectioners' sugar

Direction

- In a bowl, combine vanilla extract, egg, butter and brownie mix until thoroughly incorporated. Chill while covered until the firm, about no less than an hour.
- Set oven to 175°C (350°F) and start preheating. Use parchment paper to line baking sheets. In a shallow bowl, add the confectioners' sugar.
- Spoon about a tablespoon dough for each cookie and roll to form a ball. Roll in the confectioners' sugar and arrange 2 inches apart onto the lined baking sheets.
- Bake at 175°C (350°F) for 12-14 minutes until cracking on the tops. Allow to cool for 5 minutes on baking sheets, then transfer to racks and let cool entirely.

Nutrition Information

- Calories: 88 calories;
- Cholesterol: 9
- Protein: 0.8
- Total Fat: 3.3
- Sodium: 61
- Total Carbohydrate: 14.5

504. Snow Balls In A Jar

Serving: 24 | Prep: | Cook: | Ready in:

Ingredients

- 1/2 cup confectioners' sugar
- 2 cups all-purpose flour
- 1 cup chopped pecans

Direction

- Mix the confectioners' sugar with flour in a medium bowl. Put into a 1-quart canning jar. Place the chopped pecans over. Cover with the lid and attach a tag with the instructions:
- Snow Balls, Makes four dozen. Set the oven to 325°F (165°C) to preheat. Grease cookie sheets. Beat together 3/4 cup of shortening with 1/4 cup of margarine in a medium bowl. Mix in 2 teaspoons of vanilla. Put in the whole contents of the jar and stir thoroughly. Roll to shape dough into one-inch balls and put them on the greased cookie sheet. Bake for 20-25 minutes, until browned lightly. Let it cool and roll in confectioners' sugar.

Nutrition Information

- Calories: 79 calories;
- Total Fat: 3.4
- Sodium: < 1
- Total Carbohydrate: 11.1
- Cholesterol: 0
- Protein: 1.5

505. Snow Flakes

Serving: 72 | Prep: 20mins | Cook: 10mins | Ready in:

Ingredients

- 1 cup butter flavored shortening
- 1 (3 ounce) package cream cheese, softened
- 1 cup white sugar
- 1 egg yolk
- 1 teaspoon vanilla extract
- 1 teaspoon orange zest
- 2 1/2 cups all-purpose flour
- 1/2 teaspoon salt

- 1/4 teaspoon ground cinnamon

Direction

- Set the oven to 350°F (175°C), and start preheating.
- Cream sugar, cream cheese and shortening together in a medium bowl. Beat in orange zest, vanilla and egg yolk. Keep beating until fluffy and light. Slowly mix in cinnamon, salt and flour. Fill the cookie press; then shape the cookies on ungreased cookie sheet.
- Bake in the preheated oven for 10 - 12 minutes. Take away from cookie sheet, and allow to cool on wire racks.

Nutrition Information

- Calories: 58 calories;
- Total Fat: 3.5
- Sodium: 20
- Total Carbohydrate: 6.1
- Cholesterol: 4
- Protein: 0.6

506. Snowballs II

Serving: 30 | Prep: 30mins | Cook: 15mins | Ready in:

Ingredients

- 1 cup butter
- 1/2 cup confectioners' sugar
- 1/4 teaspoon salt
- 1 teaspoon vanilla extract
- 2 1/4 cups all-purpose flour
- 1 cup chopped pecans
- 1/3 cup confectioners' sugar for dusting, or as needed
- 1/4 cup finely crushed peppermint candy canes (optional)

Direction

- Start preheating the oven to 350°F (175°C).
- Cream vanilla, 1/2 cup of the confectioners' sugar, and butter. Mix in salt, pecans, and flour. Form about 1 tablespoon or so of the dough into balls and arrange on an ungreased cookie sheet.
- Bake in prepared oven for about 15 minutes until bottoms are golden. Do not let these cookies overbrown: it's better to undercook them than overcook them. While cookies are still hot, roll them in confectioners' sugar. Once cooled, roll them in confectioners' sugar again.

Nutrition Information

- Calories: 135 calories;
- Total Fat: 8.8
- Sodium: 64
- Total Carbohydrate: 13
- Cholesterol: 16
- Protein: 1.4

507. Soft Christmas Cookies

Serving: 48 | Prep: 20mins | Cook: 8mins | Ready in:

Ingredients

- 3 3/4 cups all-purpose flour
- 1 teaspoon baking powder
- 1/2 teaspoon salt
- 1 cup margarine, softened
- 1 1/2 cups white sugar
- 2 eggs
- 2 teaspoons vanilla extract

Direction

- Sift together salt, baking powder, and flour; put aside. Cream together the sugar and margarine in a big bowl until fluffy and light. Whisk in eggs, 1 egg each time, and then mix in vanilla. Slowly mix in the sifted ingredients

until completely incorporated. Put a cover on the dough and refrigerate for 2 hours.
- Turn the oven to 400°F (200°C) to preheat. Coat the baking sheets with oil. On a surface scattered with flour, roll a bit of the chilled dough until having 1/4-in. thickness. Use cookie cutters to cut out shapes.
- Bake in the preheated oven for 6-8 minutes until just turning brown around the edges. Transfer from cookie sheets to wire racks to cool.

Nutrition Information

- Calories: 97 calories;
- Total Carbohydrate: 13.8
- Cholesterol: 8
- Protein: 1.3
- Total Fat: 4
- Sodium: 81

508. Sour Cream Cut Outs

Serving: 24 | Prep: 25mins | Cook: 10mins | Ready in:

Ingredients

- 1 cup butter, softened
- 1 cup white sugar
- 2 eggs
- 1 cup sour cream
- 1 1/2 teaspoons vanilla extract
- 1 teaspoon baking soda
- 1 teaspoon baking powder
- 1/2 teaspoon salt
- 6 1/2 cups cake flour

Direction

- Prepare the oven by preheating to 375°F (190°C).
- Cream the sugar and butter in a large bowl until smooth. Whisk in 1 egg at a time, then mix in the vanilla and sour cream. Whisk in salt and baking powder and soda; slowly whisk in flour to make a dough that is stiff enough to roll out. Less or more flour may be needed.
- On a lightly floured surface, roll out the dough and use cookie cutters to cut into shapes. Transfer the cookies to ungreased cookie sheets with 2-inch apart.
- Place in the preheated oven and bake for 10 minutes or until the center looks dry and firm. Cookies should remain white, so be cautious not to overbake.

Nutrition Information

- Calories: 268 calories;
- Total Fat: 10.4
- Sodium: 187
- Total Carbohydrate: 39.1
- Cholesterol: 40
- Protein: 4.1

509. Sour Cream Spritz

Serving: 96 | Prep: 20mins | Cook: 12mins | Ready in:

Ingredients

- 1 cup butter, softened
- 3/4 cup white sugar
- 1 egg yolk
- 1/3 cup sour cream
- 1 teaspoon vanilla extract
- 2 3/4 cups all-purpose flour
- 1 teaspoon ground cinnamon
- 1/2 teaspoon salt
- 1/2 teaspoon baking soda

Direction

- Prepare the oven by preheating to 375°F (190°C).
- Cream the sugar and butter. Whisk in vanilla, sour cream, and egg yolk. Combine baking

soda, salt, cinnamon, and flour in another bowl. Whisk the flour mixture into the butter mixture. Transfer the dough to a cookie press and onto ungreased baking sheets, press cookies.
- Place in the preheated oven and bake for 10-12 minutes until golden. Cool on sheet for 5 minutes before taking it to a wire rack to cool fully.

Nutrition Information

- Calories: 38 calories;
- Cholesterol: 8
- Protein: 0.4
- Total Fat: 2.2
- Sodium: 33
- Total Carbohydrate: 4.4

510. Speculaas Cookies Or Spicy Sinterklass Cakes

Serving: 30 | Prep: 15mins | Cook: 15mins | Ready in:

Ingredients

- 2 tablespoons milk
- 2/3 cup dark brown sugar
- 2 cups sifted all-purpose flour
- 1 teaspoon ground cloves
- 1 teaspoon ground cinnamon
- 1/2 teaspoon ground nutmeg
- 1/2 teaspoon ground ginger
- 1/4 teaspoon baking powder
- 1/4 teaspoon salt
- 2 tablespoons chopped slivered almonds
- 2 tablespoons chopped candied citron
- 2/3 cup butter
- 1/2 cup slivered almonds

Direction

- Dissolve brown sugar in milk in a large bowl. Mix salt, baking powder, ginger, nutmeg, cinnamon, cloves and flour. Mix the dry ingredients into the milk and sugar. Stir in candied citron and 2 tablespoons of almonds. Slice in butter until it begins to form a dough. Knead on a surface that is lightly floured until smooth. Cover the dough and refrigerate for about one hour for easier handling.
- Preheat an oven to 175 degrees C (350 degrees F). Lightly sprinkle a wooden speculaas mold with cornstarch. Firmly push dough into the mold. Move a knife around edges to chop off the excess dough. Carefully lift the dough out of mold or tap out on a cookie sheet. Push the remaining almond slivers into the cookies and match the designs.
- Bake for about 15 minutes in prepared oven until edges start to darken. In case the cookies are more than half inch thick, bake for up to 30 minutes at 150 degrees C (300 degrees F). Let the cookies cool on wire racks to crisp. Keep for up to a month in an airtight container at lukewarm. Flavor gets better with age.

Nutrition Information

- Calories: 97 calories;
- Total Fat: 5.4
- Sodium: 56
- Total Carbohydrate: 10.9
- Cholesterol: 11
- Protein: 1.4

511. Spicy Ginger Cookies

Serving: 48 | Prep: 20mins | Cook: 10mins | Ready in:

Ingredients

- 2 cups lightly packed brown sugar
- 1 cup butter-flavored shortening, melted
- 1/2 cup unsalted butter, melted
- 1/2 cup molasses
- 2 eggs
- 1 tablespoon baking soda

- 1 tablespoon ground cinnamon
- 1 tablespoon ground ginger
- 1 teaspoon salt
- 1 teaspoon ground cloves
- 1/2 teaspoon cayenne pepper
- 4 cups all-purpose flour
- 1/2 cup coarse sugar crystals, or as needed

Direction

- Set the oven to 375°F (190°C) and start preheating.
- In a large bowl, whisk together cayenne pepper, cloves, salt, ginger, cinnamon, baking soda, eggs, molasses, butter, shortening and brown sugar until mixture is glossy; fold in flour until dough is just-blended.
- In a shallow bowl, pour coarse sugar. Roll the dough into 48 balls, coat balls with sugar and arrange on prepared baking sheet 2 inches apart.
- Bake in the preheated oven for about 9 minutes until the upper surface of the cookies crack.

Nutrition Information

- Calories: 151 calories;
- Total Fat: 6.7
- Sodium: 129
- Total Carbohydrate: 21.8
- Cholesterol: 13
- Protein: 1.4

512. Spoon Cookies

Serving: 6 | Prep: | Cook: | Ready in:

Ingredients

- 1 cup butter
- 1 cup white sugar
- 2 teaspoons vanilla extract
- 6 eggs
- 4 teaspoons baking powder
- 5 cups all-purpose flour
- 1 (1.75 ounce) package multicolored sprinkles (jimmies)
- 2 cups confectioners' sugar
- 1/4 cup milk

Direction

- Set oven to 350°F (175°C). Line baking sheets with parchment paper.
- Whip the butter or margarine and white sugar until fluffy and light. Whip in the vanilla with eggs and stir well. Mix in the flour and baking powder. Drop dough by rounded spoonful onto the prepared baking sheets. Whisk milk into the confectioners' sugar, 1 tablespoon at a time in a small bowl until it has a drizzling consistency.
- Bake for about 10 minutes at 350°F (175°C). Cool the cookies then sprinkle with confectioners' sugar and milk glaze then scatter with candy sprinkles.

Nutrition Information

- Calories: 1056 calories;
- Sodium: 621
- Total Carbohydrate: 160.5
- Cholesterol: 268
- Protein: 17.8
- Total Fat: 38.6

513. Springerle I

Serving: 60 | Prep: | Cook: | Ready in:

Ingredients

- 4 eggs
- 2 tablespoons butter
- 2 teaspoons baking powder
- 1/4 teaspoon salt
- 2 cups white sugar

- 4 cups all-purpose flour
- 1/4 cup anise seed

Direction

- In large mixing bowl, beat eggs until very light.
- Put in butter and sugar. Cream together until fluffy and light.
- Sift salt, flour and baking powder. Put in the dry ingredients, then combine.
- Knead the dough until it becomes smooth. If necessary, put in additional flour to make a smooth dough.
- Cover the dough; let chill in the fridge for at least 2 hours.
- On the slightly floured board, roll the dough to 1/2-inch thickness. Using springerle roller, roll the dough again to create designs. Cut at the border. On the clean tea towel, sprinkle anise seed and arrange cookies on it. Let stand overnight (do not cover) to dry.
- Bake at 325°F (170°C) for 12-15 mins.
- Let cool completely. Preserve in a tight tin container; the longer cookies are preserved, the more anise flavor they take up.

Nutrition Information

- Calories: 66 calories;
- Sodium: 34
- Total Carbohydrate: 13.3
- Cholesterol: 13
- Protein: 1.4
- Total Fat: 0.9

514. Springerle II

Serving: 36 | Prep: | Cook: | Ready in:

Ingredients

- 4 eggs
- 2 cups white sugar

- 1 teaspoon anise extract
- 2 tablespoons anise seed
- 4 1/2 cups cake flour

Direction

- Whisk eggs until puffy and light, slowly adding sugar (for about 15 minutes). Note: It is important to not under beat.
- Fold in flour and extract.
- Roll out the dough into about 3/8- inch on a lightly floured surface. To imprint the design firmly onto the dough, use the rolling pin.
- Slice cookies separately and spread with anise seeds on the greased baking sheet. Let cookies rest overnight, with cover, to make it dry.
- Start preheating the oven at 375°F (190°C).
- Put cookies into the oven and lower the temperature to 300°F (150°C). Bake for 15 minutes just until light yellow. Do not let it brown.
- Keep the cookies for a minimum of 2 to 3 weeks because these are a stiff cookie. You can put in a slice of apple to "soften" back up or maybe a slice of bread. Replenish bread or apple every 2 to 3 days.

Nutrition Information

- Calories: 117 calories;
- Cholesterol: 21
- Protein: 2.2
- Total Fat: 0.8
- Sodium: 8
- Total Carbohydrate: 25.3

515. Springerle V

Serving: 60 | Prep: | Cook: | Ready in:

Ingredients

- 4 eggs
- 1 pound confectioners' sugar

- 2 teaspoons anise extract
- 4 1/4 cups sifted all-purpose flour
- 2 teaspoons baking powder

Direction

- Whip eggs in big bowl on high speed of an electric mixer, till light. Lower speed; put in confectioners' sugar and anise extract. Keep whipping at medium moderate speed to combine thoroughly. Sift baking powder and flour together; mix to egg mixture, dough will become quite firm.
- Unroll dough to 3/8-inch thick. Use a springerle board to imprint and slice apart. Arrange cookies on cookie sheet and sit overnight with no cover.
- Heat an oven to 175°C or 350°F. Let cookies bake, about 7 - 10 minutes.

Nutrition Information

- Calories: 67 calories;
- Total Fat: 0.4
- Sodium: 21
- Total Carbohydrate: 14.4
- Cholesterol: 12
- Protein: 1.3

516. Springerle VII

Serving: 72 | Prep: 15mins | Cook: 10mins | Ready in:

Ingredients

- 4 eggs, separated
- 1 pound confectioners' sugar
- 1 teaspoon baking powder
- 1/4 teaspoon anise oil
- 4 cups all-purpose flour

Direction

- Whip egg whites in large bowl until stiff. Beat in yolks, 1 at a time, beating well before adding the next. Stir in anise oil, baking powder and confectioners' sugar. Mix in flour, one cup at a time, mixing well before adding the next, until fairly stiff. Roll dough out on the lightly floured surface to 1/2-in. thick. Flour a springerle rolling pin and carefully roll it over the dough, leaving the imprints. Cut the cookies along the design lines; arrange on lightly greased cookie sheet, about 1-in. apart. Allow cookies to stand to dry in a cool place overnight.
- Start preheating oven to 325°F (165°C). Bake cookies until bottoms are browned lightly, about 8-10 mins.

Nutrition Information

- Calories: 54 calories;
- Total Fat: 0.4
- Sodium: 9
- Total Carbohydrate: 11.6
- Cholesterol: 10
- Protein: 1.1

517. Spumoni Chocolate Chip Cookies

Serving: 24 | Prep: 20mins | Cook: 10mins | Ready in:

Ingredients

- 2 1/4 cups all-purpose flour
- 1 teaspoon baking soda
- 1 cup butter, softened
- 1/4 cup white sugar
- 3/4 cup packed brown sugar
- 1 (3.4 ounce) package instant pistachio pudding mix
- 2 eggs
- 1 teaspoon vanilla extract
- 1 (12 ounce) bag semi-sweet chocolate chips
- 1/2 cup chopped maraschino cherries
- 1/4 cup chopped pistachios

Direction

- Set oven to 175°C (350°F) and start preheating. Sift baking soda and flour and put aside.
- In a big bowl, beat brown sugar, white sugar and butter until smooth. Mix in instant pudding mix until thoroughly blended. Beat in eggs, one at a time; mix in vanilla. Beat in the dry mixture. Fold in pistachios, cherries and chocolate chips. Scoop by big spoonfuls and place onto ungreased baking pans.
- Bake at 175°C (350°F) for 10 minutes until cookies turn light brown in color.

Nutrition Information

- Calories: 247 calories;
- Total Carbohydrate: 32.2
- Cholesterol: 36
- Protein: 2.7
- Total Fat: 13.1
- Sodium: 179

518. Storybook Gingerbread Men

Serving: 5 | Prep: | Cook: | Ready in:

Ingredients

- 1/2 cup shortening
- 1/2 cup packed brown sugar
- 3 1/4 cups sifted all-purpose flour
- 1 teaspoon salt
- 1 teaspoon baking soda
- 1/2 teaspoon ground cinnamon
- 1/2 teaspoon ground ginger
- 3/4 cup molasses
- 1/4 cup water

Direction

- Cream the sugar and shortening. Combine and sift together spices, soda, flour, and salt and mix it into the creamed mixture, adding alternately with water and molasses. Allow it to chill for 60 minutes.
- Set the oven to 350°F or 180°C for preheating.
- Roll out dough into 1/4-inch thick. Cut the dough using the large 6-8 inches gingerbread men cookie cutters. Grease the cookie sheet lightly. Transfer the cookies into the prepared cookie sheet using a broad spatula.
- Position the pan above the oven's center. Let it bake for 12 minutes until the cookies spring back lightly in the center. Be sure not to overcook the cookies since they won't stay soft. Transfer them on wire racks to cool completely. This recipe makes up to 10 men with 6-8-inches tall.

Nutrition Information

- Calories: 704 calories;
- Protein: 8.4
- Total Fat: 21.4
- Sodium: 743
- Total Carbohydrate: 120.7
- Cholesterol: 0

519. Strufoli I

Serving: 8 | Prep: | Cook: | Ready in:

Ingredients

- 4 eggs
- 2 1/2 cups all-purpose flour
- 16 ounces honey
- 1/2 vanilla bean, halved lengthwise
- 4 tablespoons chopped semisweet chocolate
- 1/2 cup blanched slivered almonds
- 1 (1.75 ounce) package multicolored sprinkles (jimmies)
- 1 cup vegetable oil for frying
- 1/3 cup confectioners' sugar for decoration

Direction

- In a bowl, add eggs and beat until triple in volume. Gradually put in flour until well mixed without using all of the flour. The dough should be still somewhat sticky.
- Remove to a board coated with flour. Cut off a piece of dough at a time. Roll piece of dough between your hands to make pencil shapes, using a little flour if necessary.
- Cut into 1/4 inch pieces and arrange each piece on a cloth dusted with flour. Heat oil in a big pan on top of the stove to 190°C or 375°F. Deep-fry about 1/2 cup pieces at a time while turning continuously until golden. Drain pieces and put aside. Dough will start to turn brown rapidly after a few batches, this is the time to replace oil.
- Bring honey with vanilla bean in a big pan to a boil, then get rid of bean. Into hot honey, put deep-fried pieces and toss to coat all. Allow to cool and stir in multi-colored jimmies, nuts and chocolate. Put on a plate while shaping firmly into tall cone, then sprinkle confectioners' sugar over top.

Nutrition Information

- Calories: 492 calories;
- Protein: 9.2
- Total Fat: 12
- Sodium: 40
- Total Carbohydrate: 90.8
- Cholesterol: 93

520. Sugar Cookies IV

Serving: 30 | Prep: | Cook: |Ready in:

Ingredients

- 1 1/2 cups confectioners' sugar
- 1 cup butter
- 1 egg
- 1 teaspoon vanilla extract
- 1/2 teaspoon almond extract
- 2 1/2 cups all-purpose flour
- 1 teaspoon baking soda
- 1 teaspoon cream of tartar
- 1/3 cup granulated sugar for decoration

Direction

- Combine egg, butter or margarine, vanilla and almond extract, and confectioners' sugar. Whisk in cream of tartar, baking soda, and flour.
- Shape mixture into a big ball, wrap in plastic wrap, and refrigerate for a minimum of 3 hours.
- Turn oven to 375°F (190°C) to preheat.
- Split dough in half. Roll each half to 3/16-inch thick on a board lightly coated with flour. Use 2" to 2 1/2" cookie cutters to cut out your favorite shapes. Scatter top of cookies with granulated sugar. Arrange cookies on lightly greased cookie sheets. Bake cookies for 6 to 8 minutes or until light brown on the edges.

Nutrition Information

- Calories: 127 calories;
- Cholesterol: 22
- Protein: 1.4
- Total Fat: 6.4
- Sodium: 88
- Total Carbohydrate: 16.2

521. Sugar Cookies XII

Serving: 36 | Prep: | Cook: |Ready in:

Ingredients

- 3 cups white sugar
- 2 cups lard
- 4 eggs
- 2 teaspoons vanilla extract
- 2 cups buttermilk
- 8 cups all-purpose flour

- 2 tablespoons baking powder
- 3/4 tablespoon baking soda
- 1 1/2 teaspoons salt

Direction

- Beat lard and sugar in a large bowl until smooth. Beat in 1 egg at a time; mix in buttermilk and vanilla. Mix together salt, baking soda, baking powder and flour. Mix to creamed mixture. Let it chill with cover for 2 hours at least.
- Turn on the oven to 375°F (190°C) to preheat.
- Roll the dough out on a lightly floured surface so that it is 1/4-inch thick. Use cookie cutters to cut into desired shapes. Transfer onto ungreased cookie sheets.
- Put into the prepped oven to bake for 12-15 minutes. Take them off the baking sheets and let them cool on wire racks.

Nutrition Information

- Calories: 283 calories;
- Total Fat: 12.3
- Sodium: 274
- Total Carbohydrate: 38.8
- Cholesterol: 32
- Protein: 4

522. Sugar Cookies With Buttercream Frosting

Serving: 60 | Prep: 15mins | Cook: 5mins | Ready in:

Ingredients

- 1 cup butter
- 1 cup white sugar
- 2 eggs
- 1/2 teaspoon vanilla extract
- 3 1/4 cups all-purpose flour
- 1/2 teaspoon baking powder
- 1/2 teaspoon baking soda
- 1/2 teaspoon salt
- 1/2 cup shortening
- 1 pound confectioners' sugar
- 5 tablespoons water
- 1/4 teaspoon salt
- 1/2 teaspoon vanilla extract
- 1/4 teaspoon butter flavored extract

Direction

- Combine vanilla, eggs, sugar and butter in a big bowl using an electric mixer until light and fluffy. Mix the salt, baking powder, baking soda and flour; mix flour mixture gradually into butter mixture until well combined with a sturdy spoon. Refrigerate dough for 2 hours.
- Set the oven to 400°F (200°C) to preheat. Shape the dough to 1/4-inch thickness on a lightly floured surface. Slice into shapes you like with cookie cutters. Put cookies 2 inches apart onto ungreased cookie trays.
- Bake in the preheated oven for 4 to 6 minutes. Take cookies out of the pan and let cool on wire racks.
- Whip butter flavoring, vanilla extract, salt, water, confectioners' sugar and shortening with an electric mixer until fluffy. Frost cookies after they have fully cooled.

Nutrition Information

- Calories: 112 calories;
- Sodium: 68
- Total Carbohydrate: 16.1
- Cholesterol: 14
- Protein: 0.9
- Total Fat: 5

523. Sugar Free Christmas Cutouts

Serving: 24 | Prep: | Cook: | Ready in:

Ingredients

- 1/2 cup shortening
- 3 tablespoons sugar substitute with aspartame (such as Equal packets)
- 1 egg
- 2 1/2 cups cake flour
- 1/2 teaspoon salt
- 2 teaspoons baking powder
- 1/2 cup skim milk
- 2 tablespoons water
- 1 teaspoon vanilla extract

Direction

- Cream shortening. Add egg and sugar substitute; beat well. Mix dry ingredients in another bowl. Add water, vanilla and milk. Add flour mixture; mix well.
- Chill dough for 2-4 hours.
- Preheat an oven to 165°C/325°F.
- Roll to 1/8-in. thick; cut cookies. Bake it for 8-10 minutes and cool; keep them in airtight container.

Nutrition Information

- Calories: 104 calories;
- Total Fat: 4.6
- Sodium: 95
- Total Carbohydrate: 12
- Cholesterol: 8
- Protein: 3.3

524. Sugar And Spice Cookies

Serving: 50 | Prep: 20mins | Cook: 10mins | Ready in:

Ingredients

- 1 3/4 cups all-purpose flour
- 1 teaspoon baking powder
- 1 teaspoon ground cinnamon
- 1/4 teaspoon ground nutmeg
- 1 pinch ground cloves
- 1/2 cup softened butter
- 1 cup packed brown sugar
- 1 egg
- 1/2 teaspoon vanilla extract

Direction

- Mix together cloves, nutmeg, cinnamon, baking powder and flour in a bowl.
- Use an electric mixer to cream together brown sugar and butter till smooth in a big bowl; beat vanilla extract and egg into butter mixture. In small amount, add flour mixture to butter mixture; beat each addition till blended. Shape dough into a ball; use plastic wrap to wrap. Refrigerate for a minimum of 1 hour or to a maximum of 3 days.
- Preheat oven to 175°C/350°F then grease baking sheets.
- Roll out dough into approximately 1/8-in. thickness with a rolling pin on a floured work surface; use 2-in. cookie cutters to cut. Transfer the cut cookies onto the prepped baking sheets.
- In preheated oven, bake for 10-12 minutes till edges start to brown; cool cookies for 1 minute on baking sheet. Transfer to a wire rack; fully cool.

Nutrition Information

- Calories: 51 calories;
- Cholesterol: 9
- Protein: 0.6
- Total Fat: 2
- Sodium: 26
- Total Carbohydrate: 7.8

525. Swedish Rye Cookies

Serving: 12 | Prep: | Cook: | Ready in:

Ingredients

- 1/2 cup butter

- 1/4 cup white sugar
- 1/2 cup rye flour
- 1 cup all-purpose flour
- 1/8 teaspoon baking powder
- 1/4 teaspoon salt
- 3 tablespoons water

Direction

- Heat oven to 190 degrees C (375 degrees F).
- Mix the sugar and butter until it becomes light and fluffy. Add salt, rye flour, all-purpose flour and baking powder. Mix properly and moisten dough with enough water.
- Spread the dough out on a floured board. The cookies would be crispier if the dough is thinner. Use a floured glass or cutter to divide into 2 1/2 inch rounds. Cut a small hole at the center with a thimble, so it could be hanged on a tree when done.
- Bake on a dry cooking sheet at 190 deg C (375 deg F) or until slightly brown in color. Leave it to cool and hang on a tree using a yarn or ribbon.

Nutrition Information

- Calories: 137 calories;
- Sodium: 108
- Total Carbohydrate: 15.5
- Cholesterol: 20
- Protein: 1.5
- Total Fat: 7.8

526. Swedish Spritzs

Serving: 12 | Prep: | Cook: | Ready in:

Ingredients

- 1 cup butter, softened
- 1 cup white sugar
- 1 egg
- 1 1/2 teaspoons almond extract
- 1 pinch salt
- 1 1/4 cups all-purpose flour

Direction

- Cream in almond extract, salt, egg, sugar and butter. Margarine could be used in place of butter. Mix in 1 1/4 cup of sifted flour thoroughly.
- Make long strips by placing dough in a cookie press.
- Lightly sprinkle oil on a cookie sheet, and place the strips on it.
- Let it bake in an oven set at 175 deg C (350 deg F) for at least 10 minutes until slightly brown. Check at 8 minutes. Remove from the oven and cut into cookies of 2 or 3 inches size immediately. The cooking will take a few minutes longer if baking is done on an air bake cookie sheet.

Nutrition Information

- Calories: 255 calories;
- Total Fat: 15.9
- Sodium: 115
- Total Carbohydrate: 26.6
- Cholesterol: 56
- Protein: 2

527. Swedish Wedding Cakes

Serving: 24 | Prep: 25mins | Cook: 10mins | Ready in:

Ingredients

- 1/4 cup margarine
- 2/3 cup white sugar
- 1 egg, beaten
- 1 (8 ounce) package dates, pitted and finely chopped
- 1 teaspoon vanilla extract
- 2 cups crispy rice cereal
- 3/4 cup walnuts, finely chopped

- 1 cup sweetened flaked coconut

Direction

- In a saucepan, mix together dates, egg, sugar and margarine, then cook the mixture on medium heat for 7-10 minutes, until thick. Take away from the heat and stir in vanilla.
- In a big bowl, mix together walnuts and crispy rice cereal, then stir in the date mixture and blend well.
- Working rapidly, shape the date and cereal mixture into balls 1 inch in size, then roll these balls in the coconut. Keep in a tightly sealed container in a cool area without refrigerating.

Nutrition Information

- Calories: 115 calories;
- Total Fat: 5.4
- Sodium: 51
- Total Carbohydrate: 16.7
- Cholesterol: 7
- Protein: 1.3

528. Swiss Hazelnut Taler

Serving: 156 | Prep: 1hours | Cook: 10mins | Ready in:

Ingredients

- 1 cup shelled hazelnuts
- 2 cups all-purpose flour
- 1 teaspoon baking powder
- 1 pinch salt
- 3/4 cup potato starch
- 1 cup confectioners' sugar
- 1/2 teaspoon vanilla extract
- 1 1/8 cups butter
- 1/4 cup unsweetened cocoa powder
- 1/4 cup white sugar

Direction

- Prepare the oven by preheating to 350°F (175°C). Place the hazelnuts on a baking sheet then spread in one layer. Place in the preheated oven and roast for about 10 minutes until scented and toasted. Put to a damp towel, then cover the nuts and lightly scrub to get rid most of the skins. Let nuts to fully cool. Once the hazelnuts are cool, place to a blender or food processor. Then cover and process until ground, even though not too nice since this will give a more appealing texture.
- Mix confectioner's sugar, potato starch, salt, baking powder, flour and ground hazelnuts in a large bowl. Mix in the butter and vanilla; massage all by hand until it turns the smooth and equally blended dough. Split into 8 portions and turn each one into a log about 1 inch in diameter. Combine white sugar and cocoa powder, place on plate. Roll each dough in the cocoa and sugar mixture. Use plastic wrap or waxed paper to wrap and transfer in the freezer for about 45 minutes until firm.
- Prepare the oven by preheating to 375°F (190°C). Cut the rolls of cookie dough into a thickness of 1/4-inch slices and put the cookies 1 inch apart on baking sheets.
- Place in the preheated oven and bake for about 10 minutes until the middles look dry and the bottoms are lightly toasted.

Nutrition Information

- Calories: 30 calories;
- Cholesterol: 4
- Protein: 0.3
- Total Fat: 1.9
- Sodium: 13
- Total Carbohydrate: 3.1

529. Tender Crisp Sugar Cookies

Serving: 60 | Prep: 25mins | Cook: 10mins | Ready in:

Ingredients

- 1 1/2 cups butter
- 1 1/2 cups shortening
- 1 1/2 cups white sugar
- 1 1/2 cups confectioners' sugar
- 4 1/2 teaspoons vanilla extract
- 3 eggs
- 6 3/4 cups all-purpose flour
- 1 1/2 teaspoons baking soda
- 1 1/2 teaspoons cream of tartar
- 1/2 teaspoon salt

Direction

- Cream the shortening, sugars and butter together until the texture of the mixture is fluffy and light. Add in the vanilla and eggs and whisk everything together. Sift all the dry ingredients and mix it into the creamed mixture until well-combined.
- Form the dough mixture into balls that are 1 inch in size. Coat each of the dough balls with decorator sprinkles, or colored or regular sugar. Coat a cookie sheet with a little bit of oil then put in the coated dough balls. Use the bottom of a water glass to flatten each dough ball a little.
- Put it in the preheated 375°F (190°C) oven and let it bake for 10-12 minutes. For bigger cookies, let it bake for 15 minutes in a preheated 350°F (175°C) oven.

Nutrition Information

- Calories: 173 calories;
- Cholesterol: 22
- Protein: 1.8
- Total Fat: 10.1
- Sodium: 87
- Total Carbohydrate: 18.8

530. The Best Rolled Sugar Cookies

Serving: 60 | Prep: 20mins | Cook: 8mins | Ready in:

Ingredients

- 1 1/2 cups butter, softened
- 2 cups white sugar
- 4 eggs
- 1 teaspoon vanilla extract
- 5 cups all-purpose flour
- 2 teaspoons baking powder
- 1 teaspoon salt

Direction

- Cream together sugar and butter in a large bowl until smooth. Then beat in vanilla and eggs. Mix in salt, baking powder, and flour. Cover the bowl and refrigerate the dough for at least 1 hour (or overnight).
- Preheat an oven to 200 degrees C (400 degrees F). On a floured surface, roll out the dough to about 1/4 to 1/2 inch thick. Use any cookie cutter to cut into shapes. Transfer the cookies into ungreased cookie sheets, placing one inch apart.
- Bake for about 6 to 8 minutes in prepped oven and then cool completely.

Nutrition Information

- Calories: 109 calories;
- Total Fat: 5
- Sodium: 93
- Total Carbohydrate: 14.7
- Cholesterol: 25
- Protein: 1.5

531. The Cookie Jar

Serving: 12 | Prep: 15mins | Cook: 10mins | Ready in:

Ingredients

- 1 1/4 cups all-purpose flour
- 1/2 cup brown sugar
- 4 ounces chocolate chips
- 4 ounces white chocolate chips
- 1/4 cup white sugar
- 1/2 teaspoon baking soda
- 1/2 teaspoon salt
- 1/2 cup butter, softened
- 1 egg

Direction

- Set oven to preheat at 190°C (375°F).
- Whisk together salt, baking soda, white sugar, white chocolate chips, chocolate chips, brown sugar and flour in a bowl. Mix the egg and butter into the mixture of flour until dough is just combined; on a baking sheet, drop spoonfuls of the dough.
- In preheated oven, bake until edges are light brown, for about 10 minutes.

Nutrition Information

- Calories: 270 calories;
- Cholesterol: 38
- Protein: 3
- Total Fat: 14.3
- Sodium: 223
- Total Carbohydrate: 34.3

532. Tina's Shortbread Chocolate Chip Cookies

Serving: 12 | Prep: | Cook: | Ready in:

Ingredients

- 1 3/4 cups all-purpose flour
- 1/2 teaspoon baking powder
- 1/4 teaspoon salt
- 1 cup unsalted butter
- 1/2 cup white sugar
- 3/4 cup semisweet chocolate chips
- 1/2 cup chopped walnuts

Direction

- Set oven to preheat at 150°C (300°F).
- Sift the salt, baking powder and flour together, put aside. Cream together the sugar and butter until fluffy in a medium bowl. Mix in the dry ingredients slowly, then stir in the chocolate chips and walnuts.
- Scoop or roll the dough into balls the size of walnuts. Put them 1 1/2 inches apart from each other onto unprepared cookie sheets. Slightly flatten out the cookies. Bake until lightly golden brown, for 15 to 20 minutes. Take out of the sheets to let cool on racks.

Nutrition Information

- Calories: 317 calories;
- Total Fat: 21.9
- Sodium: 72
- Total Carbohydrate: 29.6
- Cholesterol: 41
- Protein: 3.2

533. Tiny Tarts

Serving: 12 | Prep: 30mins | Cook: 30mins | Ready in:

Ingredients

- 1/2 cup butter, softened
- 1 (3 ounce) package cream cheese, softened
- 1 cup all-purpose flour
- 1 egg
- 3/4 cup packed brown sugar
- 1 tablespoon margarine, melted
- 1/2 cup chopped pecans

Direction

- Heat the oven to 165°C (325°F) beforehand.

- Beating cream cheese and softened butter or margarine till combined thoroughly. Stirring in flour.
- In twenty four of 1-3/4-inch mini muffin cup (ungreased), evenly pressing up the sides and into the bottom of each cup with a rounded teaspoon of pastry.
- For making The Filling: Beating the egg and mixing in chopped pecans, melted butter or margarine and brown sugar.
- Filling approximately a heaping teaspoon pecan filling into each muffin cup lined with pastry. Allow to bake for approximately 30 minutes at 165°C (325°F) or till filling is puffed and pastry is golden. Let it sit in the muffin cups to slightly cool down, then remove to a wire rack for completely cooling down.

Nutrition Information

- Calories: 228 calories;
- Total Carbohydrate: 22.3
- Cholesterol: 44
- Protein: 2.7
- Total Fat: 14.8
- Sodium: 96

534. Tyler's Raspberry Thumbprints With White Chocolate Glaze

Serving: 48 | Prep: 20mins | Cook: 15mins | Ready in:

Ingredients

- 1/2 cup butter, softened
- 1/2 cup sour cream
- 1 cup white sugar
- 2 tablespoons milk
- 2 eggs
- 2 2/3 cups all-purpose flour
- 2 cups rolled oats
- 1 teaspoon baking soda
- 5 ounces white chocolate, chopped
- 2/3 cup raspberry preserves
- 1 tablespoon butter
- 1/2 (1 ounce) square white chocolate
- 1 cup confectioners' sugar
- 2 tablespoons milk

Direction

- Preheat an oven to 175°C/350°F.
- Cream sugar and 1/2 cup butter till smooth in big bowl; blend eggs, 2 tbsp. milk and sour cream in. Mix baking soda, oats and flour; mix into creamed mixture slowly. Mix chopped white chocolate in finally; by rounded spoonfuls, drop on prepped cookie sheet. Press dent in middle of every cookie with finger or thumb; use 1/2 tsp. raspberry preserves to fill dent.
- In preheated oven, bake for 8-10 minutes. Cool cookies for 5 minutes on baking sheet; transfer to wire rack then completely cool.
- Glaze: Cook 1/2-oz. white chocolate and 1 tbsp. butter on high in microwave-safe bowl, mixing every 15-sec till smooth; beat milk and confectioners' sugar in slowly till icing has drizzling consistency. Drizzle on cooled cookies.

Nutrition Information

- Calories: 122 calories;
- Protein: 1.8
- Total Fat: 4.3
- Sodium: 50
- Total Carbohydrate: 19.3
- Cholesterol: 16

535. Vanilla Kifli

Serving: 15 | Prep: | Cook: | Ready in:

Ingredients

- 3/4 cup unsalted butter, softened
- 1/2 cup white sugar
- 1 teaspoon vanilla extract
- 2 egg yolks
- 2 cups all-purpose flour
- 1/2 cup vanilla sugar
- 2 (1 ounce) squares semisweet chocolate, chopped

Direction

- Combine the butter and sugar in a large mixing bowl and cream them together. Add in the vanilla and egg yolks, beating them in then add the flour little by little while continuing to beat.
- Shape the mixture into a ball and cover it then leave it to stand for 2 hours at room temperature.
- The oven should be preheated to 375° F (190° C).
- To shape them into crescents, take about 1 Tbsp. of dough and roll it in between your palms. Continue to roll them until you have formed a 3-inch length rope that is about 1/2 inch thick, then bend the rope for it to form a crescent. Do this again with the rest of the dough then place them on cookie sheets that are ungreased, with 1-inch space in between the doughs.
- Bake the crescent doughs for about 10 to 12 minutes until the cookies have turned white in color. Leave them to cool for 5 minutes on cookie sheets so they won't break. Carefully roll the cookies in vanilla sugar (you may find this in bulk food stores) while they are still warm. Do this again with the rest of the cookies then let the cookies cool completely
- Set a double boiler over low heat and melt the chocolate on it. Once the cookies have cooled, dip their tips in the melted chocolate and set them to dry on a waxed paper.

Nutrition Information

- Calories: 220 calories;
- Total Carbohydrate: 28.3
- Cholesterol: 52
- Protein: 2.4
- Total Fat: 11.2
- Sodium: 3

536. Vanille Kipferl I

Serving: 18 | Prep: 30mins | Cook: 8mins | Ready in:

Ingredients

- 2 cups all-purpose flour
- 1/3 cup white sugar
- 3/4 cup ground almonds
- 1 cup unsalted butter
- 1/4 cup vanilla sugar
- 1/4 cup confectioners' sugar

Direction

- Preheat the oven to 170 degrees C (325 degrees F). Use the parchment paper to line a baking sheet.
- Mix the ground almonds, a third cup of sugar and flour. Chop in the butter using pastry blender, and then quickly knead it into dough.
- Form the dough into log shapes and chop off half-an-in. pieces. Form each piece into a crescent and add onto the prepped baking sheet.
- Bake in the preheated oven for 8-10 minutes till the edges turn golden-brown. Allow it to cool down for 60 seconds and carefully roll in the vanilla sugar mixture.

Nutrition Information

- Calories: 207 calories;
- Sodium: 2
- Total Carbohydrate: 20
- Cholesterol: 27
- Protein: 2.8
- Total Fat: 13.4

537. Vanillekipferl

Serving: 60 | Prep: 30mins | Cook: 40mins | Ready in:

Ingredients

- Cookies:
- 2 1/3 cups all-purpose flour
- 1 1/4 cups almond flour
- 1/2 cup white sugar
- 2 tablespoons white sugar
- 1 cup butter, softened
- 2 tablespoons butter, softened
- 3 egg yolks
- Vanilla Sugar:
- 1/2 cup white sugar
- 1 tablespoon white sugar
- 3 whole vanilla beans

Direction

- In a bowl, mix half cup plus 2 tablespoons of white sugar, almond flour and all-purpose flour together. Put egg yolks and a cup plus 2 tablespoons of butter; in bowl, knead using your hands till a smooth dough create.
- Split dough into 4 portions and shape every portion into rectangle. With plastic wrap, wrap every rectangle. Refrigerate dough to chill for a minimum of an hour or overnight till firm.
- In food processor, put half cup plus a tablespoon of white sugar. Halve every vanilla bean lengthwise and using back of knife, scoop seeds from every half; put to sugar. Pulse till seeds are equally dispersed. Into shallow bowl, put the vanilla sugar.
- Preheat an oven to 175 °C or 350 °F. Line parchment paper on a big baking sheet.
- Slice a dough rectangle making 6 even portions, maintaining the rest of the dough refrigerated. On a slightly floured area, roll every portion smoothly into a half-inch-thick cylinder. Slice every log crosswise into 2 inches portions and slowly pinch or roll every portion ends into points. Bend every portion into crescent and put to prepped baking sheet, place approximately an-inch away.
- In the prepped oven, bake for 10 to 12 minutes till bases are slightly golden yet surfaces remain light in color. Take out of oven and allow to sit for 2 minutes.
- In the vanilla sugar, turn warm cookies, brushing extra sugar off. Turn cookies out onto wire rack to cool fully. Baking in batches, redo with the rest of the dough.

Nutrition Information

- Calories: 84 calories;
- Total Fat: 5
- Sodium: 25
- Total Carbohydrate: 8.9
- Cholesterol: 19
- Protein: 1.2

538. Vegan Chocolate Spelt Biscotti

Serving: 24 | Prep: 30mins | Cook: 1hours5mins | Ready in:

Ingredients

- 1/4 cup chia seeds
- 1 cup hot water
- 1/2 cup raw sugar
- 1/2 cup olive oil
- 1/3 cup coffee-flavored liqueur (such as Kahlua®)
- 1/4 cup water
- 1/4 cup agave nectar
- 1 tablespoon lecithin
- 1 tablespoon almond extract
- 1 teaspoon vanilla extract
- 1/2 teaspoon salt
- 2 cups spelt flour
- 1 1/2 cups cocoa powder
- 2 teaspoons baking powder
- 1 cup chocolate chips

- 1/2 cup pecans
- 1/2 cup cocoa nibs (optional)

Direction

- Set the oven to 300°F (150°C) and start preheating. Line parchment paper on 2 baking sheets.
- Combine chia seeds and hot water in a blender. Allow chia seeds to sit in hot water for 5 minutes until well soaked. Add salt, vanilla extract, almond extract, lecithin, agave nectar, water, coffee-flavored liqueur, olive oil and sugar into chia seeds; blend on high speed until mixture is smooth.
- In a bowl, combine baking powder, cocoa powder and flour. Slowly stir in chia seed mixture to the flour mixture until dough is just mixed; fold in cocoa nibs, pecans and chocolate chips.
- Separate dough in 2 halves and spoon each half on to prepared baking sheets, remember to shape dough into 2 2x12 inch logs with wet hands.
- Bake in preheated oven for about 40 minutes until light brown in color. Remove baking sheet from the oven and allow to cool for 10 minutes.
- Lower oven temperature to 275°F (135°C)
- Slice logs into 3/4 inch thick slices diagonally. Arrange slices on their sides on parchment-paper-lined baking sheets.
- Bake in prepared oven for about 25 minutes until dry.

Nutrition Information

- Calories: 208 calories;
- Cholesterol: 0
- Protein: 3.2
- Total Fat: 11.7
- Sodium: 98
- Total Carbohydrate: 25.1

539. Viennese Crescent Holiday Cookies

Serving: 48 | Prep: 15mins | Cook: 10mins | Ready in:

Ingredients

- 2 cups all-purpose flour
- 1 cup butter
- 1 cup hazelnuts, ground
- 1/2 cup sifted confectioners' sugar
- 1/8 teaspoon salt
- 1 teaspoon vanilla extract
- 2 cups sifted confectioners' sugar
- 1 vanilla bean

Direction

- Start preheating the oven to 375°F (190°C).
- Combine vanilla, salt, half cup of the confectioners' sugar, nuts, butter and flour in the large mixing bowl. Mix until they are thoroughly blended, using your hand. Form the dough into ball. Cover and chill in the refrigerator for 60 mins.
- In the meantime, put sugar into a small container or bowl. Split the vanilla bean lengthwise with the sharp chef's knife. Scrape out the seeds, then mix into sugar. Divide the pod into 2-inch pieces. Mix into the sugar.
- Remove the dough from refrigerator. Shape into 1-inch balls. Form each ball into the 3-inches long small roll. Put the rolls 2-inches apart on an unoiled cookie sheet, then bend each one to create the crescent shape.
- Bake in prepared oven for 10-12 mins or until they are set but not brown.
- Allow to stand one minute. Remove it from the cookie sheets. Arrange the hot cookies on the large sheet of aluminum foil. Top with the prepared sugar mixture. Gently flip to coat both sides. Let cool completely. Keep in the airtight container at the room temperature. Use more vanilla flavored sugar to coat, just before enjoying.

Nutrition Information

- Calories: 95 calories;
- Total Fat: 5.3
- Sodium: 33
- Total Carbohydrate: 11.2
- Cholesterol: 10
- Protein: 0.9

---

540. Wainachsrollen

Serving: 24 | Prep: 20mins | Cook: 8mins | Ready in:

Ingredients

- 1 cup butter, melted
- 1 cup lard, melted
- 1 cup white sugar
- 1 cup packed brown sugar
- 3 egg
- 4 1/2 cups all-purpose flour
- 2 teaspoons baking soda
- 1 teaspoon salt
- 1 teaspoon ground cinnamon
- 8 ounces chopped almonds

Direction

- Mix eggs, brown sugar, white sugar, melted lard and melted butter together in a large bowl. Stir till well-blended. Mix in almonds, cinnamon, salt, baking soda and flour. Roll the dough into two logs around 2 1/2 in. in diameter; use waxed paper to wrap tightly; place in the refrigerator for 8 hours or overnight.
- Set the oven at 350°F (175°C) and start preheating. Take the dough logs away from the fridge; allow to rest for around 5 minutes at room temperature.
- Cut the dough into around 1/4-in.-thick slices. (The thinner you cut them, the crispier the cookies will become.) Bake for 8-10 minutes in the preheated oven, or till it starting to brown on the edges. Let cool on wire racks.

Nutrition Information

- Calories: 360 calories;
- Sodium: 268
- Total Carbohydrate: 37.2
- Cholesterol: 52
- Protein: 5.3
- Total Fat: 21.8

---

541. Walnut Cheesecake Cookies

Serving: 12 | Prep: | Cook: | Ready in:

Ingredients

- 1/2 cup butter, softened
- 1 (3 ounce) package cream cheese
- 1 egg, separated
- 1 teaspoon vanilla extract
- 1 teaspoon lemon zest
- 1/4 teaspoon salt
- 1 cup sifted confectioners' sugar
- 1 cup sifted all-purpose flour
- 1 cup finely chopped walnuts
- 1/4 cup apricot preserves

Direction

- Cream salt, lemon peel, vanilla, egg yolk, cream cheese and butter until fluffy. Combine in confectioners' sugar gradually; then combine in flour to make stiff dough.
- Chill dough for 2 hours.
- Set oven to 325°F (165°C) and start preheating.
- Form dough into 30 - one inch balls.
- Whisk egg white until foamy. Coat balls with egg white; roll in chopped nuts. Place on clean and dry cookie sheet, 2 inches apart, and make a depression in each with your thumb
- Bake until cookies start browning on the bottoms for 12-15 minutes. Take out of the wire rack carefully and fill each depression

with half teaspoon of apricot preserves or your favorite jam while hot.

Nutrition Information

- Calories: 260 calories;
- Total Fat: 17
- Sodium: 130
- Total Carbohydrate: 24.6
- Cholesterol: 44
- Protein: 3.7

542. Walnut Tassies

Serving: 36 | Prep: 20mins | Cook: 25mins | Ready in:

Ingredients

- 1/2 pound sweet butter
- 6 ounces cream cheese, softened
- 2 cups all-purpose flour
- Filling:
- 1 1/2 cups dark brown sugar
- 1 cup chopped walnuts
- 3 tablespoons butter, melted
- 3 eggs
- 2 teaspoons vanilla extract

Direction

- Start preheating the oven to 350°F (175°C).
- With an electric mixer, beat cream cheese and sweet butter together in a bowl until creamy and smooth. Slowly stir flour into the butter until a dough is formed. Roll dough into 1-inch balls and transfer into 3/4 -inch muffin cups. Press the dough into the bottom and sides of each muffin cup.
- Combine vanilla extract, eggs, melted butter, walnuts, and brown sugar in a different bowl. Scoop 1 teaspoon walnut filling into the dough cups.
- Bake in the prepared oven for about 25 minutes until edges of cookies seem lightly browned and the filling is heated through.

Nutrition Information

- Calories: 159 calories;
- Total Fat: 10.4
- Sodium: 66
- Total Carbohydrate: 14.9
- Cholesterol: 37
- Protein: 2.2

543. White Chocolate Hazelnut Spread Bars

Serving: 16 | Prep: 20mins | Cook: 26mins | Ready in:

Ingredients

- cooking spray
- 1 (18.25 ounce) package white cake mix
- 1/2 cup 2% milk
- 1/2 cup butter, melted
- 3 (1 ounce) packages instant vanilla pudding mix
- 1 1/2 cups sliced almonds, divided
- 1 cup white chocolate chips
- 6 ounces white baking chocolate (such as Baker's®), chopped and divided
- 3/4 cup chopped hazelnuts, divided
- 1 1/2 cups chocolate hazelnut spread

Direction

- Set the oven to 350°F or 175°C for preheating. Use an aluminum foil to line a 9x13-inch baking sheet and coat the foil with cooking spray.
- In a large bowl, mix the melted butter, white cake mix, vanilla pudding mix, and milk. Use the electric mixer and beat the mixture until thick and well-blended. Divide the dough into halves.

- Spread 2 large sheets of waxed paper and place 1 piece of dough in between. Roll the dough into a 9x13-inch rectangle. Remove the waxed paper and transfer the dough into the baking pan, pressing it into the pan's bottom.
- Transfer the pan inside the preheated oven and allow it to bake for 10 minutes until the dough is pale golden. Shower half of the sliced almonds, hazelnuts, white baking chocolate, and white chocolate chips and press it on top of the soft dough.
- Heat the chocolate hazelnut spread in a small microwave-safe bowl on medium-high heat. Heat and stir for 1 minute until melted. Spread all over the dough.
- Prepare 2 large sheets of waxed paper and place the second piece of the dough in between. Roll the dough into a 9x13-inch rectangle. Remove the waxed paper and put it on top of the dough with chocolate hazelnut spread. Top it with the remaining sliced of almonds, hazelnuts, white baking chocolates, and white chocolate chips. Use a spatula to push into the dough.
- Place it inside the preheated oven and bake for 15 minutes until the dough is golden brown. Allow it to cool for 60 minutes. Place it in a refrigerator and chill for 3-4 hours until firm. Cut it into bars.

Nutrition Information

- Calories: 543 calories;
- Total Fat: 31.8
- Sodium: 376
- Total Carbohydrate: 59.7
- Cholesterol: 20
- Protein: 7.5

544. White Chocolate Holiday Spritz Cookies

Serving: 50 | Prep: 20mins | Cook: 6mins | Ready in:

Ingredients

- 1 cup unsalted butter, softened
- 1 egg
- 2 teaspoons vanilla extract
- 3/4 cup confectioners' sugar
- 2 1/4 cups all-purpose flour
- salt
- 1 (12 ounce) package white chocolate chips
- 3/4 cup multicolored candy sprinkles (jimmies), as desired

Direction

- Preheat an oven to 190°C/375°F; lightly grease/line parchment paper on 2 cookie sheets.
- Cream butter till fluffy and light colored in mixing bowl; beat vanilla and egg in till smooth. If desired, add food coloring. Mix salt, flour and confectioners' sugar in slowly to create smooth dough.
- Put dough in cookie press cylinder with 1-in. sawtooth ribbon disk then press dough to long strips on prepped cookie sheets. Score strips every 2-in. using paring knife dipped in flour.
- In preheated oven, bake for 6 minutes till edges are slightly golden. Take out of oven; slightly cool. While still warm, cut along score lines. Put on wire racks; completely cool.
- Line parchment paper on baking sheet. Melt white chocolate chips in top of double boiler on medium heat/in microwave. If desired, add food coloring. Spread white chocolate icing on bottom of a cookie; put bottom of 2nd cookie in icing to make a sandwich. Put cookie sandwich on prepped baking sheet. Repeat to make leftover cookies; refrigerate for 10 minutes on baking sheet to set icing. Remove; dip cookie ends in white chocolate then in candy sprinkles. Put cookies on wax paper till white chocolate sets.

Nutrition Information

- Calories: 114 calories;
- Protein: 1.3

- Total Fat: 6.8
- Sodium: 9
- Total Carbohydrate: 12.2
- Cholesterol: 14

545. White Chocolate Thumbprint Cookies

Serving: 72 | Prep: 20mins | Cook: 20mins | Ready in:

Ingredients

- 1 pound butter, softened
- 1 1/2 cups white sugar
- 1 teaspoon vanilla extract
- 4 cups all-purpose flour
- 2 teaspoons baking powder
- 1 cup chopped walnuts (optional)
- 1 (8 ounce) jar seedless raspberry jam
- 3 (1.55 ounce) bars white chocolate, chopped
- 1 tablespoon vegetable shortening

Direction

- Beat vanilla extract, sugar and butter till smooth and creamy in bowl. Mix baking powder and flour in another bowl; beat flour mixture slowly into creamed butter mixture till dough is smooth then fold walnuts into dough. Refrigerate the dough for an hour.
- Preheat an oven to 165°C/325°F.
- Roll out cookie dough to 6 dozen small balls; put on baking sheet, 2-in. apart. Use your thumb to press middle of each ball to make small well. Use jam to fill depressions.
- In preheated oven, bake for 18 minutes till cookies are light golden brown.
- Melt shortening and white chocolate in top of double boiler above simmering water, frequently mixing and scraping sides down with rubber spatula to prevent scorching then drizzle melted white chocolate mixture on cookies.
- Cool cookies for 5 minutes on sheet. Transfer to wire rack; completely cool.

Nutrition Information

- Calories: 117 calories;
- Cholesterol: 14
- Protein: 1.1
- Total Fat: 7
- Sodium: 52
- Total Carbohydrate: 12.8

546. White Chocolate And Cranberry Cookies

Serving: 24 | Prep: 15mins | Cook: 10mins | Ready in:

Ingredients

- 1/2 cup butter, softened
- 1/2 cup packed brown sugar
- 1/2 cup white sugar
- 1 egg
- 1 tablespoon brandy
- 1 1/2 cups all-purpose flour
- 1/2 teaspoon baking soda
- 3/4 cup white chocolate chips
- 1 cup dried cranberries

Direction

- Set the oven to 190°C or 375°F to preheat. Grease cookie sheets.
- Cream white sugar, brown sugar and butter together in a big bowl until the mixture is smooth. Beat in brandy and egg. Mix together baking soda and flour, then stir into sugar mixture. Blend in cranberries and chocolate chips. Drop on prepped cookie sheets with heaping spoonfuls of batter.
- In the preheated oven, bake about 8-10 minutes. To get the best results, remove cookies while they are still doughy. Let cookies cool for about 1 minute on cookie sheets prior to moving them to wire racks to cool thoroughly.

Nutrition Information

- Calories: 147 calories;
- Sodium: 64
- Total Carbohydrate: 21.9
- Cholesterol: 19
- Protein: 1.5
- Total Fat: 6.1

547. Whole Wheat Ginger Snaps

Serving: 60 | Prep: 10mins | Cook: 15mins | Ready in:

Ingredients

- 1 cup butter or margarine
- 1 1/2 cups white sugar
- 2 eggs, beaten
- 1 cup molasses
- 4 cups whole wheat flour
- 1 tablespoon baking soda
- 2 teaspoons baking powder
- 1 tablespoon ground ginger
- 1 1/2 teaspoons ground nutmeg
- 1 1/2 teaspoons ground cinnamon
- 1 1/2 teaspoons ground cloves
- 1 1/2 teaspoons ground allspice
- 1 cup white sugar for decoration

Direction

- Set an oven to 175°C (350°F) and started preheating. Coat the cookie sheets with cooking spray.
- Cream 1 1/2 cups of sugar and butter together in a large bowl until they are smooth. Combine in eggs, then molasses. Mix allspice, cloves, cinnamon, nutmeg, ginger, baking powder, baking soda and the whole wheat flour, and if you desire lots of spice, heap the measures. Stir the dry ingredients into the molasses mixture until just combined.
- Roll the dough to form into small balls, then dip the top of each ball in the rest of white sugar. On the cookie sheets, arrange the cookies roughly 2 inches apart.
- In the prepared oven, bake until the tops crack, 10-15 minutes. Bake shorter time for chewy cookies and longer for crispy cookies. Transfer onto wire racks and cool.

Nutrition Information

- Calories: 106 calories;
- Sodium: 97
- Total Carbohydrate: 18.5
- Cholesterol: 14
- Protein: 1.4
- Total Fat: 3.4

548. Working Mom's Hamentashen

Serving: 24 | Prep: 10mins | Cook: 15mins | Ready in:

Ingredients

- 1 (18.25 ounce) package moist yellow cake mix
- 1 cup all-purpose flour
- 2 eggs
- 2 tablespoons water
- 1 cup fruit preserves, any flavor

Direction

- Heat oven to 190 degrees c/375 degrees F. Grease the cookie sheets.
- Mix flour and cake mix in a big bowl. Mix in water and eggs to make a stiff dough. Roll out dough on a lightly floured surface to 1/8-in. thick. Cut to 3-in. round circles. Put on prepped cookie sheets, 2-in. apart. Put a tsp. of filling in the middle of every cookie. Pinch sides to make 3 corners. Moisten with water if needed.

- Bake in the preheated oven for 6-8 minutes until light brown. Cool cookies for 1 minute on cookie sheet. Transfer to wire racks. Completely cool.

Nutrition Information

- Calories: 155 calories;
- Total Fat: 3
- Sodium: 152
- Total Carbohydrate: 29.9
- Cholesterol: 16
- Protein: 2.1

549. Yum Yum Squares

Serving: 25 | Prep: | Cook: | Ready in:

Ingredients

- 1 1/2 cups all-purpose flour
- 2 tablespoons brown sugar
- 1/2 cup white sugar
- 1/2 cup butter
- 1 1/2 cups packed brown sugar
- 2 eggs, beaten
- 1 cup flaked coconut
- 1/2 cup chopped walnuts

Direction

- Turn on the oven to 375°F (195°C) to preheat. Prepare a 9x9 inch baking pan and grease.
- Combine white sugar, brown sugar and flour in a medium bowl. Cut in 1/2 cup of butter until the mixture becomes coarse crumbs. Transfer onto the prepared pan and pat into the bottom.
- Mix together brown sugar and eggs in the same bowl; mix in walnuts and coconut until gooey. Transfer to crust layer and spread out evenly. Put into the oven to bake for 25-35 minutes until all are golden brown.

Nutrition Information

- Calories: 164 calories;
- Total Fat: 6.5
- Sodium: 44
- Total Carbohydrate: 25.6
- Cholesterol: 25
- Protein: 1.8

Chapter 6: Awesome Holiday Cookie Recipes

***

550. After Dinner Mint Delights

Serving: 4-1/2 dozen. | Prep: 35mins | Cook: 10mins | Ready in:

Ingredients

- 1 cup butter, softened
- 1/2 cup confectioners' sugar
- 1-1/2 teaspoons peppermint extract
- 1/2 teaspoon vanilla extract
- 1/4 teaspoon salt
- Green food coloring, optional
- 2-1/4 cups all-purpose flour
- GLAZE:
- 2 cups (12 ounces) semisweet chocolate chips
- 2 tablespoons shortening
- Green pearl dust, optional

Direction

- Cream confectioners' sugar and butter in one big bowl till fluffy and light. Whip salt, several

drops of food coloring if wished and extracts. Slowly put in flour and combine thoroughly.
- Form to balls, an-inch in size; put on not greased baking sheets, 2-inch away. Pat with glass dipped in sugar onto quarter-inch thickness. Bake till set, about 10 to 12 minutes at 375°. Transfer onto wire racks to fully cool.
- Liquify shortening and chips in metal bowl or double boiler above hot water; mix till smooth. Dunk the cookies into chocolate glaze, letting excess drip off. Put to set on a waxed paper, chill if need to be. Brush pearl dust on tops. Keep refrigerated in airtight container.

Nutrition Information

- Calories: 90 calories
- Cholesterol: 9mg cholesterol
- Protein: 1g protein.
- Total Fat: 6g fat (3g saturated fat)
- Sodium: 39mg sodium
- Fiber: 1g fiber)
- Total Carbohydrate: 9g carbohydrate (5g sugars

551. Almond Chocolate Cookies

Serving: 6-1/2 dozen. | Prep: 15mins | Cook: 10mins | Ready in:

Ingredients

- 1 cup butter, softened
- 3/4 cup packed brown sugar
- 2/3 cup sugar
- 2 eggs
- 2 to 3 teaspoons almond extract
- 1 teaspoon vanilla extract
- 2-1/4 cups all-purpose flour
- 1/2 cup baking cocoa
- 1 teaspoon baking soda

Direction

- Cream sugars and butter together in a big bowl until fluffy and light. Add eggs, 1 each time, whisk thoroughly between additions. Whisk in extracts. Mix together baking soda, cocoa, and flour; slowly add to the creamed mixture and stir thoroughly.
- Drop on non-oiled cookie sheets by rounded teaspoonfuls, 2 inches apart. Bake at 375° until the edges firm up, 7-9 minutes. Transfer to wire racks to cool.

Nutrition Information

- Calories: 105 calories
- Protein: 1g protein.
- Total Fat: 5g fat (3g saturated fat)
- Sodium: 85mg sodium
- Fiber: 0 fiber)
- Total Carbohydrate: 14g carbohydrate (8g sugars
- Cholesterol: 23mg cholesterol

552. Almond Crescent Cookies

Serving: 24 | Prep: 45mins | Cook: 15mins | Ready in:

Ingredients

- 1/2 cup salted butter, at room temperature
- 1/3 cup confectioners' sugar, plus extra for dusting
- 1 teaspoon vanilla extract
- 1 teaspoon almond extract
- 1/8 teaspoon salt
- 3/4 cup all-purpose flour, sifted
- 2 tablespoons all-purpose flour, sifted
- 1/2 cup almonds, finely chopped

Direction

- Preheat the oven to 325°F (165°C).
- In a bowl, beat confectioners' sugar and butter with an electric mixer until creamy and smooth. Put in salt, almond extract and vanilla

extract; briefly mix to blend. Slowly mix 3/4 cup plus 2 tablespoons of flour into the creamed butter; put in almonds, and stir until the dough is just blended.
- Form the dough into tiny crescents; arrange 2 inches apart on an ungreased baking sheet.
- Bake cookies in the preheated oven in about 15 minutes, until the edges become golden. Cool down for 5 minutes on baking sheet, then add onto a wire rack and cool completely.
- Once cooled, roll cookies into sifted confectioners' sugar.

Nutrition Information

- Calories: 70 calories;
- Protein: 0.9
- Total Fat: 4.9
- Sodium: 40
- Total Carbohydrate: 5.6
- Cholesterol: 10

553. Almond Macaroons

Serving: Makes about 3 dozen | Prep: | Cook: | Ready in:

Ingredients

- 3 large egg whites
- Zest of 1 large lemon
- 1 cup sugar
- 1 1/2 cups blanched finely ground almonds
- Cooking spray, butter, or margarine for greasing pans

Direction

- Preparation: Heat oven beforehand to 275°F. Beat the egg whites in an electric mixer till they can hold soft peaks. Add the lemon zest into the egg whites. Add in the sugar gradually and beat till the whites are very stiff and shiny but not dry. Fold the ground almonds into the mixture.
- Use aluminum foil to cover 2 baking sheets then grease or spray them. With 2 teaspoons, use 1 to take a heaping teaspoon of batter and use the other one to scoop it off onto the baking sheet. Put the cookies about 1 to 1 1/2 inches apart. Repeat the step with the remaining dough.
- Bake till the cookies are slightly brown and firm, for about 20 to 30 minutes. Let them cool down for 5 to 10 minutes then take the cookies out of the baking sheets, put onto a rack. Once cooled, keep in an air-tight container for storage.

Nutrition Information

- Calories: 269
- Protein: 7 g(14%)
- Total Fat: 14 g(22%)
- Saturated Fat: 1 g(5%)
- Sodium: 22 mg(1%)
- Fiber: 4 g(14%)
- Total Carbohydrate: 32 g(11%)

554. Almond Meringue Cookies

Serving: 36 | Prep: 15mins | Cook: 15mins | Ready in:

Ingredients

- 11 ounces ground almonds
- 3 egg whites
- 1 cup confectioners' sugar
- 1 teaspoon grated lemon zest
- 3/4 teaspoon ground cinnamon

Direction

- Set the oven at 325°F (165°C) and start preheating. Lightly coat cookie sheets with grease and flour.
- Whip egg whites in a large bowl till it forms soft peaks. Slowly sprinkle in sugar; continue

- to whip till the egg whites hold a stiff peak, around 5 minutes. Set 1/2 cup of the egg whites aside. Put cinnamon and lemon zest into the rest of the meringue; fold in almonds till everything is blended evenly.
- Drop mounds onto the prepared sheets, by spoonfuls. Place a smaller dollop of the reserved meringue on top of each cookie.
- Bake in the preheated oven for 15 minutes, till golden brown. Take the cookies away from the baking sheets; place on wire racks to cool.

Nutrition Information

- Calories: 66 calories;
- Total Fat: 4.5
- Sodium: 5
- Total Carbohydrate: 5.5
- Cholesterol: 0
- Protein: 2

555. Almond Sugar Cookies

Serving: about 4-1/2 dozen. | Prep: 20mins | Cook: 10mins | Ready in:

Ingredients

- 1 cup butter, softened
- 3/4 cup sugar
- 1 teaspoon almond extract
- 2 cups all-purpose flour
- 1/2 teaspoon baking powder
- 1/4 teaspoon salt
- Additional sugar
- GLAZE:
- 1 cup confectioners' sugar
- 1-1/2 teaspoons almond extract
- 2 to 3 teaspoons water
- Green food coloring, optional
- Sliced almonds, toasted

Direction

- Mix together sugar and butter in a large bowl until fluffy and light. Whip in almond extract. Mix together salt, baking powder and flour; put into creamed mixture gradually and stir thoroughly. Form into balls of 1-inch.
- On ungreased baking sheets, arrange dough balls 2 inches apart from each other. Use cooking spray to coat bottom of one glass; dip in sugar. Use the prepped glass to flatten cookies; if necessary, dip the glass again into the sugar.
- Put into the oven to bake at 400 degrees until the edges turn light brown or for 7-9 minutes. Allow to cool for 1 minute; then transfer to wire racks.
- Beat together almond extract, confectioners' sugar and sufficient water in a small bowl to reach glaze consistency. Use food coloring to tint to your liking; drizzle onto cookies. Use almonds to sprinkle over.

Nutrition Information

- Calories:
- Cholesterol:
- Protein:
- Total Fat:
- Sodium:
- Fiber:
- Total Carbohydrate:

556. Ambrosia Bites

Serving: 6 dozen. | Prep: 30mins | Cook: 10mins | Ready in:

Ingredients

- 1 cup butter, softened
- 1 cup sugar
- 1 cup packed brown sugar
- 2 large eggs
- 1 tablespoon grated lemon zest
- 1 tablespoon grated orange zest

- 1 teaspoon vanilla extract
- 2 cups all-purpose flour
- 1-1/2 cups quick-cooking oats
- 1-1/2 teaspoons baking soda
- 1 teaspoon salt
- 1 teaspoon baking powder
- 1 cup chopped walnuts
- 1 cup raisins
- 1 cup chopped dates
- 1 cup sweetened shredded coconut

Direction

- Cream sugars and butter together in a large bowl until fluffy and light. Beat in vanilla, zest and eggs. Mix baking powder, salt, baking soda, oats and flour together; slowly add into creamed mixture until well incorporated. Stir in the rest of the ingredients.
- Drop heaping tablespoonfuls of batter onto baking sheets that were ungreased, keeping a 3-inch distance away from each other. Bake at 375 degrees until golden brown or 8 to 10 minutes. Bring over to wire racks to cool.

Nutrition Information

- Calories:
- Protein:
- Total Fat:
- Sodium:
- Fiber:
- Total Carbohydrate:
- Cholesterol:

557. Anise Butter Cookies

Serving: 5 dozen. | Prep: 30mins | Cook: 40mins | Ready in:

Ingredients

- 2 cups butter, softened
- 1-3/4 cups sugar, divided
- 2 eggs
- 1/4 cup thawed orange juice concentrate
- 4 teaspoons aniseed, crushed
- 6 cups all-purpose flour
- 3 teaspoons baking powder
- 1/2 teaspoon salt
- 1 teaspoon ground cinnamon

Direction

- Set oven to preheat at 350°. Cream together butter and 1-1/2 cups sugar in a large bowl till fluffy and light. Add eggs into the mix, one by one, beat well after each time you add eggs. Beat orange juice concentrate and aniseed into the mix. Mix together the salt, baking powder and flour; add them into the creamed mixture slowly and combine thoroughly.
- Roll out the dough to 1/4-in thick on a lightly floured surface. Use a floured 2-1/2-in. round cookie cutter to cut the dough. Put them 1 in. apart onto ungreased baking sheets.
- Mix together remaining sugar and cinnamon; sprinkle them atop the cookies. Bake until golden brown for about 12-15 minutes. Take out to wire racks.

Nutrition Information

- Calories: 253 calories
- Protein: 3g protein.
- Total Fat: 13g fat (8g saturated fat)
- Sodium: 208mg sodium
- Fiber: 1g fiber)
- Total Carbohydrate: 32g carbohydrate (13g sugars
- Cholesterol: 47mg cholesterol

558. Anise Cutout Cookies

Serving: about 5 dozen. | Prep: 20mins | Cook: 15mins | Ready in:

Ingredients

- 2 cups shortening
- 1 cup sugar
- 2 large eggs
- 2 teaspoons aniseed
- 6 cups all-purpose flour
- 1 tablespoon baking powder
- 1 teaspoon salt
- 1/4 cup apple juice
- 1/2 cup sugar
- 1 teaspoon ground cinnamon

Direction

- Beat shortening with sugar in a bowl until fluffy; put in aniseed and eggs. Mix salt, baking powder and flour; put into the whipped mixture. Pour in apple juice and stir well.
- Knead on a floured surface for about 4-5 minutes until well combined. Shape dough to 1/2-in. thickness; slice into 2-in. shapes. Put on greased baking trays.
- Bake for 12-16 minutes at 375° or until lightly browned. Mix cinnamon and sugar; toss cookies in the mixture while still warm. Let cool on wire racks.

Nutrition Information

- Calories: 254 calories
- Total Carbohydrate: 29g carbohydrate (10g sugars
- Cholesterol: 14mg cholesterol
- Protein: 3g protein.
- Total Fat: 13g fat (3g saturated fat)
- Sodium: 124mg sodium
- Fiber: 1g fiber)

559. Anise Spritz Cookies

Serving: 8 dozen. | Prep: 15mins | Cook: 10mins | Ready in:

Ingredients

- 1 cup butter, softened
- 2/3 cup sugar
- 1 egg
- 1 teaspoon anise extract
- 1/2 teaspoon vanilla extract
- 2-1/4 cups all-purpose flour
- 1 teaspoon baking powder
- Red and green sprinkles

Direction

- Beat sugar and butter in a big bowl until fluffy and light. Mix in extracts and egg. Mix together baking powder and flour; pour into the beaten mixture, a little at a time.
- Press cookie dough with a cookie press inserted with disk that you like, placing an inch apart onto baking sheets without grease. Use sprinkles for decorations. Bake in a 375-degree oven until the cookies set, or about 7 to 8 minutes. Transfer to wire racks.

Nutrition Information

- Calories: 34 calories
- Total Carbohydrate: 4g carbohydrate (1g sugars
- Cholesterol: 7mg cholesterol
- Protein: 0 protein.
- Total Fat: 2g fat (1g saturated fat)
- Sodium: 18mg sodium
- Fiber: 0 fiber)

560. Apple Butter Cookies

Serving: about 2-1/2 dozen. | Prep: 20mins | Cook: 15mins | Ready in:

Ingredients

- 1/4 cup butter, softened
- 1 cup packed brown sugar
- 1 large egg
- 1/2 cup quick-cooking oats

- 1/2 cup apple butter
- 1 cup all-purpose flour
- 1/2 teaspoon baking soda
- 1/2 teaspoon baking powder
- 1/2 teaspoon salt
- 2 tablespoons whole milk
- 1/2 cup chopped nuts
- 1/2 cup raisins

Direction

- In the small-sized bowl, cream the sugar and butter. Beat in the apple butter, oats and egg. Mix the dry ingredients; slowly put into the creamed mixture with milk; beat till blended. Stir in the raisins and nuts. Cover and refrigerate till easy to handle.
- Drop by teaspoonfuls to the lightly greased baking sheets. Bake at 350 degrees till set or for 15 minutes. Take out onto the wire racks.

Nutrition Information

- Calories: 185 calories
- Total Carbohydrate: 31g carbohydrate (21g sugars
- Cholesterol: 23mg cholesterol
- Protein: 3g protein.
- Total Fat: 6g fat (2g saturated fat)
- Sodium: 177mg sodium
- Fiber: 1g fiber)

561. Apple Crisp Crescents

Serving: 3 dozen. | Prep: 30mins | Cook: 20mins | Ready in:

Ingredients

- 2 cups all-purpose flour
- 1/8 teaspoon salt
- 1 cup cold butter
- 1 large egg, separated
- 2/3 cup sour cream
- 1/2 teaspoon vanilla extract
- 1 cup finely chopped peeled tart apple
- 1/3 cup finely chopped walnuts
- 1/4 cup raisins, chopped
- 2/3 cup sugar
- 1 teaspoon ground cinnamon

Direction

- Combine salt and flour in a large bowl; add in a slice of butter until mixture forms a coarse crumbs. Beat together in a small bowl the vanilla, sour cream and egg yolk; add into the crumb mixture and combine well. Place inside the refrigerator, covered, for 4 hours or overnight. Split the dough into thirds. Spin each portion into a 10-inch circle on a surface that is lightly floured. Blend the cinnamon, sugar, raisins, walnuts and apple; drizzle 1/2 cup over each circle. Slice into 12 wedges. Turn each wedge from the wide end and put point side down 1 inch away on a baking sheet that is greased. To form crescents, curl ends. Beat egg until foamy; then sweep on top of crescents. Place inside the oven for 18- 20 minutes at 350 degrees F or until lightly brown in color. Let it cool on wire racks. Use an airtight container to store.

Nutrition Information

- Calories: 107 calories
- Fiber: 0 fiber)
- Total Carbohydrate: 11g carbohydrate (5g sugars
- Cholesterol: 22mg cholesterol
- Protein: 1g protein.
- Total Fat: 7g fat (4g saturated fat)
- Sodium: 48mg sodium

562. Apricot Tea Cookies

Serving: About 4 dozen. | Prep: 35mins | Cook: 20mins | Ready in:

Ingredients

- 1-1/4 cups all-purpose flour
- 6 tablespoons sugar
- 1/8 teaspoon salt
- 4 ounces cream cheese
- 1/2 cup cold butter, cubed
- 1 tablespoon sour cream
- FILLING:
- 1-1/4 cups chopped dried apricots
- 1/2 cup sugar
- 5 tablespoons orange juice
- GLAZE:
- 1 cup confectioners' sugar
- 4 teaspoons water

Direction

- Mix salt, sugar and flour in a large bowl. Cut in butter and cream cheese until mixture looks like coarse crumbs. Add sour cream; use a fork to toss until dough forms a ball. Chill in the fridge with a cover for at least an hour.
- In the meantime, mix the filling ingredients in a large saucepan; boil the mixture. Lower the heat; simmer with a cover for 10 minutes. Simmer without a cover while stirring occasionally until most liquid is absorbed or for 7-9 more minutes. Cool.
- Separate dough in 1/2. Roll each part out on a well-floured surface into a 10-in. square; cut each into 2-in. squares. Fill about half teaspoon of filling into each square's center. Take 2 opposite corners of square to the center; firmly pinch to seal.
- Arrange on greased baking sheets. Bake for 18-20 minutes at 325° or until edges turn light brown. Transfer to wire racks to cool. Mix glaze ingredients; drizzle over cooled cookies.

Nutrition Information

- Calories: 141 calories
- Protein: 1g protein.
- Total Fat: 6g fat (3g saturated fat)
- Sodium: 70mg sodium
- Fiber: 1g fiber)
- Total Carbohydrate: 22g carbohydrate (15g sugars
- Cholesterol: 16mg cholesterol

563. Apricot Thumbprints

Serving: 3 dozen. | Prep: 20mins | Cook: 10mins | Ready in:

Ingredients

- 2 tablespoons butter, softened
- 1/2 cup packed brown sugar
- 1 egg
- 1 teaspoon vanilla extract
- 2 cups Quick Cookie Mix
- 1 egg white, lightly beaten
- 3/4 cup finely chopped cashews
- 1/3 cup apricot preserves

Direction

- Cream brown sugar and butter in a small bowl till crumbly. Whisk in vanilla and egg. Slowly add cookie mix and combine thoroughly.
- In separate shallow bowls, put cashews and egg white. Form dough into 1-in. balls. Dunk in egg white, then toss in cashews.
- Put 1 inch away on ungreased baking sheets. Create an indentation in the middle of every cookie using the end of a wooden spoon handle. Stuff with preserves. Bake at 350° till set, about 10 to 12 minutes. Transfer to wire racks to cool. Keep in an airtight container.

Nutrition Information

- Calories: 79 calories
- Cholesterol: 13mg cholesterol
- Protein: 1g protein.
- Total Fat: 4g fat (2g saturated fat)
- Sodium: 97mg sodium
- Fiber: 0 fiber)

- Total Carbohydrate: 10g carbohydrate (4g sugars

564. Apricot Hazelnut Triangles

Serving: about 2-1/2 dozen. | Prep: 25mins | Cook: 30mins | Ready in:

Ingredients

- 1/3 cup butter, softened
- 1 cup sugar, divided
- 1 large egg
- 1 teaspoon vanilla extract
- 1-1/4 cups all-purpose flour
- 1/2 teaspoon baking powder
- 3 tablespoons apricot preserves or flavor of your choice
- 1/3 cup butter, melted
- 2 tablespoons water
- 3/4 cup finely chopped hazelnuts or nuts of your choice
- 7 ounces dark chocolate candy coating, melted

Direction

- Prepare the oven by preheating to 350°F. Beat 1/2 cup sugar and cream butter in a small bowl until fluffy and light. Mix in vanilla and egg. Combine baking powder and flour in another bowl; slowly stir into creamed mixture.
- Place dough into an 8-inch square baking pan, greased then press; spread preserves. Beat remaining sugar, water, and dissolved butter in a small bowl; mix in hazelnuts. Place over preserves and spread.
- Place in the preheated oven and bake for 30-35 minutes or until edges are golden brown and the middle is set. Take to a wire rack and cool for 15 minutes. Slice into sixteen 2-inch squares. Slice squares into triangles. Take to wire racks to fully cool.
- Sink one side of each triangle halfway into dissolved chocolate; let excess to drip off. Set on waxed paper; allow to stand until set. Keep in an airtight container.

Nutrition Information

- Calories: 132 calories
- Sodium: 41mg sodium
- Fiber: 1g fiber)
- Total Carbohydrate: 16g carbohydrate (11g sugars
- Cholesterol: 16mg cholesterol
- Protein: 1g protein.
- Total Fat: 7g fat (4g saturated fat)

565. Behr Track Cookie Bars

Serving: about 4 dozen | Prep: 30mins | Cook: 10mins | Ready in:

Ingredients

- 1-1/2 cups all-purpose flour
- 2/3 cup confectioners' sugar
- 1/3 cup baking cocoa
- 1/4 teaspoon salt
- 1 cup butter, melted
- CARAMEL LAYER:
- 1 package (13 ounces) caramels
- 3 tablespoons heavy whipping cream
- 1-1/2 cups lightly crushed pretzels
- PEANUT BUTTER LAYER:
- 1 cup creamy peanut butter
- 1/4 cup butter, softened
- 1/2 cup confectioners' sugar
- CHOCOLATE LAYER:
- 2 cups (12 ounces) semisweet chocolate chips
- 3 tablespoons shortening

Direction

- Prepare the oven by preheating it to 350°F. Beat salt, cocoa, sugar and flour together. Mix

in butter. On a greased 13x9-inch baking pan compress mixture onto the base of the pan. Put inside the oven and bake for 10-15 minutes. Cool down entirely.
- On high setting, microwave cream and caramels, covered, mixing occasionally for 3-5 minutes until it melts. Pour onto crust and distribute evenly; coat with crushed pretzels. Put in refrigerator until it sets.
- In the meantime, mix butter and peanut butter; beat confectioners' sugar in until smooth. Spread evenly over the pretzels. Put back in fridge.
- Dissolve shortening and chocolate chips in the microwave; mix until smooth in consistency. Pour over peanut butter layer and distribute evenly. Before slicing into bars, chill in refrigerator for 15 minutes.

Nutrition Information

- Calories: 185 calories
- Protein: 3g protein.
- Total Fat: 12g fat (5g saturated fat)
- Sodium: 134mg sodium
- Fiber: 1g fiber)
- Total Carbohydrate: 20g carbohydrate (12g sugars
- Cholesterol: 14mg cholesterol

566. Best Sour Cream Sugar Cookies

Serving: 2 dozen. | Prep: 20mins | Cook: 10mins | Ready in:

Ingredients

- 1/3 cup butter, softened
- 2/3 cup sugar
- 1 large egg
- 1/3 cup sour cream
- 1/8 teaspoon lemon extract
- 1-2/3 cups all-purpose flour
- 3/4 teaspoon baking powder
- 1/8 teaspoon baking soda
- 1/8 teaspoon ground nutmeg
- Colored sugar or sprinkles, optional

Direction

- Cream sugar and butter together in a small bowl until fluffy and light. Whisk in extract, sour cream, and egg. Mix together nutmeg, baking soda, baking powder, and flour; slowly add to the creamed mixture and stir thoroughly.
- Halve the dough. Form one portion into a roll with a 5-inch length. Wrap plastic around the dough, put in a resealable plastic freezer bag. You can freeze the dough for a maximum of 3 months. Put a cover on the leftover dough and chill until easy to work with, 60 mins.
- Roll the dough on a lightly floured surface until the thickness is 1/4 inch. With a floured 2 1/2-inch cookie cutter, cut the dough. Put on a greased cookie sheet, 1-inch separately. Sprinkle sprinkles or colored sugar over top if you like.
- Bake at 375° until turning light brown on the bottoms, 8-10 minutes. Let cool for 1 minute, and then transfer to a wire rack to fully cool.
- When using the frozen cookie dough: Take the dough out of the freezer about 60 minutes before baking. Remove the wrap and slice into 12 slices. Place on a greased cookie sheet, 1-inch separately. Sprinkle sprinkles or colored sugar over top if you like.
- Bake at 375° until turning light brown on the bottoms, 8-10 minutes. Transfer to a wire rack to cool.

Nutrition Information

- Calories: 85 calories
- Total Carbohydrate: 12g carbohydrate (6g sugars
- Cholesterol: 18mg cholesterol
- Protein: 1g protein. Diabetic Exchanges: 1 starch
- Total Fat: 3g fat (2g saturated fat)

- Sodium: 41mg sodium
- Fiber: 0 fiber)

567. Best Ever Sugar Cookies

Serving: 4 dozen. | Prep: 30mins | Cook: 10mins | Ready in:

Ingredients

- 1 cup butter, softened
- 3 ounces cream cheese, softened
- 1 cup sugar
- 1 large egg yolk
- 1/2 teaspoon vanilla extract
- 1/4 teaspoon almond extract
- 2-1/4 cups all-purpose flour
- 1/2 teaspoon salt
- 1/4 teaspoon baking soda
- 1/8 teaspoon ground nutmeg
- ICING:
- 3-3/4 cups confectioners' sugar
- 1/3 cup water
- 4 teaspoons meringue powder
- Assorted colors of liquid food coloring

Direction

- Cream the sugar, cream cheese and butter in a big bowl until fluffy and light. Whip in egg yolk and extracts. Mix the nutmeg, baking soda, salt and flour; put into creamed mixture gradually. Cover and chill for 3 hours or until easy to handle.
- Shape dough into 1/8-in. thickness on a lightly floured surface. Slice with floured 2-1/2-in. cookie cutters.
- Put 1 in. apart on ungreased baking trays. Bake for 8 to 10 mins at 375° or until edges start to brown. Let cool for 2 minutes before taking out from pans to wire racks to cool completely.
- To make icing, mix the meringue powder, water and confectioners' sugar in a small bowl; whip on low speed just until blended. Whip on high for 4 minutes or until it creates soft peaks. Put damp paper towels or plastic wrap on top to cover between uses.
- Pipe or spread icing over cookies quickly; let sit at room temperature for a few hours to dry or until set. Use toothpicks or small new paintbrushes and food coloring to create patterns on the cookies. Let sit until set. Put in an airtight container to store.

Nutrition Information

- Calories: 116 calories
- Cholesterol: 16mg cholesterol
- Protein: 1g protein. Diabetic Exchanges: 1 starch
- Total Fat: 5g fat (3g saturated fat)
- Sodium: 66mg sodium
- Fiber: 0 fiber)
- Total Carbohydrate: 18g carbohydrate (13g sugars

568. Black Forest Thumbprint Cookies

Serving: 5 dozen. | Prep: 25mins | Cook: 10mins | Ready in:

Ingredients

- 1 cup butter, softened
- 1-1/3 cups sugar
- 2 egg yolks
- 1/4 cup 2% milk
- 1 teaspoon almond extract
- 2 cups all-purpose flour
- 2/3 cup baking cocoa
- 1/2 teaspoon salt
- FILLING:
- 1/2 cup dried cherries
- 1/2 cup cherry spreadable fruit
- 2 teaspoons Amaretto
- 1 teaspoon grated lemon peel
- 2 egg whites, lightly beaten

- 1-1/4 cups chopped almonds

Direction

- Cream sugar and butter in a big bowl until fluffy and light. Beat in extract and milk with egg yolks. Mix the salt, cocoa and flour; put into the creamed mixture gradually and stir well. Cover and refrigerate for an hour.
- Mix the lemon peel, Amaretto, spreadable fruit and cherries in a food processor. Cover then pulse until chopped. Put aside. In separate shallow bowls, put almonds and egg whites. Roll the dough into 1-inch balls. Coat in eggs white, and roll in almonds.
- Arrange 1 inch apart on ungreased baking sheets. Make an indentation in the middle of each cookie with the end of a wooden spoon handle. Fill with cherry mixture. Bake for 10 to 12 minutes at 350°, or until set. Transfer to cool on wire racks. Store in an airtight container.

Nutrition Information

- Calories: 90 calories
- Fiber: 1g fiber)
- Total Carbohydrate: 11g carbohydrate (7g sugars
- Cholesterol: 15mg cholesterol
- Protein: 1g protein.
- Total Fat: 5g fat (2g saturated fat)
- Sodium: 44mg sodium

569. Black Walnut Butter Cookies

Serving: 6 dozen. | Prep: 20mins | Cook: 20mins | Ready in:

Ingredients

- 3/4 cup butter, softened
- 1 cup all-purpose flour
- 1/2 cup cornstarch
- 1/2 cup confectioners' sugar
- 1/2 cup chopped black walnuts or walnuts
- Additional confectioners' sugar

Direction

- Cream the butter in a bowl. Mix together confectioners' sugar, cornstarch and flour; add to the butter and stir thoroughly. Mix in walnuts.
- Shape into 3/4-inch balls by rolling. Put on lightly oil-coated baking sheets by 1-inch apart.
- Bake at 300° until set, or for 20-25 minutes. Transfer to wire racks to cool. Dust more confectioners' sugar over.

Nutrition Information

- Calories: 70 calories
- Fiber: 0 fiber)
- Total Carbohydrate: 6g carbohydrate (2g sugars
- Cholesterol: 10mg cholesterol
- Protein: 1g protein.
- Total Fat: 5g fat (2g saturated fat)
- Sodium: 39mg sodium

570. Blackberry Peekaboo Cookies

Serving: about 3 dozen | Prep: 15mins | Cook: 10mins | Ready in:

Ingredients

- 1/2 cup butter, softened
- 1/2 cup shortening
- 2 cups packed brown sugar
- 2 large eggs
- 1 teaspoon vanilla extract
- 4 cups all-purpose flour
- 1-1/2 teaspoons baking soda
- 1-1/2 teaspoons salt

- 3/4 cup seedless blackberry spreadable fruit

Direction

- Cream brown sugar, shortening, and butter together until fluffy and light. Add eggs, 1 egg each time, whisking thoroughly between each addition. Whisk in vanilla. Combine salt, baking soda, and flour in a separate bowl; slowly whisk into the creamed mixture. Split the dough into 2 portions. Form each portion into a disc, use plastic to wrap. Chill for 30 minutes until firm enough to roll.
- Turn the oven to 350° to preheat. On a surface lightly scattered with flour, roll out each dough portion into 1/8-inch thickness. Use a floured 2-inch round cookie cutter to cut the dough out. On cookie sheets lined with parchment paper, put 1/2 of the circles. Spread into the middle of each circle with 1 teaspoon of the spreadable fruit; put the leftover circles on top, gently pinch the edge to seal.
- Bake for 10-12 minutes until light brown. Transfer from the pans to wire racks to cool.

Nutrition Information

- Calories: 162 calories
- Protein: 2g protein.
- Total Fat: 6g fat (2g saturated fat)
- Sodium: 179mg sodium
- Fiber: 0 fiber)
- Total Carbohydrate: 26g carbohydrate (15g sugars
- Cholesterol: 17mg cholesterol

571. Blue Moon Crescent Cookies

Serving: about 2-1/2 dozen. | Prep: 15mins | Cook: 15mins | Ready in:

Ingredients

- 1 cup butter, softened
- 1/2 cup sugar
- 2 teaspoons grated lemon zest
- 1 teaspoon lemon juice
- 1/2 teaspoon vanilla extract
- 1/2 teaspoon ground cinnamon
- 1/4 teaspoon salt
- 2 cups all-purpose flour
- 1 cup dried blueberries
- Confectioners' sugar

Direction

- Prepare the oven by preheating to 350°F. Cream the sugar and butter in a big bowl until fluffy and light. Add in the salt, cinnamon, vanilla, lemon zest and juice. Slowly whisk the flour into the creamed mixture then mix in the blueberries. Turn tablespoonfuls of dough into crescent shapes. On a baking sheet that is not greased, place it two inches apart. Place inside the oven and bake for 15 to 18 minutes or until the edges are lightly brown in color. Let it cool for two minutes on pans. Transfer it to wire racks and let it fully cool down. Sprinkle cookies with confectioners' sugar.

Nutrition Information

- Calories:
- Total Carbohydrate:
- Cholesterol:
- Protein:
- Total Fat:
- Sodium:
- Fiber:

572. Brandy Snap Cannoli

Serving: about 2 dozen. | Prep: 01hours30mins | Cook: 5mins | Ready in:

Ingredients

- 1/2 cup butter, cubed
- 1/2 cup sugar
- 3 tablespoons molasses
- 1 teaspoon ground ginger
- 1/4 teaspoon salt
- 1 cup all-purpose flour
- 2 tablespoons brandy
- FILLING:
- 1-1/2 cups ricotta cheese
- 3 tablespoons grated orange zest
- 3 tablespoons sugar, divided
- 1-1/2 cups miniature semisweet chocolate chips, divided
- 1-1/2 cups heavy whipping cream

Direction

- Mix the first 5 ingredients in a small saucepan. Cook and stir until butter is melted over medium heat. Take off heat. Mix in brandy and flour; keep warm.
- Drop tablespoonfuls of batter on well-greased or parchment paper-lined baking sheet. Make 4-inchcircle by spreading each batter. Bake until edges begins to turn brown or for 5 to 6 minutes at 350 degrees. Allow to cool just until cookie begins to firm or for about a minute.
- Do this step quickly. Loosen every cookie and shape by curling around a metal cannoli tube. Remove cookies from the tubes and allow to cool on wire racks.
- Make the filling by mixing 1 tablespoon of sugar, orange zest and ricotta in a big bowl. Mix 1/2 cup chocolate chips in. Beat the cream until get soft peaks formed on medium speed in a small bowl. Put the remaining sugar gradually while beating on high until get stiff peaks formed. Fold into ricotta mixture then put in the refrigerator until serving.
- Pipe the filling into cannoli shells just prior to serving. Dunk ends in the leftover chocolate chips.

Nutrition Information

- Calories: 230 calories
- Cholesterol: 40mg cholesterol
- Protein: 3g protein.
- Total Fat: 15g fat (10g saturated fat)
- Sodium: 85mg sodium
- Fiber: 1g fiber)
- Total Carbohydrate: 22g carbohydrate (15g sugars

573. Brown Butter Spice Cookies

Serving: about 2 dozen. | Prep: 20mins | Cook: 10mins | Ready in:

Ingredients

- 1/2 cup unsalted butter, cubed
- 1 cup packed brown sugar
- 1 large egg
- 1 tablespoon spiced rum
- 1-1/4 cups all-purpose flour
- 1-1/2 teaspoons ground cinnamon
- 1/2 teaspoon baking soda
- 1/4 teaspoon salt
- 1/4 teaspoon ground ginger
- 1/4 teaspoon ground nutmeg
- 1/2 cup dark chocolate chips

Direction

- In a small heavy saucepan, add butter. Cook butter over medium heat until golden brown, 5-7 minutes; let it cool slightly.
- In a large bowl, beat brown sugar and browned butter until blended. Crack in egg, then rum. Blend together nutmeg, ginger, salt, baking soda, cinnamon and the flour; slowly add to brown sugar mixture and stir well. Mix in chips. Cover and put in refrigerator for at least 30 minutes.
- On baking sheets coated with cooking spray, drop the mixture by rounded tablespoonfuls, keeping 2 in. apart. Bake at 350° until bottoms are lightly browned, 10-12 minutes. Transfer to wire racks to cool.

Nutrition Information

- Calories: 111 calories
- Total Fat: 5g fat (3g saturated fat)
- Sodium: 54mg sodium
- Fiber: 1g fiber)
- Total Carbohydrate: 16g carbohydrate (11g sugars
- Cholesterol: 17mg cholesterol
- Protein: 1g protein.

574. Brown Sugar Cutout Cookies

Serving: 7-1/2 dozen. | Prep: 55mins | Cook: 10mins | Ready in:

Ingredients

- 1 cup butter, softened
- 2 cups packed dark brown sugar
- 3 large eggs
- 6 tablespoons cold water
- 3 tablespoons canola oil
- 1 teaspoon vanilla extract
- 6 cups all-purpose flour
- 1 teaspoon cream of tartar
- 1 teaspoon baking soda
- 1/2 teaspoon salt
- ICING:
- 1 cup butter, softened
- 4 teaspoons meringue powder
- 3 teaspoons cream of tartar
- 1/2 teaspoon salt
- 4 cups confectioners' sugar
- 4 to 6 tablespoons water

Direction

- Beat butter with brown sugar in a big bowl until light and fluffy. Whip in vanilla, oil, water and eggs. Mix salt, baking soda, cream of tartar and flour in a separate bowl; combine into creamed mixture slowly.
- Split dough into 4 parts. Roll each into a disk; cover in plastic. Chill for 2 hours or until firm enough to roll.
- Set oven to 350° to preheat. Shape each portion of dough to 1/8-in. thickness on a lightly floured surface. Punch out cookies with a floured 2-1/4-in. fluted square cookie cutter. Place 1 in. apart on greased baking trays.
- Bake until bottoms are light brown, 7 to 9 mins. Take them out of the pans to wire racks to cool completely.
- To make icing, whip salt, cream of tartar, meringue powder and butter in a small bowl until combined. Alternately whip in confectioners' sugar with enough water to reach a spreading consistency. Put over cookies. Let sit until set.

Nutrition Information

- Calories:
- Fiber:
- Total Carbohydrate:
- Cholesterol:
- Protein:
- Total Fat:
- Sodium:

575. Brown Sugar Cutouts

Serving: About 6 dozen. | Prep: 35mins | Cook: 10mins | Ready in:

Ingredients

- 1 cup butter, softened
- 2 cups packed brown sugar
- 3 eggs
- 2 teaspoons grated lemon peel
- 3 cups all-purpose flour
- 1 teaspoon baking soda
- 1 teaspoon ground ginger
- FROSTING:
- 1-1/2 cups confectioners' sugar

- 1/2 teaspoon vanilla extract
- 2 to 3 tablespoons half-and-half cream
- Green food coloring, optional

Direction

- In a large bowl, cream brown sugar and butter till fluffy and light. Beat in lemon peel and eggs. Mix together ginger, baking soda and flour; slowly put into the creamed mixture; mix properly. Separate the dough in half. Form each into a ball; flatten into a disk. Wrap in plastic; keep in a refrigerator till easy to handle, or for 2 hours.
- Roll to form one portion of the dough into 1/8-in. thickness on a lightly floured work surface. Using floured 2-in. cookie cutters to cut. Arrange on ungreased baking sheets, 2 in. apart. Repeat.
- Bake till golden brown, at 350°, 8-10 minutes. Transfer onto wire racks to cool.
- To make frosting, in a small bowl, mix enough cream, vanilla and confectioners' sugar to reach the spreading consistency. If desired, add food coloring to all or some of the frosting. Decorate the cookies.

Nutrition Information

- Calories: 156 calories
- Total Fat: 6g fat (3g saturated fat)
- Sodium: 97mg sodium
- Fiber: 0 fiber)
- Total Carbohydrate: 25g carbohydrate (17g sugars
- Cholesterol: 32mg cholesterol
- Protein: 2g protein.

---

576. Brownie Biscotti

Serving: 30 | Prep: 30mins | Cook: 45mins | Ready in:

Ingredients

- 1/3 cup butter, softened
- 2/3 cup white sugar
- 2 eggs
- 1 teaspoon vanilla extract
- 1 3/4 cups all-purpose flour
- 1/3 cup unsweetened cocoa powder
- 2 teaspoons baking powder
- 1/2 cup miniature semisweet chocolate chips
- 1/4 cup chopped walnuts
- 1 egg yolk, beaten
- 1 tablespoon water

Direction

- Preheat the oven to 190°C or 375°Fahrenheit. Grease or line parchment paper on baking sheets.
- Cream sugar and butter in a big bowl until smooth. Whisk in one egg at a time then mix in vanilla. Mix baking powder, cocoa, and flour together; combine with the creamed mixture until well incorporated. Use your hands to mix in the last bit since the dough is going to be stiff. Stir in walnuts and chocolate chips.
- Evenly halve the dough then form into 9-in by 2-in by 1-in loaves; put 4-in apart on a baking sheet. Brush with yolk and water mixture.
- Bake in the preheated oven for 20-25 minutes or until firm. Cool for half an hour on the baking sheet.
- Diagonally cut the loaves into one-inch slices using a serrated knife. Place the slices on their side back to the baking sheet. Bake for 10-15 minutes per side or until dry. Completely cool then place in an airtight container to store.

Nutrition Information

- Calories: 91 calories;
- Cholesterol: 25
- Protein: 1.7
- Total Fat: 4.2
- Sodium: 53
- Total Carbohydrate: 12.6

577. Brownie Bourbon Bites

Serving: about 2 dozen. | Prep: 25mins | Cook: 10mins | Ready in:

Ingredients

- 1/2 cup butter, softened
- 1/2 cup packed brown sugar
- 1/4 cup bourbon
- 1 cup all-purpose flour
- 3 tablespoons baking cocoa
- 1/2 cup miniature semisweet chocolate chips
- 1 cup coarsely chopped pecans

Direction

- Cream brown sugar and butter till fluffy and light in small bowl; beat bourbon in. Mix cocoa and flour; add to creamed mixture slowly. Beat till smooth; mix chocolate chips in. Cover; refrigerate for 1-2 hours.
- Form to 1/2-in balls then roll in pecans; put on ungreased baking sheets, 2-in. apart. Bake for 8-10 minutes at 350° till cookies set; cool for 5 minutes. Transfer from pans carefully onto wire racks; completely cool. Keep in airtight container.

Nutrition Information

- Calories: 110 calories
- Total Carbohydrate: 10g carbohydrate (6g sugars
- Cholesterol: 9mg cholesterol
- Protein: 1g protein.
- Total Fat: 7g fat (3g saturated fat)
- Sodium: 35mg sodium
- Fiber: 1g fiber)

578. Butter Ball Chiffons

Serving: 5 dozen. | Prep: 15mins | Cook: 15mins | Ready in:

Ingredients

- 1 cup butter, softened
- 1/4 cup confectioners' sugar
- 1 package (3.4 ounces) instant lemon pudding mix
- 2 teaspoons water
- 1 teaspoon vanilla extract
- 2 cups all-purpose flour
- 1 cup chopped pecans or walnuts
- 2 Heath candy bars (1.4 ounces each), chopped

Direction

- Start preheating the oven to 325°. Cream the confectioners' sugar and butter in a small bowl until fluffy and light. Whisk in vanilla, water and pudding mix. Put in flour gradually. Whisk in chopped candy bars and nuts.
- Roll the mixture into 1-inch balls. Arrange 2 inches apart on ungreased baking sheets. Bake until lightly browned, 12-15 minutes. Let cool for 3 min., then transfer to wire racks.

Nutrition Information

- Calories: 141 calories
- Protein: 1g protein.
- Total Fat: 10g fat (4g saturated fat)
- Sodium: 107mg sodium
- Fiber: 1g fiber)
- Total Carbohydrate: 13g carbohydrate (5g sugars
- Cholesterol: 17mg cholesterol

579. Butter Cookies

Serving: | Prep: | Cook: | Ready in:

Ingredients

- 1 1/2 sticks butter at room temperature
- 1 1/2 cups flour
- 3/4 teaspoon baking soda
- 1 cup light brown sugar

- 1 egg
- 1 teaspoon vanilla extract
- A pinch of salt
- 1/2 cup chopped walnuts (optional)

Direction

- Mix salt, baking soda and flour in medium-sized bowl. Beat vanilla, sugar and egg in another bowl; add butter to sugar and egg mixture. Beat till fluffy and light. Add to dry ingredients; mix till blended. You can add 1/2 cup coarsely chopped walnuts at this point.
- Divide the cookie dough to 2 parts; roll in wax paper. Freeze for 4 hours – overnight. Cut frozen dough carefully into 1/4-in. thick slices with serrated knife. Bake for 10-12 minutes at 350° on cookie sheet; creates 2 dozen cookies.

Nutrition Information

580. Butterscotch Eggnog Stars

Serving: about 3 dozen. | Prep: 25mins | Cook: 10mins | Ready in:

Ingredients

- 2/3 cup butter, softened
- 1 cup sugar
- 1 egg
- 1/4 cup eggnog
- 2 cups all-purpose flour
- 3/4 teaspoon baking powder
- 1/4 teaspoon salt
- 1/4 teaspoon ground nutmeg
- 1/2 cup crushed hard butterscotch candies
- OPTIONAL ICING:
- 1-1/2 cups confectioners' sugar
- 1/4 teaspoon rum extract
- 2 to 3 tablespoons eggnog
- Yellow colored sugar

Direction

- Cream butter with sugar in a big bowl until fluffy and light. Whip in eggnog and egg. Stir the nutmeg, salt, baking powder and flour; put into creamed mixture gradually and stir well. Split dough in half.
- Shape one portion at a time to 1/4-in. thickness on a lightly floured surface. Slice with a floured 3-1/2-in. star cutter. Slice out centers with a 1-1/2-in. star cutter. Line baking trays using foil; grease foil.
- On greased baking trays, put big star cutouts. Scatter a teaspoon candy in middle of each. Keep working with leftover dough; roll small cutouts again (optional).
- Bake for 6-8 minutes at 375° or until golden brown on the edges. Let cool on baking trays for 5 minutes. Take out foil and cookies carefully from baking trays onto wire racks to cool.
- To make icing (optional), whip rum extract, confectioners' sugar and enough eggnog to reach a drizzling consistency. Drizzle on top of cooled cookies (optional). Scatter with colored sugar (optional). Let sit until firmed up.

Nutrition Information

- Calories: 91 calories
- Sodium: 67mg sodium
- Fiber: 0 fiber)
- Total Carbohydrate: 13g carbohydrate (8g sugars
- Cholesterol: 16mg cholesterol
- Protein: 1g protein.
- Total Fat: 4g fat (2g saturated fat)

581. Butterscotch Shortbread

Serving: 4-1/2 dozen. | Prep: 30mins | Cook: 10mins | Ready in:

Ingredients

- 1 cup butter, softened
- 1/2 cup confectioners' sugar
- 1 teaspoon vanilla extract
- 1-3/4 cups all-purpose flour
- 1/2 cup cornstarch
- 1/4 teaspoon salt
- 1/2 cup butterscotch chips, finely chopped
- 1/2 cup milk chocolate English toffee bits

Direction

- Beat confectioners' sugar and butter in a big bowl till fluffy and light. Whip vanilla in. Mix cornstarch, salt and flour, put into creamed mixture gradually; mixing thoroughly. Fold toffee bits and butterscotch chips in. Chill for an hour with cover or till easily handled.
- Set the oven to 350 degrees to preheat. Roll dough out on a surface slightly dusted with flour into 1/4-inch-thick. Use a 2-inch fluted round cookie cutter covered in flour to cut dough out. Arrange on grease-free baking sheets spacing an-inch apart.
- Bake till pale brown, about 10 to 12 minutes. Transfer onto wire racks.

Nutrition Information

- Calories: 76 calories
- Protein: 1g protein. Diabetic Exchanges: 1 fat
- Total Fat: 5g fat (3g saturated fat)
- Sodium: 45mg sodium
- Fiber: 0 fiber)
- Total Carbohydrate: 8g carbohydrate (1g sugars
- Cholesterol: 10mg cholesterol

582. Buttersweets

Serving: 32 cookies. | Prep: 20mins | Cook: 10mins | Ready in:

Ingredients

- 1 tube (18 ounces) refrigerated chocolate chip cookie dough
- 3 ounces cream cheese, softened
- 3/4 cup confectioners' sugar
- 1/4 cup chopped maraschino cherries
- 1 drop red food coloring, optional
- 1/2 cup semisweet chocolate chips
- 2 tablespoons butter

Direction

- Use a sharp knife to cut cookie dough into 8 even slices. Quarter each slice again and roll each into balls. Arrange on grease-free baking sheets with 2 inches apart. Bake at 375 degrees until turn golden brown, about 10 minutes. Make a deep impression in the center of each cookie instantly with the back of a small spoon or small melon baller. Allow to cool about 5 minutes, then transfer to wire racks to cool thoroughly. In the meantime, cream sugar and cream cheese together in a bowl. Use paper towels to pat cherries dry, then stir into creamed mixture with cherries and food coloring, if wanted. Put down the center of each cookie with a teaspoonful of filling. Melt butter and chocolate chips in a heavy saucepan on low heat while stirring sometimes. Drizzle over cookies and keep in the fridge.

Nutrition Information

- Calories: 225 calories
- Cholesterol: 17mg cholesterol
- Protein: 2g protein.
- Total Fat: 11g fat (5g saturated fat)
- Sodium: 99mg sodium
- Fiber: 1g fiber)
- Total Carbohydrate: 30g carbohydrate (22g sugars

583. Buttery Potato Chip Cookies

Serving: 4-1/2 dozen. | Prep: 15mins | Cook: 10mins | Ready in:

Ingredients

- 2 cups butter, softened
- 1 cup sugar
- 1 teaspoon vanilla extract
- 3-1/2 cups all-purpose flour
- 2 cups crushed potato chips
- 3/4 cup chopped walnuts

Direction

- Preheat an oven to 350°. Cream sugar and butter till fluffy and light in big bowl; beat vanilla in. Add flour slowly to creamed mixture; stir well. Mix walnuts and potato chips in.
- By rounded tablespoonfuls, drop on ungreased baking sheets, 2-in. apart. Bake till lightly browned, about 10-12 minutes. Cool for 2 minutes. Transfer from pans onto wire racks.

Nutrition Information

- Calories: 126 calories
- Total Fat: 9g fat (5g saturated fat)
- Sodium: 67mg sodium
- Fiber: 0 fiber)
- Total Carbohydrate: 11g carbohydrate (4g sugars
- Cholesterol: 18mg cholesterol
- Protein: 1g protein.

584. Calypso Cups

Serving: 4 dozen. | Prep: 30mins | Cook: 15mins | Ready in:

Ingredients

- 1 cup butter, softened
- 6 ounces cream cheese, softened
- 2 cups all-purpose flour
- FILLING:
- 1 egg, lightly beaten
- 1 can (8 ounces) crushed pineapple, undrained
- 1/2 cup sweetened shredded coconut
- 1/2 cup sugar
- 1-1/2 teaspoons cornstarch
- FROSTING:
- 2 cups confectioners' sugar
- 1/2 cup shortening
- 1 teaspoon vanilla extract
- 3 to 5 tablespoons 2% milk
- Chopped walnuts and/or additional coconut, optional

Direction

- Whisk cream cheese and butter until smooth in a large bowl. Whisk in flour gradually. Chill in the fridge with a cover until firm enough to shape or for an hour.
- Set the oven to 350° and start preheating. Form dough into 1-in. balls; put in greased mini-muffin cups. Evenly press onto bottoms and up sides of cups.
- In a small bowl, combine filling ingredients; scoop into cups. Bake until edges turn light brown or for 15-20 minutes. Completely cool in pans on wire racks.
- To prepare frosting, whisk enough milk, vanilla, shortening and confectioners' sugar to achieve the consistency as preferred. Take cups out of pans. Add frosting on top. Top with walnuts and/or coconut if preferred.

Nutrition Information

- Calories:
- Fiber:
- Total Carbohydrate:
- Cholesterol:
- Protein:
- Total Fat:
- Sodium:

585. Candied Cherry Hermits

Serving: about 3-1/2 dozen. | Prep: 15mins | Cook: 10mins |Ready in:

Ingredients

- 1/2 cup butter, softened
- 1 cup packed brown sugar
- 2 eggs
- 1-1/2 cups all-purpose flour
- 1 to 2 teaspoons ground cinnamon
- 1/2 teaspoon baking soda
- 1 cup chopped pecans
- 3/4 cup raisins, chopped
- 3/4 cup candied cherries, chopped

Direction

- Cream brown sugar and butter till fluffy and light in big bowl; one by one, add eggs, beating well with every addition. Mix baking soda, cinnamon and flour; add to creamed mixture slowly. Stir well; mix cherries, raisins and pecans in.
- By rounded tablespoonfuls, drop on ungreased baking sheets, 2-in. apart. Bake for 10-12 minutes at 375° till golden brown. Transfer to wire racks; cool.

Nutrition Information

- Calories: 191 calories
- Total Carbohydrate: 27g carbohydrate (18g sugars
- Cholesterol: 32mg cholesterol
- Protein: 2g protein.
- Total Fat: 9g fat (3g saturated fat)
- Sodium: 90mg sodium
- Fiber: 1g fiber)

586. Candy Cane Blossom Cookies

Serving: 4 dozen. | Prep: 45mins | Cook: 10mins |Ready in:

Ingredients

- 48 milk chocolate kisses, candy cane kisses or miniature chocolate-covered peppermint patties, unwrapped
- 4 candy canes
- 1 cup butter, softened
- 1 cup sugar
- 1 egg
- 1 tablespoon 2% milk
- 1 teaspoon vanilla extract
- 3 cups all-purpose flour
- 2 teaspoons baking powder
- 1/4 teaspoon salt

Direction

- In a covered container, freeze kisses for at least an hour. Put candy canes in a food processor; process until crushed finely.
- Set the oven to 350° and start preheating. Cream sugar and butter until fluffy and light in a large bowl. Whisk in vanilla, milk and egg. Beat salt, baking powder and flour in another bowl; whisk into creamed mixture gradually.
- Form into 1-in. balls; roll into crushed candy canes. Arrange 2 inches apart on baking sheets lined with parchment paper.
- Bake until bottoms turn golden brown or for 10-12 minutes. Press a kiss into each cookie's center immediately. Place cookies on wire racks to cool.

Nutrition Information

- Calories: 109 calories
- Sodium: 69mg sodium
- Fiber: 0 fiber)
- Total Carbohydrate: 15g carbohydrate (8g sugars

- Cholesterol: 15mg cholesterol
- Protein: 1g protein.
- Total Fat: 5g fat (3g saturated fat)

587. Caramel Chocolate Cookies

Serving: 24 | Prep: | Cook: | Ready in:

Ingredients

- 1 cup white sugar
- 1 cup packed brown sugar
- 1 cup margarine
- 2 teaspoons vanilla extract
- 2 eggs
- 2 1/2 cups all-purpose flour
- 3/4 cup unsweetened cocoa powder
- 1 teaspoon baking soda
- 1 cup chopped pecans
- 48 chocolate covered caramel candies
- 1 tablespoon white sugar
- 4 ounces vanilla flavored confectioners' coating

Direction

- Mix margarine, brown sugar and a cup sugar in a big bowl and whip until light; put in eggs and vanilla, mix well.
- Mix baking soda, cocoa and flour in a small bowl, stir well. Put into sugar mixtures; mix well. Stir in half cup pecans. Chill for half an hour.
- Set oven to 375°F (190°C) to preheat.
- Cover a caramel candy completely with 1 tablespoon of dough. Mix 1 tbsp. sugar and leftover 1/2 cup pecans in a small bowl. Push one side of each ball into pecan mix. Put nut side up on cookie trays. Bake for 7-10 minutes. Let cool. Melt candy coating and sprinkle on top of cooled cookies.

Nutrition Information

- Calories: 281 calories;
- Sodium: 165
- Total Carbohydrate: 36.9
- Cholesterol: 17
- Protein: 3.4
- Total Fat: 14.4

588. Caroling Fortune Cookies

Serving: 1 dozen. | Prep: 20mins | Cook: 10mins | Ready in:

Ingredients

- 12 strips of green and red glossy paper (about 5-1/2 inches x 1/2 inch)
- Nontoxic black marker
- 2 egg whites
- 1/3 cup sugar
- 2 tablespoons confectioners' sugar
- 1/3 cup cake flour
- 2 tablespoons canola oil
- 1 tablespoon butter, melted
- 1 teaspoon vanilla extract
- Pinch salt

Direction

- Use a marker to print the Christmas carol titles or any holiday wishes onto the paper strips; then put aside.
- Whisk egg whites in a small bowl until foamy. Put in sugars; whisk thoroughly. Stir in salt, vanilla, butter, oil, and flour until smooth.
- Drop 6 tablespoonfuls onto a baking sheet coated with cooking spray and flour, approximately 3 inches apart. Spread each into a 3 1/2-inch circle using the back of the spoon (bake 6 cookies at a time). Bake at 300 degrees until lightly browned, 6-8 minutes.
- Loosen the cookies from the baking sheet. Bake 1 more minute to soften. Then remove cookies, one at a time, keeping the others in the oven (keep them warm to shape). Fold the cookie slowly in half; then put in a fortune.

Fold in half again and gather the points together. Put into the muffin cups to cool and maintain the shape. Repeat with the rest of the cookies.

Nutrition Information

- Calories:
- Total Carbohydrate:
- Cholesterol:
- Protein:
- Total Fat:
- Sodium:
- Fiber:

589. Cashew Cookies

Serving: 36 | Prep: 10mins | Cook: 15mins | Ready in:

Ingredients

- 1/2 cup butter, softened
- 1 cup brown sugar
- 1 egg
- 1/3 cup sour cream
- 1 teaspoon vanilla extract
- 2 cups all-purpose flour
- 3/4 teaspoon baking powder
- 3/4 teaspoon baking soda
- 1/4 teaspoon salt
- 1 3/4 cups chopped cashews
- 1/2 cup butter
- 3 tablespoons heavy whipping cream
- 2 cups confectioners' sugar
- 1 teaspoon vanilla extract

Direction

- Preheat the oven to 175°C or 350°F. Grease the cookie sheets.
- Cream together the sugar and half cup butter in a big bowl till fluffy and light. Put the egg, beating thoroughly, then mix in the 1 teaspoon vanilla and sour cream. Put together the salt, baking soda, baking powder and flour; slowly mix into the creamed mixture. Fold cashew pieces in. Onto the prepped cookie sheets, drop by rounded spoonfuls.
- In the prepped oven, bake for 12 to 15 minutes. Let cookies cool down on baking sheet for 5 minutes prior taking to a wire rack to fully cool.
- For the frosting, in a saucepan over medium heat, liquefy half cup butter. Cook till butter becomes light brown in color, keep from burning. Take off heat and mix in the cream. Slowly beat in the confectioners' sugar and a teaspoon vanilla till smooth. Scatter onto cooled cookies.

Nutrition Information

- Calories: 162 calories;
- Total Carbohydrate: 18.3
- Cholesterol: 21
- Protein: 2.1
- Total Fat: 9.3
- Sodium: 136

590. Cashew Sandwich Cookies

Serving: 4 dozen. | Prep: 30mins | Cook: 10mins | Ready in:

Ingredients

- 1 cup butter, softened
- 3/4 cup sugar
- 2 large eggs yolks
- 1/2 cup sour cream
- 1 teaspoon vanilla extract
- 1 teaspoon lemon juice
- 3 cups all-purpose flour
- FILLING:
- 2 cups (12 ounces) semisweet chocolate chips
- 1/2 cup butter, cubed

- 1 can (10 ounces) salted cashews, finely chopped
- Confectioners' sugar, optional

Direction

- Cream sugar and butter in a big bowl till fluffy and light. Whisk in the lemon juice, vanilla, sour cream and egg yolks. Slowly put flour and mix thoroughly. Put cover and refrigerate for a minimum of 2 hours till easy to handle.
- Roll dough out to 1/8-inch thickness on a lightly floured surface. Slice with a 2-inch circle cookie cutter. On ungreased baking sheets, put the sliced dough 1 inch away from each other. Bake at 350° for 11 to 13 minutes till edges are browned lightly. Let cool on wire racks.
- For the filling, in a microwave-safe bowl, liquefy butter and chocolate chips; mix till smooth. Mix in cashews. Scatter on the base of half of the cookies; on each cookie, put another cookie over. Sprinkle confectioners' sugar if wished.

Nutrition Information

- Calories: 337 calories
- Sodium: 198mg sodium
- Fiber: 2g fiber)
- Total Carbohydrate: 30g carbohydrate (15g sugars
- Cholesterol: 52mg cholesterol
- Protein: 5g protein.
- Total Fat: 23g fat (12g saturated fat)

591. Cashew Tassie Cups

Serving: 2 dozen. | Prep: 20mins | Cook: 20mins | Ready in:

Ingredients

- 1/2 cup butter, softened
- 3 ounces cream cheese, softened
- 1 cup all-purpose flour
- FILLING:
- 2/3 cup coarsely chopped cashews
- 1/2 cup packed brown sugar
- 1 large egg
- 1 teaspoon vanilla extract

Direction

- Whisk cream cheese and butter in a small bowl till smooth; mix in flour. Form into 1-inch balls. Force dough onto the bottom and up the sides of ungreased mini muffin cups. Put a spoonful of cashews into shells; reserve.
- Whisk the vanilla, egg and brown sugar in a separate small bowl till incorporated; spoon atop nuts. Bake at 350° till pastry is golden brown and filling is set, about 20 to 25 minutes. Allow to cool for 10 minute prior to transfer from pans to wire racks.

Nutrition Information

- Calories: 215 calories
- Sodium: 156mg sodium
- Fiber: 1g fiber)
- Total Carbohydrate: 20g carbohydrate (10g sugars
- Cholesterol: 46mg cholesterol
- Protein: 3g protein.
- Total Fat: 14g fat (7g saturated fat)

592. Chai Chocolate Chip Shortbread

Serving: 4 dozen. | Prep: 35mins | Cook: 15mins | Ready in:

Ingredients

- 1-3/4 cups all-purpose flour
- 1/2 cup sugar
- 1/3 cup cornstarch
- 1/4 cup vanilla chai tea latte mix

- 1 cup cold butter, cubed
- 1/2 teaspoon vanilla extract
- 3/4 cup finely chopped almonds
- 1/3 cup miniature semisweet chocolate chips
- 4 ounces semisweet chocolate, melted

Direction

- In a food processor, put latte mix, cornstarch, sugar and flour; blend until combined. Put in vanilla and butter; process to cut butter into pea-sized pieces. Put in chocolate chips and almonds; blend until combined.
- Lightly flour a surface and turn out the dough; knead to form a ball. Split into 6 dough pieces; wrap each with plastic wrap. Put in the refrigerator for no less than half an hour, until the dough is firm enough to be rolled.
- Set oven to 375 degrees and start preheating. Lightly dust a surface with flour; roll each dough piece into a circle of 5 inches. Slice into 8 wedges. Place onto unprepared baking sheets, laying 2 inches from each other.
- Bake in preheated oven until edges start to turn brown, about 15 to 18 minutes. Keep in baking sheets for a minute to cool then transfer to wire racks. Melt chocolate and drizzle over top; let sit to set. Keep in a tightly sealed container to store.

Nutrition Information

- Calories:
- Fiber:
- Total Carbohydrate:
- Cholesterol:
- Protein:
- Total Fat:
- Sodium:

593. Cherry & Macadamia Nut Cookies

Serving: about 3-1/2 dozen. | Prep: 20mins | Cook: 10mins | Ready in:

Ingredients

- 1 cup unsalted butter, softened
- 1/2 cup plus 1 cup confectioners' sugar, divided
- 1/2 teaspoon salt
- 3 teaspoons vanilla extract
- 2 cups cake flour
- 1/2 cup all-purpose flour
- 2/3 cup dried cherries, chopped
- 2/3 cup macadamia nuts, toasted and finely chopped

Direction

- Set oven at 350°F and start preheating. Whisk butter with half a cup of confectioners' sugar and salt in a big bowl until light and fluffy. Mix in vanilla. Combine flours in another bowl, add them little by little into creamed mixture. Mix in nuts and cherries.
- Take level tablespoons of dough and form balls, place them 1 inch away from another on uncoated baking trays. Put the trays in the preheated oven and bake just until the bottoms start to turn brown, about 8 to 10 minutes. Let cool in the trays for 10 minutes.
- Add the rest of confectioners' sugar to a small bowl. Plunge cooled cookies into sugar and roll gently, take them back to wire racks and let cool completely. Roll cookies in sugar once more time right before serving.

Nutrition Information

- Calories:
- Sodium:
- Fiber:
- Total Carbohydrate:
- Cholesterol:
- Protein:

- Total Fat:

594. Cherry Almond Chews

Serving: about 7 dozen. | Prep: 15mins | Cook: 15mins | Ready in:

Ingredients

- 1 cup shortening
- 1 cup sugar
- 1 cup packed brown sugar
- 2 eggs
- 3/4 teaspoon almond extract
- 2-1/2 cups all-purpose flour
- 1 teaspoon baking soda
- 1 teaspoon salt
- 2-1/2 cups sweetened shredded coconut
- 3/4 cup chopped almonds or pecans, optional
- 1 jar (16 ounces) maraschino cherries, drained and halved

Direction

- Cream shortening with sugars in a big bowl until fluffy and light. Put in one egg at a time, whisking well after each. Whip in extract. Mix salt, baking soda and flour; Put into the creamed mixture gradually and stir well. Mix in nuts (optional) and coconut.
- Put by rounded teaspoonfuls 2 in. apart onto lightly greased baking trays. Put a cherry half in the middle of each. Bake for 12-14 minutes at 350° or until slightly browned. Take out to wire racks to cool.

Nutrition Information

- Calories: 152 calories
- Protein: 1g protein.
- Total Fat: 7g fat (3g saturated fat)
- Sodium: 106mg sodium
- Fiber: 0 fiber)

- Total Carbohydrate: 22g carbohydrate (16g sugars
- Cholesterol: 10mg cholesterol

595. Cherry Bonbon Cookies

Serving: 2 dozen. | Prep: 15mins | Cook: 20mins | Ready in:

Ingredients

- 1/2 cup butter, softened
- 3/4 cup confectioners' sugar
- 2 tablespoons milk
- 1 teaspoon vanilla extract
- 1-1/2 cups all-purpose flour
- 1/8 teaspoon salt
- 24 maraschino cherries
- GLAZE:
- 1 cup confectioners' sugar
- 1 tablespoon butter, melted
- 2 tablespoons maraschino cherry juice
- Additional confectioners' sugar

Direction

- Heat the oven beforehand to 350 degrees. Cream the sugar and butter until fluffy and light in a big bowl. Put vanilla and milk. Mix salt and flour; put in the creamed mixture gradually.
- Cut the dough into 24 parts. Form a ball by shaping every part around one cherry. Put them on baking sheets without grease. Bake until lightly browned or for 18 to 20 minutes. Allow to cool by putting on wire racks.
- For the glaze, mix cherry juice, butter and sugar until smooth. Sprinkle on top of the cookies. Dust using confectioners' sugar.

Nutrition Information

- Calories: 113 calories
- Cholesterol: 12mg cholesterol

- Protein: 1g protein.
- Total Fat: 4g fat (3g saturated fat)
- Sodium: 48mg sodium
- Fiber: 0 fiber)
- Total Carbohydrate: 18g carbohydrate (12g sugars

596. Cherry Cookies

Serving: 20 | Prep: | Cook: | Ready in:

Ingredients

- 1/2 cup packed brown sugar
- 1 cup white sugar
- 3/4 cup soy margarine
- 2 egg whites
- 1 teaspoon imitation vanilla extract
- 1 cup white spelt flour
- 1 cup whole wheat flour
- 1 teaspoon baking soda
- 1/2 teaspoon salt
- 1 cup dried cherries

Direction

- Set oven to 300°F (150°C) to preheat.
- Whisk soy margarine with white sugar and brown sugar in a medium bowl. Whisk in egg until well combined.
- Combine salt, baking soda, wheat flour and spelt flour in a separate bowl. Stir into sugar mixture until well combined. Finally, mix in dried cherries.
- Drop cookie batter from a teaspoon onto a lightly greased cookie sheet. Bake cookies for 13 minutes in the preheated oven.

Nutrition Information

- Calories: 186 calories;
- Sodium: 209
- Total Carbohydrate: 29.3
- Cholesterol: 0

- Protein: 2.5
- Total Fat: 7

597. Cherry Kiss Cookies

Serving: 4-1/2 dozen. | Prep: 20mins | Cook: 10mins | Ready in:

Ingredients

- 1 cup butter, softened
- 1 cup confectioners' sugar
- 1/2 teaspoon salt
- 2 teaspoons maraschino cherry juice
- 1/2 teaspoon almond extract
- 6 drops red food coloring, optional
- 2-1/4 cups all-purpose flour
- 1/2 cup chopped maraschino cherries
- 54 milk chocolate kisses, unwrapped

Direction

- Preheat an oven to 350°. Beat salt, confectioners' sugar and butter in a large bowl until blended, then beat in food coloring (if using), extract and cherry juice. Slowly beat in flour. Mix in cherries.
- Gather the dough to form 1-inch balls. Transfer onto greased baking sheets placing 1 inch apart.
- Bake for 8 to 10 minutes or until the bottoms are light brown. Immediately push down a chocolate kiss into the middle of every cookie (the cookie should crack around edges). Let it cool for 2 minutes on the pans. Transfer onto wire racks to cool.

Nutrition Information

- Calories: 85 calories
- Total Fat: 5g fat (3g saturated fat)
- Sodium: 51mg sodium
- Fiber: 0 fiber)

- Total Carbohydrate: 10g carbohydrate (5g sugars
- Cholesterol: 10mg cholesterol
- Protein: 1g protein.

598. Cherry Pecan Chews

Serving: 3 dozen. | Prep: 30mins | Cook: 25mins | Ready in:

Ingredients

- 3/4 cup cake flour
- 1/2 cup butter, melted
- 1 teaspoon vanilla extract
- 3/4 cup finely chopped pecans
- 6 tablespoons finely chopped red candied cherries
- 6 tablespoons finely chopped candied pineapple
- 3 egg whites
- 1/2 teaspoon salt
- 3/4 cup granulated sugar
- 1/2 cup confectioners' sugar

Direction

- Whisk together the flour, butter and vanilla in a large bowl till incorporated. Stir pecans and fruits into the mixture. Beat together egg whites and salt in another large bowl on medium speed until it form soft peaks. Add granulated sugar slowly into the mix, beat on high till it forms stiff glossy peaks and sugar dissolves. Fold it into the flour mixture.
- Spread the mixture into a 9-inch greased square baking pan. Bake until golden brown, at 350° for about 25-30 minutes. Let it cool down on a wire rack. Cover and chill in refrigerator overnight.
- Slice it into squares and roll them in confectioners' sugar. For storage, keep in an airtight container.

Nutrition Information

- Calories: 84 calories
- Sodium: 57mg sodium
- Fiber: 0 fiber)
- Total Carbohydrate: 11g carbohydrate (8g sugars
- Cholesterol: 7mg cholesterol
- Protein: 1g protein.
- Total Fat: 4g fat (2g saturated fat)

599. Cherry Surprise Cookies

Serving: 36-40 cookies. | Prep: 10mins | Cook: 10mins | Ready in:

Ingredients

- 2 cups Basic Cookie Dough
- 36 to 40 chocolate stars or chocolate kisses
- 36 to 40 candied cherry halves

Direction

- By heaping teaspoonfuls, drop cookie dough onto greased baking sheets, 2-in. apart. Put a chocolate star on top of each; wrap dough around it. Put candied cherry half over each; bake at 375° till bottoms are lightly browned or for 10-12 minutes. Transfer to wire racks; cool.

Nutrition Information

- Calories:
- Cholesterol:
- Protein:
- Total Fat:
- Sodium:
- Fiber:
- Total Carbohydrate:

600. Cherry Chocolate Coconut Meringues

Serving: 3 dozen. | Prep: 15mins | Cook: 25mins | Ready in:

Ingredients

- 3 large egg whites
- 1/2 teaspoon almond extract
- Dash salt
- 1/3 cup sugar
- 2/3 cup confectioners' sugar
- 1/4 cup baking cocoa
- 1-1/4 cups unsweetened finely shredded coconut
- 1/2 cup dried cherries, finely chopped

Direction

- In a big bowl, put the egg whites and allow it to stand for 30 minutes at room temperature.
- Add the salt and extract and beat it on medium speed until it forms soft peaks. Slowly add the sugar, one tablespoon at a time, then beat it on high until the sugar dissolves and forms stiff glossy peaks. Mix together the cocoa and confectioner's sugar, then beat it into the egg white mixture. Fold in cherries and coconut.
- Drop it by rounded tablespoonfuls onto the cooking spray coated baking trays, placed 2 inches apart, then let it bake for 25 to 28 minutes at 325 degrees or until it becomes firm to the touch. Allow it to fully cool on the pans on wire racks. Store it in an airtight container.

Nutrition Information

- Calories: 42 calories
- Total Carbohydrate: 6g carbohydrate (5g sugars
- Cholesterol: 0 cholesterol
- Protein: 1g protein. Diabetic Exchanges: 1/2 starch.
- Total Fat: 2g fat (1g saturated fat)
- Sodium: 10mg sodium
- Fiber: 1g fiber)

601. Chevron Ornament Cookies

Serving: about 2 dozen | Prep: 45mins | Cook: 10mins | Ready in:

Ingredients

- 1-1/2 cups butter, softened
- 2 cups sugar
- 2 large eggs
- 2 teaspoons vanilla extract
- 5 cups all-purpose flour
- 1-1/2 teaspoons baking powder
- 1 teaspoon salt
- 1/2 teaspoon baking soda
- 1/8 to 1/4 teaspoon paste food coloring

Direction

- Cream sugar and butter till fluffy and light; beat in vanilla and eggs. Whisk baking soda, salt, baking powder and flour in another bowl; beat into creamed mixture. Halve dough. Put preferred food coloring in 1 portion or different colors for every portion. Form into 2 1-in. thick 9x4-in. rectangles; freeze for about 30 minutes till firm.
- Cut rectangles crosswise to 1/8-in. slices using a sharp knife; stack alternate colored slices side by side, brushing water between slices to adhere, to make 2 new rectangles. Trim off uneven dough. Roll portions to 1/2-in. thick between 2 waxed paper pieces; freeze for about 15 minutes till firm.
- Preheat an oven to 350°. Diagonally cut rectangles to 1/2-in. slices with a sharp knife. Turn every other slice, upside down, to make chevron pattern, brushing between slices with water to adhere. Roll to 1/4-in. thick between waxed paper sheets.
- Cut using preferred cookie cutters; put onto ungreased baking sheets, 2-in. apart. Bake for

10-12 minutes till set. Cool for 1-2 minutes. Transfer from pans onto wire racks; fully cool.

Nutrition Information

- Calories: 269 calories
- Protein: 3g protein.
- Total Fat: 12g fat (7g saturated fat)
- Sodium: 253mg sodium
- Fiber: 1g fiber)
- Total Carbohydrate: 37g carbohydrate (17g sugars
- Cholesterol: 46mg cholesterol

602. Chewy Almond Cookies

Serving: 4-1/2 dozen. | Prep: 15mins | Cook: 10mins | Ready in:

Ingredients

- 3 tablespoons butter
- 1 cup packed brown sugar
- 1 large egg
- 1/4 teaspoon vanilla extract
- 1/4 teaspoon almond extract
- 1-1/2 cups all-purpose flour
- 1/4 teaspoon baking soda
- 1/4 teaspoon ground cinnamon
- 1/2 cup sliced almonds

Direction

- In the big bowl, whip the brown sugar and butter till crumbly. Whip in extracts and egg. Mix cinnamon, baking soda and flour; slowly put into butter mixture and stir well. Form into 2 6-inch rolls; wrap each of them in the plastic wrap. Keep in the refrigerator overnight.
- Remove the wrap; chop into a-quarter-inch slices. Position 2 inches apart onto the greased baking sheets. Sprinkle the almonds on top.
- Bake at 350 degrees till turning brown a bit or for 7 to 10 minutes. Let cool down for 2 to 3 minutes prior to transferring onto the wire racks.

Nutrition Information

- Calories: 80 calories
- Protein: 1g protein.
- Total Fat: 2g fat (1g saturated fat)
- Sodium: 30mg sodium
- Fiber: 0 fiber)
- Total Carbohydrate: 14g carbohydrate (8g sugars
- Cholesterol: 11mg cholesterol

603. Chewy Chocolate Cookies

Serving: 45 | Prep: | Cook: 20mins | Ready in:

Ingredients

- ¾ cup all-purpose flour
- ¾ cup whole-wheat pastry flour
- 3 tablespoons unsweetened cocoa powder
- ½ teaspoon baking soda
- ½ teaspoon salt
- 6 large egg whites
- ¾ cup granulated sugar
- 1½ cups packed dark brown sugar
- 1 tablespoon vanilla extract
- 3 ounces unsweetened chocolate, chopped and melted (see Tip)

Direction

- Set the rack in the middle of the oven; prepare by preheating to 350°F. Use a silicone baking mat or parchment paper to line a large baking sheet.
- In a medium bowl, combine salt, baking soda, cocoa powder, whole-wheat and all-purpose flour. In a large bowl, use an electric mixer to whisk egg whites for about 1 minute until

foamy. Whisk in granulated sugar in a steady, slow stream. Scrape down the sides then whisk in 1 tablespoon at a time of brown sugar. Whisk for about 3 minutes until smooth. Whisk in melted chocolate and vanilla. Mix in the dry ingredients using a wooden spoon until blended.
- Place the batter by the tablespoonful onto the prepared baking sheet with 1 1/2-inch space apart.
- Bake the cookies for 10-12 minutes until flat but springy, with slightly cracked tops. Let them cool on the pan for 5 minutes then place onto a wire rack and fully cool. Before baking another batch, allow the pan to cool first for a few minutes; replace parchment paper once burned or torn.

Nutrition Information

- Calories: 72 calories;
- Sugar: 11
- Protein: 1
- Saturated Fat: 1
- Fiber: 1
- Cholesterol: 0
- Total Fat: 1
- Sodium: 50
- Total Carbohydrate: 14

604. Chewy Fruit Cookies

Serving: 3 dozen. | Prep: 20mins | Cook: 15mins | Ready in:

Ingredients

- 1/2 cup shortening
- 1 cup packed brown sugar
- 1 egg
- 1/4 cup buttermilk
- 1-3/4 cups all-purpose flour
- 1/2 teaspoon salt
- 1/2 teaspoon baking soda
- 1 cup halved candied cherries
- 1 cup chopped dates
- 3/4 cup chopped pecans
- 36 pecan halves

Direction

- Cream brown sugar and shortening in a large bowl until fluffy and light. Beat in buttermilk and egg. Mix baking soda, salt and flour. Slowly add to the creamed mixture and combine thoroughly. Mix in the chopped pecans, dates and cherries.
- Transfer onto lightly greased baking sheets by heaping tablespoonfuls two inch apart. Add a pecan half on top of each. Bake for 12 to 15 minutes at 350° or until turned golden brown. Transfer onto wire racks.

Nutrition Information

- Calories: 114 calories
- Cholesterol: 6mg cholesterol
- Protein: 1g protein.
- Total Fat: 6g fat (1g saturated fat)
- Sodium: 60mg sodium
- Fiber: 1g fiber)
- Total Carbohydrate: 15g carbohydrate (9g sugars

605. Chocolate Almond Crescents

Serving: 6 dozen. | Prep: 20mins | Cook: 10mins | Ready in:

Ingredients

- 1-1/4 cups butter, softened
- 2/3 cup sugar
- 2 cups finely chopped almonds
- 1-1/2 teaspoons vanilla extract
- 2 cups all-purpose flour
- 1/2 cup baking cocoa

- 1/8 teaspoon salt
- 1-1/4 cups semisweet chocolate chips, melted
- 1 to 2 tablespoons confectioners' sugar
- Sweetened shredded coconut, optional

Direction

- Cream sugar and butter together in a big bowl until fluffy and light. Beat in vanilla and almonds. Whisk together salt, cocoa and flour in a separate bowl, then beat into the creamed mixture gradually. Chill with a cover until firm enough to shape, about 2 hours.
- Set the oven to 350 degrees to preheat. Form 2 tsp. of dough into logs with the length of 2 inches, then shape each into a crescent. Put on ungreased baking sheets with 2 inches apart. Bake until set, about 10 to 12 minutes. Transfer from pans to wire rack to completely cool.
- Dip into the melted chocolate with halfway of cookies, the let excess chocolate drip off. Arrange coated cookies on waxed paper. Sprinkle coconut over top if you want. Allow to stand until set, then use waxed paper to cover the dipped sides of cookies. Use confectioners' sugar to sprinkle over the undipped sides. Keep between pieces of waxed paper in airtight containers.

Nutrition Information

- Calories: 85 calories
- Total Carbohydrate: 7g carbohydrate (4g sugars
- Cholesterol: 8mg cholesterol
- Protein: 1g protein.
- Total Fat: 6g fat (3g saturated fat)
- Sodium: 27mg sodium
- Fiber: 1g fiber)

606. Chocolate Almond Drops

Serving: 4 dozen. | Prep: 20mins | Cook: 10mins |Ready in:

Ingredients

- 2 cups (12 ounces) semisweet chocolate chips
- 1 can (14 ounces) sweetened condensed milk
- 1 cup granola without raisins
- 1/2 cup sliced almonds
- 3 cups (18 ounces) miniature semisweet chocolate chips

Direction

- Melt milk and chocolate chips, occasionally mixing, in heavy saucepan on low heat. Take off heat; mix almonds and granola in. Refrigerate for 1 hour till firm enough to roll.
- Form mixture to 1-in. balls; roll in mini chocolate chips. Refrigerate for 2 hours till firm, covered. Keep in the fridge.

Nutrition Information

- Calories: 127 calories
- Sodium: 13mg sodium
- Fiber: 2g fiber)
- Total Carbohydrate: 18g carbohydrate (15g sugars
- Cholesterol: 3mg cholesterol
- Protein: 2g protein.
- Total Fat: 7g fat (4g saturated fat)

607. Chocolate Almond Wafers

Serving: about 4-1/2 dozen. | Prep: 20mins | Cook: 10mins |Ready in:

Ingredients

- 3/4 cup butter, softened
- 3/4 cup sugar
- 1 large egg
- 1 teaspoon vanilla extract
- 1-1/4 cups all-purpose flour
- 2/3 cup baking cocoa
- 1 teaspoon baking powder
- 3/4 cup sliced almonds

- 2/3 cup ground almonds

Direction

- Cream sugar and butter in big bowl till fluffy and light. Whip in vanilla and egg. Mix cocoa, baking powder and flour; slowly put to creamed mixture and combine thoroughly. Mix sliced almonds in.
- Form dough making a log, 14-inches in size. Roll into the ground almonds. Encase using plastic. Chill till firm, about 2 hours.
- Remove wrap and slice to make quarter-inch pieces. Put on not greased baking sheets, an-inch away. Bake for 9 to 11 minutes at 375° or till set. Transfer onto wire racks.

Nutrition Information

- Calories: 60 calories
- Cholesterol: 10mg cholesterol
- Protein: 1g protein.
- Total Fat: 4g fat (2g saturated fat)
- Sodium: 26mg sodium
- Fiber: 1g fiber)
- Total Carbohydrate: 6g carbohydrate (3g sugars

608. Chocolate Cake Mix Cookies

Serving: 4 dozen. | Prep: 15mins | Cook: 10mins | Ready in:

Ingredients

- 1 package (8 ounces) cream cheese, softened
- 1/2 cup butter, softened
- 1 egg
- 1 teaspoon vanilla extract
- 1 package chocolate cake mix (regular size)
- 1 cup semisweet chocolate chips
- 1 cup peanut butter chips

Direction

- Set oven to preheat at 375°. Beat together butter and cream cheese till smooth in a large bowl. Beat in vanilla and egg. Add the cake mix into the mixture; beat until incorporated on low speed. Stir in peanut butter chips and chocolate.
- On the greased baking sheets, drop rounded tablespoonfuls of the dough 2 in. apart. Bake until set, or 10-12 minutes. Allow to cool for 3 minutes, then take out and transfer to wire racks. Keep in an airtight container.

Nutrition Information

- Calories: 113 calories
- Fiber: 1g fiber)
- Total Carbohydrate: 13g carbohydrate (9g sugars
- Cholesterol: 15mg cholesterol
- Protein: 2g protein. Diabetic Exchanges: 1 starch
- Total Fat: 7g fat (4g saturated fat)
- Sodium: 111mg sodium

609. Chocolate Caramel Kiss Cookies

Serving: about 2 dozen. | Prep: 15mins | Cook: 10mins | Ready in:

Ingredients

- 1/2 cup butter, softened
- 1/2 cup packed brown sugar
- 1 cup granulated sugar, divided
- 1 large egg plus 1 large egg yolk
- 1-1/2 teaspoons vanilla extract
- 1-1/4 cups all-purpose flour
- 3/4 cup baking cocoa
- 1 teaspoon baking soda
- 1 teaspoon ground cinnamon
- 3/4 teaspoon salt

- 24 caramel-filled milk chocolate kisses

Direction

- Heat the oven beforehand to 350 degrees. Cream half cup of granulated sugar, brown sugar and butter until fluffy and light. Stir in vanilla, egg yolk and egg. Whisk the next 5 ingredients in a different bowl then beat into the creamed mixture gradually.
- Form rounded tablespoons of dough into balls. Roll in the leftover sugar. Put on baking sheets without grease, leaving 2-inch space apart. Bake for 8 to 10 minutes until edges begin to turn brown. Press a chocolate kiss immediately in the middle of every cookie, crack will form around edges. Allow to cool on pans for 2 minutes. Allow to cool by moving to wire racks.

Nutrition Information

- Calories: 143 calories
- Cholesterol: 27mg cholesterol
- Protein: 2g protein.
- Total Fat: 6g fat (3g saturated fat)
- Sodium: 170mg sodium
- Fiber: 1g fiber)
- Total Carbohydrate: 23g carbohydrate (15g sugars

610. Chocolate Cherry Cookies

Serving: 4 dozen. | Prep: 25mins | Cook: 10mins | Ready in:

Ingredients

- 1/2 cup butter, softened
- 1 cup sugar
- 1 egg
- 2 teaspoons maraschino cherry juice
- 1-1/2 teaspoons vanilla extract
- 1-1/2 cups all-purpose flour
- 1/2 cup baking cocoa
- 1/4 teaspoon salt
- 1/4 teaspoon baking powder
- 1/4 teaspoon baking soda
- 24 maraschino cherries, drained and halved
- FROSTING:
- 1 cup (6 ounces) semisweet chocolate chips
- 1/2 cup sweetened condensed milk
- 1 teaspoon maraschino cherry juice

Direction

- Cream sugar and butter in big bowl; beat vanilla, cherry juice and egg in. Mix baking soda, baking powder, salt, cocoa and flour; add to creamed mixture slowly.
- Roll to 1-in. balls; put on ungreased baking sheets, 2-in. apart. Make indentation in middle of each with the end of a wooden spoon. Put a cherry half in every indentation.
- Melt milk and chocolate chips, constantly mixing, in small saucepan on low heat. Take off heat; mix cherry juice in till blended. Put 1 tsp. on each cherry, the frosting will spread on cookies while baking. Bake for 9-11 minutes at 350° till set. Transfer to wire racks; cool.

Nutrition Information

- Calories: 167 calories
- Protein: 2g protein. Diabetic Exchanges: 1-1/2 starch
- Total Fat: 7g fat (4g saturated fat)
- Sodium: 92mg sodium
- Fiber: 1g fiber)
- Total Carbohydrate: 26g carbohydrate (19g sugars
- Cholesterol: 21mg cholesterol

611. Chocolate Chip Cherry Oatmeal Cookies

Serving: 15 cookies. | Prep: 20mins | Cook: 15mins | Ready in:

Ingredients

- 1/2 cup butter, softened
- 2/3 cup packed brown sugar
- 1/3 cup sugar
- 1 large egg
- 1 teaspoon vanilla extract
- 1 cup all-purpose flour
- 3/4 cup quick-cooking oats
- 3/4 teaspoon baking soda
- 1/2 teaspoon salt
- 2/3 cup dried cherries, chopped
- 1/2 cup semisweet chocolate chips

Direction

- In a small bowl, cream together the butter and sugars until fluffy and light. Beat vanilla and egg into the mixture. Combine the salt, baking soda, oats and flour; add them into the creamed mixture slowly and combine thoroughly. Mix in the chocolate chips and cherries.
- On ungreased baking sheets, drop scant 1/4 cupfuls and place it 3 in. apart. Bake to a golden brown at 350° or for 14-16 minutes. Allow to cool for 1 minute, then take out of baking sheets to wire racks. Keep in an airtight container for storage.

Nutrition Information

- Calories: 203 calories
- Cholesterol: 30mg cholesterol
- Protein: 2g protein. Diabetic Exchanges: 2 starch
- Total Fat: 8g fat (5g saturated fat)
- Sodium: 194mg sodium
- Fiber: 1g fiber
- Total Carbohydrate: 31g carbohydrate (21g sugars

612. Chocolate Chip Meringue Cookies

Serving: 20 | Prep: 25mins | Cook: 30mins | Ready in:

Ingredients

- 2/3 cup granulated sugar
- 2 teaspoons cornstarch
- 3 egg whites, at room temperature
- 1/2 teaspoon white vinegar
- 1/2 cup mini semi-sweet chocolate chips
- 3 tablespoons unsweetened cocoa powder
- Garnish:
- Cocoa powder (optional)

Direction

- Heat the oven beforehand to 150°C or 300°F. Use parchment paper to line 2 big baking sheets.
- Whisk cornstarch and sugar together in a small bowl then leave aside.
- Use an electric mixer to beat egg whites until foamy in a big bowl. Beat in vinegar until get soft peaks formed for about 2 minutes on medium speed. Beat in sugar mixture until get stiff glossy peaks formed on high speed, putting 15ml or 1 tablespoon at a time for about 2 to 3 minutes. Fold in cocoa powder and chocolate chips until just combined.
- By tablespoonfuls, drop about 15ml on baking sheets that were prepared, leaving about 2.5cm or 1-inch space apart. Bake until cookies are dry to touch while rotating the pans halfway through or for 30 minutes. Transfer cookies onto cooling racks from sheets. If desired, sprinkle cocoa powder. Allow to cool completely; keep in airtight containers.

Nutrition Information

- Calories: 52 calories;
- Total Fat: 1.4
- Sodium: 9
- Total Carbohydrate: 10.2
- Cholesterol: 0

- Protein: 0.9

613. Chocolate Chip Oat Cookies

Serving: 3-1/2 dozen. | Prep: 25mins | Cook: 10mins | Ready in:

Ingredients

- 1 cup packed brown sugar
- 2 large eggs
- 1/2 cup whole milk
- 3/4 cup vegetable oil
- 1 teaspoon vanilla extract
- 2 cups all-purpose flour
- 1 teaspoon baking soda
- 1 teaspoon salt
- 1 teaspoon ground cinnamon
- 1 teaspoon ground nutmeg
- 2 cups old-fashioned oats
- 1/2 cup semisweet chocolate chips
- 1/2 cup raisins

Direction

- In a bowl, mix together vanilla, eggs, oil, milk and brown sugar; mix well. Mix together the nutmeg, baking soda, salt, cinnamon and flour; mix them into the batter. Mix in raisins, chocolate chips and oats. Let it sit for 5-10 minutes. Onto greased baking sheets, drop teaspoonfuls of the dough. Bake to a light brown, at 350° for 10-12 minutes. Take out to wire racks right away.

Nutrition Information

- Calories: 221 calories
- Sodium: 187mg sodium
- Fiber: 1g fiber)
- Total Carbohydrate: 30g carbohydrate (15g sugars
- Cholesterol: 21mg cholesterol

- Protein: 3g protein.
- Total Fat: 10g fat (2g saturated fat)

614. Chocolate Chip Peanut Butter Cookies

Serving: Makes 40-50 cookies | Prep: | Cook: | Ready in:

Ingredients

- 1/2 cup (1 stick) unsalted butter, softened to room temperature, plus more for greasing
- 3/4 cup creamy peanut butter
- 1/2 cup sugar
- 1/2 cup brown sugar
- 2 large eggs
- 1 teaspoon vanilla extract
- 2 cups all-purpose flour
- 1/2 teaspoon baking powder
- 1/2 teaspoon baking soda
- 1/2 teaspoon salt
- 2 cups (12-ounce package) semisweet chocolate chips
- 1/2 cup peanut butter chips
- 1/2 cup dry-roasted peanuts

Direction

- Put oven rack in center position; preheat oven to 350°F. Rub 2 cookie sheets lightly with butter/use nonstick baking sheets; put aside.
- Use electric mixer/wooden spoon to beat sugars, peanut butter and butter till creamy and smooth in big bowl. Add vanilla and eggs; beat. Add salt, baking soda, baking powder and flour; beat till blended well at low speed. Add peanuts, peanut butter chips and chocolate chips; thoroughly mix.
- Scoop dough portion with teaspoon; use your hands to roll every portion to ball. Put balls, 5 rows with 3 cookies per row, on each cookie sheet; use fork tines/heel of your hand to flatten balls to spread them to 1 1/2-in. in diameter. One cookie sheet at a time, bake

each batch for 10 minutes; cookies should start to brown and be firm to touch.
- Take out of oven; cool for 3 minutes on sheet. Use spatula to transfer to cooling rack; cool for 1-2 minutes on cookie sheet then reuse dough so it won't melt. Keep in airtight container.
- Keep 1/2 cup chocolate chips when stirring batter if you want chocolate coating over each cookie. Press 5 chocolate chips lightly over each cookie when they're formed and put on cookie sheets. Gently spread partly melted chocolate chips over each cookie using a knife when cookies are out of the oven to create thin chocolate layer then cool as instructed.

Nutrition Information

- Calories: 145
- Fiber: 1 g(4%)
- Total Carbohydrate: 15 g(5%)
- Cholesterol: 14 mg(5%)
- Protein: 3 g(6%)
- Total Fat: 9 g(14%)
- Saturated Fat: 4 g(18%)
- Sodium: 50 mg(2%)

615. Chocolate Chip Pistachio Cookies

Serving: 30 | Prep: | Cook: | Ready in:

Ingredients

- 3 1/4 cups all-purpose flour
- 2 teaspoons baking powder
- 1 teaspoon salt
- 1 cup butter
- 1 cup white sugar
- 2 eggs
- 2 tablespoons milk
- 1 teaspoon vanilla extract
- 1/4 cup chopped walnuts
- 1 (3 ounce) package instant pistachio pudding mix
- 1 cup semisweet chocolate chips
- 1/2 cup white chocolate chips
- 1/3 cup confectioners' sugar for decoration

Direction

- Set oven to preheat at 190°C (375°F). Grease cookie sheets lightly.
- Sift the salt, baking powder and flour together, put them aside. Cream the sugar and butter together in a medium bowl. Add eggs, milk and vanilla, mix well after each time you add an ingredient. Add the dry ingredients into the mixture and mix until it creates a stiff dough. Save 1/4 of the dough in a small bowl. To the saved dough in the bowl, add in the nuts. Add the 3/4 cup of chocolate chips and pudding mix to the rest of the dough (big portion of dough); mix till incorporated.
- Make walnut sized balls out of the rolled pudding flavored dough, and place them onto the prepared cookie sheets, put them 1 1/2 inches apart. Use the bottom of a glass dipped in sugar or your hand to flatten out the balls. Make marble sized balls out of the rolled dough from the small bowl, top each of the flattened cookies with a marble sized ball. After that, place 1 of the white chocolate chips on top of each cookie.
- In the preheated oven, bake until cookies are set, or for 8 to 10 minutes. Take them out of the baking sheet to cool down on wire racks. Once cooled, dust them with confectioners' sugar if you want.

Nutrition Information

- Calories: 204 calories;
- Total Fat: 10.1
- Sodium: 210
- Total Carbohydrate: 26.9
- Cholesterol: 29
- Protein: 2.5

616. Chocolate Coconut Neapolitans

Serving: 5-1/2 dozen. | Prep: 30mins | Cook: 15mins | Ready in:

Ingredients

- 1 cup butter, softened
- 1-1/2 cups sugar
- 1 egg
- 1 teaspoon vanilla extract
- 2-1/2 cups all-purpose flour
- 1-1/2 teaspoons baking powder
- 1/2 teaspoon salt
- 1 teaspoon almond extract
- 4 drops red food coloring
- 1/2 cup sweetened shredded coconut, finely chopped
- 4-1/2 teaspoons chocolate syrup
- 1/2 cup semisweet chocolate chips
- 1-1/2 teaspoons shortening

Direction

- Line waxed paper on 9x5-in. loaf pan; put aside. Cream sugar and butter till fluffy and light in a big bowl; beat in vanilla and egg. Mix salt, baking powder and flour. Add to creamed mixture slowly; stir well.
- Divide dough to thirds. In 1 portion, add red food coloring and almond extract; evenly spread in prepped pan. Put coconut in 2nd portion; evenly spread on 1st layer. Put chocolate syrup in 3rd portion; spread on 2nd layer. Use foil to cover; freeze it for 4 hours to overnight.
- Unwrap loaf; halve lengthwise. Cut each portion widthwise to 1/4-in. slices; put on ungreased baking sheets, 2-in. apart. Bake at 350° till edges brown lightly or for 12-14 minutes. Transfer to wire racks; cool.
- Melt shortening and chocolate chips in a microwave; mix till smooth. In chocolate, dip 1 end of every cookie; let extra drip off. Put on waxed paper; let stand till set.

Nutrition Information

- Calories: 72 calories
- Protein: 1g protein.
- Total Fat: 4g fat (2g saturated fat)
- Sodium: 58mg sodium
- Fiber: 0 fiber)
- Total Carbohydrate: 10g carbohydrate (6g sugars
- Cholesterol: 11mg cholesterol

617. Chocolate Double Chip Cookies

Serving: about 6 dozen. | Prep: 25mins | Cook: 10mins | Ready in:

Ingredients

- 2 cups (12 ounces) semisweet chocolate chips
- 1/2 cup butter
- 3 eggs
- 1/2 cup sugar
- 2 teaspoons vanilla extract
- 2-1/4 cups all-purpose flour
- 1 teaspoon baking soda
- 1/2 teaspoon salt
- 1 package (10 ounces) vanilla or white chips

Direction

- In a heavy saucepan or microwave, melt butter and chocolate chips; mix till smooth. Take off the heat; allow to cool for 10 minutes. In a bowl, beat together the vanilla, sugar and eggs until light. Add in the chocolate mixture and combine well. Combine salt, baking soda and flour; add to the creamed mixture slowly. Mix in the vanilla chips (the batter will get sticky). Drop rounded tablespoonfuls of the mixture onto ungreased baking sheets 2 in. apart.
- Bake at 350° until set or 10-12 minutes. Allow to cool for 2 minutes before transferring from pans to wire racks.

Nutrition Information

- Calories: 100 calories
- Cholesterol: 13mg cholesterol
- Protein: 1g protein.
- Total Fat: 6g fat (3g saturated fat)
- Sodium: 50mg sodium
- Fiber: 1g fiber)
- Total Carbohydrate: 13g carbohydrate (9g sugars

618. Chocolate Drops

Serving: 48 | Prep: | Cook: | Ready in:

Ingredients

- 2 cups butterscotch chips
- 2 cups semisweet chocolate chips
- 2 cups salted peanuts
- 2 cups crushed, rippled potato chips

Direction

- Melt chocolate chips and butterscotch chips in a microwave-safe bowl for 4 minutes on the medium setting, whisking sometimes. Take out of the microwave and fold in potato chips and peanuts.
- Drop onto wax paper by heaping spoonfuls. Allow to stand until firm, 60 minutes.

Nutrition Information

- Calories: 127 calories;
- Cholesterol: 0
- Protein: 2
- Total Fat: 8.2
- Sodium: 75
- Total Carbohydrate: 11.8

619. Chocolate Fruit N Nut Cookies

Serving: about 2 dozen. | Prep: 25mins | Cook: 10mins | Ready in:

Ingredients

- 6 tablespoons butter, cubed
- 1/3 cup milk
- 1/4 cup sugar
- 2 tablespoons honey
- 1 cup sliced almonds
- 1/2 cup mixed candied fruit, finely chopped
- 1/4 cup all-purpose flour
- 3/4 cup semisweet chocolate chips
- 2 tablespoons shortening

Direction

- Mix honey, sugar, milk and butter in saucepan. Let mixture come to full boil. Take off from heat, then mix in fruit and almonds. Mix in flour till combined. Drop on baking sheets coated with grease and flour, by tablespoonfuls, spacing 3-inch apart. Smear batter using a spoon, making circles of 2-1/2-inch. Bake about 6 to 9 minutes at 350 degrees or till pale brown on edges. Cool about a minute on pans, then remove to waxed paper carefully and let cool fully. In a small-size saucepan, mix shortening and chocolate chips for coating. Cook on low heat to melt. Smear a teaspoonful on top of every cookie bottom. Once chocolate nearly sets, use a cake decorating comb or fork to draw wavy lines. Keep in fridge.

Nutrition Information

- Calories: 92 calories
- Protein: 1g protein.
- Total Fat: 5g fat (1g saturated fat)
- Sodium: 7mg sodium
- Fiber: 1g fiber)
- Total Carbohydrate: 13g carbohydrate (10g sugars

- Cholesterol: 0 cholesterol

620. Chocolate Gingerbread Cookie Mix

Serving: 3 dozen. | Prep: 45mins | Cook: 10mins | Ready in:

Ingredients

- 2-1/2 cups all-purpose flour
- 2/3 cup sugar
- 1 teaspoon ground ginger
- 1/2 teaspoon baking soda
- 1/4 teaspoon salt
- 1/4 teaspoon ground nutmeg
- 1-1/2 cups semisweet chocolate chips
- ADDITIONAL INGREDIENTS:
- 1/2 cup butter, cubed
- 1/2 cup molasses
- 1/4 cup water

Direction

- Mix the first six ingredients in a large bowl. Place the mixture inside the resealable plastic bag. In a separate bag, place the chocolate chips. Put both bags inside the cookie tin. The ingredients can make 1 batch of gingerbread cookies.
- To make the cookies, mix water, butter, chocolate chips, and molasses in a large saucepan. Cook the mixture over low heat, stirring constantly until both butter and chips are melted. Remove the mixture from the heat. Add the dry ingredients and mix until soft dough forms. Place the dough in a bowl, cover, and store it inside the fridge for 2 hours until easy to handle.
- Lightly dust the working surface with flour. Roll out dough into 1/4-inch thick. Dip the 3 1/2 gingerbread cookie cutter in flour and use it to cut the dough. Transfer the dough in an ungreased baking pan, arranging them 2-inches apart from each other. Reroll any scraps. Set the oven to 375°F and bake for 8-10 minutes until all set. Let the cookies cool on pans for 1-2 minutes before transferring on wire racks to cool completely.

Nutrition Information

- Calories: 115 calories
- Sodium: 54mg sodium
- Fiber: 1g fiber)
- Total Carbohydrate: 18g carbohydrate (10g sugars
- Cholesterol: 7mg cholesterol
- Protein: 1g protein. Diabetic Exchanges: 1 starch
- Total Fat: 5g fat (3g saturated fat)

621. Chocolate Gingersnaps

Serving: about 3-1/2 dozen. | Prep: 45mins | Cook: 10mins | Ready in:

Ingredients

- 1/2 cup butter, softened
- 1/2 cup packed light brown sugar
- 1/4 cup molasses
- 1 tablespoon water
- 2 teaspoons minced fresh gingerroot
- 1-1/2 cups all-purpose flour
- 1 tablespoon baking cocoa
- 1-1/4 teaspoons ground ginger
- 1 teaspoon baking soda
- 1 teaspoon ground cinnamon
- 1/4 teaspoon ground nutmeg
- 1/4 teaspoon ground cloves
- 7 ounces semisweet chocolate, finely chopped
- 1/4 cup course sugar

Direction

- Beat butter and brown sugar in a large bowl until light and fluffy. Beat in gingerroot, water, and molasses. Combine cloves, nutmeg,

cinnamon, baking soda, ginger, cocoa, and flour; slowly put into the cream mixture and mix thoroughly. Blend in chocolate. Chill, covered, until easy to handle, 2 hours.
- Form mixture into 1-inch balls; coat with sugar. Arrange the balls 2 inches apart on greased baking sheets.
- Bake for 10 to 12 minutes at 350° until surface starts to crack. Allow to cool for 2 minutes before transferring to wire racks.

Nutrition Information

- Calories: 80 calories
- Protein: 1g protein.
- Total Fat: 4g fat (2g saturated fat)
- Sodium: 47mg sodium
- Fiber: 0 fiber)
- Total Carbohydrate: 9g carbohydrate (6g sugars
- Cholesterol: 6mg cholesterol

622. Chocolate Hazelnut Shortbread

Serving: about 7-1/2 dozen. | Prep: 30mins | Cook: 10mins | Ready in:

Ingredients

- 1 cup butter, softened
- 1/3 cup Nutella
- 1 cup confectioners' sugar
- 1 large egg
- 3-3/4 cups all-purpose flour
- 1 teaspoon ground cinnamon
- Dash salt
- 1/2 cup finely chopped hazelnuts
- Additional confectioners' sugar, optional

Direction

- Heat the oven beforehand to 350 degrees. Cream confectioners' sugar, Nutella and butter until fluffy and light then stir in egg. Whisk salt, cinnamon and flour in a different bowl; mix in the creamed mixture gradually. Put hazelnuts and stir well.
- Cut the dough into 2 parts and form into disk. Make 1/8-inch thickness dough by rolling on a lightly floured surface. Cut the dough using 2 1/4-inch scalloped round cookie cutter with flour; put on baking sheets without grease, leaving 1-inch space apart. Bake for 8 to 10 minutes until bottoms turn light brown. Allow to cool by putting transferring to wire racks from pans. Dust confectioners' sugar if desired.

Nutrition Information

- Calories: 51 calories
- Sodium: 33mg sodium
- Fiber: 0 fiber)
- Total Carbohydrate: 6g carbohydrate (2g sugars
- Cholesterol: 7mg cholesterol
- Protein: 1g protein.
- Total Fat: 3g fat (1g saturated fat)

623. Chocolate Hazelnut Tassies

Serving: 3 dozen. | Prep: 25mins | Cook: 20mins | Ready in:

Ingredients

- 1 cup butter, softened
- 6 ounces cream cheese, softened
- 1 tablespoon sugar
- 2 teaspoons grated lemon peel
- 2 cups all-purpose flour
- FILLING:
- 1/4 cup Nutella
- 1/2 cup packed brown sugar
- 1 large egg
- 1 tablespoon butter, melted

- 1 teaspoon vanilla extract
- 1/2 cup finely chopped hazelnuts
- 1/4 cup miniature semisweet chocolate chips

Direction

- In a large bowl, cream lemon peel, sugar, cream cheese, and butter. Beat in flour. Form into 36 balls. Use floured fingers to press onto the bottom and up the sides of ungreased miniature muffin cups.
- To make the filling, beat vanilla, butter, egg, brown sugar, and Nutella in a small bowl until blended. Stir in chocolate chips and hazelnuts. Fill prepared cups until 3/4 full.
- Bake for 16 to 18 minutes at 375° until firm. Let cool on wire racks for 10 minutes. Carefully transfer from pans to wire racks. Place in an airtight container.

Nutrition Information

- Calories: 130 calories
- Sodium: 56mg sodium
- Fiber: 0 fiber)
- Total Carbohydrate: 11g carbohydrate (5g sugars
- Cholesterol: 25mg cholesterol
- Protein: 2g protein.
- Total Fat: 9g fat (5g saturated fat)

624. Chocolate Hazelnut Thumbprints

Serving: about 6 dozen. | Prep: 20mins | Cook: 10mins | Ready in:

Ingredients

- 2/3 cup butter, softened
- 1/2 cup sugar
- 1 egg plus 1 egg yolk
- 1/2 teaspoon vanilla extract
- 1-1/2 cups all-purpose flour
- 1/4 cup baking cocoa
- 1/2 teaspoon salt
- 2/3 cup ground hazelnuts
- 1/2 cup raspberry preserves
- Confectioners' sugar

Direction

- Beat sugar and butter in a large bowl until fluffy and light. Stir in the vanilla and egg yolk; blend well. Mix the salt, cocoa and flour; stir a third at a time to creamed mixture, whisking well after every addition. Mix in nuts. Turn dough into 1-inch balls; set 2-inch apart on baking sheets that are not greased. Make a 1/2-in-deep indention in the middle of each ball using the end of a wooden spoon handle; stuff with 1/4 teaspoon of preserves. Bake in the oven for 10-12 minutes at 350°F or until set. Take to wire racks and cool. Light sprinkle with confectioner sugar just prior to serving.

Nutrition Information

- Calories: 84 calories
- Sodium: 68mg sodium
- Fiber: 0 fiber)
- Total Carbohydrate: 10g carbohydrate (6g sugars
- Cholesterol: 21mg cholesterol
- Protein: 1g protein.
- Total Fat: 5g fat (2g saturated fat)

625. Chocolate Island Cookies

Serving: about 4 dozen. | Prep: 15mins | Cook: 15mins | Ready in:

Ingredients

- 1/2 cup shortening
- 1 cup packed brown sugar
- 1 egg

- 3 ounces unsweetened chocolate, melted and cooled
- 1/4 cup strong brewed coffee
- 2 cups all-purpose flour
- 1/2 teaspoon baking soda
- 1/2 teaspoon salt
- 2/3 cup buttermilk
- 1/3 cup sweetened shredded coconut
- FROSTING:
- 1-1/2 ounces unsweetened chocolate, melted and cooled
- 1/4 cup sour cream
- 1 tablespoon butter, softened
- 1 to 1-1/2 cups confectioners' sugar
- 2/3 cup sweetened shredded coconut

Direction

- Cream sugar and shortening together in a big bowl until fluffy and light. Whisk in coffee, chocolate, and egg. Mix together salt, baking soda, and flour; slowly add to the creamed mixture alternating with buttermilk, thoroughly stirring between additions. Mix in coconut.
- Drop onto non-oiled cookie sheets by tablespoonfuls, 2 inches separately. Bake at 375° until turning brown around the edges, 12-15 minutes. Transfer to wire racks to cool.
- To make the frosting, in a small bowl, mix together butter, sour cream, and chocolate until smooth. Add a sufficient amount of sugar to reach spreading consistency. Frost the cooled cookies. Sprinkle coconut over top.

Nutrition Information

- Calories: 175 calories
- Sodium: 56mg sodium
- Fiber: 1g fiber)
- Total Carbohydrate: 25g carbohydrate (16g sugars
- Cholesterol: 12mg cholesterol
- Protein: 2g protein.
- Total Fat: 8g fat (4g saturated fat)

626. Chocolate Lebkuchen

Serving: 50 | Prep: 15mins | Cook: 45mins | Ready in:

Ingredients

- 1 1/4 cups white sugar
- 3/4 cup honey
- 2 tablespoons water
- 2 cups semisweet chocolate chips
- 1 cup chopped almonds
- 1/2 cup candied mixed fruit, chopped
- 2 eggs, beaten
- 1/4 cup orange juice
- 2 3/4 cups all-purpose flour
- 2 teaspoons ground cinnamon
- 1 teaspoon ground cloves
- 2 teaspoons ground cardamom
- 1 teaspoon baking soda
- 1 teaspoon baking powder
- 1 1/2 cups confectioners' sugar
- 2 1/2 tablespoons orange juice
- 1/4 cup green decorator sugar
- 1/4 cup cinnamon red hot candies

Direction

- Mix in a large saucepan the water, honey, and sugar. Make to a rolling simmer, then separate from heat and reserve to cool. Mix in a medium bowl the orange juice, eggs, candied fruit, almonds, chocolate chips, and honey mixture. Strain together the baking powder and soda, cardamom, cloves, cinnamon, and flour; add into the fruit and nut mixture. Cover the bowl tightly, and keep in the refrigerator for 2-3 days to enhance the flavors.
- Prepare the oven by preheating to 325°F (165°C). Prepare a 10x15 inch jellyroll pan that is greased and floured. Place the dough into the prepared pan and equally spread. Place in the preheated oven and bake for 35-40 minutes. Let it cool then frost with the orange frosting.
- For orange frosting, place them in a small bowl the confectioner's sugar, and whisk in

the orange juice 1 tablespoon at a time until you achieve the consistency you want. Place over the cooled bars then spread. Slice bars into diamond shapes and top with cinnamon candies then dust with the green sugar.

Nutrition Information

- Calories: 135 calories;
- Total Fat: 3.3
- Sodium: 39
- Total Carbohydrate: 26.5
- Cholesterol: 7
- Protein: 1.7

627. Chocolate Lover's Drop Cookies

Serving: 5 dozen. | Prep: 15mins | Cook: 10mins | Ready in:

Ingredients

- 1 cup butter, softened
- 2 cups sugar
- 3/4 cup buttermilk
- 1 egg
- 2 teaspoons vanilla extract
- 2-1/4 cups all-purpose flour
- 2/3 cup baking cocoa
- 1 teaspoon baking soda
- 1/2 teaspoon salt
- 1 package (10 ounces) 60% cacao bittersweet chocolate baking chips
- 1 cup ground walnuts

Direction

- Cream sugar and butter in a large bowl until fluffy and light. Mix in the vanilla, egg and buttermilk until it turns smooth. Mix salt, baking soda, cocoa, and flour; then slowly add to creamed mixture and combine well. Mix in walnuts and chocolate chips. Place inside the refrigerator for 1 hour, covered. Onto ungreased baking sheets, drop dough by heaping teaspoonfuls. Place inside the oven and bake for 10-12 minutes at 350 degrees F or until edges are solid. Send to wire racks.

Nutrition Information

- Calories: 111 calories
- Protein: 1g protein.
- Total Fat: 6g fat (3g saturated fat)
- Sodium: 67mg sodium
- Fiber: 1g fiber)
- Total Carbohydrate: 15g carbohydrate (10g sugars
- Cholesterol: 12mg cholesterol

628. Chocolate Maple Cookies

Serving: 4 dozen. | Prep: 15mins | Cook: 10mins | Ready in:

Ingredients

- 1-1/4 cups shortening
- 1-1/2 cups packed brown sugar
- 5 eggs
- 1 teaspoon vanilla extract
- 1/2 teaspoon maple flavoring
- 2-1/2 cups all-purpose flour
- 3/4 teaspoon baking soda
- 1/2 teaspoon salt
- FROSTING:
- 2 ounces semisweet chocolate
- 1 tablespoon butter
- 1-1/2 cups confectioners' sugar
- 1/4 cup milk

Direction

- Beat brown sugar and cream shortening in a large bowl until fluffy and light. Put in eggs, one at a time, mixing well after every addition. Mix in maple flavoring and vanilla. Mix salt, baking soda and the flour; gently add to the creamed mixture and combine well. Put teaspoonfuls 2-inch apart onto a greased baking sheets. Place in the oven and bake for 8-10 minutes at 350°F or until edges start to brown. Take to wire racks to cool. To make frosting, melt butter and chocolate in a microwave; mix until smooth. Mix in milk and confectioner's sugar until become smooth. Place over cooled cookies and spread.

Nutrition Information

- Calories: 248 calories
- Protein: 3g protein.
- Total Fat: 12g fat (3g saturated fat)
- Sodium: 113mg sodium
- Fiber: 0 fiber)
- Total Carbohydrate: 32g carbohydrate (21g sugars
- Cholesterol: 46mg cholesterol

629. Chocolate Marshmallow Meltaways

Serving: 3 dozen. | Prep: 20mins | Cook: 10mins | Ready in:

Ingredients

- 1/2 cup butter-flavored shortening
- 3/4 cup sugar
- 1 egg
- 1/4 cup 2% milk
- 1 teaspoon vanilla extract
- 1-3/4 cups all-purpose flour
- 1/2 cup baking cocoa
- 1/2 teaspoon salt
- 1/2 teaspoon baking soda
- 18 large marshmallows, halved
- FROSTING:
- 3 tablespoons butter, softened
- 3 cups confectioners' sugar
- 3 tablespoons baking cocoa
- 1/8 teaspoon salt
- 4 to 6 tablespoons 2% milk

Direction

- Cream sugar and shortening in a large bowl until fluffy and light. Mix in vanilla, milk and egg. Mix the baking soda, salt, cocoa and flour; gently add to the creamed mixture and combine well.
- Into ungreased baking sheets, drop by tablespoonfuls 2-inch apart. Place in the oven and bake for 8 minutes at 350°F. Press down a marshmallow half, cut side down, onto each cookie; bake for 2 more minutes. Take out to wire racks to cool.
- Beat salt, cocoa, confectioner's sugar and butter in a small bowl until smooth. Mix in enough milk to reach a spreading consistency. Then frost cookies.

Nutrition Information

- Calories: 261 calories
- Total Carbohydrate: 46g carbohydrate (31g sugars
- Cholesterol: 18mg cholesterol
- Protein: 3g protein.
- Total Fat: 8g fat (3g saturated fat)
- Sodium: 147mg sodium
- Fiber: 1g fiber)

630. Chocolate Orange Checkerboard Cookies

Serving: about 3-1/2 dozen. | Prep: 30mins | Cook: 10mins | Ready in:

Ingredients

- 1-1/4 cups butter, softened
- 1-1/2 cups confectioners' sugar
- 1/4 teaspoon salt
- 1 large egg

- 1 teaspoon vanilla extract
- 3 cups cake flour
- 1-1/2 cups finely chopped pecans
- 1/4 cup baking cocoa
- 1 teaspoon grated orange zest
- 1/2 teaspoon orange extract

Direction

- Cream salt, confectioners' sugar and butter in a big bowl until combined. Whip in vanilla and egg. Stir in flour gradually. Mix in pecans.
- Split dough in half. Stir baking cocoa into one half; stir extract and orange zest into leftover half.
- Form each portion into a 5-1/2x2x2-in. block. Cover each block with plastic; chill 30 minutes.
- Unfold dough; slice each block into quarters lengthwise, creating 4 5-1/2x1x1-in. sticks. Alter 2 of the chocolate sticks with 2 of the orange sticks, creating 2 checkerboard blocks. Push sticks together gently to adhere. Cover in plastic again; chill 2 hours or until set.
- Set oven to 350° to preheat. Unfold and slice dough into 1/4-in. slices crosswise. Put 1 in. apart on ungreased baking trays. Bake for 9-11 minutes or until firm. Take out from pans to wire racks to cool.

Nutrition Information

- Calories:
- Protein:
- Total Fat:
- Sodium:
- Fiber:
- Total Carbohydrate:
- Cholesterol:

631. Chocolate Orange Cookies

Serving: 36 | Prep: 30mins | Cook: 10mins | Ready in:

Ingredients

- 1 (1 ounce) square unsweetened chocolate
- 3/4 cup butter
- 3/4 cup white sugar
- 1 egg
- 1 teaspoon vanilla extract
- 1 1/2 cups all-purpose flour
- 1 teaspoon baking powder
- 1 pinch salt
- 1 tablespoon orange zest

Direction

- Preheat an oven to 175°C/350°F. Melt unsweetened chocolate in microwave-safe dish, frequently mixing till smooth; put aside.
- Cream sugar and butter together till smooth in a medium bowl; beat in vanilla and egg. Mix salt, baking powder and flour; mix into creamed mixture, then divide dough to 2. On 1 half, mix orange zest, then melted chocolate into other half. To make about 1-in. diameter ball, use a bit of each mixture.
- In preheated oven, bake till center is set or for 8-10 minutes; cool on wire racks.

Nutrition Information

- Calories: 75 calories;
- Sodium: 47
- Total Carbohydrate: 8.5
- Cholesterol: 15
- Protein: 0.9
- Total Fat: 4.4

632. Chocolate Peanut Butter Thumbprints

Serving: about 3 dozen. | Prep: 35mins | Cook: 15mins | Ready in:

Ingredients

- 1 cup butter-flavored shortening

- 1 cup sugar
- 2 egg yolks
- 2 tablespoons milk
- 2 ounces unsweetened chocolate, melted and cooled
- 1 teaspoon vanilla extract
- 2 cups all-purpose flour
- 1/2 teaspoon salt
- 2/3 cup miniature semisweet chocolate chips
- FILLING:
- 1/3 cup creamy peanut butter
- 2 tablespoons butter-flavored shortening
- 1 cup plus 2 tablespoons confectioners' sugar
- 2 tablespoons milk
- 1/2 teaspoon vanilla extract

Direction

- Cream sugar and shortening in big bowl; beat vanilla, melted chocolate, milk and egg yolks in. Mix salt and flour; add to chocolate mixture slowly. Mix chocolate chips in; roll to 1-in. balls.
- Put on greased baking sheets, 2-in. apart. Make an indentation in middle of every ball with the end of wooden spoon handle; bake for 11-13 minutes at 350° till firm. Transfer to wire racks; completely cool.
- Meanwhile, for filling: Beat shortening and peanut butter till combined in small bowl; beat vanilla, milk and confectioners' sugar in till smooth. Use filling to fill cookies; keep in airtight container.

Nutrition Information

- Calories: 135 calories
- Fiber: 0 fiber)
- Total Carbohydrate: 15g carbohydrate (10g sugars
- Cholesterol: 10mg cholesterol
- Protein: 1g protein. Diabetic Exchanges: 1 starch
- Total Fat: 8g fat (2g saturated fat)
- Sodium: 41mg sodium

633. Chocolate Peppermint Pinwheels

Serving: 4 dozen. | Prep: 0mins | Cook: 10mins | Ready in:

Ingredients

- 1 cup shortening
- 1-1/2 cups sugar
- 2 eggs
- 2 tablespoons milk
- 2 teaspoons peppermint extract
- 2-1/2 cups all-purpose flour
- 1/2 teaspoon salt
- 1/2 teaspoon baking powder
- 2 ounces unsweetened chocolate, melted

Direction

- Cream sugar and shortening in a large bowl until fluffy and light. Beat in the extract, milk and eggs. Mix baking powder, salt and flour. Slowly transfer to the creamed mixture and combine thoroughly. Separate the dough in half. Place chocolate onto one portion and combine thoroughly.
- Roll every portion in between waxed paper to form a 16x7-inch rectangle of approximately 1/4-inch thick. Take out the top sheet of the waxed paper. Put the plain dough on top of chocolate dough. Then roll up jelly-roll style beginning with a long side. Encase in plastic and then chill for two hours or until firm.
- Unwrap the dough and chop into 1/4-inch slices. Transfer on greased baking sheets placing two inch apart. Bake for 8 to 10 minutes at 375° or until browned lightly. Transfer to wire racks and cool.

Nutrition Information

- Calories: 92 calories
- Sodium: 32mg sodium
- Fiber: 0 fiber)

- Total Carbohydrate: 11g carbohydrate (6g sugars
- Cholesterol: 9mg cholesterol
- Protein: 1g protein.
- Total Fat: 5g fat (1g saturated fat)

634. Chocolate Peppermint Snaps

Serving: about 5 dozen. | Prep: 25mins | Cook: 15mins | Ready in:

Ingredients

- 2 cups (12 ounces) semisweet chocolate chips, divided
- 1 large egg
- 1 cup sugar, divided
- 1/2 cup canola oil
- 1/4 cup corn syrup
- 1 teaspoon peppermint extract
- 1 teaspoon vanilla extract
- 2 cups all-purpose flour
- 1 teaspoon baking soda
- 1/4 teaspoon salt
- 1/3 cup coarsely crushed peppermint candies

Direction

- Preheat an oven to 350°. Melt 1 cup of chocolate chips in a microwave; mix till smooth. Cool. Beat extracts, corn syrup, oil, 2/3 cup sugar and egg till combined in another bowl; beat in melted chocolate. Whisk salt, baking soda and flour in another bowl; beat into peppermint mixture slowly. Fold in leftover chocolate chips and candies.
- Put leftover sugar into shallow bowl. Form dough to 1-in. balls and roll in sugar; put onto parchment paper-lined baking sheets, 2 in. apart. Bake for 12-15 minutes till cookies set and tops are cracked. Cool for 1 minute on pans. Transfer to wire racks; cool.

Nutrition Information

- Calories: 79 calories
- Total Fat: 4g fat (1g saturated fat)
- Sodium: 34mg sodium
- Fiber: 0 fiber)
- Total Carbohydrate: 12g carbohydrate (8g sugars
- Cholesterol: 3mg cholesterol
- Protein: 1g protein.

635. Chocolate Pretzel Cookies

Serving: 4 dozen. | Prep: 30mins | Cook: 5mins | Ready in:

Ingredients

- 1/2 cup butter, softened
- 2/3 cup sugar
- 1 egg
- 2 ounces unsweetened chocolate, melted and cooled
- 2 teaspoons vanilla extract
- 1-3/4 cups all-purpose flour
- 1/2 teaspoon salt
- MOCHA GLAZE:
- 1 cup (6 ounces) semisweet chocolate chips
- 1 teaspoon shortening
- 1 teaspoon light corn syrup
- 1 cup confectioners' sugar
- 4 to 5 tablespoons strong brewed coffee
- 2 ounces white baking chocolate

Direction

- Beat butter with sugar in a large bowl until light and fluffy. Add vanilla, chocolate, and eggs and mix well. Combine salt and flour. Slowly bring into the creamed mixture; stir well. Chill, covered, until firm, 60 minutes.
- Cut dough into 4 portions; shape each into a 6-inch roll. Cut each roll into slices of 1/2-inch thick; roll each into a 9-inch rope. Arrange

ropes on oiled baking sheets; shape ropes into pretzel shapes, keeping a 2-inch distance between each. Bake for 5 to 7 minutes at 400° until set. Allow to cool for 1 minute before transferring to wire racks to cool entirely.
- To make glaze, melt corn syrup, shortening, and chocolate chips in a microwaveable bowl; whisk until no lumps remain. Mix in confectioners' sugar and enough coffee until a smooth glaze is formed.
- Dip pretzels into glaze; drip off excess. Arrange pretzels on waxed paper until glaze is firm. Melt white chocolate. Drizzle melted chocolate over pretzels; drip off excess. Allow to rest until chocolate is entirely set. Store pretzels in an airtight container.

Nutrition Information

- Calories: 161 calories
- Protein: 2g protein.
- Total Fat: 7g fat (4g saturated fat)
- Sodium: 93mg sodium
- Fiber: 1g fiber)
- Total Carbohydrate: 23g carbohydrate (15g sugars
- Cholesterol: 19mg cholesterol

636. Chocolate Pretzels

Serving: 24 | Prep: 10mins | Cook: 2mins | Ready in:

Ingredients

- 24 circular pretzels
- 24 milk chocolate candy kisses
- 1 (1.69 ounce) package mini candy-coated chocolates

Direction

- Set the oven to 350°F (175°C) and start preheating.
- Arrange pretzels on baking sheets. Unwrap candy kisses; put one in each pretzel's center.
- Transfer to the prepared oven for 1-2 minutes until kisses melt. Take out of the oven; put a candy-coated chocolate in each pretzel's center. Chill in the fridge until set.

Nutrition Information

- Calories: 62 calories;
- Total Fat: 1.9
- Sodium: 70
- Total Carbohydrate: 9.7
- Cholesterol: 1
- Protein: 1.2

637. Chocolate Thumbprints Cookies

Serving: about 2-1/2 dozen. | Prep: 25mins | Cook: 10mins | Ready in:

Ingredients

- 1/2 cup butter, softened
- 2/3 cup sugar
- 1 egg, separated
- 2 tablespoons milk
- 1 teaspoon vanilla extract
- 1 cup all-purpose flour
- 1/3 cup baking cocoa
- 1/4 teaspoon salt
- 1 cup finely chopped walnuts
- FILLING:
- 1/2 cup confectioners' sugar
- 1 tablespoon butter, softened
- 2 teaspoons milk
- 1/4 teaspoon vanilla extract
- 24 milk chocolate kisses

Direction

- Cream sugar and butter in big bowl till fluffy and light. Whip in milk, vanilla and egg yolk. Mix cocoa, salt and flour; slowly put to the creamed mixture and combine thoroughly.

- Chill with cover for an hour or till easy to hold.
- Beat egg white in small bowl till frothy. Form dough to an-inch balls; dunk in egg white, then turn in nuts. Put on oiled baking sheets. Create a depression in middle of every cookie with the handle of wooden spoon. Bake for 10 to 12 minutes at 350° or till middle is set.
- For filling, mix vanilla, milk, butter and confectioners' sugar; mix till smooth. Pipe or spoon quarter teaspoon to every warm cookie; slowly push one chocolate kiss in the middle. Cautiously transfer from the pans onto wire racks to let cool.

Nutrition Information

- Calories: 117 calories
- Total Carbohydrate: 13g carbohydrate (8g sugars
- Cholesterol: 16mg cholesterol
- Protein: 2g protein.
- Total Fat: 7g fat (3g saturated fat)
- Sodium: 52mg sodium
- Fiber: 1g fiber)

638. Chocolate Almond Thumbprints

Serving: about 5-1/2 dozen. | Prep: 45mins | Cook: 10mins | Ready in:

Ingredients

- 1-1/2 cups butter, softened
- 1/2 cup sugar
- 1/2 cup packed brown sugar
- 2 large eggs
- 1 teaspoon almond extract
- 2-1/2 cups all-purpose flour
- 1/2 cup baking cocoa
- 1/2 teaspoon salt
- 1 cup ground almonds
- FILLING:
- 6 ounces semisweet chocolate, chopped
- 3/4 cup almond paste
- 2 cups confectioners' sugar
- 1/4 cup water
- 4 teaspoons meringue powder

Direction

- Cream sugars and butter till fluffy and light in a big bowl; beat in extract and eggs. Mix salt, cocoa and flour. Add to creamed mixture slowly; stir well.
- Put almonds into shallow bowl. Roll dough to 1-in. balls, then roll in almonds; put on greased baking sheets, 2-in. apart. Make an indentation in middle of each using end of wooden spoon handle; bake at 350° till firm or for 10-12 minutes. Transfer to wire racks; fully cool.
- Melt chocolate in small microwave-safe bowl; mix till smooth. Slightly cool. Add almond paste; beat till crumbly. Beat in meringue powder, water and confectioners' sugar till smooth; pipe filling into cookies, about 1 1/4 tsp. on each. Keep in an airtight container.

Nutrition Information

- Calories: 119 calories
- Sodium: 53mg sodium
- Fiber: 1g fiber)
- Total Carbohydrate: 14g carbohydrate (9g sugars
- Cholesterol: 18mg cholesterol
- Protein: 2g protein. Diabetic Exchanges: 1 starch
- Total Fat: 7g fat (3g saturated fat)

639. Chocolate Cherry Sandwich Cookies

Serving: 3-1/2 dozen. | Prep: 35mins | Cook: 0mins | Ready in:

Ingredients

- 4 ounces cream cheese, softened
- 1/2 cup confectioners' sugar
- 1/2 cup finely chopped maraschino cherries, drained
- 1/4 teaspoon almond extract
- 1 package (12 ounces) vanilla wafers
- 18 ounces milk chocolate candy coating, melted
- Red nonpareils or red colored sugar

Direction

- Beat confectioners' sugar and cream cheese until it becomes smooth in a small bowl. Mix in extract and cherries. Spread a teaspoon of cream cheese mixture on half of the wafers' bottoms. Use leftover wafers to cover. Put in the refrigerator until filling is firm or for an hour.
- Immerse the sandwiches in the candy coating. Let the excess drip off the sandwich. Put on waxed paper and use nonpareils to sprinkle. Let rest until set. Keep in the refrigerator in an airtight container.

Nutrition Information

- Calories:
- Total Fat:
- Sodium:
- Fiber:
- Total Carbohydrate:
- Cholesterol:
- Protein:

640. Chocolate Cherry Thumbprint Cookies

Serving: 2-1/2 dozen. | Prep: 50mins | Cook: 10mins | Ready in:

Ingredients

- 3/4 cup butter, softened
- 1/2 cup sugar
- 1 large egg yolk
- 1 teaspoon vanilla extract
- 1-1/2 cups all-purpose flour
- 1/4 cup baking cocoa
- FILLING:
- 1 cup confectioners' sugar
- 1/4 cup butter, softened
- 1 tablespoon maraschino cherry juice
- TOPPING:
- 30 maraschino cherries, patted dry
- 1/4 cup semisweet chocolate chips
- 1-1/2 teaspoons shortening

Direction

- Heat the oven beforehand to 350 degrees. Cream the sugar and butter until fluffy and light in a big bowl. Beat in vanilla and egg yolk. Whisk cocoa and flour in a separate bowl then beat into the creamed mixture gradually.
- Form into 1-inch balls then put them on baking sheets with grease, leaving 2-inch space apart. Use the end of a wooden spoon handle to press a deep indentation in the middle of each of the dough. Bake until firm or for 7 to 9 minutes. Allow it to cool by putting it on wire racks.
- Make the filling by beating cherry juice, butter and confectioners' sugar in a small bowl. Put 1/2 teaspoon of filling in each cookie and put cherry on top. Melt shortening and chocolate chips in a microwave. Mix until it becomes smooth; drizzle on top of cookies. Let rest until set.

Nutrition Information

- Calories: 84 calories
- Cholesterol: 14mg cholesterol
- Protein: 1g protein.
- Total Fat: 4g fat (3g saturated fat)
- Sodium: 27mg sodium
- Fiber: 0 fiber)

- Total Carbohydrate: 11g carbohydrate (8g sugars

641. Chocolate Covered Cherry Delights

Serving: 4 dozen. | Prep: 35mins | Cook: 10mins | Ready in:

Ingredients

- 1 cup butter, softened
- 1-1/2 cups sugar
- 1/3 cup maraschino cherry juice
- 1 teaspoon vanilla extract
- 3 cups all-purpose flour
- 1/2 cup baking cocoa
- 1 cup sweetened shredded coconut
- 3/4 cup chopped maraschino cherries, drained and patted dry
- 1/2 cup miniature semisweet chocolate chips
- TOPPING:
- 3/4 cup vanilla frosting
- 48 maraschino cherries with stems, drained and patted dry
- 1 cup miniature semisweet chocolate chips
- 1 teaspoon shortening

Direction

- Set oven to 375° to preheat. Whip butter with sugar in a big bowl until combined. Gradually whip in vanilla and cherry juice. Mix flour and cocoa in a separate bowl; whip into creamed mixture gradually. Mix in chocolate chips, cherries and coconut.
- Roll dough into 48 balls (about 1-1/4 in.); put 2 inches apart on ungreased baking trays. Push a deep indentation in center of each using the end of a wooden spoon handle. Bake until firm and bottoms are slightly browned, or for 9-11 minutes. Take out from pans to wire racks to cool completely.
- Frost each cookie with 3/4 teaspoon frosting. Put cherries on top. Microwave chocolate chips with shortening to melt; mix until smooth. Scoop on top of cherries. Let sit until firm.

Nutrition Information

- Calories: 160 calories
- Protein: 1g protein.
- Total Fat: 7g fat (4g saturated fat)
- Sodium: 47mg sodium
- Fiber: 1g fiber)
- Total Carbohydrate: 25g carbohydrate (17g sugars
- Cholesterol: 10mg cholesterol

642. Chocolate Covered Maraschino Cherry Cookies

Serving: 2 dozen. | Prep: 45mins | Cook: 15mins | Ready in:

Ingredients

- 24 maraschino cherries
- 1/2 cup butter, softened
- 3/4 cup packed brown sugar
- 1 tablespoon maraschino cherry juice
- 1 teaspoon vanilla extract
- 1-1/2 cups all-purpose flour
- 1/8 teaspoon salt
- 1 cup milk chocolate chips, divided
- 1/2 teaspoon shortening

Direction

- Use paper towels to pat cherries to remove extra moisture; put aside. Cream brown sugar and butter till fluffy and light in big bowl; beat vanilla and cherry juice in. Mix salt and flour; add to creamed mixture slowly. Stir well. Cover; refrigerate till dough is easy to handle, about 1 hour.
- Put a chocolate chip into every maraschino cherry; wrap 1 tbsp. dough around every

cherry. Put on ungreased baking sheets, 1-in. apart.
- Bake for 15-17 minutes till set and edges lightly brown at 350°; transfer to wire racks then cool.
- Melt shortening and leftover chips in microwave; mix till smooth. Dip cookies' tops in melted chocolate; let excess drip off. Put on waxed paper; stand till set. Keep in airtight container.

Nutrition Information

- Calories:
- Sodium:
- Fiber:
- Total Carbohydrate:
- Cholesterol:
- Protein:
- Total Fat:

643. Chocolate Dipped Cookies

Serving: 4-1/2 dozen. | Prep: 25mins | Cook: 10mins | Ready in:

Ingredients

- 1/2 cup butter, softened
- 3/4 cup sugar
- 1 large egg
- 1 teaspoon vanilla extract
- 1 cup all-purpose flour
- 1/3 cup baking cocoa
- 1/2 teaspoon baking soda
- 1/4 teaspoon salt
- 1/2 cup chopped almonds
- 1/2 cup miniature semisweet chocolate chips
- 12 ounces white candy coating disks, melted
- 12 ounces dark chocolate candy coating disks, melted
- 2 ounces milk chocolate candy coating disks, melted

Direction

- Cream sugar and butter in a large bowl. Whisk in vanilla and egg. Mix salt, baking soda, cocoa and flour; add to the creamed mixture gradually. Stir in chocolate chips and almonds. Chill in the fridge with a cover for 2 hours. Separate dough in 1/2. Form into 2 8-in. rolls; use plastic wrap to wrap each. Chill in the fridge until firm or for 3 hours.
- Unwrap; slice into 1/4-in. slices. Transfer to the greased baking sheets, 2 in. apart. Bake for 8-10 minutes at 350° or until set. Transfer to wire racks to cool.
- Coat 1/2 of cookies with white coating; let excess drip off. Arrange on waxed paper. Do the same with the rest of the cookies in dark chocolate coating.
- In a resealable plastic bag, place milk chocolate coating; create a small hole in one of the bag's corners. Pipe designs on cookies. Allow to stand for half an hour or until set.

Nutrition Information

- Calories: 247 calories
- Sodium: 82mg sodium
- Fiber: 1g fiber)
- Total Carbohydrate: 31g carbohydrate (25g sugars
- Cholesterol: 17mg cholesterol
- Protein: 2g protein.
- Total Fat: 14g fat (10g saturated fat)

644. Chocolate Dipped Macaroons

Serving: Makes about 5 dozen | Prep: | Cook: | Ready in:

Ingredients

- 5 large egg whites
- 1/2 vanilla bean, split lengthwise
- 1 1/3 cups sugar

- 4 cups long-shred unsweetened coconut (about 6 ounces), lightly toasted
- 3/4 cup slivered almonds, toasted, cooled, ground
- 12 ounces bittersweet (not unsweetened) or semisweet chocolate, finely chopped

Direction

- Heat the oven to 275°F. Line parchment paper on 2 big baking sheets. In a big bowl, put the egg whites; scratch in vanilla bean seeds. Whip egg whites with electric mixer to form soft peaks. Slowly put in the sugar, whipping for 5 minutes till meringue turn extremely thick, resembles marshmallow creme. Fold coconut in, then the almonds. Drop rounded tablespoonfuls of batter on prepped sheets, gapping piles 1 1/2-inch away.
- Let macaroons bake for 25 minutes till light beige on the outer and looks dry, insides will still remain soft. Turn the baking sheets onto racks; let macaroons cool fully. Turn the macaroons onto work counter; line the pans again with clean parchment.
- In double boiler top above the simmering water, put the chocolate. Mix chocolate till smooth; take from above water. Dunk a macaroon bottom to liquified chocolate to quarter-inch depth. Put, chocolate side facing down, on prepped sheet. Redo dipping with the rest of macaroons. Refrigerate to firm the chocolate, for an hour. May be done 3 days in advance. Store in refrigerator with cover. Rest macaroons for an hour at room temperature prior to serving.

Nutrition Information

- Calories: 272
- Saturated Fat: 10 g(50%)
- Sodium: 24 mg(1%)
- Fiber: 4 g(14%)
- Total Carbohydrate: 34 g(11%)
- Protein: 4 g(8%)
- Total Fat: 16 g(24%)

645. Chocolate Dipped Orange Spritz

Serving: 4 dozen. | Prep: 20mins | Cook: 10mins | Ready in:

Ingredients

- 3/4 cup butter, softened
- 1 cup sugar
- 1 large egg
- 2 tablespoons orange juice
- 4 teaspoons grated orange zest
- 2-3/4 cups all-purpose flour
- 1 teaspoon baking powder
- 1/4 teaspoon salt
- 1/2 cup ground walnuts
- 1 cup semisweet chocolate chips
- 1 tablespoon shortening

Direction

- Preheat an oven to 350°. Cream sugar and butter till fluffy and light in a bowl; beat in egg, zest and orange juice slowly. Whisk salt, baking powder and flour in another bowl. Add to creamed mixture slowly, stirring well.
- Press long dough strips onto ungreased baking sheets using a cookie press with bar disk; cut ends to release from the disk. Cut every strip to 3-in. lengths; you don't have to separate them.
- Bake till set, do not brown, or 8-10 minutes; if needed, re-cut cookies. Transfer from pans onto wire racks; fully cool.
- In a shallow bowl, put walnuts. Melt shortening and chocolate chips in a microwave; mix till smooth. In chocolate, dip each cookie halfway; let extra drip off. Sprinkle walnuts. Put on waxed paper; let stand till set.

Nutrition Information

- Calories: 99 calories

- Total Fat: 5g fat (3g saturated fat)
- Sodium: 43mg sodium
- Fiber: 1g fiber)
- Total Carbohydrate: 12g carbohydrate (6g sugars
- Cholesterol: 12mg cholesterol
- Protein: 1g protein. Diabetic Exchanges: 1 starch

- Calories: 136 calories
- Cholesterol: 20mg cholesterol
- Protein: 1g protein.
- Total Fat: 8g fat (5g saturated fat)
- Sodium: 89mg sodium
- Fiber: 0 fiber)
- Total Carbohydrate: 16g carbohydrate (10g sugars

646. Chocolate Dipped Spritz

Serving: about 6 dozen. | Prep: 25mins | Cook: 10mins | Ready in:

Ingredients

- 1 cup butter, softened
- 3/4 cup sugar
- 1 egg
- 1 teaspoon vanilla extract
- 2-1/4 cups all-purpose flour
- 1/2 teaspoon salt
- 1/4 teaspoon baking powder
- 11 ounces dark, white or milk chocolate candy coating, coarsely chopped
- Crushed peppermint candies

Direction

- Cream together sugar and butter in a big bowl until fluffy and light. Whisk in vanilla and egg. Mix together baking powder, salt, and flour; slowly add to the creamed mixture.
- With a cookie press that can fit your desired disk, press the dough onto non-oiled cookie sheets, 2 inches separately. Bake at 375° until set without turning brown, 7-9 minutes. Transfer to wire racks to cool.
- Melt candy coating in a microwave-safe bowl; dip each cookie to coat halfway. Sprinkle crushed candies over top. Put on waxed paper to set.

Nutrition Information

647. Chocolate Dipped Triple Ginger Cookies

Serving: about 3 dozen. | Prep: 35mins | Cook: 10mins | Ready in:

Ingredients

- 1 cup shortening
- 1/2 cup sugar
- 1/2 cup packed brown sugar
- 1 large egg
- 1 cup molasses
- 2 tablespoons finely chopped crystallized ginger
- 2 teaspoons grated fresh gingerroot
- 4-2/3 cups all-purpose flour
- 1-1/2 teaspoons baking powder
- 3/4 teaspoon baking soda
- 2 teaspoons ground ginger
- 1/2 teaspoon salt
- 1/2 teaspoon ground cinnamon
- 1/2 teaspoon ground nutmeg
- 2 packages (10 ounces each) 60% cacao bittersweet chocolate baking chips, melted
- 4 ounces white baking chocolate, melted

Direction

- Cream sugars and shortening together in a big bowl until fluffy and light. Whisk in eggs, and then molasses, crystallized ginger, and gingerroot. Stir seasonings, baking soda, baking powder, and flour together in a separate bowl; slowly whisk into the creamed mixture.

- Split the dough into 2 portions. Form each portion into a disk, wrap with plastic. Chill until firm enough to roll, 60 minutes.
- Turn the oven to 375° to preheat. Roll each dough portion on a lightly floured surface until the thickness is 1/8-inch. With a floured 2 1/2-inch round or 3-inch gingerbread man cookie cutter, cut the dough. Put on non-oiled cookie sheets, 2 inches separately. Bake until set, 8-10 minutes. Transfer from the pans to wire racks to fully cool.
- In melted dark chocolate, dip each cookie to coat halfway, letting the excess fall off. Put on waxed paper and allow to sit until set. Drizzle melted white chocolate over top, allow to sit until set.

Nutrition Information

- Calories:
- Sodium:
- Fiber:
- Total Carbohydrate:
- Cholesterol:
- Protein:
- Total Fat:

648. Chocolate Mint Cookie Cups

Serving: about 3 dozen. | Prep: 45mins | Cook: 10mins | Ready in:

Ingredients

- 1/2 cup butter, softened
- 1 cup sugar
- 1 large egg
- 1 teaspoon peppermint extract
- 1-1/2 cups all-purpose flour
- 1/2 cup baking cocoa
- 1/4 teaspoon baking soda
- 1/4 teaspoon baking powder
- 1/4 teaspoon salt
- TOPPING:
- 1 cup (6 ounces) semisweet chocolate chips
- 1/2 cup heavy whipping cream
- 1/4 cup white baking chips
- Green paste food coloring, optional

Direction

- Set the oven to 350 degrees to preheat. Beat sugar and butter in a big bowl till fluffy and light. Whip in extract and egg. Mix the salt, baking powder, baking soda, cocoa and flour, then put into creamed mixture gradually; stir thoroughly.
- Form to balls of 1-inch, then arrange in miniature muffin cups lined with paper. Bake till set, about 8 to 10 minutes. Transfer onto wire racks. Cool fully.
- In a small-size bowl, put the chocolate chips. Let the cream come just to boil in small saucepan. Add on top of chocolate, then whip till smooth. Let come to room temperature, while mixing from time to time. Chill for 20 minutes, till ganache attains the piping consistency. Pipe on top of cookies.
- Liquified white baking chips in microwavable bowl for a minute at 50% power, then mix till smooth. Tint using green food coloring If wished. Pipe on tops.

Nutrition Information

- Calories: 115 calories
- Sodium: 57mg sodium
- Fiber: 1g fiber)
- Total Carbohydrate: 15g carbohydrate (9g sugars
- Cholesterol: 17mg cholesterol
- Protein: 1g protein.
- Total Fat: 6g fat (4g saturated fat)

649. Chocolate Mint Hearts

Serving: 2 dozen. | Prep: 25mins | Cook: 10mins | Ready in:

Ingredients

- 1 package (10 ounces) mint chocolate chips, divided
- 1/4 cup butter, softened
- 1/3 cup sugar
- 1 large egg
- 1/2 teaspoon vanilla extract
- 1-1/4 cups all-purpose flour
- 3/4 teaspoon baking powder
- 1/4 teaspoon salt
- 1/4 teaspoon baking soda
- 1/4 cup shortening
- Colored sprinkles, optional

Direction

- Microwave half cup chocolate chips to melt in a microwaveable bowl; stir. Let cool slightly. Cream butter with sugar in a small bowl. Whip in the melted chocolate, vanilla and egg. Mix the baking soda, salt, baking powder and flour; put into creamed mixture gradually and stir well.
- Cover and chill for 1-2 hours or until easy to handle. Shape dough to 1/4-in. thickness on a lightly floured surface. Slice out cookies with a floured 2-1/2-in. heart-shaped cookie cutter. Put 2 in. apart on ungreased baking trays. Bake for 7-10 minutes at 350° or until firm. Take out to wire racks to cool completely.
- Microwave shortening and leftover chocolate chips to melt; mix until smooth. Plunge each cookie halfway into chocolate mixture; let excess fall off. Dust chocolate with sprinkles (optional). Put on waxed paper; chill until firm.

Nutrition Information

- Calories: 131 calories
- Fiber: 1g fiber)
- Total Carbohydrate: 15g carbohydrate (10g sugars
- Cholesterol: 14mg cholesterol
- Protein: 2g protein.
- Total Fat: 7g fat (4g saturated fat)
- Sodium: 67mg sodium

650. Chocolate Raspberry Cutout Cookies

Serving: 4 dozen. | Prep: 45mins | Cook: 10mins | Ready in:

Ingredients

- 1 cup unsalted butter, softened
- 1 cup superfine sugar
- 1 large egg
- 1 large egg yolk
- 2 teaspoons vanilla extract
- 2-1/4 cups all-purpose flour
- 1/4 cup baking cocoa
- 1/2 teaspoon salt
- 1/4 teaspoon baking powder
- 1/4 teaspoon ground cinnamon
- FROSTING:
- 1-1/2 cups frozen unsweetened raspberries, thawed
- 6 tablespoons butter, softened
- 4 cups confectioners' sugar
- Gold and pearl dragees

Direction

- Cream sugar and butter till fluffy and light in big bowl; beat vanilla, yolk and egg in. Mix cinnamon, baking powder, cocoa, salt and flour; add to creamed mixture slowly. Stir well.
- Halve dough; form each portion into ball. Flatten into disk; use plastic to wrap. Refrigerate for an hour.
- Roll one dough portion to 1/4-in. thick on lightly floured surface; use floured 3-in. heart-shaped cookie cutter to cut. Put on greased

baking sheets, 1-in. apart. Repeat with leftover dough.
- Bake for 6-8 minutes at 375° till lightly browned; cool for a minute. Transfer from pans onto wire racks; completely cool.
- Frosting: Through sieve, press raspberries; discard seeds. Cream raspberry puree, confectioners' sugar and butter till creamy and smooth in big bowl. Frost and decorate cookies with dragees as desired. Keep in airtight container in the fridge.

Nutrition Information

- Calories: 128 calories
- Sodium: 39mg sodium
- Fiber: 0 fiber)
- Total Carbohydrate: 19g carbohydrate (14g sugars
- Cholesterol: 22mg cholesterol
- Protein: 1g protein.
- Total Fat: 6g fat (3g saturated fat)

651. Chocolate Tipped Butter Cookies

Serving: about 3-1/2 dozen. | Prep: 20mins | Cook: 15mins | Ready in:

Ingredients

- 1 cup butter, softened
- 1/2 cup confectioners' sugar
- 1 teaspoon vanilla extract
- 2 cups all-purpose flour
- CHOCOLATE COATING:
- 1 cup (6 ounces) semisweet chocolate chips
- 1 tablespoon shortening
- 1/2 cup finely chopped pecans

Direction

- Cream sugar and butter together in a bowl. Add vanilla, stir thoroughly. Slowly add flour, thoroughly stir. Put on a cover and refrigerate for 60 minutes. Form the dough into 2 1/2x1/2-inch sticks by tablespoonfuls. Put on non-oiled cookie sheets, 2-inch separately. With a fork, flatten 3/4 of each stick lengthwise. Bake at 350° until set, 14-16 minutes. Keep on cookie sheets to cool. Melt shortening and chocolate chips until smooth; dip each cookie with the round end into the chocolate mixture. Sprinkle nuts over top. Put on waxed paper to firm up.

Nutrition Information

- Calories: 97 calories
- Protein: 1g protein.
- Total Fat: 7g fat (4g saturated fat)
- Sodium: 35mg sodium
- Fiber: 1g fiber)
- Total Carbohydrate: 9g carbohydrate (4g sugars
- Cholesterol: 12mg cholesterol

652. Christmas Cookie Train

Serving: 6 cookies. | Prep: 30mins | Cook: 10mins | Ready in:

Ingredients

- 1/2 tube refrigerated peanut butter cookie dough
- 1/4 cup all-purpose flour
- 6 tablespoons butter, softened
- 3 cups confectioners' sugar
- 3 tablespoons whole milk
- 2 teaspoons vanilla extract
- Green, red, yellow and brown paste food coloring
- Assorted decorations: Peppermint candies, M&M's, mini vanilla wafers, animal crackers and red shoestring licorice

Direction

- Whisk flour and cookie dough until combined in a small bowl. Roll dough to 1/8-in. thickness on a lightly floured surface. Cut out 6 4x3-in. rectangles with a sharp knife; reserve scraps.
- Arrange rectangles on clean and dry baking sheets, 2 inches apart. Reroll dough scraps; for cowcatcher, cut out a 1-1/2-in. triangle, for smokestack, a 1-1/4x1/2-in. rectangle and for engine cab, a 2x1-1/2-in. rectangle. Attach to one rectangle; press seams gently to seal.
- Bake for 7-9 minutes at 350° or until edges turn golden brown. Place them on wire racks; cool.
- To prepare frosting: whisk vanilla, milk, confectioners' sugar and butter in a small bowl until creamy. Put 1 cup aside. Tint 1 tablespoon frosting yellow, 3 tablespoons red and 3 tablespoons green. Tint the rest of frosting brown.
- Put 2 tablespoons of white frosting aside. Spread the rest of white frosting over cookies, leaving a 2-1/2x1-1/2-in. rectangles in three passenger cars' centers and 2-1/2x2-in. rectangles in the two animal cars' centers. Frost the engine.
- Attach peppermint candy wheels and train cars with a small amount of reserved frosting on a 35x8-in. covered board.
- Add couplings between the cars and a headlight above cowcatcher with M&M's and frosting. Add M&M's for smoke coming out of smokestack. For passenger faces, use vanilla wafers; garnish with colored frosting. Add licorice bars and animal crackers to the animal cars. Garnish train as preferred with the rest of frosting.

Nutrition Information

- Calories:
- Cholesterol:
- Protein:
- Total Fat:
- Sodium:
- Fiber:
- Total Carbohydrate:

653. Christmas Cookies In A Jar

Serving: 3 dozen. | Prep: 15mins | Cook: 10mins | Ready in:

Ingredients

- 1/3 cup sugar
- 1/3 cup packed brown sugar
- 3/4 cup all-purpose flour
- 1/2 teaspoon baking powder
- 1/8 teaspoon baking soda
- 1/8 teaspoon salt
- 1 cup quick-cooking oats
- 1 cup dried cranberries
- 1 cup vanilla or white chips
- ADDITIONAL INGREDIENTS:
- 1/2 cup butter, melted
- 1 egg
- 1 teaspoon vanilla extract

Direction

- In a 1-qt. glass jar, layer in the sugar, then brown sugar, pack each layer well. Mix together the salt, baking soda, baking powder and flour, then spoon this mixture into jar. Place chips, cranberries and oats on top. For storage, cover and keep in a cool, dry place for 6 months at most.
- For the cookies: Add cookie mix to a large bowl; mix to combine. Beat vanilla, egg and butter into the mixture. Refrigerate, covered, for 30 minutes.
- On ungreased baking sheets, drop tablespoonfuls of the dough 2 in. apart. Bake until browned at 375° for 8-10 minutes. Transfer to wire racks to cool down.

Nutrition Information

- Calories: 188 calories
- Sodium: 102mg sodium
- Fiber: 1g fiber)
- Total Carbohydrate: 26g carbohydrate (13g sugars
- Cholesterol: 27mg cholesterol
- Protein: 2g protein.
- Total Fat: 9g fat (5g saturated fat)

654. Christmas Eve Mice

Serving: | Prep: 25mins | Cook: 0mins | Ready in:

Ingredients

- 24 double-stuffed Oreo cookies
- 1 cup (6 ounces) semisweet chocolate chips
- 2 teaspoons shortening
- 24 red maraschino cherries with stems, well drained
- 24 milk chocolate kisses
- 48 sliced almonds
- 1 small tube green decorative icing gel
- 1 small tube red decorative icing gel

Direction

- Twist cookies apart carefully and put aside the halves attached with cream filling. Reserve the plain halves for another use.
- Melt shortening and chocolate chips in a microwave, then stir until mixture is smooth. Dip each cherry in the melted chocolate by holing its stem, then press it on the bottom of a chocolate kiss. Put on the cream filling of cookie with the stem of cherry extending beyond the edge of cookie.
- To make ears, put between cherry and kiss with slivered almonds, then chill until set. Pipe holly leaves on the cream using green gel. Pipe holly berries between leaves using red gel. Keep in a tightly sealed container at room temperature.

Nutrition Information

- Calories: 151 calories
- Sodium: 50mg sodium
- Fiber: 1g fiber)
- Total Carbohydrate: 20g carbohydrate (15g sugars
- Cholesterol: 1mg cholesterol
- Protein: 2g protein.
- Total Fat: 8g fat (3g saturated fat)

655. Christmas Lights Sugar Cookies

Serving: 4 dozen cookies. | Prep: 25mins | Cook: 10mins | Ready in:

Ingredients

- 1 cup butter, softened
- 1-1/2 cups confectioners' sugar
- 1 large egg
- 1 teaspoon vanilla extract
- 1/2 teaspoon almond extract
- 2-1/2 cups all-purpose flour
- 1 teaspoon baking soda
- 1 teaspoon cream of tartar
- DECORATING:
- 1/3 cup light corn syrup
- Assorted sprinkles
- Shoestring licorice
- 1/3 cup sweetened shredded coconut
- 28 miniature semisweet chocolate chips
- 14 red M&M's miniature baking bits
- 28 miniature marshmallows, halved

Direction

- Whisk together powdered sugar and butter in a large mixing bowl until fluffy and light. Beat in extracts and egg. Mix cream of tartar, baking soda, and flour; slowly mix into creamed mixture until well combined. Cut dough in half. Freeze, covered, for 25 minutes or until easy to work with.

- To make lights: flatten one piece of dough to 1/8-inch thickness on a work surface lightly coated with flour. Use a 3 1/2-inch light-shaped cookie cutter coated with flour to cut out shapes. Arrange cookies 2 inches apart on ungreased baking sheets. Poke a 1/2-inch hole from the top of each cookie using a plastic straw.
- Bake cookies for 6 to 8 minutes at 350° until edges turn brown lightly. Reopen holes in cookies with a plastic straw. Transfer to wire racks to cool entirely.
- To make Santas: roll the rest of dough into an 11x8-inch rectangle directly on an ungreased baking sheet. Cut dough vertically into 2 strips without separating. Divide each strip into 7 triangles (no separating).
- Bake for 10 to 13 minutes at 350° until edges turn brown lightly. Allow to cool for 2 minutes; cut around to separate cookies. Transfer cookies from the pan to wire rack to cool entirely.
- To decorate: microwave corn syrup until thinned, for 6 to 8 seconds. Brush corn syrup over the surface of the cookies, working with a couple of cookies at a time. Decorate with sprinkles to make lights, as desired. Thread licorice through holes.
- Press coconut onto faces of Santas for beards. Attach baking bits for noses and chocolate chips for eyes. To make hats, scatter top of cookies with sprinkles; attach marshmallow halves for pom-poms.

Nutrition Information

- Calories:
- Total Carbohydrate:
- Cholesterol:
- Protein:
- Total Fat:
- Sodium:
- Fiber:

656. Christmas Mice Cookies

Serving: 1-1/2 dozen. | Prep: 30mins | Cook: 0mins | Ready in:

Ingredients

- 2/3 cup semisweet chocolate chips
- 2 cups chocolate wafer crumbs, divided
- 1/3 cup sour cream
- 36 red nonpareils
- 1/4 cup sliced almonds
- 18 pieces black shoestring licorice (2 inches each)

Direction

- Melt chocolate chips in a microwave; whisk until smooth. Mix in sour cream and 1 cup wafer crumbs. Cover and chill until firm enough to handle, 60 minutes.
- In a shallow bowl, put the leftover wafer crumbs. To make 1 mouse, roll approximately 1 tablespoon crumb mixture into a ball; taper one end to make it look like a mouse. Coat the mouse with wafer crumbs. Attach licorice pieces to make the tails, sliced almonds to make the ears, and nonpareils to make the eyes. Put in an airtight container and store in the fridge.

Nutrition Information

- Calories: 135 calories
- Total Fat: 5g fat (2g saturated fat)
- Sodium: 89mg sodium
- Fiber: 1g fiber)
- Total Carbohydrate: 22g carbohydrate (11g sugars
- Cholesterol: 3mg cholesterol
- Protein: 2g protein. Diabetic Exchanges: 1-1/2 starch

657. Christmas Molasses Cookies

Serving: 6-7 dozen (2-1/2-inch cookies). | Prep: 25mins | Cook: 12mins | Ready in:

Ingredients

- 3/4 cup sugar
- 2/3 cup butter, softened
- 1/4 cup orange juice
- 1/2 cup dark corn syrup
- 1/2 cup dark molasses
- 4-1/2 cups all-purpose flour
- 2 teaspoons ground ginger
- 1 teaspoon baking soda
- 1 teaspoon salt
- 1/2 teaspoon ground cloves
- 1/2 teaspoon ground nutmeg
- 1/2 teaspoon ground allspice

Direction

- Cream butter and sugar in a bowl; blend in molasses, corn syrup and orange juice. Mix dry ingredients; add to creamed mixture. Stir well; chill for 3-4 hours or overnight. A portion at a time, roll dough to 1/4-in. thick on lightly floured surface; cut into preferred shapes. Put on greased baking sheets, 2-in. apart. Bake for 12-14 minutes at 350°; if baked for 12 minutes, cookies will be chewy and soft and crunchy if longer.

Nutrition Information

- Calories: 111 calories
- Fiber: 0 fiber)
- Total Carbohydrate: 20g carbohydrate (8g sugars
- Cholesterol: 8mg cholesterol
- Protein: 1g protein.
- Total Fat: 3g fat (2g saturated fat)
- Sodium: 123mg sodium

658. Christmas Wreath Cookies

Serving: 7 dozen. | Prep: 60mins | Cook: 10mins | Ready in:

Ingredients

- 2 cups butter, softened
- 3 cups confectioners' sugar
- 2 eggs
- 2 teaspoons vanilla extract
- 5 cups all-purpose flour
- 2 teaspoons baking soda
- 2 teaspoons cream of tartar
- FROSTING:
- 8 cups confectioners' sugar
- 1 cup shortening
- 2 teaspoons maple flavoring
- 1/2 to 2/3 cup 2% milk
- 1/4 to 1/2 teaspoon red food coloring
- 1/2 teaspoon green food coloring

Direction

- Cream confectioners' sugar and butter together in a big bowl until fluffy and light. Whisk in vanilla and eggs. Mix together cream of tartar, baking soda, and flour; slowly add to the creamed mixture and stir thoroughly. Quarter the dough. Put a cover on and chill until easy to work with, 1-2 hours.
- Roll one portion out on a lightly floured surface until the thickness is 1/4 inch. With a floured 2 1/2-inch round cookie cutter, cut the dough. Put on cookie sheets lined with parchment paper, 1 inch apart; cut out the middles with a floured 1-inch round cookie cutter.
- Bake at 375° until it turns light brown, 8-10 minutes. Let cool for 2 minutes, then transfer to wire racks to fully cool. Continue with the rest of the dough.
- To make the frosting, mix a sufficient amount of milk to reach piping consistency, maple flavoring, shortening, and confectioners' sugar together in a big bowl.

- In a small bowl, put 3/4 cup frosting; add red food coloring to tint. Tint the leftover frosting green. Pipe the green frosting over the cookies with a #13 star tip. On the wreaths, pipe red frosting with a #2 round tip to make bows.

Nutrition Information

- Calories: 151 calories
- Sodium: 63mg sodium
- Fiber: 0 fiber)
- Total Carbohydrate: 21g carbohydrate (15g sugars
- Cholesterol: 17mg cholesterol
- Protein: 1g protein.
- Total Fat: 7g fat (3g saturated fat)

659. Cinnamon Chocolate Minties

Serving: about 4 dozen. | Prep: 45mins | Cook: 10mins | Ready in:

Ingredients

- 1/2 cup butter, softened
- 1/2 cup sugar
- 1/2 cup packed brown sugar
- 1 egg
- 1 teaspoon vanilla extract
- 1-1/2 cups all-purpose flour
- 1/3 cup baking cocoa
- 1 teaspoon ground cinnamon
- 1/4 teaspoon baking soda
- 1/3 cup coarsely crushed soft peppermint candies
- 1/3 cup dark chocolate chips
- DRIZZLE:
- 1/2 cup semisweet chocolate chips
- 1/2 teaspoon canola oil
- 2 teaspoons finely crushed soft peppermint candies

Direction

- Set oven to 350° to preheat. Cream butter with sugars in a small bowl until fluffy and light. Whip in egg and vanilla. Whisk baking soda, cinnamon, cocoa and flour; put into creamed mixture slowly and stir well. Fold in dark chocolate chips and candies.
- Roll into 1-in. balls; put 1 in. apart on baking trays that are greased. Flatten lightly. Bake for 6-8 minutes or until firm. Take out to wire racks to cool fully.
- Melt semisweet chips with oil in a small bowl; mix until smooth. Sprinkle on top of cookies. Scatter with candies. Let sit until firm. Put in an airtight container to store.

Nutrition Information

- Calories: 73 calories
- Sodium: 23mg sodium
- Fiber: 0 fiber)
- Total Carbohydrate: 11g carbohydrate (7g sugars
- Cholesterol: 9mg cholesterol
- Protein: 1g protein. Diabetic Exchanges: 1/2 starch
- Total Fat: 3g fat (2g saturated fat)

660. Cinnamon White & Dark Chocolate Chip Cookies

Serving: 1 batch (about 4 cups mix). | Prep: 15mins | Cook: 10mins | Ready in:

Ingredients

- 1-2/3 cups all-purpose flour
- 1 teaspoon ground cinnamon
- 3/4 teaspoon baking soda
- 1/4 teaspoon salt
- 3/4 cup dark chocolate chips
- 1/2 cup granulated sugar
- 1/2 cup packed light brown sugar
- 3/4 cup white baking chips
- ADDITIONAL INGREDIENTS:

- 3/4 cup butter, softened
- 2 large eggs
- 1 teaspoon vanilla extract

Direction

- Whisk together the salt, baking soda, cinnamon and flour. In the following order, layer into a 1-qt. glass jar the flour mixture, chocolate chips, granulated sugar, brown sugar and white baking chips.
- To make the cookies: Set oven to preheat at 350°. Cream the butter till fluffy and light. Beat eggs and vanilla into the mixture. Add the cookie mixture; blend thoroughly. Drop rounded tablespoonfuls of the dough 2 in. apart from each other onto baking sheets lined with parchment paper. Bake till the edges start to brown, for 7-9 minutes. Let them cool down on pans for 1 minute, then transfer to wire racks to cool thoroughly.

Nutrition Information

- Calories: 83 calories
- Total Carbohydrate: 10g carbohydrate (7g sugars
- Cholesterol: 14mg cholesterol
- Protein: 1g protein.
- Total Fat: 5g fat (3g saturated fat)
- Sodium: 55mg sodium
- Fiber: 0 fiber)

661. Classic Crisp Sugar Cookies

Serving: 6 dozen. | Prep: 15mins | Cook: 10mins | Ready in:

Ingredients

- 1-1/2 cups Domino® or C&H® Pure Cane Granulated Sugar
- 1/2 cup butter, softened
- 1/2 cup shortening
- 2 eggs
- 3 tablespoons sour cream
- 1 teaspoon vanilla extract
- 3 cups all-purpose flour
- 1/2 teaspoon baking soda
- 1/2 teaspoon salt
- Domino® or C&H® Pure Cane Powdered Sugar
- Additional Domino® or C&H® Pure Cane Granulated Sugar

Direction

- Cream shortening, butter and sugar till fluffy and light in big bowl; one by one, add eggs. Beat vanilla and sour cream in. Mix salt, baking soda and flour; add to creamed mixture slowly. Stir well. Cover; refrigerate till dough becomes easy to handle, about a minimum of 30 minutes.
- Roll dough out to 1/8-in. thick on powdered sugar-covered surface. Use floured 2 1/2-in. cookie cutters to cut; put on ungreased baking sheets, 1-in. apart. Sprinkle granulated sugar over; bake for 7-8 minutes at 350° till edges lightly brown. Transfer to wire racks; cool.

Nutrition Information

- Calories:
- Protein:
- Total Fat:
- Sodium:
- Fiber:
- Total Carbohydrate:
- Cholesterol:

662. Cocoa Brownie Cookies

Serving: 16 cookies. | Prep: 15mins | Cook: 10mins | Ready in:

Ingredients

- 1/2 cup butter, softened
- 1 cup packed brown sugar
- 3 large eggs
- 8 ounces semisweet chocolate, melted and slightly cooled
- 1 teaspoon vanilla extract
- 1-1/4 cups all-purpose flour
- 1/4 cup baking cocoa
- 1/2 teaspoon baking powder
- Dash salt
- 1 cup semisweet chocolate chunks

Direction

- Preheat an oven to 350°. Cream brown sugar and butter till fluffy and light in big bowl; one by one, beat eggs in, beating well with every addition. Beat vanilla and chocolate in. Whisk salt, baking powder, cocoa and flour in small bowl; mix into creamed mixture. Fold chocolate chunks in.
- By 1/4 cupfuls, drop dough on lightly greased baking sheets, 3-in. apart. Spread each to 3-in. diameter then bake till cookies are just set and tops are cracked, about 9-11 minutes. Cool for 2 minutes on pans; transfer to wire racks then cool.

Nutrition Information

- Calories:
- Sodium:
- Fiber:
- Total Carbohydrate:
- Cholesterol:
- Protein:
- Total Fat:

663. Coconut Cherry Sandies

Serving: about 7 dozen. | Prep: 30mins | Cook: 10mins | Ready in:

Ingredients

- 1 cup butter, softened
- 1-1/3 cups sugar
- 1/2 cup packed brown sugar
- 1 cup plus 4 teaspoons canola oil, divided
- 2 large eggs
- 1 teaspoon almond extract
- 4-1/2 cups all-purpose flour
- 1 teaspoon salt
- 1 teaspoon baking soda
- 1-1/3 cups sweetened shredded coconut, toasted
- 1-1/3 cups chopped pistachios
- 1-1/3 cups chopped dried cherries
- 1-1/3 cups white baking chips

Direction

- Preheat an oven to 350°. Cream sugars and butters till fluffy and light in a big bowl; beat in extract, eggs and 1 cup oil. Whisk baking soda, salt and flour in another bowl; beat into creamed mixture slowly. Mix in cherries, pistachios and coconut.
- By tablespoonfuls, drop on ungreased baking sheets, 2-in. apart; use glass dipped in sugar to slightly flatten. Bake till set for 8-10 minutes. Transfer to wire racks; fully cool.
- Melt leftover oil and baking chips in a microwave; mix till smooth. Drizzle on cookies; stand till set.

Nutrition Information

- Calories:
- Total Carbohydrate:
- Cholesterol:
- Protein:
- Total Fat:
- Sodium:
- Fiber:

664. Coconut Christmas Mice

Serving: about 3 dozen. | Prep: 45mins | Cook: 0mins | Ready in:

Ingredients

- 3 cups sweetened shredded coconut
- 2 cups confectioners' sugar
- 1/3 cup sweetened condensed milk
- 1/4 cup sliced almonds
- 2 teaspoons miniature semisweet chocolate chips
- 38 pieces black shoestring licorice (2 inches each)

Direction

- In a food processor, pulse milk, confectioners' sugar and coconut until the coconut is finely chopped. Roll 1 tablespoon coconut mixture into a ball for each mouse, taper one end to look like a mouse. Attach licorice pieces for tails, miniature chocolate chips for eyes, and sliced almonds for ears. Put in an airtight container to store.

Nutrition Information

- Calories: 79 calories
- Total Carbohydrate: 13g carbohydrate (11g sugars
- Cholesterol: 1mg cholesterol
- Protein: 1g protein.
- Total Fat: 3g fat (3g saturated fat)
- Sodium: 25mg sodium
- Fiber: 0 fiber)

665. Coconut Cranberry Yummies

Serving: 5 dozen. | Prep: 15mins | Cook: 10mins | Ready in:

Ingredients

- 1 can (14 ounces) sweetened condensed milk
- 1 package (14 ounces) sweetened shredded coconut
- 1 cup white baking chips
- 1/4 cup ground almonds
- 1 teaspoon almond extract
- 1 cup chopped fresh or frozen cranberries

Direction

- Combine the first five ingredients in a large bowl; stir well. Mix in cranberries.
- Drop 3 inch apart onto parchment paper-lined baking sheets by tablespoonfuls; carefully form into mounds.
- Bake at 325° until edges turn light brown, about 10-12 minutes. Allow to cool for 3 minutes before taking out from pans to wire racks to cool entirely.

Nutrition Information

- Calories: 74 calories
- Total Fat: 4g fat (3g saturated fat)
- Sodium: 28mg sodium
- Fiber: 0 fiber)
- Total Carbohydrate: 9g carbohydrate (8g sugars
- Cholesterol: 3mg cholesterol
- Protein: 1g protein. Diabetic Exchanges: 1/2 starch

666. Coconut Pecan Joys

Serving: 4 dozen. | Prep: 15mins | Cook: 10mins | Ready in:

Ingredients

- 4 egg whites
- 1 teaspoon vanilla extract
- 1/8 teaspoon lemon juice
- 3/4 cup sugar

- 1 package (7 ounces) sweetened shredded coconut
- 1/4 cup chopped pecans
- 1/4 cup semisweet chocolate chips

Direction

- Whip the lemon juice, vanilla and egg whites in a big bowl until it creates soft peaks. Slowly put in 1 tablespoon sugar at a time, whipping until it forms stiff peaks and sugar dissolves. Fold in chocolate chips, pecans and coconut.
- Put by rounded tablespoonfuls 2 in. apart onto greased baking trays. Bake for 10-12 minutes at 350° or until slightly browned. Take out to wire racks to cool. Put in an airtight container to store.

Nutrition Information

- Calories: 43 calories
- Protein: 1g protein. Diabetic Exchanges: 1/2 starch.
- Total Fat: 2g fat (1g saturated fat)
- Sodium: 16mg sodium
- Fiber: 0 fiber)
- Total Carbohydrate: 6g carbohydrate (5g sugars
- Cholesterol: 0 cholesterol

667. Coconut Macadamia Biscotti

Serving: about 2-1/2 dozen. | Prep: 20mins | Cook: 55mins | Ready in:

Ingredients

- 6 tablespoons butter, softened
- 3/4 cup sugar
- 1/3 cup canola oil
- 3 large eggs
- 2 teaspoons vanilla extract
- 1 teaspoon coconut extract
- 3-1/4 cups all-purpose flour
- 1-3/4 teaspoons baking powder
- 1/4 teaspoon salt
- 1 cup sweetened shredded coconut, toasted and finely chopped
- 1 cup macadamia nuts, coarsely chopped
- 2 cups (12 ounces) semisweet chocolate chips
- 2 tablespoons shortening

Direction

- Heat the oven beforehand to 350 degrees. Beat oil, sugar and butter until blended in a big bowl. Beat in extracts and eggs. Whisk salt, baking powder and flour in a different bowl; mix in the creamed mixture gradually. Mix in nuts and coconut.
- Divide the dough into 2. Shape each part into 8x3-inch rectangle on baking sheets lined with parchment paper. Bake until set for about 25 minutes.
- Transfer pans onto wire racks; put baked rectangles into cutting board once cool enough to handle. Slice crosswise into half inch slices using a serrated knife. Put back to pans with the cut side down.
- Bake until golden brown or for 15 to 18 minutes on each side. Allow to cool completely by transferring to wire racks from pans.
- Melt shortening and chocolate chips in a microwave then mix until smooth. Dunk each cookie in the mixture halfway through; let the excess drip. Put on waxed paper until set then keep in an airtight container.

Nutrition Information

- Calories:
- Protein:
- Total Fat:
- Sodium:
- Fiber:
- Total Carbohydrate:
- Cholesterol:

668. Cookie Jar Gingersnaps

Serving: 3 dozen. | Prep: 20mins | Cook: 15mins | Ready in:

Ingredients

- 3/4 cup shortening
- 1 cup plus 2 tablespoons sugar, divided
- 1 large egg
- 1/4 cup molasses
- 2 cups all-purpose flour
- 2 teaspoons baking soda
- 1-1/2 teaspoons ground ginger
- 1 teaspoon ground cinnamon
- 1/2 teaspoon salt

Direction

- Set the oven at 350° and start preheating. Cream 1 cup of sugar and shortening till fluffy and light. Whisk in molasses and egg. Mix together the first five ingredients in another bowl; slowly add to the creamed mixture; stir properly.
- Roll level tablespoonfuls of dough into balls. Dip one side into the remaining sugar; arrange 2 in. apart on greased baking sheets, sugary side up. Bake for 12-15 minutes, or till crinkly and lightly browned. Take away and place on wire racks to cool.

Nutrition Information

- Calories: 92 calories
- Cholesterol: 5mg cholesterol
- Protein: 1g protein.
- Total Fat: 4g fat (1g saturated fat)
- Sodium: 106mg sodium
- Fiber: 0 fiber)
- Total Carbohydrate: 13g carbohydrate (7g sugars

669. Cookie Pops

Serving: 20 | Prep: | Cook: |Ready in:

Ingredients

- 3/4 cup white sugar
- 3/4 cup packed brown sugar
- 3/4 cup butter, softened
- 1 teaspoon vanilla extract
- 2 eggs
- 1 1/2 cups all-purpose flour
- 1 teaspoon baking soda
- 1/2 teaspoon salt
- 2 cups rolled oats
- 1 cup candy-coated milk chocolate pieces
- 20 lollipop sticks

Direction

- Cream butter, brown sugar and white sugar in a big bowl. Stir in eggs and vanilla; blend well. Sift flour, salt, and baking soda together, then add to the butter mixture. Lastly, stir in rolled oats.
- Chill the dough for an hour.
- Set oven to preheat at 350°F (175°C).
- Mold dough to create 2-inch balls. Put them on a cookie sheet. Slightly press them down. Poke a lollipop stick into the center of each ball. Don't overcrowd the cookie sheet as the dough balls will expand a bit. Bake until golden brown for 8-12 minutes. Let them cool for a minute. Place the small candies to form a smiling face design. You now have firm but chewy cookies.

Nutrition Information

- Calories: 245 calories;
- Total Fat: 10.2
- Sodium: 186
- Total Carbohydrate: 35.7
- Cholesterol: 38
- Protein: 3.2

670. Cookies With Pecans

Serving: about 3-1/2 dozen. | Prep: 15mins | Cook: 10mins | Ready in:

Ingredients

- 1/3 cup butter, softened
- 1/3 cup shortening
- 1/2 cup sugar
- 1/2 cup packed brown sugar
- 1 egg
- 1 teaspoon vanilla extract
- 1-1/2 cups self-rising flour
- 1/2 cup chopped pecans

Direction

- Cream sugars, shortening and butter until fluffy and light in a large bowl. Whisk in vanilla and egg. Add flour gradually and combine well. Stir in pecans.
- Drop onto clean and dry baking sheets by rounded teaspoonfuls, 2 inches apart. Bake for 9-11 minutes at 375° or until edges turn light brown. Cool for 1-2 minutes; transfer to wire racks.

Nutrition Information

- Calories: 144 calories
- Total Carbohydrate: 17g carbohydrate (10g sugars
- Cholesterol: 18mg cholesterol
- Protein: 1g protein.
- Total Fat: 8g fat (3g saturated fat)
- Sodium: 137mg sodium
- Fiber: 0 fiber)

671. Cornmeal Lime Cookies

Serving: 8 dozen. | Prep: 45mins | Cook: 12mins | Ready in:

Ingredients

- 1 cup butter, softened
- 1/2 cup sugar
- 1/2 cup packed brown sugar
- 1 large egg
- 1/4 cup lime juice
- 4-1/2 teaspoons grated lime zest
- 2 cups all-purpose flour
- 1 cup yellow cornmeal
- GLAZE:
- 2 cups confectioners' sugar
- 3 tablespoons lime juice
- Holiday sprinkles

Direction

- Cream sugars and butter till fluffy and light in a big bowl; beat in zest, lime juice and egg. Mix cornmeal and flour. Add to creamed mixture slowly; stir well.
- Form into 2 12-in. rolls; wrap each in plastic. Refrigerate for 30 minutes. Form each roll to square-shaped log; freeze till firm or 1 hour.
- Preheat an oven to 350°. Unwrap the logs; cut to 3/8-in. pieces. Put onto parchment paper-lined baking sheets, 1-in. apart; bake till set or 11-14 minutes. Transfer to wire racks; fully cool.
- Mix lime juice and confectioners' sugar; spread on cookies. Decorate using sprinkles; let stand till set.

Nutrition Information

- Calories:
- Cholesterol:
- Protein:
- Total Fat:
- Sodium:
- Fiber:
- Total Carbohydrate:

672. Cran Orange Cookies

Serving: 6 dozen. | Prep: 30mins | Cook: 15mins | Ready in:

Ingredients

- 1 cup butter, softened
- 1 cup sugar
- 1/2 cup packed brown sugar
- 1 large egg
- 2 tablespoons orange juice
- 1 teaspoon grated orange zest
- 2-1/2 cups all-purpose flour
- 1/2 teaspoon salt
- 1/2 teaspoon baking soda
- 2 cups chopped fresh or frozen cranberries
- 1/2 cup chopped walnuts
- ICING:
- 1-1/2 cups confectioners' sugar
- 2 tablespoons orange juice
- 1/2 teaspoon grated orange zest

Direction

- In a large bowl, cream sugars and butter until fluffy and light. Beat in the zest, orange juice and egg. Combine the baking soda, salt and flour; add to the creamed mixture gradually and thoroughly mix. Mix in walnuts and cranberries.
- On greased baking sheets, drop by tablespoonfuls placing 2 inches apart. Bake at 375° for around 12 to 14 minutes or until edges are browned lightly. Take away to wire racks for cooling.
- Combine icing ingredients; spread over cooled cookies.

Nutrition Information

- Calories: 72 calories
- Total Fat: 3g fat (2g saturated fat)
- Sodium: 45mg sodium
- Fiber: 0 fiber)
- Total Carbohydrate: 11g carbohydrate (7g sugars
- Cholesterol: 10mg cholesterol
- Protein: 1g protein. Diabetic Exchanges: 1/2 starch

673. Cran Orange Oatmeal Cookies

Serving: 4 dozen. | Prep: 20mins | Cook: 15mins | Ready in:

Ingredients

- 1 cup butter, softened
- 1 cup packed brown sugar
- 1/2 cup sugar
- 1 large egg
- 1 tablespoon grated orange zest
- 1-1/2 teaspoons orange extract
- 1-3/4 cups all-purpose flour
- 1 teaspoon baking powder
- 1/4 teaspoon baking soda
- 2 cups old-fashioned oats
- 1 cup dried cranberries
- 1 cup sweetened shredded coconut

Direction

- In a large bowl, cream sugars and butter until fluffy and light. Beat in the extract, orange zest and egg.
- Combine baking soda, baking powder and flour; add to creamed mixture gradually and mix well. Mix in the coconut, cranberries and oats. Form into balls of 1-inch; on ungreased baking sheets, place 2-inch apart.
- Bake at 375° for around 11 to 13 minutes or until bottoms are browned. Take away to wire racks. Place in airtight container for storing.

Nutrition Information

- Calories: 107 calories
- Fiber: 1g fiber)

- Total Carbohydrate: 15g carbohydrate (9g sugars
- Cholesterol: 14mg cholesterol
- Protein: 1g protein.
- Total Fat: 5g fat (3g saturated fat)
- Sodium: 50mg sodium

674. Cranberry Almond Macaroons

Serving: 11 cookies. | Prep: 15mins | Cook: 10mins | Ready in:

Ingredients

- 2 egg whites
- 1/4 teaspoon almond extract
- Sugar substitute equivalent to 2 tablespoons sugar
- 1 cup sweetened shredded coconut
- 1/4 cup dried cranberries, chopped
- 1/4 cup chopped almonds
- 1/4 cup semisweet chocolate chips, melted

Direction

- Add egg whites into a small bowl; let it sit for 30 minutes at room temperature. Add extract into the egg whites; beat on medium speed till it can hold soft peaks. Beat in the sugar substitute gradually on high speed till it can make stiff glossy peaks. Fold the coconut, cranberries and almonds into the mixture.
- Onto a baking sheet covered with cooking spray, drop rounded tablespoonfuls 2 in. apart. Bake until set, at 325° for 10-15 minutes. Let them cool down for 15 minutes then take out of pan carefully to a wire rack.
- Onto each cookie's bottoms, spread about 1 teaspoon melted chocolate. Put chocolate side up onto waxed paper; let sit till set.

Nutrition Information

- Calories: 91 calories
- Sodium: 33mg sodium
- Fiber: 1g fiber)
- Total Carbohydrate: 10g carbohydrate (7g sugars
- Cholesterol: 0 cholesterol
- Protein: 2g protein. Diabetic Exchanges: 1 fat
- Total Fat: 6g fat (3g saturated fat)

675. Cranberry Chocolate Cookies With A Kick

Serving: 2 dozen. | Prep: 20mins | Cook: 10mins | Ready in:

Ingredients

- 1 cup dried cranberries
- 1/4 cup coffee liqueur or strong brewed coffee
- 1-1/4 cups semisweet chocolate chunks
- 1/4 cup unsalted butter, cubed
- 2 large eggs
- 3/4 cup packed brown sugar
- 3 teaspoons vanilla extract
- 1 cup all-purpose flour
- 1/2 teaspoon baking powder
- 1/2 teaspoon salt
- 1/2 teaspoon ground cinnamon
- 1/2 teaspoon freshly ground pepper
- 1/8 to 1/4 teaspoon cayenne pepper

Direction

- Preheat the oven to 350°. Mix liqueur and cranberries in a small saucepan. Heat to simmer and take out from the heat. Microwave on high butter and chocolate in a microwave-safe bowl in 30-second intervals until they are melted. Mix until the mixture is smooth (should be thick). Let cool a bit.
- Beat vanilla, brown sugar and eggs on high in a large bowl for about 3 minutes until thickened. Then beat in the chocolate mixture. Whisk seasonings, salt, baking powder and flour in another bowl and fold into the sugar

mixture until mixed. Then fold in the cranberry mixture.
- Transfer onto baking sheets lined with parchment paper by dropping rounded tablespoonfuls and placing 2 inches apart. Bake for about 10 to 12 minutes or until the tops are crackly and the cookies are shiny. Let cool for 2 minutes on pans. Transfer to wire racks and cool.

Nutrition Information

- Calories:
- Sodium:
- Fiber:
- Total Carbohydrate:
- Cholesterol:
- Protein:
- Total Fat:

676. Cranberry Cookies With Browned Butter Glaze

Serving: about 4-1/2 dozen. | Prep: 40mins | Cook: 10mins | Ready in:

Ingredients

- 1/2 cup butter, softened
- 1 cup sugar
- 3/4 cup packed brown sugar
- 1 large egg
- 2 tablespoons orange juice
- 3 cups all-purpose flour
- 1 teaspoon baking powder
- 1/2 teaspoon salt
- 1/4 teaspoon baking soda
- 1/4 cup 2% milk
- 2-1/2 cups coarsely chopped fresh cranberries
- 1 cup white baking chips
- 1 cup chopped pecans or walnuts
- GLAZE:
- 1/3 cup butter, cubed
- 2 cups confectioners' sugar
- 1-1/2 teaspoons vanilla extract
- 3 to 4 tablespoons water

Direction

- Set oven to 375 degrees and start preheating. Beat sugars and butter in a big bowl until they form a fluffy and light mixture. Beat in orange juice and egg. Combine baking soda, salt, baking powder and flour in a separate bowl; pour into beaten mixture alternating with milk. Mix in pecans, baking chips and cranberries.
- Scoop by level tablespoonfuls of dough and place onto greased baking sheets, laying 1 inch from each other. Bake in preheated oven until lightly browned, about 10 to 12 minutes. Take out of the pans and place on wire racks until fully cool.
- To make the glaze, heat butter in a small heavy saucepan over medium heat until melted. Heat while stirring continuously until the butter turns golden brown, about 5 to 7 minutes. Take away from the heat. Mix in vanilla, confectioners' sugar and enough water to achieve a drizzling texture. Drizzle onto cookies. Allow to set.

Nutrition Information

- Calories: 130 calories
- Cholesterol: 12mg cholesterol
- Protein: 1g protein.
- Total Fat: 5g fat (3g saturated fat)
- Sodium: 66mg sodium
- Fiber: 1g fiber)
- Total Carbohydrate: 19g carbohydrate (13g sugars

677. Cranberry Crispies

Serving: 2-1/2 dozen. | Prep: 10mins | Cook: 10mins | Ready in:

Ingredients

- 1 package (15.6 ounces) cranberry-orange quick bread mix
- 1/2 cup butter, melted
- 1/2 cup finely chopped walnuts
- 1 egg
- 1/2 cup dried cranberries

Direction

- Combine egg, walnuts, butter, and bread mix in a large bowl. Mix in cranberries. Shape mixture into 1 1/4-inch balls. Arrange them 3 inches apart on unoiled baking sheets. Press the balls to a thickness of 1/8 inch thick using a glass dipped in sugar.
- Bake for 10 to 12 minutes at 350° until top turns light golden brown. Transfer to wire racks to cool.

Nutrition Information

- Calories: 223 calories
- Cholesterol: 36mg cholesterol
- Protein: 3g protein.
- Total Fat: 12g fat (5g saturated fat)
- Sodium: 205mg sodium
- Fiber: 1g fiber)
- Total Carbohydrate: 26g carbohydrate (16g sugars

678. Cranberry Drop Cookies

Serving: 5 dozen. | Prep: 15mins | Cook: 15mins | Ready in:

Ingredients

- 1/2 cup butter, softened
- 1 cup sugar
- 1 cup packed brown sugar
- 1 egg
- 1/4 cup milk
- 2 tablespoons lemon juice
- 3 cups all-purpose flour
- 1 teaspoon baking powder
- 1/2 teaspoon salt
- 1/4 teaspoon baking soda
- 1 package (12 ounces) fresh or frozen cranberries, chopped
- 1 cup chopped walnuts

Direction

- Cream sugars and butter until fluffy and light in a large bowl. Whisk in egg. Whisk in lemon juice and milk. Mix dry ingredients; add to creamed mixture; combine well. Stir in nuts and cranberries.
- Drop onto greased baking sheets, 2 in. apart, by heaping teaspoonfuls. Bake for 13-15 minutes at 375° or until golden brown. Cool on wire racks.

Nutrition Information

- Calories: 160 calories
- Total Fat: 6g fat (2g saturated fat)
- Sodium: 100mg sodium
- Fiber: 1g fiber)
- Total Carbohydrate: 25g carbohydrate (15g sugars
- Cholesterol: 16mg cholesterol
- Protein: 3g protein.

679. Cranberry Orange Pinwheels

Serving: 80 cookies. | Prep: 60mins | Cook: 10mins | Ready in:

Ingredients

- 1 cup butter, softened
- 1-1/2 cups sugar
- 2 large eggs
- 2 teaspoons grated orange zest
- 3 cups all-purpose flour

- 1/2 teaspoon baking powder
- 1/2 teaspoon salt
- 1 cup fresh or frozen cranberries, thawed
- 1 cup chopped pecans
- 1/4 cup packed brown sugar

Direction

- In a large bowl, cream sugar and butter till fluffy and light. Add eggs, one at a time; after each addition, beating well. Beat in orange zest.
- Combine the salt, baking powder and flour; add to the creamed mixture gradually and mix well.
- Split dough in half. Allow 1 hour to refrigerate, covered or until easy to handle.
- In the meantime, in a food processor, combine the brown sugar, pecans and cranberries. Process while covering until chopped finely; put aside.
- Between two sheets of waxed paper, roll out one portion of dough into a 10-inch square. Take away top sheet; spread dough together with half of the cranberry mixture to within half an inch of edges. Roll up jelly-roll style tightly. Use plastic to wrap. Repeat with the rest of the dough and cranberry mixture. Allow 4 hours or overnight to chill in refrigerator.
- Unwrap rolls and cut into slices of 1/4-inch. On ungreased baking sheets, place 2 inches apart. Bake at 375° for nearly 8 to 10 minutes or until edges are browned lightly. Take away to wire racks. Place in an airtight container for storing.

Nutrition Information

- Calories: 67 calories
- Cholesterol: 11mg cholesterol
- Protein: 1g protein. Diabetic Exchanges: 1 fat
- Total Fat: 4g fat (2g saturated fat)
- Sodium: 36mg sodium
- Fiber: 0 fiber)
- Total Carbohydrate: 8g carbohydrate (5g sugars

680. Cranberry Pecan Cookies

Serving: about 3-1/2 dozen. | Prep: 10mins | Cook: 10mins | Ready in:

Ingredients

- 1 tube (16-1/2 ounces) refrigerated sugar cookie dough, softened
- 1 cup chopped pecans
- 2/3 cup white baking chips
- 2/3 cup dried cranberries
- 1 teaspoon vanilla extract

Direction

- Set oven to preheat at 350°. In a large bowl, combine vanilla, cranberries, chips, pecans and cookie dough. On ungreased baking sheets, drop the dough by tablespoonfuls 2 in. apart from each other.
- Bake until light brown, or 10-12 minutes. Allow to cool for 2 minutes before taking out of from pans to wire racks. Keep in an airtight container.

Nutrition Information

- Calories: 87 calories
- Total Fat: 5g fat (1g saturated fat)
- Sodium: 50mg sodium
- Fiber: 0 fiber)
- Total Carbohydrate: 10g carbohydrate (5g sugars
- Cholesterol: 4mg cholesterol
- Protein: 1g protein.

681. Cranberry Pecan Oatmeal Cookies

Serving: about 5 dozen. | Prep: 25mins | Cook: 15mins | Ready in:

Ingredients

- 1/2 cup butter, softened
- 1/2 cup sugar
- 1/2 cup packed brown sugar
- 1 large egg
- 1/2 teaspoon vanilla extract
- 1 cup all-purpose flour
- 3/4 teaspoon ground cinnamon
- 1/2 teaspoon salt
- 1/2 teaspoon baking powder
- 1/2 teaspoon baking soda
- 1-1/2 cups old-fashioned or quick-cooking oats
- 1 cup dried cranberries, coarsely chopped
- 1 cup chopped pecans

Direction

- Preheat the oven to 350 degrees. Cream the sugars and butter till fluffy and light; beat in the vanilla and egg. In a separate bowl, whisk the baking soda, baking powder, salt, cinnamon and flour together; slowly beat to the creamed mixture. Stir in the leftover ingredients.
- Drop by tablespoonfuls 1 inch apart to the ungreased baking sheets. Bake for 12 to 15 minutes till light golden brown. Let cool down on the pans for 2 minutes. Take out onto the wire racks to cool down.

Nutrition Information

- Calories: 62 calories
- Protein: 1g protein.
- Total Fat: 3g fat (1g saturated fat)
- Sodium: 47mg sodium
- Fiber: 1g fiber)
- Total Carbohydrate: 8g carbohydrate (5g sugars
- Cholesterol: 7mg cholesterol

682. Cranberry Pecan Sandies

Serving: 2-1/2 to 3 dozen. | Prep: 20mins | Cook: 15mins | Ready in:

Ingredients

- 1 package (15.6 ounces) cranberry-orange quick bread mix
- 1/2 cup butter, melted
- 1 egg
- 2 tablespoons orange juice
- 3/4 cup chopped pecans
- 30 to 36 pecan halves
- ORANGE GLAZE:
- 1 cup confectioners' sugar
- 3 to 4 teaspoons orange juice

Direction

- In a large bowl, combine the butter, bread mix, orange juice and egg. Mix in chopped pecans. Roll into balls of 1-inch. On ungreased baking sheets, place 2 inches apart. Use the bottom of a glass coated with cooking spray to flatten them. In the center of each cookie, press a pecan half.
- Bake at 350° for nearly 12 to 14 minutes or till browned lightly. Allow 1 minute to cool before taking away to wire racks. In a small bowl, whisk confectioners' sugar together with enough orange juice to achieve the consistency you desired.

Nutrition Information

- Calories: 129 calories
- Protein: 1g protein.
- Total Fat: 8g fat (2g saturated fat)
- Sodium: 90mg sodium
- Fiber: 1g fiber)
- Total Carbohydrate: 14g carbohydrate (9g sugars

- Cholesterol: 16mg cholesterol

683. Cranberry And Pistachio Biscotti

Serving: about 2-1/2 dozen. | Prep: 25mins | Cook: 30mins | Ready in:

Ingredients

- 3/4 cup sugar
- 1/4 cup canola oil
- 2 large eggs
- 2 teaspoons vanilla extract
- 1 teaspoon almond extract
- 1-3/4 cups all-purpose flour
- 1 teaspoon baking powder
- 1/4 teaspoon salt
- 2/3 cup chopped pistachios
- 1/2 cup dried cranberries

Direction

- Beat oil and sugar in a small bowl until combined. Beat in eggs, then the extracts. Combine salt, baking powder and flour; gently put into sugar mixture and stir well (dough will become stiff). Mix in cranberries and pistachios.
- Split dough into half. Form each half into a 12-inch x 2-inch rectangle on a baking sheet lined with parchment paper using your hands dusted with flour. Bake at 350° until set, about 18-22 minutes.
- On wire rack, place the pan. Once cool enough to handle, bring to a cutting board; use a serrated knife to cut 3/4-inch slices of diagonally. Place on ungreased baking sheets, cut side down. Bake until firm, about 12-14 minutes. Take out to wire racks to cool. Put in an airtight container to store.

Nutrition Information

- Calories: 85 calories
- Total Carbohydrate: 12g carbohydrate (6g sugars
- Cholesterol: 13mg cholesterol
- Protein: 2g protein. Diabetic Exchanges: 1 starch.
- Total Fat: 3g fat (0 saturated fat)
- Sodium: 46mg sodium
- Fiber: 1g fiber)

684. Cranberry Cashew Drop Cookies

Serving: 4-1/2 dozen. | Prep: 20mins | Cook: 10mins | Ready in:

Ingredients

- 1 cup butter, softened
- 1 cup packed brown sugar
- 1/2 cup sugar
- 2 large eggs
- 1 teaspoon vanilla extract
- 2-1/4 cups all-purpose flour
- 1 teaspoon baking soda
- 1 teaspoon salt
- 1 package (10 to 12 ounces) white baking chips
- 1 cup chopped cashews
- 1 cup dried cranberries

Direction

- Beat sugars and butter in a large bowl to form a fluffy and light mixture. Add vanilla and eggs and beat. Mix together salt, baking soda and flour; pour little by little into beaten mixture and whisk thoroughly. Mix in cranberries, cashews and chips.
- Scoop by rounded tablespoonfuls and place onto baking sheets without grease, laying 2 in. from each other. Bake in 350-degree oven until cookies turn golden brown, about 9 to 11 minutes. Transfer to wire racks and allow to cool.

Nutrition Information

- Calories: 124 calories
- Sodium: 116mg sodium
- Fiber: 0 fiber)
- Total Carbohydrate: 16g carbohydrate (11g sugars
- Cholesterol: 17mg cholesterol
- Protein: 2g protein. Diabetic Exchanges: 1 starch
- Total Fat: 6g fat (3g saturated fat)

685. Cranberry Chocolate Chip Cookie Mix

Serving: 2-1/2 dozen. | Prep: 15mins | Cook: 10mins | Ready in:

Ingredients

- 1-1/4 cups all-purpose flour
- 1 teaspoon baking soda
- 1/2 teaspoon salt
- 1/2 teaspoon ground cinnamon
- 3/4 cup packed brown sugar
- 1 cup (6 ounces) semisweet chocolate chips
- 1/2 cup dried cranberries
- 1/2 cup chopped walnuts
- 1/2 cup quick-cooking oats
- ADDITIONAL INGREDIENTS:
- 2/3 cup butter, softened
- 1 egg
- 3/4 teaspoon vanilla extract

Direction

- Mix together cinnamon, salt, baking soda and flour in a small bowl. Place flour mixture, brown sugar, half a cup chocolate chips, cranberries, walnuts, oats and remaining chips in layers into a 1-quart glass container. Keep covered in a cool and dry place for no longer than 6 months. This will make a batch of 4 cups in total.
- To make cookies: Set oven to 350 degrees and start preheating. Beat vanilla, egg and butter in a big bowl until combined. Pour in cookie mix and stir thoroughly.
- Scoop dough by rounded tablespoonfuls and place 2 inches apart onto unprepared cookie sheets. Bake until cookies turn golden brown, about 10 to 15 minutes. Transfer to wire racks.

Nutrition Information

- Calories: 129 calories
- Total Carbohydrate: 16g carbohydrate (10g sugars
- Cholesterol: 18mg cholesterol
- Protein: 2g protein. Diabetic Exchanges: 1-1/2 fat
- Total Fat: 7g fat (4g saturated fat)
- Sodium: 115mg sodium
- Fiber: 1g fiber)

686. Cranberry Pistachio Cookie Cups

Serving: 2 dozen. | Prep: 45mins | Cook: 20mins | Ready in:

Ingredients

- 1/2 cup butter, softened
- 3 ounces cream cheese, softened
- 2 tablespoons sugar
- 1/2 teaspoon grated orange zest
- 1 cup all-purpose flour
- FILLING:
- 1 large egg
- 1 cup confectioners' sugar
- 1 tablespoon butter, melted
- 1/2 cup pistachios, chopped
- 1/3 cup dried cranberries

Direction

- In a large bowl, cream orange peel, sugar, cream cheese, and butter until fluffy and light. Put in flour; combine well. Cover and let cool in the refrigerator for 1 hour, until easy to work with.
- Blend butter, confectioners' sugar, and egg in a small bowl. Mix in cranberries and pistachios. Form the dough into 24 balls. Press on bottom and up the sides of ungreased miniature muffin cups. Spoon the filling into cups.
- Bake for 20 to 25 minutes at 350° until firm. Let chill for 10 minutes before transferring from pans to wire racks to cool fully. Preserve in an airtight container.

Nutrition Information

- Calories: 116 calories
- Cholesterol: 24mg cholesterol
- Protein: 2g protein. Diabetic Exchanges: 1 starch
- Total Fat: 7g fat (4g saturated fat)
- Sodium: 55mg sodium
- Fiber: 1g fiber)
- Total Carbohydrate: 12g carbohydrate (7g sugars

687. Cranberry White Chocolate Cookies

Serving: about 7 dozen. | Prep: 25mins | Cook: 10mins | Ready in:

Ingredients

- 1 cup butter, softened
- 3/4 cup sugar
- 3/4 cup packed brown sugar
- 2 large eggs
- 1/3 cup cranberry juice
- 1 teaspoon vanilla extract
- 3 cups all-purpose flour
- 2 teaspoons baking powder
- 1/2 teaspoon salt
- 2 cups dried cranberries
- 2 cups vanilla or white chips
- GLAZE:
- 2 cups vanilla or white chips
- 2 tablespoons plus 1-1/2 teaspoons shortening

Direction

- Beat sugars and butter in a large bowl until fluffy and light. Beat in vanilla, cranberry juice, and eggs. In a different bowl, mix salt, baking powder, and flour; slowly pour to creamed mixture and blend well. Fold in vanilla chips and cranberries.
- Drop by rounded teaspoonfuls, keeping 2-inch distance, onto greased baking sheets. Bake for 10 to 12 minutes at 350°, until edges turn brown. Let cool for 2 minutes before transferring to wire racks to cool fully.
- To make the glaze, microwave shortening, and vanilla chips at 70% power until melted; stir until smooth. Drizzle onto cookies.

Nutrition Information

- Calories: 103 calories
- Sodium: 47mg sodium
- Fiber: 0 fiber)
- Total Carbohydrate: 14g carbohydrate (10g sugars
- Cholesterol: 11mg cholesterol
- Protein: 1g protein. Diabetic Exchanges: 1 starch
- Total Fat: 5g fat (3g saturated fat)

688. Cream Cheese Cutouts

Serving: about 7 dozen. | Prep: 15mins | Cook: 10mins | Ready in:

Ingredients

- 1 cup butter, softened
- 3 ounces cream cheese, softened
- 1 cup sugar

- 1/4 teaspoon salt
- 1 large egg
- 1 teaspoon vanilla extract
- 2-1/2 cups all-purpose flour
- FROSTING:
- 3 cups confectioners' sugar
- 1/3 cup butter, softened
- 1-1/2 teaspoons vanilla extract
- 2 to 3 tablespoons 2% milk
- Food coloring, optional
- Assorted sprinkles or candies

Direction

- Whisk cream cheese, butter, salt, and sugar in a large mixing bowl until fluffy and light. Beat in vanilla and egg. Slowly beat in flour. Cover and chill until dough is firm enough to handle, for 1 to 2 hours.
- Preheat your oven to 375°. Roll dough to a thickness of 1/8 inch on a work surface lightly dusted with flour. Cut dough using floured cookies cutters. Lay cookies on ungreased baking sheets; separate each cookie about 1 inch.
- Bake cookies in the preheated oven until edges are lightly browned, approximately 7 to 8 minutes. Allow cookies to cool for 1 minutes on pans. Transfer to wire racks to cool entirely.
- In a small bowl, beat butter, vanilla, confectioners' sugar, and enough milk to achieve desired consistency. Mix in food coloring (if using). Garnish cookies with frosting and sprinkles.

Nutrition Information

- Calories: 70 calories
- Total Fat: 3g fat (2g saturated fat)
- Sodium: 32mg sodium
- Fiber: 0 fiber)
- Total Carbohydrate: 10g carbohydrate (6g sugars
- Cholesterol: 11mg cholesterol
- Protein: 1g protein.

689. Cream Cheese Slice And Bake Cookies

Serving: about 5-1/2 dozen. | Prep: 25mins | Cook: 15mins | Ready in:

Ingredients

- 1 cup butter, softened
- 3 ounces cream cheese, softened
- 1 cup sugar
- 1 large egg
- 1/2 teaspoon rum extract
- 1/4 teaspoon vanilla extract
- 3 cups all-purpose flour
- 1/2 teaspoon salt
- 1/2 teaspoon baking powder
- 1/4 teaspoon baking soda
- 1/2 teaspoon ground nutmeg
- 1 cup finely chopped almonds

Direction

- Cream butter, cream cheese and sugar until fluffy and light in a large bowl. Whisk in extracts and egg. Mix nutmeg, baking soda, salt, baking powder and flour; add to creamed mixture gradually; combine well.
- Form into 2 9-in. rolls. Roll each in almonds; use plastic to wrap. Refrigerate until firm or for 2 hours.
- Slice into 1/4-in. slices. Arrange 2 inches apart on baking sheets lined with parchment paper. Bake at 375° until bottoms turn light brown or for 11-13 minutes. Cool for a minute; place on wire racks.

Nutrition Information

- Calories: 74 calories
- Protein: 1g protein. Diabetic Exchanges: 1 fat
- Total Fat: 4g fat (2g saturated fat)
- Sodium: 50mg sodium
- Fiber: 0 fiber)

- Total Carbohydrate: 8g carbohydrate (3g sugars
- Cholesterol: 12mg cholesterol

690. Cream Filberts

Serving: about 5 dozen. | Prep: 25mins | Cook: 15mins | Ready in:

Ingredients

- 1 cup shortening
- 3/4 cup sugar
- 1 egg
- 1 teaspoon vanilla extract
- 2-1/2 cups all-purpose flour
- 1/2 teaspoon baking powder
- 1/8 teaspoon salt
- 3/4 cup whole hazelnuts
- GLAZE:
- 2 cups confectioners' sugar
- 3 tablespoons water
- 2 teaspoons vanilla extract
- Granulated sugar or about 60 crushed sugar cubes

Direction

- Beat sugar and cream shortening in a large bowl until fluffy and light. Mix in vanilla and egg. Mix the dry ingredients and slowly stir to creamed mixture.
- Turn heaping teaspoonfuls of dough into balls; push a hazelnut into each and reshape balls. Set 2-inch apart on baking sheets that is not greased.
- Place in the oven and bake for 12-15 minutes at 375°F or until lightly browned. Take to wire rack and cool. Mix vanilla, water and confectioner's sugar in a bowl until smooth; sink top of cookies in glaze. Dust with sugar.

Nutrition Information

- Calories: 84 calories
- Protein: 1g protein.
- Total Fat: 4g fat (1g saturated fat)
- Sodium: 9mg sodium
- Fiber: 0 fiber)
- Total Carbohydrate: 11g carbohydrate (6g sugars
- Cholesterol: 4mg cholesterol

691. Creepy Spiders

Serving: about 2 dozen. | Prep: 30mins | Cook: 10mins | Ready in:

Ingredients

- 1 package chocolate fudge cake mix (regular size)
- 1/2 cup butter, melted
- 1 egg
- 1 can (16 ounces) chocolate frosting
- Shoestring black licorice, cut into 1-1/2 inch pieces
- 1/4 cup red-hot candies

Direction

- Mix the butter, egg and cake mix together in a big bowl (the texture of the dough is going to be stiff). Form the dough mixture into balls that are 1 inch in size.
- On baking sheets that are not greased, put in the dough balls 2 inches away from each other. Put it in a 350° oven and let it bake for 10-12 minutes or until the doughs have set. Let the baked cookies cool down for 1 minute, then remove them from pans and place them onto wire racks.
- Coat the bottom side of 1/2 of each of the baked cookies evenly with a heaping teaspoonful of the frosting. Use 4 licorice pieces to create the spider legs on each side of the cookies; put the remaining 1/2 of the baked cookies over the prepared bottom cookies. Use the frosting to stick 2 red-hot

candies on top of the spider to serve as the eyes.

Nutrition Information

- Calories: 206 calories
- Sodium: 243mg sodium
- Fiber: 1g fiber)
- Total Carbohydrate: 31g carbohydrate (22g sugars
- Cholesterol: 18mg cholesterol
- Protein: 2g protein.
- Total Fat: 9g fat (4g saturated fat)

692. Crisp Lemon Cookies

Serving: about 4-1/2 dozen. | Prep: 30mins | Cook: 15mins | Ready in:

Ingredients

- 1-1/3 cups butter, softened
- 2 cups confectioners' sugar
- 2 tablespoons lemon juice
- 2 teaspoons grated lemon peel
- 1/2 teaspoon vanilla extract
- 3 cups all-purpose flour
- 1/4 cup sugar
- 3/4 cup vanilla or white chips, melted

Direction

- Cream together butter and confectioners' sugar in a large bowl until fluffy and light. Beat in the vanilla, peel and lemon juice. Slowly put in flour and stir well.
- Form dough into 1-in. balls. On ungreased baking sheets, arrange the balls 2 in. apart. Use cooking spray to grease the bottom of a glass; dip in sugar. Use glass to flatten cookies, dipping in sugar again if desired.
- Bake at 325° until edges are lightly browned, 11-13 minutes. Move to wire racks to cool down. Drizzle over the cookies with melted vanilla chips.

Nutrition Information

- Calories: 99 calories
- Sodium: 34mg sodium
- Fiber: 0 fiber)
- Total Carbohydrate: 12g carbohydrate (7g sugars
- Cholesterol: 12mg cholesterol
- Protein: 1g protein. Diabetic Exchanges: 1 starch
- Total Fat: 5g fat (3g saturated fat)

693. Crispy Coconut Balls

Serving: about 3 dozen. | Prep: 20mins | Cook: 0mins | Ready in:

Ingredients

- 1/4 cup butter, cubed
- 40 large marshmallows or 4 cups miniature marshmallows
- 5 cups crisp rice cereal
- 1 cup sweetened shredded coconut

Direction

- In a saucepan, melt butter on low heat. Put in marshmallows and cook while stirring continuously, until marshmallows have melted. Take away from the heat and stir in cereal until coated well. Form the mixture into balls, 1 inch in size using your hands coated with butter. Roll balls in the coconut and press gently to coat well.

Nutrition Information

- Calories: 127 calories
- Fiber: 0 fiber)
- Total Carbohydrate: 22g carbohydrate (11g sugars
- Cholesterol: 7mg cholesterol

- Protein: 1g protein.
- Total Fat: 4g fat (3g saturated fat)
- Sodium: 118mg sodium

694. Crispy Gingerbread

Serving: One small gingerbread house approximately 8 in. x 10-in. | Prep: 15mins | Cook: 10mins | Ready in:

Ingredients

- 1-1/2 cups dark corn syrup
- 1-1/3 cups packed dark brown sugar
- 1 cup butter
- 7 cups all-purpose flour
- 1 tablespoon ground cinnamon
- 1-1/2 teaspoons ground ginger
- 1 teaspoon ground cloves
- 1/2 teaspoon ground nutmeg
- 1/2 teaspoon salt

Direction

- Mix together the sugar, butter, and corn syrup into a big pot. On medium heat, cook-stir until butter dissolves. Transfer in a big bowl.
- Mix together the dry ingredients. Slowly mix in the dry mixture into the sugar mixture to form a stiff dough. Keep in the chiller for a minimum of 1 hour. On an oiled baking pan, roll out the dough into 1/8-inch thickness. Cut out to desired shapes. Take out the scraps of dough.
- On 350° heat, bake until edges turn lightly brown, 10 to 15 minutes. Cool, 5 minutes before removing to pans and transferring onto wire racks to completely cool.

Nutrition Information

- Calories:
- Total Fat:
- Sodium:
- Fiber:

- Total Carbohydrate:
- Cholesterol:
- Protein:

695. Cutout Sugar Cookies

Serving: about 2-1/2 dozen (3-inch cookies). | Prep: 30mins | Cook: 10mins | Ready in:

Ingredients

- 1 cup butter, softened
- 1-1/2 cups confectioners' sugar
- 1 egg
- 1 teaspoon vanilla extract
- 1/2 teaspoon almond extract
- 2-1/2 cups all-purpose flour
- 1 teaspoon baking soda
- 1 teaspoon cream of tartar
- ICING:
- 1/2 cup butter, softened
- 1/2 cup shortening
- 1-1/2 teaspoons vanilla extract
- 1/4 teaspoon salt
- 5-1/2 cups confectioners' sugar
- 4 to 5 tablespoons milk
- Food coloring

Direction

- Beat sugar and butter together in a large mixing bowl until fluffy and light. Beat in extracts and egg. Mix cream of tartar, baking soda, and flour; slowly mix into creamed mixture to combine. Refrigerate, covered, for 2 to 3 hours or until easy to work with.
- Roll dough out to a thickness of 1/4 inch on a work surface dusted with flour. Cut dough into your favorite shapes. Arrange cookies 1 inch apart on buttered baking sheet. Bake cookies for 6 to 8 minutes at 375° until edges start browning. Transfer cookies to wire racks and allow to cool completely.
- To make icing, beat shortening and butter together in a mixing bowl. Beat in salt and

vanilla. Slowly add sugar, 1 cup per batch, beating well between additions. Beat in milk until fluffy and light. Add enough coloring to tint icing with desired color; frost cookies with icing.

Nutrition Information

- Calories:
- Sodium:
- Fiber:
- Total Carbohydrate:
- Cholesterol:
- Protein:
- Total Fat:

696. Daria's Best Ever Sugar Cookies

Serving: about 13-1/2 dozen. | Prep: 02hours00mins | Cook: 10mins | Ready in:

Ingredients

- 1/2 cup almond paste
- 4 large egg yolks
- 2 cups butter, softened
- 1-3/4 cups sugar
- 1/2 teaspoon salt
- 3-3/4 cups all-purpose flour
- FROSTING:
- 3-3/4 cups confectioners' sugar
- 3 tablespoons meringue powder
- 1/3 cup water
- Food coloring, coarse sugar and assorted sprinkles, optional

Direction

- Whip egg yolks and almond paste in a big bowl till crumbly. Put the sugar, salt and butter; whip till fluffy and light. Slowly put the flour and combine thoroughly. Distribute to parts; form each part into one ball, then pat into a flat round. Encase using plastic and chill for 1 to 2 hours or till handleable.
- Heat the oven to 375°. Roll a dough portion on a slightly floured counter into thickness of quarter-inch. Use a 2-1/2-inches, floured cookie cutter to cut the dough. Arrange on unoiled baking sheets, spacing 2-inches apart. Redo with the rest of dough.
- Bake till edges start to turn brown for 6 to 8 minutes. Allow 2 minutes to cool prior to transferring from pans onto wire racks to fully cool.
- For icing, whip meringue powder, water and confectioners' sugar for 5 minutes till fluffy. Tint the icing if wished. Ice the cookies; jazz up using sprinkles and coarse sugar if wished. Rest till set. Keep in airtight container.

Nutrition Information

- Calories: 55 calories
- Cholesterol: 11mg cholesterol
- Protein: 1g protein. Diabetic Exchanges: 1/2 starch.
- Total Fat: 3g fat (1g saturated fat)
- Sodium: 25mg sodium
- Fiber: 0 fiber)
- Total Carbohydrate: 7g carbohydrate (5g sugars

697. Date Nut Pinwheels

Serving: about 9 dozen. | Prep: 30mins | Cook: 10mins | Ready in:

Ingredients

- 1 cup butter, softened
- 1 cup sugar
- 1 cup packed brown sugar
- 2 large eggs
- 4 cups all-purpose flour
- 1/2 teaspoon baking soda
- FILLING:

- 2 packages (8 ounces each) pitted dates
- 1 cup water
- 1/2 cup sugar
- 1/2 cup chopped walnuts

Direction

- Cream sugars and butter in a big bowl until the mixture is fluffy and light. Beat in the eggs. Whip baking soda and flour in another bowl; beat into the creamed mixture little by little. Chop the dough into 3 parts. Form each part into a disk; use plastic to cover. Put in the fridge for 1 hour or until the dough is firm enough to roll.
- To make the filling, in a big saucepan, put sugar, water and dates. Boil. Lower the heat; simmer without a cover until the dates become tender and there is almost no liquid left. Mix in walnuts; let it fully cool.
- Put each part of the dough in the middle of 2 waxed paper sheets, roll them to form a 12x10-inch rectangle. Put in the fridge for half an hour. Discard the waxed paper sheets. Spread each rectangle with one-third of the filling. Roll the rectangles up tightly, beginning with the long side and following jelly-roll style. Use plastic to cover. Put in the fridge until they are firm.
- Set the oven at 350° to preheat. Remove the plastic, chop the dough into 1/3 -inch slices crosswise. Arrange them on baking sheets coated with cooking spray, 2 inches apart. Bake for 10-12 minutes or until the dough is set. Transfer them from pans to wire racks to cool.

Nutrition Information

- Calories: 67 calories
- Sodium: 21mg sodium
- Fiber: 1g fiber)
- Total Carbohydrate: 12g carbohydrate (7g sugars
- Cholesterol: 8mg cholesterol
- Protein: 1g protein.
- Total Fat: 2g fat (1g saturated fat)

698. Decorated Butter Cookies

Serving: 4 dozen. | Prep: 20mins | Cook: 10mins | Ready in:

Ingredients

- 1 cup butter, softened
- 1/2 cup sugar
- 1/2 cup packed brown sugar
- 1 egg
- 1 teaspoon vanilla extract
- 2 cups all-purpose flour
- 2 teaspoons cream of tartar
- 1 teaspoon baking soda
- 1/8 teaspoon salt
- Colored sprinkles, colored sugar, ground nuts and/or chocolate sprinkles

Direction

- Cream the sugars and butter until fluffy and light in a small bowl. Beat in vanilla and egg. Mix salt, baking soda, cream of tartar and flour; put in the creamed mixture gradually. Stir well. Cover and put in the refrigerator until easy to handle or for an hour.
- Make 1-inch balls by rolling the dough. Put on baking sheets without grease, leaving 2-inch space apart. Flatten using a glass dipped in sugar then sprinkle using nuts, colored sugar or sprinkles.
- Bake until lightly browned or for 10 to 12 minutes at 350 degrees. Allow to cool by putting on wire racks.

Nutrition Information

- Calories: 142 calories
- Sodium: 147mg sodium
- Fiber: 0 fiber)
- Total Carbohydrate: 17g carbohydrate (9g sugars
- Cholesterol: 29mg cholesterol

- Protein: 1g protein.
- Total Fat: 8g fat (5g saturated fat)

699. Decorated Sugar Cookie Cutouts

Serving: 6 dozen. | Prep: 01hours15mins | Cook: 15mins | Ready in:

Ingredients

- 1-1/2 cups unsalted butter, softened
- 2 cups sugar
- 2 large eggs
- 2 large egg yolks
- 4 teaspoons vanilla extract
- 2 teaspoons almond extract
- 4 cups all-purpose flour
- 1 teaspoon baking powder
- 1 teaspoon salt
- ROYAL ICING:
- 3-3/4 cups confectioners' sugar
- 7 tablespoons water
- 1/4 cup meringue powder
- 1 teaspoon light corn syrup
- 1 to 2 drops clear vanilla extract, optional
- Assorted food coloring, optional
- DECORATIONS:
- Assorted candy coating disks, melted
- Colored sprinkles, optional

Direction

- Cream sugar and butter in a big bowl till fluffy and light. Whip in egg yolks, extracts and eggs. Mix the baking powder, salt and flour; slowly put into creamed mixture and combine thoroughly. Split the dough in half. Form every portion into a ball, then pat into a flat round. Encase in plastic and chill for an hour.
- Roll a dough portion on a slightly floured counter into 1/4-inch-thick. Use a 2-1/2-inches, floured cookie cutter to cut dough. Arrange on oiled baking sheets, 2 inches away. Redo.
- Bake for 13 to 16 minutes at 350° or till pale brown. Transfer onto wire racks and fully cool.
- For frosting, mix corn syrup, meringue powder, water and confectioners' sugar in a big bowl. If wished, put the extract and color using food coloring; whip on low speed to barely combine. Whip for 4 to 5 minutes on high to form firm peaks. Cover unused icing always using moist cloth. If need be, whip on high speed once more to bring back to its texture. Ice the cookies. Rest till firm.
- To jazz up cookies, in a sealable, small plastic bags, put the liquified candy coating; snip off a small hole from corner of every bag. Jazz cookies up as wished.

Nutrition Information

- Calories:
- Cholesterol:
- Protein:
- Total Fat:
- Sodium:
- Fiber:
- Total Carbohydrate:

700. Deluxe Sugar Cookies

Serving: 5 dozen (2-inch cookies). | Prep: 20mins | Cook: 10mins | Ready in:

Ingredients

- 1 cup butter, softened
- 1-1/2 cups confectioners' sugar
- 1 large egg, beaten
- 1 teaspoon vanilla extract
- 1/2 teaspoon almond extract
- 2-1/2 cups all-purpose flour
- 1 teaspoon baking soda
- 1 teaspoon cream of tartar

Direction

- Whisk butter and sugar in a large mixing bowl until fluffy and light. Whisk in extracts and egg. Mix cream of tartar, baking soda, and flour together; slowly mix into the creamed mixture until combined. Refrigerate until easy to work with, for a minimum of 1 hour.
- Cut dough into 4 equal pieces. Flatten dough to a thickness of 1/8 inch on a work surface lightly coated with confectioners' sugar. Cut dough into desired shapes. Arrange cookies on ungreased baking sheets. Repeat the steps with the rest of dough. Bake for 7 to 8 minutes at 350° until edges start browning. Transfer cookies to wire cooling racks; allow to cool.

Nutrition Information

- Calories: 118 calories
- Protein: 1g protein.
- Total Fat: 6g fat (4g saturated fat)
- Sodium: 106mg sodium
- Fiber: 0 fiber)
- Total Carbohydrate: 14g carbohydrate (6g sugars
- Cholesterol: 23mg cholesterol

701. Diamond Almond Bars

Serving: 5 dozen. | Prep: 20mins | Cook: 25mins | Ready in:

Ingredients

- 1 cup butter, softened
- 1 cup plus 1 tablespoon sugar, divided
- 1 large egg, separated
- 1 teaspoon almond extract
- 2 cups all-purpose flour
- 1/2 cup blanched sliced almonds
- 1/4 teaspoon ground cinnamon

Direction

- Cream 1 cup sugar and butter together in a big bowl until fluffy and light. Whisk in extract and egg yolk. Slowly add flour to the creamed mixture and thoroughly stir.
- Press into an oil-coated 15x10x1-inch baking pan. Whisk egg white until frothy; brush over the dough. Put almonds on top. Mix together the leftover sugar and cinnamon; sprinkle over the top.
- Bake at 350° until turning light brown, 25-30 minutes (do not over bake). Put on a wire rack to cool, 10 minutes. Slice into bars with a diamond shape. Let fully cool.

Nutrition Information

- Calories: 64 calories
- Sodium: 23mg sodium
- Fiber: 0 fiber)
- Total Carbohydrate: 7g carbohydrate (4g sugars
- Cholesterol: 12mg cholesterol
- Protein: 1g protein. Diabetic Exchanges: 1/2 starch
- Total Fat: 4g fat (2g saturated fat)

702. Dipped Lemon Spritz

Serving: 6 dozen. | Prep: 50mins | Cook: 10mins | Ready in:

Ingredients

- 2/3 cup plus 2 tablespoons sugar
- 2 teaspoons grated lemon peel
- 1 cup unsalted butter, softened
- 1 egg
- 2 teaspoons lemon juice
- 1 teaspoon vanilla extract
- 2-1/2 cups all-purpose flour
- 1/4 teaspoon baking powder
- Dash salt
- 1 package (12 ounces) dark chocolate chips

Direction

- Set oven to 350° to preheat. Mix sugar with lemon peel in a small food processor; cover and pulse until blended. Cream butter with 2/3 cup lemon-sugar in a big bowl until fluffy and light. Whip in vanilla, lemon juice and egg. Mix salt, baking powder and flour; put into creamed mixture gradually and stir well.
- Shape dough into long strips on ungreased baking trays with a cookie press fitted with a 1-1/2-in. bar disk. Slice each strip into squares (you don't need to separate the pieces).
- Bake until set or for 8-10 minutes (do not brown). Take out to wire racks until fully cooled.
- Microwave chocolate to melt; mix until smooth. Diagonally plunge cookies in chocolate, let excess fall off. Put on waxed paper; scatter chocolate with leftover lemon-sugar. Let sit until firm. Put in an airtight container to store at room temperature or put in the freezer for up to 3 months.

Nutrition Information

- Calories: 83 calories
- Total Fat: 5g fat (3g saturated fat)
- Sodium: 5mg sodium
- Fiber: 0 fiber)
- Total Carbohydrate: 10g carbohydrate (5g sugars
- Cholesterol: 10mg cholesterol
- Protein: 1g protein.

703. Dipped Spice Cookies

Serving: about 3-1/2 dozen. | Prep: 25mins | Cook: 10mins | Ready in:

Ingredients

- 1/2 tube refrigerated sugar cookie dough, softened
- 1/2 cup all-purpose flour
- 1/4 cup packed brown sugar
- 1 tablespoon orange juice
- 3/4 teaspoon ground cinnamon
- 1/2 teaspoon ground ginger
- 1/2 teaspoon grated orange zest
- 1/2 cup semisweet chocolate chips
- 4 teaspoons shortening
- 1/4 cup finely chopped walnuts

Direction

- In a large bowl, beat orange zest, ginger, cinnamon, orange juice, brown sugar, flour, and cookie dough until combined. Form teaspoonfuls of dough into 2-inch logs. Arrange on ungreased baking sheets, 2 inches apart.
- Bake for 8 to 10 minutes at 350° until edges turn golden brown. Bring to wire racks to cool.
- Heat shortening and chocolate chips in a microwave-safe bowl until melted; stir until smooth. Plunge one end of each cookie into the melted chocolate, letting the excess to drip off; scatter walnuts over. Arrange on waxed paper; allow to stand until firm.

Nutrition Information

- Calories: 110 calories
- Protein: 1g protein.
- Total Fat: 5g fat (2g saturated fat)
- Sodium: 53mg sodium
- Fiber: 1g fiber)
- Total Carbohydrate: 15g carbohydrate (8g sugars
- Cholesterol: 4mg cholesterol

704. Double Butterscotch Cookies

Serving: about 7 dozen. | Prep: 20mins | Cook: 10mins | Ready in:

Ingredients

- 1/2 cup butter, softened
- 1/2 cup shortening
- 4 cups packed brown sugar
- 4 large eggs
- 1 tablespoon vanilla extract
- 6 cups all-purpose flour
- 3 teaspoons baking soda
- 3 teaspoons cream of tartar
- 1 teaspoon salt
- 1 package English toffee bits (10 ounces) or almond brickle chips (7-1/2 ounces)
- 1 cup finely chopped pecans

Direction

- Beat brown sugar, shortening and butter till mixture looks like wet sand or for 2 minutes in a big bowl. One by one, add eggs; beat well after each addition. Beat in vanilla. Mix salt, cream of tartar, baking soda and flour; add to brown sugar mixture slowly. Mix well; mix in pecans and toffee bits.
- Form into 3 14-in. rolls; it'll be a bit crumbly. Wrap each in a plastic wrap; refrigerate till firm or for 4 hours.
- Unwrap; cut to 1/2-in. slices. Put on greased baking sheets, 2-in. apart; bake at 375° till lightly browned or for 9-11 minutes. Cool for 1-2 minutes. Transfer from pans onto wire racks; fully cool.

Nutrition Information

- Calories: 248 calories
- Total Carbohydrate: 39g carbohydrate (25g sugars
- Cholesterol: 28mg cholesterol
- Protein: 3g protein.
- Total Fat: 9g fat (3g saturated fat)
- Sodium: 221mg sodium
- Fiber: 1g fiber)

705. Double Dipped Shortbread Cookies

Serving: about 2-1/2 dozen. | Prep: 15mins | Cook: 10mins | Ready in:

Ingredients

- 3/4 cup butter, softened
- 1-1/2 cups confectioners' sugar
- 3 ounces semisweet chocolate, melted and cooled
- 1 teaspoon vanilla extract
- 1-1/2 cups all-purpose flour
- 2 teaspoons baking cocoa
- 1/8 teaspoon salt
- 3 ounces semisweet chocolate, chopped
- 1/4 cup heavy whipping cream
- 4 ounces white baking chocolate, chopped

Direction

- Cream the confectioners' sugar and butter until fluffy and light. Stir in vanilla and melted chocolate. Whisk salt, cocoa and flour in a different bowl then put in the creamed mixture gradually. Form rounded tablespoons of dough to 2-inch-long logs. Put in baking sheets without grease, leaving 2-inch space apart. Store in the refrigerator with cover for an hour.
- Heat the oven beforehand to 350 degrees. Bake cookies for 8 to 10 minutes until edges are set. Allow to cool for 2 minutes on pans. Let to cool completely by putting on wire racks.
- Melt semisweet chocolate with cream in a microwave and mix until smooth. Dip each cookie in the chocolate halfway through. Let the excess drip off then put on waxed paper. Melt white chocolate in the microwave then stir until smooth. Drizzle melted white chocolate on cookies and let rest until set.

Nutrition Information

- Calories: 137 calories
- Sodium: 47mg sodium

- Fiber: 0 fiber)
- Total Carbohydrate: 14g carbohydrate (9g sugars
- Cholesterol: 14mg cholesterol
- Protein: 1g protein.
- Total Fat: 8g fat (5g saturated fat)

706. Double Drizzled Biscotti

Serving: about 3 dozen. | Prep: 25mins | Cook: 30mins | Ready in:

Ingredients

- 3/4 cup butter, softened
- 1 cup sugar
- 3 large eggs
- 1 teaspoon almond extract
- 1 teaspoon vanilla extract
- 3 cups all-purpose flour
- 2 tablespoons aniseed
- 1-1/2 teaspoons baking powder
- 1/4 teaspoon salt
- 1 cup chopped walnuts
- 1/3 cup semisweet chocolate chips
- 2 teaspoons shortening, divided
- 1/3 cup white baking chips

Direction

- Set the oven to 350° and start preheating. Cream sugar and butter until fluffy and light in a large bowl. Whisk in extracts and eggs. Beat salt, baking powder, aniseed and flour in a small bowl; whisk into creamed mixture gradually. Stir in walnuts.
- Separate dough in 1/2. Form each portion into a 14x2-in. rectangle on a clean and dry baking sheet. Bake until firm to the touch or for 15-20 minutes.
- Cool on wire racks on pans until it becomes cool enough that you can handle. Place baked rectangles on a cutting board. Cut into 1/2-in. slices diagonally with a serrated knife. Place on clean and dry baking sheets with cut side down. Bake until golden brown or for 6-7 minutes per side. Transfer from pans to wire racks; completely cool.
- Melt a teaspoon shortening and semisweet chips in a microwave; stir until smooth. Drizzle over biscotti. Melt the rest of shortening and white chips in a microwave; stir until smooth. Drizzle over biscotti.

Nutrition Information

- Calories: 126 calories
- Protein: 2g protein.
- Total Fat: 7g fat (3g saturated fat)
- Sodium: 61mg sodium
- Fiber: 1g fiber)
- Total Carbohydrate: 14g carbohydrate (7g sugars
- Cholesterol: 25mg cholesterol

707. Dried Cherry Biscotti

Serving: 2-1/2 dozen. | Prep: 25mins | Cook: 25mins | Ready in:

Ingredients

- 2 tablespoons butter, softened
- 1/2 cup sugar
- 4 egg whites
- 2 teaspoons almond extract
- 2 cups all-purpose flour
- 2 teaspoons baking powder
- 1/4 teaspoon salt
- 1/2 cup dried cherries
- 1/4 cup chopped almonds, toasted
- 2 teaspoons confectioners' sugar

Direction

- Beat sugar and butter till crumbly in small bowl; beat extract and egg whites in. Mix salt, baking powder and flour; add to sugar

mixture slowly. Mix almonds and cherries in; it will be stiff.
- Press in 8-in. square baking dish coated in cooking spray. Bake for 15-20 minutes till lightly browned at 375°; cool for 5 minutes. Transfer from pan onto cutting board. Use a serrated knife to cut biscotti in half. Cut every half to 1/2-in. slices.
- Put slices on baking sheets coated in cooking spray, cut side down. Bake till light golden brown, 8-10 minutes, turning once. Transfer to wire racks; cool. Sprinkle confectioners' sugar over.

Nutrition Information

- Calories: 135 calories
- Fiber: 1g fiber)
- Total Carbohydrate: 24g carbohydrate (10g sugars
- Cholesterol: 4mg cholesterol
- Protein: 3g protein. Diabetic Exchanges: 1-1/2 starch
- Total Fat: 3g fat (1g saturated fat)
- Sodium: 123mg sodium

708. Drizzled Gingerbread Biscotti

Serving: 3-1/2 dozen. | Prep: 35mins | Cook: 40mins | Ready in:

Ingredients

- 7 tablespoons butter, softened
- 1 cup sugar
- 3 large eggs
- 1/3 cup molasses
- 2 teaspoons vanilla extract
- 2-1/2 cups all-purpose flour
- 1 cup whole wheat flour
- 5 teaspoons ground ginger
- 2 teaspoons ground cinnamon
- 1-1/2 teaspoons ground cloves
- 1/2 teaspoon coarsely ground pepper
- 1/4 teaspoon ground nutmeg
- 1 tablespoon baking powder
- 1/2 teaspoon salt
- 1/2 cup finely chopped crystallized ginger
- 1-1/4 cups white baking chips
- 1-1/2 teaspoons shortening
- Red Hots

Direction

- Heat oven to 375°. Whisk the sugar and butter together into a big bowl until fluffy and light. Stir in the vanilla, eggs, and molasses. Beat the spices, salt, baking powder, and flour into a separate bowl. Slowly pour the flour mixture into the butter mixture; mix. Beat in the crystallized ginger.
- Split the dough into half. Mold each dough half to 14x2 inch rectangle on an ungreased baking pan. For 20 to 25 minutes, bake until firm when touched.
- Allow rectangles to cool on pans before transferring to wire racks until easily handle. Place on a chopping board. Cur to 1/2 inch diagonal slices with the serrated knife. Position the chopped rectangle vertically 1-inch apart on the ungreased baking pans. For 12 to 14 minutes, bake turns to a golden brown. Take out from baking pans and transfer onto wire racks for complete cooling.
- Heat the shortening and baking chips in the microwave, stirring until mixture is smooth. Season over the biscotti. Use Red hots for decoration.

Nutrition Information

- Calories: 124 calories
- Protein: 2g protein.
- Total Fat: 4g fat (2g saturated fat)
- Sodium: 90mg sodium
- Fiber: 1g fiber)
- Total Carbohydrate: 20g carbohydrate (11g sugars
- Cholesterol: 19mg cholesterol

709. Dutch Speculaas

Serving: about 2-1/2 dozen. | Prep: 40mins | Cook: 10mins | Ready in:

Ingredients

- 1 cup butter, softened
- 1 cup packed dark brown sugar
- 2 large eggs
- 1 tablespoon molasses
- 2 teaspoons grated orange zest
- 3-1/2 cups all-purpose flour
- 1/2 cup finely ground almonds
- 3 teaspoons ground cinnamon
- 1 teaspoon baking powder
- 1/2 teaspoon ground nutmeg
- 1/2 teaspoon ground cloves
- 1/4 teaspoon white pepper
- 1/4 teaspoon ground ginger
- 1/4 teaspoon ground cardamom

Direction

- Cream brown sugar and butter together in a big bowl until fluffy and light. Whisk in orange zest, molasses, and eggs. Mix together cardamom, ginger, pepper, cloves, nutmeg, baking powder, cinnamon, ground almonds, and flour. Slowly add to the creamed mixture and stir thoroughly. Put a cover on and chill until easy to work with, about a minimum of 4 hours.
- Turn the oven to 350° to preheat. Roll a little dough on a surface lined with parchment paper until the thickness is 1/8 inch. Press floured cookie stamp into the dough to make designs, then use a floured 3-inch cookie cutters to cut, leaving 1 inch between cookies. Take out the excess dough and roll the scraps again if you like.
- Remove the dough on the parchment paper to a baking sheet. If the dough is warm, put the cookie sheet in the fridge for 10-15 minutes until firm. Bake at 350° for 8-10 minutes until it turns light brown around the edges. Transfer from the pans to wire racks to cool.

Nutrition Information

- Calories: 151 calories
- Fiber: 1g fiber)
- Total Carbohydrate: 19g carbohydrate (8g sugars
- Cholesterol: 30mg cholesterol
- Protein: 2g protein.
- Total Fat: 7g fat (4g saturated fat)
- Sodium: 65mg sodium

710. Dutch Spice Cookies

Serving: 40 cookies. | Prep: 20mins | Cook: 10mins | Ready in:

Ingredients

- 3/4 cup butter, softened
- 1 cup packed brown sugar
- 2-1/4 cups all-purpose flour
- 2 teaspoons ground cinnamon
- 1/2 teaspoon ground mace
- 1/2 teaspoon crushed aniseed
- 1/4 teaspoon each ground ginger, nutmeg and cloves
- 1/4 teaspoon baking powder
- 1/8 teaspoon salt
- 3 tablespoons 2% milk
- 1 cup finely chopped slivered almonds

Direction

- Cream brown sugar and butter till fluffy and light in a big bowl. Mix salt, baking powder, spices and flour. Add to creamed mixture slowly; stir well. Mix in almonds and milk.
- Roll dough between 2 waxed paper sheets to 16x10-in. rectangle; cut to 2-in. squares. Use waxed paper to cover; refrigerate for 30 minutes.

- Put squares on ungreased baking sheets, 1-in. apart; bake at 375° till firm or for 8-10 minutes. Transfer to wire racks; cool.

Nutrition Information

- Calories: 187 calories
- Fiber: 1g fiber)
- Total Carbohydrate: 23g carbohydrate (11g sugars
- Cholesterol: 19mg cholesterol
- Protein: 3g protein.
- Total Fat: 10g fat (5g saturated fat)
- Sodium: 95mg sodium

711. Easy Bizcochitos

Serving: 3 dozen. | Prep: 25mins | Cook: 10mins | Ready in:

Ingredients

- 1 package (17-1/2 ounces) sugar cookie mix
- 1/4 cup all-purpose flour
- 2 teaspoons grated orange zest
- 1 teaspoon aniseed, crushed
- 1/2 cup butter, melted
- 1 large egg, lightly beaten
- 1 teaspoon vanilla extract
- 1/4 cup sugar
- 1 teaspoon ground cinnamon

Direction

- Mix together aniseed, orange zest, flour and cookie mix together in a big bowl, then stir in vanilla, egg and melted butter until combined.
- Halve the dough then form each into a disk, use plastic to wrap disk. Chill until firm enough to roll, about an hour.
- Set the oven to 375 degrees to preheat. Roll each dough portion on a surface coated lightly with flour to the thickness of 1/4 inch, then use a 2-inch cookie cutter coated with flour to cut dough out.
- Arrange on grease-free baking sheet, spacing 1 inch apart. Combine together cinnamon and sugar in a small bowl, then sprinkle over cookies. Bake until edges turn light brown, about 6 to 9 minutes. Transfer to wire rack to cool.

Nutrition Information

- Calories: 93 calories
- Cholesterol: 13mg cholesterol
- Protein: 1g protein.
- Total Fat: 4g fat (2g saturated fat)
- Sodium: 52mg sodium
- Fiber: 0 fiber)
- Total Carbohydrate: 13g carbohydrate (8g sugars

712. Easy Chocolate Gingerbread Cutouts

Serving: about 3 dozen. | Prep: 25mins | Cook: 10mins | Ready in:

Ingredients

- 2 large eggs
- 1/3 cup canola oil
- 1/3 cup molasses
- 1 package chocolate cake mix (regular size)
- 3/4 cup plus 2 tablespoons all-purpose flour
- 2-1/2 teaspoons ground ginger
- Baking cocoa
- Raisins
- Vanilla frosting and Red-Hots

Direction

- Whisk the molasses, eggs, and oil into a big bowl until well blended. Beat flour, ginger, and cake mix into a separate bowl. Slowly stir into the egg mixture.

- Mold the dough to a disk and use plastic to wrap. Keep in the refrigerator until dough becomes firm to roll for 3 to 4 hours.
- Heat oven to 375 degrees. Roll out the dough into 1/8-inch thick on a lightly floured working surface. Use a 3-1/2-inch cookie cutter to cut out gingerbread man from the dough. Put into the greased baking sheets, 1-inch apart. Use the raisins for the eyes.
- For 8 to 10 minutes, bake until firm at the edges. Take out from the pans and transfer onto wire racks to completely cool. Use the frosting and candies to decorate, if desired.

Nutrition Information

- Calories:
- Protein:
- Total Fat:
- Sodium:
- Fiber:
- Total Carbohydrate:
- Cholesterol:

713. Ellen's Edible Gingerbread House

Serving: 1 house. | Prep: 03hours00mins | Cook: 15mins | Ready in:

Ingredients

- DOUGH:
- 1/2 cup butter, softened
- 3/4 cup packed dark brown sugar
- 3/4 cup dark molasses
- 1 egg
- 2 teaspoons ground ginger
- 1 teaspoon ground cloves
- 1/4 teaspoon salt
- 3-1/2 to 4 cups all-purpose flour
- ICING:
- 3-3/4 to 4 cups confectioners' sugar
- 3 tablespoons meringue powder
- 5 to 6 tablespoons warm water
- Pastry bag
- Round pastry tip # 12
- Green paste food coloring
- Spice jars
- CANDIES: Starlight mints, caramels, red-hot candies, colored sprinkles, red shoestring licorice, Tootsie rolls, Sixlets, sticks striped-fruit gum, Fruit Roll-Ups
- OTHER DECORATIONS: Ice cream sugar cones, cutout butter cookie, pretzel stick, miniature pretzels

Direction

- Beat brown sugar and butter in a large bowl until fluffy and light. Stir in egg, salt, molasses, ginger, and cloves. Pour the flour, 1 cup at a time, and whisk until it forms like a ball.
- Place the dough on a floured working surface. Knead the dough until smooth but not sticky, adding more flour if it's still sticky. Cover the dough and let it chill for few hours or overnight.
- Cut out the patterns. Line the baking pan with a lightly greased foil. Place a damp towel on the counter and lay the prepared pan over it to prevent it from slipping. Place half of the dough into the baking pan. Roll the dough into a 1/8-inch thick rectangle using a floured rolling pin. Position the cutout patterns 1/2-inch apart from the dough. Using a sharp knife or pizza cutter, cut out two of each of the patterns. Remove the pattern and the dough scraps, reserving the scraps and re-roll for later use.
- Let it bake inside the oven with a temperature of 350°F for 15 minutes until all edges start to brown. Make sure not to overbake. Once the pan is removed from the oven, immediately lay the patterns on the dough. Trace the edges of the pattern, trimming the excess cookie if necessary. Allow it to cool for 10 minutes until the cookies start to set. Gently remove to wire racks allowing to cool completely. Do the same with the remaining dough and patterns.

Reserve the dough scraps since it can be used to decorate the house.
- Whisk meringue powder, 4 tbsp. of water, and confectioners' sugar in a bowl at low speed until the mixture is well-blended. Whisk it on high speed for 8-10 minutes, adding water 1 tbsp. at a time if necessary, until stiff peaks are formed. Lay the damp paper towel over the bowl, covering it securely until they are ready to use.
- To make the house frame, make sure that the baked cookie pieces are capable of fitting together. If not, trim the cookies using a serrated knife. Fill the pastry bag with icing. Using its round pastry tip, pipe a 3/8-inch wide strip of icing into the bottom edge of the front piece. Place it into the covered board, positioning it 3-inches away from the front edge of the base. Use spice jars to prop the frames for 2-3 minutes until the icing sets completely. Remove the jars.
- For adding the back part and its sides, pipe icing along the side edge of the front piece and along the lower edge of one side piece. Position the cookie pieces right angle to each other. Make sure that they were connected tightly. Do the same with the other side. Line an icing along the bottom and side edges of the back piece. Align the pieces with the other assembled pieces. Line the icing along the inside edges and corners of the assembled cookie pieces for its strong stability.
- For the house roof, work with one side at a time. Pipe the icing along the top edges of the sides, front, and back pieces. Attach the roof piece carefully so that the roof's peak is now even with the points of the back and front pieces (there will be a tiny overhang back and front.) Do the same steps for the other roof piece and allow it to dry completely.
- For final touches and decorations, attach mints into the roof using an icing. For the chimney, pile caramels along the side of the house, using icing as its mortar. Top the chimney with an icing "smoke plume"
- To assemble the trees and wreath, tint the icing with green food coloring. Frost the butter cookie and sugar cones and garnish it with red-hots and sprinkles. Assemble the trees, fence, shutters, doorway, wreath, mailbox, logs, walkways, and windows. Use candies and other decorations.

Nutrition Information

- Calories:
- Sodium:
- Fiber:
- Total Carbohydrate:
- Cholesterol:
- Protein:
- Total Fat:

714. Fancy Butter Cookies

Serving: about 5 dozen. | Prep: 25mins | Cook: 15mins | Ready in:

Ingredients

- 1 cup plus 3 tablespoons butter, softened, divided
- 1/2 cup confectioners' sugar
- 2 cups all-purpose flour
- 1 teaspoon vanilla extract
- 1 cup (6 ounces) semisweet chocolate chips
- 1/2 cup finely chopped pecans or walnuts

Direction

- Beat confectioners' sugar and 1 cup of butter until fluffy and light in a large bowl. Put in vanilla and flour; combine well. Leave in the fridge, covered, for 60 minutes.
- Form 1/4 cupful of dough into logs of 1/2" thickness. Slice logs into 2 1/2" pieces; arrange on unoiled baking sheets. Bake at 350 degrees until light brown, or for 12 to 14 minutes. Transfer to wire racks to cool.
- Microwave or heat the rest of the butter and chocolate in a heavy saucepan until melted; whisk until smooth. Dip one end of each

cookie into chocolate, then dip in nuts; arrange over waxed paper until chocolate is firm.

Nutrition Information

- Calories: 143 calories
- Sodium: 74mg sodium
- Fiber: 1g fiber)
- Total Carbohydrate: 12g carbohydrate (5g sugars
- Cholesterol: 19mg cholesterol
- Protein: 1g protein.
- Total Fat: 10g fat (6g saturated fat)

715. Fancy Sugar Cookies

Serving: about 1-1/2 dozen. | Prep: 30mins | Cook: 8mins | Ready in:

Ingredients

- 1-1/2 cups Domino® or C&H® Pure Cane Granulated Sugar
- 1 cup butter-flavored shortening
- 2 eggs
- 3 tablespoons sour cream
- 1 teaspoon vanilla extract
- 1/2 teaspoon lemon extract
- 3 cups all-purpose flour
- 1/2 teaspoon baking soda
- 1/2 teaspoon salt
- Domino® or C&H® Pure Cane Powdered Sugar
- COLORED SUGAR CRYSTALS:
- 2 tablespoons Domino® or C&H® Pure Cane Granulated Sugar
- 1 to 2 drops food coloring

Direction

- Cream the sugar and shortening until fluffy and light in a big bowl. Put eggs in, 1 at a time. Stir well before putting the next. Beat in lemon extract, vanilla and sour cream. Mix salt, baking soda and flour then put in the creamed mixture. Stir well. Cover and put in the refrigerator until easy to handle or for a minimum of 30 minutes.
- Roll out 1/2 of the dough into 1/8-inch thickness on a surface covered with powder sugar. Cut using 2 1/2-inch floured cookie cutters. Put on cookie sheets with grease, leaving 1 inch space apart. Roll the rest of the dough out to 1/8 inch thickness then slice into lattice-style strips. Criss-cross the strips in lattice style on top of the cutout cookies, pressing its ends lightly to the cookies. Trim the strips if needed. Collect the scraps then roll and cut them again.
- To make the colored sugar crystals, mix food coloring and sugar using the back of a spoon to blend. Sprinkle over the cookies with lattice on top. Bake until it turns lightly browned or for 7 to 8 minutes at 350 degrees. Transfer to wire racks; cool.

Nutrition Information

- Calories:
- Total Carbohydrate:
- Cholesterol:
- Protein:
- Total Fat:
- Sodium:
- Fiber:

716. Favorite Molasses Cookies

Serving: 6 dozen. | Prep: 15mins | Cook: 10mins | Ready in:

Ingredients

- 3/4 cup butter, softened
- 1 cup sugar
- 1/4 cup molasses
- 1 egg

- 2 cups all-purpose flour
- 2 teaspoons baking powder
- 1/2 teaspoon baking soda
- 1 teaspoon ground cinnamon
- 1/2 teaspoon ground cloves
- 1/2 teaspoon ground ginger

Direction

- Cream sugar and butter in a bowl. Whisk in egg and molasses. Mix the dry ingredients; slowly put to the creamed mixture. Refrigerate for an hour or till firm.
- Form into 1-inch balls; put on oiled baking sheets. Press flat using a glass dipped in sugar. Allow to bake for 8 to 10 minutes at 375° or till lightly browned. Let cool on wire racks.

Nutrition Information

- Calories: 89 calories
- Cholesterol: 16mg cholesterol
- Protein: 1g protein.
- Total Fat: 4g fat (2g saturated fat)
- Sodium: 81mg sodium
- Fiber: 0 fiber)
- Total Carbohydrate: 13g carbohydrate (7g sugars

717. Festive Cranberry Oat Cookies

Serving: about 4 dozen. | Prep: 15mins | Cook: 10mins | Ready in:

Ingredients

- 2/3 cup butter, softened
- 2/3 cup brown sugar
- 2 eggs
- 1-1/2 cups all-purpose flour
- 1-1/2 cups old-fashioned oats
- 1 teaspoon baking soda
- 1 teaspoon ground cinnamon
- 1/2 teaspoon salt
- 1-1/4 cups dried cranberries
- 1 cup chopped pecans, toasted
- 2/3 cup vanilla or white chips

Direction

- Cream brown sugar and butter in a bowl. Add eggs; combine well. Mix dry ingredients; add to creamed mixture gradually. Stir in the rest of the ingredients. Drop onto clean and dry baking sheets by tablespoonfuls, 3-in. apart. Bake 10-12 minutes at 375° or until golden brown. Place on wire racks to cool.

Nutrition Information

- Calories: 200 calories
- Cholesterol: 32mg cholesterol
- Protein: 3g protein.
- Total Fat: 11g fat (5g saturated fat)
- Sodium: 165mg sodium
- Fiber: 2g fiber)
- Total Carbohydrate: 24g carbohydrate (10g sugars

718. Fig Filled Cookies

Serving: About 2-1/2 dozen. | Prep: 35mins | Cook: 10mins | Ready in:

Ingredients

- 1/2 cup butter, softened
- 1/4 cup sugar
- 1/4 cup packed brown sugar
- 1 egg
- 1 teaspoon vanilla extract
- 1-3/4 cups all-purpose flour
- 1/2 teaspoon baking soda
- 1/4 teaspoon salt
- FILLING:
- 2/3 cup finely chopped raisins
- 1/2 cup finely chopped dates

- 1/2 cup finely chopped dried figs
- 1/2 cup orange juice
- 1/3 cup finely chopped dried cherries or cranberries
- 2 teaspoons sugar
- 1 teaspoon grated lemon peel
- 1/4 teaspoon ground cinnamon
- 1/2 cup finely chopped pecans
- GLAZE:
- 3/4 cup confectioners' sugar
- 2 to 3 teaspoons lemon juice

Direction

- Cream sugars and butter together in a big bowl. Whisk in vanilla and egg. Mix together salt, baking soda, and flour; mix into the creamed mixture. Halve the dough. Chill with a cover for a minimum of 3 hours.
- Mix the first 8 filling ingredients together in a saucepan. Boil it. Lower the heat, simmer without a cover until the fruit is soft and absorbs the liquid, whisking sometimes, 4-6 minutes. Take away from heat, mix in pecans. Let cool until reaching room temperature.
- Between 2 waxed paper pieces, roll out each dough portion into a 10x8-inch rectangle. Slice each into two 10x4-inch rectangles. In the middle of each rectangle, spread 1/2 cup filling. Beginning from the long side, fold the dough over the filling; fold the other side over the top. Seal the edges and seams by pinching. Put on cookie sheets lined with parchment papers, the seam-side down.
- Bake at 375° until turning light brown, 10-15 minutes. Diagonally slice each rectangle into strips, 1-inch each. Transfer to wire racks to cool. Mix together the glaze ingredients and drizzle the glaze over cookies.

Nutrition Information

- Calories: 259 calories
- Sodium: 151mg sodium
- Fiber: 2g fiber)
- Total Carbohydrate: 42g carbohydrate (27g sugars
- Cholesterol: 31mg cholesterol
- Protein: 3g protein.
- Total Fat: 10g fat (4g saturated fat)

719. Filled Chocolate Spritz

Serving: about 2 dozen. | Prep: 15mins | Cook: 10mins | Ready in:

Ingredients

- 3/4 cup semisweet chocolate chips
- 1/4 cup butter, cubed
- 1/2 cup packed brown sugar
- 2 large eggs, lightly beaten
- 1 teaspoon vanilla extract
- 1-1/2 cups all-purpose flour
- 1/8 teaspoon baking soda
- PEPPERMINT FILLING:
- 1/4 cup butter, softened
- 3/4 cup confectioners' sugar
- 1 tablespoon whole milk
- 1/2 teaspoon peppermint extract
- 3 to 4 drops green food coloring
- GLAZE:
- 2/3 cup milk chocolate chips
- 1 teaspoon shortening

Direction

- Melt chocolate chips in a big microwaveable bowl; mix until smooth. Mix in the vanilla, eggs, brown sugar and butter. Put in flour and baking soda and stir well. Chill, covered, for 30 minutes or until easy to handle.
- Push dough 2 in. apart onto ungreased baking trays with a cookie press fitted with the disk of your choice. Bake for 6-8 minutes at 375° or until firm. Take out to wire racks to cool.
- Mix filling ingredients in a small bowl; mix until smooth. Put evenly on the bottoms of half of the cookies; garnish with the leftover cookies.
- Melt milk chocolate chips with shortening in a

microwave; mix until smooth. Sprinkle on top of cookies. Let sit until firm.

Nutrition Information

- Calories: 152 calories
- Protein: 2g protein.
- Total Fat: 7g fat (4g saturated fat)
- Sodium: 57mg sodium
- Fiber: 1g fiber)
- Total Carbohydrate: 20g carbohydrate (14g sugars
- Cholesterol: 29mg cholesterol

720. Flourless Peanut Butter Cookies

Serving: 6 | Prep: | Cook: | Ready in:

Ingredients

- 1 cup peanut butter
- 1 cup white sugar
- 1 egg

Direction

- Preheat oven to 180 degrees C or 350 degrees F
- Mix the ingredients and drop by teaspoonfuls onto the cookie sheet. Bake for 8 minutes. Allow to cool down. Double the recipe as you wish because the recipe doesn't make a big amount.

Nutrition Information

- Calories: 394 calories;
- Total Fat: 22.5
- Sodium: 209
- Total Carbohydrate: 41.8
- Cholesterol: 31
- Protein: 11.8

721. French Noisette Cups

Serving: 2 dozen. | Prep: 20mins | Cook: 20mins | Ready in:

Ingredients

- 1/2 cup butter, softened
- 3 ounces cream cheese, softened
- 1 cup all-purpose flour
- 1-1/3 cups hazelnuts
- 2/3 cup packed brown sugar
- 1 egg
- 1 tablespoon butter, melted
- 1 teaspoon vanilla extract

Direction

- Cream cheese and butter in a large bowl. Mix in flour. Cover and keep in the refrigerator for 30 minutes or until simple to handle.
- Prepare the oven by preheating to 350°F. In a 15x10x1- inch baking pan, place the hazelnuts and spread. Place in the preheated oven and bake for 7-10 minutes or until scented and lightly browned, whisking occasionally. Use tea towel to wrap hazelnuts to get rid of skins; loosen skin by rubbing. Set 24 hazelnuts aside for topping.
- Form dough into 24 balls. Push evenly on bottom using floured fingers, and up the sides of mini-muffin cups that are not greased.
- In a food processor, combine remaining hazelnuts and brown sugar; process until hazelnuts are nicely ground. Beat vanilla, liquify butter and egg in a small bowl; mix in hazelnut mixture. Then stuff cups with 2 teaspoons; place a reserved hazelnut on each top.
- Bake in the oven for 18-22 minutes or until set. Take to wire racks to cool.

Nutrition Information

- Calories: 156 calories

- Total Fat: 12g fat (4g saturated fat)
- Sodium: 50mg sodium
- Fiber: 1g fiber)
- Total Carbohydrate: 12g carbohydrate (6g sugars
- Cholesterol: 23mg cholesterol
- Protein: 2g protein.

722. French Toast Spirals

Serving: 4 dozen. | Prep: 30mins | Cook: 15mins | Ready in:

Ingredients

- 1 cup butter, softened
- 3/4 cup confectioners' sugar
- 1/4 cup granulated sugar
- 1 large egg
- 2 tablespoons maple syrup
- 1 teaspoon vanilla extract
- 2-1/2 cups all-purpose flour
- 1/2 teaspoon salt
- 1/2 teaspoon ground cinnamon
- FILLING:
- 1/3 cup butter, softened
- 3 tablespoons all-purpose flour
- 3 tablespoons brown sugar
- 2 tablespoons maple syrup
- 1 teaspoon instant coffee granules
- Confectioners' sugar, optional

Direction

- Cream sugars and butter until fluffy and light. Whisk in vanilla, maple syrup and egg. Beat cinnamon, salt and flour in another bowl; beat into creamed mixture gradually. Roll dough between 2 sheets of waxed paper into a 12-in. square on a baking sheet. Chill in the fridge for half an hour.
- To prepare filling, whisk the first 5 ingredients until blended. Discard top sheet of waxed paper; place filling on top and spread to within 1/4-in. of edges over dough. Tightly roll up with waxed paper jelly-roll style; remove paper as you roll. Use plastic to wrap. Chill in the fridge for about 2 hours until firm.
- Set the oven to 375° and start preheating. Unwrap; slice dough crosswise into 1/4-in. slices. Arrange on baking sheets lined with parchment paper, 2 inches apart. Bake for 12-14 minutes until edges turn light brown. Cool for 5 minutes on pan. Transfer to wire racks to finish cooling. If preferred, sprinkle with confectioners' sugar.

Nutrition Information

- Calories:
- Total Fat:
- Sodium:
- Fiber:
- Total Carbohydrate:
- Cholesterol:
- Protein:

723. Frieda's Molasses Cookies

Serving: 6-7 dozen. | Prep: 30mins | Cook: 10mins | Ready in:

Ingredients

- 1 cup shortening
- 1 cup sugar
- 1 cup light molasses or sorghum
- 1/3 cup boiling water
- 1 tablespoon white vinegar
- 5 cups all-purpose flour
- 2 teaspoons baking soda
- 1 teaspoon ground ginger
- 1 teaspoon ground cinnamon
- 1/4 teaspoon salt

Direction

- Cream sugar and shortening till fluffy and light in a bowl; beat in vinegar, water and molasses. Mix salt, cinnamon, ginger, baking soda and flour; whisk into creamed mixture. Cover; chill it for 3 hours.
- Roll dough to 1/4-in. thick on a lightly floured surface; use decorative cutter or drinking glass or 2 1/2-in. cookie cutter dipped in flour to cut; put on greased baking sheets; bake for 8 minutes at 375° till edges brown lightly; don't overbake.

Nutrition Information

- Calories: 158 calories
- Fiber: 1g fiber)
- Total Carbohydrate: 25g carbohydrate (11g sugars
- Cholesterol: 0 cholesterol
- Protein: 2g protein.
- Total Fat: 6g fat (1g saturated fat)
- Sodium: 90mg sodium

724. Frosted Anise Cookies

Serving: 3-1/2 dozen. | Prep: 30mins | Cook: 10mins | Ready in:

Ingredients

- 1 cup butter, softened
- 1-1/2 cups sugar
- 1 large egg
- 1 teaspoon anise extract
- 2-3/4 cups all-purpose flour
- 1 teaspoon baking soda
- 1/2 teaspoon baking powder
- 1 can (16 ounces) vanilla frosting
- Holiday sprinkles

Direction

- Cream together the butter and sugar in a large bowl till fluffy and light. Beat egg and extract into the mixture. Mix together the baking powder, baking soda and flour; add them to the creamed mixture and combine thoroughly.
- Drop tablespoonfuls of the dough 2 in. apart onto baking sheets that are ungreased. Bake at 375° until golden brown, about 9-11 minutes. Take them out to wire racks to cool thoroughly.
- Frost cookies and decorate with sprinkles. Let sit till set. For storage, keep in an airtight container.

Nutrition Information

- Calories:
- Sodium:
- Fiber:
- Total Carbohydrate:
- Cholesterol:
- Protein:
- Total Fat:

725. Frosted Cashew Cookies

Serving: about 3 dozen. | Prep: 20mins | Cook: 10mins | Ready in:

Ingredients

- 1/2 cup butter, softened
- 1 cup packed brown sugar
- 1 large egg
- 1/3 cup sour cream
- 1/2 teaspoon vanilla extract
- 2 cups all-purpose flour
- 3/4 teaspoon each baking powder, baking soda and salt
- 1-1/2 cups salted cashews, coarsely chopped
- BROWNED BUTTER FROSTING:
- 1/2 cup butter, cubed
- 3 tablespoons half-and-half cream
- 1/4 teaspoon vanilla extract
- 2 cups confectioners' sugar
- Additional cashew halves, optional

Direction

- Cream the brown sugar and butter in a bowl. Whisk in vanilla, sour cream and egg; mix thoroughly. Mix together the salt, baking soda, baking powder and flour; put into creamed mixture and combine thoroughly. Mix in cashews.
- On greased baking sheets, drop by tablespoonfuls 2 inches away. Bake at 375° till lightly browned, about 8 to 10 minutes. Allow to cool on a wire rack.
- For the frosting, in a small saucepan, brown butter lightly. Take away from heat; put in vanilla and cream. Whisk in confectioners' sugar till smooth and thick. Frost the cookies. If wished, put a cashew half atop each serving.

Nutrition Information

- Calories: 348 calories
- Total Fat: 19g fat (9g saturated fat)
- Sodium: 381mg sodium
- Fiber: 1g fiber)
- Total Carbohydrate: 40g carbohydrate (26g sugars
- Cholesterol: 43mg cholesterol
- Protein: 5g protein.

726. Frosted Cherry Chip Cookies

Serving: 3-1/2 dozen. | Prep: 60mins | Cook: 15mins | Ready in:

Ingredients

- 1 jar (10 ounces) maraschino cherries
- 6 tablespoons butter, softened
- 1 cup sugar
- 1 egg
- 1 teaspoon vanilla extract
- 2 cups all-purpose flour
- 1/2 teaspoon baking soda
- 1/2 teaspoon salt
- 1/2 cup sour cream
- FROSTING:
- 3-1/2 cups confectioners' sugar
- 1/2 cup sour cream
- Red colored sugar, optional

Direction

- Let the cherries drain and save 1 tablespoon of juice for frosting. Slice the cherries and pat dry; put aside. Cream the sugar and butter in a big bowl. Stir in vanilla and egg. Mix salt, baking soda and flour then put alternately with the sour cream into the creamed mixture. Mix in the cherries.
- Drop by tablespoonfuls on baking sheets with grease, leaving 2-inchspaces apart. Bake until lightly browned or for 12 to 15 minutes at 350 degrees. Allow to cool by moving to wire racks.
- For the frosting, combine the reserved cherry juice, sour cream and confectioners' sugar until smooth in a bowl. Pour mixture over cookies and if desired, use colored sugar to sprinkle on top.

Nutrition Information

- Calories: 115 calories
- Protein: 1g protein.
- Total Fat: 3g fat (2g saturated fat)
- Sodium: 64mg sodium
- Fiber: 0 fiber)
- Total Carbohydrate: 22g carbohydrate (17g sugars
- Cholesterol: 13mg cholesterol

727. Frosted Cutout Sugar Cookies

Serving: 5 dozen. | Prep: 30mins | Cook: 10mins | Ready in:

Ingredients

- 3 cups all-purpose flour
- 1 cup granulated sugar
- 1 teaspoon baking soda
- 1/4 teaspoon salt
- 1/2 cup shortening
- 1/2 cup cold butter
- 2 large eggs
- 1 tablespoon whole milk
- 1 teaspoon vanilla extract
- FROSTING:
- 1/2 cup butter, softened
- 4 cups confectioners' sugar
- 1 teaspoon vanilla extract
- 2 to 4 tablespoons half-and-half cream
- Food coloring, optional
- Colored sugar, optional
- Decorating candies, optional

Direction

- Mix salt, baking soda, granulated sugar and flour; cut butter and shortening in till crumbly. Whisk vanilla, milk and eggs in another bowl; add to flour mixture. Stir well then divide dough to 3 balls. Cover; refrigerate for 2 hours till easy to handle.
- Preheat an oven to 325°; take one dough portion out of the fridge at a time. Roll dough to 1/4-in. thick on lightly floured surface. Use floured 2-in. cookie cutter to cut; put on ungreased baking sheets, 1-in. apart. Repeat with leftover dough.
- Bake for 8-10 minutes till edges lightly brown. Cool for 1 minute; transfer to wire racks. Completely cool.
- Frosting: Cream vanilla, confectioners' sugar, butter and enough cream to get spreading consistency. Tint with food coloring if desired; frost cookies. If desired, decorate with candies and colored sugar.

Nutrition Information

- Calories: 112 calories
- Fiber: 0 fiber)
- Total Carbohydrate: 16g carbohydrate (11g sugars
- Cholesterol: 15mg cholesterol
- Protein: 1g protein.
- Total Fat: 5g fat (2g saturated fat)
- Sodium: 58mg sodium

728. Frosted Ginger Creams

Serving: about 4 dozen. | Prep: 20mins | Cook: 10mins | Ready in:

Ingredients

- 1/4 cup shortening
- 1/2 cup sugar
- 1 egg
- 1/3 cup molasses
- 2 cups all-purpose flour
- 1 teaspoon ground ginger
- 1/2 teaspoon baking soda
- 1/2 teaspoon salt
- 1/2 teaspoon ground cinnamon
- 1/2 teaspoon ground cloves
- 1/3 cup water
- FROSTING:
- 1-1/2 ounces cream cheese, softened
- 3 tablespoons butter, softened
- 1 cup plus 3 tablespoons confectioners' sugar
- 1/2 teaspoon vanilla extract
- 1 to 2 teaspoons lemon juice

Direction

- Cream sugar and shortening in a big bowl; stir in molasses and egg. Mix cloves, flour, cinnamon, ginger, salt, and baking soda; stir into the creamed mixture gradually alternating with water to make a soft dough.
- Drop heaping teaspoonfuls of batter on greased baking sheets, two inches apart. Bake for 7-8 minutes in a 400 degrees oven or until cracked on top. Cool on wire racks.
- Beat confectioners' sugar, butter, and cream cheese together in a small bowl until fluffy and

light; stir in vanilla and just enough lemon juice to get the spreading consistency. Spread frosting over the cookies, then keep in the refrigerator.

Nutrition Information

- Calories: 130 calories
- Total Carbohydrate: 21g carbohydrate (13g sugars
- Cholesterol: 15mg cholesterol
- Protein: 1g protein.
- Total Fat: 4g fat (2g saturated fat)
- Sodium: 100mg sodium
- Fiber: 0 fiber)

729. Frosted Gingerbread Nut Cookies

Serving: 5 dozen. | Prep: 15mins | Cook: 10mins | Ready in:

Ingredients

- 1/2 cup butter, softened
- 2/3 cup sugar
- 1 egg
- 1/2 cup molasses
- 2-3/4 cups all-purpose flour
- 1 teaspoon baking soda
- 1 teaspoon ground cinnamon
- 1 teaspoon ground ginger
- 1/2 teaspoon salt
- 1/4 teaspoon ground cloves
- 1/2 cup buttermilk
- 1/2 cup chopped walnuts
- FROSTING:
- 1-1/2 cups confectioners' sugar
- 4-1/2 teaspoons butter, softened
- 1/2 teaspoon vanilla extract
- 2 to 3 tablespoons half-and-half cream
- Walnuts halves, optional

Direction

- Cream sugar and butter in a large bowl until fluffy and light. Stir in molasses and egg. Mix baking soda, cloves, ginger, salt, cinnamon, and flour. Add the dry ingredients into the creamed mixture, adding it alternately with buttermilk. Be sure to whisk the mixture every after addition. Sprinkle the chopped walnuts.
- Grease the baking sheets. Place tablespoonfuls of the dough into the prepared baking dish, arranging them 2-inches apart from each other. Let it bake inside the oven with a temperature of 350°F for 10-12 minutes until all edges are set. Allow it to cool on wire racks.
- Prepare the frosting. In a small bowl, mix butter, vanilla, confectioners' sugar, and enough cream to reach desired consistency of the frosting. Decorate it into the cooled cookies and top each with a walnut half if preferred.

Nutrition Information

- Calories: 74 calories
- Protein: 1g protein.
- Total Fat: 3g fat (1g saturated fat)
- Sodium: 64mg sodium
- Fiber: 0 fiber)
- Total Carbohydrate: 12g carbohydrate (7g sugars
- Cholesterol: 9mg cholesterol

730. Frosted Oatmeal Cookies

Serving: about 4 dozen. | Prep: 45mins | Cook: 10mins | Ready in:

Ingredients

- 1 cup butter, softened
- 2 cups packed brown sugar
- 2 large eggs
- 2 cups all-purpose flour
- 2 cups quick-cooking oats
- 1 teaspoon baking soda
- 1 teaspoon salt

- 1 teaspoon ground allspice
- 1 teaspoon ground cinnamon
- 1/4 teaspoon ground cloves
- 1 cup raisins
- 1 cup chopped pecans, optional
- FROSTING:
- 5 cups confectioners' sugar
- 1/4 cup butter, melted
- 1/3 to 1/2 cup 2% milk
- White sprinkles, optional

Direction

- Cream brown sugar and butter until fluffy and light. Whisk in eggs. Beat the next 7 ingredients in another bowl; whisk into creamed mixture gradually. Stir in raisins and pecans if preferred. Separate dough into 1/2. Form each into a disk; use plastic to wrap. Chill in the fridge for about an hour until it reaches the firmness that you can roll.
- Set the oven to 350° and start preheating. Roll each dough portion to 1/4-in. thickness on a lightly floured surface. Use a floured 2-3/4-in. round cookie cutter to cut. Arrange on greased baking sheets 2 in. apart. Bake for 7-9 minutes until light brown. Cool for 2 minutes; place cookies on wire racks to completely cool.
- To prepare frosting, whisk enough milk, butter and confectioners' sugar to achieve the consistency that you can spread. Spread over cookies. If preferred, sprinkle with white sprinkles.

Nutrition Information

- Calories: 164 calories
- Fiber: 1g fiber)
- Total Carbohydrate: 29g carbohydrate (22g sugars
- Cholesterol: 20mg cholesterol
- Protein: 1g protein.
- Total Fat: 5g fat (3g saturated fat)
- Sodium: 116mg sodium

731. Frosted Peanut Butter Cookies

Serving: about 2 dozen. | Prep: 20mins | Cook: 10mins | Ready in:

Ingredients

- 1 package (17-1/2 ounces) peanut butter cookie mix
- 2 cups confectioners' sugar
- 1/4 cup baking cocoa
- 1/4 cup hot water
- 1 teaspoon vanilla extract
- Sliced almonds or pecan halves

Direction

- Follow package directions to prep cookie dough in big bowl; form to 1-in. balls. Put on ungreased baking sheets, 2-in. apart.
- Bake for 8-10 minutes at 375° till edges are golden brown; cool for 1 minute. Transfer to wire racks.
- Frosting: Mix vanilla, water, cocoa and confectioners' sugar in big bowl; spread on cookies. Put nuts on.

Nutrition Information

- Calories:
- Sodium:
- Fiber:
- Total Carbohydrate:
- Cholesterol:
- Protein:
- Total Fat:

732. Frosted Pumpkin Cookies

Serving: 6-1/2 dozen. | Prep: 25mins | Cook: 15mins | Ready in:

Ingredients

- 1 cup shortening
- 2 cups packed brown sugar
- 1 can (15 ounces) solid-pack pumpkin
- 4 cups all-purpose flour
- 2 teaspoons baking powder
- 2 teaspoons baking soda
- 2 teaspoons ground cinnamon
- 1/8 teaspoon salt
- 1 cup chopped pecans
- 1 cup chopped dates
- CARAMEL FROSTING:
- 1/2 cup butter, cubed
- 1-1/2 cups packed brown sugar
- 1/4 cup 2% milk
- 1 teaspoon maple flavoring
- 1/2 teaspoon vanilla extract
- 2 to 2-1/2 cups confectioners' sugar

Direction

- Cream brown sugar and shortening until fluffy and light in a large bowl. Beat in pumpkin. Mix salt, cinnamon, baking powder, flour and baking soda; add to pumpkin mixture gradually; mix well. Stir in dates and pecans.
- Drop onto a clean and dry baking sheet by rounded teaspoonfuls 2 in. apart. Bake at 375° until firm or for 13-15 minutes.
- In the meantime, to prepare frosting: In a small saucepan, combine milk, brown sugar and butter. Bring to boiling while stirring constantly over medium heat; boil for 3 minutes. Take out of the heat; stir in vanilla and maple flavoring.
- Cool slightly; whisk in enough confectioners' sugar to reach the consistency that you can spread. Transfer cookies to wire racks; frost while they are warm.

Nutrition Information

- Calories: 249 calories
- Protein: 2g protein.
- Total Fat: 10g fat (3g saturated fat)
- Sodium: 125mg sodium
- Fiber: 1g fiber)
- Total Carbohydrate: 40g carbohydrate (29g sugars
- Cholesterol: 7mg cholesterol

733. Frosted Sour Cream Cutouts

Serving: 5-1/2 dozen. | Prep: 30mins | Cook: 10mins | Ready in:

Ingredients

- 1/2 cup butter, softened
- 1 cup sugar
- 1 egg
- 1/2 cup sour cream
- 1 teaspoon vanilla extract
- 3-1/2 cups all-purpose flour
- 1 teaspoon baking soda
- 1/2 teaspoon salt
- FROSTING:
- 1/4 cup cold milk
- 3 tablespoons instant vanilla pudding mix
- 1/4 cup butter, softened
- 2-1/2 cups confectioners' sugar
- 1 teaspoon vanilla extract
- Food coloring, optional
- Edible glitter

Direction

- Beat butter and sugar in a large mixing bowl. Beat in vanilla, sour cream, and egg. Mix salt, baking soda, and flour together; slow mix into creamed mixture. Refrigerate, covered, for 1 hour or until easy to work with.
- Flatten dough to a thickness of 1/8 inch on a work surface heavily coated with confectioners' sugar. Cut dough using 2 1/2-inch cookie cutter. Arrange cookies 1 inch apart on buttered baking sheets. Bake for 8 to 10 minutes at 375° until lightly browned. Instantly transfer to wire racks to cool.

- To make frosting, beat pudding mix and milk together until smooth; put to one side; beat butter in a large mixing bowl. Add pudding mixture and beat well. Slowly add vanilla, confectioners' sugar, and food coloring (if using); beat on high speed until fluffy and light. Pipe frosting onto cookies and garnish with edible glitter.

Nutrition Information

- Calories:
- Cholesterol:
- Protein:
- Total Fat:
- Sodium:
- Fiber:
- Total Carbohydrate:

734. Fruit Filled Spritz Cookies

Serving: about 7-1/2 dozen. | Prep: 30mins | Cook: 15mins | Ready in:

Ingredients

- 1-1/2 cups chopped dates
- 1 cup water
- 1/2 cup sugar
- 2 teaspoons orange juice
- 2 teaspoons grated orange zest
- 1 cup maraschino cherries, chopped
- 1/2 cup sweetened shredded coconut
- 1/2 cup ground nuts
- DOUGH:
- 1 cup butter, softened
- 1 cup sugar
- 1/2 cup packed brown sugar
- 3 large eggs
- 1/2 teaspoon almond extract
- 1/2 teaspoon vanilla extract
- 4 cups all-purpose flour
- 1/2 teaspoon baking soda
- 1/2 teaspoon salt
- Confectioners' sugar, optional

Direction

- Mix the first 5 ingredients in a small saucepan; boil the mixture, stirring constantly. Lower the heat; cook while stirring until thickened or for 8 minutes. Completely cool. Stir in nuts, coconut and cherries; put aside.
- Ceram sugars and butter until fluffy and light in a large bowl. Whisk in extracts and eggs. Mix salt, baking soda and flour; add to creamed mixture gradually; combine well.
- Press a 12-in.-long strip of dough with a cookie press fitted with a bar disk onto a clean and dry baking sheet. Add fruit filling on top and spread. Press another strip over filling. Cut into 1-in. pieces (you do not have to separate pieces). Do the same with the rest of filling and dough.
- Bake for 12-15 minutes at 375° or until edges turn golden. Recut into pieces if needed. Transfer to wire racks to cool. Sprinkle with confectioners' sugar if preferred.

Nutrition Information

- Calories: 77 calories
- Total Fat: 3g fat (2g saturated fat)
- Sodium: 45mg sodium
- Fiber: 0 fiber)
- Total Carbohydrate: 12g carbohydrate (7g sugars
- Cholesterol: 12mg cholesterol
- Protein: 1g protein.

735. Fruitcake Cookies With Rum Glaze

Serving: about 4 dozen. | Prep: 45mins | Cook: 15mins | Ready in:

Ingredients

- 1 cup golden raisins
- 3/4 cup dried cherries
- 1/2 cup diced dried apricots
- 3/4 cup water
- 1/4 cup rum or additional water
- 3/4 cup chopped pecans
- 1/3 cup diced crystallized ginger
- 1/3 cup diced candied orange peel
- 1 cup butter, softened
- 2 cups sugar, divided
- 2 large eggs
- 1-1/2 teaspoons rum extract
- 3-1/2 cups all-purpose flour
- 1 teaspoon baking soda
- 1/2 teaspoon salt
- GLAZE:
- 3 cups confectioners' sugar
- 3 to 5 tablespoons 2% milk
- 3 tablespoons rum or additional milk

Direction

- Boil first 5 ingredients in small saucepan. Lower heat; simmer, uncovered, for 12-15 minutes till liquid is nearly absorbed. Fully cool; mix in orange peel, ginger and pecans.
- Preheat an oven to 350°. Cream 1 1/2 cups sugar and butter till fluffy and light; beat in extract and eggs. Whisk salt, baking soda and flour together in another bowl; beat into creamed mixture slowly. Mix in fruit mixture.
- In a shallow bowl, put leftover sugar. Form 2 tbsp. dough to balls; to lightly coat, toss in sugar. Put onto parchment paper-lined baking sheets, 2-in. apart.
- Bake for 11-13 minutes till just set and golden brown. Transfer from pans onto wire racks; fully cool.
- Stir glaze ingredients; drizzle on cookies.

Nutrition Information

- Calories: 176 calories
- Fiber: 1g fiber)
- Total Carbohydrate: 31g carbohydrate (21g sugars
- Cholesterol: 18mg cholesterol
- Protein: 2g protein.
- Total Fat: 5g fat (3g saturated fat)
- Sodium: 92mg sodium

736. Fudge Filled Toffee Cookies

Serving: 5-1/2 dozen. | Prep: 25mins | Cook: 15mins | Ready in:

Ingredients

- 1/2 cup butter, softened
- 1/2 cup sugar
- 1/2 cup confectioners' sugar
- 1/2 cup canola oil
- 1 egg
- 1/2 teaspoon almond extract
- 1/4 teaspoon coconut extract
- 1-3/4 cups all-purpose flour
- 1/2 cup whole wheat flour
- 1/2 teaspoon salt
- 1/2 teaspoon baking soda
- 1/2 teaspoon cream of tartar
- 3/4 cup milk chocolate English toffee bits
- 2/3 cup chopped pecans
- 2/3 cup sweetened shredded coconut
- Additional sugar
- FILLING:
- 1-1/2 cups semisweet chocolate chips, melted
- 3/4 cup sweetened condensed milk
- 1-1/2 teaspoons vanilla extract
- 1-1/4 cups pecan halves

Direction

- Cream sugars and butter in a big bowl until the mixture is fluffy and light. Beat in extracts, egg and oil. Mix cream of tartar, baking soda, salt and flours together; put into creamed mixture gradually and blend well. Stir in coconut, pecans and toffee bits. Put into the fridge with a cover for an hour or until easy to handle.

- Set the oven at 350° to preheat. Round dough into 1-inch balls; roll in sugar. Put 2-inch apart on ungreased baking sheets. Make an indentation in the center of each with the end of a wooden spoon handle.
- Mix vanilla, milk and melted chocolate in a big bowl until smooth. Fill the center of each cookie with 1 teaspoon of the chocolate mixture. Put a pecan half on top.
- Bake for 12-14 minutes or until the cookies are lightly browned. Transfer to a wire rack to cool.

Nutrition Information

- Calories: 248 calories
- Cholesterol: 18mg cholesterol
- Protein: 3g protein.
- Total Fat: 16g fat (6g saturated fat)
- Sodium: 131mg sodium
- Fiber: 2g fiber)
- Total Carbohydrate: 25g carbohydrate (17g sugars

737. Fudge Topped Orange Cookies

Serving: 2 dozen. | Prep: 15mins | Cook: 20mins | Ready in:

Ingredients

- 3/4 cup butter, softened
- 1 cup sugar
- 1 large egg
- 2 large egg yolks
- 2 teaspoons grated orange zest
- 1-1/2 teaspoons orange extract
- 2 cups all-purpose flour
- 1 teaspoon ground ginger
- 1/2 teaspoon baking soda
- TOPPING:
- 1 jar (7 ounces) marshmallow creme
- 3/4 cup sugar
- 1/3 cup evaporated milk
- 2 tablespoons butter
- 1/8 teaspoon salt
- 1 cup (6 ounces) semisweet chocolate chips
- 1/2 teaspoon vanilla extract

Direction

- In a big bowl, cream the sugar and butter till fluffy and light. Whip in orange extract, orange zest, egg yolks and egg. Mix baking soda, ginger and flour; slowly put into the creamed mixture and stir well.
- Drop by the rounded tablespoonfuls 2 inches apart to the ungreased baking sheets. Bake at 300 degrees till they turn golden brown or for 20 to 22 minutes. Transfer onto the wire racks to cool down.
- In a big saucepan, mix salt, butter, milk, sugar and marshmallow crème. Boil to a rolling boil on medium heat; boil for 5 minutes, whisk continuously. Take it off the heat. Put in the vanilla and chocolate chips; whisk till the chips have been melted. Spread on tops of the cookies.

Nutrition Information

- Calories: 458 calories
- Total Carbohydrate: 69g carbohydrate (48g sugars
- Cholesterol: 91mg cholesterol
- Protein: 4g protein.
- Total Fat: 19g fat (12g saturated fat)
- Sodium: 241mg sodium
- Fiber: 1g fiber)

738. Fudgy Pinwheel Cookies

Serving: 4 dozen. | Prep: 25mins | Cook: 10mins | Ready in:

Ingredients

- 1/2 cup butter, softened

- 1/2 cup packed brown sugar
- 1 large egg yolk
- 1/2 teaspoon vanilla extract
- 1 cup all-purpose flour
- 1/2 teaspoon salt
- 1/4 teaspoon baking powder
- FILLING:
- 1 cup (6 ounces) semisweet chocolate chips
- 1 tablespoon shortening
- 1 cup finely chopped walnuts
- 1/3 cup sweetened condensed milk
- 1 teaspoon vanilla extract

Direction

- In the big bowl, cream the brown sugar and butter till fluffy and light. Whip in the vanilla and egg yolk. In the small-sized bowl, stir the baking powder, salt and flour; slowly whip to the creamed mixture.
- Roll the dough between two sheets of the waxed paper into one 12x10-inch rectangle; move onto the baking sheet. Keep in the refrigerator for half an hour.
- In the small-sized microwave safe bowl, melt the shortening and chocolate chips; whisk till smooth. Whisk in the vanilla, milk and walnuts. Peel the top sheet of waxed paper; spread the dough with the filling. Use the waxed paper to form the dough, roll the dough up securely like the jelly-roll, and begin with one long side. Wrap in the plastic; keep in the refrigerator till firm or for 2 hours.
- Pre-heat the oven to 375 degrees. Remove the wrap and chop the dough crosswise into a-quarter-inch slices. Position 2 inches apart on the greased baking sheets. Bake till set or for 7 to 9 minutes. Let cool down for 60 seconds prior to taking out of the pans onto the wire racks.

Nutrition Information

- Calories: 125 calories
- Cholesterol: 16mg cholesterol
- Protein: 2g protein. Diabetic Exchanges: 1 starch
- Total Fat: 8g fat (3g saturated fat)
- Sodium: 71mg sodium
- Fiber: 1g fiber)
- Total Carbohydrate: 13g carbohydrate (9g sugars

739. Full Of Chips Cookies

Serving: about 4 dozen. | Prep: 15mins | Cook: 10mins | Ready in:

Ingredients

- 1 cup butter-flavored shortening
- 3/4 cup sugar
- 3/4 cup packed brown sugar
- 2 eggs
- 1 teaspoon vanilla extract
- 2-1/4 cups all-purpose flour
- 1 teaspoon baking soda
- 3/4 teaspoon salt
- 1/3 cup each semisweet chocolate chips, peanut butter chips, butterscotch chips and vanilla or white chips
- 1/3 cup milk chocolate M&M's
- 1/3 cup Reese's pieces candy

Direction

- Beat sugars and shortening in a big bowl until the mixture is fluffy and light. Pour in eggs, one at a time and beat thoroughly between additions. Add vanilla and beat. Mix together salt, baking soda and flour; pour little by little into beaten mixture and stir thoroughly. Mix in candy and chips.
- Scoop dough by rounded tablespoonfuls and place 2 inches apart onto unprepared baking sheets. Bake in 375-degree oven until edges turn light brown, about 7 to 9 minutes. Transfer to wire racks and let cool.

Nutrition Information

- Calories: 253 calories

- Total Carbohydrate: 32g carbohydrate (20g sugars
- Cholesterol: 19mg cholesterol
- Protein: 3g protein.
- Total Fat: 13g fat (5g saturated fat)
- Sodium: 152mg sodium
- Fiber: 1g fiber)

740. German Chocolate Tassies

Serving: about 2-1/2 dozen. | Prep: 30mins | Cook: 20mins | Ready in:

Ingredients

- 2/3 cup butter, softened
- 4 ounces cream cheese, softened
- 1/2 cup granulated sugar
- 2 teaspoons vanilla extract
- 1 cup all-purpose flour
- 1/2 cup baking cocoa
- Dash salt
- FILLING:
- 1/2 cup pecan halves, toasted
- 1/4 cup sweetened shredded coconut, toasted
- 1/2 cup packed brown sugar
- 1 large egg
- 1 tablespoon butter, melted
- 1 teaspoon vanilla extract
- 1/8 teaspoon salt
- 2 ounces semisweet chocolate, melted

Direction

- Beat cream cheese, sugar and butter till fluffy and light. Whip vanilla in. Mix cocoa, salt and flour in a separate bowl and whip into creamed mixture slowly. Chill for half an hour, with cover.
- Set the oven to 350 degrees to preheat. Form the dough to balls of 1-inch then evenly pat on up sides and bottom of grease-free mini-muffin cups.
- In food processor, pulse coconut and pecans to fine chop. Whip salt, vanilla, butter, egg and brown sugar in small bowl. Whip chocolate in. Mix in mixture of pecan. Fill every cup with 1 rounded teaspoon of filling. Bake for 17 to 20 minutes, till filling sets. Cool down for five minutes in pans. Transfer onto wire racks and cool fully.

Nutrition Information

- Calories: 129 calories
- Sodium: 68mg sodium
- Fiber: 1g fiber)
- Total Carbohydrate: 12g carbohydrate (8g sugars
- Cholesterol: 22mg cholesterol
- Protein: 2g protein.
- Total Fat: 8g fat (4g saturated fat)

741. German Chocolate Thumbprints

Serving: 4 dozen. | Prep: 45mins | Cook: 10mins | Ready in:

Ingredients

- 1/2 cup semisweet chocolate chips
- 1 tablespoon shortening
- 1/2 cup butter, softened
- 3/4 cup sugar
- 1 egg
- 1 tablespoon strong brewed coffee
- 1 teaspoon vanilla extract
- 2 cups all-purpose flour
- 1 tablespoon baking cocoa
- 1 teaspoon baking powder
- 1/4 teaspoon salt
- FILLING:
- 3/4 cup sweetened shredded coconut, toasted
- 3/4 cup chopped pecans, toasted
- 1 teaspoon vanilla extract
- 4 to 6 tablespoons sweetened condensed milk

- DRIZZLE:
- 1/2 cup semisweet chocolate chips
- 1 tablespoon shortening

Direction

- Melt shortening and chips in a microwave, whisk until smooth. Put aside. Cream sugar and butter together in a big bowl until fluffy and light. Whisk in the melted chocolate mixture, vanilla, coffee, and egg. Mix together salt, baking powder, cocoa, and flour; slowly add to the creamed mixture and stir thoroughly.
- Roll into balls, 1 inch each. Put on oil-coated cookie sheets, 2 inches apart. In the middle of each ball, form a dent with the end of a wooden spoon handle. Bake at 350° until firm, 6-8 minutes. Transfer to wire racks to fully cool.
- In the meantime, to prepare the filling, mix vanilla, pecans, and coconut together in a small bowl. Mix in a sufficient amount of milk to make a stiff mixture. Fill rounded teaspoonful of the filling into each cookie. Melt shortening and chips; whisk until smooth. Drizzle over the cookies. Put in an airtight container to store.

Nutrition Information

- Calories: 97 calories
- Sodium: 42mg sodium
- Fiber: 1g fiber)
- Total Carbohydrate: 11g carbohydrate (7g sugars
- Cholesterol: 10mg cholesterol
- Protein: 1g protein.
- Total Fat: 6g fat (3g saturated fat)

742. German Christmas Cookies

Serving: 12 dozen. | Prep: 30mins | Cook: 10mins | Ready in:

Ingredients

- 2 cups all-purpose flour
- 1 cup granulated sugar
- 1 teaspoon ground cinnamon
- 1/2 teaspoon baking soda
- 1/2 teaspoon ground cloves
- 1/4 teaspoon ground nutmeg
- 1/4 teaspoon ground allspice
- 2 large eggs
- 1/2 cup butter, melted
- 1/2 teaspoon grated lemon peel
- 1/2 teaspoon anise extract
- 1-1/2 cups chopped almonds
- 1/2 cup chopped candied citron
- Confectioners' sugar

Direction

- Preheat the oven to 350 degrees. Mix the first 7 ingredients together. Mix lemon extract, eggs, lemon peel, and butter in a separate bowl; mix into the dry ingredients until just moistened. Fold in citron and almonds.
- Form into half-inch balls then arrange on greased baking sheets an inch apart. Bake for 8-10 minutes until set. In confectioners' sugar, dredge the warm cookies then place on wire racks to cool. Store cookies in an airtight container.

Nutrition Information

- Calories: 29 calories
- Total Carbohydrate: 4g carbohydrate (2g sugars
- Cholesterol: 4mg cholesterol
- Protein: 1g protein.
- Total Fat: 1g fat (0 saturated fat)
- Sodium: 13mg sodium
- Fiber: 0 fiber)

743. Ginger Diamonds

Serving: 7 dozen. | Prep: 20mins | Cook: 10mins | Ready in:

Ingredients

- 1 cup shortening
- 1-1/2 cups sugar
- 1/2 cup molasses
- 2 eggs
- 3-1/2 cups all-purpose flour
- 1 teaspoon baking soda
- 1 teaspoon ground cinnamon
- 1 teaspoon ground cloves
- 1/2 teaspoon salt
- 1/2 teaspoon ground ginger
- Additional sugar

Direction

- Cream sugar and shortening till fluffy and light in a big bowl; beat in molasses. One by one, add eggs; beat well after each addition. Mix ginger, salt, cloves, cinnamon, baking soda and flour. Add to creamed mixture slowly; mix well. Cover; refrigerate till easy to handle or for 30 minutes.
- Halve dough; roll each portion out to 1/4-in. thick on lightly floured surface. In 1 direction, create cuts 1 1/2-in. apart with a sharp knife; in opposite direction, create diagonal cuts 1 1/2-in. apart. Sprinkle extra sugar generously.
- Put on ungreased baking sheets, 1-in. apart; bake at 350° till edges are golden brown or for 10-11 minutes. Transfer to wire racks; cool.

Nutrition Information

- Calories: 121 calories
- Fiber: 0 fiber)
- Total Carbohydrate: 18g carbohydrate (9g sugars
- Cholesterol: 10mg cholesterol
- Protein: 1g protein.
- Total Fat: 5g fat (1g saturated fat)
- Sodium: 63mg sodium

744. Ginger Shortbread Cookies

Serving: 36 cookies | Prep: | Cook: |Ready in:

Ingredients

- 2 1/3 cups unbleached all purpose flour
- 3/4 cup powdered sugar
- 2 teaspoons ground ginger
- 1/4 teaspoon salt
- 1/4 cup coarsely chopped crystallized ginger (about 1 1/2 ounces)
- 1 tablespoon sugar
- 1 cup (2 sticks) unsalted butter, room temperature
- 2 teaspoons grated lemon peel
- 1/2 teaspoon lemon extract
- 1/2 teaspoon vanilla extract
- Additional powdered sugar (optional)

Direction

- Mix salt, ground ginger, 3/4 cup powdered sugar and flour in a medium bowl. Mix 1 tbsp. sugar and crystallized ginger on work surface; finely chop.
- Beat butter using electric mixer till light in a big bowl. Add extracts and lemon peel; beat in the crystallized ginger mixture. In 4 additions, beat dry ingredients into the butter mixture.
- Put dough on floured work surface; halve dough. Roll every half to 6-in. log. Form each log to 2x1x6-in. long rectangular log, then wrap in plastic; refrigerate for 2 hours.
- Preheat an oven to 325°F. Butter 2 big baking sheets lightly. Cut every dough log to 1/3-in. thick cookies; put cookies on prepped baking sheets, 1-in. apart. They'll slightly spread while baking. Bake cookies for about 24 minutes till edges are pale golden. Cool

cookies for 3 minutes on baking sheets. Put cookies on racks using metal spatula. If desired, sift extra powdered sugar on warm cookies; fully cool. Can be done ahead; keep at room temperature in airtight container for up to 1 week.

Nutrition Information

- Calories: 90
- Fiber: 0 g(1%)
- Total Carbohydrate: 10 g(3%)
- Cholesterol: 14 mg(5%)
- Protein: 1 g(2%)
- Total Fat: 5 g(8%)
- Saturated Fat: 3 g(16%)
- Sodium: 18 mg(1%)

745. Ginger Macadamia Nut Snowballs

Serving: about 5 dozen. | Prep: 25mins | Cook: 15mins | Ready in:

Ingredients

- 1 cup butter, softened
- 3/4 cup plus 1-1/2 cups confectioners' sugar, divided
- 2 teaspoons grated lemon peel
- 2 teaspoons lemon extract
- 2-1/4 cups cake flour
- 1 cup chopped macadamia nuts
- 1 cup chopped crystallized ginger

Direction

- Cream 3/4 cup confectioners' sugar and butter till blended in a big bowl; beat in lemon extract and lemon peel. Beat flour slowly into creamed mixture; mix in ginger and macadamia nuts. Refrigerate till easy to handle or for 1 hour.
- Form dough to 1-in. balls; put onto parchment paper-lined baking sheets, 2-in. apart. Bake at 350° till lightly browned or for 14-16 minutes.
- In leftover confectioners' sugar, roll warm cookies; cool on wire racks. Roll cookies in confectioners' sugar again when cool.

Nutrition Information

- Calories:
- Protein:
- Total Fat:
- Sodium:
- Fiber:
- Total Carbohydrate:
- Cholesterol:

746. Gingerbread Barn

Serving: 1 barn and about 2 dozen large cookies. | Prep: 3mins | Cook: 50mins | Ready in:

Ingredients

- DOUGH:
- 2-1/4 cups shortening
- 2 cups sugar
- 2 large eggs
- 1 cup molasses
- 2/3 cup light corn syrup
- 2 teaspoons ground ginger
- 1-1/2 teaspoons ground cinnamon
- 1 teaspoon ground cloves
- 8-1/2 to 9 cups all-purpose flour
- Heavy-duty cardboard
- Muffin tin
- ICING AND ASSEMBLY:
- 1-1/2 cups butter, softened
- 1-1/2 cups shortening
- 3/4 cup water
- 3 tablespoons vanilla extract
- 12 cups confectioners' sugar
- 17-inch x 22-inch display base—heavy-duty cardboard or cutting board or piece of

- plywood, covered with foil wrapping or aluminum foil
- Serrated knife or emery board
- Red, green and black liquid or paste food coloring
- Small new paintbrush
- Pastry bags or heavy-duty resealable plastic bags
- Pastry tips — #10 round, #5 round and #67 leaf
- Spice bottles
- Heavy-duty cardboard
- Masking tape
- 1 package (9.5 ounces) Triscuit crackers
- Cardboard roll from wrapping paper (about 10 inches long x 2-1/2 inches in diameter)
- 2 cups oyster crackers
- Thin butter ring cookie
- Decorating candies and sugars
- Thin red ribbon, optional
- Thin pretzel sticks
- Sugar ice cream cones
- Spearmint candies or marshmallows
- Black and white jelly beans

Direction

- Whisk the sugar and shortening into a mixing bowl until mixture is fluffy. Whisk in the corn syrup, cinnamon, eggs, cloves, ginger, and molasses until well combined. Slowly add the flour, a cup for each time, until dough can be easily molded into a ball. Roll out on a lightly floured working surface, kneading until the dough is not sticky and smooth; add additional flour if necessary. Keep in the chiller with cover for several hours to overnight.
- Use cardboard to make all templates for the barn. Cut the windows and throw away. Cut 2 pieces of side walls (8 1/2 inches by 5 3/4 inch) for the barn. If you want side windows, cut and throw away 5 pieces of windows, 1 by 1 1/2-inch, 1 inch starting from the bottom and 3/4 starting from each side with a 1/2 inch between the windows. (Note: Roof is not assembled from t gingerbread. But on the cardboard.). Cut patterns for barn animals, if desired. Use an animal cookie cutter to cut out shapes later.
- Using the foil, line the baking sheets, greasing foil lightly. To prevent from slipping, lay out a wet towel on the working surface and put over the pan on the towel. Roll out directly 1/6 of dough onto the prepared baking sheet with the use of a lightly floured rolling pin. Roll dough until form into a rectangle of a 1/4 inch thickness. Place the barn template into the dough. Cut out pattern following the quantities labeled on each of the patterns with a pizza cutter or sharp knife. Remove extra dough. Keep in the refrigerator with cover to reserve. Roll again before using.
- Draw outline to label the windows and doors as indicated on the template with a knife. Be cautious not to slice straight ahead through the dough. Outline vertical lines for the siding of the barn, if preferred. Cut windows out as indicated on the pattern.
- On 350 degrees, bake cookies until brown on the edges, 12 to 14 minutes. Take out from the oven and quickly replace barn templates on the cookies. If needed, trim the extra cookies off around the edges. For 10 minutes, allow cookies to cool until just firm. Gently take out and transfer to wire racks for cooling completely. Do again with the rest of the dough and templates.
- For the silo's roof, cut out gingerbread circle of 5 inches. Prepare a standard size of the muffin tin and turn upside down. Using cooking spray, spray the one cup bottom. Using the sides of the cup, roll over and down the circle to shape, pressing the cracks to stick together and cutting off the extra dough. On 350 degrees, bake until color turns golden brown, 10 minutes. Allow cooling on tins, 10 minutes. Take out carefully to transfer into wire racks for complete cooling.
- For the gingerbread people and barn animals, cut out shapes from the extra dough. On 350 degrees, bake cows and people, 12 to 14 minutes and chicken, pig, and dog, 6 to 7 minutes.

- For the icing: Whisk shortening and butter into a big bowl. Pour in vanilla and water, whisking until mixture is smooth. Gently whisk in the sugar until well mixed. Tightly cover in between uses, use a damp paper towel to place over the bowl.
- Assembling barn frames: Prepare cookie pieces to assure it will fit snugly together. Carefully file using an emery board or serrated knife to allow fit perfectly.
- Mix 4 teaspoons of water and a 1/2 teaspoon of red food coloring together. Carefully paint at the front, sides, and back of the barn using a small-sized paintbrush. Allow to completely dry overnight.
- Prepare pastry bag by fitting a no. 10 tip and filling 2/3 icing into the bag. Start piping into the barn's back lining a wide icing strip at the back-piece bottom edge. Place on the base 7 inches from one short corner. Put it vertically and use spice bottle for support for 3 to 4 hours until firm.
- Adding the front and sides of the barn: On the one side piece lower corner and back piece side corner, pipe icing. Position pieces into a right angle, assuring that pieces tightly adhere together. Support using spice bottles. Do again on the other barn's side. To strengthen more, pipe icing on the inside edge of each piece and corners.
- On the sides and bottom edge of the front piece, pipe icing, and place together with the other positioned pieces. Use additional spice bottle for support. Allow to completely dry.
- Assembling roof of the barn: Cut out 2 pieces label as A of 10-1/2 by 3-1/2 inch on thick cardboard. Cut 2 pieces label as B of 10-1/2 by 2-1/2 inch. Tape the one long corner of the piece A and B roof using masking tape; do it again. To form a roof peak center, taping together both A of pieces.
- On the top edges of the diagonal front edge and back edge of the barn, pipe icing. Gently put the roof into the diagonal to form an equal peak of the roof with points of back and front. (An overhang of a 3/4 inch at the front and back will be formed). Cut into half the Triscuits to make the shingles of the roof. Adhere the Triscuits with icing into the roof cardboard in rows, starting on the bottom row and overlap slightly on each row and alternate the seams of shingles. Do it again on the other side. Cut crackers into narrow strips and adhere to the roof peak's center.
- Preparation for silo: Using icing, coat the roll of cardboard. Cover the entire silo using oyster crackers, pressing on the one side into the icing. Pipe icing on the silo's top corner. Gently push cookie silo roof towards the silo. Pipe icing on the silo's lower corner, standing it vertically at the barn's edge.
- Decorating the barn: Draw the windows and doors outline with no. 5 tip attached on a pastry bag with white icing. Tint green food coloring into a section of the icing. For the wreath, using the leaf-shaped tip, decorate the butter ring cookie. If preferred, put candies for decoration or a ribbon. Place the wreath on the barn using the icing.
- Mix together a 1/2 teaspoon of water and a small tint of green food coloring. Paint mixture on the shutters. Use the icing to adhere to the small window sides onto the front of the barn. Outline icicles into the barn and roofs silo using the icing. If preferred, create snow by frosting the surroundings of the barn and base.
- For the barn fence: On preferred angles, use pretzel sticks to overlap each end. Use icing dabs to stick intersections together. For 1 hour, allow icing to dry until firm. (For an alternative, use white glue to stick together the pretzels). Position the fence around the barn and use icing as glue.
- For the finishing touches: With a serrated knife, carefully mold and slice the sugar ice cream cones into your desired heights for the trees.
- Add green food coloring to tint a section of the icing. With a leaf-shaped tip, decorate the trees. You can use marshmallows to decorate with the leaf-shaped tip or spearmint candies as shrubs. Allow frosting to dry before arranging and adhere to the base using the icing, as preferred.

- For the markings on barn animals, thin a bit of icing with water and tint it using black food coloring. As preferred, draw marking onto animals. Let it dry. Surround the barn with animals and secure each position of animals using dabs of the icing.
- For the creation of the path: Cut in lengthwise half the jellybeans. Place seam down and stick into the board using the icing.

Nutrition Information

- Calories:
- Sodium:
- Fiber:
- Total Carbohydrate:
- Cholesterol:
- Protein:
- Total Fat:

747. Gingerbread Boys

Serving: 60 | Prep: 15mins | Cook: 10mins | Ready in:

Ingredients

- 1 cup butter, softened
- 1 1/2 cups white sugar
- 1 egg
- 1 1/2 tablespoons orange zest
- 2 tablespoons dark corn syrup
- 3 cups all-purpose flour
- 2 teaspoons baking soda
- 2 teaspoons ground cinnamon
- 1 teaspoon ground ginger
- 1/2 teaspoon ground cloves
- 1/2 teaspoon salt

Direction

- Cream together sugar and butter; beat in egg until well blended. Stir in dark corn syrup and orange peel. Mix in cinnamon, ground cloves, baking soda, ginger, salt, and flour; stir until mixture is well blended. For 2 hours up to overnight, keep the dough in the chiller.
- Heat oven to 375°F (190°C) and prepare cookie sheets by greasing. Lightly flour the working surface and roll out the dough into 1/4-in thick. Use a cookie cutter to cut dough into preferred shapes. Transfer cut out cookies into the greased cookie sheets, 1 inch apart.
- Place into the heated oven and bake cookies until toasted lightly on edges and firm, 10-12 minutes.

Nutrition Information

- Calories: 73 calories;
- Total Fat: 3.2
- Sodium: 86
- Total Carbohydrate: 10.4
- Cholesterol: 11
- Protein: 0.8

748. Gingerbread Christmas Cutouts

Serving: about 2 dozen. | Prep: 15mins | Cook: 10mins | Ready in:

Ingredients

- 1/2 cup butter, softened
- 1/2 cup packed brown sugar
- 1/2 cup molasses
- 1 egg
- 3 cups all-purpose flour
- 1 teaspoon baking soda
- 1 teaspoon ground ginger
- 1/2 teaspoon salt
- 1/4 teaspoon ground cinnamon
- 1/8 teaspoon ground cloves
- 1 to 2 tablespoons cold water

Direction

- Cream brown sugar and butter in a large bowl until fluffy and light. Stir in egg and molasses. In a separate bowl, mix baking soda, cloves, cinnamon, flour, salt, and ginger. Add the dry ingredients gradually into the creamed mixture, adding them alternately with water. Cover and store it inside the refrigerator for 1 hour or until easy to handle.
- Dust the surface with flour. Lay the dough into the surface and roll it out up to 1/4-inch thick. Coat the rocking horse cookie cutter with flour. You can use other cutters according to your liking and use it to cut the dough. Transfer the dough in a greased baking sheet, arranging them 2-inches apart from each other.
- Allow it to bake inside the oven with a temperature of 350°F for 9-11 minutes until all edges are firm. Cool it completely by transferring them on wire racks.

Nutrition Information

- Calories: 130 calories
- Cholesterol: 19mg cholesterol
- Protein: 2g protein. Diabetic Exchanges: 1 starch
- Total Fat: 4g fat (2g saturated fat)
- Sodium: 136mg sodium
- Fiber: 0 fiber)
- Total Carbohydrate: 21g carbohydrate (8g sugars

749. Gingerbread Cookie Bites

Serving: about 3 dozen. | Prep: 30mins | Cook: 10mins | Ready in:

Ingredients

- 1 package (14-1/2 ounces) gingerbread cake/cookie mix
- 1/2 cup butter, softened
- 1/4 cup sugar
- 1 large egg
- 2 tablespoons all-purpose flour
- 1 tablespoon water
- 1/4 teaspoon ground ginger, optional
- FILLING:
- 4 ounces cream cheese, softened
- 1/4 cup butter, softened
- 1/2 teaspoon vanilla extract
- 1-3/4 cups confectioners' sugar
- Ground cinnamon and nutmeg
- Crystallized ginger, chopped, optional

Direction

- Mix the flour, sugar, cookie mix, water, butter, egg, and ginger (if desired) until combined into a big bowl. Keep in refrigerator until mixture is firm or for 30 minutes.
- Heat oven to 350°. Mold the dough to 1-inch balls. Put into ungreased mini-muffin tins, pressing onto the bottoms then up towards the sides of the tin evenly. For 10 to 12 minutes, bake until edges turn lightly golden. For 2 minutes, cool cookies in pans. Take out and transfer onto wire racks to complete cooling.
- To make the filling: Whisk butter, vanilla, cream cheese into a big bowl until incorporated. Slowly stir in the confectioner's sugar until the mixture is smooth. Spread to the cookie cups. Season nutmeg, cinnamon, and crystallized ginger (if desired). Store in a tightly sealed container and keep in the refrigerator.

Nutrition Information

- Calories:
- Protein:
- Total Fat:
- Sodium:
- Fiber:
- Total Carbohydrate:
- Cholesterol:

750. Gingerbread Cookie Wreath

Serving: 1 wreath. | Prep: 40mins | Cook: 25mins | Ready in:

Ingredients

- 1 package (14-1/2 ounces) gingerbread cake/cookie mix or 2 cups gingerbread cookie dough of your choice
- Musical note cookie cutter (4 inches)
- Holly leaf cookie cutter (1-1/2 inches)
- 1/2 pound white candy coating, melted
- 1/4 cup green colored sugar
- Pastry bag or small heavy-duty resealable plastic bag
- Pastry tip-#3 round
- 15 red-hot candies

Direction

- Following the packaging instruction to prepare the cookie mix. Scoop 1/4 cup of dough to reserve. Roll the rest of the dough out to 9-1/2-inch round in a greased baking sheet. On the middle of the 9-1/2-inch round, use a sharp knife to cut out a 4-in. round. Take out the 4-inch round and put together on the reserved dough. On 375°, bake, 12 to 15 minutes, the 9-1/2-inch round until corners are firm (Do not overcook). Let it cool, 1 minute before transferring into the wire rack to completely cool.
- Roll the reserved dough into 1/2 inch thick. Cut 10 pieces of holly leaves and 5 pieces of musical notes out. Put onto a greased baking sheet, 2 inches apart. On 375°, cook until corners are firm, 10 to 12 minutes. Take out and transfer to wire racks for cooling.
- Dip into candy coating the half body of holly leaves and season the green sugar over. Put into the ring. Prepare the pastry bag by cutting a small hole on the edge; fill the rest of the candy coating. At the cookie's back, to connect into the wreath. Outline the corners of the notes and create small dots over the holly leaves using the icing to adhere to the candies. Let the coating to completely set for 30 minutes.

Nutrition Information

- Calories: 215 calories
- Sodium: 194mg sodium
- Fiber: 0 fiber
- Total Carbohydrate: 33g carbohydrate (14g sugars
- Cholesterol: 3mg cholesterol
- Protein: 2g protein.
- Total Fat: 9g fat (4g saturated fat)

751. Gingerbread Cookies With Buttercream Icing

Serving: 1-1/2 dozen. | Prep: 30mins | Cook: 10mins | Ready in:

Ingredients

- 2/3 cup shortening
- 1 cup sugar
- 1 large egg
- 1/4 cup molasses
- 2 cups all-purpose flour
- 1 teaspoon baking soda
- 1 teaspoon salt
- 1 teaspoon each ground cinnamon, cloves and ginger
- ICING:
- 3 cups confectioners' sugar
- 1/3 cup butter, softened
- 1 teaspoon vanilla extract
- 1/4 teaspoon lemon extract
- 1/4 teaspoon butter flavoring
- 3 to 4 tablespoons milk

Direction

- Whisk the sugar and shortening into a big bowl until fluffy and light. Stir in the molasses and egg. Mix together the baking soda, spices,

flour, and salt. Slowly pour into the butter mixture, stirring well to combine. Keep in the refrigerator, 2 hours to overnight.
- Roll out the dough into 1/4-inch thick on the lightly floured working surface. Cut out desired cookie shapes using a 3-1/2-inch floured cookie cutter. Put into an ungreased baking pan, 2-inches apart. On 350° temperature of the oven, bake until edges turn brown, 8 to 10 minutes. Take out from pans and cool onto wire racks.
- To make the icing, whisk the butter, flavoring, confectioner's sugar, and extracts into a bowl. Slowly beat in milk until desired consistency will be achieved. Frost the cookies.

Nutrition Information

- Calories:
- Protein:
- Total Fat:
- Sodium:
- Fiber:
- Total Carbohydrate:
- Cholesterol:

752. Gingerbread Crisp Cutouts

Serving: 4-1/2 dozen. | Prep: 25mins | Cook: 10mins | Ready in:

Ingredients

- 1/2 cup shortening
- 1/2 cup sugar
- 1/2 cup molasses
- 1 large egg
- 2-1/4 cups all-purpose flour
- 1-1/2 teaspoons ground cinnamon
- 1 teaspoon baking powder
- 1 teaspoon ground ginger
- 1 teaspoon ground cloves
- 1/2 teaspoon salt
- 1/2 teaspoon baking soda
- 1/2 teaspoon ground nutmeg

Direction

- Cream the sugar and shortening in a huge bowl until fluffy and light. Stir in egg and molasses. In a separate bowl, combine all of the dry ingredients. Pour the dry mixture into the creamed mixture and mix it thoroughly until soft dough forms. Cover the dough and store it inside the refrigerator for 1 hour until it's easy and firm enough to handle.
- Dust the working surface with flour and lay the dough. Roll it out into 1/8-inch thick. Dip 2 1/2 cookie cutters in flour and use it to cut the dough. Transfer the dough into the greased baking pan.
- Set the oven to 350°F and bake the cookies for 8-10 minutes until all of its edges are lightly browned. Transfer the cookies on wire racks and allow them to cool completely.

Nutrition Information

- Calories:
- Sodium:
- Fiber:
- Total Carbohydrate:
- Cholesterol:
- Protein:
- Total Fat:

753. Gingerbread Cutout Cookies

Serving: 5 dozen. | Prep: 30mins | Cook: 10mins | Ready in:

Ingredients

- 3/4 cup butter, softened
- 1 cup packed brown sugar
- 1 egg

- 3/4 cup molasses
- 4 cups all-purpose flour
- 2 teaspoons ground ginger
- 1-1/2 teaspoons baking soda
- 1-1/2 teaspoons ground cinnamon
- 3/4 teaspoon ground cloves
- 1/4 teaspoon salt
- Vanilla frosting of your choice
- Red and green paste food coloring

Direction

- Whisk the brown sugar and butter into a big bowl until fluffy and light. Stir in molasses and egg. Mix together the baking soda, salt, cinnamon, ginger, flour, and cloves. Stir in into the butter mixture until well combined. Keep in refrigerator until easily handled, 4 hours to overnight.
- Roll out the dough into 1/8-inch thick on the lightly floured flat working surface. Cut out cookies using a floured 2 1/2-inch cookie cutters. Put into ungreased baking pans, 1-inch apart.
- Place in oven at 350° temperature; bake until firm at the edges, 8 to 10 minutes. Take out from the oven and transfer onto wire racks; cool. Tint frosting with red and green food coloring. Use colored frosting for decorating the cookies.

Nutrition Information

- Calories: 77 calories
- Sodium: 69mg sodium
- Fiber: 0 fiber)
- Total Carbohydrate: 13g carbohydrate (6g sugars
- Cholesterol: 10mg cholesterol
- Protein: 1g protein.
- Total Fat: 2g fat (1g saturated fat)

754. Gingerbread House Cookies

Serving: 4 dozen. | Prep: 40mins | Cook: 10mins | Ready in:

Ingredients

- 1 cup shortening
- 1/2 cup sugar
- 1/2 cup packed brown sugar
- 2 large eggs
- 1 cup molasses
- 1 to 1-1/2 teaspoons grated orange zest
- 5-1/2 cups all-purpose flour
- 3 teaspoons baking soda
- 3/4 teaspoon salt
- 3/4 teaspoon ground ginger
- 3/4 teaspoon ground cinnamon
- 1/2 teaspoon ground nutmeg
- 1/2 cup water
- Frosting and food coloring of your choice

Direction

- Whisk sugar and shortening into the big bowl until fluffy and light. Beat in eggs, one by one, stirring thoroughly after every addition. Whisk in orange zest and molasses. Mix together the baking soda, spices, flour, and salt. Combine into the butter mixture interchangeably with water, stirring thoroughly after every addition. Keep in the refrigerator with cover, 3 hours until mixture can handled easily.
- Roll the dough out into 1/4-inch thick on a lightly floured working surface. Using the 3-1/2-inch gingerbread house cutter, cut out the shapes from the dough.
- Put into the prepared baking pans, 1-inch apart. On 350° heat, bake the cookies until edges turn firm. For 2 minutes, cool on pans before transferring cookies onto wire racks. Decorate the cookies using the colored frosting with your preference.

Nutrition Information

- Calories: 127 calories
- Sodium: 85mg sodium
- Fiber: 0 fiber)
- Total Carbohydrate: 20g carbohydrate (9g sugars
- Cholesterol: 9mg cholesterol
- Protein: 2g protein.
- Total Fat: 4g fat (1g saturated fat)

755. Gingerbread Oatmeal Cookies

Serving: about 1-1/2 dozen. | Prep: 10mins | Cook: 15mins | Ready in:

Ingredients

- 3/4 cup all-purpose flour
- 1/2 teaspoon baking soda
- 1/2 teaspoon salt
- 1/2 teaspoon ground ginger
- 1/4 teaspoon baking powder
- 1 cup Biscoff creamy cookie spread, room temperature
- 1/2 cup unsalted butter
- 1/2 cup granulated sugar
- 1/2 cup packed brown sugar
- 1 large egg
- 1 teaspoon vanilla extract
- 1 cup quick-cooking oats

Direction

- Heat oven to 350°. Beat the initial five ingredients together. Whisk the sugars, butter, and cookie spread into a separate bowl until fluffy and light. Stir in vanilla and egg. Slowly stir in the flour mixture and mix in the oats. Keep in refrigerator for a minimum of 3 hours.
- Bring the dough to room temperature. Drop dough mounds with a medium cookie scoop into the parchment-lined baking pans. For 15 to 18 minutes, bake until cookies turn lightly brown, turning the pans midway through the baking time. For 5 minutes, cool the cookies on the pans. Take out the cookies from the pans and transfer onto wire racks; cool completely.

Nutrition Information

- Calories: 210 calories
- Sodium: 113mg sodium
- Fiber: 1g fiber)
- Total Carbohydrate: 26g carbohydrate (17g sugars
- Cholesterol: 24mg cholesterol
- Protein: 2g protein.
- Total Fat: 11g fat (4g saturated fat)

756. Gingerbread Rings

Serving: about 5 dozen. | Prep: 40mins | Cook: 10mins | Ready in:

Ingredients

- 1 cup shortening
- 2 cups sugar
- 2 egg yolks
- 1 cup water
- 1 cup light molasses
- 8 cups all-purpose flour
- 2 teaspoons baking soda
- 1-1/2 teaspoons ground ginger
- 1 teaspoon ground cinnamon
- 1 teaspoon ground allspice
- 3/4 teaspoon salt
- FROSTING:
- 2-1/2 cups sugar
- 1/2 cup water
- 1/2 teaspoon light corn syrup
- 2 egg whites
- 1 teaspoon vanilla extract
- Red and green decorating gel, optional

Direction

- Cream the sugar and shortening into a mixing bowl. Whisk in molasses, egg yolks, and water. Mix together the dry ingredients and slowly pour into creamed mixture. Keep in the refrigerator with cover until mixture can be handled easily, 2 hours. Roll the dough out to 1/4 inch thick on a lightly floured flat working surface. Using a 2- 3/4 inch dough cutter, cut the dough. Take out and throw away the centers. Transfer the cut-out dough into the ungreased baking sheets, 2 inches apart. Place in oven with 350°, baking until cookies are set, 10 minutes. Transfer to wire racks. Mix together the corn syrup, sugar, and water in a heavy pot; boil. Heat mixture until a candy thermometer says 238° for 5 minutes. Separate from heat. Whisk the vanilla and egg whites in a mixing bowl until mixture form soft peaks. Slowly pour the sugar mixture, beating the mixture on high speed until thickened, 7 to 8 minutes. Frost the cookies. If desired, decorate the cookies.

Nutrition Information

- Calories: 332 calories
- Sodium: 152mg sodium
- Fiber: 1g fiber)
- Total Carbohydrate: 63g carbohydrate (36g sugars
- Cholesterol: 14mg cholesterol
- Protein: 4g protein.
- Total Fat: 7g fat (2g saturated fat)

757. Gingerbread Snowflakes

Serving: Makes about 4 dozen cookies | Prep: 1.5hours | Cook: 2.25hours | Ready in:

Ingredients

- 2/3 cup molasses (not robust)
- 2/3 cup packed dark brown sugar
- 1 tablespoon ground ginger
- 1 1/2 teaspoons ground cinnamon
- 1/2 teaspoon ground allspice
- 1/2 teaspoon ground cloves
- 2 teaspoons baking soda
- 2 sticks (1 cup) unsalted butter, cut into tablespoon pieces
- 1 large egg, lightly beaten
- 3 3/4 to 4 cups all-purpose flour
- 1/2 teaspoon salt
- Decorating icing
- 1 metal offset spatula
- 1 pastry bag fitted with 1/8- to 1/4-inch plain tip
- assorted 2- to 3-inch cookie cutters (preferably snowflake-shaped); a metal offset spatula; a pastry bag fitted with 1/8- to 1/4-inch plain tip (optional)

Direction

- Boil the mixture of brown sugar, spices, and molasses, stirring it occasionally, in a 4-5-quart heavy saucepan over medium heat. Take off from heat. Add the baking soda. Once the mixture foams up, stir in butter, 3 pieces at a time and melting it first before adding the next butter. After melting all the butter, whisk in the egg until well-combined. Stir in salt and 3 3/4 cups flour.
- Set the oven to 325 degrees F for preheating.
- Dust the working surface lightly with flour to prevent the dough from sticking. Knead the dough for 30-60 seconds while dusting with the remaining 1/4 cup of flour as necessary to prevent from sticking until soft and easy to handle. Divide the dough into halves, reserving the other half at room temperature and completely wrapped with a plastic wrap.
- Roll the remaining half of the dough into a 14-inch round and 1/8-inch thick on a lightly floured surface. Use a cutter to cut out cookies as many as possible and use an offset spatula to transfer them on 2 buttered large baking pans. Be sure to arrange the cookies 1-inch apart from each other.
- Position the pans in upper and lower thirds of the oven. Bake the cookies for 10-12 minutes,

switching the position of the pans halfway through baking. Watch carefully until the end of the baking, making sure not to burn the cookies. Place the cookies to wire racks and allow them to cool completely. Do the same with the remaining half of the dough and scraps making as many cookies as possible.
- Fill the pastry bag (if using) with icing and use it to pipe or spread to decorate the cookies.
- You can store the cookies inside a sealed container and keep it at room temperature for 3 weeks.

Nutrition Information

---

758. Gingerbread Spritz

Serving: about 11-1/2 dozen. | Prep: 30mins | Cook: 10mins | Ready in:

Ingredients

- 1 cup butter, softened
- 1-1/2 cups sugar
- 1 egg
- 1/2 cup molasses
- 1-1/2 teaspoons vanilla extract
- 4 cups all-purpose flour
- 1 teaspoon baking soda
- 1 teaspoon ground ginger
- 1/2 teaspoon ground cinnamon
- 1/2 teaspoon ground cloves
- 1/4 teaspoon salt
- Colored sugar or multicolored jimmies

Direction

- Whisk the sugar and butter into a large bowl until fluffy and light. Stir in vanilla, egg, and molasses. Mix together the baking soda, cinnamon, flour, salt, cloves, and ginger. Gently stir in the flour mixture into the butter mixture until well combined.
- Press the dough into 1-inch on the ungreased baking sheet with a cookie press inserted with a disk of your preference. Season the jimmies or colored sugar.
- On 400°, bake until done (Color of cookies must not be brown), 6 to 8 minutes. Place on wire racks. Keep in a tightly sealed container.

Nutrition Information

- Calories: 37 calories
- Protein: 0 protein.
- Total Fat: 1g fat (1g saturated fat)
- Sodium: 24mg sodium
- Fiber: 0 fiber)
- Total Carbohydrate: 6g carbohydrate (3g sugars
- Cholesterol: 5mg cholesterol

---

759. Gingerbread Star Tree

Serving: 1 gingerbread tree and 3 dozen small star cookies. | Prep: 02hours00mins | Cook: 15mins | Ready in:

Ingredients

- DOUGH:
- 1-1/3 cups packed brown sugar
- 1-1/3 cups molasses
- 2 cups cold butter, cubed
- 2 eggs, lightly beaten
- 8 cups all-purpose flour
- 3 tablespoons ground ginger
- 2 tablespoons ground cinnamon
- 4 teaspoons baking soda
- 2 teaspoons ground allspice
- 2 teaspoons ground cloves
- 1 teaspoon salt
- 1 teaspoon ground cardamom
- ROYAL ICING AND DECORATIONS:
- 7-1/2 cups confectioners' sugar, divided
- 6 tablespoons meringue powder, divided
- 10 tablespoons warm water, divided
- Confectioners' sugar

- Candy of your choice
- Dark chocolate and white candy coating, melted
- EQUIPMENT:
- Pencil
- Ruler
- Waxed paper
- Scissors
- Cookie cutters—round (2-1/2 inches, 2 inches and 1-1/2 inches) and star-shaped (3 inches, 2 inches and 1 inch)
- #1 round or #101 petal pastry tip

Direction

- Prepare the template for the star: On a waxed paper, use the ruler and pencil to draw five-pointed stars with the following measurements:
- 8-1/2 in., 8 in., 7-1/2 in., 7-1/4 in., 6-3/4 in., 6 in. and 4-1/2 in
- Label each star template using its measurements. Use the scissors to cut the star out. Put aside.
- Preparation of dough: On medium heat, combine molasses and brown sugar into a big pot; bring to boil while constantly stirring. Take from heat and beat in the butter until dissolved. Whisk in the eggs until combined. Mix the rest of the dough ingredients and beat into the brown sugar mixture. Split the dough to four portions.
- Prepare for large stars: Roll the portion out into 1/4 inch thick on a lightly floured flat working surface. With the use of the templates, cut out two 8-in. stars, two 7-1/4-in. stars, one 8-1/2-in. star, one 6-3/4-in. star, one 7-1/2-in. star, one 4-1/2-in. star and two 6-in. stars. Put the cut-out stars into the greased baking sheets. On 325°, bake until stars are set, 12 to 15 minutes. Transfer onto wire racks; cool.
- Preparation of small stars and circles: (A) Use the floured 2-1/2-inch round cookie cutter to cut out 2 pieces of circles. Using the 2-inch round cookie cutter floured, cut out 12 pieces of circles. Use the 1-1/2-inch round cookie cutter floured to cut out 2 pieces of circles. (B) Use a star-shaped cookie cutter floured to cut on the remaining dough. Roll again the dough scraps. Put into the greased baking sheets. On 325°, bake until set, 10 to 12 minutes. Transfer into the wire racks; cool.
- Preparation for icing: Mix together the 3 tablespoons meringue powder, 5 tablespoons water, and 3-3/4 cups confectioners' sugar into a big mixing bowl. On low speed, whisk mixture until just blended. For 4 to 5 minutes, whisk on high speed until mixture form stiff peaks. Keep a damp cloth over icing at all times. Whisk the icing again on high if needed to restore the texture if needed.
- Assembling: With the use of the round cookies and icing, create six 2-in. sandwich cookies, one 1-1/2-in. sandwich cookie, and one 2-1/2-in. sandwich cookie. Set aside until sandwich cookies set, 15 minutes. Put the 8-1/2 in. star cookie into the serving plate. Spread a little icing in the middle of the star and place the 8-in star on top. (A) Spread a little icing in the middle of the star and place the 2-1/2-in round cookie sandwich on top. (B) Spread a little icing in the middle of the cookie sandwich and place the leftover 8-in star on top. Set aside until set, 15 minutes. Do the steps again with the rest of the sandwich cookies, stars, and icing. Build the tree beginning with the largest stars and sandwich cookies. Add each star after and allow to stand until set, 15 minutes.
- Decorating the tree: Do the second set of icing. Make a small hole by cutting at the corner of a plastic or pastry bag and then insert the small pastry tip. Add the icing into the bag to fill. Decorate as desired the tree using the icing, confectioner's sugar, and candy. Decorate with your preference the 2-in star cookie. Place star at the top of the tree using icing to adhere.
- Decorating the small star cookie: Coat cookies by dipping into the melted candy. Transfer on the waxed paper. Set aside until set. Season edible glitter into white cookies. If desired, keep some of the cookies plain. Slowly put the

cookies on the branches of the tree and on the serving plate.

Nutrition Information

- Calories:
- Sodium:
- Fiber:
- Total Carbohydrate:
- Cholesterol:
- Protein:
- Total Fat:

760. Gingerbread Teddy Bears

Serving: 8 cookies. | Prep: 40mins | Cook: 10mins | Ready in:

Ingredients

- 1 cup butter, cubed
- 2/3 cup packed brown sugar
- 2/3 cup molasses
- 1 egg, lightly beaten
- 1-1/2 teaspoons vanilla extract
- 4 cups all-purpose flour
- 1-1/2 teaspoons ground cinnamon
- 1 teaspoon ground ginger
- 3/4 teaspoon baking soda
- 1/2 teaspoon ground cloves
- Miniature chocolate chips
- Red decorating frosting

Direction

- Mix together the molasses, butter, and brown sugar into the small pot. On medium heat, cook with cover until sugar melts. Transfer to a big bowl and set aside for 10 minutes. Mix in the vanilla and egg. Mix together the baking soda, ginger, cinnamon, cloves, and flour. Slowly pour into the butter mixture; whisk well. Keep in the refrigerator with cover for 2 hours up to overnight.
- Heat oven to 350°. Mold the dough to 8 pieces ball of 2 inches, eight pieces balls of 1 inch, 32 pieces ball of a 1/2 inch, and 16 pieces balls of 3/8 inch. To make the 8 bear's bodies, put the 2-inch balls into three baking sheets lined with foil. Flatten each ball into 1/2 inch thick. Put the 1-inch balls for the head position; flatten each into 1/2 inch thick. Use the four pieces of 1/2 inch balls to attach on the bears for the legs and arms. Use the 2 pieces 3/8-inch balls to attach on the bear for the ears. Use chocolate chips for the buttons, eyes, and nose.
- For 10 to 12 minutes, bake until done. For 10 minutes, cool and carefully remove from sheets to transfer onto wire racks; completely cool. Outline bows on the bears using the frosting.

Nutrition Information

- Calories:
- Protein:
- Total Fat:
- Sodium:
- Fiber:
- Total Carbohydrate:
- Cholesterol:

761. Gingerbread Tree Recipe

Serving: 33 cookies. | Prep: 01hours30mins | Cook: 10mins | Ready in:

Ingredients

- 2 cups butter, softened
- 2 cups sugar
- 2 large eggs
- 2 cups light molasses
- 1/4 cup white vinegar
- 10 cups all-purpose flour
- 4 teaspoons ground ginger
- 1 tablespoon baking soda
- 2 teaspoons ground cinnamon

- 2 teaspoons ground cloves
- 1 container (3 ounces) cinnamon Red Hot candies (about 1/3 cup)
- Confectioners' sugar, optional
- Clear Contact paper (optional)
- 10-inch flat serving plate
- Patterns

Direction

- Whisk the sugar and butter into a big bowl until fluffy into a big bowl. Stir in the vinegar, egg, and molasses until well combined. Mix together the baking soda, cloves, flour, ginger, and cinnamon. Slowly mix into the butter mixture. Keep in chill with cover, overnight.
- Preparing of star template: Draw each of the star sizes on the waxed paper and cut the template. To preserve the templates, copy the template and cover both sides using contact paper and cut. Roll out dough portion into 1/4-inch thick on a lightly floured working surface. Keep in the refrigerator.
- Cutting the stars out: Cut around the star templates with the use of the sharp knife. There must be 33 cookies in total for two pieces of treetop stars; three-star pieces of 1-4 and 9; four-star pieces of 5-8. Put into prepared baking sheets, 12 inches apart. On the middle of each treetop stars, push a red-hot candy, pressing until red hots stick into the stars. Create two indentions as indicated on the template of one number 9 star (to adhere treetop star in position).
- Bake: Bake all the cookies at 350° until edges turns lightly brown; for treetop stars, 5 minutes; for numbers 6-9, 8 to 10 minutes; for numbers 1-5, 11 to 12 minutes. For 5 minutes, allow cooling onto the baking pans. Take out and transfer on wire racks to completely cool.
- Assembling: Begin on the star number 1, pile up the stars into the serving plate, alternating the position of star points. To make a tree that looks natural, position sizes of star in alternate pattern with the following order: 1-1-2-1-2-3-2-3-4-5-4-5-5-6-5-6-6-7-6-7-7-8-7-8-8-9-8-9-9 (including the indentions). Put the two treetops stars onto the indentions and lean back to back. Sprinkle trees using the confectioner's sugar, if preferred. Serve and pass whole tree.

Nutrition Information

- Calories:
- Total Carbohydrate:
- Cholesterol:
- Protein:
- Total Fat:
- Sodium:
- Fiber:

762. Gingerbread Yule Logs

Serving: 1 dozen. | Prep: 20mins | Cook: 25mins | Ready in:

Ingredients

- 3-1/3 cups all-purpose flour
- 1-1/2 teaspoons ground cinnamon
- 3/4 teaspoon ground ginger
- 1/2 teaspoon baking powder
- 1/4 teaspoon salt
- 3/4 cup light corn syrup
- 2/3 cup packed light brown sugar
- 1/2 cup butter, cubed
- 4 ounces cream cheese, softened
- 3/4 cup Nutella
- 1-1/2 teaspoons grated lime zest, optional
- DRIZZLE:
- 3/4 cup confectioners' sugar
- 2 tablespoons water or lime juice
- Holiday sprinkles, optional

Direction

- Beat the initial five ingredients into a small sized bowl. Mix together the brown sugar, butter, and corn syrup into a big pot. Heat on medium heat, stirring until butter dissolves.

- Pour mixture into a big bowl. Gently stir in the flour mixture to the corn syrup mixture. Whisk in the cream cheese. Mold the dough to disk and use plastic to wrap. For 30 minutes, keep in refrigerator until dough can be easily rolled.
- Heat oven to 350°. Roll out the dough to an 18x22-inch rectangle on a parchment paper. Slice to 3 pieces 12x6-inches rectangle.
- Combine the Nutella and lime zest (if desired) into a small sized bowl. Spread Nutella mixture over the rectangles. Roll the dough up using jelly-roll style, beginning on the long side. Seal by pinching the seams. Cut in crosswise each of the rolls into four pieces of logs. Transfer logs into oiled baking sheets, seam side down. Draw stroke into the log using fork tines to create a bark-like appearance.
- For 20 to 25 minutes, bake until edges and bottom of the log is lightly brown. Take out from the pans and transfer on wire racks for complete cooling.
- Combine the water and confectioner's sugar into a small sized bowl. Sprinkle on top of the cookies. Use sprinkles for decorating the cookies, if preferred. Set aside to set.

Nutrition Information

- Calories: 459 calories
- Protein: 5g protein.
- Total Fat: 17g fat (8g saturated fat)
- Sodium: 185mg sodium
- Fiber: 2g fiber)
- Total Carbohydrate: 75g carbohydrate (47g sugars
- Cholesterol: 30mg cholesterol

763. Gingersnap Cream Cookie Cups

Serving: 2-1/2 dozen. | Prep: 35mins | Cook: 10mins | Ready in:

Ingredients

- 1-1/2 cups all-purpose flour
- 1/2 cup whole wheat flour
- 1/3 cup sugar
- 1-1/2 teaspoons ground ginger
- 1 teaspoon baking soda
- 1 teaspoon ground cinnamon
- 1/2 teaspoon salt
- 1 large egg
- 1/4 cup canola oil
- 1/4 cup unsweetened applesauce
- 1/4 cup molasses
- FILLING:
- 4 ounces reduced-fat cream cheese
- 1/2 cup confectioners' sugar
- 3/4 teaspoon vanilla extract
- 1/2 cup heavy whipping cream, whipped

Direction

- In a large bowl, mix together salt, cinnamon, baking soda, ginger, sugar and flours. In another bowl, mix molasses, applesauce, oil and egg; transfer into dry ingredients. Mix till it forms a ball-shaped dough. Roll to shape into 1-in. balls. Press up the sides and onto the bottoms of miniature muffin cups coated with cooking spray.
- Bake at 350° till golden brown, or for 10-12 minutes. Allow to cool for 5 minutes; take away from the pans and place on wire racks to cool completely.
- For the filling, beat vanilla, confectioners' sugar and cream cheese till smooth in a small bowl; fold in whipped cream. Into each cup, spoon 2 teaspoons of the mixture.

Nutrition Information

- Calories: 97 calories

- Total Carbohydrate: 13g carbohydrate (6g sugars
- Cholesterol: 15mg cholesterol
- Protein: 2g protein. Diabetic Exchanges: 1 starch
- Total Fat: 4g fat (2g saturated fat)
- Sodium: 102mg sodium
- Fiber: 0 fiber)

764. Glazed Apple Cookies

Serving: 18 | Prep: | Cook: | Ready in:

Ingredients

- 1/2 cup shortening
- 1 1/3 cups packed brown sugar
- 1 egg
- 2 cups sifted all-purpose flour
- 1 teaspoon baking soda
- 1/2 teaspoon salt
- 1 teaspoon ground cinnamon
- 1/2 teaspoon ground cloves
- 1/4 teaspoon ground nutmeg
- 1 cup chopped walnuts (optional)
- 1 cup apples - peeled, cored and finely diced
- 1 cup raisins
- 1/4 cup milk
- 1 1/2 cups sifted confectioners' sugar
- 1 tablespoon butter
- 1/2 teaspoon vanilla extract
- 2 1/2 tablespoons half-and-half cream

Direction

- Beat together brown sugar and shortening until fluffy and light. Beat in the egg and mix well.
- Mix together nutmeg, baking soda, cinnamon, salt, cloves and flour.
- Mix 1/2 the dry ingredients into creamed mixture. Mix in raisins, apple and nuts, then mix in milk and the other half of dry ingredients. Combine thoroughly.
- Use a tablespoon to drop the mixture onto a lightly greased baking sheet, spacing 1 1/2 inches apart. Bake for 10-12 minutes in an oven preheated at 400 degrees. While still warm, transfer cookies to racks and spread the glaze on top.
- For the Glaze: Mix together vanilla, butter, powdered sugar and the right amount of cream to give the glaze a spreadable consistency. Beat till smooth. Spread atop the warm cookies.

Nutrition Information

- Calories: 289 calories;
- Total Fat: 11.4
- Sodium: 151
- Total Carbohydrate: 45.7
- Cholesterol: 13
- Protein: 3.3

765. Glazed Butter Cookies

Serving: about 3 dozen. | Prep: 20mins | Cook: 10mins | Ready in:

Ingredients

- 1/2 cup butter, softened
- 3/4 cup sugar
- 1 egg
- 3/4 teaspoon vanilla extract
- 1-3/4 cups all-purpose flour
- 1/2 teaspoon baking powder
- 1/4 teaspoon salt
- GLAZE:
- 1 cup confectioners' sugar
- 1 to 2 tablespoons milk
- Red, green and yellow liquid or paste food coloring

Direction

- Cream the sugar and butter until fluffy and light in a small bowl. Beat vanilla and egg in. Mix the dry ingredients and put in the creamed mixture gradually. Cover and put in the refrigerator until easy to handle or for an hour.
- Make 1/8-inch thickness dough by rolling on a lightly floured surface. Cut the dough using 2 1/2-inch cookie cutters; put on baking sheets without grease, leaving 1-inch apart. Bake until lightly browned or for 8 to 10 minutes at 350 degrees. Allow to cool by putting on wire racks.
- Mix milk and confectioners' sugar until smooth in a small bowl. Mix in food coloring then pour on top of the cooled cookies lightly. Allow to rest until set.

Nutrition Information

- Calories: 152 calories
- Protein: 2g protein.
- Total Fat: 5g fat (3g saturated fat)
- Sodium: 100mg sodium
- Fiber: 0 fiber)
- Total Carbohydrate: 24g carbohydrate (15g sugars
- Cholesterol: 26mg cholesterol

766. Glazed Cherry Bon Bon Cookies

Serving: 3 dozen. | Prep: 20mins | Cook: 15mins | Ready in:

Ingredients

- 36 maraschino cherries
- 1 cup butter, softened
- 1-1/2 cups confectioners' sugar
- 1 tablespoon 2% milk
- 3 teaspoons vanilla extract
- 2-3/4 cups all-purpose flour
- 1/4 teaspoon salt
- CHRISTMAS GLAZE:
- 1-1/4 cups confectioners' sugar
- 1 to 2 tablespoons water
- Red and green liquid food coloring
- Colored sprinkles
- CHOCOLATE GLAZE:
- 1 ounce unsweetened chocolate, melted
- 1 teaspoon vanilla extract
- 1 cup confectioners' sugar
- 1 to 2 tablespoons water
- 1/2 cup chopped pecans or walnuts

Direction

- Use paper towels to pat dry the cherries. Cream the confectioners' sugar and butter until fluffy and light in a big bowl. Beat in vanilla and milk. Mix salt and flour then put into creamed mixture gradually. Stir well.
- Form a circle by forming a tablespoonful of dough around each cherry. Put on baking sheets without grease, leaving 2 inches space apart. Bake until the bottoms turn brown or for 14 to 16 minutes at 350 degrees. Allow to cool by putting on wire racks.
- To make the Christmas glaze: Combine enough water and confectioners' sugar in a small bowl to achieve the consistency of dipping. Put 1/2 of the glaze in a separate bowl then tint one bowl with red color and green color on the other. Dunk the top of 9 cookies in the green glaze and another 9 in the red glaze. Use sprinkles to decorate then let it rest until set.
- To make the chocolate glaze: Combine enough water and confectioners' sugar in a small bowl to achieve the consistency of the dipping. Mix in vanilla and chocolate. Dunk the top of the rest of the cookies in the glaze. Use nuts to sprinkle then let it rest until set.

Nutrition Information

- Calories: 155 calories
- Sodium: 53mg sodium
- Fiber: 1g fiber)

- Total Carbohydrate: 23g carbohydrate (15g sugars
- Cholesterol: 13mg cholesterol
- Protein: 1g protein.
- Total Fat: 7g fat (4g saturated fat)

767. Glazed Maple Shortbread Cookies

Serving: 1-1/2 dozen. | Prep: 25mins | Cook: 20mins | Ready in:

Ingredients

- 1 cup butter, softened
- 1/4 cup sugar
- 3 tablespoons cornstarch
- 1 teaspoon maple flavoring
- 1-3/4 cups all-purpose flour
- GLAZE:
- 3/4 cup plus 1 tablespoon confectioners' sugar
- 1/3 cup maple syrup

Direction

- Whisk cornstarch, sugar and butter in a large bowl until blended. Whisk in flavoring. Whisk in flour gradually.
- Form dough into a disk; use plastic to wrap. Keep in the fridge for about 45 minutes until firm enough to roll.
- Set the oven to 325° and start preheating. Roll dough to 1/4-in. thickness on a lightly floured surface. Use a floured 2-3/4-in. leaf-shaped cookie cutter to cut. Arrange on baking sheets lined with parchment paper, an inch apart.
- Bake for 20-25 minutes until edges turn light brown. Take out of pans and place on wire racks to completely cool.
- Mix maple syrup and confectioners' sugar in a small bowl until smooth. Place on top of cookies and spread. Allow to stand until set.

Nutrition Information

- Calories:
- Protein:
- Total Fat:
- Sodium:
- Fiber:
- Total Carbohydrate:
- Cholesterol:

768. Gluten Free Almond Crispies

Serving: about 3 dozen. | Prep: 20mins | Cook: 10mins | Ready in:

Ingredients

- 1/3 cup maple syrup
- 1/4 cup canola oil
- 1 tablespoon water
- 1 teaspoon almond extract
- 1 cup brown rice flour
- 1/2 cup almond flour
- 1/4 cup sugar
- 1 teaspoon baking powder
- 1 teaspoon ground cinnamon
- 1/8 teaspoon salt
- 1/2 cup finely chopped almonds

Direction

- Whip the extract, water, oil and syrup in a small bowl until well combined. Mix the salt, cinnamon, baking powder, sugar and flours; whip into syrup mixture gradually until combined. Mix in almonds.
- Put by heaping teaspoonfuls onto baking trays lined with parchment paper; flatten slightly. Bake for 10-12 minutes at 350° or until lightly browned on the bottoms. Let cool for a minute before transferring from pans to wire racks.

Nutrition Information

- Calories: 54 calories

- Cholesterol: 0 cholesterol
- Protein: 1g protein. Diabetic Exchanges: 1/2 starch
- Total Fat: 3g fat (0 saturated fat)
- Sodium: 18mg sodium
- Fiber: 1g fiber)
- Total Carbohydrate: 6g carbohydrate (3g sugars

769. Gluten Free Peanut Butter Kiss Cookies

Serving: 4 dozen. | Prep: 20mins | Cook: 10mins | Ready in:

Ingredients

- 1/4 cup butter-flavored shortening
- 1-1/4 cups packed brown sugar
- 3/4 cup creamy peanut butter
- 1 large egg
- 1/4 cup unsweetened applesauce
- 3 teaspoons vanilla extract
- 1 cup white rice flour
- 1/2 cup potato starch
- 1/4 cup tapioca flour
- 1 teaspoon baking powder
- 3/4 teaspoon baking soda
- 1/4 teaspoon salt
- 48 milk chocolate kisses, unwrapped

Direction

- Beat peanut butter, brown sugar and shortening till blended in big bowl; beat vanilla, applesauce and egg in, it might look curdled. Whisk salt, baking soda, baking powder, tapioca flour, potato starch and rice flour in another bowl; beat into creamed mixture slowly. Refrigerate for 1 hour, covered.
- Preheat an oven to 375°. Form dough to 48 1-in. balls; put on ungreased baking sheets, 2-in. apart. Bake till slightly cracked for 9-11 minutes; press chocolate kiss immediately into middle of every cookie. Cool for 2 minutes on pans. Transfer to wire racks; cool.

Nutrition Information

- Calories: 98 calories
- Protein: 2g protein. Diabetic Exchanges: 1 starch
- Total Fat: 5g fat (2g saturated fat)
- Sodium: 67mg sodium
- Fiber: 0 fiber)
- Total Carbohydrate: 13g carbohydrate (8g sugars
- Cholesterol: 5mg cholesterol

770. Gluten Free Sugar Cookies

Serving: 40 | Prep: 20mins | Cook: 10mins | Ready in:

Ingredients

- Cookies:
- 2 1/2 cups gluten-free flour
- 1 teaspoon baking powder
- 1/2 teaspoon salt
- 1 cup white sugar
- 3/4 cup butter, softened
- 1 teaspoon vanilla extract
- 2 eggs
- Icing:
- 1/4 cup cream cheese, softened
- 1/4 cup butter, softened
- 1 teaspoon vanilla extract
- 1 1/2 cups confectioners' sugar

Direction

- In a bowl, combine the baking powder, salt and flour together. Use an electric mixer to mix 3/4 cup of butter, 1 teaspoon of vanilla extract and white sugar together in another bowl; whisk in the eggs one by one until the mixture is smooth in consistency. Add the

prepared butter mixture into the flour mixture and mix everything together; shape the dough mixture into a ball. Use a plastic wrap to enwrap the dough ball then keep it in the fridge for 1 hour.
- Preheat the oven to 325°F (165°C).
- Put the chilled dough ball onto a clean surface that is covered with a little bit of flour and roll it out; use cookie cutters to cut the rolled out dough into shapes. Put the cut-out cookies onto a baking sheet.
- Put it in the preheated oven and let it bake for about 10 minutes until the edges of the cookies are starting to turn brown in color. Allow the baked cookies to cool down on the baking sheet for 2 minutes then place the cookies onto a wire rack to let it fully cool down.
- Use an electric mixer to beat 1/4 cup of butter, 1 teaspoon of vanilla extract and cream cheese together in a bowl until it is smooth in consistency. Gradually mix in the confectioners' sugar until the icing mixture is smooth in consistency. Spread the prepared icing mixture evenly over each cooled down cookie.

Nutrition Information

- Calories: 88 calories;
- Total Fat: 5.4
- Sodium: 82
- Total Carbohydrate: 9.8
- Cholesterol: 23
- Protein: 0.5

771. Goblin Chewies

Serving: about 6 dozen. | Prep: 30mins | Cook: 10mins | Ready in:

Ingredients

- 1 cup shortening
- 1 cup packed brown sugar
- 1 cup sugar
- 2 large eggs
- 1 teaspoon vanilla extract
- 2 cups all-purpose flour
- 1 teaspoon baking soda
- 1/2 teaspoon baking powder
- 1/2 teaspoon salt
- 1-1/2 cups old-fashioned oats
- 1 cup crisp rice cereal
- 1 cup diced candy orange slices
- 1 cup (6 ounces) semisweet chocolate chips or raisins
- Additional raisins or chocolate chips and candy orange slices

Direction

- In the bowl, cream the sugars and shortening. Put in the vanilla and eggs; stir them well. Mix salt, baking powder, baking soda and flour; put into the creamed mixture. Stir in the raisins/chips, slices of orange, cereal and oats.
- Drop by tablespoonfuls 2 inches apart to the greased baking sheets. Flatten slightly using the fork. Decorate with orange slice mouths and chocolate chip or raisin eyes. Bake at 350 degrees for 10 to 14 minutes. Let cool down on the wire racks.

Nutrition Information

- Calories:
- Cholesterol:
- Protein:
- Total Fat:
- Sodium:
- Fiber:
- Total Carbohydrate:

772. Golden Raisin Cookies

Serving: about 6 dozen. | Prep: 25mins | Cook: 10mins | Ready in:

Ingredients

- 1 cup butter, softened
- 1-1/2 cups sugar
- 1 tablespoon lemon juice
- 2 eggs
- 3-1/2 cups all-purpose flour
- 1-1/2 teaspoons cream of tartar
- 1-1/2 teaspoons baking soda
- 1 package (15 ounces) golden raisins (2-1/2 cups)

Direction

- Cream sugar and butter in a bowl. Add eggs and lemon juice. Mix dry ingredients; add to creamed mixture gradually. Stir in raisins. Roll into 1-in. balls.
- Arrange on greased baking sheets; use a floured fork to make them flat. Bake for 8-10 minutes at 400° or until browned lightly.

Nutrition Information

- Calories: 161 calories
- Cholesterol: 25mg cholesterol
- Protein: 2g protein.
- Total Fat: 5g fat (3g saturated fat)
- Sodium: 109mg sodium
- Fiber: 1g fiber)
- Total Carbohydrate: 27g carbohydrate (16g sugars

---

773. Golden Thumbprints

Serving: 1-1/2 dozen. | Prep: 30mins | Cook: 15mins | Ready in:

Ingredients

- 3 tablespoons butter, softened
- 3 tablespoons brown sugar blend
- 2 tablespoons canola oil
- 1 egg yolk
- 1/2 teaspoon vanilla extract
- 1 cup all-purpose flour
- 1/4 teaspoon salt
- 9 red or green candied cherries, halved

Direction

- Beat brown sugar blend and butter till well blended in a small bowl; beat in vanilla, egg yolk and oil. Mix salt and flour. Add to butter mixture slowly; mix well.
- Form into scant 1-in. balls. Put on ungreased baking sheets, 2-in. apart; slightly flatten. Bake for 5 minutes at 375°; remove from oven.
- Carefully create indentation in middle of each using end of wooden spoon handle; cookie edges will crack. Use candied cherry half to fill each; bake till edges are lightly browned or 6-8 minutes more. Transfer to wire racks.

Nutrition Information

- Calories: 75 calories
- Total Fat: 4g fat (1g saturated fat)
- Sodium: 55mg sodium
- Fiber: 0 fiber)
- Total Carbohydrate: 9g carbohydrate (4g sugars
- Cholesterol: 17mg cholesterol
- Protein: 1g protein. Diabetic Exchanges: 1/2 starch

---

774. Good Fortune & Cheer Cookies

Serving: 1-1/2 dozen. | Prep: 30mins | Cook: 5mins | Ready in:

Ingredients

- 6 tablespoons butter, softened
- 1/3 cup sugar
- 2 large egg whites
- 1/2 teaspoon vanilla extract
- 1/2 teaspoon rum extract

- 2/3 cup all-purpose flour
- 3 ounces white baking chocolate, chopped
- Crushed peppermint candies
- Red, white and green nonpareils

Direction

- Write the fortunes on 3x1/2-inch strips of paper; then put aside. Draw two 3-inch circles on a parchment paper sheet using a pencil. On a baking sheet, place the paper with the pencil mark down; then put aside.
- Whisk the extracts, egg whites, sugar, and butter in a large bowl until thoroughly combined. Add flour; stir thoroughly (the batter will become thick). Spread a scant tablespoonful of the batter over each circle. Bake at 400 degrees until the edges are lightly browned, 4-5 minutes.
- Slide the parchment paper onto a work surface. Cover a cookie with a kitchen towel to keep it warm. In the center of the other cookie, put a fortune; use a thin spatula to loosen the cookie from the parchment paper. Fold the cookie in half over the fortune so that the edges meet; gather the edges and hold for 3 seconds.
- Put the center of cookie over the rim of a glass; then press the ends down gently to bend the cookie. Let cool for a minute, then transfer to a wire rack. Repeat with the second cookie. Put back into the oven for a minute to soften if the cookies become too cool to fold. Repeat with the rest of the fortunes and batter.
- Melt the chocolate in a microwave; mix until smooth. Plunge the cookies partly or sprinkle as wanted; put on the waxed paper. Dust with nonpareils and crushed candies. Allow to stand until set. Put into an airtight container.

Nutrition Information

- Calories:
- Cholesterol:
- Protein:
- Total Fat:
- Sodium:
- Fiber:
- Total Carbohydrate:

775. Grandma's Christmas Spice Cutouts

Serving: about 7 dozen. | Prep: 01hours20mins | Cook: 10mins | Ready in:

Ingredients

- 2 cups molasses
- 2 cups dark corn syrup
- 1/2 cup shortening, melted
- 2 tablespoons white vinegar
- 1 tablespoon cold water
- 10 cups all-purpose flour
- 1 teaspoon baking soda
- 1 teaspoon powdered star anise
- 1/4 teaspoon ground cloves
- 1/8 teaspoon ground cinnamon
- 1/8 teaspoon ground nutmeg
- Dash salt

Direction

- Mix initial 5 ingredients. Whisk leftover ingredients together; add to molasses mixture. Stir well; refrigerate for 3 hours or overnight, covered.
- Preheat an oven to 375°. Roll dough to 1/8-in. thick on lightly floured surface; use floured cookie cutters to cut to desired shapes. Put on greased baking sheets, 1-in. apart; bake for 10-12 minutes till set. Transfer to wire racks; cool.

Nutrition Information

- Calories: 109 calories
- Protein: 2g protein. Diabetic Exchanges: 1-1/2 starch.
- Total Fat: 1g fat (0 saturated fat)
- Sodium: 47mg sodium
- Fiber: 0 fiber)

- Total Carbohydrate: 23g carbohydrate (12g sugars
- Cholesterol: 0 cholesterol

776. Grandma's Sugar Cookies

Serving: 24 | Prep: | Cook: | Ready in:

Ingredients

- 1 cup packed brown sugar
- 1 cup white sugar
- 4 eggs, beaten
- 1 cup shortening
- 5 cups all-purpose flour
- 1 tablespoon baking powder
- 1 teaspoon baking soda
- 2 teaspoons ground cinnamon
- 1 teaspoon ground nutmeg
- 1 cup buttermilk
- 1/2 cup colored sugar for decoration

Direction

- Heat the oven beforehand to 175°C or 350°F.
- Cream the shortening, eggs, white sugar and brown sugar in a big bowl. Sift the nutmeg, cinnamon, baking soda, baking powder and flour together. Put the buttermilk alternately with the dry ingredients.
- Make walnut sized balls by rolling the dough and if desired, roll the balls in colored sugar. Put on an unprepared cookie sheet, leaving 2-inch space apart. Bake it in the preheated oven for 10 to 13 minutes. Allow to cool by putting on wire racks.

Nutrition Information

- Calories: 271 calories;
- Sodium: 139
- Total Carbohydrate: 42.3
- Cholesterol: 31
- Protein: 4.1

- Total Fat: 9.8

777. Harveys Coconut Macaroons

Serving: about 4 dozen. | Prep: 15mins | Cook: 15mins | Ready in:

Ingredients

- 1 cup sweetened shredded coconut
- 3-1/2 cups almond paste
- 1 cup all-purpose flour
- 2/3 cup sugar
- 5 large eggs
- 1/2 cup chopped walnuts
- Red candied cherries, halved

Direction

- Preheat the oven to 350°. Blend coconut in blender or food processor till chopped finely; put aside. Whip almond paste till crumbled. Slowly put in sugar, coconut and flour; combine thoroughly. Put in eggs, 1 by 1, whipping thoroughly after every increment; whip till smooth. Mix nuts in.
- Make a small hole in pastry bag tip or in food-safe plastic bag corner; fit a big star tip. Turn the dough onto bag. Pipe cookies, about an-inch in diameter, spacing 2-inches away on baking sheets lined with parchment paper. Put cherries on top. Bake for 15 to 20 minutes, till golden brown. Cool down for 5 minutes prior to transferring onto wire racks.

Nutrition Information

- Calories: 121 calories
- Fiber: 1g fiber)
- Total Carbohydrate: 14g carbohydrate (10g sugars
- Cholesterol: 19mg cholesterol
- Protein: 3g protein.

- Total Fat: 7g fat (1g saturated fat)
- Sodium: 14mg sodium

778. Hazelnut Chocolate Chip Pizzelle

Serving: 3 dozen. | Prep: 15mins | Cook: 5mins | Ready in:

Ingredients

- 4 large eggs
- 1 cup sugar
- 3/4 cup butter, melted
- 2 cups all-purpose flour
- 1/2 cup finely chopped hazelnuts, toasted
- 1/2 cup miniature semisweet chocolate chips

Direction

- Whisk butter, sugar and eggs in a large bowl until smooth. Slowly stir in flour and blend well. Add in chocolate chips and hazelnuts then fold.
- Place in the preheated pizzelle iron and bake based on the manufacturer's instructions until golden brown. Take to wire racks to cool. Keep in an airtight container.

Nutrition Information

- Calories: 110 calories
- Sodium: 35mg sodium
- Fiber: 0 fiber)
- Total Carbohydrate: 13g carbohydrate (7g sugars
- Cholesterol: 34mg cholesterol
- Protein: 2g protein.
- Total Fat: 6g fat (3g saturated fat)

779. Hazelnut Chocolate Cookies

Serving: 2 dozen. | Prep: 20mins | Cook: 15mins | Ready in:

Ingredients

- 1/2 cup butter, softened
- 6 tablespoons sugar
- 1 teaspoon vanilla extract
- 3/4 cup cake flour
- 1/4 cup baking cocoa
- 3/4 cup ground hazelnuts (about 3 ounces)
- 24 whole hazelnuts, toasted and skins removed
- Confectioners' sugar

Direction

- Prepare the oven by preheating to 325°F. Beat sugar and cream butter in a bowl until fluffy and light. Mix in vanilla. Combine cocoa and flour in a separate bowl; slowly stir into creamed mixture. Mix in ground hazelnuts.
- Form dough into twenty-four 1-inch balls; set 2-inch apart on baking sheets that are not greased. Put a whole hazelnut onto the middle of each and press. Place in the preheated oven and bake for 15-19 minutes or until firm to the touch. Let cool on pans for 2 minutes. Take from pans to wire racks to fully cool. Sprinkle cookies with confectioner's sugar.

Nutrition Information

- Calories:
- Cholesterol:
- Protein:
- Total Fat:
- Sodium:
- Fiber:
- Total Carbohydrate:

780. Hazelnut Crescents

Serving: about 10 dozen. | Prep: 30mins | Cook: 15mins | Ready in:

Ingredients

- 1 cup butter, softened
- 1/4 cup sugar
- 1 teaspoon vanilla extract
- 2 cups all-purpose flour
- 1 cup whole hazelnuts, ground
- Confectioners' sugar

Direction

- Beat sugar and cream butter in a large bowl until fluffy and light. Mix in vanilla. Slowly stir in flour and blend well. Add in nuts. Keep in the refrigerator for 2 hours, covered, or until simple to handle.
- Form dough by teaspoonfuls into 2-inch rolls. Make into crescents. Set 2-inch apart on baking sheets that are not greased.
- Place in the oven and bake for 12 minutes at 350°F or until lightly browned. Let cool for 2 minutes prior taking from pans to wire racks. Sprinkle with confectioner's sugar.

Nutrition Information

- Calories:
- Sodium:
- Fiber:
- Total Carbohydrate:
- Cholesterol:
- Protein:
- Total Fat:

781. Hazelnut Shortbread Hearts

Serving: 7-1/2 dozen. | Prep: 30mins | Cook: 20mins | Ready in:

Ingredients

- 1-1/2 cups butter, softened
- 1 cup confectioners' sugar
- 3 teaspoons vanilla extract
- 3 cups all-purpose flour
- 1 cup ground toasted hazelnuts
- 4 ounces bittersweet chocolate, melted
- 2 ounces white baking chocolate, melted

Direction

- Cream the confectioners' sugar and butter until fluffy and light in a big bowl then mix the vanilla in. Mix hazelnuts and flour then put into the creamed mixture gradually. Stir well. Cover and put in the refrigerator until easy to handle or for an hour.
- Make 1/4-inch thickness dough by rolling it out on a lightly floured surface. Use a 2-inch floured heat-shaped cookie cutter to cut the dough; put on baking sheets without grease, 1 inch apart.
- Bake until it turns light brown or for 18 to 20 minutes at 325 degrees. Before letting it completely cool into wire racks, allow it to cool for a minute in the pans.
- Use bittersweet and white chocolate to drizzle on top of the cookies then let rest until it is set. Keep it in an airtight container.

Nutrition Information

- Calories: 63 calories
- Sodium: 22mg sodium
- Fiber: 0 fiber)
- Total Carbohydrate: 6g carbohydrate (2g sugars
- Cholesterol: 8mg cholesterol
- Protein: 1g protein. Diabetic Exchanges: 1/2 starch
- Total Fat: 4g fat (2g saturated fat)

782. Hazelnut Mocha Bonbon Cookies

Serving: 3-1/2 dozen. | Prep: 40mins | Cook: 10mins | Ready in:

Ingredients

- 1/2 cup butter, softened
- 3/4 cup confectioners' sugar
- 3 teaspoons vanilla extract
- 2 teaspoons instant espresso powder
- 1-1/2 cups all-purpose flour
- 1/8 teaspoon salt
- 42 whole hazelnuts
- ESPRESSO GLAZE:
- 1-1/2 cups confectioners' sugar
- 3/4 teaspoon instant espresso powder
- 1-1/2 teaspoons vanilla extract
- 4 to 5 tablespoons heavy whipping cream
- CHOCOLATE GLAZE:
- 1-1/2 cups confectioners' sugar
- 2 ounces unsweetened chocolate, melted
- 2 tablespoons heavy whipping cream
- Chocolate and gold jimmies

Direction

- Cream confectioners' sugar and butter together in a big bowl until fluffy and light. Mix together espresso powder and vanilla until dissolved. Pour into the creamed mixture. Mix together salt and flour; slowly add to the creamed mixture and stir thoroughly.
- Form one heaping teaspoon dough around each hazelnut to make a ball. Put on non-oiled cookie sheets, 2 inches apart. Bake at 350° until the bottoms turn brown, 8-10 minutes. Transfer to wire racks to cool.
- To make the espresso glaze: In a small bowl, put confectioners' sugar. Mix together vanilla and espresso powder until dissolved; add to the bowl. Mix in a sufficient amount of cream to reach a dipping consistency; put aside. To make the chocolate glaze: Mix together cream, chocolate, and confectioners' sugar.
- In the espresso glaze, dip 1/2 of the cookies. In the chocolate glaze, dip the rest of the cookies, letting the excess fall off. Put on waxed paper and sprinkle jimmies over. Allow to sit until set.

Nutrition Information

- Calories: 103 calories
- Sodium: 24mg sodium
- Fiber: 0 fiber)
- Total Carbohydrate: 15g carbohydrate (10g sugars
- Cholesterol: 11mg cholesterol
- Protein: 1g protein.
- Total Fat: 5g fat (3g saturated fat)

783. Holiday Bells

Serving: 1-1/2 dozen. | Prep: 35mins | Cook: 10mins | Ready in:

Ingredients

- 1/2 tube refrigerated sugar cookie dough, softened
- 1/4 cup all-purpose flour
- 1 tablespoon brown sugar
- 2-1/4 teaspoons maraschino cherry juice
- 1/2 teaspoon butter, softened
- 1/4 cup finely chopped pecans
- 5 red or green maraschino cherries, quartered

Direction

- Whip cookie dough with flour in a small bowl until incorporated. Shape out on a lightly floured surface to 1/8-in. thickness. Slice out with a floured 2-1/2-in. round cookie cutter. Put 2 in. apart on ungreased baking trays.
- Mix the butter, cherry juice and brown sugar in a small bowl. Mix in pecans. Put half teaspoonful in the middle of each cookie. Form into a bell by folding edges of dough to meet on top of filling; crimp edges together.

- For clapper, put a piece of cherry at open end of each bell. Bake for 7-9 minutes at 350° or until slightly browned on the edges. Take out to wire racks right away.

Nutrition Information

- Calories: 87 calories
- Cholesterol: 4mg cholesterol
- Protein: 1g protein.
- Total Fat: 4g fat (1g saturated fat)
- Sodium: 61mg sodium
- Fiber: 0 fiber)
- Total Carbohydrate: 12g carbohydrate (5g sugars

784. Holiday Biscotti

Serving: 2 dozen. | Prep: 20mins | Cook: 50mins | Ready in:

Ingredients

- 1/2 cup butter, softened
- 1 cup sugar
- 3 large eggs
- 2 teaspoons vanilla extract
- 1 teaspoon orange extract
- 3 cups all-purpose flour
- 2 teaspoons baking powder
- 1/2 teaspoon salt
- 2/3 cup dried cranberries, coarsely chopped
- 2/3 cup pistachios, coarsely chopped
- 2 tablespoons grated orange zest

Direction

- In a bowl, cream sugar and butter together. Add eggs, one at a time; after each addition, beating well. Mix in extracts. Combine salt, baking powder and flour; add to creamed mixture gradually and mix well (dough will be sticky). Blend in orange zest, pistachios and cranberries. Allow 30 minutes for chilling.
- Split dough in half. On a floured surface, shape each half into a loaf of 1 and a half to 2-inch diameter. On an ungreased baking sheet, place the dough. Bake at 350° for around 30 to 35 minutes.
- Allow 5 minutes for cooling. Diagonally cut into thick slices of 3/4-inch. On an ungreased baking sheet, place the slices with cut side down. Bake for nearly 9 to 10 minutes. Turn slices over. Bake for an addition of 10 minutes or until they have the color of golden brown. Cool on wire rack. Place in an airtight container for storing.

Nutrition Information

- Calories: 164 calories
- Fiber: 1g fiber)
- Total Carbohydrate: 24g carbohydrate (11g sugars
- Cholesterol: 37mg cholesterol
- Protein: 3g protein.
- Total Fat: 6g fat (3g saturated fat)
- Sodium: 144mg sodium

785. Holiday Butter Mint Cookies

Serving: 4-1/2 dozen. | Prep: 15mins | Cook: 15mins | Ready in:

Ingredients

- 1 cup butter, softened
- 1/4 cup confectioners' sugar
- 1 tablespoon water
- 2 teaspoons mint extract
- 2 cups all-purpose flour
- 3/4 cup crushed butter mints, divided

Direction

- Set the oven to 325° and start preheating. Cream confectioners' sugar and butter until

fluffy and light. Whisk in extract and water. Whisk flour into creamed mixture gradually. Stir in 1/4 cup crushed mints.
- Form into 1-in. balls. Arrange on clean and dry baking sheets, 2 in. apart; make it flat slightly. Bake until bottoms turn light brown or for 12-15 minutes.
- Coat warm cookies with the rest of crushed mints. Place on wire racks to cool.

Nutrition Information

- Calories: 56 calories
- Total Fat: 3g fat (2g saturated fat)
- Sodium: 30mg sodium
- Fiber: 0 fiber)
- Total Carbohydrate: 6g carbohydrate (2g sugars
- Cholesterol: 9mg cholesterol
- Protein: 1g protein.

786. Holiday Eggnog Snickerdoodles

Serving: 7-1/2 dozen. | Prep: 01hours30mins | Cook: 10mins | Ready in:

Ingredients

- 1/2 cup butter, softened
- 1/2 cup shortening
- 2 cups plus 1/3 cup sugar, divided
- 1 large egg
- 1 teaspoon rum extract
- 1/2 cup evaporated milk
- 1/2 cup refrigerated French vanilla nondairy creamer
- 5-1/2 cups all-purpose flour
- 1 teaspoon salt
- 1 teaspoon baking soda
- 1/2 teaspoon ground nutmeg
- ICING:
- 1 cup confectioners' sugar
- 5 to 6 teaspoons refrigerated French vanilla nondairy creamer

Direction

- Preheat an oven to 350°. Cream 2 cups sugar, shortening and butter till fluffy and light in a big bowl; beat in extract and egg. Mix creamer and milk in a small bowl. Whisk baking soda, salt and flour in another bowl; slowly add to creamed mixture alternately with milk mixture; beat well after each addition.
- Mix leftover sugar and nutmeg in a small bowl. Form dough to 1-in. balls, then roll in nutmeg mixture; put on ungreased baking sheets, 2-in. apart. Use bottom of a glass to slightly flatten.
- Bake till lightly browned or 10-12 minutes; cool for 2 minutes on pans. Transfer to wire racks; fully cool.
- Icing: Mix confectioners' sugar with enough creamer to get desired consistency in a small bowl; pipe snowflake designs as desired on cookies.

Nutrition Information

- Calories: 77 calories
- Cholesterol: 5mg cholesterol
- Protein: 1g protein.
- Total Fat: 2g fat (1g saturated fat)
- Sodium: 50mg sodium
- Fiber: 0 fiber)
- Total Carbohydrate: 13g carbohydrate (7g sugars

787. Holiday Meringue Miniatures

Serving: about 7 dozen. | Prep: 20mins | Cook: 60mins | Ready in:

Ingredients

- 2 large egg whites, room temperature
- 1/2 teaspoon white vinegar
- Dash salt
- 1/2 teaspoon almond extract
- 1/2 teaspoon vanilla extract
- 1/2 cup granulated sugar
- Red gel food coloring

Direction

- Heat the oven beforehand to 225 degrees. Beat egg whites with salt and vinegar until doubled in volume and foamy on medium speed. Mix the extracts in. Put sugar in gradually, 1 tablespoon at a time. Every time after you add, beat the mixture on high until sugar dissolves. Keep on beating until get stiff glossy peaks formed.
- Put a half inch round tip in the pastry bag. Inside the length of pastry bag, paint 5 stripes of red food coloring, then put meringue in pastry bag. Pipe dollops onto the parchment-lined baking sheets, leaving 1-inch space apart.
- Bake until set and dry for an hour. Turn the oven off and leave the meringues inside for an hour, keeping the oven door closed. Take out and allow to cool completely on baking sheets. Take the meringues out of parchment paper and keep at room temperature in an airtight container.

Nutrition Information

- Calories: 5 calories
- Fiber: 0 fiber)
- Total Carbohydrate: 1g carbohydrate (1g sugars
- Cholesterol: 0 cholesterol
- Protein: 0 protein. Diabetic Exchanges: 1 free food.
- Total Fat: 0 fat (0 saturated fat)
- Sodium: 19mg sodium

788. Holiday Miniatures

Serving: 10 dozen. | Prep: 01hours10mins | Cook: 10mins | Ready in:

Ingredients

- 1 cup butter, softened
- 1/4 cup sugar
- 1 teaspoon vanilla extract
- 1 teaspoon lemon juice
- 2 cups plus 2 tablespoons all-purpose flour
- 1 pound white candy coating, coarsely chopped
- Colored sugar and/or nonpareils

Direction

- Cream sugar and butter until fluffy and light in a large bowl. Whisk in lemon juice and vanilla. Add flour to creamed mixture gradually; combine well. Separate dough in 1/2. Use plastic to wrap; chill in the fridge for half an hour or until you can handle it easily.
- Roll each portion of dough out on a lightly floured surface to 1/4-in. thickness. Use floured 1-in. cookie cutters to cut. Arrange on clean and dry baking sheets, 1 in. apart.
- Bake 10-12 minutes at 350° or until browned lightly. Transfer to wire racks; cool.
- Melt candy coating in a microwave; stir until smooth. Coat cookies with coating; let excess drip off. Arrange on baking sheets lined with waxed paper. Top with colored sugar and/or nonpareils. Chill in the fridge for half an hour or until set.

Nutrition Information

- Calories: 86 calories
- Protein: 1g protein.
- Total Fat: 5g fat (4g saturated fat)
- Sodium: 31mg sodium
- Fiber: 0 fiber)
- Total Carbohydrate: 10g carbohydrate (6g sugars
- Cholesterol: 8mg cholesterol

789. Holiday Pinwheels

Serving: 4-1/2 dozen. | Prep: 30mins | Cook: 10mins | Ready in:

Ingredients

- 1 cup butter, softened
- 1-1/4 cups sugar
- 2 large eggs
- 1/4 cup light corn syrup
- 1 tablespoon vanilla extract
- 3 cups all-purpose flour
- 3/4 teaspoon baking powder
- 1/2 teaspoon baking soda
- 1/2 teaspoon salt
- 1/2 teaspoon peppermint extract
- Green food coloring

Direction

- In a big bowl, cream sugar and butter. Put in one egg at a time, beating properly after each addition. Then beat in vanilla and corn syrup. Whisk the baking powder, baking soda, salt, and flour together; slowly pour into creamed mixture. Halve the dough. For one portion, add food coloring and peppermint extract. Wrap plastic around each portion; let refrigerate for 2 hours or till firm.
- On the baking sheet, roll out each portion between 2 waxed paper sheets into a 14x9-inch rectangle. Let refrigerate for 30 minutes. Take away the waxed paper. Position plain rectangle over green rectangle. Roll up tightly in jelly-roll style, beginning with a long side; then wrap in plastic. Let refrigerate for 2 hours or up to firm.
- Unwrap then divide into quarter-inch slices. Set 2-inch apart on the greased baking sheets. Allow to bake at 350° for about 8-10 minutes, or until set. Allow to cool for 2 minutes before transferring to wire racks.

Nutrition Information

- Calories: 161 calories
- Sodium: 155mg sodium
- Fiber: 0 fiber)
- Total Carbohydrate: 22g carbohydrate (11g sugars
- Cholesterol: 34mg cholesterol
- Protein: 2g protein.
- Total Fat: 7g fat (4g saturated fat)

790. Holiday Sandwich Cookies

Serving: 50-55 cookies. | Prep: 20mins | Cook: 0mins | Ready in:

Ingredients

- 6 ounces white or milk chocolate candy coating, coarsely chopped
- 50 to 55 Oreo cookies
- Sprinkles

Direction

- Melt 2 oz. of candy coating in a microwave, whisking until smooth. Spread over the tops of 1/3 of the cookies; use sprinkles to garnish as you like. Put onto waxed paper till set. Continue with the rest of the toppings, cookies, and coating.

Nutrition Information

- Calories: 65 calories
- Cholesterol: 0 cholesterol
- Protein: 1g protein.
- Total Fat: 3g fat (1g saturated fat)
- Sodium: 67mg sodium
- Fiber: 0 fiber)
- Total Carbohydrate: 9g carbohydrate (6g sugars

791. Holiday Shortbread

Serving: about 3-1/2 dozen. | Prep: 20mins | Cook: 15mins |Ready in:

Ingredients

- 2 cups butter, softened
- 1 cup sugar
- 1 teaspoon vanilla extract
- 4 cups all-purpose flour
- Colored sugar, optional

Direction

- Cream the sugar and butter together in a big bowl until fluffy and light. Whisk in vanilla. Slowly add flour; whisk until the dough turns into a ball.
- Roll the dough on a lightly floured surface until the thickness is 1/2-inch. Slice into 1 1/2-inch diamonds, squares and if you like, triangles. Put on unoiled baking sheets. If you like, sprinkle colored sugar over.
- Bake at 325° until turning light brown around the edges, or for 14-18 minutes. Put on wire racks to cool.

Nutrition Information

- Calories: 138 calories
- Protein: 1g protein. Diabetic Exchanges: 1-1/2 fat
- Total Fat: 9g fat (5g saturated fat)
- Sodium: 62mg sodium
- Fiber: 0 fiber)
- Total Carbohydrate: 14g carbohydrate (5g sugars
- Cholesterol: 23mg cholesterol

792. Holiday Spritz Wreaths

Serving: about 5 dozen. | Prep: 25mins | Cook: 10mins |Ready in:

Ingredients

- 1/3 cup sugar blend
- 1/4 cup butter, softened
- 3 tablespoons canola oil
- 2 eggs
- 1/2 teaspoon vanilla extract
- 1-3/4 cups all-purpose flour
- 1/2 teaspoon baking powder
- 1/4 teaspoon salt
- 1/4 teaspoon ground allspice
- 1/8 teaspoon baking soda
- 6 drops green food coloring
- 1/4 cup holiday sprinkles

Direction

- Whisk oil, butter and sugar blend until well blended in a large bowl. Whisk in extract and eggs. Mix baking soda, allspice, salt, baking powder and flour; add to butter mixture gradually; combine well. Whisk in food coloring.
- Press dough with a cookie press fitted with a wreath-shaped disk onto clean and dry baking sheets, an inch apart. Garnish with holiday sprinkles.
- Bake for 7-10 minutes at 375° or until set (do not brown). Transfer to wire racks.

Nutrition Information

- Calories: 37 calories
- Cholesterol: 9mg cholesterol
- Protein: 1g protein. Diabetic Exchanges: 1/2 starch.
- Total Fat: 2g fat (1g saturated fat)
- Sodium: 25mg sodium
- Fiber: 0 fiber)
- Total Carbohydrate: 5g carbohydrate (1g sugars

793. Homemade Honey Grahams

Serving: 32 cookies | Prep: 15mins | Cook: 10mins | Ready in:

Ingredients

- 1 cup whole wheat flour
- 3/4 cup all-purpose flour
- 1/2 cup toasted wheat germ
- 2 tablespoons dark brown sugar
- 1 teaspoon baking powder
- 1 teaspoon ground cinnamon
- 1/2 teaspoon salt
- 1/2 teaspoon baking soda
- 6 tablespoons cold butter, cubed
- 1/4 cup honey
- 4 tablespoons ice water

Direction

- Beat together first eight ingredients; add butter and slice repeatedly using 2 knives until the mixture is crumbly. Pour water and honey in another bowl, beat together and slowly add to dry ingredients using a fork to toss, stop when the dough remains together when pressed.
- Halve the dough. Roll each portion into a disk; cover with plastic wrap. Place in refrigerator in 30 minutes, until firm enough to roll.
- Start preheating oven to 350deg; Roll each piece into an 8-in. square on a lightly floured surface. Cut each into sixteen 2-in. squares with a fluted pastry wheel or a knife. If desired, use fork to prick holes. Prepare the parchment paper-lined baking sheet, place each piece 1 in. apart.
- Bake for 10 to 12 minutes until edges are light brown. Take out of pans, let it cool on wire racks. Keep in an airtight container.

Nutrition Information

- Calories: 60 calories
- Fiber: 1g fiber)
- Total Carbohydrate: 9g carbohydrate (3g sugars
- Cholesterol: 6mg cholesterol
- Protein: 1g protein. Diabetic Exchanges: 1/2 starch
- Total Fat: 2g fat (1g saturated fat)
- Sodium: 89mg sodium

794. Homemade Lemon Sugar Cookies

Serving: about 13 dozen. | Prep: 30mins | Cook: 10mins | Ready in:

Ingredients

- 2 cups butter, softened
- 4 cups confectioners' sugar
- 4 large eggs
- 3 tablespoons lemon juice
- 3 tablespoons half-and-half cream
- 2 teaspoons grated lemon zest
- 6-1/2 cups all-purpose flour
- 1 teaspoon baking soda
- 1/4 teaspoon salt
- Sugar

Direction

- Cream confectioners' sugar and butter till fluffy and light in big bowl; one by one, add eggs, beating well with every addition. Beat lemon zest, cream and lemon juice in. Mix salt, baking soda and flour; add to creamed mixture slowly. Cover; refrigerate till easy to handle, about 2 hours.
- Roll out to 1/8-in. thick on lightly floured surface; use 2 1/2-in. cookie cutters that are dipped in flour to cut. Put on ungreased baking sheets, 1-in. apart; sprinkle sugar over. Bake for 8-10 minutes at 350° till lightly browned. Transfer to wire racks; cool.

Nutrition Information

- Calories: 108 calories
- Sodium: 75mg sodium
- Fiber: 0 fiber)
- Total Carbohydrate: 14g carbohydrate (6g sugars
- Cholesterol: 24mg cholesterol
- Protein: 1g protein.
- Total Fat: 5g fat (3g saturated fat)

795. Homemade Macaroon Kisses

Serving: 4 dozen. | Prep: 45mins | Cook: 10mins | Ready in:

Ingredients

- 1/3 cup butter, softened
- 3 ounces cream cheese, softened
- 3/4 cup sugar
- 1 large egg yolk
- 2 teaspoons almond extract
- 1-1/2 cups all-purpose flour
- 2 teaspoons baking powder
- 1/2 teaspoon salt
- 5 cups sweetened shredded coconut, divided
- 48 milk chocolate kisses
- Coarse sugar

Direction

- Cream sugar, cream cheese and butter till fluffy and light in big bowl; beat extract and egg yolk in. Mix salt, baking powder and flour; add to creamed mixture slowly. Stir well; mix 3 cups coconut in. Cover; refrigerate till dough becomes easy to handle, 1 hour.
- Preheat an oven to 350°; form to 1-in. balls. Roll in leftover coconut; put on ungreased baking sheets, 2-in. apart.
- Bake till lightly browned, about 10-12 minutes; press chocolate kiss immediately in middle of every cookie. Sprinkle coarse sugar over; cool till chocolate is soft on pan, about 2-3 minutes. Transfer to wire racks; completely cool.

Nutrition Information

- Calories: 120 calories
- Sodium: 85mg sodium
- Fiber: 1g fiber)
- Total Carbohydrate: 14g carbohydrate (9g sugars
- Cholesterol: 11mg cholesterol
- Protein: 1g protein.
- Total Fat: 7g fat (5g saturated fat)

796. Honey Crunch Cookies

Serving: about 5 dozen. | Prep: 20mins | Cook: 10mins | Ready in:

Ingredients

- 2 cups all-purpose flour
- 2 teaspoons baking powder
- 1/2 teaspoon salt
- 1 cup butter, softened
- 1 cup honey
- 2 large eggs
- 1 cup sweetened shredded coconut
- 1 cup butterscotch chips
- 4 cups crisp rice cereal

Direction

- Sift together salt, baking powder, and flour; put aside. Cream the butter in a big bowl until fluffy and light. Pour in honey, a small amount each time, thoroughly whisking between additions.
- Add eggs, 1 egg each time, thoroughly whisking between additions. The mixture will seem curdled. Slowly add the dry ingredients, whisk until moist. Fold in cereal, chips, and coconut. Drop onto oil-coated cookie sheets by teaspoonfuls, 2 inches separately.

- Bake at 350° until turning golden brown, 12-14 minutes. Transfer to wire racks.

Nutrition Information

- Calories: 196 calories
- Total Carbohydrate: 25g carbohydrate (15g sugars
- Cholesterol: 31mg cholesterol
- Protein: 2g protein.
- Total Fat: 10g fat (7g saturated fat)
- Sodium: 181mg sodium
- Fiber: 0 fiber)

797. Honey Date Pumpkin Cookies

Serving: 5 dozen. | Prep: 25mins | Cook: 15mins | Ready in:

Ingredients

- 3/4 cup butter, softened
- 1-1/3 cups sugar
- 1/4 cup honey
- 1 large egg
- 1 cup canned pumpkin
- 1 teaspoon milk
- 2-1/2 cups all-purpose flour
- 1 teaspoon baking powder
- 3/4 teaspoon salt
- 3/4 cup chopped dates
- 3/4 cup chopped pecans
- 2 tablespoons poppy seeds
- FROSTING:
- 3 ounces cream cheese, softened
- 1/4 cup butter, softened
- 2 cups confectioners' sugar
- 2 tablespoons heavy whipping cream
- 1 teaspoon vanilla extract

Direction

- Cream sugar and butter together in a big bowl until fluffy and light. Slowly whisk in egg and honey. Add milk and pumpkin, whisk thoroughly. Mix together salt, baking powder, and flour; slowly add to the creamed mixture and stir thoroughly. Mix in poppy seeds, pecans, and dates.
- Onto cookie sheets lined with parchment, drop rounded tablespoonfuls of the batter, about 2-inch separately. Bake at 350° until the edges turn light brown, about 12-15 minutes. Transfer to wire racks to fully cool.
- To prepare the frosting, whisk confectioners' sugar, butter, and cream cheese in a big bowl until fluffy and light. Whisk in vanilla and cream until smooth. Frost the cookies. Put in an airtight container to store in the fridge.

Nutrition Information

- Calories: 110 calories
- Cholesterol: 14mg cholesterol
- Protein: 1g protein.
- Total Fat: 5g fat (2g saturated fat)
- Sodium: 64mg sodium
- Fiber: 1g fiber)
- Total Carbohydrate: 16g carbohydrate (11g sugars

798. Ice Cream Kolachkes

Serving: 10 dozen. | Prep: 60mins | Cook: 15mins | Ready in:

Ingredients

- 2 cups butter, softened
- 1 pint vanilla ice cream, softened
- 4 cups all-purpose flour
- 2 tablespoons sugar
- 2 cans (12 ounces each) apricot and/or raspberry cake and pastry filling
- 1 to 2 tablespoons confectioners' sugar, optional

Direction

- Beat ice cream and butter until combined in a bowl of heavy-duty stand mixer. The mixture will seem curdled. Put sugar and flour then stir well. Cut the dough into 4 parts. Cover and put in the refrigerator until easy to handle or for 2 hours.
- Heat the oven beforehand to 350 degrees. Roll one part of the dough into a 12x10-inch rectangle on a lightly floured surface. Slice the dough into 2-inch squares. In the middle of each square, put 1 teaspoonful of filling overlap the 2 opposite corners of dough on top of the filling. Seal by pinching tightly. Put on ungreased baking sheets, leaving 2-inchspace apart. Repeat with the rest of the dough and filling.
- Bake it until bottoms are lightly browned or for 11 to 14 minutes. Allow to cool for a minute before transferring to wire racks from the pans. If desired, use confectioners' sugar and sprinkle on top.

Nutrition Information

- Calories: 60 calories
- Fiber: 0 fiber)
- Total Carbohydrate: 7g carbohydrate (2g sugars
- Cholesterol: 9mg cholesterol
- Protein: 1g protein.
- Total Fat: 3g fat (2g saturated fat)
- Sodium: 27mg sodium

799. Icebox Sugar Cookies

Serving: about 8 dozen. | Prep: 20mins | Cook: 10mins | Ready in:

Ingredients

- 1 cup butter, softened
- 2 cups sugar
- 2 large eggs
- 1 teaspoon vanilla extract
- 3-1/2 cups all-purpose flour
- 1 teaspoon baking soda
- 1/2 teaspoon salt

Direction

- Cream sugar and butter in a bowl. Whisk in vanilla and eggs. Mix salt, baking soda, and flour; put them gradually into the creamed mixture. Form the dough into three 10-inch long rolls on a lightly floured surface. Use waxed paper to wrap each roll tightly. Let chill until firm, or for an hour.
- Slice into 3/8-inch slices; then transfer onto baking sheets coated with cooking spray. Dust with sugar. Bake at 375 degrees until lightly browned, or for 8-10 minutes. Place onto the wire racks to cool.

Nutrition Information

- Calories: 102 calories
- Sodium: 92mg sodium
- Fiber: 0 fiber)
- Total Carbohydrate: 15g carbohydrate (8g sugars
- Cholesterol: 19mg cholesterol
- Protein: 1g protein.
- Total Fat: 4g fat (2g saturated fat)

800. Iced Orange Cutouts

Serving: about 4 dozen. | Prep: 45mins | Cook: 10mins | Ready in:

Ingredients

- 2-1/2 cups all-purpose flour
- 1/3 cup sugar
- 1 to 2 tablespoons grated orange zest
- 1 cup cold butter, cubed
- 2 to 4 tablespoons ice water

- ICING:
- 3 cups confectioners' sugar
- 1/4 cup orange juice
- 1 tablespoon grated orange zest

Direction

- Whisk flour, orange zest, and sugar; cut in butter until crumbly. Pour ice water gradually, use a fork to toss until the dough holds together when pressed. Gently knead until the dough forms. Next, divide into 2 equal parts. Form each into a disk and wrap in plastic. Let them chill for 60 minutes.
- Set the oven at 350° to preheat. Gently roll the dough on a lightly floured surface to 1/8-in. thickness. Use a floured 2-1/4-in. round cookie cutter to cut. On ungreased baking sheets, arrange 1 in. apart. Then bake for around 10-12 minutes, until the bottoms are light brown. Transfer from pans to wire racks to cool totally.
- To make the icing: Combine confectioners' sugar, orange zest and juice until smooth. Then spread over the cookies. Allow to sit at room temperature until set.

Nutrition Information

- Calories: 89 calories
- Sodium: 30mg sodium
- Fiber: 0 fiber)
- Total Carbohydrate: 13g carbohydrate (9g sugars
- Cholesterol: 10mg cholesterol
- Protein: 1g protein.
- Total Fat: 4g fat (2g saturated fat)

801. Italian Lemon Cookies

Serving: 3 dozen. | Prep: 30mins | Cook: 15mins | Ready in:

Ingredients

- 1 cup butter, softened
- 1/2 cup sugar
- 3 eggs, separated
- 2 teaspoons grated lemon peel
- 2-1/2 cups all-purpose flour
- Colored sugar

Direction

- Cream sugar and butter together in a big bowl until fluffy and light. Whisk in lemon peel and egg yolks. Slowly whisk in flour. Cover and chill until firm enough to shape, 60 minutes.
- Turn the oven to 350° to preheat. Form the dough into 6-inch ropes by level tablespoons. Form each rope into an "S" shape, then coil each end to reach the middle. Put on non-oiled cookie sheets, 2 inches apart. Beat egg whites; brush over the cookies. Sprinkle colored sugar over.
- Bake until it turns brown on the bottom, 12-14 minutes. Transfer from the pans to wire racks to cool.

Nutrition Information

- Calories:
- Total Fat:
- Sodium:
- Fiber:
- Total Carbohydrate:
- Cholesterol:
- Protein:

802. Italian Sesame Cookies

Serving: 8 dozen. | Prep: 35mins | Cook: 10mins | Ready in:

Ingredients

- 1/2 cup butter, softened
- 1 cup sugar
- 3 eggs

- 1 teaspoon vanilla extract
- 3 cups all-purpose flour
- 3 teaspoons baking powder
- 1/2 teaspoon salt
- 1-3/4 cups sesame seeds
- 3/4 cup 2% milk

Direction

- Cream sugar and butter together in a big bowl until fluffy and light. Add eggs, 1 each time, whisking thoroughly between additions. Add vanilla. Mix together salt, baking powder, and flour; slowly add to the creamed mixture and stir thoroughly.
- On a lightly floured surface, invert the dough; knead until smooth, 10-12 times. Split the dough into 8 parts. Shape each part into a 24-inch log. Slice the logs into 2-inch pieces.
- In different shallow bowls, put milk and sesame seeds. Plunge pieces in the milk, then in the sesame seeds. Put on oil-coated cookie sheets, 2 inches apart. Bake at 350° until it turns light brown on the bottoms and set, 7-9 minutes. Let cool for 2 minutes, then transfer from the pans to wire racks.

Nutrition Information

- Calories: 45 calories
- Total Carbohydrate: 6g carbohydrate (2g sugars
- Cholesterol: 9mg cholesterol
- Protein: 1g protein. Diabetic Exchanges: 1/2 starch.
- Total Fat: 2g fat (1g saturated fat)
- Sodium: 35mg sodium
- Fiber: 0 fiber)

803. Italian Spumoni Cookies

Serving: 4 dozen. | Prep: 30mins | Cook: 10mins | Ready in:

Ingredients

- 2 tubes (16-1/2 ounces each) refrigerated sugar cookie dough
- 1 cup all-purpose flour, divided
- 1/4 cup chopped maraschino cherries
- 4 to 6 drops red food coloring, optional
- 2 tablespoons baking cocoa
- 2 teaspoons hazelnut liqueur
- 1/3 cup chopped pistachios
- 4 to 6 drops green food coloring, optional

Direction

- Allow the cookie dough to stand for 5 to 10 minutes at room temperature to make it soft. Beat the 3/4 cup of flour and cookie dough in a big bowl, until blended. Split the dough into 3 parts.
- Add red food coloring (optional), cherries and the leftover flour to 1 part. Add the liqueur and cocoa to the 2nd part. Add green food coloring (optional) and pistachios to the leftover part.
- Roll each part in between the 2 pieces of waxed paper to an 8x6-inch rectangle. Take off the waxed paper. On a piece of plastic wrap, put the cherry rectangle. Layer it with chocolate and pistachio rectangles, then gently press together. Use plastic wrap to wrap it and let it chill in the fridge overnight.
- Set an oven to preheat to 375 degrees. Slice the chilled dough in 1/2 widthwise. Put 1 rectangle back into the fridge. Slice the leftover rectangle to 1/4-inch pieces. Put it on the baking trays that are ungreased and place it 1-inch apart. Redo the process with the leftover dough.
- Let it bake until it becomes set or for 8 to 10 minutes. Allow to cool for 2 minutes prior to transferring to wire racks. Keep it in an airtight container.

Nutrition Information

- Calories: 103 calories
- Total Fat: 4g fat (1g saturated fat)

- Sodium: 87mg sodium
- Fiber: 0 fiber)
- Total Carbohydrate: 14g carbohydrate (5g sugars
- Cholesterol: 6mg cholesterol
- Protein: 1g protein.

804. Jam Filled Wreaths & Hearts

Serving: about 3 dozen wreaths or 4 dozen hearts. | Prep: 25mins | Cook: 10mins | Ready in:

Ingredients

- 3/4 cup butter, softened
- 1 cup sugar
- 2 large eggs
- 1-1/2 cups all-purpose flour
- 1 teaspoon baking powder
- 1 teaspoon ground cinnamon
- 1/2 teaspoon ground allspice
- 1 cup quick-cooking oats
- 3/4 cup finely chopped nuts
- 1 jar (18 ounces) seedless raspberry jam
- Confectioners' sugar

Direction

- Cream sugar and butter in a bowl. Add eggs, one by one; beat well after each addition. Mix allspice, cinnamon, baking powder and flour; add to creamed mixture. Mix in nuts and oats; stir well. Refrigerate till dough gets easy to handle or for 3 hours.
- Roll dough to 1/8-in. thick on floured surface; cut with 2-in. heart-shaped or 2 1/2-in. round cookie cutter; cut out the center of 1/2 cookies using heart-shaped or 1-in. round cookie cutter. Put window and solid cookies onto lightly greased baking sheets.
- Bake it at 400° till lightly browned or for 6-8 minutes; cool on wire racks.
- On bottoms of solid cookies, spread 1 tsp. jam; put window cookies over. Dust using confectioners' sugar; if desired, use extra jam to fill centers.

Nutrition Information

- Calories:
- Protein:
- Total Fat:
- Sodium:
- Fiber:
- Total Carbohydrate:
- Cholesterol:

805. Jelly Topped Sugar Cookies

Serving: about 3-1/2 dozen. | Prep: 20mins | Cook: 10mins | Ready in:

Ingredients

- 3/4 cup sugar
- 3/4 cup canola oil
- 2 eggs
- 2 teaspoons vanilla extract
- 1 teaspoon lemon extract
- 1 teaspoon grated lemon peel
- 2 cups all-purpose flour
- 2 teaspoons baking powder
- 1/2 teaspoon salt
- 1/2 cup jam or jelly

Direction

- Whisk together oil and sugar in a large mixing bowl until incorporated. Whisk in lemon peel, extracts, and eggs. Mix together salt, baking powder, and flour; slowly mix into sugar mixture until well combined.
- Drop mixture onto ungreased baking sheets by rounded tablespoonfuls, separating cookies 2 inches apart. Apply cooking spray over the bottom of a glass; press the bottom of the glass into sugar to coat. Press cookies with the

prepared glass, re-dipping the glass in sugar if necessary.
- Spread 1/4 teaspoon jelly down the center of each cookie. Bake cookies for 8 to 10 minutes at 400° until firm. Transfer to wire racks and allow to cool.

Nutrition Information

- Calories: 84 calories
- Total Carbohydrate: 11g carbohydrate (6g sugars
- Cholesterol: 10mg cholesterol
- Protein: 1g protein.
- Total Fat: 4g fat (1g saturated fat)
- Sodium: 52mg sodium
- Fiber: 0 fiber)

806. Kipplens

Serving: 12 dozen. | Prep: 15mins | Cook: 20mins |Ready in:

Ingredients

- 2 cups butter, softened
- 1 cup sugar
- 2 teaspoons vanilla extract
- 5 cups all-purpose flour
- 2 cups chopped pecans
- 1/4 teaspoon salt
- Confectioners' sugar

Direction

- Cream sugar and butter together in a big bowl until fluffy and light; whisk in vanilla. Add salt, pecans, and flour; stir thoroughly. Roll the dough into 1-inch balls and put on non-oiled cookie sheets.
- Bake at 325° until it turns light brown, 17-20 minutes. Let the cookies cool a bit, then roll them in confectioners' sugar.

Nutrition Information

- Calories: 110 calories
- Protein: 1g protein.
- Total Fat: 8g fat (3g saturated fat)
- Sodium: 60mg sodium
- Fiber: 1g fiber)
- Total Carbohydrate: 10g carbohydrate (3g sugars
- Cholesterol: 14mg cholesterol

807. Kris Humphries' Mom's Small Chocolate Chip Butter Cookies

Serving: 4-1/2 dozen. | Prep: 25mins | Cook: 10mins | Ready in:

Ingredients

- 1 cup butter, softened
- 1 cup sugar
- 1 egg
- 2 teaspoons vanilla extract
- 2-1/2 cups all-purpose flour
- 1/4 teaspoon salt
- 1-1/4 cups semisweet chocolate chips

Direction

- Cream sugar and butter until fluffy and light in a large bowl. Whisk in vanilla and egg. Mix salt and flour; add to creamed mixture gradually; combine well. Stir in chocolate chips.
- Drop onto greased baking sheets by rounded teaspoonfuls, 2 inches apart. Make them flat slightly, using a glass dipped in sugar. Bake for 7-8 minutes at 375° or until bottom turn brown. Transfer to wire racks. Keep in an airtight container.

Nutrition Information

- Calories: 86 calories
- Total Fat: 5g fat (3g saturated fat)
- Sodium: 40mg sodium
- Fiber: 0 fiber)
- Total Carbohydrate: 11g carbohydrate (6g sugars
- Cholesterol: 12mg cholesterol
- Protein: 1g protein.

808. Lace Cookies With Chocolate Middles

Serving: 2 dozen sandwich cookies. | Prep: 60mins | Cook: 10mins | Ready in:

Ingredients

- 1/2 cup butter, softened
- 1 cup sugar
- 1 egg
- 1 teaspoon vanilla extract
- 1 cup quick-cooking oats
- 3 tablespoons all-purpose flour
- 1/2 teaspoon salt
- 2 cups (12 ounces) semisweet chocolate chips, melted

Direction

- In the big bowl, cream the sugar and butter till fluffy and light. Beat in the vanilla and egg. Mix the salt, flour and oats; slowly put into the creamed mixture and stir them well.
- Drop by teaspoonfuls 3 inches apart to the baking sheets which are lined with parchment paper.
- Bake at 350 degrees till golden brown or for 8 to 10 minutes. Let cool down totally on the pans prior to gently taking out onto the wire racks.
- Spread the melted chocolate on bottoms of 1/2 of cookies; add the leftover cookies on top. Keep stored in an airtight container.

Nutrition Information

- Calories: 152 calories
- Total Fat: 8g fat (5g saturated fat)
- Sodium: 81mg sodium
- Fiber: 1g fiber)
- Total Carbohydrate: 20g carbohydrate (16g sugars
- Cholesterol: 19mg cholesterol
- Protein: 1g protein. Diabetic Exchanges: 1-1/2 fat

809. Lactose Free Chocolate Chip Cookies

Serving: 3 dozen. | Prep: 15mins | Cook: 15mins | Ready in:

Ingredients

- 1 cup maple syrup
- 3/4 cup sugar
- 1/2 cup canola oil
- 1/2 cup unsweetened applesauce
- 3-1/2 teaspoons vanilla extract
- 3/4 teaspoon molasses
- 3 cups all-purpose flour
- 3 teaspoons baking powder
- 1-1/2 teaspoons baking soda
- 3/4 teaspoon salt
- 1 package (10 ounces) dairy-free semisweet chocolate chips

Direction

- In a large bowl, beat the molasses, vanilla, applesauce, oil, sugar and syrup until well combined. Combine the salt, baking soda, baking powder and flour; add to the syrup mixture slowly and combine well. Mix in the chocolate chips. Refrigerate, covered, for 1 hour.
- On baking sheets lightly sprayed with cooking spray, drop heaping tablespoonfuls of the dough 2 in. apart. Bake for 11-13 minutes at

350° or until edges are light brown. Transfer to wire racks.

Nutrition Information

- Calories: 147 calories
- Total Fat: 6g fat (2g saturated fat)
- Sodium: 136mg sodium
- Fiber: 1g fiber)
- Total Carbohydrate: 23g carbohydrate (14g sugars
- Cholesterol: 0 cholesterol
- Protein: 2g protein. Diabetic Exchanges: 1-1/2 starch

810. Lemon Lover's Cookies

Serving: About 3-1/2 dozen. | Prep: 20mins | Cook: 10mins | Ready in:

Ingredients

- 3/4 cup butter, softened
- 1/3 cup confectioners' sugar
- 2 teaspoons lemon juice
- 1 cup all-purpose flour
- 1/2 cup cornstarch
- 1 teaspoon grated lemon peel
- LEMON FROSTING:
- 1/4 cup butter, softened
- 1 cup confectioners' sugar
- 2 teaspoons lemon juice
- 1 teaspoon grated lemon peel
- GARNISH:
- Additional grated lemon peel, optional

Direction

- Cream sugar and butter in a small bowl for 5 minutes, until fluffy and light, then beat in lemon juice. Mix together lemon peel, cornstarch and flour, then put into the creamed mixture gradually and blend well.
- Form into a roll, 1 1/2 inches in size; use plastic to wrap then chill until firm, or about an hour. Unwrap and cut into slices, 1/4 inch each. Arrange slices onto baking sheets coated with grease, 2 inches apart.
- Bake at 350 degrees until edges turn golden brown, or about 10 to 12 minutes. Transfer gently to wire racks to cool thoroughly.
- Beat butter in a small bowl until fluffy. Put in lemon peel, lemon juice and confectioners' sugar, then beat the mixture until smooth. Spread over cooled cookies and use more lemon peel to sprinkle over if you want. Allow to stand until set; keep in an airtight container to store.

Nutrition Information

- Calories: 73 calories
- Total Carbohydrate: 8g carbohydrate (4g sugars
- Cholesterol: 12mg cholesterol
- Protein: 0 protein.
- Total Fat: 5g fat (3g saturated fat)
- Sodium: 33mg sodium
- Fiber: 0 fiber)

811. Lemon Pistachio Wreaths

Serving: 1-1/2 dozen. | Prep: 30mins | Cook: 10mins | Ready in:

Ingredients

- 1/2 cup plus 2 tablespoons butter, softened
- 1/2 cup plus 1 tablespoon sugar
- 2 large egg yolks
- 5 teaspoons grated lemon peel
- 1 teaspoon vanilla extract
- 1 cup all-purpose flour
- 3/4 cup plus 1 tablespoon cornstarch
- 1 teaspoon baking powder
- 1/4 teaspoon salt
- 1-3/4 cups confectioners' sugar

- 6 to 8 teaspoons lemon juice
- 1-1/4 cups pistachios, toasted and finely chopped

Direction

- Cream the sugar and butter in a small bowl, until it becomes fluffy and light. Beat in the vanilla, lemon peel and egg yolks. Mix together the salt, baking powder, cornstarch and flour. Slowly add to the creamed mixture and stir well.
- Form it into a ball and flatten to a disk. Use plastic to wrap it and let it chill in the fridge for an hour.
- Roll the dough to 1/8-inch thick on a surface that's lightly floured. Slice it using a 2 1/2-inch doughnut cutter that's floured. Put it on the greased baking trays and place it 2 inches apart.
- Let it bake for 10 to 12 minutes at 350 degrees or until it turns light brown, then transfer to wire racks to fully cool.
- Beat enough lemon juice and confectioners' sugar in a small bowl to reach your preferred consistency. Spread on top of the cookies and sprinkle pistachios on top. Allow to stand until it becomes set. Keep it in an airtight container.

Nutrition Information

- Calories: 230 calories
- Protein: 3g protein.
- Total Fat: 11g fat (5g saturated fat)
- Sodium: 138mg sodium
- Fiber: 1g fiber)
- Total Carbohydrate: 31g carbohydrate (18g sugars
- Cholesterol: 39mg cholesterol

812. Lemon Poppy Seed Cookies

Serving: 3-1/2 dozen. | Prep: 20mins | Cook: 15mins | Ready in:

Ingredients

- 1/2 cup poppy seed filling
- 2 teaspoons lemon juice
- 1 cup butter, softened
- 1-1/2 cups sugar
- 3 egg yolks
- 1 tablespoon grated lemon peel
- 2 teaspoons lemon extract
- 1 teaspoon vanilla extract
- 3-1/2 cups all-purpose flour
- 2 teaspoons baking powder
- 1-1/4 teaspoons baking soda
- 3/4 cup buttermilk
- FROSTING:
- 3 cups confectioners' sugar
- 2 tablespoons butter, softened
- 1/4 cup 2% milk
- 2 teaspoons lemon extract
- 1 teaspoon grated lemon peel
- Poppy seeds, optional

Direction

- Mix together lemon juice and poppy seed filling in a small bowl, then put aside. Cream sugar and butter together in a big bowl until fluffy and light, then beat in extracts, lemon peel and egg yolks. Mix together baking soda, baking powder and flour, and then put into the creamed mixture gradually together with buttermilk, alternately, while beating well between additions.
- Drop on baking sheets coated with grease with tablespoonfuls of batter. Use the end of a wooden spoon handle to create an indentation in the center of each with the depth of 1/2 inch. Fill into the indentation with approximately 1/2 tsp. of the poppy seed filling, and then put a teaspoonful of dough on top.

- Bake at 350 degrees until edges turn golden brown, about 14 to 16 minutes. Transfer to wire racks to cool.
- To make frosting, beat together lemon peel, extract, milk, butter and confectioners' sugar until combined, then spread over cookies. Use poppy seeds to sprinkle over cookies if you want.

Nutrition Information

- Calories: 163 calories
- Total Fat: 6g fat (3g saturated fat)
- Sodium: 115mg sodium
- Fiber: 0 fiber)
- Total Carbohydrate: 26g carbohydrate (15g sugars
- Cholesterol: 29mg cholesterol
- Protein: 2g protein.

813. Lemon Shortbread Cookies

Serving: 10 | Prep: 20mins | Cook: 20mins | Ready in:

Ingredients

- 1/4 cup packed brown sugar
- 2 teaspoons finely grated lemon zest
- 1/2 teaspoon lemon extract
- 1/4 teaspoon vanilla extract
- 1 cup all-purpose flour
- 1/4 teaspoon salt
- 1/2 cup butter, room temperature

Direction

- Combine brown sugar and butter in a medium-sized bowl using an electric mixer until blended. Mix in vanilla extract, lemon extract, and lemon zest.
- Mix into the butter mixture with salt and flour. Move the mixture to plastic wrap or waxed paper. Form into a disk (if using cutters) or roll into a disk (to slice to cookies); wrap the dough and chill for 30 minutes.
- Start preheating the oven to 325°F (170°C).
- On a surface lightly scattered with flour, roll out the dough to 1/4 inch thick. Use a 2-inch round cutter to cut out cookies and put on non-oiled cookie sheets 2" separately. (Or slice cookies and put on the cookie sheets). Collect and roll the scraps again.
- Put in the preheated oven and bake for 20-25 minutes until the edges turn lightly golden but not brown. Allow it to sit on the cookie sheet for 2 minutes. Transfer to a rack to fully cool down.

Nutrition Information

- Calories: 149 calories;
- Total Fat: 9.3
- Sodium: 125
- Total Carbohydrate: 15
- Cholesterol: 24
- Protein: 1.4

814. Lemon Shortbread Trees

Serving: 3-1/2 dozen. | Prep: 45mins | Cook: 10mins | Ready in:

Ingredients

- 1 cup butter, softened
- 1/2 cup confectioners' sugar
- 1/2 cup cornstarch
- 2 tablespoons grated lemon peel
- 1 tablespoon lemon juice
- 2 cups all-purpose flour
- 22 pretzel sticks
- ROYAL ICING:
- 2-1/2 cups confectioners' sugar
- 10 teaspoons water
- 4 teaspoons meringue powder
- Red and green paste food coloring
- Assorted sprinkles

Direction

- Cream together cornstarch, confectioners' sugar and butter in a big bowl until fluffy and light. Beat in lemon juice and peel, then put in flour gradually, mixing well.
- Split dough into 2 portions and form each into 2 logs, 6 inches length. Flatten top and push in sides at an angle to make a 2x2x 1-1/2 triangle, then use plastic wrap to wrap. Refrigerate until firm, or for 4 hours.
- Take off the plastic wrap and slice into slices, 1/4 inch size, then arrange on grease-free baking sheets by 2 inches apart. Break the pretzels sticks into 2 equal parts then press into short side of each cookie to make tree trunk. Bake at 350 degrees until set, or for 10 to 12 minutes. Transfer to wire racks to cool.
- Mix together meringue powder, water and confectioners' sugar in a big bowl, then beat the mixture on low speed just until blended. Beat on high speed until hold stiff peaks, or for 4 to 5 minutes. Take out 1 cup of icing and tint red. Tint the rest of icing green. Use a wet cloth to cover unused icing at all times. Frost and decorate cookies as wished. Allow to dry at room temperature for a few hours, or until firm. Keep in an airtight container.

Nutrition Information

- Calories: 97 calories
- Total Fat: 4g fat (3g saturated fat)
- Sodium: 37mg sodium
- Fiber: 0 fiber)
- Total Carbohydrate: 14g carbohydrate (8g sugars
- Cholesterol: 11mg cholesterol
- Protein: 1g protein.

---

815. Lemon Snowballs Cookie

Serving: about 3 dozen. | Prep: 20mins | Cook: 10mins | Ready in:

Ingredients

- 1/2 cup butter, softened
- 2/3 cup sugar
- 1 large egg
- 1/4 cup lemon juice
- 1 tablespoon grated lemon zest
- 1-3/4 cups all-purpose flour
- 1/4 teaspoon baking soda
- 1/4 teaspoon cream of tartar
- 1/4 teaspoon salt
- 1/2 cup finely chopped almonds
- Confectioners' sugar

Direction

- Cream together egg, sugar and butter in a bowl until well combined. Put in zest and lemon juice. Mix together salt, cream of tartar, baking soda and flour. Put in almonds, then cover and chill the dough for a minimum of an hour to overnight.
- Roll dough into balls, 1 inch in size and arrange onto ungreased baking sheet. Bake at 350 degrees until bottoms are browned slightly, or about 10 to 12 minutes. The cookies will not brown on top.
- Transfer to wire racks instantly and allow to cool for 5 minutes, then roll in confectioners' sugar.

Nutrition Information

- Calories: 144 calories
- Protein: 2g protein.
- Total Fat: 7g fat (3g saturated fat)
- Sodium: 106mg sodium
- Fiber: 1g fiber)
- Total Carbohydrate: 18g carbohydrate (8g sugars
- Cholesterol: 25mg cholesterol

816. Lemon Stars

Serving: 9 dozen. | Prep: 45mins | Cook: 10mins | Ready in:

Ingredients

- 1/2 cup butter-flavored shortening
- 1 cup sugar
- 1 egg
- 1-1/2 teaspoons lemon extract
- 1/2 cup sour cream
- 1 teaspoon grated lemon peel
- 2-3/4 cups all-purpose flour
- 1/2 teaspoon baking soda
- 1/2 teaspoon salt
- FROSTING:
- 1-1/2 cups confectioners' sugar
- 6 tablespoons butter, softened
- 3/4 teaspoon lemon extract
- 3 drops yellow food coloring, optional
- 3 to 4 tablespoons 2% milk
- Yellow colored sugar, optional

Direction

- Cream together the shortening and sugar in a big bowl until the consistency is fluffy and light. Add in egg and extract and beat them together. Stir in the peel and sour cream. Whisk the flour together with salt and baking soda; add the dry mixture little by little to the creamed mixture and incorporate thoroughly. Split the dough into three balls; cover and keep in the fridge for 3 hours or until the dough can easily be handled.
- Take one part of dough out from the fridge at a time. Dust your work area lightly with flour and roll out the dough to a quarter-in. thickness. Shape using a floured 2-in. star cookie cutter. Arrange the patterned dough an inch apart on baking sheets that's ungreased.
- Let them bake at 375° for 6 to 8 minutes or until the edges turns brown lightly. Transfer on wire racks to cool.
- For preparing the frosting, beat the butter together with the extract, confectioners' sugar, food coloring (if preferred) in a small bowl. You may add enough milk to achieve a spreading consistency. Decorate the cookies using the frosting; scatter with colored sugar if preferred.

Nutrition Information

- Calories: 43 calories
- Protein: 0 protein.
- Total Fat: 2g fat (1g saturated fat)
- Sodium: 23mg sodium
- Fiber: 0 fiber)
- Total Carbohydrate: 6g carbohydrate (4g sugars
- Cholesterol: 4mg cholesterol

817. Lemon Thins

Serving: 30 | Prep: | Cook: 30mins | Ready in:

Ingredients

- 1¼ cups whole-wheat pastry flour or all-purpose flour
- ⅓ cup cornstarch
- 1½ teaspoons baking powder
- ¼ teaspoon salt
- ¾ cup sugar, divided
- 2 tablespoons butter, softened
- 2 tablespoons canola oil
- 1 large egg white
- 1½ teaspoons freshly grated lemon zest
- 1 teaspoon vanilla extract
- 3 tablespoons lemon juice

Direction

- Set the oven to 350 degrees F. Coat cooking spray onto 2 baking sheets.
- In a mixing bowl, whisk together salt, baking powder, cornstarch and flour. Beat in another mixing bowl with electric mixer the oil, butter and 1/2 cup of sugar on moderate speed until

fluffy. Put in vanilla, lemon zest and egg white, then beat until smooth. Beat in lemon juice. Put the flour mixture into the wet mixture, then fold in using a rubber spatula just until blended.
- Drop the dough onto prepared baking sheet by teaspoonfuls, placing 2 inches apart. Put in a saucer the remaining 1/4 cup sugar. Coat cooking spray onto the bottom of a wide-bottomed glass and dip it in the sugar. Flatten the dough into 2 1/2-in. circles using the glass while dipping the glass into sugar each time.
- Bake cookies for 8-10 minutes until just beginning to brown around the edges. Put to a flat surface, not a rack, to crisp.

Nutrition Information

- Calories: 60 calories;
- Saturated Fat: 1
- Sugar: 5
- Protein: 1
- Total Fat: 2
- Sodium: 46
- Fiber: 0
- Cholesterol: 2
- Total Carbohydrate: 11

818. Lemon Cream Sandwich Cookies

Serving: Makes about 24 cookies | Prep: | Cook: | Ready in:

Ingredients

- 1 1/2 tablespoons finely grated lemon peel
- 1/8 teaspoon salt
- 1/2 cup (1 stick) unsalted butter, at room temperature
- 2 cups (packed) powdered sugar
- 1/2 cup fresh lemon juice
- 1 tablespoon finely grated lemon peel
- 3 3/4 cups all purpose flour
- 1 teaspoon salt
- 1/2 teaspoon baking soda
- 1 cup (2 sticks) unsalted butter, room temperature
- 1 1/2 cups sugar
- 2 large eggs
- 2 large egg yolks

Direction

- Preparing filling: Mash salt and lemon peel in medium bowl to form paste using back of spoon. Add butter; beat till fluffy using electric mixer. Add sugar in 4 batches; beat after every addition till blended.
- Cookies: Boil lemon peel and lemon juice in small saucepan for about 4 minutes till it reduces to 2 tbsp.; put into small bowl. Cool. Sift baking soda, salt and flour into medium bowl.
- Beat butter using electric mixer till fluffy in a big bowl. Add sugar; beat till blended. One by one, beat in eggs; beat in yolks, then beat in the lemon juice mixture. Add the dry ingredients; mix to blend well. Cover the dough; chill for at least 4 hours up to1 day till firm.
- Preheat an oven to 375°F. Line parchment paper on 2 baking sheets. Roll out 1/3 dough to scant 3/8-in. thick on lightly floured surface. Cut out cookies with 2-in. round cutter. Put cookies on prepped baking sheets; bake cookies one sheet at a time for about 12 minutes till golden at edges. Cool cookies for 5 minutes. Put onto racks; fully cool. Repeat with leftover dough.
- Spread flat side of a cookie with 2 tsp. filling; put another cookie over, flat side down. To create more sandwich cookies, repeat process. You can make it 2 days ahead; keep airtight in the fridge.

Nutrition Information

- Calories: 272
- Sodium: 144 mg(6%)
- Fiber: 1 g(2%)
- Total Carbohydrate: 38 g(13%)

- Cholesterol: 61 mg(20%)
- Protein: 3 g(6%)
- Total Fat: 12 g(19%)
- Saturated Fat: 8 g(38%)

819. Lemon Lime Butter Cookies

Serving: 3-1/2 dozen. | Prep: 20mins | Cook: 20mins | Ready in:

Ingredients

- 3/4 cup butter, softened
- 1 cup confectioners' sugar
- 3 tablespoons grated lime zest
- 1 tablespoon grated lemon zest
- 1/4 cup lemon juice
- 2 cups all-purpose flour

Direction

- Whisk confectioners' sugar and butter in a small bowl until blended. Whisk in lemon juice and citrus zest. Whisk in flour gradually.
- Form into a disk; use plastic to wrap. Chill in the fridge for 2 hours or until firm enough for you to roll.
- Set the oven to 325° and start preheating. Roll dough to 1/8-in. thickness on a lightly floured surface. Use a floured 2-in. round cookie cutter to cut. Arrange on clean and dry baking sheets, an inch apart.
- Bake until it turns light brown on edges or for 16-19 minutes. Take out of pan and place on wire racks to cool.

Nutrition Information

- Calories:
- Protein:
- Total Fat:
- Sodium:
- Fiber:
- Total Carbohydrate:
- Cholesterol:

820. Lemony Bonbon Cookies

Serving: 2 dozen. | Prep: 15mins | Cook: 15mins | Ready in:

Ingredients

- 1/2 cup butter, softened
- 1/3 cup confectioners' sugar
- 1 tablespoon lemon juice
- 3/4 cup all-purpose flour
- 1/3 cup cornstarch
- 24 pecan halves
- ICING:
- 1-1/4 cups confectioners' sugar
- 1-1/2 teaspoons butter, softened
- 3 to 4 teaspoons lemon juice

Direction

- Cream confectioners' sugar and butter together in a small bowl until fluffy and light, then beat in lemon juice. Mix together cornstarch and flour, then put into the creamed mixture gradually and blend well. Place a cover and refrigerate about 2 hours.
- Form the dough into balls 1 inch in size. On 2 ungreased baking sheets, arrange pecan halves, then place a dough ball on top of each pecan half and use the bottom of a small glass to flatten.
- Bake about 14-16 minutes at 350 degrees, until set. Transfer to wire racks and allow to cool thoroughly.
- To make icing, mix together butter, confectioners' sugar and enough amount of lemon juice to obtain spreading consistency, then spread icing over cookies. Allow to stand until set.

Nutrition Information

- Calories: 97 calories
- Sodium: 29mg sodium
- Fiber: 0 fiber)
- Total Carbohydrate: 13g carbohydrate (8g sugars
- Cholesterol: 11mg cholesterol
- Protein: 1g protein.
- Total Fat: 5g fat (3g saturated fat)

821. Lemony Coconut Bars

Serving: 2 dozen. | Prep: 25mins | Cook: 25mins | Ready in:

Ingredients

- 1/2 cup butter, softened
- 1/2 cup packed light brown sugar
- 1-1/2 cups all-purpose flour
- FILLING:
- 2 large eggs
- 1 cup packed light brown sugar
- 1/2 teaspoon grated lemon peel
- 1/2 teaspoon vanilla extract
- 1/4 teaspoon lemon extract
- 2 tablespoons all-purpose flour
- 1/2 teaspoon baking powder
- 1/4 teaspoon salt
- 1-1/2 cups sweetened shredded coconut
- 1 cup chopped pecans or walnuts
- GLAZE:
- 1 cup confectioners' sugar
- 1 tablespoon butter, melted
- 1/2 teaspoon grated lemon peel
- 3 tablespoons lemon juice

Direction

- Set oven to 350 degrees and start preheating. Beat sugar and butter in a bowl until creamy and light; slowly mix in flour, beating thoroughly.
- Grease a 13x9-inch baking pan and pat mixture onto the bottom of the prepared pan. Bake in preheated oven for 8 to 10 minutes until edges turn golden brown. Place on a wire rack to cool.
- To make filling, cream extracts, lemon peel, brown sugar and eggs until incorporated. Combine salt, baking powder and flour in a small bowl and mix into egg mixture. Fold in pecans and coconut. Layer on top of crust.
- Bake for 17 to 20 minutes until golden browned. Let cool on a wire rack for 10 minutes. In the meantime, mix ingredients for glazing until smooth and sprinkle on top of warm filling. Wait until fully cool before cutting into bars.

Nutrition Information

- Calories: 208 calories
- Protein: 2g protein.
- Total Fat: 10g fat (5g saturated fat)
- Sodium: 96mg sodium
- Fiber: 1g fiber)
- Total Carbohydrate: 29g carbohydrate (21g sugars
- Cholesterol: 27mg cholesterol

822. Lime Christmas Tea Cookies

Serving: about 4 dozen. | Prep: 60mins | Cook: 10mins | Ready in:

Ingredients

- 1 cup butter, softened
- 1/2 cup sugar
- 2 teaspoons grated lime zest
- 1/4 cup lime juice
- 1 teaspoon vanilla extract
- 2-3/4 cups all-purpose flour
- 10 to 12 drops green food coloring
- 3/4 cup finely chopped pistachios
- ICING:
- 3-3/4 to 4 cups confectioners' sugar
- 5 to 6 tablespoons warm water

- 3 tablespoons meringue powder
- Green food coloring, optional

Direction

- Cream the sugar and butter in a big bowl, until it becomes fluffy and light. Beat in the vanilla, lime juice and lime zest. Slowly add the flour and stir it well. Beat in the food coloring, then mix in the pistachios. Put cover and let it chill in the fridge for 4 hours or until it becomes easy to handle.
- Roll out the dough on a surface that's lightly floured to a 1/4-inch thick. Cut it using a 2 1/2-inch tree-shaped cookie cutter that's floured. Put it on the ungreased baking trays and place it 1-inch apart. Let it bake for 8 to 10 minutes at 350 degrees or until it becomes set. Let it cool for 5 minutes prior to taking it out of the pans and transferring to wire racks to fully cool.
- Mix together the meringue powder, water and confectioner's sugar in a big bowl, then beat it on low speed just until combined. Beat it on high until it forms stiff peaks, about 4 to 5 minutes. Split it in half. Tint one part with green color if preferred. Store the unused icing covered with damp cloth all the time. Beat again on high speed if needed to bring back the texture.
- Decorate and frost the cookies as your preference. Allow to stand at room temperature for a couple of hours or until the frosting becomes firm and dry. Keep it in an airtight container.

Nutrition Information

- Calories: 191 calories
- Fiber: 1g fiber)
- Total Carbohydrate: 22g carbohydrate (9g sugars
- Cholesterol: 24mg cholesterol
- Protein: 3g protein.
- Total Fat: 11g fat (6g saturated fat)
- Sodium: 104mg sodium

823. Linzer Cookies

Serving: 16 | Prep: 20mins | Cook: 35mins | Ready in:

Ingredients

- DOUGH:
- 1 1/2 cups all-purpose flour
- 3/4 teaspoon baking powder
- 1/2 teaspoon salt
- 5/8 cup butter
- 1/2 cup brown sugar
- 1 teaspoon ground cinnamon
- 1 tablespoon lemon zest
- 1 egg
- 1 teaspoon vanilla extract
- 1 cup finely chopped almonds
- FILLING:
- 1/4 cup chopped dried apricots
- 1/2 cup apricot preserves
- 2 teaspoons lemon juice
- GLAZE:
- 1 egg white
- 2 tablespoons finely chopped almonds
- 1 tablespoon coarse granulated sugar

Direction

- Sift salt, baking powder and flour together; set aside. Cream cinnamon, brown sugar and butter together in a medium bowl until fluffy and light. Mix in vanilla, egg and lemon zest; stir in a cup of chopped almonds then combine with the sifted ingredients. Press two-thirds of the dough on a parchment-lined or greased 8-by-8-inch baking pan. Roll the remaining dough to an 8-in square in the middle of two waxed paper sheets. Place all of the dough for at least 2 hours in the refrigerator.
- Meanwhile, put apricots in a small pot; pour in water to cover. Boil and cook for 3 minutes. Take off the heat then let it sit to cool. Drain the excess liquid from the apricots then combine with lemon juice and preserves.
- Preheat the oven to 175°C or 350°Fahrenheit. Evenly spread the apricot filling on top of the

chilled crust, keeping a quarter-inch border on the sides. Slice the chilled dough square to half-inch strips. Make a lattice design on top of the filling using the strips. Trim the corners to fit then push the edges on the border. Brush egg white then sprinkle coarse sugar and the remaining chopped almonds on top.
- Bake in the preheated oven for 15-20 minutes until the crust is golden brown and the filling is bubbly. Completely cool then slice into squares.

Nutrition Information

- Calories: 228 calories;
- Total Fat: 13.4
- Sodium: 154
- Total Carbohydrate: 24.5
- Cholesterol: 31
- Protein: 4.5

824. Macadamia Almond Delights

Serving: 4 dozen. | Prep: 15mins | Cook: 15mins | Ready in:

Ingredients

- 2/3 cup butter, softened
- 2/3 cup shortening
- 1 cup sugar
- 1 cup packed brown sugar
- 2 eggs
- 2 teaspoons vanilla extract
- 1 cup almond paste
- 3 cups plus 3 tablespoons all-purpose flour
- 1 teaspoon baking soda
- 1 teaspoon salt
- 1-1/2 cups macadamia nuts, chopped
- 1 package (11 ounces) vanilla or white chips

Direction

- Beat sugar, shortening and butter in a big bowl until fluffy and light. Whisk in 1 egg at a time until completely blended before adding another one. Mix in almond paste and vanilla. Mix the salt, baking soda and flour together, mix them little by little into creamed mixture until well combined. Mix in chips and nuts.
- Drop by heaping tablespoonfuls 2 inch away from each other on uncoated baking trays. Set oven at 350°F and bake until they turns light brown, about 12 to 15 minutes. Take to wire racks and let cool.

Nutrition Information

- Calories: 401 calories
- Sodium: 246mg sodium
- Fiber: 2g fiber)
- Total Carbohydrate: 43g carbohydrate (19g sugars
- Cholesterol: 34mg cholesterol
- Protein: 5g protein.
- Total Fat: 24g fat (8g saturated fat)

825. Macadamia Coffee Bean Cookies

Serving: about 2-1/2 dozen. | Prep: 20mins | Cook: 10mins | Ready in:

Ingredients

- 1 package (17-1/2 ounces) double chocolate chunk cookie mix
- 1 large egg
- 1/4 cup canola oil
- 2 tablespoons water
- 1-1/2 cups chocolate-covered coffee beans, finely chopped
- 1 cup macadamia nuts, chopped

Direction

- Whip the water, oil, egg and cookie mix in a big bowl until combined. Mix in coffee beans and nuts.
- Put by tablespoonfuls 2 in. apart onto baking trays that are greased. Bake for 8-10 minutes at 375° or until firm. Take out to wire racks to cool. Put in an airtight container to store.

Nutrition Information

- Calories: 148 calories
- Sodium: 82mg sodium
- Fiber: 1g fiber)
- Total Carbohydrate: 17g carbohydrate (8g sugars
- Cholesterol: 7mg cholesterol
- Protein: 2g protein.
- Total Fat: 9g fat (2g saturated fat)

826. Magic Stars

Serving: about 2-1/2 dozen. | Prep: 20mins | Cook: 10mins | Ready in:

Ingredients

- 1 cup refrigerated Holiday Cookie Dough
- 3/4 cup sweetened shredded coconut, toasted
- 1/2 cup graham cracker crumbs
- 1/2 cup miniature semisweet chocolate chips
- 1/4 cup sweetened condensed milk
- Additional miniature semisweet chocolate chips, optional

Direction

- Allow cookie dough to stand at room temperature to soften, about 5 to 10 minutes. Mix together milk, chocolate chips, cracker crumbs, coconut and dough in a big bowl. Place a cover and chill until easy to handle, about an hour.
- Roll dough on a surface floured lightly to the thickness of 1/8 inch. Use a 3-inch star-shaped cookie cutter that floured to cut.
- Arrange on baking sheets coated with cooking spray with 1 inch apart. Bake at 350 degrees until edges are browned slightly, about 8 to 10 minutes. Allow to cool about 2 minutes before moving to wire racks.
- Melt additional chocolate chips if you want frosting, stir until smooth. Frost cooled cookies.

Nutrition Information

- Calories: 71 calories
- Protein: 1g protein. Diabetic Exchanges: 1 fat
- Total Fat: 4g fat (3g saturated fat)
- Sodium: 40mg sodium
- Fiber: 0 fiber)
- Total Carbohydrate: 8g carbohydrate (5g sugars
- Cholesterol: 7mg cholesterol

827. Maple Macadamia Nut Cookies

Serving: About 4-1/2 dozen. | Prep: 20mins | Cook: 10mins | Ready in:

Ingredients

- 1-1/4 cups butter, softened
- 1-1/2 cups confectioners' sugar
- 1 egg
- 2 tablespoons maple flavoring
- 1 teaspoon vanilla extract
- 2 cups all-purpose flour
- 1 teaspoon baking soda
- 1 teaspoon cream of tartar
- 2 cups quick-cooking oats
- 3/4 cup white baking chips
- 3/4 cup milk chocolate chips
- 3/4 cup chopped macadamia nuts
- MAPLE ICING:
- 1-1/2 cups confectioners' sugar
- 1/4 cup heavy whipping cream
- 3 teaspoons maple flavoring

- 1 teaspoon vanilla extract
- 1/8 teaspoon salt

Direction

- Beat butter with confectioners' sugar in a big bowl. Mix in the vanilla, maple flavoring and egg. Mix the cream of tartar, baking soda and flour together; add them little by little to the creamed mixture. Mix in nuts, chips and oats,
- Grease baking sheets. Drop by heaping teaspoonfuls 2 inches apart from another on the prepared baking sheets. Set oven at 350° and start baking until cookies turn light brown, or for 10 to 12 minutes. Take them to wire racks and let cool. Mix icing ingredients together in a bowl until smooth. Drizzle icing on top of cookies. Keep in the fridge

Nutrition Information

- Calories: 278 calories
- Protein: 3g protein.
- Total Fat: 16g fat (8g saturated fat)
- Sodium: 165mg sodium
- Fiber: 1g fiber)
- Total Carbohydrate: 30g carbohydrate (15g sugars
- Cholesterol: 36mg cholesterol

828. Maple Walnut Biscotti

Serving: 20 | Prep: 20mins | Cook: 40mins | Ready in:

Ingredients

- Biscotti:
- 3 1/2 cups all-purpose flour
- 1 teaspoon baking powder
- 1/2 teaspoon salt
- 1/2 cup butter, softened
- 1/2 cup white sugar
- 2 eggs
- 1/2 cup maple syrup
- 1 teaspoon maple extract
- 1 cup chopped walnuts
- Maple Glaze:
- 1 tablespoon melted butter
- 1/4 cup maple syrup
- 3/4 cup confectioners' sugar

Direction

- Preheat oven to 350 °F (175 °C). On a baking sheet, line with parchment paper.
- In a bowl, sift salt, baking powder, and flour together.
- In a large bowl, beat softened butter and sugar using an electric mixer until smooth. Beat into butter mixture with one egg until blended completely, then beat in maple extract, half a cup maple syrup, and the rest of egg. Stir flour mixture into butter mixture just till dough forms; fold in walnuts just till combined.
- Split dough in half. Form each portion of dough into a log the length of a baking sheet; and on the prepared baking sheet, place the dough. Flatten each log into a rectangle of 1-inch tall and 3-inch wide.
- In the preheated oven, bake for approximately 30 minutes until slightly cracked on top and browned lightly on the bottom. Take out of the oven to cool for nearly 15 minutes, but still keep oven on.
- Diagonally slice logs into thick slices of half an inch; and on the baking sheet, lay slices on their sides.
- In the preheated oven, bake biscotti for around 8 minutes until crisp on the outside and browned lightly. Take out of the oven; allow a few minutes for cooling.
- In a bowl, stir 1/4 cup maple syrup and 1 tablespoon melted butter together. Gradually stir confectioners' sugar into the mixture till smooth. Use a spoon to lightly drizzle maple glaze over warm biscotti.

Nutrition Information

- Calories: 239 calories;
- Sodium: 128

- Total Carbohydrate: 35
- Cholesterol: 32
- Protein: 3.8
- Total Fat: 9.7

829. Mayan Chocolate Biscotti

Serving: 2 dozen. | Prep: 35mins | Cook: 40mins | Ready in:

Ingredients

- 1/2 cup butter, softened
- 3/4 cup sugar
- 2 large eggs
- 1-1/2 teaspoons coffee liqueur
- 1-1/2 teaspoons vanilla extract
- 2 cups all-purpose flour
- 1-1/2 teaspoons ground ancho chili pepper
- 1/2 teaspoon baking soda
- 1/2 teaspoon baking powder
- 1/2 teaspoon ground cinnamon
- 1/8 teaspoon salt
- 1-1/2 cups chopped pecans
- 1 cup (6 ounces) semisweet chocolate chips
- 1 ounce 53% cacao dark baking chocolate, grated

Direction

- Cream sugar and butter in a large bowl until fluffy and light. Place in the eggs, one at a time, and beat thoroughly well after every addition. Mix in vanilla and coffee liqueur. Mix salt, cinnamon, baking powder, baking soda, chili pepper and flour. Gradually transfer to the creamed mixture and combine thoroughly. Mix in grated chocolate, chocolate chips and pecans.
- Divide the dough in half. Form each half into a 10x2-inch rectangle onto a baking sheet that is not greased. Bake for about 20 to 25 minutes at 350° or until lightly browned and set.
- Put the pans onto wire racks. Once cooled enough to handle, place onto cutting board and slice diagonally into 3/4-inch pieces using a serrated knife. Transfer onto ungreased baking sheets with the cut side down.
- Bake for about 8 to 10 minutes per side or until turned golden brown. Transfer to wire racks and cool completely. Keep in an airtight container.

Nutrition Information

- Calories: 191 calories
- Sodium: 81mg sodium
- Fiber: 1g fiber)
- Total Carbohydrate: 21g carbohydrate (11g sugars
- Cholesterol: 28mg cholesterol
- Protein: 3g protein.
- Total Fat: 12g fat (4g saturated fat)

830. Midnight Moon Pies

Serving: 2 dozen. | Prep: 20mins | Cook: 10mins | Ready in:

Ingredients

- 2/3 cup dark chocolate chips
- 1/2 cup butter, cubed
- 2 cups all-purpose flour
- 2/3 cup sugar
- 1/3 cup packed brown sugar
- 1/4 cup baking cocoa
- 1/2 teaspoon baking soda
- 1/4 teaspoon salt
- 1 egg, beaten
- 1/2 cup buttermilk
- 1 teaspoon vanilla extract
- 1/4 teaspoon almond extract
- FILLING:
- 2/3 cup dark chocolate chips
- 1/4 cup butter, cubed
- 4 ounces cream cheese, softened
- 1 jar (7 ounces) marshmallow creme
- 1/4 teaspoon almond extract

- 1 cup miniature semisweet chocolate chips

Direction

- Melt butter and chocolate chips in microwave; mix till smooth then cool.
- Mix salt, baking soda, cocoa, sugars and flour in big bowl. Mix cooled chocolate mixture, extracts, buttermilk and egg; add to dry ingredients. Beat till batter is just moist, it will be very thick.
- Drop with small scoop/ by tablespoonfuls on parchment paper-lined baking sheets, 2-in. apart.
- Bake for 8-10 minutes till edges set at 350°; cool for 2 minutes. Transfer from pans onto wire racks; completely cool.
- Filling: Melt butter and chocolate chips; mix till smooth. Cool. Beat almond extract, marshmallow crème and cream cheese till smooth in small bowl; beat cooled chocolate mixture in. Spread 1 heaping tsp. filling on bottoms of 1/2 of the cookies; top using leftover cookies.
- In mini chocolate chips, roll sides of cookies; keep in the fridge.

Nutrition Information

- Calories: 279 calories
- Fiber: 1g fiber)
- Total Carbohydrate: 37g carbohydrate (25g sugars
- Cholesterol: 29mg cholesterol
- Protein: 3g protein.
- Total Fat: 14g fat (9g saturated fat)
- Sodium: 122mg sodium

831. Mini Baklava

Serving: about 2-1/2 dozen. | Prep: 20mins | Cook: 10mins | Ready in:

Ingredients

- 1/2 cup butter
- 1/4 cup sugar
- 1 teaspoon ground cinnamon
- 1 cup finely chopped pecans
- 1 cup finely chopped walnuts
- 2 packages (1.90 ounces each) frozen miniature phyllo tart shells
- Honey

Direction

- Preheat an oven to 350°. Melt butter in a small saucepan on medium heat; mix in cinnamon and sugar. Boil. Lower heat. Add walnuts and pecans, tossing to cover; simmer, with no cover, for 5-10 minutes till nuts are toasted lightly.
- Put phyllo shells onto parchment paper-lined baking sheet. Evenly scoop butter sauce and nut mixture into shells; bake for 9-11 minutes till golden brown. Cool fully on pan onto wire rack. Into each shell, drizzle a honey drop; stand till serving, with cover. If desired, serve with extra honey.

Nutrition Information

- Calories: 105 calories
- Total Carbohydrate: 5g carbohydrate (2g sugars
- Cholesterol: 8mg cholesterol
- Protein: 1g protein.
- Total Fat: 9g fat (2g saturated fat)
- Sodium: 33mg sodium
- Fiber: 1g fiber)

832. Mini Cinnamon Roll Cookies

Serving: about 2-1/2 dozen. | Prep: 60mins | Cook: 10mins | Ready in:

Ingredients

- 1 cup butter, softened
- 1-3/4 cups sugar, divided
- 3 large egg yolks
- 1 tablespoon plus 1 teaspoon honey, divided
- 1 teaspoon vanilla extract
- 2-1/2 cups all-purpose flour
- 1 teaspoon baking powder
- 1/2 teaspoon salt
- 1/2 teaspoon cream of tartar
- 1 tablespoon ground cinnamon
- 8 ounces white baking chocolate, chopped

Direction

- Cream 1 1/4 cups sugar and butter till fluffy and light in a big bowl. Beat vanilla, 1 tablespoon honey and egg yolks in. Mix cream of tartar, baking powder, salt and flour. Add to creamed mixture slowly; stir well.
- Form a heaping tablespoonful dough to 6-in. log. Mix leftover sugar and cinnamon in shallow bowl. Roll the log in cinnamon sugar. Coil log loosely to spiral shape; put on greased baking sheet and repeat, putting cookies 1-in. apart then sprinkle leftover cinnamon sugar on.
- Bake till set or for 8-10 minutes at 350°. Transfer to wire racks; completely cool. Melt leftover honey and baking chocolate in small bowl; mix till smooth. Drizzle on cookies. Stand till set. Keep in airtight container.

Nutrition Information

- Calories: 189 calories
- Sodium: 105mg sodium
- Fiber: 0 fiber)
- Total Carbohydrate: 25g carbohydrate (17g sugars
- Cholesterol: 38mg cholesterol
- Protein: 2g protein.
- Total Fat: 9g fat (6g saturated fat)

833. Mint Chocolate Snaps

Serving: about 6 dozen. | Prep: 20mins | Cook: 15mins | Ready in:

Ingredients

- 1 cup (6 ounces) semisweet chocolate chips
- 1/2 cup plus 1-1/2 tablespoons shortening
- 3/4 cup sugar
- 1 egg
- 1/4 cup light corn syrup
- 1 teaspoon peppermint extract
- 1 teaspoon vanilla extract
- 2 cups all-purpose flour
- 1 teaspoon baking soda
- 1/4 teaspoon salt
- 1/4 cup crushed peppermint candy
- Additional sugar

Direction

- Melt chocolate chips in a double boiler. Put off the heat. Beat shortening until creamed in a large bowl. Slowly add sugar, beating until light and fluffy. Add melted chocolate; beat well. Add extracts, corn syrup, and egg; stir well.
- Mix together salt, baking soda, and flour; mix into batter. Fold candy into the mixture. Form mixture into 1-inch balls and roll in sugar. Arrange in ungreased baking sheets, keeping a distance of 3 inches between each ball.
- Bake for 12 to 15 minutes at 350°. Allow to cool for 5 minutes before transferring cookies to a wire rack.

Nutrition Information

- Calories: 50 calories
- Protein: 1g protein.
- Total Fat: 2g fat (1g saturated fat)
- Sodium: 26mg sodium
- Fiber: 0 fiber)
- Total Carbohydrate: 7g carbohydrate (4g sugars
- Cholesterol: 2mg cholesterol

834. Mint Chocolate Wafers

Serving: 10 dozen. | Prep: 60mins | Cook: 10mins | Ready in:

Ingredients

- 1 large egg
- 1/3 cup water
- 3 tablespoons canola oil
- 1 package chocolate fudge cake mix (regular size)
- 1/2 cup cake flour
- COATING:
- 4 cups (24 ounces) semisweet chocolate chips
- 1/4 cup shortening
- 1/2 teaspoon peppermint extract
- Sprinkles

Direction

- Beat oil, water and egg until mixed in a big bowl. Beat in flour and cake mix gradually.
- Halve the dough. Form each into a disk then wrap with plastic. Put in the refrigerator until it becomes firm enough to roll or for 2 hours.
- Heat the oven beforehand to 350 degrees. Roll each portion of the dough, making 1/8-inch thickness on a lightly floured surface. Cut the dough using a 1 1/2-inch floured round cookie cutter. Put on baking sheets with grease, leaving 1 inch space apart.
- Bake it until it becomes firm or for 8 to 10 minutes. Allow to completely cool by transferring to wire racks from pans.
- Melt shortening and chocolate chips in top of a double broiler or a metal bowl over hot water. Mix until it becomes smooth. Mix extract in. Spread chocolate mixture on the cookies. Put on baking sheets lined with waxed paper then use sprinkles to decorate. Keep in the refrigerator until set.

Nutrition Information

- Calories:
- Sodium:
- Fiber:
- Total Carbohydrate:
- Cholesterol:
- Protein:
- Total Fat:

835. Minty Meringue Drops

Serving: about 2-1/2 dozen. | Prep: 20mins | Cook: 30mins | Ready in:

Ingredients

- 2 egg whites
- 1/4 teaspoon cream of tartar
- 3/4 cup sugar
- 1/8 teaspoon vanilla extract
- 2 to 6 drops green food coloring, optional
- 1 package (10 ounces) mint chocolate chips

Direction

- Coat baking sheets lightly with grease or use parchment paper to line them, then put aside.
- Beat egg whites in a big bowl until foamy. Put in cream of tartar while beating until forming soft peaks. Beat in 1 tbsp. of sugar at a time gradually, until forming stiff peaks. Beat in food coloring and vanilla, if wanted. Stir in chocolate chips.
- Drop on prepped baking sheets with rounded tablespoonfuls of mixture, spaced 2 inches apart. Bake at 250 degrees until dry to the touch, about 30 to 35 minutes. Transfer to wire racks to cool then keep in an airtight container.

Nutrition Information

- Calories: 134 calories
- Total Fat: 5g fat (3g saturated fat)
- Sodium: 7mg sodium

- Fiber: 1g fiber)
- Total Carbohydrate: 22g carbohydrate (20g sugars
- Cholesterol: 0 cholesterol
- Protein: 0 protein.

836. Mocha Butterscotch Cookies

Serving: 40 cookies. | Prep: 20mins | Cook: 10mins | Ready in:

Ingredients

- 1 package (12 ounces) dark chocolate chips
- 2 tablespoons butter
- 2 tablespoons instant coffee granules
- 3 eggs
- 1 cup sugar
- 1/4 cup packed brown sugar
- 2 teaspoons vanilla extract
- 3/4 cup all-purpose flour
- 1 teaspoon baking powder
- 1/2 teaspoon salt
- 1 cup butterscotch chips

Direction

- Heat coffee granules, butter and chocolate chips in a small saucepan to dissolve coffee, and melt butter and chocolate; put aside and allow to cool.
- Beat sugars and eggs in a big bowl to form a light mixture. Put in chocolate mixture and vanilla; mix until smooth. Mix together salt, baking powder and flour; blend into the egg mixture until combined. Mix in butterscotch chips and you will have a sticky dough.
- Scoop by heaping tablespoonfuls of dough and place 2 inches apart onto baking sheets lined with parchment paper. Bake in 325-degree oven until edges set and the center remains lightly soft texture (cookies will look cracked). Transfer to a wire rack. Keep in a tightly sealed container to store.

Nutrition Information

- Calories: 122 calories
- Total Carbohydrate: 17g carbohydrate (10g sugars
- Cholesterol: 17mg cholesterol
- Protein: 2g protein.
- Total Fat: 5g fat (4g saturated fat)
- Sodium: 53mg sodium
- Fiber: 0 fiber)

837. Mocha Fudge Cookies

Serving: 18-1/2 dozen. | Prep: 30mins | Cook: 10mins | Ready in:

Ingredients

- 4 cups (24 ounces) semisweet chocolate chips, divided
- 2 cups butter
- 3 cups sugar
- 3 cups packed brown sugar
- 1 cup baking cocoa
- 1 tablespoon instant coffee granules
- 8 eggs, lightly beaten
- 3 tablespoons vanilla extract
- 8 cups all-purpose flour
- 2 teaspoons baking powder
- 1 teaspoon salt
- 1-1/2 cups chopped walnuts

Direction

- Melt butter and 2 cups of chocolate chips in a large microwave-safe bowl; mix till smooth. Combine the coffee, cocoa and sugars; add them into the chocolate mixture. Mix the vanilla and eggs into the mixture. Combine the salt, baking powder and flour; add them into the chocolate mixture slowly and combine thoroughly. Mix in the remaining chocolate chips and walnuts.

- On ungreased baking sheets, drop rounded teaspoonfuls of the dough 2 in. apart. Bake till edges are set at 350° or for 10-11 minutes. Transfer to wire racks to cool down.

Nutrition Information

- Calories: 153 calories
- Sodium: 70mg sodium
- Fiber: 1g fiber)
- Total Carbohydrate: 23g carbohydrate (15g sugars
- Cholesterol: 24mg cholesterol
- Protein: 2g protein.
- Total Fat: 7g fat (3g saturated fat)

838. Mocha Nut Balls

Serving: 4-1/2 dozen. | Prep: 20mins | Cook: 15mins | Ready in:

Ingredients

- 1 cup butter, softened
- 1/2 cup sugar
- 2 teaspoons vanilla extract
- 1-3/4 cups all-purpose flour
- 1/3 cup baking cocoa
- 1 tablespoon instant coffee granules
- 1 cup finely chopped pecans or walnuts
- Confectioners' sugar

Direction

- Turn the oven to 325° to preheat. Cream sugar and butter together in a big bowl until fluffy and light. Whisk in vanilla. Mix coffee granules, cocoa, and flour together in a separate bowl; slowly whisk into the creamed mixture. Mix in pecans. Form the dough into 1-inch balls; put on non-oiled cookie sheets, 2 inches separately.
- Bake until set, 14-16 minutes. Leave in the pans to cool for 1-2 minutes. In confectioners' sugar, roll the warm cookies. Put on wire racks to cool.

Nutrition Information

- Calories: 69 calories
- Total Fat: 5g fat (2g saturated fat)
- Sodium: 24mg sodium
- Fiber: 0 fiber)
- Total Carbohydrate: 6g carbohydrate (2g sugars
- Cholesterol: 9mg cholesterol
- Protein: 1g protein. Diabetic Exchanges: 1 fat

839. Mocha Pecan Butter Balls

Serving: 4 dozen. | Prep: 15mins | Cook: 15mins | Ready in:

Ingredients

- 2/3 cup butter, softened
- 3 ounces cream cheese, softened
- 1/3 cup confectioners' sugar
- 2 teaspoons vanilla extract
- 1-3/4 cups all-purpose flour
- 2/3 cup instant chocolate drink mix
- 1 teaspoon instant coffee granules
- 1/4 teaspoon salt
- 1 cup finely chopped pecans
- Additional confectioners' sugar

Direction

- Cream confectioners' sugar, cream cheese and butter till fluffy and light in a big bowl; beat in vanilla. Mix salt, coffee granules, drink mix and flour. Add to creamed mixture slowly; mix well. Mix in pecans; cover. Refrigerate till easy to handle or for 1 hour.
- Roll to 1-in. balls; put on ungreased baking sheets, 1-in. apart. Bake at 350° till firm or for 15-18 minutes; cool for 1-2 minutes on pan. In

confectioners' sugar, roll warm cookies; cool on wire racks.

Nutrition Information

- Calories: 172 calories
- Sodium: 111mg sodium
- Fiber: 1g fiber)
- Total Carbohydrate: 20g carbohydrate (11g sugars
- Cholesterol: 18mg cholesterol
- Protein: 2g protein.
- Total Fat: 10g fat (4g saturated fat)

---

840. Molasses Cookie Mix

Serving: about 4 dozen per batch. | Prep: 10mins | Cook: 0mins | Ready in:

Ingredients

- 6 cups all-purpose flour
- 3 cups sugar
- 1 tablespoon baking soda
- 1 tablespoon baking powder
- 1 tablespoon ground ginger
- 1 tablespoon ground cinnamon
- 1-1/2 teaspoons ground nutmeg
- 3/4 teaspoon ground cloves
- 1/2 teaspoon ground allspice
- ADDITIONAL INGREDIENTS (for each batch):
- 3/4 cup butter, softened
- 1 egg
- 1/4 cup molasses
- Additional sugar

Direction

- Mix the initial 9 ingredients in a big bowl. Distribute into 3 batches; keep in a dry, cool place in airtight containers for up to 6 months. Makes a total of 9 cups for 3 batches.

- For cookies: preheat the oven to 375°. Cream butter in a big bowl till fluffy and light. Put the molasses and egg; combine thoroughly. Put 3 cups of the cookie mix; whisk till smooth.
- Form into an-inch rounds and turn in sugar. On unoiled baking sheets, set 2-inch away. Allow to bake for 9 to 11 minutes or till top cracks and edges are firm. Let cool on wire racks.

Nutrition Information

- Calories: 67 calories
- Protein: 1g protein.
- Total Fat: 3g fat (1g saturated fat)
- Sodium: 70mg sodium
- Fiber: 0 fiber)
- Total Carbohydrate: 9g carbohydrate (5g sugars
- Cholesterol: 4mg cholesterol

---

841. Molasses Sugar Cookies

Serving: 72 | Prep: 25mins | Cook: 15mins | Ready in:

Ingredients

- 1 1/2 cups shortening
- 2 cups white sugar
- 1/2 cup molasses
- 2 eggs
- 4 cups all-purpose flour
- 4 teaspoons baking soda
- 2 teaspoons ground cinnamon
- 1 teaspoon ground cloves
- 1 teaspoon ground ginger
- 1 teaspoon salt

Direction

- In a big pan, liquify the shortening on stove, and allow to cool.
- Put the molasses, eggs and sugar, whisk thoroughly.

- Sift the dry ingredients together in another bowl and put to pan. Combine thoroughly and refrigerate for 3 hours or overnight.
- Shape into walnut-size rounds. Roll in granulated sugar. On oiled cookie sheet, put approximately 2-inch away.
- Allow to bake for 8 to 10 minutes at 190°C or 375°F.
- Keep in an airtight container to prevent from becoming too crisp. In case they lose the softness. Put a fresh bread slice in the container with cookies for a couple of hours up or overnight to make them soft once more.

Nutrition Information

- Calories: 93 calories;
- Total Fat: 4.5
- Sodium: 105
- Total Carbohydrate: 12.7
- Cholesterol: 5
- Protein: 0.9

842. Mom's Old Fashioned Cutouts

Serving: 5 dozen. | Prep: 50mins | Cook: 10mins | Ready in:

Ingredients

- 1 cup butter, softened
- 1-1/2 cups sugar
- 1 large egg
- 1/2 cup sour cream
- 1 teaspoon vanilla extract
- 4 cups all-purpose flour, sifted
- 1 teaspoon baking powder
- 1/2 teaspoon baking soda
- 1/2 teaspoon salt
- 1/2 teaspoon ground cinnamon or ground nutmeg
- 2 cups confectioners' sugar
- 1 teaspoon vanilla extract
- 1/4 teaspoon salt
- 3 to 4 tablespoons heavy whipping cream
- Food coloring, optional

Direction

- Cream butter with sugar in a big bowl until fluffy and light. Whip in the egg, sour cream and vanilla. Combine the cinnamon, salt, baking soda, baking powder and flour in a separate bowl; whip into creamed mixture gradually.
- Spit dough into 3 portions. Roll each into a disk; cover in plastic. Chill for 30 minutes or until easy to handle.
- Shape each portion of dough to 1/4-in. thickness on a lightly floured surface. Slice with a floured 3-in. cookie cutter. Put 2 in. apart on greased baking trays.
- Bake for 10-12 minutes at 350° or until slightly browned. Take out to wire racks to cool completely.
- Combine the salt, vanilla, confectioners' sugar and enough cream to reach desired consistency in a small bowl. Dye with food coloring (optional). Garnish cookies as preferred.

Nutrition Information

- Calories:
- Sodium:
- Fiber:
- Total Carbohydrate:
- Cholesterol:
- Protein:
- Total Fat:

843. Mom's Soft Raisin Cookies

Serving: 6 dozen. | Prep: 25mins | Cook: 15mins | Ready in:

Ingredients

- 1 cup water
- 2 cups raisins
- 1 cup shortening
- 1-3/4 cups sugar
- 2 large eggs
- 1 teaspoon vanilla extract
- 3-1/2 cups all-purpose flour
- 1 teaspoon baking powder
- 1 teaspoon baking soda
- 1 teaspoon salt
- 1/2 teaspoon ground cinnamon
- 1/2 teaspoon ground nutmeg
- 1/2 cup chopped walnuts

Direction

- Mix in small saucepan with raisins and water; boil. Let cook for three minutes; take off heat and cool, avoid draining.
- Preheat the oven to 350°. Cream sugar and shortening in big bowl till fluffy and light. Whip in vanilla and eggs. Mix spices, salt, baking soda, baking powder and flour; slowly put to creamed mixture and combine thoroughly. Mix in raisins and nuts.
- Drop to oiled baking sheets by teaspoonfuls, spacing about 2-inches apart. Bake till golden brown, for 12 to 14 minutes. Transfer onto wire racks to let cool.

Nutrition Information

- Calories: 170 calories
- Fiber: 1g fiber)
- Total Carbohydrate: 26g carbohydrate (15g sugars
- Cholesterol: 12mg cholesterol
- Protein: 2g protein.
- Total Fat: 7g fat (2g saturated fat)
- Sodium: 116mg sodium

844. Nativity Molasses Cookies

Serving: 5 dozen. | Prep: 01hours15mins | Cook: 10mins | Ready in:

Ingredients

- 1/2 cup shortening
- 1/2 cup sugar
- 1 egg yolk
- 1/2 cup water
- 1/2 cup molasses
- 3-1/4 cups all-purpose flour
- 1 teaspoon baking soda
- 1/2 teaspoon salt
- 1/2 teaspoon ground ginger
- 1/2 teaspoon ground cinnamon
- 1/2 teaspoon ground cloves
- ICING:
- 3/4 cup sugar
- 1 egg white
- 1/3 cup water
- 1/8 teaspoon cream of tartar

Direction

- Cream sugar and shortening till fluffy and light in a big bowl; beat in molasses, water and egg yolk. Mix cloves, cinnamon, ginger, salt, baking soda and flour; add to creamed mixture slowly. Stir well; cover. Refrigerate till easy to handle or for 2 hours.
- Roll dough to 1/8-in. thick on a lightly floured surface; use 2 1/2-in. floured Nativity-themed cookie cutters to cut. Put on ungreased baking sheets, 1-in. apart. Bake till edges are firm or for 10-12 minutes at 350°. Put on wire racks; fully cool.
- Mix the icing ingredients in a heavy saucepan placed over low heat. Beat on low speed for a minute using a portable mixer. Keep beating on low heat for 8-10 minutes till the frosting reaches 160°. Put in a small bowl; beat at high speed for 7 minutes till icing makes stiff peaks. Spread on cookies; fully dry.

Nutrition Information

- Calories:
- Protein:
- Total Fat:
- Sodium:
- Fiber:
- Total Carbohydrate:
- Cholesterol:

845. Nice 'n' Soft Sugar Cookies

Serving: about 3 dozen. | Prep: 01hours45mins | Cook: 5mins | Ready in:

Ingredients

- 1 cup butter, softened
- 1-1/2 cups confectioners' sugar
- 1 large egg
- 1-1/2 teaspoons vanilla extract
- 2-1/2 cups self-rising flour
- ICING:
- 2-1/2 cups confectioners' sugar
- 1/4 cup water
- 4 teaspoons meringue powder
- 1/4 cup light corn syrup
- Food coloring of choice
- Colored sugar and sprinkles, optional

Direction

- Cream confectioners' sugar and butter till fluffy and light; whip in vanilla and egg. Slowly whip flour in. Split the dough in half. Encase every dough with plastic; chill till set enough to roll, for about 2 hours.
- Heat an oven to 375°. Form every dough portion on a floured counter into 3/16-inch-thick. Use a 3-inches, floured cookie cutter to cut the dough. Arrange on unoiled baking sheets 2-inches away. Bake for 5 to 7 minutes till set. Cool for 2 minutes on pans; transfer onto wire racks and fully cool.
- Whip water, meringue powder and confectioners' sugar at low speed to blend; whip for 4 minutes on high to form soft peaks. Put in the corn syrup; whip for a minute.
- Color using food coloring as preferred. Always use damp cloth to keep unused icing covered; if need be, whip once more on high speed to bring back the texture. Spread or pipe icing over cookies; jazz up as wished. Allow to dry.

Nutrition Information

- Calories: 138 calories
- Sodium: 150mg sodium
- Fiber: 0 fiber)
- Total Carbohydrate: 22g carbohydrate (15g sugars
- Cholesterol: 19mg cholesterol
- Protein: 1g protein.
- Total Fat: 5g fat (3g saturated fat)

846. No Bake Cookie Butter Blossoms

Serving: about 2-1/2 dozen. | Prep: 25mins | Cook: 0mins | Ready in:

Ingredients

- 1 cup Biscoff creamy cookie spread
- 1/2 cup corn syrup
- 3 cups Rice Krispies
- 32 milk chocolate kisses

Direction

- Mix corn syrup and cookie spread in a large saucepan. Cook while stirring until blended over low heat. Take out of the heat; stir in Rice Krispies until coated. Form level tablespoons of mixture into balls; arrange onto waxed paper. Press a kiss into center of each cookie immediately. Allow to stand until set.

Nutrition Information

- Calories: 93 calories
- Total Carbohydrate: 14g carbohydrate (10g sugars
- Cholesterol: 1mg cholesterol
- Protein: 1g protein.
- Total Fat: 4g fat (1g saturated fat)
- Sodium: 22mg sodium
- Fiber: 0 fiber)

847. No Bake Peanut Butter Snowballs

Serving: about 8-1/2 dozen. | Prep: 45mins | Cook: 0mins | Ready in:

Ingredients

- 2 cups chunky peanut butter
- 1-1/2 cups heavy whipping cream
- 2 packages (11 ounces each) vanilla wafers, finely crushed
- 1-1/2 cups chopped salted peanuts
- 2 cups confectioners' sugar

Direction

- Beat cream and peanut butter till blended in big bowl; mix peanuts and wafers in slowly.
- Form dough to 1-in. balls then roll in confectioners' sugar; put on waxed paper-lined baking sheets. In confectioners' sugar, reroll balls; refrigerate for 2 hours. Keep between waxed paper pieces in airtight container in fridge. Before serving, reroll in confectioners' sugar if desired.

Nutrition Information

- Calories:
- Protein:
- Total Fat:
- Sodium:
- Fiber:
- Total Carbohydrate:
- Cholesterol:

848. Nut Filled Horns

Serving: 10 dozen. | Prep: 25mins | Cook: 15mins | Ready in:

Ingredients

- 2 cups butter, softened
- 2 packages (8 ounces each) cream cheese, softened
- 2 egg yolks
- 4-1/2 cups all-purpose flour
- 2 teaspoons baking powder
- FILLING:
- 4 cups finely chopped walnuts
- 1-1/2 to 2 cups sugar
- 6 tablespoons evaporated milk
- 1-1/2 teaspoons vanilla extract

Direction

- Cream the cream cheese and butter till fluffy and light in a big bowl; add egg yolks. Mix baking powder and flour. Add to creamed mixture slowly; stir well. Cover; chill overnight.
- Mix filling ingredients, it'll be thick, in a small bowl. Divide dough to fourths; it'll be sticky. Roll each portion out to 12x10-in. rectangle on well-sugared surface; cut to 2-in. squares. Put 1 tsp. filling in middle of every square. Fold over 2 opposing corners; tightly seal.
- Put on ungreased baking sheets, 2-in. apart; bake till lightly browned for 15-18 minutes at 350°. Transfer to wire racks; cool.

Nutrition Information

- Calories: 175 calories

- Total Fat: 12g fat (5g saturated fat)
- Sodium: 88mg sodium
- Fiber: 1g fiber)
- Total Carbohydrate: 13g carbohydrate (5g sugars
- Cholesterol: 28mg cholesterol
- Protein: 4g protein.

849. Nutmeg Meltaways

Serving: about 5 dozen. | Prep: 15mins | Cook: 20mins | Ready in:

Ingredients

- 1 cup butter, softened
- 1/2 cup sugar
- 1 teaspoon vanilla extract
- 2 cups all-purpose flour
- 3/4 cup ground almonds (about 3 ounces), toasted
- 1 cup confectioners' sugar
- 1 tablespoon ground nutmeg

Direction

- Cream vanilla, sugar, and butter together in a big bowl until fluffy and light. Slowly add flour and stir thoroughly. Mix in almonds. Form into 1-inch balls.
- Put on non-oiled cookie sheets, 2 inches apart. Bake at 300° until it turns light brown on the bottoms, 18-20 minutes. Put on wire racks to cool.
- Mix nutmeg and confectioners' sugar together in a shallow bowl. In the sugar mixture, lightly roll the cooled cookies.

Nutrition Information

- Calories: 128 calories
- Sodium: 62mg sodium
- Fiber: 1g fiber)

- Total Carbohydrate: 14g carbohydrate (7g sugars
- Cholesterol: 16mg cholesterol
- Protein: 1g protein.
- Total Fat: 7g fat (4g saturated fat)

850. Nutmeg Sugar Crisps

Serving: about 6 dozen. | Prep: 15mins | Cook: 10mins | Ready in:

Ingredients

- 1 cup butter, softened
- 3/4 cup sugar
- 1/2 cup confectioners' sugar
- 1 egg
- 1 teaspoon vanilla extract
- 2-1/2 cups all-purpose flour
- 1/2 teaspoon baking soda
- 1/2 teaspoon cream of tartar
- 1/4 to 1/2 teaspoon ground nutmeg
- 1/8 teaspoon salt

Direction

- Cream sugars and butter in bowl. Whip in vanilla and egg; combine thoroughly. Mix salt, nutmeg, cream of tartar, baking soda and flour; put into creamed mixture and combine thoroughly. Chill about an hour.
- Form into balls of 3/4-inch; arrange on oiled baking sheets spacing 2-inches apart. Use a glass dipped in sugar to flatten. Bake about 10 to 12 minutes at 350° or till pale brown. Let cool onto wire racks.

Nutrition Information

- Calories: 101 calories
- Protein: 1g protein.
- Total Fat: 5g fat (3g saturated fat)
- Sodium: 79mg sodium
- Fiber: 0 fiber)

- Total Carbohydrate: 13g carbohydrate (6g sugars
- Cholesterol: 20mg cholesterol

851. Nuts About You Cookie Sticks

Serving: about 2-1/2 dozen. | Prep: 5mins | Cook: 5mins | Ready in:

Ingredients

- 1 cup semisweet chocolate chips
- 1 tablespoon shortening
- 2 tablespoons creamy peanut butter
- 1 can (13-1/2 ounces) Pirouette cookies
- 1/2 cup chopped nuts

Direction

- Melt the peanut butter, shortening and chocolate chips in a microwave. Mix until it becomes smooth. Dunk 1 end of each cookie in the chocolate mixture and let the excess drip off. Sprinkle using nuts and put it on waxed paper. Let rest until set.

Nutrition Information

- Calories: 111 calories
- Protein: 1g protein.
- Total Fat: 7g fat (3g saturated fat)
- Sodium: 34mg sodium
- Fiber: 1g fiber)
- Total Carbohydrate: 13g carbohydrate (8g sugars
- Cholesterol: 5mg cholesterol

852. Nutty Chocolate Batons

Serving: 8 dozen. | Prep: 45mins | Cook: 10mins | Ready in:

Ingredients

- 3/4 cup butter, softened
- 1/3 cup sugar
- 1/3 cup almond paste
- 1 large egg yolk
- 1-2/3 cups all-purpose flour
- 1 cup (6 ounces) semisweet chocolate chips
- 1/2 cup pistachios, finely chopped and toasted

Direction

- Cream the almond paste, sugar and butter in a small bowl, until it becomes fluffy and light, then beat in the egg yolk. Slowly add the flour and stir well. Form it into a ball and flatten to a disk. Use plastic to wrap it and let it chill in the fridge for 2 hours or until it becomes easy to handle.
- Split the dough to 8 even portions, then split each portion to 1/2. Roll each 1/2 on a surface that's lightly floured to a 12-inch rope, then slice each rope to two inches length. Put it on the baking trays that was greased and place it 2 inches apart. Let it bake for 6 to 8 minutes at 350 degrees or until the edges turn light brown in color. Transfer to wire racks to fully cool.
- Melt the chocolate chips in the microwave and mix it until it becomes smooth. Dunk the ends of each cookie on the chocolate, then dredge it in the pistachios. Allow to stand on waxed paper until it becomes set. Keep it in an airtight container.

Nutrition Information

- Calories: 39 calories
- Cholesterol: 6mg cholesterol
- Protein: 1g protein. Diabetic Exchanges: 1/2 starch.
- Total Fat: 3g fat (1g saturated fat)
- Sodium: 13mg sodium
- Fiber: 0 fiber)
- Total Carbohydrate: 4g carbohydrate (2g sugars

853. Nutty Maple Cookies

Serving: 3 dozen. | Prep: 35mins | Cook: 10mins | Ready in:

Ingredients

- 2/3 cup butter, softened
- 1/3 cup confectioners' sugar
- 1 tablespoon water
- 1 teaspoon maple flavoring
- 1-3/4 cups all-purpose flour
- 1/2 teaspoon salt
- 1 cup chopped walnuts
- FROSTING:
- 1/4 cup butter, softened
- 1-1/2 cups confectioners' sugar
- 2 tablespoons heavy whipping cream
- 1 teaspoon maple flavoring
- Additional chopped walnuts, optional

Direction

- Cream confectioners' sugar and butter till fluffy and light in a big bowl; beat in flavoring and water. Mix salt and flour. Add to creamed mixture slowly; stir well. Mix in walnuts.
- Roll to 1-in. balls; use a fork to flatten to 1/2-in. thick. Put on ungreased baking sheets, 2-in. apart; bake at 350° till lightly browned or for 10-12 minutes. Cool on wire racks.
- Frosting: Beat flavoring, cream, confectioners' sugar and butter till smooth in a small bowl; frost cookies. If desired, sprinkle extra walnuts.

Nutrition Information

- Calories: 112 calories
- Sodium: 66mg sodium
- Fiber: 0 fiber)
- Total Carbohydrate: 11g carbohydrate (6g sugars
- Cholesterol: 13mg cholesterol
- Protein: 2g protein. Diabetic Exchanges: 1 starch
- Total Fat: 7g fat (3g saturated fat)

854. Oat & Coconut Icebox Cookies

Serving: about 3-1/2 dozen. | Prep: 20mins | Cook: 10mins | Ready in:

Ingredients

- 1/2 cup butter, softened
- 1/2 cup shortening
- 1 cup granulated sugar
- 1 cup packed brown sugar
- 2 large eggs
- 1 teaspoon vanilla extract
- 1-1/2 cups all-purpose flour
- 1 teaspoon baking soda
- 1 teaspoon salt
- 3 cups old-fashioned oats
- 1/2 cup sweetened shredded coconut
- 1/2 cup chopped walnuts

Direction

- Mash sugars, shortening and butter till fluffy and light. Whip in vanilla and eggs. Whip salt, baking soda and flour in a separate bowl; slowly whip into the creamed mixture. Mix in walnuts, coconut and oats.
- Split dough in 2. Form each into a lengthy roll, 10-inch in size. Wrap with plastic; chill to overnight.
- Preheat the oven to 375 °. Remove wrap and slice dough crosswise making half-inch pieces. Put on unoiled baking sheets, 2-inch away. Bake for 8 to 10 minutes, till edges start to brown. Let cool for 2 minutes prior to transferring from pans onto the wire racks.

Nutrition Information

- Calories: 142 calories
- Sodium: 117mg sodium
- Fiber: 1g fiber)
- Total Carbohydrate: 19g carbohydrate (11g sugars
- Cholesterol: 15mg cholesterol
- Protein: 2g protein.
- Total Fat: 7g fat (3g saturated fat)

855. Oatmeal Peanut Butter Chip Cookies

Serving: about 3-1/2 dozen. | Prep: 15mins | Cook: 20mins | Ready in:

Ingredients

- 3/4 cup butter, softened
- 1 cup packed brown sugar
- 1/2 cup sugar
- 2 eggs
- 1 teaspoon vanilla extract
- 3 cups quick-cooking oats
- 1-1/2 cups all-purpose flour
- 1/2 teaspoon baking soda
- 1/4 teaspoon salt
- 3/4 cup raisins
- 3/4 cup peanut butter chips or Reese's pieces

Direction

- Cream sugars and butter till fluffy and light in big bowl; beat vanilla and eggs in. Mix salt, baking soda, flour and oats; add to creamed mixture slowly. Stir well; mix candy and raisins in. By tablespoonfuls, drop on ungreased baking sheets. Cover; freeze.
- Put frozen cookie dough balls in big resealable plastic freezer bag; keeps for up to 3 months, frozen.
- Using: put dough balls on greased baking sheets, 2-in. apart; bake for 18-22 minutes at 350° till golden brown. Transfer to wire racks; cool.

Nutrition Information

- Calories: 348 calories
- Protein: 6g protein.
- Total Fat: 13g fat (8g saturated fat)
- Sodium: 208mg sodium
- Fiber: 2g fiber)
- Total Carbohydrate: 52g carbohydrate (31g sugars
- Cholesterol: 53mg cholesterol

856. Oatmeal Pecan Cookie Mix

Serving: about 3 dozen. | Prep: 15mins | Cook: 0mins | Ready in:

Ingredients

- 1 cup all-purpose flour
- 1/2 cup sugar
- 1/2 teaspoon baking soda
- 1/2 teaspoon baking powder
- 1/2 cup packed brown sugar
- 3/4 cup old-fashioned oats
- 1/2 cup chopped pecans
- 1 cup crisp rice cereal
- ADDITIONAL INGREDIENTS:
- 1/2 cup butter, softened
- 1 egg
- 1 teaspoon vanilla extract

Direction

- Mix baking powder, baking soda, sugar, and flour together in a small bowl. Place rice cereal, pecans, oats, brown sugar, and flour mixture in a 1-quart glass jar, fully packing between each layer. Put the lid on jar and place in a dry, cool place to store for a maximum of 6 months. Yield: 1 batch (approximately 4 cups in total).
- For the cookies: Turn the oven to 350° to preheat. Cream the butter in a big bowl until

fluffy and light. Whisk in vanilla and egg. Slowly pour in the cookie mix.
- Drop on oil-coated cookie sheets by rounded teaspoonfuls, 2-inch separately. Bake until turning golden brown, 8-10 minutes. Let cool for 2 minutes, and then transfer from the pans to wire racks.

Nutrition Information

- Calories: 160 calories
- Sodium: 118mg sodium
- Fiber: 1g fiber)
- Total Carbohydrate: 21g carbohydrate (12g sugars
- Cholesterol: 25mg cholesterol
- Protein: 2g protein.
- Total Fat: 8g fat (3g saturated fat)

857. Oatmeal Sandwich Cookies

Serving: about 4-1/2 dozen. | Prep: 25mins | Cook: 10mins | Ready in:

Ingredients

- 1-1/2 cups shortening
- 2-2/3 cups packed brown sugar
- 4 large eggs
- 2 teaspoons vanilla extract
- 2-1/4 cups all-purpose flour
- 2 teaspoons ground cinnamon
- 1-1/2 teaspoons baking soda
- 1 teaspoon salt
- 1/2 teaspoon ground nutmeg
- 4 cups old-fashioned oats
- FILLING:
- 3/4 cup shortening
- 3 cups confectioners' sugar
- 1 jar (7 ounces) marshmallow creme
- 1 to 3 tablespoons 2% milk

Direction

- Set oven to 350 degrees and start preheating. Cream brown sugar and shortening until fluffy and light. Beat vanilla and eggs into the mixture. Whisk the next 5 ingredients in a separate bowl; slowly beat into creamed mixture. Mix in oats.
- Drop rounded teaspoonfuls of dough onto baking sheets that were lightly greased, keeping a 2-inch distance away from each other. Bake for 10 to 12 minutes until golden brown. Transfer to wire racks to cool.
- Cream marshmallow crème, confectioners' sugar and shortening to make filling. Pour in an adequate amount of milk until spreadable. Spread bottoms of 1/2 of cookies with the filling; cover with the rest of the cookies.

Nutrition Information

- Calories: 201 calories
- Protein: 2g protein.
- Total Fat: 9g fat (2g saturated fat)
- Sodium: 90mg sodium
- Fiber: 1g fiber)
- Total Carbohydrate: 28g carbohydrate (20g sugars
- Cholesterol: 14mg cholesterol

858. Old Fashioned Gingersnaps

Serving: about 4 dozen. | Prep: 15mins | Cook: 10mins | Ready in:

Ingredients

- 3/4 cup butter, softened
- 1 cup sugar
- 1 large egg
- 1/4 cup molasses
- 2 cups all-purpose flour
- 2 teaspoons baking soda
- 1 teaspoon ground cinnamon
- 1 teaspoon ground cloves

- 1 teaspoon ground ginger
- 1/4 teaspoon salt
- Additional sugar

Direction

- Cream sugar and butter together in a bowl. Whisk in molasses and egg. Mix together salt, ginger, cloves, cinnamon, baking soda, and flour; slowly add to the creamed mixture. Refrigerate.
- Roll into 1 1/4-inch balls and dip into sugar. Put on non-oiled cookie sheets, 2 inches apart. Bake at 375° until set and the surface cracks, about 10 minutes. Put on wire racks to cool.

Nutrition Information

- Calories: 150 calories
- Cholesterol: 29mg cholesterol
- Protein: 1g protein.
- Total Fat: 8g fat (5g saturated fat)
- Sodium: 211mg sodium
- Fiber: 0 fiber)
- Total Carbohydrate: 19g carbohydrate (10g sugars

859. Old Fashioned Mincemeat Cookies

Serving: 4 dozen. | Prep: 20mins | Cook: 10mins | Ready in:

Ingredients

- 1/2 cup butter, softened
- 1 cup sugar, divided
- 1 egg
- 1 teaspoon vanilla extract
- 1-3/4 cups all-purpose flour
- 1-1/2 teaspoons baking powder
- 1/4 teaspoon salt
- 1 package (9 ounces) condensed mincemeat, cut into small pieces
- 1 egg white, lightly beaten

Direction

- Cream 3/4 cup of sugar and butter in a big bowl until the mixture is fluffy and light. Beat in vanilla and egg. Mix salt, baking powder and flour; put little by little into creamed mixture and blend well. Mix in mincemeat. Put into the fridge for 2 hours with a cover.
- Round the dough into 1-inch balls; dunk into egg white then dip into remaining sugar to coat. Arrange on baking sheets coated with cooking spray, the sugar side up and the space between 2 balls is 2 inches. Bake for 10-12 minutes at 375° or until the dough is set. Transfer to wire racks.

Nutrition Information

- Calories:
- Protein:
- Total Fat:
- Sodium:
- Fiber:
- Total Carbohydrate:
- Cholesterol:

860. Old Fashioned Oatmeal Cookies

Serving: 5 dozen. | Prep: 30mins | Cook: 10mins | Ready in:

Ingredients

- 1 cup raisins
- 1 cup water
- 3/4 cup shortening
- 1-1/2 cups sugar
- 2 large eggs
- 1 teaspoon vanilla extract
- 2-1/2 cups all-purpose flour
- 1 teaspoon baking soda

- 1 teaspoon salt
- 1 teaspoon ground cinnamon
- 1/2 teaspoon baking powder
- 1/4 teaspoon ground cloves
- 2 cups quick-cooking oats
- 1/2 cup chopped walnuts, optional

Direction

- Cook raisins for about 15 minutes in water on medium heat in a saucepan until plump. Drain, putting liquid aside. Add enough water to liquid until you get half a cup. Cream vanilla, eggs, sugar and shortening in a bowl. Stir in raisin liquid. Blend in dry ingredients. Mix in oats and raisins. Put in nuts as preferred.
- Drop teaspoonfuls of dough onto ungreased baking sheets, keeping about 2-inch distance away from each other. Bake at 375 degrees until light brown or for 10-12 minutes.

Nutrition Information

- Calories: 161 calories
- Fiber: 1g fiber)
- Total Carbohydrate: 25g carbohydrate (13g sugars
- Cholesterol: 14mg cholesterol
- Protein: 2g protein.
- Total Fat: 6g fat (1g saturated fat)
- Sodium: 133mg sodium

861. Old Fashioned Oatmeal Raisin Cookies

Serving: 7 dozen. | Prep: 10mins | Cook: 60mins | Ready in:

Ingredients

- 3/4 cup canola oil
- 1/4 cup packed brown sugar
- 2 large eggs
- 1/2 cup 2% milk
- 1 package spice cake mix (regular size)
- 2 cups old-fashioned oats
- 2-1/2 cups raisins
- 1 cup chopped pecans

Direction

- Beat brown sugar and oil in a large bowl until combined. Beat in eggs, followed by milk. Mix together oats and cake mix; slowly add into brown sugar mixture and combine thoroughly. Fold pecans and raisins into the mixture.
- Drop tablespoonfuls of dough onto baking sheets that were greased, keeping a 2-inch distance away from each other. Bake at 350 degrees until golden brown or 10 to 12 minutes. Allow to cool for 60 seconds, then move onto wire racks.

Nutrition Information

- Calories: 79 calories
- Total Fat: 4g fat (1g saturated fat)
- Sodium: 50mg sodium
- Fiber: 1g fiber)
- Total Carbohydrate: 10g carbohydrate (6g sugars
- Cholesterol: 7mg cholesterol
- Protein: 1g protein.

862. Olive Oil Cookies

Serving: about 2 dozen. | Prep: 15mins | Cook: 10mins | Ready in:

Ingredients

- 3/4 cup sugar
- 1/2 cup olive oil
- 1 egg
- 1/4 cup honey
- 1/4 teaspoon lemon extract

- 1 cup all-purpose flour
- 1 cup whole wheat flour
- 2 tablespoons minced fresh rosemary
- 2 teaspoons grated lemon peel
- 1-1/2 teaspoons baking soda
- 1/4 teaspoon plus 2 teaspoons sea salt, divided

Direction

- Beat oil and sugar till blended in big bowl; beat egg in then lemon extract and honey. Mix 1/4 tsp. salt, lemon peel, baking soda, rosemary and flours; add to sugar mixture slowly. Mix till just combined.
- Drop by tablespoonfuls on parchment paper-lined baking sheets, 2-in. apart. Sprinkle leftover sea salt on tops; bake for 9-12 minutes till lightly browned at 350°. Transfer to wire racks; keep in airtight container.

Nutrition Information

- Calories: 114 calories
- Protein: 2g protein. Diabetic Exchanges: 1 starch
- Total Fat: 5g fat (1g saturated fat)
- Sodium: 303mg sodium
- Fiber: 1g fiber)
- Total Carbohydrate: 17g carbohydrate (9g sugars
- Cholesterol: 9mg cholesterol

863. Orange Cocoa Sandies

Serving: about 2 dozen. | Prep: 15mins | Cook: 15mins | Ready in:

Ingredients

- 1/2 cup butter, softened
- 1/2 cup confectioners' sugar
- 1/2 teaspoon orange extract
- 1 cup all-purpose flour
- 2 tablespoons baking cocoa
- 1/2 cup finely chopped pecans
- Additional confectioners' sugar

Direction

- Preheat an oven to 350°. Beat extract, 1/2 cup confectioners' sugar and butter till blended in a big bowl. Whisk cocoa and flour in another bowl; beat into butter mixture slowly. Mix in pecans.
- Form dough to 1-in. balls; put on ungreased baking sheets, 1-in. apart. Bake till set or 12-14 minutes; cool for 1-2 minutes on pans. In confectioners' sugar, roll warm cookies; cool on wire racks. Reroll cookies after cooling in confectioner's sugar, if desired.

Nutrition Information

- Calories: 91 calories
- Total Fat: 6g fat (3g saturated fat)
- Sodium: 29mg sodium
- Fiber: 1g fiber)
- Total Carbohydrate: 8g carbohydrate (3g sugars
- Cholesterol: 11mg cholesterol
- Protein: 1g protein. Diabetic Exchanges: 1 fat

864. Orange Marmalade Linzer Tarts

Serving: 2-1/2 dozen. | Prep: 25mins | Cook: 10mins | Ready in:

Ingredients

- 1-1/2 cups all-purpose flour, divided
- 1 cup chopped almonds, toasted
- 1/2 teaspoon baking powder
- 1/4 teaspoon salt
- 1/2 cup unsalted butter, softened
- 2/3 cup sugar
- 4 large egg yolks

- 1/2 teaspoon almond extract
- 1/2 teaspoon grated lemon peel
- 3/4 cup orange marmalade
- 2 teaspoons confectioners' sugar

Direction

- Mix almonds and 1/2 cup flour, cover, pulse till almonds and finely ground in a food processor. Put in leftover flour, salt and baking powder; cover. Process till just combined.
- Cream sugar and butter till fluffy and light in a small bowl; beat in lemon peel, extract and egg yolks. Add almond mixture slowly to creamed mixture; stir well.
- Halve dough. Form each to a ball; flatten to disk. Wrap in plastic; refrigerate for 1 hour.
- Preheat an oven to 350°. Roll 1 dough portion to 1/8-in thick on floured surface; use 2-in. floured round cookie cutter to cut it. Cut out centers of 1/2 cookies with 1-in. floured round cookie cutter. Put cutout and solid cookies on greased baking sheets, 1-in. apart.
- Bake till edges are lightly browned or 6-8 minutes; cool for 5 minutes. Transfer to wire racks; fully cool. Repeat with leftover dough.
- Spread bottoms of solid cookies with 1 tsp. marmalade. Sprinkle confectioners' sugar on cutout cookies; put over marmalade. Keep in airtight container.

Nutrition Information

- Calories:
- Protein:
- Total Fat:
- Sodium:
- Fiber:
- Total Carbohydrate:
- Cholesterol:

---

865.   Orange Sugar Cookies

Serving: 24 | Prep: 15mins | Cook: 10mins | Ready in:

Ingredients

- 1 cup shortening
- 2 cups white sugar
- 3 eggs
- 1 tablespoon orange zest
- 3/8 cup orange juice
- 1 tablespoon vanilla extract
- 5 1/2 cups all-purpose flour
- 2 teaspoons baking powder
- 1 teaspoon salt

Direction

- Cream together in a large bowl the sugar and shortening. One at a time, add in the eggs, then mix in the orange zest, vanilla and orange juice. Mix together the salt, baking powder and flour then mix into the creamed mixture until well combined. Place inside the refrigerator for overnight, covered.
- Prepare the oven by preheating to 375°F (190°C). Roll the dough out to a thickness of 1/4 inch on a surface that is lightly floured. Use stamps or cookie cutters to cut into shapes. On unprepared cookie sheet, place cookies 1 inch apart.
- Place inside the preheated oven and bake for 8-10 minutes. Let cookies cool for 5 minutes on baking sheet then remove to wire racks to fully cool.

Nutrition Information

- Calories: 259 calories;
- Total Fat: 9.5
- Sodium: 135
- Total Carbohydrate: 39.2
- Cholesterol: 31
- Protein: 3.8

866. Orange Cranberry Nut Tarts

Serving: 4 dozen. | Prep: 50mins | Cook: 10mins | Ready in:

Ingredients

- 1/2 cup butter, softened
- 1 cup sugar
- 1 large egg
- 4 teaspoons grated orange zest
- 1/4 cup orange juice
- 2 tablespoons evaporated milk or 2% milk
- 3 cups all-purpose flour
- 3 teaspoons baking powder
- 1/4 teaspoon salt
- FILLING:
- 1 can (14 ounces) whole-berry cranberry sauce
- 1/2 cup sugar
- 2 tablespoons orange juice
- 1 cup chopped walnuts
- 4 ounces white baking chocolate, melted

Direction

- Cream sugar and butter in a large bowl until fluffy and light. Add egg and beat until blended. Beat in milk, orange juice, and orange zest. Whisk salt, baking powder, and flour in another bowl; gradually beat the mixture into the creamed mixture.
- Split dough into 3 parts. Form each on a slightly floured counter to make a 10-inches long log. Encase with plastic; chill till firm, for overnight.
- For filling, mix sugar, orange juice and cranberry sauce in small saucepan. Boil, mixing continuously; cook and mix for 2 minutes. Take off heat; cool fully. Mix walnuts in.
- Preheat the oven to 375°. Remove wrap of every dough portion and slice crosswise to make 16 pieces. Press on bases and up sides of mini-muffin cups that are greased. Put 2 teaspoons cranberry mixture in each.
- Bake till edges turn pale golden, for 8 to 10 minutes. Cool for 10 minutes in pans. Transfer to cool fully onto wire racks. Sprinkle liquified white chocolate over; rest till set.

Nutrition Information

- Calories: 113 calories
- Cholesterol: 9mg cholesterol
- Protein: 2g protein.
- Total Fat: 4g fat (2g saturated fat)
- Sodium: 60mg sodium
- Fiber: 1g fiber)
- Total Carbohydrate: 18g carbohydrate (10g sugars

867. Orange Cranberry Shortbread

Serving: 2 dozen. | Prep: 25mins | Cook: 15mins | Ready in:

Ingredients

- 1 cup dried cranberries, finely chopped
- 3 tablespoons orange liqueur
- 1 tablespoon grated orange zest
- 1-1/2 teaspoons vanilla extract
- 1-1/2 cups butter, softened
- 1/2 cup sugar
- 1/2 cup packed light brown sugar
- 3-1/2 cups all-purpose flour
- 1 teaspoon ground cinnamon
- 1/2 teaspoon salt
- 1/4 teaspoon ground ginger
- 1/8 teaspoon ground cloves
- Gold colored or coarse white sugar, optional

Direction

- Toss cranberries with vanilla, orange zest and liqueur in a small bowl. Allow to stand with a cover, 1 hour.

- Cream sugars and butter in a large bowl until fluffy and light. Pour in cranberry mixture; beat barely until blended. In another bowl, combine cloves, ginger, salt, cinnamon, and flour; gently beat into creamed mixture.
- Split dough into half. Form each into a disk; use plastic to wrap. Refrigerate until firm enough to roll, about 30 minutes.
- Set the oven to 350° to preheat. , Roll each half of dough to 1/2-inch thickness on a surface light dusted with flour. Cut using floured 2-3/4-inch cookie cutter. Arrange 1 inch apart on ungreased baking sheets. If desired, dust with colored or coarse sugar. Before baking, refrigerate for 10 minutes.
- Bake until edges turn to light brown, 12-15 minutes. Take out of pans to wire racks to cool down.

Nutrition Information

- Calories: 229 calories
- Protein: 2g protein.
- Total Fat: 12g fat (7g saturated fat)
- Sodium: 143mg sodium
- Fiber: 1g fiber)
- Total Carbohydrate: 29g carbohydrate (14g sugars
- Cholesterol: 31mg cholesterol

868. Outrageous Chocolate Mint Cookies

Serving: 3 dozen. | Prep: 20mins | Cook: 10mins | Ready in:

Ingredients

- 1 cup 60% cacao bittersweet chocolate baking chips
- 1/4 cup butter, cubed
- 2 large eggs
- 3/4 cup packed brown sugar
- 1 teaspoon vanilla extract
- 2/3 cup all-purpose flour
- 1/2 teaspoon baking powder
- 1/2 teaspoon salt
- 1 cup (6 ounces) semisweet chocolate chips
- 36 mint Andes candies, chopped

Direction

- Set the oven to 350 degrees to preheat. Melt butter and bittersweet chocolate chips in a microwave, then stir until smooth. Allow to cool a bit. Beat eggs with brown sugar in a big bowl. Stir in chocolate mixture and vanilla. Mix together salt, baking powder and flour, then put into the chocolate mixture slowly. Stir in candies and semisweet chocolate chips.
- Drop on baking sheets coated with grease by teaspoonfuls, 3 inches apart. Bake until edges are set, about 8 to 10 minutes. Allow to cool about 2 minutes prior to transferring from pans to wire racks. Keep in an airtight container for storage.

Nutrition Information

- Calories: 111 calories
- Sodium: 47mg sodium
- Fiber: 1g fiber)
- Total Carbohydrate: 15g carbohydrate (12g sugars
- Cholesterol: 15mg cholesterol
- Protein: 1g protein.
- Total Fat: 6g fat (4g saturated fat)

869. Panforte Cookie Cups

Serving: 2 dozen. | Prep: 25mins | Cook: 20mins | Ready in:

Ingredients

- 1/2 cup butter, softened
- 3 ounces cream cheese, softened
- 2 tablespoons sugar
- 1 cup all-purpose flour

- 1/2 teaspoon ground allspice
- FILLING:
- 3/4 cup confectioners' sugar
- 1 large egg
- 3 tablespoons chopped pecans
- 3 tablespoons chopped dates
- 3 tablespoons dried cranberries
- 3 tablespoons grated semisweet chocolate
- 2 tablespoons chopped candied orange peel
- 2 tablespoons chopped crystallized ginger
- Additional confectioners' sugar, optional

Direction

- In a large bowl, cream sugar, cream cheese and butter together till fluffy and light. Combine allspice and flour; mix into the creamed mixture just till combined. Allow 1 hour to refrigerate, covered or till easy to handle.
- In the meantime, in a small bowl, combine the egg, confectioners' sugar, dates, pecans, chocolate, cranberries, ginger and orange peel. Roll dough into balls of 1-inch; in 24 greased miniature muffin cups, press dough onto the bottoms and up the sides. In each cup, place 1 teaspoon filling.
- Bake at 350° for nearly 18 to 22 minutes or until edges have the color of golden brown. Allow 10 minutes to cool before taking away from pans to wire racks. If you want, use additional confectioners' sugar for dusting.

Nutrition Information

- Calories: 112 calories
- Sodium: 45mg sodium
- Fiber: 0 fiber)
- Total Carbohydrate: 13g carbohydrate (8g sugars
- Cholesterol: 23mg cholesterol
- Protein: 1g protein. Diabetic Exchanges: 1 starch
- Total Fat: 6g fat (3g saturated fat)

870. Peanut Butter Blossom Cookies

Serving: about 3 dozen. | Prep: 15mins | Cook: 10mins | Ready in:

Ingredients

- 1/2 cup butter, softened
- 1/2 cup creamy peanut butter
- 1/2 cup sugar
- 1/2 cup packed brown sugar
- 1 large egg
- 1-1/4 cups all-purpose flour
- 3/4 teaspoon baking soda
- 1/2 teaspoon baking powder
- 1/4 teaspoon salt
- 36 milk chocolate kisses

Direction

- Preheat an oven to 350°. Cream sugars, peanut butter and butter till fluffy and light; beat egg in. sift salt, baking powder, baking soda and flour in another bowl; beat it into peanut butter mixture.
- By level tablespoonfuls, drop on ungreased baking sheets, 2-in. apart. Bake for 10-12 minutes till light brown. Take out of oven; push chocolate kiss immediately over each cookie. Cool for 2 minutes in pans. Transfer from pans onto wire racks; completely cool.

Nutrition Information

- Calories: 106 calories
- Total Fat: 6g fat (3g saturated fat)
- Sodium: 92mg sodium
- Fiber: 0 fiber)
- Total Carbohydrate: 13g carbohydrate (9g sugars
- Cholesterol: 13mg cholesterol
- Protein: 2g protein.

871. Peanut Butter Chip Cookie

Serving: about 5 dozen. | Prep: 20mins | Cook: 15mins | Ready in:

Ingredients

- 1 cup butter, softened
- 1/2 cup peanut butter
- 1 cup sugar
- 1 cup packed brown sugar
- 2 eggs
- 1 tablespoon maple syrup
- 2 teaspoons vanilla extract
- 2 cups all-purpose flour
- 3/4 cup quick-cooking oats
- 1-1/2 teaspoons baking powder
- 1 teaspoon baking soda
- 1 teaspoon salt
- 1 package (10 ounces) peanut butter chips

Direction

- Cream together the sugars, peanut butter and butter in a large bowl until fluffy and light. Add in one egg at a time, beat properly after each addition. Beat in vanilla and syrup. Combine salt, baking soda, baking powder, oats and flour; slowly add the dry mixture to creamed mixture, mix properly. Stir in peanut butter chips.
- Drop by heaping tablespoonfuls onto ungreased baking sheets 2 inch apart. Bake at 325° for 15 to 18 minutes or until cookies turn golden brown. Cool for a minutes prior to transferring to cool completely on wire racks. Can be frozen up to 6 months.

Nutrition Information

- Calories:
- Protein:
- Total Fat:
- Sodium:
- Fiber:
- Total Carbohydrate:
- Cholesterol:

872. Peanut Butter Cookies

Serving: 48 | Prep: | Cook: 30mins | Ready in:

Ingredients

- 2 cups packed light brown sugar
- ½ cup natural peanut butter
- ¼ cup canola oil
- 2 large eggs
- 2 teaspoons vanilla extract
- 5 teaspoons water
- 2 cups all-purpose flour
- ⅔ cup whole-wheat flour
- 1 teaspoon baking powder
- 1 teaspoon baking soda
- ½ teaspoon salt
- ⅓ cup chopped peanuts

Direction

- Preheat an oven to 350°F; use cooking spray to coat 3 baking sheets.
- Mix vanilla, eggs, oil, peanut butter and brown sugar in mixing bowl; add water. Use electric mixer to beat till smooth. Mix salt, baking soda, baking powder, whole-wheat and all-purpose flours in small bowl. Mix dry ingredients into brown-sugar mixture till just combined.
- Between your palms, roll dough to 1-in. balls; put on prepped baking sheets, 2-in. apart. Use fork to flatten cookies, dipping into flour if it starts to stick to dough. Sprinkle peanuts; use your fingers to lightly press them into dough.
- One sheet at a time, bake cookies for 8-10 minutes till golden. Put on wire rack; cool.

Nutrition Information

- Calories: 97 calories;
- Sodium: 75

- Cholesterol: 8
- Sugar: 9
- Protein: 2
- Total Fat: 3
- Saturated Fat: 0
- Fiber: 1
- Total Carbohydrate: 15

873. Peanut Butter Treats

Serving: 4-1/2 dozen. | Prep: 15mins | Cook: 15mins | Ready in:

Ingredients

- 2 cups peanut butter
- 1-1/4 cups sugar
- 2 eggs
- 52 milk chocolate stars or kisses

Direction

- Cream sugar and peanut butter until fluffy and light in a big bowl. Add in one egg at a time, beat properly after each addition (the dough will become sticky). Using floured hands, roll tablespoonfuls into 1-1/4 inch balls. Arrange dough on ungreased baking sheets 2 inch apart.
- Bake at 350° for 14 to 16 minutes until the tops crack. Transfer into wire racks, Force a chocolate star in the middle of every cookie right away.

Nutrition Information

- Calories: 200 calories
- Sodium: 101mg sodium
- Fiber: 1g fiber)
- Total Carbohydrate: 18g carbohydrate (15g sugars
- Cholesterol: 18mg cholesterol
- Protein: 6g protein.
- Total Fat: 13g fat (4g saturated fat)

874. Peanut Butter Filled Cookies

Serving: 2-1/2 dozen. | Prep: 25mins | Cook: 10mins | Ready in:

Ingredients

- 1/2 cup butter, softened
- 1/4 cup peanut butter
- 1/2 cup sugar
- 1/2 cup packed brown sugar
- 1 egg
- 1 teaspoon vanilla extract
- 1-1/4 cups all-purpose flour
- 1/2 cup baking cocoa
- 1/2 teaspoon baking soda
- FILLING:
- 3/4 cup confectioners' sugar
- 3/4 cup peanut butter
- Additional confectioners' sugar

Direction

- Preheat an oven to 375°. Cream sugars, peanut butter and butter till fluffy and light in big bowl; beat vanilla and egg in. Mix baking soda, cocoa and flour; add to creamed mixture slowly. Stir well.
- Mix peanut butter and confectioners' sugar in small bowl; roll to 30 balls. Form tablespoonfuls dough around the filling to completely cover; put on ungreased baking sheets, 2-in. apart. Use glass to flatten.
- Bake till set for 6-8 minutes; transfer to wire racks. Use extra confectioners' sugar to dust.

Nutrition Information

- Calories: 141 calories
- Sodium: 86mg sodium
- Fiber: 1g fiber)

- Total Carbohydrate: 16g carbohydrate (10g sugars
- Cholesterol: 15mg cholesterol
- Protein: 3g protein. Diabetic Exchanges: 1 starch
- Total Fat: 8g fat (3g saturated fat)

875. Peanut Chocolate Chip Cookies

Serving: 7-8 dozen. | Prep: 20mins | Cook: 10mins | Ready in:

Ingredients

- 1 cup butter, softened
- 1 cup sugar
- 1 cup packed brown sugar
- 2 large eggs
- 1 teaspoon vanilla extract
- 1 cup creamy peanut butter
- 2 cups all-purpose flour
- 2 teaspoons baking powder
- 1/2 teaspoon salt
- 1 cup Spanish peanuts
- 1 cup (6 ounces) semisweet chocolate chips

Direction

- Beat sugars and butter in a big bowl. Put in eggs, 1 at a time, mixing thoroughly between additions. Put in vanilla and mix until the mixture is fluffy. Beat in peanut butter. Mix together the dry ingredients and pour little by little into the batter. Mix in chips and peanuts. Scoop the batter by teaspoonfuls onto baking sheets coated with grease. Bake for approximately 8 minutes at 350 degrees.

Nutrition Information

- Calories: 174 calories
- Fiber: 1g fiber)

- Total Carbohydrate: 19g carbohydrate (13g sugars
- Cholesterol: 12mg cholesterol
- Protein: 3g protein.
- Total Fat: 10g fat (4g saturated fat)
- Sodium: 137mg sodium

876. Peanut Oat Cookies

Serving: about 8 dozen. | Prep: 25mins | Cook: 10mins | Ready in:

Ingredients

- 1-1/4 cups butter-flavored shortening
- 1-1/4 cups chunky peanut butter
- 1-1/2 cups packed brown sugar
- 1 cup sugar
- 3 eggs
- 4-1/2 cups old-fashioned oats
- 2 teaspoons baking soda
- 1 package (11-1/2 ounces) milk chocolate chips
- 1 cup chopped peanuts

Direction

- In the big bowl, cream sugars, peanut butter and shortening till fluffy and light. Put in the eggs, 1 at a time, beat well after each of the additions. Mix the baking soda and oats; slowly put into the creamed mixture and stir them well. Stir in the peanuts and chocolate chips.
- Drop by tablespoonfuls 2 inches apart to the greased baking sheets. Bake at 350 degrees till golden brown or for 10 to 12 minutes. Transfer onto the wire racks to cool down.

Nutrition Information

- Calories: 210 calories
- Protein: 4g protein.
- Total Fat: 13g fat (4g saturated fat)

- Sodium: 97mg sodium
- Fiber: 2g fiber)
- Total Carbohydrate: 22g carbohydrate (15g sugars
- Cholesterol: 15mg cholesterol

877. Pecan Horns

Serving: 4 dozen. | Prep: 25mins | Cook: 25mins | Ready in:

Ingredients

- 2 cups all-purpose flour
- 4-1/2 teaspoons sugar
- 1/2 teaspoon salt
- 1 cup cold butter, cubed
- 1 large egg plus 1 large egg yolk
- 1 teaspoon vanilla extract
- FILLING/TOPPING:
- 1-1/2 cups ground pecans, divided
- 1/2 cup sugar, divided
- 1/4 teaspoon grated lemon zest
- 1/4 cup milk
- 1 large egg white, beaten

Direction

- Mix salt, sugar and flour in a big bowl; cut in butter till mixture looks like coarse crumbs. Mix vanilla, yolk and egg; add to flour mixture. Form dough to ball; chill till easy to handle or for 1 hour.
- Filling: Meanwhile, mix milk, zest, 1/4 cup sugar and 1 1/4 cups pecans; put aside. Divide dough to 4 portions; form each to 12 balls. Flatten every ball to 2 1/2-in. circle; put scant teaspoon filling on top of each. Fold dough on top of filling; seal edges. To make crescents, curve ends.
- Put on ungreased baking sheets. Mix leftover sugar and pecans. Brush tops with egg white; sprinkle pecan mixture. Bake at 350° till lightly browned or for 17-20 minutes. Transfer to wire racks; fully cool.

Nutrition Information

- Calories: 165 calories
- Protein: 3g protein.
- Total Fat: 11g fat (5g saturated fat)
- Sodium: 133mg sodium
- Fiber: 1g fiber)
- Total Carbohydrate: 14g carbohydrate (5g sugars
- Cholesterol: 39mg cholesterol

878. Pecan Meltaways

Serving: Makes 3 dozen cookies or 18 servings, 2 cookies each. | Prep: 20mins | Cook: | Ready in:

Ingredients

- 1-1/2 cups PLANTERS Pecan Halves, divided
- 3/4 cup (1-1/2 sticks) margarine or butter, softened
- 1/3 cup firmly packed brown sugar
- 1-1/4 cups flour
- 1 tsp. vanilla
- 1/4 tsp. salt

Direction

- Turn the oven to 350°F to preheat. Put aside 36 of the pecan halves to use for garnishing; finely chop the leftover pecans.
- In a big bowl, use an electric mixer to whisk sugar and margarine on medium speed until fluffy and light. Mix in salt, chopped pecans, vanilla and flour. Form the dough into 36 balls with a diameter of 1-inch each. Put on baking sheets by 2-in. apart; use a floured glass to flatten. In the middle of each cookie, press 1 pecan half.
- Bake until turning golden around the edges, or for 10-12 minutes. Take out of the baking sheets; put on wire racks to fully cool. Put in

an airtight container to store at room temperature.

Nutrition Information

- Calories: 180
- Total Carbohydrate: 12 g
- Cholesterol: 0 mg
- Total Fat: 15 g
- Fiber: 1 g
- Sodium: 125 mg
- Sugar: 4 g
- Protein: 2 g
- Saturated Fat: 2 g

879. Pecan Pie Cookies

Serving: 24 | Prep: 20mins | Cook: 10mins | Ready in:

Ingredients

- 1/4 cup butter
- 1/2 cup confectioners' sugar
- 3 tablespoons light corn syrup
- 3/4 cup finely chopped pecans
- 2 cups all-purpose flour
- 1 teaspoon baking powder
- 1 cup brown sugar, packed
- 3/4 cup butter, softened
- 1 egg
- 1 teaspoon vanilla extract

Direction

- In a pot, melt a quarter cup of butter; mix in corn syrup and confectioners' sugar until the sugar dissolves. On medium heat, boil the mixture while mixing often; mix in pecans until well blended. Chill the mixture for half an hour.
- Preheat the oven to 175°C or 350°Fahrenheit. In a bowl, sift baking powder and flour together; set aside.
- Using an electric mixer on medium speed, beat vanilla extract, egg, 3/4 cup butter and brown sugar for 2 minutes in a big bowl until the mixture is creamy. Mix in the flour mixture gradually until well combined. Pinch and roll a tbsp. of dough into a ball.
- Press the dough into the bottom of an ungreased cupcake pan cup. With your thumb, push the dough to make a small piecrust shape with 1/4 inch walls up the sides of the cupcake cup. Repeat with the remaining dough. Place a teaspoon of the prepared pecan to fill each little crust.
- Bake for 10-13 minutes in the preheated oven until the cookie shells are pale brown. Watch carefully after 10 minutes. Cool the cookies for 5 minutes in the cupcake pans; completely cool on a wire rack.

Nutrition Information

- Calories: 185 calories;
- Total Fat: 10.4
- Sodium: 82
- Total Carbohydrate: 22.1
- Cholesterol: 28
- Protein: 1.7

880. Pecan Pie Thumbprints

Serving: 4-1/2 dozen. | Prep: 30mins | Cook: 10mins | Ready in:

Ingredients

- 1 cup butter, softened
- 1/2 cup sugar
- 2 large eggs, separated
- 1/2 cup dark corn syrup
- 2-1/2 cups all-purpose flour
- FILLING:
- 1/4 cup plus 2 tablespoons confectioners' sugar
- 3 tablespoons butter

- 2 tablespoons dark corn syrup
- 1/4 cup plus 2 tablespoons finely chopped pecans

Direction

- Cream sugar and butter till fluffy and light in a big bowl; beat in corn syrup and egg yolks. Beat in flour slowly; refrigerate, covered, for 30 minutes till firm enough to roll.
- Filling: Mix corn syrup, butter and confectioners' sugar in a small saucepan and boil on medium heat, mixing occasionally. Take off heat; mix in pecans. Take out of pan; refrigerate for 30 minutes till cold.
- Preheat an oven to 375°. Form dough to 1-in. balls; put onto parchment paper-lined baking sheets, 2-in. apart. Whisk egg whites in a small bowl; brush on tops.
- Bake for 5 minutes; take out of oven. Use end of wooden spoon handle to gently press an indentation in middle of each cookie; use scant 1/2 tsp. pecan mixture to fill each. Bake for 4-5 minutes more till edges are light brown.
- Cool for 5 minutes on pans. Transfer to wire racks; cool.

Nutrition Information

- Calories: 86 calories
- Sodium: 37mg sodium
- Fiber: 0 fiber)
- Total Carbohydrate: 10g carbohydrate (4g sugars
- Cholesterol: 18mg cholesterol
- Protein: 1g protein.
- Total Fat: 5g fat (3g saturated fat)

881. Pecan Topped Sugar Cookies

Serving: about 3-1/2 dozen. | Prep: 25mins | Cook: 10mins | Ready in:

Ingredients

- 1 can (8 ounces) almond paste
- 3 ounces cream cheese, softened
- 1/4 cup sweetened shredded coconut
- 1 tube (18 ounces) refrigerated sugar cookie dough
- 1 cup pecan halves

Direction

- Whip cream cheese and almond paste in one bowl. Put in the coconut; combine thoroughly. Slice cookie dough to half-inch pieces; distribute each piece into 4 portions.
- Form into balls. Arrange on oiled baking sheets, 2-inches away. Form half teaspoonfuls mixture of almond into balls; put 1 on every dough ball. Press pecans lightly in tops.
- Bake for 10 to 12 minutes at 350° or till pale brown. Transfer onto wire racks and let cool.

Nutrition Information

- Calories: 211 calories
- Fiber: 1g fiber)
- Total Carbohydrate: 21g carbohydrate (9g sugars
- Cholesterol: 12mg cholesterol
- Protein: 3g protein.
- Total Fat: 14g fat (3g saturated fat)
- Sodium: 118mg sodium

882. Peppermint Biscotti

Serving: about 3-1/2 dozen. | Prep: 60mins | Cook: 15mins | Ready in:

Ingredients

- 3/4 cup butter, softened
- 3/4 cup sugar
- 3 large eggs
- 2 teaspoons peppermint extract
- 3-1/4 cups all-purpose flour

- 1 teaspoon baking powder
- 1/4 teaspoon salt
- 1 cup crushed peppermint candies
- FROSTING:
- 2 cups (12 ounces) semisweet chocolate chips
- 2 tablespoons shortening
- 1/2 cup crushed peppermint candies

Direction

- Beat sugar and butter in a big bowl. Put in eggs, one by one, whipping thoroughly after every increment. Whip extract in. Mix baking powder salt and flour and mix peppermint candy in. Put into creamed mixture slowly, while whipping till combined; the dough will become stiff.
- Split dough in 1/2. Form every part to a rectangle measuring 12x2-1/2-inch on a grease-free baking sheet. Bake till golden brown, about 25 minutes to half an hour at 350°. Transfer onto wire racks carefully and let cool down, about 15 minutes. Remove onto a chopping board and use a sharp knife to slice diagonally to 1/2-inch pieces. Put on grease-free baking sheets with cut side facing down. Bake till firm, about 12 to 15 minutes. Transfer onto wire racks and cool down.
- Melt the shortening and chocolate chips in a microwavable bowl and mix till smooth. Dunk an end of every biscotti in liquified chocolate, let excess drip off then scatter candy over. Put onto a waxed paper and rest till set. Keep in airtight container.

Nutrition Information

- Calories: 121 calories
- Protein: 2g protein.
- Total Fat: 5g fat (3g saturated fat)
- Sodium: 63mg sodium
- Fiber: 1g fiber)
- Total Carbohydrate: 17g carbohydrate (8g sugars
- Cholesterol: 24mg cholesterol

883. Peppermint Candy Cane Cookies

Serving: 3 dozen. | Prep: 25mins | Cook: 10mins | Ready in:

Ingredients

- 1/2 tube refrigerated sugar cookie dough, softened
- 2 tablespoons all-purpose flour
- 1/2 teaspoon peppermint extract
- 1/2 teaspoon red food coloring

Direction

- Beat extract, flour and cookie dough till smooth in a big bowl. Halve dough; mix food coloring into 1 portion.
- Form 1 tsp. white dough to 6-in. rope. Form 1 tsp. red dough to 6-in. rope. Put ropes side by side; lightly press together, then twist.
- Put onto ungreased baking sheet; to make handle of cane, curve top of cookie. Repeat with leftover dough, putting cookies on baking sheets, 2-in. apart.
- Bake at 350° till set or for 8-10 minutes; cool for 2 minutes. Transfer to wire racks carefully.

Nutrition Information

- Calories: 33 calories
- Sodium: 30mg sodium
- Fiber: 0 fiber)
- Total Carbohydrate: 5g carbohydrate (2g sugars
- Cholesterol: 2mg cholesterol
- Protein: 0 protein.
- Total Fat: 1g fat (0 saturated fat)

884. Peppermint Meltaways

Serving: about 2-1/2 dozen. | Prep: 30mins | Cook: 10mins | Ready in:

Ingredients

- 1 cup butter, softened
- 1/2 cup confectioners' sugar
- 1/2 teaspoon peppermint extract
- 1-1/4 cups all-purpose flour
- 1/2 cup cornstarch
- FROSTING:
- 2 tablespoons butter, softened
- 2 tablespoons 2% milk
- 1/4 teaspoon peppermint extract
- 2 to 3 drops red food coloring, optional
- 1-1/2 cups confectioners' sugar
- 1/2 cup crushed peppermint candies

Direction

- Cream confectioners' sugar and butter till fluffy and light in a small bowl. Whisk in extract. Blend cornstarch with flour together in another bowl; slowly whisk into the creamed mixture. Refrigerate with a cover till firm enough to handle, or for 30 minutes.
- Set the oven at 350° and start preheating. Form the dough into 1-in. balls; place on ungreased baking sheets, 2 in. apart. Bake till the bottoms are lightly browned or for 9 to 11 minutes. Take away from the pans and place on wire racks to completely cool.
- Beat butter in a small bowl till creamy. Whisk in extract, milk and food coloring if desired. Slowly whisk in confectioners' sugar till smooth. Spread over the cookies; sprinkle crushed candies over. Place in an airtight container for storing.

Nutrition Information

- Calories: 126 calories
- Cholesterol: 18mg cholesterol
- Protein: 1g protein.
- Total Fat: 7g fat (4g saturated fat)
- Sodium: 56mg sodium
- Fiber: 0 fiber)
- Total Carbohydrate: 15g carbohydrate (9g sugars

885. Peppermint Ribbon Cookies

Serving: 8 dozen. | Prep: 35mins | Cook: 10mins | Ready in:

Ingredients

- 1 cup butter, softened
- 1-1/4 cups sugar
- 1 egg
- 1 teaspoon vanilla extract
- 1/4 teaspoon peppermint extract
- 2-1/4 cups all-purpose flour
- 1-1/4 teaspoons baking powder
- 1/4 teaspoon salt
- 7 to 9 drops each red and green food coloring

Direction

- Line waxed paper on a loaf pan, 8x4-inch in size; reserve. Mash sugar and butter in a big bowl till fluffy and light. Beat in peppermint extract, vanilla and egg. Mix salt, baking powder and flour; slowly put to the creamed mixture and combine thoroughly.
- Split dough into 3 portions. Put red food coloring to a part; scatter equally into the prepped pan. Scatter another part on top of the initial layer. Put green food coloring to the final portion; scatter on top of the second layer. Put on plastic wrap to cover; chill overnight.
- Pull dough out from pan with waxed paper. Slowly remove waxed paper. Slice dough into 3 parts lengthwise. Slice every part into quarter-inch slices.
- Put on unoiled baking sheets, 2-inch away. Bake for 7 to 9 minutes at 350° or till firm and edges are browned slightly. Let cool for a

minute prior to transferring onto wire racks. Keep in airtight container.

Nutrition Information

- Calories: 41 calories
- Protein: 0 protein.
- Total Fat: 2g fat (1g saturated fat)
- Sodium: 27mg sodium
- Fiber: 0 fiber)
- Total Carbohydrate: 5g carbohydrate (3g sugars
- Cholesterol: 8mg cholesterol

886. Peppermint Kissed Fudge Mallow Cookies

Serving: 2 dozen. | Prep: 30mins | Cook: 10mins | Ready in:

Ingredients

- 1/3 cup reduced-fat plain yogurt
- 5 tablespoons butter, melted
- 3/4 teaspoon peppermint extract
- 1 cup all-purpose flour
- 3/4 cup sugar
- 1/2 cup baking cocoa
- 1/4 teaspoon salt
- 1/4 teaspoon baking soda
- 12 large marshmallows, cut in half lengthwise
- CHOCOLATE GLAZE:
- 2 tablespoons semisweet chocolate chips
- 3/4 cup confectioners' sugar
- 3 tablespoons baking cocoa
- 3 tablespoons fat-free milk
- 1/4 teaspoon peppermint extract
- 1/4 cup crushed peppermint candies

Direction

- Beat together the yogurt, butter and extract till well incorporated in a large bowl. Mix together the flour, baking soda, cocoa, salt and sugar; add them into the yogurt mixture slowly and combine thoroughly.
- Drop tablespoonfuls of the mixture onto baking sheets sprayed using cooking spray. Bake for about 8 minutes at 350°. Add a marshmallow half on top of each cookie; bake until marshmallow is puffed, for another 1-2 minutes. Let them cool down for 2 minutes then take out of pans to wire racks to cool fully.
- To make glaze, melt chocolate chips in a microwave; stir till smooth. Mix together confectioners' sugar and cocoa in a small bowl. Stir milk and extract into the mix till smooth. Stir melted chocolate slowly into the mix. Drizzle on top of marshmallows; sprinkle using candies.

Nutrition Information

- Calories: 109 calories
- Total Fat: 3g fat (2g saturated fat)
- Sodium: 60mg sodium
- Fiber: 1g fiber)
- Total Carbohydrate: 20g carbohydrate (13g sugars
- Cholesterol: 7mg cholesterol
- Protein: 1g protein.

887. Pfeffernuesse Cookies

Serving: 10 dozen. | Prep: 35mins | Cook: 15mins | Ready in:

Ingredients

- 1/2 cup molasses
- 1/4 cup honey
- 1/4 cup butter, cubed
- 1/4 cup shortening
- 2 large eggs
- 1-1/2 teaspoons anise extract
- 4 cups all-purpose flour
- 3/4 cup sugar

- 1/2 cup packed brown sugar
- 2 teaspoons ground cinnamon
- 1-1/2 teaspoons baking soda
- 1 teaspoon ground ginger
- 1 teaspoon ground cardamom
- 1 teaspoon ground nutmeg
- 1 teaspoon ground cloves
- 3/4 teaspoon coarsely ground pepper
- 1/2 teaspoon salt
- 1 cup confectioners' sugar

Direction

- Mix together shortening, butter, honey and molasses in a small saucepan, then cook and stir the mixture on moderate heat until melted. Take away from the heat and allow to cool to room temperature. Stir in extract and eggs.
- Mix together salt, pepper, cloves, nutmeg, cardamom, ginger, baking soda, cinnamon, brown sugar, sugar and flour. Put in molasses mixture gradually and blend well. Place a cover and chill for a minimum of 2 hours to overnight.
- Set the oven to 325 degrees to preheat. Roll dough into balls, 1 inch size. Arrange balls on baking sheets coated with grease, spaced 1 inch apart. Bake until turn golden brown, about 12 to 15 minutes. Transfer cookies to wire racks, then roll warm cookies into confectioners' sugar. Allow to cool thoroughly and put into an airtight container for storage.

Nutrition Information

- Calories: 42 calories
- Protein: 1g protein.
- Total Fat: 1g fat (0 saturated fat)
- Sodium: 31mg sodium
- Fiber: 0 fiber)
- Total Carbohydrate: 8g carbohydrate (5g sugars
- Cholesterol: 4mg cholesterol

888. Pine Nut Thumbprints

Serving: 2 dozen. | Prep: 15mins | Cook: 10mins | Ready in:

Ingredients

- 1/2 cup butter, softened
- 1/4 cup packed brown sugar
- 1 egg yolk
- 1 teaspoon grated lemon peel
- 1 teaspoon vanilla extract
- 1 cup all-purpose flour
- 1/4 teaspoon salt
- 2 tablespoons honey
- 1 tablespoon orange juice
- 3/4 cup finely chopped pine nuts
- 1/4 cup orange marmalade

Direction

- Cream the brown sugar and butter together in a small bowl. Add in the lemon peel, vanilla and egg yolk and whisk everything together. Mix the salt and flour together then slowly put it into the prepared creamed mixture. Cover the bowl and keep it in the fridge for 1 hour or until it is a lot easier to work with.
- Shape the dough mixture into balls that are 1 inch in size. Mix the orange juice and honey together in a shallow bowl. Coat each of the dough balls with the prepared honey mixture then roll it in the pine nuts. Put the pine nut-coated dough balls onto greased baking sheets 1 inch away from each other.
- Use the tip of a wooden spoon handle to create a dent in the middle of each pine nut-coated dough ball. Put it in a 350° oven and let it bake for 10-12 minutes or until the edges of each cookie turn light brown in color. Place the baked cookies onto wire racks. Put orange marmalade into the dented part in the middle of each cookie then let the cookies fully cool down.

Nutrition Information

- Calories: 102 calories
- Protein: 2g protein.
- Total Fat: 6g fat (3g saturated fat)
- Sodium: 67mg sodium
- Fiber: 0 fiber)
- Total Carbohydrate: 11g carbohydrate (6g sugars
- Cholesterol: 19mg cholesterol

889. Pistachio Cookies

Serving: Makes about 40 (1 1/2-inch) cookies | Prep: | Cook: | Ready in:

Ingredients

- 3 cups unsalted shelled natural pistachios (15 oz)
- 1 2/3 cups confectioners sugar
- 1 whole large egg
- 2 large egg yolks
- 1 tablespoon unsalted butter, melted
- 1 teaspoon rose water (preferably French)

Direction

- Preheat an oven to 300°F.
- In boiling water, blanch pistachios for 1 minute. Drain. Peel; use your fingers to slip off skins. Use paper towels to dry. Spread in shallow baking pan; bake in center of oven for 10 minutes till dry. Fully cool.
- Pulse confectioners' sugar and nuts till finely ground, not a paste, in a food processor.
- Mix yolks and whole egg with a fork in a big bowl; little by little, mix in ground pistachios till slightly sticky dough forms. Add rose water and butter; knead to mix. Shape dough to 2 disks.
- Roll 1 disk, keeping a disk covered in plastic wrap, on well-floured surface to 3/4-in. thick. Use floured cookie cutters to cut out various shapes.
- On ungreased big baking sheet, bake in center of oven for 20-25 minutes till bottoms are golden and crisp. Put cookies onto rack with a metal spatula; cool. While warm, dust with confectioners' sugar. Make extra cookies with leftover dough, rerolling scraps.
- Cookies keep for 2 days in airtight container in room temperature.

Nutrition Information

- Calories: 86
- Saturated Fat: 1 g(4%)
- Sodium: 3 mg(0%)
- Fiber: 1 g(4%)
- Total Carbohydrate: 8 g(3%)
- Cholesterol: 15 mg(5%)
- Protein: 2 g(5%)
- Total Fat: 5 g(8%)

890. Pistachio Pinwheels

Serving: 5 dozen. | Prep: 40mins | Cook: 10mins | Ready in:

Ingredients

- 1/3 cup butter, softened
- 1/3 cup sugar blend
- 2 large egg whites
- 3 tablespoons canola oil
- 1/2 teaspoon vanilla extract
- 2-3/4 cups cake flour
- 1 teaspoon baking powder
- 1/4 teaspoon salt
- Red paste food coloring
- 1/2 cup pistachios, finely chopped

Direction

- Cream the sugar and butter until fluffy and light in a big bowl then beat the vanilla, oi and egg whites in. Mix baking powder, flour and salt then put it into the butter mixture gradually. Stir well.

- Cut the dough into two parts. Put food coloring on one part. Cut plain and red doughs in half. Between 2 sheets of waxed paper, make an 8x6-inch rectangle by rolling out one part of the plain dough. Repeat with one part of the red dough. Take away the waxed paper then put the red on top of the plain dough.
- Starting with the long side, tightly roll the dough up on jelly-roll style. Roll the log in the pistachios; use plastic to wrap. Repeat with the rest of the doughs. Put it in the refrigerator until it becomes firm or for 2 hours.
- Remove the plastic cover of the logs then slice into 1/4 inch slices. Put on baking sheets without grease, 2 inches apart. Bake it until set or for 7 to 9mins. Transfer it to wire racks.

Nutrition Information

- Calories: 49 calories
- Fiber: 0 fiber)
- Total Carbohydrate: 6g carbohydrate (1g sugars
- Cholesterol: 3mg cholesterol
- Protein: 1g protein. Diabetic Exchanges: 1/2 starch
- Total Fat: 2g fat (1g saturated fat)
- Sodium: 33mg sodium

891. Pistachio Cranberry Rugelach

Serving: 4 dozen. | Prep: 30mins | Cook: 25mins | Ready in:

Ingredients

- 1 cup butter, softened
- 1 package (8 ounces) cream cheese, softened
- 1 teaspoon salt
- 1/4 cup heavy whipping cream
- 2-1/2 cups all-purpose flour
- 1 cup dried cranberries, coarsely chopped
- 1 cup finely chopped pistachios
- 1/4 cup sugar
- 1-1/4 teaspoons ground cinnamon
- 1/4 cup butter, melted
- 1-1/3 cups confectioners' sugar
- 1/2 teaspoon vanilla extract
- 1 to 2 tablespoons water

Direction

- Put the softened butter, salt and cream cheese in a big bowl, cream the mixture until incorporated; beat in cream. Beat in flour little by little.
- Divide the dough into four portions. Form each to a disk and wrap them in plastic. Place inside the fridge for half 1 hour or until easy to handle. Mix together the pistachios, cinnamon, cranberries and sugar in a small bowl; put aside.
- Work with one part of dough at a time. Roll each dough in a 12-in. circle on a lightly floured counter. Brush them up with one fourth of the melted butter. Scatter one fourth of the cranberry mixture, pressing gently on the dough to stick. Slice the dough into 12 wedges. Roll up wedges from the wide ends; arrange them 2 in. apart on the baking sheets that's greased, with the point side facing down.
- Let it bake for 20-25 minutes at 325° or until the bottoms turns brown. Take them out from pans to wire racks and allow to cool through.
- Mix together the vanilla and confectioners' sugar in a small bowl, and add enough water to reach preferred consistency. Drizzle the mixture over cookies.

Nutrition Information

- Calories: 129 calories
- Cholesterol: 19mg cholesterol
- Protein: 2g protein.
- Total Fat: 8g fat (4g saturated fat)
- Sodium: 114mg sodium
- Fiber: 1g fiber)

- Total Carbohydrate: 13g carbohydrate (7g sugars

892. Pistachio Mint Meringue Cookies

Serving: 10 dozen. | Prep: 15mins | Cook: 60mins | Ready in:

Ingredients

- 4 egg whites
- 1 teaspoon vanilla extract
- 1/4 teaspoon cream of tartar
- 1/4 teaspoon salt
- 3/4 cup sugar
- 1 package (10 to 12 ounces) white baking chips
- 1 cup chopped pistachios
- 1 cup finely crushed peppermint candies
- Additional chopped pistachios, optional

Direction

- Put egg whites in big bowl; stand for 30 minutes at room temperature.
- Preheat an oven to 225°. Add salt, cream of tartar and vanilla to egg whites; beat till foamy on medium speed. 1 tbsp. at a time, add sugar slowly, beating on high after every addition till sugar melts; beat till stiff glossy peaks form. Fold crushed candies, pistachios and baking chips in.
- By rounded teaspoonfuls, drop on parchment paper-lined baking sheets, 1-in. apart. Sprinkle extra pistachios over if desired; bake till firm to touch, about 1-1 1/4 hours. Transfer to wire racks; completely cool. Keep in airtight containers.

Nutrition Information

- Calories:
- Fiber:
- Total Carbohydrate:
- Cholesterol:
- Protein:
- Total Fat:
- Sodium:

893. Poinsettia Pinwheel Cookies

Serving: 5 dozen. | Prep: 30mins | Cook: 10mins | Ready in:

Ingredients

- 1 cup butter, softened
- 1 cup confectioners' sugar
- 1 egg
- 2 to 3 drops red food coloring
- 2-1/3 cups all-purpose flour
- 3/4 teaspoon salt
- 1/4 cup finely crushed red-hot candies
- FROSTING:
- 1 cup confectioners' sugar
- 4 teaspoons milk
- Additional red-hot candies

Direction

- Cream butter with confectioners' sugar in a big bowl. Whip in food coloring and egg. Whisk flour and salt; put into the creamed mixture slowly. Mix in red hots. Split dough in half; cover in plastic. Chill for no less than an hour or until set.
- Shape a portion of dough into a 12x10-in. rectangle on a lightly floured surface. Slice dough into 2-in. squares using a sharp knife or pastry wheel. Put 1 in. apart on gently greased baking trays. Slice through dough from each corner of square to within 1/2 in. of center. Fold alternating points of square to center to form a pinwheel; pinch gently at center alternately to seal. Keep working with leftover dough.
- Bake for 7-9 minutes at 350° or until firm. Take out to wire racks to completely cool. Mix the

confectioners' sugar with milk. Pipe half a teaspoon frosting in middle of each cookie; garnish with red-hot.

Nutrition Information

- Calories: 63 calories
- Protein: 1g protein.
- Total Fat: 3g fat (2g saturated fat)
- Sodium: 56mg sodium
- Fiber: 0 fiber)
- Total Carbohydrate: 8g carbohydrate (4g sugars
- Cholesterol: 11mg cholesterol

894. Pumpkin Cookies With Cream Cheese Frosting

Serving: 4 dozen. | Prep: 30mins | Cook: 10mins | Ready in:

Ingredients

- 1 cup butter, softened
- 2/3 cup packed brown sugar
- 1/3 cup sugar
- 1 large egg
- 1 teaspoon vanilla extract
- 1 cup canned pumpkin
- 2 cups all-purpose flour
- 1-1/2 teaspoons ground cinnamon
- 1 teaspoon baking soda
- 1/2 teaspoon salt
- 1/4 teaspoon baking powder
- 1 cup chopped walnuts
- FROSTING:
- 1/4 cup butter, softened
- 4 ounces cream cheese, softened
- 2 cups confectioners' sugar
- 1-1/2 teaspoons vanilla extract

Direction

- Cream sugars and butter until fluffy and light in a large bowl. Beat in vanilla and egg. Add pumpkin; combine well. Mix baking powder, salt, baking soda, cinnamon and flour; add to creamed mixture gradually; combine well. Stir in walnuts.
- Drop onto greased baking sheets by rounded tablespoonfuls 2 in. apart. Bake at 350° until edges turn light brown or for 8-10 minutes. Transfer to wire racks to completely cool.
- Whisk the frosting ingredients until fluffy and light in a small bowl. Frost cookies. Keep in an airtight container in the fridge.

Nutrition Information

- Calories: 125 calories
- Sodium: 97mg sodium
- Fiber: 1g fiber)
- Total Carbohydrate: 14g carbohydrate (9g sugars
- Cholesterol: 20mg cholesterol
- Protein: 2g protein. Diabetic Exchanges: 1 starch
- Total Fat: 7g fat (4g saturated fat)

895. Pumpkin Cookies With Penuche Frosting

Serving: 48 | Prep: 15mins | Cook: 12mins | Ready in:

Ingredients

- 1 cup shortening
- 1/2 cup packed brown sugar
- 1/2 cup white sugar
- 1 cup pumpkin puree
- 1 egg
- 1 teaspoon vanilla extract
- 2 cups all-purpose flour
- 1 teaspoon baking soda
- 1 teaspoon baking powder
- 1 teaspoon ground cinnamon
- 1/2 teaspoon salt

- 1 cup chopped walnuts
- 3 tablespoons butter
- 1/2 cup packed brown sugar
- 1/4 cup milk
- 2 cups confectioners' sugar

Direction

- Start preheating oven to 350°F (175°C). Coat the cookie sheets with grease.
- Cream white sugar, half cup of the brown sugar and shortening together in a large bowl. Mix in vanilla, pumpkin, and egg. Sift salt, cinnamon, baking powder, baking soda and flour together. Then stir into creamed mixture. Mix in the walnuts. Drop onto prepared baking sheets with the dough by heaping spoonfuls.
- Bake in prepared oven for 10-12 mins. Place on the wire racks to cool.
- In a small saucepan, combine half cup of brown sugar and 3 tablespoons of the butter over medium heat. Boil. Cook while stirring until slightly thickened, about one minute. Let cool slightly. Stir in milk, beat until they are smooth. Stir in two cups of confectioners' sugar gradually until the frosting has reached the preferred consistency. Spread on the cooled cookies.

Nutrition Information

- Calories: 128 calories;
- Total Fat: 6.8
- Sodium: 81
- Total Carbohydrate: 16.4
- Cholesterol: 6
- Protein: 1.2

896. Pumpkin Pecan Tassies

Serving: 2 dozen. | Prep: 20mins | Cook: 35mins | Ready in:

Ingredients

- 1/2 cup butter, softened
- 3 ounces cream cheese, softened
- 1 cup all-purpose flour
- FILLING:
- 3/4 cup packed brown sugar, divided
- 1/4 cup canned pumpkin
- 4 teaspoons plus 1 tablespoon butter, melted, divided
- 1 large egg yolk
- 1 tablespoon half-and-half cream
- 1 teaspoon vanilla extract
- 1/4 teaspoon rum extract
- 1/8 teaspoon ground cinnamon
- 1/8 teaspoon ground nutmeg
- 1/2 cup chopped pecans

Direction

- Cream together cream cheese and butter in a small bowl. Whisk in flour. Form into 24 balls. Press up the sides and onto the bottom of oil-coated miniature muffin cups using floured fingers.
- Bake at 325° until the edges turn light brown, about 8-10 minutes.
- In the meantime, mix nutmeg, cinnamon, extracts, cream, egg yolk, 4 teaspoons butter, pumpkin, and 1/2 cup brown sugar together in a bowl. Put into the warm cups. Mix together butter, the leftover brown sugar, and pecans; sprinkle over the filling.
- Bake until set and turning golden brown around the edges, about another 23-27 minutes. Let cool for 10 minutes, and then transfer from the pans to wire racks to cool.

Nutrition Information

- Calories: 244 calories
- Sodium: 127mg sodium
- Fiber: 1g fiber)
- Total Carbohydrate: 23g carbohydrate (14g sugars
- Cholesterol: 53mg cholesterol
- Protein: 2g protein.

- Total Fat: 16g fat (8g saturated fat)

897. Pumpkin Spice Cookies

Serving: about 2-1/2 dozen. | Prep: 15mins | Cook: 20mins | Ready in:

Ingredients

- 1 package yellow cake mix (regular size)
- 1/2 cup quick-cooking oats
- 2 to 2-1/2 teaspoons pumpkin pie spice
- 1 can (15 ounces) solid-pack pumpkin
- 1 large egg
- 2 tablespoons canola oil
- FROSTING:
- 3 cups confectioners' sugar
- 1 teaspoon grated orange zest
- 3 to 4 tablespoons orange juice

Direction

- Set the oven to 350° and start preheating. Mix pie spice, oats and cake mix. Beat oil, egg and pumpkin in another bowl; stir into dry ingredients until just moistened.
- Drop onto baking sheets coated with cooking spray by 2 tablespoonfuls; use the back of a spoon to flatten. Bake for 18-20 minutes until edges turn golden brown. Place on wire racks to cool.
- To prepare frosting: mix enough orange juice, orange zest and confectioners' sugar to reach the consistency as desired.
- Spread over cooled cookies.

Nutrition Information

- Calories: 118 calories
- Fiber: 1g fiber)
- Total Carbohydrate: 26g carbohydrate (18g sugars
- Cholesterol: 6mg cholesterol
- Protein: 1g protein.

- Total Fat: 2g fat (0 saturated fat)
- Sodium: 109mg sodium

898. Pumpkin Whoopie Pies

Serving: 18 | Prep: | Cook: |Ready in:

Ingredients

- 2 cups packed brown sugar
- 1 cup vegetable oil
- 1 1/2 cups solid pack pumpkin puree
- 2 eggs
- 3 cups all-purpose flour
- 1 teaspoon salt
- 1 teaspoon baking powder
- 1 teaspoon baking soda
- 1 teaspoon vanilla extract
- 1 1/2 tablespoons ground cinnamon
- 1/2 tablespoon ground ginger
- 1/2 tablespoon ground cloves
- 1 egg white
- 2 tablespoons milk
- 1 teaspoon vanilla extract
- 2 cups confectioners' sugar
- 3/4 cup shortening

Direction

- Set the oven to 350°F (175°C) and start preheating. Grease baking sheets lightly.
- Mix brown sugar and oil. Mix in eggs and pumpkin; whisk well. Add cloves, ginger, cinnamon, 1 teaspoon vanilla, baking soda, baking powder, salt and flour. Combine well.
- Drop dough by heaping teaspoons onto the greased baking sheets. Bake for 10-12 minutes at 350°F (175°C). Allow cookies to cool; fill Whoopie Pie Filling between 2 cookies to make sandwiches.
- For Whoopie Pie Filling: Whisk egg white and combine with a cup of confectioners' sugar, a teaspoon of vanilla and milk. Combine well; whisk in the remaining cup of confectioners'

sugar and the shortening. Whisk until fluffy and light.

Nutrition Information

- Calories: 425 calories;
- Cholesterol: 21
- Protein: 3.4
- Total Fat: 21.7
- Sodium: 295
- Total Carbohydrate: 55.8

899. Pumpkin Chocolate Whoopie Cookies

Serving: about 2 dozen | Prep: 25mins | Cook: 10mins | Ready in:

Ingredients

- 2 cups packed brown sugar
- 1 cup canola oil
- 2 large eggs
- 3 cups canned pumpkin
- 3 cups all-purpose flour
- 3 tablespoons pumpkin pie spice
- 1 teaspoon baking soda
- 1 teaspoon baking powder
- 1 teaspoon salt
- FILLING:
- 1 package (8 ounces) cream cheese, softened
- 1/2 cup butter, softened
- 1/2 cup miniature semisweet chocolate chips, melted
- 3 cups confectioners' sugar
- 3/4 cup miniature semisweet chocolate chips

Direction

- Set the oven to 350° and start preheating. Beat oil and brown sugar until blended in a large bowl. Whisk in eggs, then pumpkin. Whisk salt, baking powder, pie spice, baking soda and flour in another bowl; beat into sugar mixture gradually.
- Drop onto greased baking sheets by two tablespoonfuls 2 in. apart. Bake until set or for 10-12 minutes. Transfer to wire racks to completely cool.
- Beat melted chocolate, butter and cream cheese until blended in a large bowl. Beat in confectioners' sugar gradually until smooth; fold in chocolate chips. Spread on bottoms of 1/2 of the cookies; place the rest of cookies on top. Keep in the airtight containers.

Nutrition Information

- Calories:
- Total Fat:
- Sodium:
- Fiber:
- Total Carbohydrate:
- Cholesterol:
- Protein:

900. Quick Cranberry Chip Cookies

Serving: 6 dozen. | Prep: 25mins | Cook: 10mins | Ready in:

Ingredients

- 1/2 cup butter, softened
- 1/2 cup shortening
- 3/4 cup sugar
- 3/4 cup packed brown sugar
- 2 eggs
- 1 teaspoon vanilla extract
- 2-1/4 cups all-purpose flour
- 1 teaspoon baking soda
- 1/2 teaspoon salt
- 1 cup semisweet chocolate chips
- 1 cup white baking chips
- 1 cup dried cranberries
- 1 cup chopped pecans

Direction

- Start preheating the oven to 375°. Cream sugars, shortening, and butter in a big bowl until fluffy and light. Add eggs, 1 egg each time, whisking thoroughly between each addition. Whisk in vanilla. Mix together salt, baking soda, and flour; slowly add to the creamed mixture and stir thoroughly. Mix in pecans, cranberries, and chips.
- Drop onto non-oiled cookie sheets by tablespoonfuls 2 inches separately. Bake until turning golden brown, about 9-11 minutes. Let stay on the pan to cool for 2 minutes, and then transfer onto wire racks.

Nutrition Information

- Calories: 97 calories
- Total Carbohydrate: 12g carbohydrate (8g sugars
- Cholesterol: 10mg cholesterol
- Protein: 1g protein.
- Total Fat: 5g fat (2g saturated fat)
- Sodium: 48mg sodium
- Fiber: 0 fiber)

901. Quick Fruitcake Cookies

Serving: 8 dozen. | Prep: 15mins | Cook: 15mins | Ready in:

Ingredients

- 1 cup butter, softened
- 1-1/2 cups sugar
- 2 eggs
- 2-1/2 cups all-purpose flour
- 1 teaspoon baking soda
- 1 teaspoon ground cinnamon
- 1/2 teaspoon salt
- 2 cups chopped pecans
- 1 package (8 ounces) chopped dates
- 8 ounces candied cherries, halved
- 8 ounces candied pineapple, diced

Direction

- Cream sugar and butter in a large bowl. Whisk in eggs. Mix salt, cinnamon, baking soda and flour; add to creamed mixture; combine well. Fold in fruit, dates and pecans.
- Drop onto greased baking sheets, 2 in. apart, by rounded teaspoonfuls. Bake for 13-15 minutes at 325° or until browned lightly. Transfer to wire racks to cool.

Nutrition Information

- Calories: 159 calories
- Total Fat: 8g fat (3g saturated fat)
- Sodium: 98mg sodium
- Fiber: 1g fiber)
- Total Carbohydrate: 22g carbohydrate (15g sugars
- Cholesterol: 19mg cholesterol
- Protein: 2g protein.

902. Raisin Bran Chewies Cookies

Serving: 4 dozen. | Prep: 15mins | Cook: 15mins | Ready in:

Ingredients

- 1 cup shortening
- 1 cup packed brown sugar
- 1/2 cup sugar
- 2 large eggs, lightly beaten
- 2 tablespoons honey
- 2 teaspoons vanilla extract
- 2-1/4 cups all-purpose flour
- 1/2 teaspoon baking soda
- 1/4 teaspoon salt
- 3 cups Raisin Bran cereal
- 3/4 cup raisins
- 1/2 cup chopped walnuts

Direction

- In a bowl, cream sugars and shortening. Add vanilla, honey, and eggs; combine well. Mix salt, baking soda, and flour; pour to the creamed mixture. Mix in cereal. Fold in walnuts and raisins. Drop onto greased baking sheets by teaspoonfuls. Bake for 12 to 14 minutes at 350° until done.

Nutrition Information

- Calories: 232 calories
- Cholesterol: 18mg cholesterol
- Protein: 3g protein.
- Total Fat: 10g fat (2g saturated fat)
- Sodium: 106mg sodium
- Fiber: 2g fiber)
- Total Carbohydrate: 33g carbohydrate (20g sugars

903. Raisin Filled Cookies

Serving: about 3-1/2 dozen. | Prep: 30mins | Cook: 10mins | Ready in:

Ingredients

- 1 cup packed brown sugar
- 1 cup sugar
- 1 cup butter, softened
- 3 large eggs
- 2 tablespoons vanilla extract
- 5 cups all-purpose flour
- 1 teaspoon baking powder
- 1 teaspoon baking soda
- 1/4 teaspoon ground nutmeg
- 1/2 teaspoon salt
- 3 tablespoons buttermilk
- FILLING:
- 1 tablespoon cornstarch
- 3 tablespoons all-purpose flour
- 1 cup packed brown sugar
- 2 cups boiling water
- 1-1/2 cup seedless raisins

Direction

- Cream butter and sugars together in a big bowl. Add eggs, 1 egg each time, whisking thoroughly between additions. Whisk in vanilla. Mix together nutmeg, salt, baking soda, baking powder, and flour; add to the creamed mixture alternately with buttermilk. Put a cover on and chill until easy to work with.
- To make the filling, mix brown sugar, flour, and cornstarch together in a saucepan. Mix in water until smooth. Add raisins. Boil over medium heat; stir and cook until thickened, 3 minutes. Let cool.
- Roll the dough out on a floured surface until the thickness is 1/8 inch. With floured 3-inch round cookie cutters, cut the dough. Top half of the circles with 2 teaspoons filling and put another circle on top of each. Seal by pinching the edges and cut a slit in the top.
- Put on non-oiled cookie sheets, 2 inches apart. Bake at 350° until it turns light brown, 10-13 minutes. Transfer to wire racks to cool.

Nutrition Information

- Calories: 351 calories
- Fiber: 1g fiber)
- Total Carbohydrate: 62g carbohydrate (37g sugars
- Cholesterol: 54mg cholesterol
- Protein: 5g protein.
- Total Fat: 10g fat (6g saturated fat)
- Sodium: 245mg sodium

904. Raspberry & Pink Peppercorn Meringues

Serving: 4 dozen. | Prep: 15mins | Cook: 20mins | Ready in:

Ingredients

- 3 large egg whites
- 1/4 teaspoon cream of tartar
- Pinch salt
- 3/4 cup sugar
- 1 teaspoon raspberry extract
- 5 to 8 drops food coloring, optional
- 1/4 cup semisweet chocolate chips
- 1 teaspoon shortening
- 2 tablespoons whole pink peppercorns, crushed

Direction

- Put egg whites in big bow; stand for 30 minutes at room temperature. Add salt and cream of tartar; beat till soft peaks form on medium speed. 1 tbsp. at a time, add sugar slowly, beating on high till sugar melts and stiff glossy peaks form; if desired, beat food coloring and extract in.
- Cut small hole in corner of plastic/pastry bag; insert big star tip. Use egg white mixture to fill bag; pipe 1 1/4-in. diameter cookies on parchment paper-lined baking sheets. Bake for 20-25 minutes till dry and set at 300°. Turn off oven; leave meringues for 1 hour in oven. Transfer onto wire racks.
- Melt shortening and chocolate chips in microwave; mix till smooth. Drizzle on cookies; sprinkle peppercorns over. Keep in airtight container.

Nutrition Information

- Calories: 19 calories
- Total Carbohydrate: 4g carbohydrate (4g sugars
- Cholesterol: 0 cholesterol
- Protein: 0 protein.
- Total Fat: 0 fat (0 saturated fat)
- Sodium: 7mg sodium
- Fiber: 0 fiber)

905. Raspberry Almonettes

Serving: about 3-1/2 dozen. | Prep: 60mins | Cook: 15mins | Ready in:

Ingredients

- 1 cup butter, softened
- 2 cups sugar
- 2 large eggs
- 1 cup canola oil
- 2 tablespoons almond extract
- 4-1/2 cups all-purpose flour
- 1 teaspoon salt
- 1 teaspoon baking powder
- 3/4 cup sliced almonds, finely chopped
- FILLING :
- 1 package (8 ounces) cream cheese, softened
- 1/2 cup confectioners' sugar
- 1 tablespoon almond extract
- 1/4 cup red raspberry preserves

Direction

- Heat the oven beforehand to 350 degrees. Cream the sugar and butter until fluffy and light in a big bowl. Put eggs in, one at a time. Beat well before putting another. Beat in extract and oil gradually. Whisk baking powder, salt and flour in a different bowl. Stir into the creamed mixture gradually.
- Form dough into 1-inch balls. Press one side of the dough in the chopped almonds. Put into baking sheets without grease, leaving 2-inch space apart, almond side up. Use the bottom of the glass to flatten the dough to 1/4-inch thickness.
- Bake until its edges turn light brown or for 8 to 10 minutes. Allow to cool on pans for 5 minutes. Allow to completely cool by moving to wire racks.
- Make the filling by beating extract, confectioners' sugar, and cream cheese in a small bowl until smooth. On half of the cookies' bottoms, put rounded teaspoonfuls of filling. Indent the middle part of each cookie then fill using 1/4 teaspoon of preserves. Use

the remaining cookies to cover and keep in the refrigerator in an airtight container.

Nutrition Information

- Calories: 216 calories
- Fiber: 1g fiber)
- Total Carbohydrate: 23g carbohydrate (12g sugars
- Cholesterol: 26mg cholesterol
- Protein: 2g protein.
- Total Fat: 13g fat (4g saturated fat)
- Sodium: 125mg sodium

906. Raspberry Chocolate Rugelach

Serving: 32 cookies. | Prep: 40mins | Cook: 20mins | Ready in:

Ingredients

- 1/2 cup butter, softened
- 4 ounces cream cheese, softened
- 1 cup all-purpose flour
- 1/4 teaspoon salt
- FILLING:
- 1/4 cup dried currants
- 2 tablespoons sugar
- 1/2 teaspoon ground cinnamon
- 1/4 cup seedless raspberry jam
- 2/3 cup finely chopped pecans
- 1/4 cup miniature semisweet chocolate chips

Direction

- Beat cream cheese and butter in a large bowl until the mix is smooth. Mix salt and flour. Slowly transfer to the creamed mixture and combine well.
- Separate the dough in half and shape into 2 balls. Then flatten to 5-inch circles and encase with plastic. Chill for about 8 hours or overnight.
- Put the currants into a small bowl and then add boiling water to cover. Allow to sit for five minutes. Drain thoroughly and reserve. Mix cinnamon and sugar. Reserve.
- Roll 1 portion of the dough to form an 11-inch circle onto a pastry mat or a lightly floured surface. Rub with 1/2 of jam. Drizzle with currants, chocolate chips, pecans and 1/2 of cinnamon-sugar. Then gently press down.
- Slice into 16 wedges. Then roll up the wedges onto a parchment paper-lined baking sheet beginning from the wide end and put the point side down two inch apart. Curve the ends to make a crescent. Then cover and chill for 30 minutes prior to baking. Repeat this with the remaining filling and dough.
- Bake for 18 to 22 minutes at 350° or until turned golden brown. Transfer to wire racks and cool.

Nutrition Information

- Calories: 90 calories
- Cholesterol: 11mg cholesterol
- Protein: 1g protein. Diabetic Exchanges: 1 fat
- Total Fat: 6g fat (3g saturated fat)
- Sodium: 49mg sodium
- Fiber: 1g fiber)
- Total Carbohydrate: 8g carbohydrate (4g sugars

907. Raspberry Coconut Balls

Serving: about 4 dozen. | Prep: 30mins | Cook: 0mins | Ready in:

Ingredients

- 1 package (12 ounces) vanilla wafers, crushed
- 3-1/3 cups sweetened shredded coconut, divided
- 1 can (14 ounces) sweetened condensed milk
- 3 teaspoons raspberry extract
- 1 teaspoon rum extract

- 1/4 cup pink sanding sugar

Direction

- Mix 1 1/3 cups coconut and wafer crumbs; mix extracts and milk in. Mix leftover coconut and sugar in shallow bowl; form dough to 1-in. balls then roll in coconut mixture. In airtight containers, refrigerate.

Nutrition Information

- Calories: 93 calories
- Total Carbohydrate: 13g carbohydrate (11g sugars
- Cholesterol: 4mg cholesterol
- Protein: 1g protein.
- Total Fat: 4g fat (3g saturated fat)
- Sodium: 52mg sodium
- Fiber: 1g fiber)

908. Raspberry Cream Sugar Cookies

Serving: about 1-1/2 dozen. | Prep: 10mins | Cook: 10mins | Ready in:

Ingredients

- 1/2 cup white baking chips
- 1/4 cup heavy whipping cream
- 6 ounces cream cheese, softened
- 1/4 cup red raspberry preserves
- 1 package sugar cookie mix
- 1/2 cup butter, softened
- 1 large egg

Direction

- Turn oven to 350° to preheat. Melt baking chips with cream in a microwave oven; whisk until no lumps remain. Beat together cream cheese and preserves in a large mixing bowl until incorporated. Pour in melted baking chip mixture; whisk until no lumps remain. Chill until firm.
- Whisk egg, butter, and cookie mix together in a large mixing bowl until combined. Form mixture into balls approximately 1 inch in diameter; arrange balls on ungreased baking sheets, placing them 2 inches apart. Bake cookies in the preheated oven until edges turn brown lightly, for 7 to 9 minutes. Allow to cool for 5 minutes in pans. Transfer to wire rack to cool entirely.
- Spoon 1 tablespoon filling onto the bottom of 1/2 of the cookies; replace tops. Chill cookies in an airtight container.

Nutrition Information

- Calories:
- Fiber:
- Total Carbohydrate:
- Cholesterol:
- Protein:
- Total Fat:
- Sodium:

909. Raspberry Kisses

Serving: Makes 2 doz. or 12 servings, 2 cookie sandwiches each. | Prep: 10mins | Cook: | Ready in:

Ingredients

- 48 vanilla wafers
- 1/2 cup (1/2 of 8-oz. tub) PHILADELPHIA Cream Cheese Spread
- 1/4 cup seedless raspberry jam or preserves
- 1 Tbsp. powdered sugar

Direction

- Pour 1 teaspoon of cream cheese spread on every piece or 24 wafers. Put half teaspoon of jam on top.
- Cover using the rest of the wafers to make sandwiches.

- Sprinkle over using sugar.

Nutrition Information

- Calories: 120
- Saturated Fat: 2.5 g
- Fiber: 0 g
- Total Carbohydrate: 16 g
- Protein: 1 g
- Total Fat: 6 g
- Sugar: 11 g
- Cholesterol: 15 mg
- Sodium: 105 mg

910. Raspberry Meringues

Serving: 7-1/2 dozen. | Prep: 20mins | Cook: 25mins | Ready in:

Ingredients

- 3 egg whites
- 3 tablespoons plus 1 teaspoon raspberry gelatin powder
- 3/4 cup sugar
- 1 teaspoon white vinegar
- 1/8 teaspoon salt
- 2 cups (12 ounces) semisweet chocolate chips
- 1/2 cup finely chopped pecans
- TOPPING:
- 1/4 cup semisweet chocolate chips
- 1 teaspoon shortening

Direction

- In a big bowl, put egg whites; let sit for 30 minutes at room temperature.
- Whip eggs whites until soft peaks form. Put in gelatin gradually, whipping until incorporated. Slowly put in sugar, 1 tablespoon at a time, whipping until it creates stiff peaks. Whip in salt and vinegar. Fold in nuts and chocolate chips.
- Put by rounded teaspoonfuls onto parchment-lined baking trays. Bake for 20-25 minutes at 250° or until firm to the touch. Turn off the oven; let cookies sit in the oven about 1-1/2 hours with door slightly open or until cool.
- Melt chocolate chips with shortening in a microwave; mix until smooth. Sprinkle over cookies.

Nutrition Information

- Calories: 68 calories
- Sodium: 14mg sodium
- Fiber: 1g fiber)
- Total Carbohydrate: 10g carbohydrate (9g sugars
- Cholesterol: 0 cholesterol
- Protein: 1g protein.
- Total Fat: 4g fat (2g saturated fat)

911. Raspberry Nut Pinwheels

Serving: about 3-1/2 dozen. | Prep: 20mins | Cook: 10mins | Ready in:

Ingredients

- 1/2 cup butter, softened
- 1 cup sugar
- 1 large egg
- 1 teaspoon vanilla extract
- 2 cups all-purpose flour
- 1 teaspoon baking powder
- 1/4 cup seedless raspberry jam
- 3/4 cup finely chopped walnuts

Direction

- Cream the sugar and butter in a big bowl, until it becomes fluffy and light. Beat in vanilla and egg. Whisk the baking powder and flour in a separate bowl, then slowly beat into the creamed mixture.

- In between the two sheets of waxed paper, roll out the dough to a 12-inch square, then take off the waxed paper. Spread jam on the dough, then sprinkle nuts on top. Tightly roll up, the jelly roll style, then wrap it in plastic. Let it chill in the fridge for 2 hours or until it becomes firm.
- Set an oven to preheat to 375 degrees. Take the wrap off the dough and slice the dough crosswise to quarter inch pieces. Put it on the ungreased baking trays and place it 2 inches apart. Let it bake until the edges turn light brown or for 9 to 12 minutes. Transfer the pans to wire racks to let it cool.

Nutrition Information

- Calories: 79 calories
- Total Carbohydrate: 11g carbohydrate (6g sugars
- Cholesterol: 11mg cholesterol
- Protein: 1g protein.
- Total Fat: 4g fat (1g saturated fat)
- Sodium: 27mg sodium
- Fiber: 0 fiber)

912. Raspberry Pistachio Thumbprints

Serving: about 3 dozen. | Prep: 25mins | Cook: 15mins | Ready in:

Ingredients

- 1 cup butter, softened
- 1/2 cup confectioners' sugar
- 1 teaspoon vanilla extract
- 2 cups all-purpose flour
- 1/4 teaspoon salt
- 1 cup finely chopped pistachios
- 1/2 cup seedless raspberry jam
- Additional confectioners' sugar, optional

Direction

- Preheat an oven to 325°; cream confectioners' sugar and butter till fluffy and light. Beat vanilla in. Whisk salt and flour in another bowl; beat into creamed mixture slowly. Add pistachios; stir well.
- Form dough to 1-in. balls; put on ungreased baking sheets, 1-in. apart. Press deep indentation in middle of each using your thumb then fill each using 1/2 tsp. jam.
- Bake for 13-16 minutes till bottoms are light brown. Transfer from pans onto wire racks; cool. Dust with extra confectioners' sugar if desired.

Nutrition Information

- Calories: 97 calories
- Fiber: 0 fiber)
- Total Carbohydrate: 10g carbohydrate (4g sugars
- Cholesterol: 12mg cholesterol
- Protein: 1g protein.
- Total Fat: 6g fat (3g saturated fat)
- Sodium: 65mg sodium

913. Red & Green Pinwheels

Serving: 6 dozen. | Prep: 30mins | Cook: 0mins | Ready in:

Ingredients

- 10 tablespoons butter, softened
- 1/2 cup packed brown sugar
- 1/4 cup granulated sugar
- 1 large egg
- 1/2 teaspoon peppermint extract
- 2 cups all-purpose flour
- 1/2 teaspoon baking powder
- 1/2 teaspoon salt
- 1/8 teaspoon baking soda
- 1/2 teaspoon red gel food coloring
- 1/4 teaspoon green gel food coloring

Direction

- Heat the oven beforehand to 375 degrees. Cream the sugars and butter until fluffy and light. Stir in extract and egg. Whisk baking soda, salt, baking powder and flour in a different bowl then put in the creamed mixture gradually. Mix well.
- Cut the dough into 2 parts. Tint one part with green and red for the other. Cut each part into 2, making 4 doughs altogether. Roll each into 9x6-inch rectangle between sheets of waxed paper. Put in the refrigerator for 15 minutes.
- Discard the waxed paper then put one green dough on top of one red dough. Tightly roll up, starting with the long side, in jelly-roll style; wrap with plastic. Repeat then put in the refrigerator for about an hour until firm.
- Remove the wrap then slice into 1/4-inch slices crosswise. Put on baking sheets without grease, leaving 1-inch space apart. Bake for 7 to 9 minutes until set. Allow to cool by putting on wire racks.

Nutrition Information

- Calories: 36 calories
- Protein: 0 protein.
- Total Fat: 2g fat (1g saturated fat)
- Sodium: 36mg sodium
- Fiber: 0 fiber)
- Total Carbohydrate: 5g carbohydrate (2g sugars
- Cholesterol: 7mg cholesterol

914. Refrigerator Cookies

Serving: about 7 dozen. | Prep: 15mins | Cook: 10mins | Ready in:

Ingredients

- 1 cup butter, softened
- 1 cup sugar
- 2 tablespoons milk
- 1 teaspoon vanilla extract
- 2-1/2 cups all-purpose flour
- 3/4 cup chopped red and green candied cherries
- 1/2 cup finely chopped pecans

Direction

- Cream butter with sugar in a big bowl until fluffy and light. Put in milk and vanilla. Put in flour gradually and stir well. Fold in the pecans and cherries. Roll dough into 2 8-in. x 2-in. rolls; cover in waxed paper and put in the freezer.
- To use frozen dough: Uncover and let sit about 10 minutes at room temperature. Slice into 1/4-in. slices. Put 2 in. apart on ungreased baking trays. Bake for 10-12 minutes at 375° or until slightly browned. Let cool on wire racks.

Nutrition Information

- Calories: 103 calories
- Protein: 1g protein.
- Total Fat: 5g fat (3g saturated fat)
- Sodium: 47mg sodium
- Fiber: 0 fiber)
- Total Carbohydrate: 13g carbohydrate (7g sugars
- Cholesterol: 12mg cholesterol

915. Reindeer Track Cookies

Serving: about 5-1/2 dozen. | Prep: 30mins | Cook: 10mins | Ready in:

Ingredients

- 1-1/4 cups butter, softened
- 1 cup sugar
- 1 cup packed brown sugar
- 2 large eggs
- 2 teaspoons vanilla extract

- 2 cups all-purpose flour
- 3/4 cup baking cocoa
- 1 tablespoon instant espresso powder
- 1 teaspoon baking soda
- 1/2 teaspoon salt
- 2 cans (16 ounces each) vanilla frosting
- Edible silver glitter
- 1 cup whole coffee beans

Direction

- Turn the oven to 350° to preheat. Cream sugars and butter together in a big bowl until fluffy and light. Whisk in vanilla and eggs. Mix salt, baking soda, espresso powder, cocoa, and flour together in a separate bowl; slowly whisk into the creamed mixture. Chill until firm enough to shape, 60 minutes.
- Form the dough into balls by level tablespoons; put on non-oiled cookie sheets, 3 inches apart. Bake until set, 7-9 minutes. Leave on the pans to cool for 3 minutes. Transfer the cookies to wire racks to fully cool.
- Frost the cookies, sprinkle glitter over. Lightly press coffee beans into the frosting, cut sides up.

Nutrition Information

- Calories:
- Total Carbohydrate:
- Cholesterol:
- Protein:
- Total Fat:
- Sodium:
- Fiber:

916. Rosettes

Serving: about 5 dozen. | Prep: 20mins | Cook: 30mins | Ready in:

Ingredients

- 2 eggs
- 2 teaspoons sugar
- 1 cup 2% milk
- 3 teaspoons vanilla extract
- 1 cup all-purpose flour
- 1/4 teaspoon salt
- Oil for deep-fat frying
- ICING:
- 2 cups confectioners' sugar
- 1 teaspoon vanilla extract
- 1 to 3 tablespoons water

Direction

- Beat sugar and eggs in a small bowl; mix in vanilla and milk. Mix salt and flour; add to batter slowly till smooth.
- Heat 2 1/2-in. oil to 375° in electric skillet or deep fat fryer. Put rosette iron into hot oil; dip in batter, 3/4 up the iron's sides (don't let batter run on top of iron. Put in hot oil immediately; use fork to loosen rosette. Remove iron.
- Fry rosettes till golden brown or 1-2 minutes per side; put on paper towel-lined wire racks and repeat with leftover batter.
- Icing: Mix enough water, vanilla and confectioners' sugar to get dipping consistency. In icing, dip edges of rosettes; dry on wire racks.

Nutrition Information

- Calories:
- Fiber:
- Total Carbohydrate:
- Cholesterol:
- Protein:
- Total Fat:
- Sodium:

917. Rugelach

Serving: 48 | Prep: 55mins | Cook: 22mins | Ready in:

Ingredients

- 2 cups all-purpose flour
- 1/4 teaspoon salt
- 1 cup unsalted butter
- 1 (8 ounce) package cream cheese
- 1/3 cup sour cream
- 1/2 cup white sugar
- 1 tablespoon ground cinnamon
- 1 cup finely chopped walnuts
- 1/2 cup raisins

Direction

- Cut margarine/cold butter and cream cheese to bits. Pulse sour cream, cream cheese, margarine/butter, salt and flour in a food processor until crumbly.
- Shape the crumbly mixture to 4 even disks. Wrap every disk. Chill for 2 hours or up to 2 days.
- Mix finely chopped raisins/mini chocolate chips, chopped walnuts, cinnamon and sugar.
- Roll every disk to a 9-in. round. Keep the other disks chilled until it's time to roll them. Sprinkle every round with nut/sugar mixture. Lightly press into dough. Cut every round to 12 wedges with a pizza cutter/chef's knife. From wide to narrow, roll wedges. You should have a point outside the cookie. Put on ungreased baking sheets. Chill rugelach for 20 minutes prior to baking.
- Preheat the oven to 180 degrees C/350 degrees F.
- When the rugelach is chilled, bake for 22 minutes in the middle rack of the oven until lightly golden. Cool them on wire racks. Keep in airtight containers. It freezes well.
- Variations: Prior to placing filling on dough, layer apricot jam using a pastry brush along with brown sugar. Add recommended filling. You could also make a mixture of sugar and cinnamon to roll rugelach in then put them on cookie sheets.

Nutrition Information

- Calories: 101 calories;
- Total Fat: 7.4
- Sodium: 28
- Total Carbohydrate: 7.9
- Cholesterol: 16
- Protein: 1.4

918. Rum Balls

Serving: 24 | Prep: 20mins | Cook: 5mins | Ready in:

Ingredients

- 1 (12 ounce) box vanilla wafer cookies (such as Nilla®)
- 1 cup semisweet chocolate chips
- 1/4 cup light corn syrup
- 3/4 cup dark rum (such as Meyer's®)
- 1 cup confectioners' sugar, plus more for dusting

Direction

- In food processor, put the vanilla cookies and pulse till fine crumbs form.
- In saucepan, heat corn syrup and chocolate chips on low heat. Cook for 5 minutes, mixing frequently, till chocolate melts and smoothen. Take off from heat and mix in confectioners' sugar and rum till smooth. Fold cookie crumbs in; dough will become gooey.
- Put the saucepan in fridge for 15 minutes, till dough firms and becomes easy to form. Use waxed paper to cover two plates; sprinkle confectioners' sugar over.
- Form the dough making an-inch balls; put onto prepped plates. Sprinkle confectioners' sugar on rum balls. Chill for half an hour, till set.
- Take rum balls out of the fridge and place into a sealable bag, put in additional confectioners' sugar. Enclose bag and shake to cover rum balls fully in confectioners' sugar.

Nutrition Information

- Calories: 148 calories;
- Total Fat: 4.9
- Sodium: 46
- Total Carbohydrate: 22.3
- Cholesterol: 0
- Protein: 0.9

919. Sally Ann Cookies

Serving: about 6 dozen. | Prep: 30mins | Cook: 10mins | Ready in:

Ingredients

- 1-1/2 cups sugar
- 1 cup molasses
- 1/2 cup brewed coffee, room temperature
- 5 cups all-purpose flour
- 2 teaspoons baking soda
- 3/4 teaspoon salt
- 1/2 teaspoon ground nutmeg
- 1/4 teaspoon ground cloves
- 1/4 teaspoon ground ginger
- FROSTING:
- 1-1/2 cups sugar
- 1/2 cup water
- 1 teaspoon vinegar
- 1 cup miniature marshmallows
- 2 egg whites

Direction

- Mix coffee, molasses and sugar in a bowl. Combine dry ingredients together; put into sugar mixture and blend well. Put into the fridge for 2 hours.
- On a surface dusted lightly with flour, roll the dough out to reach 1/4 -inch thickness. Cut the dough using 3 to 4-inch cookie cutters. Transfer to greased baking sheets. Bake for 8-10 minutes at 350° until the dough is set. Let it cool on the wire racks.
- Meanwhile, to make the frosting, in a heavy saucepan, mix vinegar, water and sugar. Boil with a cover. Remove the cover and cook over medium-high heat until reaching the soft-ball stage (the candy thermometer indicates 234°-240°), approximately 5-10 minutes. Take the saucepan away from the heat; mix in marshmallows until smooth.
- Beat egg whites in a bowl until it is bubbly. Beat in sugar mixture gradually; beat for 7-8 minutes on high until forming stiff peaks. Top the cookies with frosting.

Nutrition Information

- Calories: 79 calories
- Sodium: 63mg sodium
- Fiber: 0 fiber)
- Total Carbohydrate: 19g carbohydrate (0 sugars
- Cholesterol: 0 cholesterol
- Protein: 1g protein. Diabetic Exchanges: 1 starch.
- Total Fat: 1g fat (0 saturated fat)

920. Salted Butterscotch & Pecan No Bakes

Serving: 4 dozen. | Prep: 25mins | Cook: 0mins | Ready in:

Ingredients

- 1-3/4 cups pecans, toasted
- 1-1/2 teaspoons kosher salt
- 1 can (14 ounces) sweetened condensed milk
- 1-1/2 cups unsweetened finely shredded coconut
- 1 package (3.4 ounces) instant butterscotch pudding mix
- 1/2 cup sugar
- 48 pecan halves, toasted

Direction

- Put salt and 1 3/4 cups pecans into a food processor; process until pecans are ground very finely. Pour into a large mixing bowl. Whisk in pudding mix, coconut, and milk until incorporated. Cover and chill until mixture is hard enough to roll, about half an hour.
- Form mixture into 48 balls about 1 inch in diameter, then roll balls in sugar to coat. Place a pecan half onto each ball, gently pressing to flatten slightly. Keep cookies in airtight containers in the fridge.

Nutrition Information

- Calories:
- Total Fat:
- Sodium:
- Fiber:
- Total Carbohydrate:
- Cholesterol:
- Protein:

921. Salted Caramel Fudge Drops

Serving: 4 dozen. | Prep: 20mins | Cook: 10mins | Ready in:

Ingredients

- 6 ounces unsweetened chocolate
- 1/3 cup butter, cubed
- 1 package (17-1/2 ounces) sugar cookie mix
- 1 large egg
- 1 can (14 ounces) sweetened condensed milk
- 1 teaspoon vanilla extract
- 48 caramel-filled chocolate candies
- Coarsely ground sea salt

Direction

- Set oven to preheat at 350°. Melt butter and unsweetened chocolate together in a microwave; stir till smooth. Let it cool down slightly. Beat together the chocolate mixture, egg, milk, vanilla and cookie mix in a large bowl. Drop tablespoonfuls of the mixture 2 inch apart onto ungreased baking sheets.
- Bake until edges are set, for about 8-10 minutes. Push a candy into each cookie's center. Let sit for 2 minutes. Sprinkle using salt. Take out of pans to wire racks to cool through.

Nutrition Information

- Calories: 135 calories
- Sodium: 58mg sodium
- Fiber: 1g fiber)
- Total Carbohydrate: 18g carbohydrate (13g sugars
- Cholesterol: 11mg cholesterol
- Protein: 2g protein.
- Total Fat: 6g fat (4g saturated fat)

922. Salted Cashew Oatmeal Cookies

Serving: 1 batch (about 4 cups mix). | Prep: 20mins | Cook: 10mins | Ready in:

Ingredients

- 1 cup all-purpose flour
- 3/4 teaspoon baking soda
- 3/4 teaspoon ground cinnamon
- 1/2 cup packed light brown sugar
- 1/2 cup sugar
- 1-1/3 cups old-fashioned oats
- 1 cup salted whole cashews
- ADDITIONAL INGREDIENTS:
- 2/3 cup butter, softened
- 3/4 teaspoon vanilla extract
- 1 large egg plus 1 large egg yolk

Direction

- Mix cinnamon, baking soda and flour. In order listed, layer flour mixture, brown sugar, granulated sugar, oats and cashews in a 1-qt. glass jar. Cover and keep in a cool dry place up to 3 months.
- For preparing cookies: Preheat the oven to 350°. Whisk vanilla extract and butter till fluffy and light. Mix in yolk and egg till well incorporated. Put in cookie mixture; combine thoroughly.
- Drop by tablespoonfuls 1-1/2 in. apart on baking sheets lined with parchment. Bake for 10 to 12 minutes till browned lightly. Take out and transfer to wire racks to cool down. Keep in an airtight container.

Nutrition Information

- Calories: 104 calories
- Protein: 2g protein.
- Total Fat: 6g fat (3g saturated fat)
- Sodium: 73mg sodium
- Fiber: 1g fiber)
- Total Carbohydrate: 12g carbohydrate (6g sugars
- Cholesterol: 19mg cholesterol

923. Santa's Coming Cookie Puzzle

Serving: 1 cookie puzzle. | Prep: 30mins | Cook: 20mins | Ready in:

Ingredients

- 1 tube (18 ounces) refrigerated sugar cookie dough, softened
- 1/2 cup all-purpose flour
- Blanched almonds
- 2-1/2 cups confectioners' sugar
- 4 to 5 tablespoons whole milk
- 1 teaspoon vanilla extract
- Assorted food coloring, decorating gels and sprinkles

Direction

- Mix flour and cookie dough together in a big bowl. On a surface lined with parchment paper, roll the dough into a rectangle, about 14x11-inch in size. Cut out puzzle shapes using cookie cutters. Slide a baking sheet under the dough and parchment paper. Refrigerate for 5-10 minutes.
- Take away the shapes, put on an unoiled baking sheet. In the middle of each shape, put an almond on its side for a handle. Bake the shapes at 350° until turning golden brown around the edges, or about 7-9 minutes. While the shapes are still warm, use the same cookie cutters to cut the shapes again to make neat edges. (If the cookies cool too fast, put back into the oven until tender). Transfer to wire racks to cool.
- Bake the large rectangular puzzle on a baking sheet lined with parchment paper until turning golden brown around the edges, or about 12-13 minutes. Immediately cut the shapes inside the puzzle again to make neat edges. Put on a wire rack to fully cool.
- Mix vanilla, milk and confectioners' sugar together in a small bowl until smooth. If you want, use food coloring to tint the frosting. Frost the shapes and puzzle, use sprinkles and decorating gel to garnish as you like. Put the puzzle shapes inside the puzzle.

Nutrition Information

- Calories: 153 calories
- Sodium: 91mg sodium
- Fiber: 0 fiber)
- Total Carbohydrate: 27g carbohydrate (17g sugars
- Cholesterol: 7mg cholesterol
- Protein: 1g protein.
- Total Fat: 5g fat (1g saturated fat)

924. Santa's Fruit & Nut Cookies

Serving: 3 dozen. | Prep: 30mins | Cook: 10mins | Ready in:

Ingredients

- 1-1/2 cups all-purpose flour
- 1/4 cup sugar
- 1-1/2 teaspoons baking powder
- 1/4 teaspoon salt
- 1/3 cup shortening
- 1/2 cup whole milk
- 1 cup chopped mixed candied fruit
- 1/2 cup chopped walnuts
- ICING:
- 1 cup confectioners' sugar
- 1 to 2 tablespoons whole milk

Direction

- Mix salt, baking powder, sugar and flour in a large bowl. Cut in shortening until crumbly. Stir in milk until just moistened. Stir in nuts and fruit.
- Pat or roll dough into a 12x6-in. rectangle on a floured surface. Cut into 4x1/2-in. strips. Shape into "S" shapes; transfer to the greased baking sheets, 1 in. apart.
- Bake for 6-8 minutes at 425° or until browned lightly. Cool on wire rack. Mix enough milk with confectioners' sugar to achieve a drizzling consistency; drizzle over cookies.

Nutrition Information

- Calories: 86 calories
- Sodium: 41mg sodium
- Fiber: 1g fiber)
- Total Carbohydrate: 15g carbohydrate (9g sugars
- Cholesterol: 0 cholesterol
- Protein: 1g protein. Diabetic Exchanges: 1 starch
- Total Fat: 3g fat (1g saturated fat)

925. Santa's Sugar Cookies

Serving: 4 dozen. | Prep: 30mins | Cook: 10mins | Ready in:

Ingredients

- 1 cup shortening
- 1-1/2 cups sugar
- 2 eggs
- 1 teaspoon vanilla extract
- 2-1/4 cups all-purpose flour
- 1 teaspoon cream of tartar
- Dash salt
- 1 package (11-1/2 ounces) milk chocolate chips, melted
- 14 peppermint candies, crushed

Direction

- Cream sugar and shortening together in a big bowl until fluffy and light. Whisk in vanilla and eggs. Mix together salt, cream of tartar, and flour; add to the creamed mixture and stir thoroughly. Put a cover on and chill until firm for a minimum of 60 minutes.
- Form the dough into 3/4-inch balls. Put on oil-coated cookie sheets, 2 inches apart. Bake at 375° until it turns light brown on the bottoms, 10-12 minutes. Transfer to wire racks to cool.
- In the melted chocolate, dip 1 end of each cookie; sprinkle crushed peppermint over. Put on waxed paper, allow to sit until set.

Nutrition Information

- Calories: 128 calories
- Total Fat: 6g fat (2g saturated fat)
- Sodium: 12mg sodium
- Fiber: 0 fiber)
- Total Carbohydrate: 16g carbohydrate (11g sugars
- Cholesterol: 10mg cholesterol
- Protein: 1g protein. Diabetic Exchanges: 1 starch

926. Santa's Wake Up Cookies

Serving: about 3-1/2 dozen. | Prep: 25mins | Cook: 10mins | Ready in:

Ingredients

- 1/3 cup butter, softened
- 1/4 cup granulated sugar
- 1/4 cup packed brown sugar
- 1/4 cup molasses
- 1 large egg
- 1 to 2 teaspoons instant espresso powder
- 1 teaspoon vanilla extract
- 1-1/2 cups all-purpose flour
- 1/2 teaspoon baking soda
- 1/4 teaspoon salt
- 1/2 cup dried cranberries, chopped
- 1/2 cup chopped pecans

Direction

- Cream molasses, sugars and butter until fluffy and light. Beat in vanilla, espresso powder and egg. In another bowl, whisk salt, baking soda and flour; beat into creamed mixture gradually. Put in pecans and cranberries; thoroughly mix.
- Form dough into balls of 1-inch; on parchment paper-lined baking sheets, place 2 inches apart. Allow 30 minutes to refrigerate.
- Preheat oven to 350°. Bake for approximately 8 to 10 minutes until set. Take away from pans to wire racks for cooling.

Nutrition Information

- Calories: 56 calories
- Cholesterol: 8mg cholesterol
- Protein: 1g protein.
- Total Fat: 3g fat (1g saturated fat)
- Sodium: 43mg sodium
- Fiber: 0 fiber)
- Total Carbohydrate: 8g carbohydrate (4g sugars

927. Scottie Cookies

Serving: 7 dozen. | Prep: 02hours30mins | Cook: 10mins | Ready in:

Ingredients

- 1/2 cup butter, softened
- 1/2 cup butter-flavored shortening
- 2 tablespoons cream cheese, softened
- 1 cup sugar
- 2 large eggs
- 1 teaspoon vanilla extract
- 1 teaspoon light corn syrup
- 4 cups cake flour
- 1 teaspoon baking powder
- 1/2 teaspoon salt
- FROSTING:
- 3 cups confectioners' sugar
- 3 tablespoons cream cheese, softened
- 4-1/2 teaspoons light corn syrup
- 3 to 4 tablespoons 2% milk
- Black liquid food coloring
- ROYAL ICING:
- 4 cups confectioners' sugar
- 6 tablespoons warm water (110° to 115°)
- 3 tablespoons meringue powder
- Red and green paste food coloring
- Assorted sprinkles

Direction

- Cream sugar, cream cheese, shortening and butter till fluffy and light in big bowl; beat corn syrup, eggs and vanilla in. Mix salt, baking powder and flour; add to creamed mixture slowly. Stir well.
- Divide dough into thirds; form each to a ball. Flatten into a disk. Use plastic to wrap; refrigerate till easy to handle, about 2 hours.
- Roll 1 dough portion to 1/4-in. thick on lightly floured surface; use floured 3-in. dog-shaped

cookie cutter to cut. Put on parchment paper-lined baking sheets, 1-in. apart. Repeat with leftover dough.
- Bake for 7-9 minutes at 375° till edges lightly brown. Transfer to wire racks; completely cool.
- Frosting: Mix corn syrup, cream cheese and confectioners' sugar in big bowl; add enough milk to get thin spreading consistency. Halve; leave one half plain and tint leftover half with black food coloring.
- Royal icing: Beat meringue powder, water and confectioners' sugar on low speed till just combined in big bowl; beat for 4-5 minutes on high till stiff peaks form. Halve; tint one portion green and the other red. Use damp cloth to keep unused icing covered always. As desired, decorate cookies with sprinkles, icing and frosting. Dry for a few hours till firm at room temperature. Keep in airtight container in the fridge.

Nutrition Information

- Calories: 99 calories
- Sodium: 35mg sodium
- Fiber: 0 fiber)
- Total Carbohydrate: 18g carbohydrate (12g sugars
- Cholesterol: 9mg cholesterol
- Protein: 1g protein. Diabetic Exchanges: 1 starch
- Total Fat: 3g fat (1g saturated fat)

928. Scrumptious Sugar Cookies

Serving: about 2-1/2 dozen. | Prep: 15mins | Cook: 10mins | Ready in:

Ingredients

- 1 cup butter, softened
- 1/2 cup butter-flavored shortening
- 1 cup sugar
- 2 eggs
- 1 teaspoon almond extract
- 1/2 teaspoon vanilla extract
- 4 cups cake flour
- 1/2 teaspoon baking powder
- 1/2 teaspoon salt
- ICING:
- 2-2/3 cups confectioners' sugar
- 6 tablespoons butter, softened
- 1 teaspoon vanilla extract
- 2 to 3 tablespoons 2% milk
- Red paste food coloring, optional
- Miniature semisweet chocolate chips and red-hot candies

Direction

- Whisk shortening, butter, and sugar together in a large mixing bowl until fluffy and light. Whisk in extracts and eggs. Mix salt, baking powder, and flour together; slowly mix into creamed mixture until combined.
- Cut dough into 3 equal portions. Press each piece of dough into a circle. Wrap each circle in plastic wrap; chill until easy to work with, for 2 hours.
- Roll 1 piece of dough out to 1/8-inch thick on a work surface lightly dusted with flour. Cut dough using a 4 1/2-inch gingerbread boy cookie cutter coated with flour; place cookies 1 inch apart on unbuttered baking sheets. Repeat the steps with the rest of dough; refrigerate and reroll scraps.
- Bake cookies for 8 to 10 minutes at 375°, until edges start browning. Transfer cookies to wire racks and allow to cool entirely.
- In a small mixing bowl, whisk together butter, vanilla, powdered sugar, and enough milk until desired consistency is reached. Color one portion of icing red if desired. Decorate cookies with red-hots, chocolate chips, and icing, if desired.

Nutrition Information

- Calories: 243 calories

- Total Carbohydrate: 32g carbohydrate (17g sugars
- Cholesterol: 36mg cholesterol
- Protein: 2g protein.
- Total Fat: 12g fat (6g saturated fat)
- Sodium: 111mg sodium
- Fiber: 0 fiber)

929. Shortbread Ornament Cookies

Serving: about 3 dozen. | Prep: 01hours30mins | Cook: 15mins | Ready in:

Ingredients

- 3 cups all-purpose flour
- 3/4 cup sugar
- 1/4 teaspoon salt
- 1-1/2 cups cold butter, cubed
- 2 tablespoons cold water
- 1/2 teaspoon rum extract
- 1/2 teaspoon almond extract
- ICING:
- 2 cups confectioners' sugar
- 2 tablespoons plus 2 teaspoons 2% milk
- Food coloring of your choice, optional
- Colored edible glitter and nonpareils

Direction

- Mix together salt, sugar and flour in a big bowl, and then slice in butter until the mixture looks like coarse crumbs. Stir in extracts and water until it forms a ball from the mixture.
- Roll dough on a surface coated lightly with flour to the thickness of 1/4 inch. Use cookie cutters coated with flour to cut the dough and arrange on grease-free baking sheets with 1 inch apart. Place a cover and chill about half an hour.
- Bake at 325 degrees until edges are browned lightly, about 15 to 18 minutes. Allow to cool for about 2 minutes prior to transferring to wire racks to cool thoroughly.
- To make icing, whisk together milk and confectioners' sugar in a big bowl. Split the mixture into small bowls and tint with food coloring if you want. Spread over cookies gently and garnish as wanted.

Nutrition Information

- Calories: 133 calories
- Total Fat: 7g fat (4g saturated fat)
- Sodium: 85mg sodium
- Fiber: 0 fiber)
- Total Carbohydrate: 17g carbohydrate (9g sugars
- Cholesterol: 19mg cholesterol
- Protein: 1g protein.

930. Silver Bells

Serving: about 4 dozen. | Prep: 20mins | Cook: 15mins | Ready in:

Ingredients

- 1-1/2 cups butter, softened
- 3 cups sugar
- 4 large eggs
- 1 teaspoon peppermint extract
- 1 teaspoon vanilla extract
- 5 cups all-purpose flour
- 2 teaspoons baking powder
- 1 teaspoon salt
- 1 package (10 to 12 ounces) white baking chips
- 1 tablespoon shortening
- Black paste food coloring, optional
- Silver edible shimmer dust or sugar

Direction

- Cream sugar and butter till fluffy and light; beat in extracts and eggs. Whisk salt, baking powder and flour in another bowl; beat into creamed mixture slowly. Divide dough to quarters. Form each to disk; wrap in plastic

- and refrigerate for about 2 hours till firm enough to roll.
- Preheat an oven to 350°. Roll each dough portion to 1/8-in. thick on lightly floured surface; use 2 1/2-in. floured bell-shaped cookie cutter to cut it. Put on greased baking sheets, 1-in. apart; bake for 12-15 minutes till edges start to brown. Transfer from pans onto wire racks; fully cool.
- Melt shortening and chips in a microwave; mix till smooth. Tint with food coloring, if desired. Spread on cookies. Allow to stand till set; brush using shimmer dust.

Nutrition Information

- Calories: 188 calories
- Fiber: 0 fiber)
- Total Carbohydrate: 26g carbohydrate (16g sugars
- Cholesterol: 32mg cholesterol
- Protein: 2g protein.
- Total Fat: 8g fat (5g saturated fat)
- Sodium: 126mg sodium

931. Simple Sugar Cookies

Serving: 18 | Prep: | Cook: |Ready in:

Ingredients

- 1/3 cup white sugar
- 1/3 cup shortening
- 1 egg
- 2/3 cup honey
- 1 teaspoon lemon extract
- 2 3/4 cups all-purpose flour
- 1 teaspoon baking soda
- 1/2 teaspoon salt

Direction

- Turn on the oven to 375°F (190°C) to preheat. Prepare cookie sheets and grease lightly.

- Combine lemon extract, honey, egg, shortening and sugar.
- Add in the remaining ingredients; stir until well-mixed.
- Roll so that the dough is 1/4-inch in thickness. Cut into shapes to your interest with cookie cutters. Transfer onto the greased cookie sheet, 1 inch away from another. Put into the oven to bake until there is no longer indentation when touched or for 7-8 minutes. Let it cool and decorate.

Nutrition Information

- Calories: 160 calories;
- Sodium: 139
- Total Carbohydrate: 28.6
- Cholesterol: 10
- Protein: 2.4
- Total Fat: 4.3

932. Sledding Teddies

Serving: 8 servings. | Prep: 03hours00mins | Cook: 15mins |Ready in:

Ingredients

- 1 cup butter, cubed
- 2/3 cup packed brown sugar
- 2/3 cup molasses
- 1 large egg
- 1-1/2 teaspoons vanilla extract
- 4 cups all-purpose flour
- 2 teaspoons ground cinnamon
- 1 teaspoon ground ginger
- 3/4 teaspoon baking soda
- 3/4 teaspoon ground cloves
- 2 tablespoons miniature semisweet chocolate chips
- FROSTING:
- 1/2 cup shortening
- 2-1/2 cups confectioners' sugar
- 2 tablespoons milk

- 1/2 teaspoon vanilla extract
- SLEDS:
- 16 candy canes (about 5-1/4 inches)
- 8 whole graham crackers
- 8 red-hot candies
- 8 cake decorator hearts

Direction

- Cook molasses, brown sugar and butter in a small saucepan on medium heat till sugar melts. Put into big bowl; allow to stand for 10 minutes, then beat in vanilla and egg. Mix cloves, baking soda, ginger, cinnamon and flour; add to butter mixture slowly. Stir well. Refrigerate for 4 hours or overnight, covered.
- Big bears: Form dough to 8 1 1/4-in. balls, 16 1-1/2x1/2-in. logs, 16 1 3/4x1/2-in. logs, 16 1/4-in. balls and 8 1-in. balls; put aside leftover dough.
- Bodies: On 3 ungreased baking sheets, put 1 1/4-in. balls; flatten to 1/2-in. thick. For heads, position 1-in. balls; flatten to 1/2-in. thick. Attach 1/4-in. balls for ears and 2 1 3/4-in. logs for the arms; for legs, don't attach 1 1/2-in. logs. Put on baking sheets separately. On each paw and on the heads for eyes, add chocolate chips.
- Small bears: Form leftover dough to 16 1x3/8-in. logs, 16 1-1/4x3/8-in. logs, 16 1/4-in. balls, 8 3/4-in. balls and 8 1-in. balls. As for big bears, put logs and bears onto 2 ungreased baking sheets; add chocolate chips.
- Bake logs and small bears for 11-13 minutes at 325° and logs and big bears for 14-16 minutes or till set; cool for 10 minutes. Remove from pans carefully onto wire racks; fully cool.
- Mix frosting ingredients in a small bowl. For sleds: To attach 2 candy canes onto bottom of every graham cracker, use frosting; let stand till set.
- To make bottom edge flat, trim bear bodies; attach big bear to back end of every sled using frosting. In front of the big bears, attach small bears. Attach big logs in the front of bears, then small logs on top for legs. For noses: On big bears, attach red hots and hearts onto small bear using dab of frosting; let stand till set.

Nutrition Information

- Calories:
- Protein:
- Total Fat:
- Sodium:
- Fiber:
- Total Carbohydrate:
- Cholesterol:

933. Slice & Bake Chocolate Pecan Cookies

Serving: 8 dozen. | Prep: 45mins | Cook: 10mins | Ready in:

Ingredients

- 1-1/2 cups butter, softened
- 2-1/4 cups confectioners' sugar
- 1 large egg
- 3 teaspoons vanilla extract
- 3-1/4 cups all-purpose flour
- 1/2 cup baking cocoa
- 1/2 teaspoon baking powder
- 1-2/3 cups chopped pecans, toasted
- 1 cup (6 ounces) semisweet chocolate chips
- 1 cup white baking chips

Direction

- Cream confectioners' sugar and butter in a large bowl until fluffy and light. Whisk in vanilla and egg. Mix baking powder, cocoa and flour; add to creamed mixture gradually; combine well. Stir in pecans.
- Form into 4 6-in. logs; use plastic to wrap. Chill in the fridge until firm or for 2 hours.
- Unwrap the dough; slice into 1/4-in. slices.
- Arrange on clean and dry baking sheets, 2

inches apart. Bake for 10-12 minutes at 375° or until firm. Transfer to wire racks to cool.
- Melt semisweet chocolate chips in a microwave; stir until smooth. Drizzle over cookies. Do the same with white chips. Allow to stand until set. Keep in an airtight container.

Nutrition Information

- Calories: 86 calories
- Protein: 1g protein. Diabetic Exchanges: 1 fat
- Total Fat: 6g fat (3g saturated fat)
- Sodium: 25mg sodium
- Fiber: 0 fiber)
- Total Carbohydrate: 9g carbohydrate (5g sugars
- Cholesterol: 10mg cholesterol

934. Slice & Bake Orange Spice Wafers

Serving: 16 dozen. | Prep: 45mins | Cook: 5mins | Ready in:

Ingredients

- 1 cup butter, softened
- 3/4 cup sugar
- 3/4 cup packed brown sugar
- 1 large egg
- 2 tablespoons light corn syrup
- 3 cups all-purpose flour
- 2 teaspoons baking soda
- 2 teaspoons ground ginger
- 2 teaspoons grated orange zest
- 1/4 teaspoon each ground allspice, cloves and nutmeg
- Additional sugar, optional

Direction

- Cream sugars and cream butter in a big bowl until fluffy and light. Mix in corn syrup and egg. Combine nutmeg, cloves, allspice, orange zest, ginger, baking soda, and flour; slowly pour into the creamed mixture and blend well.
- Form into 4 rolls, 6-inch each. Use plastic to wrap and keep in the fridge overnight.
- Unwrap and chop into 1/8-inch slices. Arrange 2 inches apart on unoiled baking trays. If wanted, sprinkle with more sugar.
- Bake for 5 to 6 minutes at 400 degrees, or until slightly browned. Transfer to wire racks to cool.

Nutrition Information

- Calories: 23 calories
- Protein: 0 protein.
- Total Fat: 1g fat (1g saturated fat)
- Sodium: 21mg sodium
- Fiber: 0 fiber)
- Total Carbohydrate: 3g carbohydrate (2g sugars
- Cholesterol: 4mg cholesterol

935. Snickerdoodles

Serving: | Prep: | Cook: | Ready in:

Ingredients

- 1/2 cup Butter unsalted softened
- 1/2 cup Shortening softened
- 1 1/2 cup Sugar
- 2 eggs
- 2 3/4 cup Flour baking sifted
- 2 teaspoons Cream of Tartar
- 1 teaspoon Baking soda
- 1/4 teaspoon Salt
- 2 teaspoon Cinnamon
- 2 tablespoon Sugar fine

Direction

- Preparation
- Set the oven to 400 degrees F to preheat.

- Use an electric mixer to mix thoroughly together eggs, 1 1/2 cups of sugar, shortening and butter in a big bowl on medium speed for 1-2 minutes, until well-blended and creamy. Sift together salt, baking soda, cream of tartar and flour, then stir into the shortening mixture.
- Stir leftover 2 tbsp. of sugar and cinnamon together in a small bowl.
- Form the dough into balls 1 1/2 inches in size, with 1 tbsp. of dough to make each ball, then roll every ball into cinnamon-sugar mixture. Arrange dough balls on grease-free cookie sheets with 2 inches apart. Bake 2 sheets at a time for 8-10 minutes while rotating the sheets halfway through, until the centers become softened yet edges of cookies are set. Remove cookies to wire racks to cool. Do the same process for leftover dough balls. Keep in an airtight container for storage.

Nutrition Information

936. Snow Day Cookies

Serving: about 2-1/2 dozen. | Prep: 25mins | Cook: 15mins | Ready in:

Ingredients

- 1 cup butter, softened
- 1-1/4 cups packed brown sugar
- 2 large eggs
- 3 teaspoons vanilla extract
- 2 teaspoons 2% milk
- 2 cups old-fashioned oats
- 1-3/4 cups all-purpose flour
- 1 teaspoon baking soda
- 1/2 teaspoon salt
- 1-1/2 cups coarsely crushed potato chips
- 1-1/2 cups coarsely crushed pretzels
- 1 cup (6 ounces) semisweet chocolate chips
- 3/4 cup milk chocolate M&M's

Direction

- Set oven to 350 degrees. Beat brown sugar and butter in a big bowl to form a fluffy and light mixture. Blend in milk, vanilla and egg. In a separate bowl, combine salt, baking soda, flour and oats; mix little by little into beaten mixture. Mix in M&M's, chocolate chips, pretzels and potato chips.
- Scoop dough by scant 1/4 cupfuls and place onto unprepared baking sheets, laying 2 inches from each other and slightly flatten. Bake in preheated oven until turning golden brown on the edges and light in the center, about 14 to 16 minutes. Allow to cool for 2 minutes on baking sheets. Transfer to wire racks and let cool.

Nutrition Information

- Calories: 226 calories
- Total Carbohydrate: 31g carbohydrate (16g sugars
- Cholesterol: 29mg cholesterol
- Protein: 3g protein.
- Total Fat: 11g fat (6g saturated fat)
- Sodium: 223mg sodium
- Fiber: 1g fiber)

937. Snow Capped Mocha Fudge Drops

Serving: about 3-1/2 dozen. | Prep: 40mins | Cook: 10mins | Ready in:

Ingredients

- 1 cup (6 ounces) semisweet chocolate chips, divided
- 1/2 cup butter, cubed
- 1 tablespoon instant coffee granules or espresso powder
- 3/4 cup sugar
- 3/4 cup packed brown sugar

- 2 large eggs
- 2 teaspoons vanilla extract
- 2 cups all-purpose flour
- 1/4 cup baking cocoa
- 1/2 teaspoon baking powder
- 1/4 teaspoon salt
- 1/2 cup chopped pecans or walnuts
- 10 ounces white candy coating, melted
- White edible glitter and/or red and green colored sugar

Direction

- Set oven to 350 degrees and start preheating. In the microwave, heat butter and half a cup of chocolate chips in a microwaveable bowl to melt butter; whisk to melt chocolate. Mix in coffee granules and wait until slightly cool.
- Mix in sugars. Beat in eggs, one at a time and vanilla until combined. Mix together salt, baking powder, cocoa and flour in a small bowl; mix into butter and chocolate mixture. Mix in the rest of chocolate chips and pecans.
- On unprepared baking sheets, place dough by tablespoonfuls, about 1 inch apart. Bake in preheated oven for 8 to10 minutes until cookies are set. Allow to cool for 2 minutes on baking sheets. Transfer to wire racks and cool entirely.
- Coat tops of cookies by dipping into melted candy coating; use colored sugar and/or glitter to sprinkle on top. Allow to set.

Nutrition Information

- Calories: 131 calories
- Total Fat: 6g fat (4g saturated fat)
- Sodium: 43mg sodium
- Fiber: 1g fiber)
- Total Carbohydrate: 19g carbohydrate (13g sugars
- Cholesterol: 15mg cholesterol
- Protein: 1g protein.

938. Snow Topped White Chocolate Macadamia Cookies

Serving: about 3 dozen. | Prep: 35mins | Cook: 15mins | Ready in:

Ingredients

- 1 tube (16-1/2 ounces) refrigerated sugar cookie dough
- 1/3 cup all-purpose flour
- 1/2 teaspoon vanilla extract
- 3/4 cup white baking chips
- 1/2 cup finely chopped macadamia nuts, toasted
- GLAZE:
- 1-1/2 cups confectioners' sugar
- 3 tablespoons 2% milk
- 1/2 teaspoon lemon extract
- 1-1/2 cups sweetened shredded coconut

Direction

- Set oven at 350°F and start preheating. Put the cookie dough in a big bowl, let rest for 5 to 10 minutes at room temperature to soften.
- Mix vanilla and flour into the dough until combined (the dough will get a little bit crumbly). Mix in nuts and baking chips. Use parchment paper to line baking trays. Form level tablespoons of dough into balls; put them 2 inches away from each other on the prepared trays.
- Let bake in preheated oven for 12 to 14 minutes until bottoms turn light brown. Take to wire racks and let cool totally.
- To make glaze: Combine extract, milk and confectioners' sugar until smooth. Plunge cookie tops into glaze. Dredge coconut over, gently patting to stick. Let rest until set.

Nutrition Information

- Calories:
- Sodium:
- Fiber:
- Total Carbohydrate:

- Cholesterol:
- Protein:
- Total Fat:

939. Snowcapped Gingerbread Biscotti

Serving: 2-1/2 dozen. | Prep: 45mins | Cook: 35mins | Ready in:

Ingredients

- 1/3 cup butter, softened
- 1 cup packed brown sugar
- 1/4 cup molasses
- 3 large eggs
- 3-1/4 cups all-purpose flour
- 3 teaspoons ground cinnamon
- 1 teaspoon ground nutmeg
- 1/2 teaspoon baking powder
- 1/2 teaspoon salt
- 1/2 teaspoon ground allspice
- 1/2 teaspoon ground cloves
- 1 cup hazelnuts, toasted and chopped
- 1/4 cup finely chopped crystallized ginger
- 1 cup butterscotch chips, melted
- 1 cup vanilla or white chips, melted

Direction

- Whisk the brown sugar and butter into a big bowl until fluffy and light. Whisk in the molasses. Stir in the eggs, one by one, whisking thoroughly after each addition. Mix together the cinnamon, salt, cloves, nutmeg, flour, allspices, and baking powder. Slowly pour flour mixture into the butter mixture, stirring well until combined. Beat in the ginger and hazelnuts.
- Portion the dough into half. Keep in the refrigerator with cover, 30 minutes.
- Mold the dough to two pieces of 10x13-inch logs on the lightly floured working surface. Place logs into oiled baking pans. On 350° heat, bake until firm when touched and light brown in color, 7 to 9 minutes.
- Place on a chopping board and cut into 1/2-inch diagonal slices using a sharp knife. Put slices on the greased baking pans, seam side down. Bake, 7 to 9 minutes a side until light brown in color. Take out and transfer onto wire racks; cool.
- On melted butterscotch chips, dip the biscotti midway, shaking off any excess. Put on a waxed paper to set. Dip partially the coated butterscotch portion of the cookie into the melted vanilla chips, shaking off any excess. Put on a waxed paper to set. Keep cookies into a tightly sealed container.

Nutrition Information

- Calories: 226 calories
- Cholesterol: 27mg cholesterol
- Protein: 4g protein.
- Total Fat: 10g fat (5g saturated fat)
- Sodium: 83mg sodium
- Fiber: 1g fiber)
- Total Carbohydrate: 31g carbohydrate (13g sugars

940. Snowman Christmas Cookies

Serving: about 4 dozen. | Prep: 45mins | Cook: 15mins | Ready in:

Ingredients

- 1 cup butter, softened
- 1 package (8 ounces) cream cheese, softened
- 2-1/4 cups sugar, divided
- 1 egg
- 1 teaspoon vanilla extract
- 1/4 teaspoon almond extract
- 3-3/4 cups all-purpose flour
- 1 teaspoon baking powder
- 1 teaspoon salt

- 50 pretzel sticks
- Decorating icing of your choice
- Orange gumdrops

Direction

- Beat cream cheese, butter with 2 cups of sugar in a large bowl until incorporated. Beat in extracts and egg. Combine salt, baking powder, and flour in a separate bowl; slowly beat into the creamed mixture. Cover and chill until firm enough to shape for a minimum of 30 minutes.
- Turn oven to 325° to preheat. Bring the remainder of sugar into a shallow bowl. For each cookie, form dough into one 1/2-inch ball, one 3/4-inch ball, and one 1-inch ball; press the balls together to make a snowman. Coat lightly with sugar. Do the same with the remainder of dough. Arrange snowmen about 2 inches apart on unoiled baking sheets.
- Break pretzel sticks into 2 parts; force into snowmen for arms. Bake snowmen in the preheated oven until bottoms are light brown, 15 to 18 minutes.
- Allow to cool for 1 minute on the pans. Transfer cookies to wire racks to cool entirely. Squeeze icing on snowmen to make mouths, buttons, eyes, and scarves. Attach gumdrops using icing for noses.

Nutrition Information

- Calories: 119 calories
- Sodium: 105mg sodium
- Fiber: 0 fiber)
- Total Carbohydrate: 16g carbohydrate (9g sugars
- Cholesterol: 19mg cholesterol
- Protein: 1g protein. Diabetic Exchanges: 1 starch
- Total Fat: 5g fat (3g saturated fat)

941. Snowman Cutouts

Serving: 2 snowmen. | Prep: 35mins | Cook: 10mins | Ready in:

Ingredients

- 1 tube (16-1/2 ounces) refrigerated sugar cookie dough
- 1/2 cup all-purpose flour
- 1/2 teaspoon almond extract
- 1 can (16 ounces) vanilla frosting
- Food coloring of your choice

Direction

- Allow the dough to sit for 5-10 minutes at room temperature until tender. Whisk extract, flour, and cookie dough together in a small bowl until blended.
- Roll the dough out on a lightly floured surface until the thickness is 1/4-inch. Cut out 2 circles with a floured 4 1/2-inch round cookie cutter. Continue with 3-inch and 3 1/2-inch round cookie cutters. Cut out two 2 1/4-inch carrots, four 1 3/4-inch mittens, and six 1-inch circles.
- On waxed paper, draw a pipe with 1 3/4-inch height and 3 1/4-inch width and a top hat with 2 1/2-inch height and 3 1/2-inch width; cut out. If needed, roll the dough scraps again. Cut out 2 pipes and 2 hats with patterns.
- Remove the pieces to oil-coated cookie sheets. Bake at 350° until turning light brown around the edges, 6-11 minutes. Transfer to wire racks to fully cool.
- Tint the frosting as you like; frost onto the cookie pieces. Allow to sit until set. Put in an airtight container to store.

Nutrition Information

- Calories: 183 calories
- Total Fat: 8g fat (2g saturated fat)
- Sodium: 91mg sodium
- Fiber: 0 fiber)
- Total Carbohydrate: 26g carbohydrate (18g sugars

- Cholesterol: 0 cholesterol
- Protein: 1g protein.

942. Snowy Mountain Cookies

Serving: about 7 dozen. | Prep: 20mins | Cook: 10mins | Ready in:

Ingredients

- 1-1/4 cups butter, softened
- 1 cup sugar
- 2 large eggs
- 1 tablespoon vanilla extract
- 4 cups all-purpose flour
- 1 teaspoon salt
- 2 cups (12 ounces) miniature semisweet chocolate chips
- 1 cup finely chopped walnuts, optional
- 1 package (12 ounces) white baking chips
- White nonpareils

Direction

- Cream the sugar and butter together until fluffy and light. Whisk in vanilla and eggs. Stir salt and flour together in a separate bowl; slowly whisk into the creamed mixture. Add walnuts (if you like) and chocolate chips; stir thoroughly. Halve the dough. Form each half into a disk; wrap plastic around. Chill for 30 minutes until firm enough to roll.
- Turn the oven to 325° to preheat. Roll each dough portion on a lightly floured surface until the thickness is 1/4 inch. With a floured 2-inch triangle-shaped cookie cutter, cut the dough. Put on non-oiled cookie sheets, 2 inches apart. Bake for 10-12 minutes until starting to turn brown around the edges. Leave in the pan to cool for 2 minutes. Transfer to wire racks to fully cool.
- In the meantime, melt white baking chips in a microwave; whisk until smooth. In the melted chips, dip the cookie tops and sprinkle nonpareils over. Allow to sit until set.

Nutrition Information

- Calories: 99 calories
- Protein: 1g protein.
- Total Fat: 5g fat (3g saturated fat)
- Sodium: 56mg sodium
- Fiber: 0 fiber)
- Total Carbohydrate: 12g carbohydrate (7g sugars
- Cholesterol: 13mg cholesterol

943. Snowy Pinecones

Serving: 16 cookies. | Prep: 01hours15mins | Cook: 0mins | Ready in:

Ingredients

- 8 cups fudge brownie fish-shaped grahams (about 24 ounces), divided
- 1 cup butter, softened
- 1 cup Nutella
- 1/2 cup Biscoff creamy cookie spread
- 3 cups plus 2 tablespoons confectioners' sugar, divided
- 8 pretzel rods, halved

Direction

- Use a food processor to pulse a cup of grahams into fine crumbs. Whip 3 cups of confectioners' sugar, cookie spread, Nutella and butter in a big bowl till no lumps remain smooth, then mix crumbs in.
- Form quarter cup if dough in cone shape around 1 pretzel rod leaving an-inch from top uncovered; arrange on baking sheets lined with waxed paper. Insert the fish grahams tail ends, flat side facing up, in a dough beginning at bottom to look like a pinecone, cutting tails off fish as necessary close the top. Trim pretzel tip with kitchen scissors and put a bit of dough over pretzel. Redo with the rest of the pretzels and dough.

- Sprinkle the rest of confectioners' sugar on pinecones. Keep in fridge in airtight container.

Nutrition Information

- Calories:
- Cholesterol:
- Protein:
- Total Fat:
- Sodium:
- Fiber:
- Total Carbohydrate:

---

944. Soft Buttermilk Sugar Cookies

Serving: about 2-1/2 dozen. | Prep: 20mins | Cook: 10mins | Ready in:

Ingredients

- 1/2 cup shortening
- 1-1/4 cups sugar, divided
- 2 eggs
- 2 teaspoons vanilla extract
- 2 cups all-purpose flour
- 2 teaspoons baking powder
- 1 teaspoon salt
- 1/2 teaspoon baking soda
- 1/2 cup buttermilk
- 1/4 teaspoon ground cinnamon

Direction

- Cream 1 cup of sugar and shortening until fluffy and light in a big bowl. Beat in vanilla and eggs. Mix baking soda, salt, baking powder and flour then put in the creamed mixture with the buttermilk alternatively. Beat well before putting the next. The batter will be moist.
- Combine the remaining sugar and cinnamon. By tablespoonfuls, drop the dough on baking sheets with grease. Use cinnamon-sugar to sprinkle over.
- Bake until edges begin to brown or for 8 to 10 minutes at 375 degrees. Put into wire racks. Keep it in an airtight container.

Nutrition Information

- Calories: 90 calories
- Total Carbohydrate: 14g carbohydrate (8g sugars
- Cholesterol: 13mg cholesterol
- Protein: 1g protein. Diabetic Exchanges: 1 starch.
- Total Fat: 3g fat (1g saturated fat)
- Sodium: 123mg sodium
- Fiber: 0 fiber)

---

945. Soft Chocolate Mint Cookies

Serving: about 3 dozen. | Prep: 15mins | Cook: 10mins | Ready in:

Ingredients

- 1/2 cup butter
- 3 ounces unsweetened chocolate
- 1/2 cup sugar
- 1/2 cup packed brown sugar
- 1 egg
- 1/4 cup buttermilk
- 1 teaspoon peppermint extract
- 1-3/4 cups all-purpose flour
- 1/2 teaspoon baking powder
- 1/4 teaspoon baking soda
- 1/4 teaspoon salt

Direction

- Melt chocolate and butter in a heavy saucepan or microwave; stir until smooth. Whisk egg and sugars in a bowl; add peppermint extract and buttermilk. Whisk in chocolate mixture.

- Mix salt, baking powder, flour and baking soda; add to sugar mixture gradually. Allow to stand until dough is firmer or for 15 minutes.
- Drop onto clean and dry baking sheets by tablespoonfuls, 3 in. apart. Bake for 8-10 minutes at 350° or until edges become firm. Cool 2 minutes; place on wire racks.

Nutrition Information

- Calories: 148 calories
- Protein: 2g protein.
- Total Fat: 6g fat (4g saturated fat)
- Sodium: 123mg sodium
- Fiber: 1g fiber)
- Total Carbohydrate: 21g carbohydrate (12g sugars
- Cholesterol: 26mg cholesterol

946. Soft Lemon Ginger Cookies

Serving: 2 dozen. | Prep: 20mins | Cook: 10mins | Ready in:

Ingredients

- 1/2 cup butter, softened
- 1 cup packed brown sugar
- 1 egg
- 3 tablespoons sour cream
- 1/2 teaspoon lemon extract
- 1/2 teaspoon vanilla extract
- 1-3/4 cups all-purpose flour
- 1 teaspoon baking soda
- 1 teaspoon cream of tartar
- 1 teaspoon ground ginger
- 1/4 teaspoon salt

Direction

- Set oven to 350° to preheat. Cream brown sugar and butter until fluffy and light in a large bowl. Beat in sour cream, egg and extracts. Combine salt, ginger, cream of tartar, baking soda, and flour; gently pour into creamed mixture and combine well.
- In ungreased baking sheets, drop by rounded teaspoonfuls 2 inches apart. Bake until lightly browned, about 10-12 minutes. Quickly remove to wire racks to cool down.

Nutrition Information

- Calories: 218 calories
- Sodium: 246mg sodium
- Fiber: 1g fiber)
- Total Carbohydrate: 32g carbohydrate (18g sugars
- Cholesterol: 41mg cholesterol
- Protein: 3g protein.
- Total Fat: 9g fat (5g saturated fat)

947. Soft Macaroons

Serving: about 6 dozen. | Prep: 10mins | Cook: 15mins | Ready in:

Ingredients

- 1 pint pineapple or orange sherbet, softened
- 2 teaspoons almond extract
- 1 package white cake mix (regular size)
- 6 cups sweetened shredded coconut

Direction

- Mix well together dry cake mix, almond extract and sherbet in a big bowl, then stir in coconut.
- Drop on baking sheets coated with grease with tablespoonfuls of batter, 2 inches apart. Bake at 350 degrees until edges are browned slightly, about 12 to 15 minutes. Transfer to wire racks to cool.

Nutrition Information

- Calories: 76 calories
- Total Carbohydrate: 11g carbohydrate (7g sugars
- Cholesterol: 0 cholesterol
- Protein: 1g protein.
- Total Fat: 4g fat (3g saturated fat)
- Sodium: 68mg sodium
- Fiber: 0 fiber)

948. Soft Sugar Cookie Puffs

Serving: about 6 dozen. | Prep: 20mins | Cook: 10mins | Ready in:

Ingredients

- 3 large eggs
- 1 cup heavy whipping cream
- 1 cup sugar
- 2 teaspoons butter, melted
- 1 teaspoon almond extract
- 4 cups all-purpose flour
- 4 teaspoons baking powder
- Assorted colored sugars, optional

Direction

- Whip eggs in bowl; put cream and whip thoroughly. Whip in butter, almond extract and sugar. Mix baking powder and flour; slowly put to mixture of sugar. Chill with cover about an hour or till handleable.
- Unroll dough on a slightly floured counter to thickness of 1/4-inch. Use floured cookie cutters of 2-1/2-inch to cut the dough. Arrange on oiled baking sheets an-inch away. Dust with colored sugars if wished, forcing sugar to dough if necessary.
- Bake about 10 to 12 minutes at 375° or till edges turn pale brown. Transfer onto wire racks and let cool.

Nutrition Information

- Calories: 104 calories
- Total Carbohydrate: 16g carbohydrate (6g sugars
- Cholesterol: 27mg cholesterol
- Protein: 2g protein.
- Total Fat: 3g fat (2g saturated fat)
- Sodium: 55mg sodium
- Fiber: 0 fiber)

949. Soft Sugar Cookies

Serving: 48 | Prep: 25mins | Cook: | Ready in:

Ingredients

- ½ cup butter, softened
- 4 ounces cream cheese, softened
- 1¾ cups sugar (see Tips)
- 1 teaspoon baking soda
- 1 teaspoon cream of tartar
- ⅛ teaspoon salt
- 3 egg yolks
- ½ teaspoon vanilla
- 1¼ cups all-purpose flour
- ½ cup white whole-wheat flour

Direction

- Set oven to 300°F to preheat. Beat cream cheese and butter in a large mixing bowl for half a minute using an electric mixer on medium to high speed. Beat in salt, cream of tartar, baking soda, and sugar until incorporated, scraping down sides of the mixing bowl occasionally. Beat in vanilla and egg yolks. Mix in as much of white whole wheat flour and all-purpose flour as you can using the mixer. Fold in the rest of flour using a wooden spoon.
- Form dough into 1-inch balls. Position balls 2 inches apart on unbuttered cookie sheets.
- Bake cookies in the preheated oven until edges are firm, for 14 to 16 minutes (do not brown edges). Allow cookies to cool on the cookie

sheet for 1 minute before removing them to a wire rack to cool.

Nutrition Information

- Calories: 73 calories;
- Saturated Fat: 2
- Sodium: 57
- Cholesterol: 19
- Total Carbohydrate: 11
- Sugar: 7
- Protein: 1
- Total Fat: 3
- Fiber: 0

950. Soft And Chewy Molasses Cookies

Serving: about 4 dozen. | Prep: 15mins | Cook: 10mins | Ready in:

Ingredients

- 1 cup plus 3 tablespoons butter, softened
- 1-1/4 cups sugar, divided
- 1/4 cup molasses
- 1 large egg
- 2-1/2 cups all-purpose flour
- 2 teaspoons baking soda
- 1 teaspoon ground cinnamon
- 1 teaspoon ground ginger
- 3/4 teaspoon ground cloves

Direction

- Cream the 1 cup sugar and butter in a big bowl. Mix in egg and molasses. Put together the cloves, ginger cinnamon, baking soda and flour; put to the creamed mixture. Combine till well incorporated.
- Form the dough into 1-1/4-inch balls. Roll the balls in leftover sugar. Put on oiled baking sheets. Flatten using a fork. Allow to bake for 10 to 12 minutes at 350° or till set.

Nutrition Information

- Calories: 180 calories
- Protein: 2g protein.
- Total Fat: 9g fat (6g saturated fat)
- Sodium: 201mg sodium
- Fiber: 0 fiber)
- Total Carbohydrate: 23g carbohydrate (12g sugars
- Cholesterol: 33mg cholesterol

951. Sour Cream Cutouts

Serving: about 6-1/2 dozen. | Prep: 30mins | Cook: 15mins | Ready in:

Ingredients

- 1 cup butter, softened
- 2 cups sugar
- 3 eggs
- 1 cup (8 ounces) sour cream
- 1 teaspoon vanilla extract
- 5-3/4 cups all-purpose flour
- 2 teaspoons baking powder
- 1/2 teaspoon baking soda
- 1/2 teaspoon salt
- 2 cans (16 ounces each) vanilla frosting
- Gel food coloring of your choice

Direction

- Cream butter with sugar in a big bowl until fluffy and light. Whip in the vanilla, sour cream and eggs. Mix the salt, baking soda, baking powder and flour; put into creamed mixture gradually and stir well. Cover and chill overnight.
- Shape dough to 1/8-in. thickness on a lightly floured surface. Slice with floured cookie cutters. Put 1 in. apart on ungreased baking trays. Bake for 12-15 minutes at 375° or until

browned lightly. Take out to wire racks to cool.
- Dye some of the frosting using food coloring; decorate cookies as you prefer.

Nutrition Information

- Calories: 109 calories
- Protein: 1g protein.
- Total Fat: 4g fat (2g saturated fat)
- Sodium: 73mg sodium
- Fiber: 0 fiber)
- Total Carbohydrate: 16g carbohydrate (9g sugars
- Cholesterol: 17mg cholesterol

952. Sour Cream Sugar Cookies

Serving: 6 | Prep: 15mins | Cook: 10mins | Ready in:

Ingredients

- Cookies:
- 1 1/2 cups white sugar
- 1 cup butter, softened
- 3 eggs
- 1 cup sour cream
- 2 teaspoons vanilla extract
- 3 1/2 cups all-purpose flour
- 2 teaspoons baking powder
- 1 teaspoon baking soda
- Frosting:
- 1/3 cup butter, softened
- 2 cups confectioners' sugar
- 2 tablespoons milk, or more as needed
- 1 1/2 teaspoons vanilla extract
- 1/4 teaspoon salt

Direction

- Use an electric mixer to beat 1 cup of butter and white sugar together until creamy in a big bowl. Put eggs in, one at a time. Stir well before putting the next. Stir 2 teaspoons of vanilla extract and sour cream in the butter mixture.
- In a bowl, mix baking soda, baking powder and flour together. Put flour mixture in the sour cream mixture. Mix well then use plastic wrap to cover the bowl. Put in the refrigerator for a minimum of 2 hours or overnight.
- Heat the oven beforehand to 175°C or 350°F. Grease two baking sheets lightly.
- Make 1/4-inch thick cookie by rolling the cookie dough on a floured surface. Slice into 3 inches round cookies. Put them on baking sheets that were prepared.
- Bake for 10 to 12 minutes until cookies spring back when lightly touched in the middle in the preheated oven. Allow to cool completely by putting on wire racks.
- Stir salt, 1 1/2 teaspoons of vanilla extract, milk, confectioners' sugar and 1/3 cup of butter together until smooth in a bowl. Spread the frosting on top of the cooled cookies.

Nutrition Information

- Calories: 1105 calories;
- Sodium: 819
- Total Carbohydrate: 148.3
- Cholesterol: 219
- Protein: 12.5
- Total Fat: 52.3

953. Special Oatmeal Chip Cookies

Serving: about 5-1/2 dozen. | Prep: 25mins | Cook: 10mins | Ready in:

Ingredients

- 1 cup butter, softened
- 1 cup peanut butter
- 1 cup sugar
- 1 cup packed brown sugar

- 2 eggs
- 1 teaspoon vanilla extract
- 3 cups old-fashioned oats
- 1 cup all-purpose flour
- 2 teaspoons ground cinnamon
- 1 teaspoon baking soda
- 1/4 teaspoon ground nutmeg
- 1-1/2 cups semisweet chocolate chips
- DRIZZLE:
- 1 cup white candy coating, melted
- 1 cup dark chocolate candy coating, melted

Direction

- Cream sugars, peanut butter, and butter together in a big bowl until fluffy and light. Add eggs, 1 each time, whisking thoroughly between additions. Whisk in vanilla. Mix together nutmeg, baking soda, cinnamon, flour, and oats; slowly add to the creamed mixture and stir thoroughly. Mix in chocolate chips.
- Roll into 1-inch balls. Put on oil-coated cookie sheets, 2 inches apart; flatten until the thickness is 1/2 inch. Bake at 350° until it turns golden brown, 10-12 minutes. Transfer to wire racks to cool.
- To make a crisscross pattern, drizzle white coating in one direction, then dark coating in the other.

Nutrition Information

- Calories:
- Sodium:
- Fiber:
- Total Carbohydrate:
- Cholesterol:
- Protein:
- Total Fat:

954. Spiced Brownie Bites

Serving: about 3-1/2 dozen. | Prep: 40mins | Cook: 15mins | Ready in:

Ingredients

- 8 ounces bittersweet chocolate, coarsely chopped
- 1/2 cup butter, cubed
- 4 large eggs
- 1 cup sugar
- 3/4 cup packed brown sugar
- 1-1/4 cups all-purpose flour
- 1/3 cup baking cocoa
- 3/4 teaspoon cayenne pepper
- 3/4 teaspoon Chinese five-spice powder
- 1/2 teaspoon salt
- GLAZE:
- 1 cup (6 ounces) semisweet chocolate chips
- 4 tablespoons butter, cubed
- 1 tablespoon light corn syrup
- Chopped crystallized ginger

Direction

- Heat the oven beforehand to 350 degrees. Melt butter and chocolate on top of double boiler or in a metal bowl over barely simmering water. Stir until smooth. Allow to cool slightly.
- Stir sugars and eggs until combined in a big bowl. Mix in chocolate mixture. Combine salt, spices, cocoa and flour in a different bowl, then put in the chocolate mixture gradually. Stir well.
- Put the mixture in to fill nearly full the mini muffin cups with grease. Bake for 12 to 15 minutes until the middle are set; avoid overbaking. Allow to cool for 5 minutes in pans. Let to cool completely by putting on wire racks.
- Melt butter and chocolate chips with corn syrup while stirring until smooth in the top of a double boiler or in a small metal bowl over barely simmering water. Take off heat. Allow to cool for about 30 minutes until slightly thickened.

- Dunk the tops of the brownies in the glaze; put ginger on top.

Nutrition Information

- Calories: 137 calories
- Cholesterol: 26mg cholesterol
- Protein: 2g protein.
- Total Fat: 7g fat (4g saturated fat)
- Sodium: 63mg sodium
- Fiber: 1g fiber)
- Total Carbohydrate: 16g carbohydrate (12g sugars

955. Spiced Christmas Cookies

Serving: 7-1/2 dozen. | Prep: 45mins | Cook: 10mins | Ready in:

Ingredients

- 2 cups molasses
- 1 cup butter, melted
- 1 cup (8 ounces) sour cream
- 1 tablespoon lemon juice
- 8 cups all-purpose flour
- 1 cup packed brown sugar
- 3 teaspoons each ground cinnamon, nutmeg and cloves
- 2-1/4 teaspoons baking soda
- 1 teaspoon grated lemon peel
- 3/4 teaspoon salt
- 3 cups chopped walnuts
- 1-2/3 cups raisins
- 1/4 cup chopped candied lemon peel
- 1/4 cup chopped candied orange peel
- FROSTING:
- 4-1/2 cups confectioners' sugar
- 1 cup heavy whipping cream
- 2 tablespoons lemon juice
- GARNISH:
- 4 cups red and/or green candied cherries, cut as desired

Direction

- Whisk lemon juice, sour cream, butter, and molasses together in a very big bowl until fully combined. Mix together salt, lemon peel, baking soda, spices, brown sugar, and flour; slowly add to the butter mixture and thoroughly stir. Mix in candied peels, raisins, and walnuts. Put on a cover and chill until easy to work with, 30 minutes.
- Quarter the dough. Roll each dough portion out on a lightly floured surface until the thickness is 1/4-inch. With a floured 2 1/4-inch round cookie cutter, cut the dough. Put on non-oiled cookie sheets, 1-inch separately. Bake at 350° until turning light brown on the bottoms, 10-12 minutes. Transfer to wire racks to cool.
- Mix together the frosting ingredients until smooth. Frost the cookies, use cherries to garnish. Put in an airtight container to store.

Nutrition Information

- Calories: 187 calories
- Total Carbohydrate: 32g carbohydrate (19g sugars
- Cholesterol: 11mg cholesterol
- Protein: 2g protein. Diabetic Exchanges: 2 starch
- Total Fat: 6g fat (2g saturated fat)
- Sodium: 81mg sodium
- Fiber: 1g fiber)

956. Spiced Molasses Doughnut Cookies

Serving: 2 dozen donut cookies plus donut hole cutouts. | Prep: 45mins | Cook: 10mins |Ready in:

Ingredients

- 1/2 cup baking cocoa
- 1/2 cup canola oil

- 1 cup packed brown sugar
- 1/2 cup molasses
- 1/4 to 1/3 cup water
- 1 large egg
- 3-1/2 cups all-purpose flour
- 3/4 teaspoon baking soda
- 1/2 teaspoon ground cinnamon
- 1/4 teaspoon ground cloves
- Pinch ground nutmeg
- Pinch salt
- FROSTING:
- 6 tablespoons butter, softened
- 3 cups confectioners' sugar
- 3 to 4 tablespoons 2% milk
- 3/4 teaspoon vanilla extract
- Pinch salt
- Assorted jimmies

Direction

- Preheat an oven to 350°. Combine oil and cocoa in a big bowl till smooth. Whisk in egg, 1/4 cup water, molasses and brown sugar. Beat salt, spices, baking soda and flour in a small bowl; slowly whisk into the cocoa mixture. If needed, put more water to create a stiff dough.
- To a slightly floured area, put the dough; knead several times, creating a smooth dough. Split dough in half; roll every piece into quarter-inch thickness. Cut using a 3-inch floured doughnut cutter. On unoiled baking sheets, put the doughnut-hole and doughnut cutouts an-inch away.
- Allow to bake for 7 to 9 minutes or till firm. Take off from pans to wire racks to cool fully.
- Whisk salt, vanilla, 3 tablespoons milk, confectioners' sugar and butter in a bowl till smooth. If needed, mix in more milk to attain spreading consistency. Scatter on top of cookies. Scatter jimmies over. Allow to sit till firm. Keep in an airtight container.

Nutrition Information

- Calories:
- Cholesterol:
- Protein:
- Total Fat:
- Sodium:
- Fiber:
- Total Carbohydrate:

957. Spicy Molasses Cookies

Serving: about 12 dozen. | Prep: 25mins | Cook: 10mins | Ready in:

Ingredients

- 1 cup shortening
- 1-1/2 cups packed brown sugar
- 1/4 cup light or dark molasses
- 3 large eggs
- 3-1/2 cups all-purpose flour
- 3 teaspoons ground cinnamon
- 1 teaspoon baking soda
- 1/2 teaspoon salt
- 1/2 teaspoon ground nutmeg
- 1/4 teaspoon ground cloves
- 1/4 teaspoon ground allspice
- 1 cup chopped walnuts, optional
- 1 cup raisins, optional

Direction

- Cream sugar and shortening in a big bowl. Put the molasses. Put the eggs, one by one, mixing thoroughly after every addition. Mix the spices and dry ingredients; put to the batter and stir gently. Mix in the raisins and nuts if wished; combine thoroughly.
- Onto oiled baking sheets, drop by teaspoonfuls. Allow to bake for 10-12 minutes at 350°. Transfer to wire racks.

Nutrition Information

- Calories: 70 calories

- Total Carbohydrate: 10g carbohydrate (5g sugars
- Cholesterol: 9mg cholesterol
- Protein: 1g protein.
- Total Fat: 3g fat (1g saturated fat)
- Sodium: 39mg sodium
- Fiber: 0 fiber)

958. Spritz Wreaths

Serving: Makes about 6 dozen cookies | Prep: | Cook: | Ready in:

Ingredients

- 1/2 preparedBasic Butter Cookie Dough at room temperature
- 1 egg white, beaten lightly with 2 teaspoons water
- green decorating sugar
- glacéed cherries, cut into slivers

Direction

- Set the oven to 350°F and start preheating.
- Pack dough into a cookie press fitted with wreath disk; press about an inch apart onto cool, clean and dry baking sheets. Brush egg-white wash lightly over cookies; top with decorating sugar. Arrange cherry slivers to form bow shapes.
- Working in batches; bake in the middle of the oven for about 12 minutes until edges turn pale golden. Cool cookies for 2 minutes on sheets and remove to racks to completely cool. (If you let cookies cool for too long on sheets, they will stick to sheets). You can place cookies between wax paper layers in airtight containers to store them up to 6 weeks frozen.

Nutrition Information

959. Star Anise Honey Cookies

Serving: 6 dozen. | Prep: 25mins | Cook: 5mins | Ready in:

Ingredients

- 1 cup sugar
- 1 cup honey
- 3 large eggs
- 5 cups all-purpose flour
- 2-1/2 teaspoons baking soda
- 1 teaspoon ground star anise

Direction

- Set an oven to 350 degrees and start preheating. Whisk honey and sugar in a large bowl until combined. Whisk in eggs. Beat star anise, baking soda, and flour in a different bowl; gradually whisk into the sugar mixture.
- Split the dough in half. Roll each portion of dough to 1/4-inch thickness on a lightly floured surface. Use a floured 1 1/2-inch star-shaped cookie cutter to slice. Put an inch apart onto baking sheets coated with cooking spray.
- Bake until the edges turn light brown, 4-6 minutes. Transfer from the pans to wire racks to cool.

Nutrition Information

- Calories:
- Total Carbohydrate:
- Cholesterol:
- Protein:
- Total Fat:
- Sodium:
- Fiber:

960. Star Sandwich Cookies

Serving: about 5 dozen. | Prep: 25mins | Cook: 10mins | Ready in:

Ingredients

- 1 cup butter, softened
- 2 cups all-purpose flour
- 1/3 cup heavy whipping cream
- Sugar
- FILLING:
- 1/2 cup butter, softened
- 1-1/2 cups confectioners' sugar
- 2 teaspoons vanilla extract
- 4 to 8 teaspoons heavy whipping cream
- Liquid or paste food coloring, optional

Direction

- Whip the cream, flour and butter in a big bowl. Chill covered for an hour or until easy to handle.
- Shape dough into 1/8-in. thickness on a lightly floured surface. Slice with a floured 2 in. star cookie cutter. Scatter tops of cookies with sugar; put on ungreased baking trays.
- Prick each cookie 3-4 times using a fork. Bake for 7-9 minutes at 375° or until firm. Take out to wire racks to cool.
- To make filling, mix the vanilla, confectioners' sugar, butter and enough cream to reach the preferred spreading consistency. Dye with food coloring (optional). Spread filling carefully on the bottom of half of the cookies; garnish with leftover cookies.

Nutrition Information

- Calories: 146 calories
- Fiber: 0 fiber)
- Total Carbohydrate: 12g carbohydrate (6g sugars
- Cholesterol: 29mg cholesterol
- Protein: 1g protein.
- Total Fat: 10g fat (6g saturated fat)
- Sodium: 94mg sodium

961. Sugar Cookie Cutouts

Serving: 36 | Prep: | Cook: | Ready in:

Ingredients

- 1 cup butter, softened
- 1 cup white sugar
- 2 eggs
- 1 teaspoon vanilla extract
- 3 3/4 cups all-purpose flour
- 2 teaspoons baking powder
- 1/4 cup heavy whipping cream
- 1/2 cup colored sugar for decoration

Direction

- Cream sugar and butter together in a medium bowl. Stir in vanilla and eggs. Sift baking powder and flour together, then add together with the heavy cream into the creamed mixture and stir. Put a cover on the dough and allow to chill until firm, 2-3 hours.
- Set an oven to 175°C (350°F) and start preheating. Coat cookie sheets with cooking spray.
- Roll out the dough on a lightly floured surface to 1/4 inch in thickness. Use cookie cutters to slice into shapes you desire. On the greased cookie sheets, arrange the cookies, an inch apart. If desired, scatter with colored sugar.
- In the prepared oven, bake until the edges and bottoms of the cookies turn light brown, for 12-14 minutes. Transfer from the baking sheet onto wire racks to cool. Place into an airtight container to store.

Nutrition Information

- Calories: 135 calories;
- Cholesterol: 26
- Protein: 1.8
- Total Fat: 6.1
- Sodium: 68
- Total Carbohydrate: 18.4

962. Sugar Diamonds

Serving: about 6 dozen. | Prep: 15mins | Cook: 30mins | Ready in:

Ingredients

- 1 cup butter, softened
- 1 cup sugar
- 1 large egg, separated
- 1/2 teaspoon vanilla extract
- 2 cups all-purpose flour
- 1/2 teaspoon ground cinnamon
- Pinch salt
- 1/2 cup chopped pecans

Direction

- Cream sugar and butter together in a bowl. Stir in vanilla and egg yolks until well-mixed. Mix salt, cinnamon and flour; combine with the cream mixture gradually.
- Scoop the mixture into a greased 15x10x1-inch baking pan. Use plastic wrap to cover the dough and press into the pan evenly; take off the wrap.
- Beat egg whites in a small bowl until foamy and use the mixture to brush over dough. Use pecans to sprinkle. Put into the oven to bake until lightly brown or for 30 minutes at 300 degrees. Slice into diamond shapes of 1 1/2 inches in size while still warm.

Nutrition Information

- Calories: 105 calories
- Fiber: 0 fiber)
- Total Carbohydrate: 11g carbohydrate (6g sugars
- Cholesterol: 20mg cholesterol
- Protein: 1g protein.
- Total Fat: 6g fat (3g saturated fat)
- Sodium: 57mg sodium

963. Sugared Cherry Jewels

Serving: about 5 dozen. | Prep: 25mins | Cook: 15mins | Ready in:

Ingredients

- 1 cup butter, softened
- 1/2 cup sugar
- 1/3 cup light corn syrup
- 2 egg yolks
- 1/2 teaspoon vanilla extract
- 2-1/2 cups all-purpose flour
- Additional sugar
- 1 jar (10 ounces) maraschino cherries, drained and halved

Direction

- Cream sugar and butter together in a big bowl until fluffy and light. Whisk in vanilla, egg yolks, and corn syrup. Slowly add the flour and stir thoroughly. Put a cover on and chill until easy to work with, 60 minutes.
- Roll into 1-inch balls; in extra sugar, roll each ball. Put on non-oiled cookie sheets, 2 inches apart. In the middle of each, form a dent using the end of a wooden spoon handle. In the middle, press a cherry half.
- Bake at 325° until it turns light brown, 14-16 minutes. Transfer to wire racks to cool.

Nutrition Information

- Calories: 132 calories
- Protein: 2g protein.
- Total Fat: 6g fat (4g saturated fat)
- Sodium: 71mg sodium
- Fiber: 0 fiber)
- Total Carbohydrate: 18g carbohydrate (9g sugars
- Cholesterol: 31mg cholesterol

964. Super Chunky Cookies

Serving: 30 | Prep: | Cook: | Ready in:

Ingredients

- 2 1/2 cups all-purpose flour
- 1 teaspoon baking soda
- 1/8 teaspoon salt
- 1 cup unsalted butter
- 3/4 cup white sugar
- 1 cup packed brown sugar
- 2 eggs
- 2 teaspoons vanilla extract
- 1 cup mini semi-sweet chocolate chips
- 1 cup milk chocolate chips
- 4 (1 ounce) squares bittersweet chocolate, cut into 1/2 inch chunks
- 2 ounces white chocolate, chopped
- 1/2 cup chopped toasted pecans
- 3/4 cup toffee baking bits

Direction

- Put 1 rack in bottom third and another in top of oven; preheat to 175°C/350°F.
- Use wire whisk to mix salt, baking soda and flour till blended thoroughly in medium bowl.
- Beat butter at medium speed till creamy for 30 seconds in medium size bowl. Add sugars; keep beating till mixture is light in color and texture for 3-4 minutes more. Use rubber spatula to scrape bowl sides down; one by one, add eggs, beating well after every addition. Beat vanilla in.
- A third at a time, beat flour mixture in at slow speed, scraping bowl sides down after every addition; use wooden spoon to mix in all white chocolate, bittersweet chocolate and chocolate chips in. Mix toffee bits and pecans in; dough will be very stiff.
- By slightly rounded tablespoonfuls, drop dough on 2 ungreased baking sheets, about 1 1/2-in. between cookies. Refrigerate leftover dough; bake cookies till edges are lightly browned and cookies are set or for 11-13 minutes. Switch baking sheets' positions for even browning halfway through baking time.
- Cool cookies for 1-3 minutes on baking sheets over wire racks. Transfer cookies onto wire racks using metal spatula; completely cool. Repeat with leftover dough.

Nutrition Information

- Calories: 280 calories;
- Total Fat: 15.4
- Sodium: 92
- Total Carbohydrate: 34.4
- Cholesterol: 35
- Protein: 2.8

965. Super Snowman Cookies

Serving: 10 cookies. | Prep: 15mins | Cook: 10mins | Ready in:

Ingredients

- 3/4 cup butter, softened
- 1 cup sugar
- 2 large eggs
- 1 teaspoon vanilla extract
- 2-3/4 cups all-purpose flour
- 1 teaspoon baking powder
- 1/2 teaspoon salt
- Miniature marshmallows, cut in half, optional
- Light corn syrup, optional
- Colored sugars, tinted frostings, cM&M's minis and pretzel sticks

Direction

- Cream butter with sugar in a big bowl until fluffy and light. Whip in vanilla and eggs. Mix the salt, baking powder and flour; put into creamed mixture gradually and stir well. Chill for an hour or until set.
- Shape dough to 1/4-in. thickness on a lightly floured surface. Slice out 10 circles using a

floured 3-in. round cookie cutter. Keep working with 2-1/2-in. and 2-in. round cookie cutters. Roll scraps again. Slice top hats from leftover dough with a paring knife (optional).
- Push together 1 circle of each size on greased baking trays to create a snowman. Keep working with leftover circles. Put one on top of each snowman if using hats.
- Bake for 8-10 minutes at 375° or until slightly browned. Let cool completely on wire racks.
- For earmuffs, plunge marshmallows in corn syrup (optional); roll in colored sugar. Let sit until dry. Frost and decorate cookies using frosting, sugars, M&M's as desired and, if using, earmuffs; attach pretzels for arms.

Nutrition Information

- Calories:
- Protein:
- Total Fat:
- Sodium:
- Fiber:
- Total Carbohydrate:
- Cholesterol:

966. Surefire Sugar Cookies

Serving: 2 dozen. | Prep: 15mins | Cook: 10mins | Ready in:

Ingredients

- 1 tube (18 ounces) refrigerated sugar cookie dough
- 1-1/2 cups semisweet chocolate chips
- 4-1/2 teaspoons shortening
- Colored sprinkles, chopped nuts or sweetened shredded coconut

Direction

- Cut and bake sugar cookies as directed on package. Allow to cool on wire racks.
- Combine shortening and chocolate chips in a microwaveable bowl. Microwave on high power until melted, for 1 to 2 minutes; whisk until no lumps remain. Immerse each cookie halfway in melted chocolate. Arrange cookies on waxed paper; instantly scatter top with coconut, nuts, or colored sprinkles. Allow to sit until chocolate is thoroughly firm.

Nutrition Information

- Calories: 300 calories
- Protein: 3g protein.
- Total Fat: 17g fat (6g saturated fat)
- Sodium: 182mg sodium
- Fiber: 2g fiber)
- Total Carbohydrate: 38g carbohydrate (23g sugars
- Cholesterol: 12mg cholesterol

967. Surprise Meringues

Serving: 12 | Prep: | Cook: | Ready in:

Ingredients

- 2 egg whites
- 1/8 teaspoon salt
- 1/8 teaspoon cream of tartar
- 3/4 cup white sugar
- 1 teaspoon vanilla extract
- 6 ounces semisweet chocolate chips

Direction

- Set oven to preheat at 300°F (150°C). Use parchment paper to line baking sheets.
- Beat together the vanilla, sugar, cream of tartar, salt and egg whites till the meringue stiffens up.
- Fold the chocolate chips into the mixture.
- Put 1 teaspoonful of meringue onto the lined cookie sheets. Bake for 25 minutes at 300°F (150°C).

Nutrition Information

- Calories: 120 calories;
- Sodium: 35
- Total Carbohydrate: 21.5
- Cholesterol: 0
- Protein: 1.2
- Total Fat: 4.3

968. Surprise Sugar Stars

Serving: 4 dozen. | Prep: 30mins | Cook: 15mins | Ready in:

Ingredients

- 1 cup butter, softened
- 1-1/4 cups sugar
- 2 eggs
- 1 teaspoon vanilla extract
- 4 cups all-purpose flour
- 2 teaspoons baking powder
- 2 teaspoons ground nutmeg
- 1 teaspoon baking soda
- 1/2 teaspoon salt
- 2/3 cup buttermilk
- 1 can (21 ounces) cherry pie filling
- ICING:
- 2 cups confectioners' sugar
- 1/2 teaspoon almond extract
- 2 to 3 tablespoons whole milk
- Colored sugar, optional

Direction

- Beat butter and sugar in a large mixing bowl until fluffy and light. Put in eggs, 1 by 1, beating well between additions. Whisk in vanilla. Mix dry ingredients together; mix alternately with buttermilk into creamed mixture, beating well between additions. Chill for 2 to 3 hours or until you can handle easily.
- Flatten dough to a thickness of 1/4 inch on a work surface coated with flour. Cut dough using a 2-inch start cookie cutter or with your favorite cutter. Arrange half of the stars on unbuttered baking sheets. In the center of each cookie, place 1 1/2 teaspoonfuls of pie filling. Place the remaining stars on tops. Pinch to seal edges; create a small slit in top of each cookie.
- Bake at 350° for 12 to 15 minutes or until cookies turn light brown. Let cookies cool on wire racks.
- To make icing, mix together extract, confectioners' sugar, and enough milk in a small bowl until desired thickness is reached. Frost cooled cookies with icing. Scatter top with colored sugar, if desired.

Nutrition Information

- Calories: 131 calories
- Protein: 2g protein.
- Total Fat: 4g fat (2g saturated fat)
- Sodium: 115mg sodium
- Fiber: 0 fiber)
- Total Carbohydrate: 22g carbohydrate (13g sugars
- Cholesterol: 19mg cholesterol

969. Swedish Spritz Cookies

Serving: 5 dozen. | Prep: 15mins | Cook: 10mins | Ready in:

Ingredients

- 1 cup butter, softened
- 2/3 cup sugar
- 1 egg
- 1/2 teaspoon almond extract
- 1/2 teaspoon vanilla extract
- 2-1/4 cups all-purpose flour
- 1 teaspoon baking powder
- Frosting

Direction

- Cream sugar and butter till fluffy and light in a big bowl; beat in extracts and egg. Mix baking powder and flour; add to creamed mixture slowly.
- Press dough to desired shapes onto ungreased baking sheets, 1-in. apart, using cookie press fitted with your preferred disk; bake at 375° till edges are lightly browned and firm or for 10-11 minutes. Transfer to wire racks; cool. As desired, frost.

Nutrition Information

- Calories: 108 calories
- Sodium: 77mg sodium
- Fiber: 0 fiber)
- Total Carbohydrate: 12g carbohydrate (4g sugars
- Cholesterol: 23mg cholesterol
- Protein: 1g protein.
- Total Fat: 6g fat (4g saturated fat)

970. Sweet Taste Of Victory Butterscotch Cookies

Serving: about 5 dozen. | Prep: 20mins | Cook: 15mins | Ready in:

Ingredients

- 1 cup butter, softened
- 1 cup sugar
- 1 cup packed brown sugar
- 3 eggs
- 3 teaspoons vanilla extract
- 3-3/4 cups all-purpose flour
- 2 teaspoons ground cinnamon
- 1 teaspoon baking soda
- 1/2 teaspoon salt
- Pinch each ground ginger, nutmeg and cloves
- 1-1/2 cups semisweet chocolate chips
- 1 cup butterscotch chips
- 1 cup chopped walnuts
- 1/2 cup brickle toffee bits

Direction

- Beat sugars and butter in a big bowl until the mixture is fluffy and light. Pour in eggs, one at a time, and beat thoroughly between additions. Add vanilla and beat. Mix together cloves, nutmeg, ginger, salt, baking soda, cinnamon and flour; pour little by little into beaten mixture and stir thoroughly. Mix in toffee bits, walnuts and chips.
- Scoop by rounded tablespoonfuls and place 2 inches apart onto ungreased baking sheets. Bake in 350-degree oven until cookies turn light brown, about 12 to 14 minutes. Transfer to wire racks and let cool.

Nutrition Information

- Calories: 142 calories
- Total Carbohydrate: 19g carbohydrate (10g sugars
- Cholesterol: 18mg cholesterol
- Protein: 2g protein. Diabetic Exchanges: 1-1/2 fat
- Total Fat: 7g fat (4g saturated fat)
- Sodium: 77mg sodium
- Fiber: 1g fiber)

971. Sweetheart Slices

Serving: about 2 dozen. | Prep: 20mins | Cook: 15mins | Ready in:

Ingredients

- 1 cup butter, softened
- 3/4 cup sugar
- 4 large egg yolks
- 3 teaspoons vanilla extract
- 2-1/2 cups all-purpose flour
- 1-1/2 teaspoons ground cinnamon
- 1/3 cup miniature semisweet chocolate chips

- Red or pink paste food coloring

Direction

- Cream sugar and butter till fluffy and light; one by one, add egg yolks, beating well with every addition. Beat vanilla in. Whisk cinnamon and flour; add to creamed mixture slowly. Stir well. Divide dough to 2 portions; 1/3 of dough and 2/3. Mix chocolate chips into bigger portion; put aside. Tint leftover dough pink.
- Roll smaller portion to 1/2-in. thick on lightly floured surface. Use 1-in. heart-shaped cookie cutter to cut; brush water on one side of hearts; stack together gently to make two 5-in. long logs. Along sides, run finger to smooth edges. Refrigerate till firm, 30 minutes.
- Divide the chocolate chip dough to 10 portions then roll each to 5-in. coil. Brush water on the outside of heart log; around heart logs, mold coils, pressing gently to adhere. Tightly wrap cookie logs in plastic; mold dough by rolling into smooth roll. Freeze till firm, 2 hours.
- Preheat an oven to 350°; cut to 1/4-in. slices. Put on parchment paper-lined baking sheets, 2-in. apart. Bake for 12-14 minutes till edges lightly brown; cool for 2 minutes on pans. Transfer to wire racks; cool.

Nutrition Information

- Calories:
- Sodium:
- Fiber:
- Total Carbohydrate:
- Cholesterol:
- Protein:
- Total Fat:

972. Tender Italian Sugar Cookies

Serving: 3 dozen. | Prep: 20mins | Cook: 10mins | Ready in:

Ingredients

- 3/4 cup shortening
- 3/4 cup sugar
- 3 large eggs
- 1 teaspoon vanilla extract
- 3 cups all-purpose flour
- 3 teaspoons baking powder
- 1/8 teaspoon salt
- ICING:
- 1/4 cup milk
- 2 tablespoons butter, melted
- 1/2 teaspoon vanilla extract
- 2-1/2 cups confectioners' sugar
- Food coloring and coarse sugar, optional

Direction

- Set the oven to 400° to preheat. Cream sugar and shortening together in a big bowl until the mixture is fluffy and light. Beat in vanilla and eggs. Mix together salt, baking powder and flour, then put into the creamed mixture gradually and blend well.
- Form the dough into balls with 1 1/2 inches in size. Arrange balls on grease-free baking sheets by 1 inch apart. Bake until browned slightly, or for 8 to 10 minutes. Transfer to wire racks to allow to cool.
- To make icing, mix together confectioners' sugar, vanilla, butter and milk until smooth in a small bowl. Tint the mixture with food coloring if you want. Dip into icing with the tops of cookies and let the excess drip off. Use coarse sugar to sprinkle if wanted. Put on waxed paper and allow to stand until set.

Nutrition Information

- Calories: 136 calories
- Total Fat: 5g fat (2g saturated fat)

- Sodium: 54mg sodium
- Fiber: 0 fiber)
- Total Carbohydrate: 21g carbohydrate (12g sugars
- Cholesterol: 20mg cholesterol
- Protein: 2g protein. Diabetic Exchanges: 1 starch

973. Tender Sugar Cookies

Serving: 5-1/2 dozen. | Prep: 30mins | Cook: 10mins | Ready in:

Ingredients

- 3/4 cup butter-flavored shortening
- 1-1/2 cups sugar
- 2 eggs
- 1/2 teaspoon almond extract
- 1/2 teaspoon vanilla extract
- 3 cups all-purpose flour
- 1 teaspoon baking powder
- 1 teaspoon baking soda
- 1/2 teaspoon salt
- 1/3 cup buttermilk
- Colored sugar and/or coarse sugar

Direction

- Cream the sugar and shortening until fluffy and light in a big bowl. Put eggs, 1 at a time. Stir well before putting the next. Stir in extracts. Mix salt, baking soda, baking powder and flour then put in the creamed mixture with the buttermilk alternately. Stir well before putting the next. Cover and put in the refrigerator for a minimum of 2 hours.
- Make 1-inch balls by rolling. Dunk the tops in the sugar. Put on baking sheets lined with parchment paper, leaving 2-inch space apart. Bake until the tops crack and lightly browned or for 9 to 11 minutes at 375 degrees. Allow to cool by putting on wire racks.

Nutrition Information

- Calories: 61 calories
- Total Carbohydrate: 9g carbohydrate (5g sugars
- Cholesterol: 6mg cholesterol
- Protein: 1g protein. Diabetic Exchanges: 1/2 starch
- Total Fat: 2g fat (1g saturated fat)
- Sodium: 47mg sodium
- Fiber: 0 fiber)

974. Toasted Anise Strips

Serving: about 2 dozen. | Prep: 15mins | Cook: 30mins | Ready in:

Ingredients

- 1/4 cup butter, softened
- 1 cup sugar
- 3 large eggs
- 1 tablespoon anise extract
- 2-1/2 cups cake flour
- 2 teaspoons baking powder
- 1/4 teaspoon salt

Direction

- Whip butter with sugar in a bowl. Put in one egg at a time, mixing thoroughly after each egg. Put in extract. Mix salt, baking powder and flour; put into whipped mixture and stir well. Put 1/2 of the batter onto a greased baking tray, shaping an 11x5-in. rectangle. Keep working with leftover batter on another baking tray. Bake for 15 minutes at 350°. Take off from baking trays; slice into 1-in. slices. Put cut side down on baking trays. Bake 15 minutes more or until lightly browned. Let cool on wire racks.

Nutrition Information

- Calories: 226 calories

- Cholesterol: 63mg cholesterol
- Protein: 4g protein.
- Total Fat: 5g fat (3g saturated fat)
- Sodium: 171mg sodium
- Fiber: 0 fiber)
- Total Carbohydrate: 39g carbohydrate (17g sugars

975. Toffee Cranberry Crisps

Serving: 5-1/2 dozen. | Prep: 15mins | Cook: 10mins | Ready in:

Ingredients

- 1 cup butter, softened
- 3/4 cup sugar
- 3/4 cup packed brown sugar
- 1 large egg
- 1 teaspoon vanilla extract
- 1-1/2 cups all-purpose flour
- 1-1/2 cups quick-cooking oats
- 1 teaspoon baking soda
- 1/4 teaspoon salt
- 1 cup dried cranberries
- 1 cup miniature semisweet chocolate chips
- 1 cup milk chocolate English toffee bits

Direction

- In a large bowl, cream sugars and butter until fluffy and light. Beat in vanilla and egg. Combine the oats, flour, salt and baking soda; add to the creamed mixture gradually and mix well. Blend in the toffee bits, chocolate chips and cranberries.
- Form into three logs of 12-inch; use plastic wrap to wrap each one. Allow 2 hours to refrigerate or till firm. Unwrap and cut into slices of half an inch. On lightly greased baking sheets, place 2 inches apart.
- Bake at 350° for around 8 to 10 minutes or until they have the color of golden brown. Take away to wire racks for cooling.

Nutrition Information

- Calories: 98 calories
- Cholesterol: 12mg cholesterol
- Protein: 1g protein.
- Total Fat: 5g fat (3g saturated fat)
- Sodium: 71mg sodium
- Fiber: 0 fiber)
- Total Carbohydrate: 13g carbohydrate (10g sugars

976. Torcetti

Serving: 6 dozen. | Prep: 30mins | Cook: 15mins | Ready in:

Ingredients

- 5 cups all-purpose flour
- 1 cup cold butter, cubed
- 1 cup shortening
- 1 package (1/4 ounce) active dry yeast
- 1/2 cup warm milk (110° to 115°)
- 2 eggs
- 1 tablespoon sugar
- 1-1/2 teaspoons vanilla extract
- 2 cups confectioners' sugar
- Additional confectioners' sugar

Direction

- In a big bowl, put flour; slice in shortening and butter until mixture forms coarse crumbs. Put aside. Mix yeast with warm milk in a big bowl to dissolve. Put in 2 cups of the crumb mixture, vanilla, sugar and eggs; whip until well combined. Whip in leftover crumb mixture gradually.
- Transfer onto a floured surface; knead for 3 to 4 minutes. Put in a greased bowl, flipping once to grease top. Cover and let sit about 1 hour in a warm place to rise until doubled.
- Punch down the dough; split into 6 portions. Roll each portion into 12 6-in. ropes, about 1/4-in. thick; roll in confectioners' sugar. Form

each rope into a loop. Grabbing both ends of loop, twist together 3 times.
- Put 2 in. apart on greased baking trays. Bake for 12-14 minutes at 375° or until golden brown. Roll warm cookies in more confectioners' sugar. Let cool on wire racks.

Nutrition Information

- Calories: 102 calories
- Fiber: 0 fiber)
- Total Carbohydrate: 12g carbohydrate (5g sugars
- Cholesterol: 13mg cholesterol
- Protein: 1g protein. Diabetic Exchanges: 1 starch
- Total Fat: 5g fat (2g saturated fat)
- Sodium: 21mg sodium

977. Trail Mix Cookie Cups

Serving: 2 dozen. | Prep: 20mins | Cook: 15mins | Ready in:

Ingredients

- 1 tube (16-1/2 ounces) refrigerated peanut butter cookie dough
- 1/2 cup creamy peanut butter
- 1/2 cup Nutella
- 1-1/2 cups trail mix

Direction

- Set the oven to 350 degrees to preheat. Form the dough to 1-1/4-inch 2 dozen balls. Pat on bottom and up sides of mini muffin cups coated in grease evenly.
- Bake till golden brown for 12 to 14 minutes. Shape the cups again with a wooden spoon end handle as need be. Cool for 15 minutes in pans. Transfer onto wire racks, and cool fully.
- Fill cups using a teaspoon Nutella and a teaspoon peanut butter. Put trail mix on top.

Nutrition Information

- Calories: 197 calories
- Total Fat: 12g fat (3g saturated fat)
- Sodium: 121mg sodium
- Fiber: 1g fiber)
- Total Carbohydrate: 20g carbohydrate (13g sugars
- Cholesterol: 3mg cholesterol
- Protein: 4g protein.

978. Treasure Cookies

Serving: 30 | Prep: | Cook: |Ready in:

Ingredients

- 1 1/2 cups graham cracker crumbs
- 1/2 cup all-purpose flour
- 2 teaspoons baking powder
- 1 (14 ounce) can sweetened condensed milk
- 1/2 cup butter, melted
- 1 1/3 cups flaked coconut
- 2 cups semisweet chocolate chips
- 1 cup chopped pecans

Direction

- Set oven to preheat at 190°C (375°F).
- In a small bowl, mix together baking powder, flour and cracker crumbs.
- In a large mixing bowl, beat together margarine and condensed milk till smooth.
- Add in cracker crumb mixture and combine well. Mix in pecans, chocolate chips, and coconut.
- Drop rounded teaspoon of the dough on a cookie sheet coated with non-stick spray. Bake until light brown, or 9-10 minutes. Store at room temperature, loosely covered.

Nutrition Information

- Calories: 188 calories;
- Sodium: 107

- Total Carbohydrate: 21.3
- Cholesterol: 13
- Protein: 2.5
- Total Fat: 11.5

979. Triple Chip Cookies

Serving: about 2-1/2 dozen. | Prep: 15mins | Cook: 10mins | Ready in:

Ingredients

- 1 tube (16-1/2 ounces) refrigerated peanut butter cookie dough
- 1 cup coarsely crushed potato chips
- 1/2 cup butterscotch chips
- 1/2 cup swirled milk chocolate and peanut butter chips

Direction

- Soften the cookie dough by letting it stand for 5-10 minutes at room temperature. In a large bowl, combine the chips and cookie dough.
- Drop by tablespoonfuls of dough onto ungreased baking sheets 2 in. apart. Bake at 350° until light brown or 10-12 minutes. Transfer to wire racks. Keep in an airtight container.

Nutrition Information

- Calories:
- Fiber:
- Total Carbohydrate:
- Cholesterol:
- Protein:
- Total Fat:
- Sodium:

980. Triple Nut Snowballs

Serving: about 6 dozen. | Prep: 15mins | Cook: 10mins | Ready in:

Ingredients

- 1 cup plus 2 tablespoons unsalted butter, softened
- 1/2 cup plus 2 cups confectioners' sugar, divided
- 1-1/2 teaspoons almond extract
- 2 cups all-purpose flour
- 1 teaspoon salt
- 1 teaspoon ground cinnamon
- 1 cup unsalted cashews
- 1 cup macadamia nuts
- 1 cup pecan halves

Direction

- Preheat an oven to 375°. Cream 1/2 cup confectioners' sugar and butter till fluffy and light; beat extract in. Whisk cinnamon, salt and flour in separate bowl; beat into creamed mixture slowly. Pulse nuts till finely ground in food processor; mix nuts into dough.
- Form to 1-in. balls; put on parchment paper-lined baking sheets, 1-in. apart. Bake for 8-10 minutes till golden brown; cool for 10 minutes on pans.
- Put leftover confectioners' sugar in small bowl; in sugar, roll slightly cooled cookies. Put cookies on wire racks; completely cool. Before serving, roll cookies again in sugar.

Nutrition Information

- Calories: 88 calories
- Total Carbohydrate: 8g carbohydrate (4g sugars
- Cholesterol: 8mg cholesterol
- Protein: 1g protein.
- Total Fat: 6g fat (2g saturated fat)
- Sodium: 40mg sodium
- Fiber: 0 fiber)

981. Two Minute Cookies

Serving: about 3 dozen. | Prep: 5mins | Cook: 10mins | Ready in:

Ingredients

- 1/2 cup butter, cubed
- 1/2 cup milk
- 2 cups sugar
- 3 cups quick-cooking oats or old-fashioned oats
- 5 tablespoons baking cocoa
- 1/2 cup raisins, chopped nuts or sweetened shredded coconut

Direction

- In the big saucepan, heat the sugar, milk and butter. Boil, stir once in a while. Boil for 60 seconds.
- Take out of heat. Stir in coconut/nuts, raisins, cocoa and oats. Drop by tablespoonfuls to the waxed paper. Let cool down.

Nutrition Information

- Calories: 203 calories
- Fiber: 2g fiber)
- Total Carbohydrate: 35g carbohydrate (24g sugars
- Cholesterol: 15mg cholesterol
- Protein: 3g protein.
- Total Fat: 6g fat (3g saturated fat)
- Sodium: 56mg sodium

982. Two Tone Christmas Cookies

Serving: 6-1/2 dozen. | Prep: 25mins | Cook: 10mins | Ready in:

Ingredients

- 1 cup butter, softened
- 1-1/2 cups sugar
- 2 egg yolks
- 2 teaspoons vanilla extract
- 1 teaspoon almond extract
- 3-1/2 cups all-purpose flour
- 1 teaspoon salt
- 1 teaspoon baking powder
- 1/2 teaspoon baking soda
- 9 drops green food coloring
- 1 tablespoon 2% milk
- 1/3 cup finely chopped pistachios
- 9 drops red food coloring
- 3 tablespoons seedless raspberry preserves
- 2 cups (12 ounces) semisweet chocolate chips, melted
- Additional chopped pistachios, optional

Direction

- Cream sugar and butter till fluffy and light in a big bowl; beat in extracts and egg yolks. Mix baking soda, baking powder, salt and flour. Add to creamed mixture slowly; mix well. Halve dough. Mix nuts, milk and green food coloring into 1 portion well. Add jam and red food coloring to other half.
- Form each portion to 8x6-in. rectangle between 2 waxed paper pieces. Lengthwise halve. Put 1 green rectangle on a plastic wrap piece. Put 1 pink rectangle over; lightly press together. Repeat, making 2nd stack. In plastic wrap, wrap each; refrigerate overnight.
- 1 at 1 time, remove a stack from fridge. Unwrap dough; lengthwise halve. Put 1 portion into fridge. Cut leftover portion to 1/8-in. slices; put on ungreased baking sheets, 1-in. apart. Bake till set for 7-9 minutes at 375°. Put onto wire racks; cool. Repeat with leftover dough.
- Drizzle melted chocolate on cooled cookies; if desired, sprinkle extra pistachios.

Nutrition Information

- Calories: 84 calories

- Fiber: 0 fiber)
- Total Carbohydrate: 12g carbohydrate (7g sugars
- Cholesterol: 12mg cholesterol
- Protein: 1g protein.
- Total Fat: 4g fat (2g saturated fat)
- Sodium: 70mg sodium

983. Vanilla Crescent Cookies

Serving: 36 | Prep: | Cook: | Ready in:

Ingredients

- 1/4 cup white sugar
- 1 vanilla bean, crushed and broken into chunks
- 1/2 cup chopped walnuts
- 1 cup unsalted butter
- 2 1/3 cups all-purpose flour
- 2 cups white sugar

Direction

- Set the oven to 350°F (175°C) and start preheating.
- In a food processor fitted with a metal blade, place vanilla beans and 1/4 cup sugar. Pulse to chop the bean; add walnuts. Pulse again until chopped finely. Take out of the food processor. Add flour and butter. Mix until blended well.
- Pinch off 1 inch square pieces of dough; form into balls. Form balls into crescent, about 2 inches long. Arrange on cookie sheets, about half inch apart.
- Bake for 10 minutes; lower the oven temperature to 300 °F; bake for 10-15 more minutes, until cookies become dry. Cool on wire racks.

Nutrition Information

- Calories: 135 calories;

- Sodium: < 1
- Total Carbohydrate: 19.3
- Cholesterol: 14
- Protein: 1.1
- Total Fat: 6.3

984. Vegan Chocolate Chip Cookies

Serving: 3-1/2 dozen. | Prep: 15mins | Cook: 10mins | Ready in:

Ingredients

- 1-1/4 cups packed dark brown sugar
- 1/2 cup canola oil
- 6 tablespoons vanilla soy milk
- 1/4 cup sugar
- 1/4 cup unsweetened applesauce
- 2 teaspoons vanilla extract
- 2-1/4 cups all-purpose flour
- 1 teaspoon baking soda
- 3/4 teaspoon salt
- 1 cup dairy-free semisweet chocolate chips
- 1/2 cup finely chopped walnuts

Direction

- Beat together the first six ingredients in a large bowl until well mixed. Combine the salt, baking soda and flour; gradually add and mix them well into the sugar mixture. Stir nuts and chocolate chips into the mixture. Refrigerate, covered for 1 hour.
- Onto baking sheets lined with parchment paper, drop rounded tablespoonfuls of the dough 2 in. apart. Bake until edges are light brown, at 375° for about 10-12 minutes. Let them cool down for 1 minute then take out of pans to wire racks.

Nutrition Information

- Calories: 111 calories

- Sodium: 76mg sodium
- Fiber: 1g fiber)
- Total Carbohydrate: 16g carbohydrate (10g sugars
- Cholesterol: 0 cholesterol
- Protein: 1g protein.
- Total Fat: 5g fat (1g saturated fat)

985. Versatile Slice 'n' Bake Cookies

Serving: 4-1/2 dozen. | Prep: 20mins | Cook: 15mins | Ready in:

Ingredients

- 1 cup butter, softened
- 1 cup sugar
- 1/4 teaspoon vanilla extract
- 1-3/4 cups all-purpose flour
- 3/4 teaspoon baking soda
- 1/4 teaspoon salt
- 2 tablespoons chopped mixed candied fruit, optional
- Nonpareils, jimmies, melted semisweet chocolate chips and chopped nuts, optional

Direction

- Cream sugar and butter together in a small bowl until fluffy and light. Whisk in vanilla. Mix together salt, baking soda, and flour; slowly add to the creamed mixture and stir thoroughly.
- Split the dough into 3 portions. Add candied fruit to 1 portion if you like. Form each portion into a 5-inch roll; put in a freezer bag. Close and freeze for a maximum of 3 months.
- When using the frozen dough: Take out of the freezer 60 minutes before baking. Remove the wrap and slice into 1/4-inch slices. Put on greased cookie sheets, 2 inches apart. If you like, sprinkle jimmies and nonpareils over.
- Bake at 350° until set, 12-14 minutes. Transfer to wire racks to cool. Frost melted chocolate chips over and if you like, sprinkle nuts over.

Nutrition Information

- Calories: 59 calories
- Sodium: 63mg sodium
- Fiber: 0 fiber)
- Total Carbohydrate: 7g carbohydrate (4g sugars
- Cholesterol: 9mg cholesterol
- Protein: 0 protein.
- Total Fat: 3g fat (2g saturated fat)

986. Vienna Triangles

Serving: 9 dozen. | Prep: 60mins | Cook: 15mins | Ready in:

Ingredients

- 3 cups all-purpose flour
- 3/4 cup confectioners' sugar
- 1/2 teaspoon salt
- 1-1/2 cups cold butter, cubed
- FILLING:
- 3 cups sliced almonds
- 1-1/2 cups sugar
- 5 laarge egg whites
- 3 tablespoons all-purpose flour
- 1 tablespoon corn syrup
- 1 teaspoon ground cinnamon
- 1/2 teaspoon almond extract
- 1/4 teaspoon baking powder
- 2/3 cup seedless raspberry jam
- COATING:
- 8 ounces semisweet chocolate, chopped
- 1 tablespoon shortening

Direction

- Mix salt, confectioners' sugar and flour in a large bowl; cut in butter until crumbly. Pat

into a greased 15x10x1-in. baking pan. Bake for 15-18 minutes at 350° or until it turns light brown. Cool on a wire rack.
- In the meantime, mix cinnamon, corn syrup, flour, egg whites, sugar and almonds in a large saucepan over low heat, cook while stirring constantly until a thermometer registers 200°. Take out of the heat; stir in baking powder and extract. Spread jam over crust; add almond mixture on top and spread.
- Bake for 15-20 minutes at 350° or until golden brown. Completely cool on a wire rack. Cut into 54 squares; cut each into 2 triangles diagonally.
- Melt shortening and chocolate in a microwave; stir until smooth. Coat 1/2 of each triangle with chocolate; let excess to drip off. Arrange on waxed paper; allow to stand until set.

Nutrition Information

- Calories: 75 calories
- Sodium: 29mg sodium
- Fiber: 1g fiber)
- Total Carbohydrate: 9g carbohydrate (5g sugars
- Cholesterol: 6mg cholesterol
- Protein: 1g protein.
- Total Fat: 4g fat (2g saturated fat)

987. Waffle Cookies

Serving: about 2-1/2 dozen. | Prep: 25mins | Cook: 10mins | Ready in:

Ingredients

- 1/4 cup butter, cubed
- 2 ounces unsweetened chocolate
- 2 eggs
- 1 teaspoon vanilla extract
- 1 cup all-purpose flour
- 3/4 cup sugar
- FROSTING:
- 2 tablespoons butter
- 1 ounce unsweetened chocolate
- 1 teaspoon vanilla extract
- 1-1/2 cups confectioners' sugar
- 7-1/2 teaspoons hot water
- Edible glitter and jimmies, optional

Direction

- Melt chocolate and butter in a microwave; stir until smooth. Place in a large bowl; completely cool. Whisk in vanilla and eggs. Mix sugar and flour; add to egg mixture gradually. Drop onto a preheated waffle iron, an inch apart, by tablespoonfuls. Bake until set or for a minute. Transfer to a wire rack to completely cool.
- To prepare frosting: melt chocolate and butter in a microwave; stir until smooth. Place in a small bowl. Whisk in vanilla. Add confectioners' sugar alternately with water gradually; whisking until smooth.
- Frost waffle cookies to within 1/4 in. of edges. Garnish with glitter and jimmies if preferred. Allow to stand until frosting is set.

Nutrition Information

- Calories: 97 calories
- Sodium: 29mg sodium
- Fiber: 0 fiber)
- Total Carbohydrate: 15g carbohydrate (11g sugars
- Cholesterol: 21mg cholesterol
- Protein: 1g protein.
- Total Fat: 4g fat (2g saturated fat)

988. Walnut Filled Pillows

Serving: 28 cookies. | Prep: 30mins | Cook: 10mins | Ready in:

Ingredients

- 1/2 cup cold butter, cubed
- 3 ounces cold cream cheese

- 1-1/4 cups all-purpose flour
- 3/4 cup ground walnuts
- 1/4 cup sugar
- 2 tablespoons whole milk
- 1/2 teaspoon vanilla or almond extract
- 1 large egg, lightly beaten
- Confectioners' sugar

Direction

- Cut cream cheese and butter into flour in a big bowl until coarse crumbs are formed; mix for 3 minutes until the mixture forms into a smooth dough. Pat dough into a rectangle; use plastic to wrap then chill for an hour or until firm. Mix vanilla, walnuts, milk, and sugar together to make the filling.
- Remove the plastic wrap then roll the dough on a lightly floured surface into a 17 1/2-in by 10-in rectangle; slice into squares measuring 2 1/2-inch. Put an even teaspoonful filling in the middle of each square; dab water on edges to moisten then fold in half. Use a fork to seal the edges; arrange on ungreased baking sheets about an inch apart. Slather with egg.
- Bake for 10-12 minutes in a 375 degrees oven or until golden brown on the edges; cool on wire racks. Sprinkle with confectioners' sugar.

Nutrition Information

- Calories: 84 calories
- Protein: 1g protein.
- Total Fat: 6g fat (3g saturated fat)
- Sodium: 45mg sodium
- Fiber: 0 fiber)
- Total Carbohydrate: 6g carbohydrate (2g sugars
- Cholesterol: 20mg cholesterol

989. White Almond No Bake Cookies

Serving: about 3-1/2 dozen. | Prep: 25mins | Cook: 5mins | Ready in:

Ingredients

- 2 cups sugar
- 1/2 cup butter, cubed
- 1/2 cup 2% milk
- 1 cup white baking chips
- 1/2 teaspoon almond extract
- 3 cups old-fashioned oats
- 1 cup dried cherries or dried cranberries, optional

Direction

- In the big saucepan, mix the milk, butter and sugar. Cook and stir on medium heat till the butter melts and the sugar dissolves. Take out of the heat. Stir in the extract and baking chips till smooth. Put in the oats, and if you want, cherries; stir till coated.
- Drop by rounded tablespoonfuls to the baking sheets which are lined with waxed paper. Keep refrigerated for roughly half an hour till set. Keep stored in the airtight container in the fridge.

Nutrition Information

- Calories: 101 calories
- Protein: 1g protein.
- Total Fat: 4g fat (2g saturated fat)
- Sodium: 23mg sodium
- Fiber: 1g fiber)
- Total Carbohydrate: 16g carbohydrate (12g sugars
- Cholesterol: 7mg cholesterol

990. White Chocolate Chip Hazelnut Cookies

Serving: 3 dozen. | Prep: 15mins | Cook: 10mins | Ready in:

Ingredients

- 1-1/4 cups whole hazelnuts, toasted, divided
- 9 tablespoons butter, softened, divided
- 1/2 cup sugar
- 1/2 cup packed brown sugar
- 1 egg
- 1 teaspoon vanilla extract
- 1-1/2 cups all-purpose flour
- 1/2 teaspoon baking soda
- 1/2 teaspoon salt
- 1 cup white baking chips

Direction

- Prepare a half cup of hazelnuts and chop it coarsely; set aside. Melt 2 tbsp. of butter and process it in a food processor together with the remaining hazelnuts. Set the mixture aside after processed, covered and it forms a crumbly paste.
- Cream the remaining butter in an empty bowl. Add sugar, egg, and vanilla and whisk until fluffy and light. Add the ground hazelnut mixture and whisk thoroughly until well-blended. Combine baking soda, salt, and flour and pour the mixture into the batter. Mix until just incorporated before adding the chopped hazelnuts and chips.
- Grease the baking sheets. Slowly drop by rounded tablespoonfuls into the baking sheets, arranging 2-inches apart. Allow it to bake inside the oven at 350°F for 10-12 minutes until lightly browned. Transfer the sheets into the wire racks and allow it cool.

Nutrition Information

- Calories:
- Sodium:
- Fiber:
- Total Carbohydrate:
- Cholesterol:
- Protein:
- Total Fat:

991. White Chocolate Cran Pecan Cookies

Serving: about 2-1/2 dozen. | Prep: 15mins | Cook: 10mins | Ready in:

Ingredients

- 1/2 cup butter, softened
- 1/2 cup sugar
- 1/2 cup packed brown sugar
- 1 egg
- 1-1/2 teaspoons vanilla extract
- 1-1/2 cups all-purpose flour
- 1/2 teaspoon baking soda
- 1 cup dried cranberries
- 3/4 cup white baking chips
- 1/2 cup chopped pecans

Direction

- Set the oven to 375° to preheat. Cream sugars and butter in a large bowl until fluffy and light. Beat in vanilla and egg. In another bowl, whip baking soda and flour; gently beat into creamed mixture. Mix in pecans, baking chips and cranberries.
- Drop 2 inch apart onto ungreased baking sheets by tablespoonfuls. Bake till light brown, 8-10 minutes. Transfer from pans to wire racks to cool.

Nutrition Information

- Calories: 128 calories
- Sodium: 50mg sodium
- Fiber: 1g fiber)
- Total Carbohydrate: 18g carbohydrate (12g sugars

- Cholesterol: 16mg cholesterol
- Protein: 1g protein.
- Total Fat: 6g fat (3g saturated fat)

992. White Chocolate Cranberry Cookies

Serving: 2 dozen. | Prep: 20mins | Cook: 10mins | Ready in:

Ingredients

- 1/3 cup butter, softened
- 1/2 cup packed brown sugar
- 1/3 cup sugar
- 1 large egg
- 1 teaspoon vanilla extract
- 1-1/2 cups all-purpose flour
- 1/2 teaspoon salt
- 1/2 teaspoon baking soda
- 3/4 cup dried cranberries
- 1/2 cup white baking chips

Direction

- Beat sugars and butter in a large bowl until crumbly, for 2 minutes. Beat in vanilla and egg. Combine baking soda, salt and flour; gently put into butter mixture and blend well. Mix in chips and cranberries.
- Drop 2 inches apart on baking sheets covered with cooking spray by heaping tablespoonfuls. Bake at 375° until turn to light brown, about 8-10 minutes. Allow to cool for 1 minute before taking out to wire racks.

Nutrition Information

- Calories: 113 calories
- Sodium: 109mg sodium
- Fiber: 0 fiber)
- Total Carbohydrate: 18g carbohydrate (10g sugars
- Cholesterol: 16mg cholesterol

- Protein: 1g protein.
- Total Fat: 4g fat (2g saturated fat)

993. White Chocolate Pumpkin Dreams

Serving: about 4-1/2 dozen. | Prep: 25mins | Cook: 15mins | Ready in:

Ingredients

- 1 cup butter, softened
- 1/2 cup sugar
- 1/2 cup packed brown sugar
- 1 egg
- 2 teaspoons vanilla extract
- 1 cup canned pumpkin
- 2 cups all-purpose flour
- 3-1/2 teaspoons pumpkin pie spice
- 1 teaspoon baking powder
- 1 teaspoon baking soda
- 1/4 teaspoon salt
- 1 package (10 to 12 ounces) white baking chips
- 1 cup chopped pecans
- PENUCHE FROSTING:
- 1/2 cup packed brown sugar
- 3 tablespoons butter
- 1/4 cup milk
- 1-1/2 to 2 cups confectioners' sugar

Direction

- Cream sugars and butter until fluffy and light in a large bowl. Beat in pumpkin, vanilla and egg. Mix dry ingredients; add to creamed mixture gradually; combine well. Stir in pecans and chips.
- Drop onto ungreased baking sheets by rounded teaspoonfuls 2 in. apart. Bake at 350° until firm or for 12-14 minutes. Place on wire racks to cool.
- To prepare frosting, in a small saucepan, mix brown sugar and butter. Bring to boiling; cook over medium heat for a minute or until slightly thickened. Stand for 10 minutes. Add

milk whisk until smooth. Whisk in enough confectioners' sugar so that it achieves the consistency as desired. Top over cooled cookies.

Nutrition Information

- Calories: 275 calories
- Protein: 3g protein.
- Total Fat: 15g fat (8g saturated fat)
- Sodium: 182mg sodium
- Fiber: 1g fiber)
- Total Carbohydrate: 34g carbohydrate (18g sugars
- Cholesterol: 32mg cholesterol

994. White Chocolate Star Sandwich Cookies

Serving: about 1 dozen. | Prep: 30mins | Cook: 10mins | Ready in:

Ingredients

- 1/2 tube refrigerated sugar cookie dough, softened
- 1/3 cup all-purpose flour
- Red sugars, nonpareils or sprinkles
- 1 ounce white baking chocolate
- 2 tablespoons cream cheese, softened
- 1 tablespoon butter, softened
- 4 drops red food coloring
- 1/2 cup confectioners' sugar

Direction

- Whisk flour and cookie dough until combined in a small bowl. On a lightly floured surface, roll out 1/8-in. thickness. Use a floured 2-3/4-in. star cookie cutter to cut. Arrange on clean and dry baking sheets, 2 inches apart.
- Garnish 1/2 cookies with nonpareils and sugars. Bake for 7-9 minutes at 350° or until edges turn golden brown. Place cookies on wire racks; cool.
- Melt white chocolate in a microwave; stir until smooth.
- Cool. Whisk food coloring, butter and cream cheese until fluffy in a small bowl. Beat in melted chocolate and confectioners' sugar gradually until smooth. Spread over the tops of plain cookies; add decorated cookies on top. Keep in the fridge.

Nutrition Information

- Calories: 124 calories
- Cholesterol: 10mg cholesterol
- Protein: 1g protein.
- Total Fat: 6g fat (2g saturated fat)
- Sodium: 87mg sodium
- Fiber: 0 fiber)
- Total Carbohydrate: 17g carbohydrate (9g sugars

995. White Chocolate Cranberry Biscotti

Serving: 2-1/2 dozen. | Prep: 15mins | Cook: 35mins | Ready in:

Ingredients

- 1/2 cup butter, softened
- 1 cup sugar
- 4 eggs
- 1 teaspoon vanilla extract
- 3 cups all-purpose flour
- 1 tablespoon baking powder
- 3/4 cup dried cranberries
- 3/4 cup vanilla or white chips

Direction

- In a large bowl, cream sugar and butter until puffy and light. Put in eggs, one each time, beating well after each addition. Beat in

vanilla. Mix baking powder and flour; slowly pour to creamed mixture and blend well. Mix in vanilla chips and cranberries. Separate dough into 3 portions.
- On ungreased baking sheets, form each portion into a 10x2-inch rectangle. Bake for 20 to 25 minutes at 350°, until lightly browned. Let cool for 5 minutes.
- Bring to a cutting board; cut diagonally, using a serrated knife, into 1-inch slices. Arrange, cut side down, on ungreased baking sheets. Bake for 15 to 20 minutes, until golden brown. Transfer to wire racks until cooled. Preserve in an airtight container.

Nutrition Information

- Calories: 281 calories
- Total Carbohydrate: 43g carbohydrate (17g sugars
- Cholesterol: 75mg cholesterol
- Protein: 5g protein.
- Total Fat: 10g fat (6g saturated fat)
- Sodium: 167mg sodium
- Fiber: 1g fiber)

996. Whoopie Cookies

Serving: about 1-1/2 dozen. | Prep: 20mins | Cook: 10mins | Ready in:

Ingredients

- 1 package devil's food cake mix (regular size)
- 1/4 cup butter, softened
- 2 large eggs
- 1 jar (7 ounces) marshmallow creme
- 4 ounces cream cheese, softened

Direction

- Beat butter and cake mix together in a big bowl until well-mixed. Beat in eggs then form the mixture into 1 inch balls. Put on ungreased baking sheets with 2 inches apart.
- Bake at 350 degrees until tops become cracked, about 7 to 9 minutes. Allow to cool about 2 minutes before transferring to wire racks to fully cool.
- Beat together cream cheese and marshmallow crème in a big bowl until mixed but (avoid over-beating). Spread on the bottoms of half of cookies with the filling, then put leftover cookies on top. Refrigerate until filling has set, about 1 to 2 hours.

Nutrition Information

- Calories: 152 calories
- Total Carbohydrate: 25g carbohydrate (16g sugars
- Cholesterol: 28mg cholesterol
- Protein: 2g protein.
- Total Fat: 5g fat (3g saturated fat)
- Sodium: 206mg sodium
- Fiber: 1g fiber)

997. Winning Cranberry Chip Cookies

Serving: about 6 dozen. | Prep: 10mins | Cook: 11mins | Ready in:

Ingredients

- 1 cup butter, softened
- 1 cup sugar
- 2 eggs
- 1 teaspoon vanilla extract
- 2-1/4 cups all-purpose flour
- 1/2 teaspoon baking powder
- 1/4 teaspoon salt
- 1-1/2 cups semisweet chocolate chips
- 1-1/2 cups dried cranberries
- 3/4 cup chopped pecans
- 1/2 cup English toffee bits or almond brickle chips, optional

Direction

- In a large bowl, cream sugar and butter. Put in vanilla and eggs; mix well. Combine salt, baking powder and flour; add to the creamed mixture gradually and mix well. Blend in cranberries, chocolate chips, pecans and toffee bits if you want (dough will be stiff).
- On ungreased baking sheets, drop by rounded tablespoonful placing 2 inches apart. Slightly flatten. Bake at 350° for nearly 11 to 14 minutes or till set and edges are browned lightly. Allow 2 minutes to cool before taking away to wire racks.

Nutrition Information

- Calories: 82 calories
- Sodium: 39mg sodium
- Fiber: 1g fiber)
- Total Carbohydrate: 10g carbohydrate (6g sugars
- Cholesterol: 13mg cholesterol
- Protein: 1g protein.
- Total Fat: 5g fat (2g saturated fat)

998. Winter Wonderland Gingerbread Cottage

Serving: 1 gingerbread cottage. | Prep: 03hours00mins | Cook: 15mins | Ready in:

Ingredients

- 1 cup butter, softened
- 1-3/4 cups packed brown sugar
- 1-1/4 cups sugar
- 2 tablespoons molasses
- 6 eggs
- 6 cups all-purpose flour
- 2 teaspoons baking soda
- 3 teaspoons ground ginger
- 1 teaspoon each ground cinnamon and allspice
- ROYAL ICING AND DECORATIONS:
- 2 pounds confectioners' sugar
- 6 tablespoons meringue powder
- 3/4 cup warm water
- Green and red gel food coloring
- 1 wooden skewer (6 inches long)
- Pastry tips—star tips #14 and 20, round tip #4 and leaf tip # 352
- 5 pieces red rope licorice, divided
- Red nonpareils, red milk chocolate M&M's, edible glitter and light bulb-shaped sprinkles
- 4 cups Crispix
- New small paintbrush
- 19 large marshmallows
- 2 tablespoons butter
- 3 cups crisp rice cereal
- Additional confectioners' sugar
- 9 miniature candy canes, divided
- 1 piece red Fruit by the Foot fruit roll (1-3/4 inches)
- Red, green and purple tiny-size Chiclets gum
- Granulated sugar and coarse sugar
- Minty Snowmen

Direction

- For the dough, cream the butter and sugars in a large bowl until fluffy and light. Stir in molasses. Beat in eggs, one at a time, whisking thoroughly every after addition. In a separate bowl, mix baking soda, spices, and flour and gradually add it into the creamed mixture. Chill for 1 hour.
- Cut the drawn patterns from the waxed paper. Line the baking sheet with a parchment paper and lay the rolled dough with having a thickness of about 1/4-inch. Cut out the house front, back, and chimney-pieces using a sharp knife. For the front house, cut a window piece and reserve the cut out for the door piece. Once the dough is baked, trim the bottom of the door piece, about 1/4-inch.
- Bake the cookies at 350°F for 15-20 minutes until they're all set. Once done, place the patterns on cutouts and cut around its edges to trim the excess. Allow it to cool on pans, about 2 minutes, before transferring it to the wire racks to cool completely.
- Cut out two 5-7/16-inches long and 5-6/16-inches high for the house sides. Reroll the

- scraps. Cut out two 7-7/16-inches long and 7-13/16-inches high for the roof. Let it bake and cool following the same directions above.
- For the icing, combine meringue powder and confectioners' sugar in a large bowl. Pour in warm water and beat for 60 seconds on a low speed. Set the electric mixer to high setting and beat for 4-5 minutes until stiff peaks form. Color 1 cup of it with green and set aside, covered. Reserve the remaining white icing.
- To assemble the house pieces, place the front of the house, front side facing down on a working surface that is lined with a wax paper. Cut the skewer into one 2 3/4-inch piece and one 2 1/4-2 1/2-inch piece to make front window panes. Attach the skewers using the icing and allow it to dry completely.
- Place the house back and sides on a working surface that is lined with a wax paper. Position the house front facing up. Pipe the shell border around the edges of the house pieces using a #14 pastry tip. Put the shell border on the front of the house and around the door opening. Decorate some snowflakes and dots in front of the house using a #4 pastry tip. Pipe front window panes and side windows over skewers.
- To make the front shutters, cut two 2 1/2-inch pieces of licorice and attach. Make at least 4 pieces of the licorice for the side shutters. Attach the pieces and let them dry.
- Pour water into the 1/4-cup of icing to thin it. Tint it with red and scatter it all over the door. Allow it to dry completely. Pipe the door using white icing. You can add a window if you want and allow it to dry. Pipe the upper part of the door and windows using the #352 pastry tip and the reserved green icing. Add the red nonpareils. Reserve the remaining green icing for the trees.
- To assemble the house, line the icing along the house sides' edges. Assemble it facing right angles in front of the house. Press it tightly to attach, propping with small cans. For the house to be more stable, pipe more icing on the inside's edges. Do the same with its back and allow it to dry completely.
- To assemble the chimney, pipe the icing on one of the adjoining sides of the chimney-piece and on one side of the chimney's front piece. Assemble each piece facing right angles to each other and transfer them in a waxed paper. For the chimney to be more stable, pipe more icing along the inside edge of the chimney. Hold it steady until it can stand on its own. Do the same with the remaining back and side pieces. Allow it to dry completely before spreading more icing over the chimney. Add M&M's over the icing.
- For the roof, pipe the reserved white icing along the top edges of the house walls. Slowly place one roof piece and prop it with cans. Repeat the same steps with others and allow it to dry. Frost the roof pieces and slowly attach the Crispix shingles and the chimney. Add snow effects on the roof and around the chimney opening using the pastry tip #4. Brush the Crispix lightly with water using the paintbrush and sprinkle edible glitter on it.
- Decorate the roof by piping a rope border along the edge of the roof using a pastry tip #20. Position the light-bulb sprinkles. Pipe all of the rope borders where the walls meet each corner, and the roof meets the house.
- For final touches, mix butter and marshmallows in a large microwavable bowl. Heat the mixture until melted. Stir in crisp rice cereal and mix. Shape it into a tree. Tint the trees with the reserved green icing using a #352 pastry tip. Shower it with edible glitter and garnish with confectioners' sugar or light-bulb sprinkles if you want.
- For the bench, cut the licorice to make five 2 1/2-inch pieces. Form C-shaped pieces by cutting curve ends from the five candy canes. Reserve the 3 curved pieces for the fence and the other 1 for the sled. Attach 1 C-shaped piece onto the bottom of one whole candy cane using an icing. Be sure that the crook is facing right and the attached piece forms one side of the bench frame. Do the same with the remaining pieces and allow it to dry. Fasten the licorice pieces into the bench frame pieces,

- propping it lightly. Dry it first before adding the icing rivets.
- Form a sled by placing the reserved straight piece in between the two whole candy canes. Bind them together using the icing. Attach the fruit by the foot and let it dry.
- Design your own path pattern on a waxed paper. Coat the pattern with icing and attach the Chiclets. Let it dry.
- Transfer the house and the path on a tray or large covered board. Add the granulated sugar for the snow drifts and sprinkle coarse sugar on its top. Position the bench, Minty Snowmen, sled, and trees, surrounding the whole house. For the fence, place the reserved candy cane into the sprinkled sugar.

Nutrition Information

- Calories:
- Total Fat:
- Sodium:
- Fiber:
- Total Carbohydrate:
- Cholesterol:
- Protein:

999.   Yule Log Cookies

Serving: 4 dozen. | Prep: 02hours00mins | Cook: 10mins | Ready in:

Ingredients

- 2/3 cup pistachios
- 2 tablespoons sugar
- 4 cups semisweet chocolate chips, divided
- 1/2 cup butter, softened
- 1-1/2 cups packed brown sugar
- 2 large eggs
- 1/4 cup whole milk
- 1 teaspoon almond extract
- 3-1/4 cups all-purpose flour
- 2 tablespoons baking cocoa
- 2 teaspoons baking powder
- 3/4 teaspoon salt
- 1 large egg white, lightly beaten
- 2 tablespoons shortening
- Ground pistachios
- MUSHROOMS:
- Miniature marshmallows
- Baking cocoa

Direction

- Process sugar and pistachios, covered, till ground in a food processor; put aside. Melt 1 cup of chocolate chips in a microwave; mix till smooth.
- Cream brown sugar and butter till fluffy and light in a big bowl; beat in almond extract, milk, melted chocolate and eggs. Mix salt, baking powder, cocoa and flour. Add to creamed mixture slowly; stir well. Mix in pistachio mixture.
- Divide dough to 8 portions then wrap in plastic; refrigerate till firm for 3 hours.
- Form each portion to 18-in. rope then cut each to 6 logs; put on greased baking sheets, 2-in. apart. At an angle, cut ends of each log. Attach removed pieces to every log, making branches, using small amount of the egg white.
- Bake for 10-12 minutes till set at 350°; transfer to wire racks.
- Melt shortening and leftover chocolate chips in a microwave; mix till smooth. Dip cookies in chocolate in batches; let excess drip off. Make strokes in chocolate to mimic bark with tines of a fork. Dust using ground pistachios.
- Mushrooms: To make a stem, pinch 1/2 of each marshmallow; flatten other 1/2 for mushroom's cap. Use cocoa to dust tops of mushrooms. With small amount of the melted chocolate, attach to cookies.
- Stand till set; keep in airtight container.

Nutrition Information

- Calories: 163 calories
- Sodium: 83mg sodium
- Fiber: 1g fiber)

- Total Carbohydrate: 23g carbohydrate (15g sugars
- Cholesterol: 14mg cholesterol
- Protein: 2g protein.
- Total Fat: 8g fat (4g saturated fat)

1000. Yummy Chocolate Double Chip Cookies

Serving: 2-1/2 dozen. | Prep: 15mins | Cook: 10mins | Ready in:

Ingredients

- 1/2 cup butter, softened
- 3/4 cup packed brown sugar
- 1 egg
- 1 teaspoon vanilla extract
- 1-1/4 cups all-purpose flour
- 1/2 teaspoon baking soda
- 1/2 teaspoon salt
- 2/3 cup semisweet chocolate chips
- 1/3 cup butterscotch chips

Direction

- Cream together butter and brown sugar in a large bowl till fluffy and light. Beat egg and vanilla into the mixture. Mix together the salt, baking soda and flour; add them gradually into the creamed mixture and combine thoroughly. Stir the chocolate and butterscotch chips into the mixture.
- Drop rounded tablespoonfuls of the dough 2 in. apart onto greased baking sheets. Bake to a golden brown at 350° or for 10-12 minutes (the tops will feel soft to touch). Let them cool down for 3 minutes, then transfer to wire racks to cool thoroughly. Keep in an airtight container.

Nutrition Information

- Calories: 101 calories

- Fiber: 0 fiber)
- Total Carbohydrate: 14g carbohydrate (7g sugars
- Cholesterol: 15mg cholesterol
- Protein: 1g protein.
- Total Fat: 5g fat (3g saturated fat)
- Sodium: 89mg sodium

1001. "Home Sweet Home" Gingerbread Cottage

Serving: 1 gingerbread cottage. | Prep: 03hours00mins | Cook: 15mins | Ready in:

Ingredients

- 1/3 cup packed brown sugar
- 1/3 cup corn syrup
- 1/4 cup butter, cubed
- 1-2/3 cups all-purpose flour
- 3/4 teaspoon ground cinnamon
- 1/2 teaspoon ground ginger
- 1/8 teaspoon salt
- Waxed paper and parchment paper
- 3 butterscotch candies, crushed
- 1-1/2 teaspoons water
- Red and green paste food coloring
- New paintbrush
- ICING AND ASSEMBLY:
- 3-3/4 cups confectioners' sugar
- 2 tablespoons meringue powder
- 1/8 teaspoon cream of tartar
- 2 tablespoons water
- Pastry tips—round tips #4 and #2, star tip #14
- Gold dragee, edible glitter, cardboard cake circle (8 inches), frosted bite-size Shredded Wheat, peppermint candy sticks, small jelly beans, milk chocolate M&M, miniature candy canes, jumbo heart sprinkles, jumbo gumdrops, red licorice, butterscotch candies, pretzel rods and jumbo peppermint stick

Direction

- For the dough, mix butter, brown sugar, and corn syrup in a small saucepan. Allow it to cook over medium heat, stirring occasionally until the butter is melted. Mix salt, cinnamon, ginger, and flour. Pour the cinnamon mixture into the brown sugar mixture and whisk well until it forms a stiff dough. Transfer the mixture in a small bowl and store inside the refrigerator for 1 hour or until fixed and easy to handle.
- Draw patterns into the waxed paper and cut it out by tracing the patterns. Lightly dust the working surface with flour and lay the dough. Roll it out to form 1/8-inch thick dough. Place the cutout patterns on top of the dough and use a sharp knife to score outlines for the windows and door. Be careful not to cut the dough all the way through. Trace lines into the dough to form bricks using a toothpick (do not include the roof and door area). Make sure to cover all the pieces to prevent them from drying out. Transfer all the cutout pieces into the baking pan lined with parchment paper. Allow it to bake inside the oven at 350 degrees F for 12-15 minutes until browned all over. After baking, immediately lay the patterns on top of the cookies and trace its edges to remove any excess. Cut the windows completely. Let it cool in the baking pans for 2 minutes before transferring the cutouts into wire racks to cool completely.
- Transfer the front of the house to a baking pan lined with parchment paper. Fill each window cutout with 1 tsp. of crushed candies. Bake it again inside the oven at 400°F for 3-4 minutes until the candy melts completely. Allow it to cool on the baking pan before removing it.
- Pour a small amount of red food coloring into the water and mix. Use a paintbrush to paint the mixture over all the cutout pieces, except for the roof and door area. Use paper towels to pat dry.
- For the icing, mix meringue powder, cream of tartar, and confectioners' sugar in a large bowl. Stir in water. Whisk the mixture at low speed until just incorporated. Whisk again on high speed for 4-5 minutes until it forms stiff peaks. Cover the icing with a damp cloth at all times.
- For the frame of the house, work with a small portion of icing at a time. Wipe icing over the bricks using your fingertip. Remove the excess by wiping the edges with paper towels.
- Lay the front of the house on a flat surface. Color the icing with green and a small amount of red. Insert a #4 pastry tip into the small hole of the corner of the pastry bag. Fill the pastry bag with white icing.
- Line the door, windows, and windowpanes with icing. Attach dragee into the door using the icing for the doorknob.
- Insert a #14-star tip into the pastry bag and fill it with green icing. Pipe garlands over the windows and wreath on the door. Insert a #2-round tip into the pastry bag and fill it with red icing. Use it to decorate berries on the garland and to put bow and berries into the wreath. You can decorate the house as you desired. Sprinkle glitter on the icing and allow it to dry completely.
- Line the base, one side of the front house, and the adjoining side wall with icing. Position the walls at right angles to each other on the cake circle. Prop the walls with small cans. For a more stable house, line the inside and outside edges with icing. Do the same steps with the second side sections and back of the house, and allow them to dry completely.
- Pipe the icing along one of the adjoining side walls and along one side of the front of the chimney. Attach the cutouts, facing right angles to each, and place them on a waxed paper. Line an icing along its inside edges for it to be more stable. Secure it with your hands tightly until it can stand on its own. Do the same with the remaining sides and let them dry completely.
- For the roof, pipe more icing on the top edges of the house. Attach the roof pieces into the icing. It must be an equal overhang in the back and front. Line the icing along the joining edges. Use cans to prop the bottoms of the roof pieces and allow it to cool completely.

- For the left roof piece, place the chimney 1 3/4-inches from the front and 1 3/4-inches down from the top. Pipe dots of icing to trace the position of the bottom chimney corners. Attach the chimney, piping more icing into its edges. Hold it steady for 1 minute until it can stand on its own and completely dried. Attach the cap of the chimney on the chimney top using an icing, leaving a small overhang on all of its sides.
- To style the roof, use a #4 tip to pipe icing along the bottom of the chimney side of the roof. Attach one row of 5 shredded wheat pieces into the icing. Cover both of the roof pieces. On one of the roof pieces, pipe icing along the top row of shredded wheat and attach the candy stick into the icing. Do the same with the other side of the roof.
- Press 4 shredded wheat pieces along the peak of the roof using an icing. Decorate the shredded pieces with jelly beans and press M&M at the front gable. Form two miniature candy canes into a heart and place it into the roof. You can add heart sprinkles and additional icing if preferred.
- Cover the cake circle with icing for the house final touches. Arrange gumdrops in front of the house for the shrubs. Spread green icing on the front of the house and use the red icing to draw berries on it.
- Place red licorice pieces in front of the door for the sidewalk. Attach butterscotch candies and use them as stepping stones. Drop a small amount of water into the licorice and shower them with glitters. Pound pretzel rods into pieces and place it in the side of the house to make it look like firewood. Cut jumbo peppermint stick into your desired length and attach it to the chimney cap for the smoke. Hold the stick securely for 60 seconds until it can stand on its own.

Nutrition Information

- Calories:
- Total Fat:
- Sodium:
- Fiber:
- Total Carbohydrate:
- Cholesterol:
- Protein:

Index

A

Almond 3,4,5,6,7,8,9,10,11,12,14,29,32,40,64,136,159,162,180,231,272,280,308,309,310,332,336,337,338,356,377,392,436,468,560

Anise 4,5,6,9,11,14,94,137,141,186,311,312,406,544,552

Apple 4,5,9,11,65,67,94,95,96,97,98,99,100,101,102,103,104,106,107,108,116,138,312,313,434

Apricot 5,9,139,140,313,314,315

B

Baking 170,300,398,531,567

Banana 5,143

Beer 4,90

Biscotti 3,5,6,7,8,9,10,11,12,13,14,32,55,119,126,130,143,148,154,159,240,281,300,322,373,382,395,396,445,470,471,500,533,564

Biscuits 3,51

Blackberry 9,318

Bran 9,13,319,512

Brie 217

Butter 3,4,5,6,7,8,9,10,11,12,13,14,17,21,24,30,31,52,55,63,70,79,80,92,95,106,127,152,153,186,198,208,214,221,230,238,245,248,254,255,256,292,311,312,318,320,323,324,325,326,342,352,364,378,390,394,400,404,410,419,425,435,437,446,457,465,475,477,481,485,493,494,495,522,531,536,544,550

C

Cake 3,4,5,6,8,9,10,19,42,61,62,63,81,86,120,185,279,286,294,339

Caramel 3,4,5,6,9,10,13,35,48,67,107,108,122,156,157,158,166,328,339,522

Cardamom 3,8,42,251

Carrot 3,42

Cashew 6,9,11,13,157,182,329,330,382,407,523

Cheddar 253

Cheese 3,4,5,6,8,9,11,13,18,22,86,115,131,139,158,170,180,184,185,253,269,302,384,385,507,516

Cherry 3,5,6,7,9,10,11,14,18,29,101,159,160,161,162,177,234,327,331,332,333,334,335,340,356,357,358,371,395,407,435,546

Chips 11,415

Chocolate 3,4,5,6,7,8,9,10,11,12,13,14,15,17,19,20,21,24,30,31,35,37,43,68,69,72,83,84,88,92,109,113,124,134,135,145,156,157,163,165,166,167,168,169,170,200,219,247,253,260,264,273,281,289,297,298,300,303,304,305,308,328,330,335,336,337,338,339,340,341,342,343,344,345,346,347,348,349,350,351,352,353,354,355,356,357,358,359,360,361,362,363,364,369,377,383,384,398,403,416,417,442,444,457,458,471,473,474,483,492,496,510,514,530,532,537,557,561,562,563,564,568

Cinnamon 3,4,5,6,10,12,38,39,96,110,175,369,473,531

Cocoa powder 341

Coconut 4,5,6,7,8,10,11,12,13,63,117,176,177,194,247,263,271,274,335,344,371,372,373,387,441,466,484,515

Coffee 7,12,222,469

Coulis 3,27

Cranberry 4,5,6,9,10,11,12,13,14,70,110,111,112,113,114,121,124,125,126,134,135,180,181,182,183,305,372,377,378,379,380,381,382,383,384,402,491,492,505,511,553,562,564,565

Cream 3,4,5,6,7,8,9,11,12,13,17,19,21,22,23,35,37,39,43,49,53,55,60,61,63,70,74,75,76,79,83,84,85,86,88,89,90,96,98,101,102,104,105,106,108,111,113,114,115,120,121,123,124,126,127,129,130,133,135,139,140,143,144,145,146,147,149,153,154,155,156,160,162,163,170,171,173,174,176,179,183,184,185,186,187,189,192,194,196,197,198,199,213,214,215,221,223,227,232,235,238,239,243,245,247,251,252,254,256,257,260,266,269,272,275,279,280,284,285,288,290,293,294,296,297,298,302,304,305,306,307,308,311,314,316,317,318,319,322,323,324,326,327,329,330,332,335,337,338,339,340,343,344,347,349,350,351,352,353,355,356,357,358,359,360,361,363,364,368,369,370,371,374,375,379,381,384,385,386,387,390,391,392,393,394,395,397,398,401,402,403,404,405,406,407,408,409,410,411,413,414,417,418,419,422,423,425,428,433,435,439,441,443,444,446,447,449,451,452,453,454,455,456,457,458,459,460,461,462,463,464,466,467,468,471,473,476,477,478,479,480,482,483,484,485,486,487,488,490,491,492,494,495,496,499,501,504,505,507,508,509,511,512,514,515,516,517,518,519,525,526,528,530,531,535,536,537,539,540,541,544,546,547,548,550,551,552,555,557,558,561,562,563,567,568

Crisps 3,4,12,14,17,52,60,482,553

Curd 3,52

D

Dark chocolate 430

Date 6,7,8,11,12,187,188,189,210,244,274,389,452

E

Egg 3,7,9,12,25,44,47,195,196,265,324,446

F

Fat 7,15,16,17,18,19,20,21,22,23,24,25,26,27,28,29,30,31,32,33,34,35,36,37,38,39,40,41,42,43,44,45,46,47,48,49,50,51,52,53,54,55,56,57,58,59,60,61,62,63,64,65,66,67,68,69,70,71,72,73,74,75,76,77,78,79,80,81,82,83,84,85,86,87,88,89,90,91,92,93,94,95,96,97,98,99,100,101,102,103,104,105,106,107,108,109,110,111,112,113,114,115,116,117,118,119,120,121,122,123,124,125,126,127,128,129,130,131,132,133,134,135,136,137,138,139,140,141,142,143,144,145,146,147,148,149,150,151,152,153,154,155,156,157,158,159,160,161,162,163,164,165,166,167,168,169,170,171,172,173,174,175,176,177,178,179,180,181,182,183,184,185,186,187,188,189,190,191,192,193,194,195,196,197,198,199,200,201,202,203,204,205,206,207,208,209,210,211,212,213,214,215,216,217,218,219,220,221,222,223,224,225,226,227,228,229,230,231,232,233,234,235,236,237,238,239,240,241,242,243,244,245,246,247,248,249,250,251,252,253,254,255,256,257,258,259,260,261,262,263,264,265,266,267,268,269,270,271,272,273,274,275,276,277,278,279,280,281,282,283,284,285,286,287,288,289,290,291,292,293,294,295,296,297,298,299,300,301,302,303,304,305,306,307,308,309,310,311,312,313,314,315,316,317,318,319,320,321,322,323,324,325,326,327,328,329,330,331,332,333,334,335,336,337,338,339,340,341,342,343,344,345,346,347,348,349,350,351,352,353,354,355,356,357,358,359,360,361,362,363,364,365,366,367,368,369,370,371,372,373,374,375,376,377,378,379,380,381,382,383,384,385,386,387,388,389,390,391,392,393,394,395,396,397,398,399,400,401,402,403,404,405,406,407,408,409,410,411,412,413,414,415,416,417,418,419,422,423,424,425,426,427,428,429,431,432,433,434,435,436,437,438,439,440,441,442,443,444,445,446,447,448,449,450,451,452,453,454,455,456,457,458,459,460,461,462,463,464,465,466,467,468,469,470,471,472,473,474,475,476,477,478,479,480,481,482,483,484,485,486,487,488,489,490,491,492,493,494,495,496,497,498,499,500,501,502,503,504,505,506,507,508,509,510,511,512,513,514,515,516,517,518,519,520,521,522,523,524,525,526,527,528,529,530,532,533,53

4,535,536,537,538,539,540,541,542,543,544,545,546,547,548,549,550,551,552,553,554,555,556,557,558,559,560,561,562,563,564,565,567,568,570

Fig 7,11,199,403

Flour 11,116,289,404,531

Fruit 3,5,6,7,8,10,11,13,46,124,154,198,201,242,337,345,399,412,413,511,524,565

Fudge 7,11,12,13,198,413,414,475,502,522,532

G

Gin 5,6,7,8,9,10,11,12,13,14,144,147,163,164,173,195,196,204,205,206,207,208,212,238,264,273,286,290,306,346,361,374,388,396,398,399,408,409,418,419,420,422,423,424,425,426,427,428,429,430,431,432,433,487,533,537,565,568

H

Ham 7,9,215,306

Hazelnut 6,7,8,9,10,12,14,170,190,217,246,250,295,303,315,347,348,442,443,444,561

Heart 3,10,12,18,25,26,30,33,35,36,38,39,363,443,456

Honey 3,7,12,14,48,81,117,209,232,450,451,452,472,544

I

Ice cream 399

Icing 4,11,25,29,30,59,74,96,164,189,220,241,278,425,438,446,520

J

Jam 5,7,12,141,221,456

Jelly 3,8,12,48,256,456

Jus 253

L

Lemon 3,4,5,6,7,11,12,13,40,50,51,52,53,54,55,56,57,60,125,192,241,387,392,450,454,459,460,461,462,463,464,465,466,537

Lime 4,7,10,12,63,227,375,465,467

Liqueur 3,7,33,220,222

M

Macadamia 3,5,9,10,11,12,13,24,135,331,373,419,468,469,470,532

Macaroon 3,4,6,7,8,9,10,12,13,40,57,186,229,247,263,309,359,377,441,451,538

Madeleines 3,54

Margarine 294

Marmalade 4,12,57,490

Marshmallow 10,44,198,351

Meat 7,231

Meringue 3,4,7,8,9,10,12,13,14,19,20,42,58,61,76,201,231,233,261,309,335,341,447,474,506,513,516,549

Mince 12,487

Mint 7,9,10,12,13,236,307,362,363,369,446,473,474,492,506,537,565,567

Molasses 6,7,10,11,12,13,14,173,237,368,402,406,477,478,479,539,543

Mushroom 7,233,568

N

Nut 6,7,8,9,10,11,12,13,14,15,16,17,18,19,20,21,22,23,24,25,26,27,28,29,30,31,32,33,34,35,36,37,38,39,40,41,42,43,44,45,46,47,48,49,50,51,52,53,54,55,56,57,58,59,60,61,62,63,64,65,66,67,68,69,70,71,72,73,74,75,76,77,78,79,80,81,82,83,84,85,86,87,88,89,90,91,92,93,94,95,96,97,98,99,100,101,102,103,104,105,106,107,108,109,110,111,112,113,114,115,116,117,118,119,120,121,122,123,124,125,126,127,128,129,130,131,132,133,134,135,136,137,138,139,140,141,142,1

43,144,145,146,147,148,149,150,151,152,153,154,155,156,157,158,159,160,161,162,163,164,165,166,167,168,169,170,171,172,173,174,175,176,177,178,179,180,181,182,183,184,185,186,187,188,189,190,191,192,193,194,195,196,197,198,199,200,201,202,203,204,205,206,207,208,209,210,211,212,213,214,215,216,217,218,219,220,221,222,223,224,225,226,227,228,229,230,231,232,233,234,235,236,237,238,239,240,241,242,243,244,245,246,247,248,249,250,251,252,253,254,255,256,257,258,259,260,261,262,263,264,265,266,267,268,269,270,271,272,273,274,275,276,277,278,279,280,281,282,283,284,285,286,287,288,289,290,291,292,293,294,295,296,297,298,299,300,301,302,303,304,305,306,307,308,309,310,311,312,313,314,315,316,317,318,319,320,321,322,323,324,325,326,327,328,329,330,331,332,333,334,335,336,337,338,339,340,341,342,343,344,345,346,347,348,349,350,351,352,353,354,355,356,357,358,359,360,361,362,363,364,365,366,367,368,369,370,371,372,373,374,375,376,377,378,379,380,381,382,383,384,385,386,387,388,389,390,391,392,393,394,395,396,397,398,399,400,401,402,403,404,405,406,407,408,409,410,411,412,413,414,415,416,417,418,419,422,423,424,425,426,427,428,429,431,432,433,434,435,436,437,438,439,440,441,442,443,444,445,446,447,448,449,450,451,452,453,454,455,456,457,458,459,460,461,462,463,464,465,466,467,468,469,470,471,472,473,474,475,476,477,478,479,480,481,482,483,484,485,486,487,488,489,490,491,492,493,494,495,496,497,498,499,500,501,502,503,504,505,506,507,508,509,510,511,512,513,514,515,516,517,518,519,520,521,522,523,524,525,526,527,528,529,530,531,532,533,534,535,536,537,538,539,540,541,542,543,544,545,546,547,548,549,550,551,552,553,554,555,556,557,558,559,560,561,562,563,564,565,567,568,570

O

Oatmeal 4,5,8,10,11,12,13,88,96,98,99,101,103,112,113,114,123,124,125,133,143,146,178,247,340,376,381,410,427,485,486,488,523,541

Oats 5,113

Oil 12,29,62,146,172,188,213,223,231,232,238,269,489,519

Olive 12,489

Orange 3,5,6,7,8,10,11,12,13,32,114,126,168,183,188,220,251,252,351,352,360,376,379,414,454,489,490,491,492,530,534

P

Pastry 5,7,116,199,399,420,424,565,569

Pear 5,132

Pecan 4,5,6,8,10,11,12,13,14,88,117,122,127,128,130,132,183,258,334,372,375,380,381,477,486,497,498,499,508,522,530,561

Peel 28,123,415,504

Pepper 3,6,7,8,10,13,20,187,200,219,244,259,260,261,262,263,281,353,354,364,500,501,502,513

Pie 4,5,12,13,68,99,117,127,128,138,264,472,498,499,509,510

Pistachio 3,8,10,11,12,13,34,269,343,382,383,460,504,505,506,517

Poppy seeds 460

Port 206,533

Potato 9,326

Praline 6,178

Pulse 41,202,300,504,520,556,557

Pumpkin 4,5,11,12,13,14,70,71,79,82,83,84,85,86,87,88,89,90,92,120,130,411,452,507,508,509,510,562

R

Raisins 399

Raspberry 3,4,7,8,9,10,13,27,33,61,213,272,298,363,513,514,515,516,517

Rhubarb 4,61

Rice 4,8,24,35,70,189,262,274,481

Royal icing 526

Rum 5,6,7,8,11,13,117,143,169,177,203,276,277,278,413,520

S

Salt 5,13,122,522,523,531

Shortbread 3,4,5,6,7,8,9,10,11,12,13,34,38,39,49,73,132,140,153,158,162,190,199,203,272,282,297,324,330,347,394,418,436,443,449,461,462,492,527

Spelt 9,300

Squash 5,133

Strawberry 3,4,45,63

Sugar 3,4,5,6,7,8,9,10,11,12,13,14,15,35,36,63,76,144,146,147,149,151,180,185,194,197,208,211,212,213,235,240,241,248,265,277,291,292,293,295,296,300,310,316,317,321,337,366,370,377,388,389,391,401,408,420,437,441,450,451,453,456,464,478,480,482,490,495,498,499,515,516,524,526,528,531,536,538,539,540,545,546,548,549,551,552

Syrup 4,74

T

Tea 3,4,5,6,8,9,12,19,63,120,185,279,313,467

Toffee 4,7,11,14,69,194,413,553

Truffle 80

Turkey 5,107,118

V

Vegan 4,7,8,9,14,74,195,265,273,300,557

W

Walnut 4,5,6,7,9,12,14,77,122,148,149,203,302,303,318,409,470,560

Wine 3,21

Z

Zest 309

Conclusion

Thank you again for downloading this book!

I hope you enjoyed reading about my book!

If you enjoyed this book, please take the time to share your thoughts and post a review on Amazon. It'd be greatly appreciated!

Write me an honest review about the book – I truly value your opinion and thoughts and I will incorporate them into my next book, which is already underway.

Thank you!

If you have any questions, **feel free to contact at:** author@ashkenazirecipes.com

Iva Alston

ashkenazirecipes.com